NOCTES AMBROSIANÆ.

BY

CHRISTOPHER NORTH.

(PROF. JOHN WILSON).

SELECTED, EDITED AND ARRANGED BY

JOHN SKELTON,

ADVOCATE.

NEW YORK:
JOHN B. ALDEN, PUBLISHER,
18 VESEY STREET.

ΧΡΗ Δ'ΕΝ ΣΥΜΠΟΣΙΩ ΚΥΛΙΚΩΝ ΠΕΡΙΝΙΣΣΟΜΕΝΑΩΝ
ΗΔΕΑ ΚΩΤΙΛΛΟΝΤΑ ΚΑΘΗΜΕΝΟΝ ΟΙΝΟΠΟΤΑΖΕΙΝ.

PHOC. *ap. Ath.*

[*This is a distich by wise old Phocylides,*
An ancient who wrote crabbed Greek in no silly days;
Meaning, " 'TIS RIGHT FOR GOOD WINE-BIBBING PEOPLE,
NOT TO LET THE JUG PACE ROUND THE BOARD LIKE A CRIPPLE;
BUT GAILY TO CHAT WHILE DISCUSSING THEIR TIPPLE."
An excellent rule of the hearty old cock'tis—
And a very fit motto to put to our Noctes.]

C. N. *ap. Ambr.*

DRAMATIS PERSONÆ.

CHRISTOPHER NORTH.
THE ETTRICK SHEPHERD.
TIMOTHY TICKLER.
THE ENGLISH OPIUM-EATER.
COLONEL CYRIL THORNTON.
MULLION, *A Gentleman from the West.*
BULLER, *An Englishman.*
THE REGISTRAR.
AMBROSE, *Mine Host.*
NATHAN GURNEY, *the Reporter for the "Noctes."*
MRS. GENTLE, *a Widow.*
MISS GENTLE.
BRONTE, *a veteran Newfoundlander.*
O'BRONTE, *a young Newfoundlander.*
A Cat, a Parrot, a Starling, a Raven, &c.
The Jug.
TAPPYTOORIE, PICARDY, SIR DAVID GAM, KING PEPIN, *and others, Servants to* AMBROSE.

The Scenes are laid at Ambrose's Tavern in Edinburgh; Buchanan Lodge, on the Firth of Forth; St. Mary's Loch; the Ettrick Forest, and elsewhere.

THE CONTENTS.

XVIII.

XIX.

XX.

XXI.

XXII.

XXIII.

XXIV.

XXV.

XXVI.

THE INTRODUCTION.

JOHN WILSON had the eagle beak, the lion-like mane of the Napiers. Mrs. Barrett Browning has said of Homer:—

> "Homer, with the broad suspense
> Of thund'rous brows, and lips intense
> Of garrulous god-innocence"—

and whenever I read the lines, the mighty presence of Christopher North rises before me. John Wilson was an immense man, physically and mentally, and yet his nature was essentially incomplete. He needed concentration. Had the tree been thoroughly pruned, the fruit would have been larger and richer. As it was, he seldom contrived to sustain the inspiration unimpaired for any time; it ran away into shallows, and spread fruitlessly over the sand. In many respects one of the truest, soundest, honestest men who ever lived, he used to grow merely declamatory at times. Amazingly humorous as the Shepherd of the "Noctes" is (there are scenes, such as the opening of the haggis and the swimming match with

Tickler while the London packet comes up the Forth, which manifest the humor of conception as well as the humor of character, in a measure that has seldom been surpassed by the greatest masters), his fun is often awkward, and his enthusiasm is apt to tire. Yet had Shakespeare written about Falstaff once a month for twenty years, might we not possibly have said the same even of him? And if the Shepherd at his best could be taken out of the "Noctes" and compressed into a compact duodecimo volume, we should have an original piece of imaginative humor, which might fitly stand for all time by the side of the portly knight. But the world is two crowded and too busy to preserve a creation which is not uniformly at its best,—which, on the contrary, is diffused and diluted through forty volumes of a magazine; and so it is possible that, not quite unwillingly, posterity will let the Shepherd die. The same in a way holds true of Christopher's own fame. The moralist has told us from of old that only the mortal part of genius returns to the dust. But then this moral part was so large a part of Wilson. He was such a magnificent man! No literary man of our time has had such muscles and sinews, such an ample chest, such perfect lungs, such a stalwart frame, such an expansive and Jove-like brow. Had he lived in the classic ages they would have made a god of him,—not because he wrote good verses, or possessed the divine gift of eloquence, but because his presence was godlike. There was a ruddy glow of health about him, too, such as the people of no nation have possessed as a nation since the culture of the body, as an art of the national life, has been neglected. The critic, therefore, who never saw Wilson, cannot rightly estimate the sources of his influence. We, on the contrary, who looked upon him, who heard him speak, know that we can never listen to his like again ; never can look upon one who, while so intellectually noble, so eloquent, so flushed with poetic life, did so nearly approach, in strength and comeliness, the type of bodily perfection. The picture of the old man eloquent in his college class-room—the old man who had breasted the flooded Awe, and cast his fly across the bleakest tarns of Lochaber—pacing restlessly to and fro like a lion in his confined cage, his grand face working with emotion while he turns to the window, through which are obscurely visible the spires and smoky gables of the ancient city, his dilated nostril yet "full of youth," his small grey eye alight with visionary fire, as he discourses (somewhat discursively, it must be owned) of truth, and beauty, and goodness, is one not to be forgotten. Had he talked the merest twaddle, the effect would have been very nearly the same: he was a living poem where the austere grandeur of the old drama was united with the humor and tenderness of modern story-tellers ; and some such feeling it was that attracted and fascinated his hearers.

It has been said by unfriendly critics that Wilson was an egotist. Montaigne and Charles Lamb were egotists ; but we do not complain of an egotism to which not the least charm of their writings is to be attributed. The truth is that the charge against Wilson rests on a misconception. Christopher North was egotistical, but Christopher North was a creation of the imagination. He represented to the world the invincible Tory champion, before whose crutch the whole breed of Radicals and Whiglings and Cockneys fled as mists before the sun. It was impossible to endow this gouty Apollo with the frailties of mortal combatants. Haughty scorn, immaculate wisdom, unassailable virtue, were the characteristics of the potent tyrant. We have as little right to say that Wilson was an egotist because Christopher North was egotistical (though, no doubt, in his old age, he could have *looked* the part admirably), as to say that Milton was immoral because he drew the devil. Men (whiggish and priggish) may continue to resent, indeed, as indelicate and unbecoming, the license of his fancy and the airy extravagance of his rhetoric; but a juster and more catholic criticism confesses that in the wide realms of literature there is room for the grotesque gambols of Puck, for Attiel's moonlight flittings, for the imaginative riot of Wilson and Heine and Jean Paul.

These sentences—written several years ago—may serve to explain how the idea of the present work first presented itself to me. My design has been to compress into a single manageable volume whatever is permanent and whatever is universal in the Comedy of the "Noctes Ambrosianæ." The "Noctes" are conceived in the true spirit of Comedy, using the word in its widest sense, and their presentation of human life is as keen, as broad, and as mellow as that of any of our dramatists. In this great play among various subordinate characters, three figures stand out with surprising force,—Christopher North, Timothy Tickler, and the Ettrick Shepherd. During these hundred-and-one ambrosial nights, what heights of the poetical imagination are scaled, what depths of the human soul are sounded, by the immortal "Three!" While the whole is bathed in an atmosphere of natural humor, of irrepressible fun, of laughter that is not the less genuine because it is at times closely akin to tears.

But the true unity of the piece is obscured by the introduction of much foreign matter. It is overlaid and smothered by protracted discussions upon topics of transient, personal, and local interest only. In the "Noctes," political events and notabilities that are no of interest to no living creature—romances which flourished for a season, poems which have been swept into oblivion—are criticised at unreasonable, or at least unreadable, length. Many of the smaller social and political portraits are first-rate of their kind,—such play of the imagination, such splendor, versatility, and, it must be added, ferocity of invective as "The Glasgow Gander," for instance, provoked by his assault on Walter Scott, are to be found nowhere else in our literature since the days of Dryden. But the "Gander" is dead; and even the most patient reader tires of controversies which, though perfectly suited to the pages of a critical journal or a party review, are entirely out of place in a permanent work of the artistic imagination.

It was clear, therefore, that if these excrescences could be conveniently detached, the true dramatic unity of the Comedy would be made manifest and emphasized; and the question then came to be,—Was such separation possible without vital injury to the whole, without reducing the entire building to mere fragmentary ruin? It appeared to me that it was possible; and this volume will enable the reader to judge whether my conviction was well founded. The operation was, I admit, a difficult and delicate one, and I cannot hope that it has been perfectly successful. Passages have been omitted which might have been retained, and passages have been retained which might have been omitted. But I have tried, as far as practicable, by preventing any dialogue from being broken into mere fragments, to preserve the current and continuity of the narrative. The *lacunæ*, I suspect, are sometimes visible to the naked eye; but on the whole I do not feel that they are likely to affect the reader's enjoyment, or that they mar the general effect—the *tout-an-sammal*, as the Shepherd would say—of an almost unique piece of dramatic humor. In what seemed to be a case of doubt, I have inclined to lean rather to the side of brevity than of prolixity. Many of the descriptive passages belong to what may be called the florid order of literary style; and these do not suffer, but on the contrary are improved, by moderate retrenchment and compression.

One of the most difficult duties devolving on a writer of books in these days is to find an appropriate and unappropriated title—to know what to call his work; and it has been suggested that an author in such straits should "request the prayers of the congregation." Even a mere editor has difficulties in his way, —as the present editor has discovered. To have called this volume the "Noctes Ambrosianæ" might have produced a false impression, seeing that it does not contain more than a third of the matter which the "Noctes" written by Professor Wilson contained. On the other hand, it is a selection made upon a definite principle; so that to have called it a volume of "Selections" would not have sufficiently indicated its scope and design. The word required was one which could be fitly applied to that portion of the work which deals with, or presents directly and dramatically to the reader, human life, and character, and passion, as distinguished from that portion of it which is *critical*, and devoted to the discussion of subjects of literary, artistic, or political interest only. The word "Comedy" (although liable from modern use or abuse to be misunderstood) ultimately appeared to me to be the most suitable; for, even if misunderstood the misunderstanding could not be very serious. It may in fact be said with perfect truth that, although the *substance* of the Discussion or Debate in which the "Three" engage is often grave, and not unfrequently pathetic, the *presentation* is essentially humorous,—the surroundings being whimsical, and the situations mirth-provoking. The "Noctes Ambrosianæ," as a characteristic product of the dramatic spirit, belongs to the Comic Muse.

The papers from which the materials of the present volume are taken, appeared in "Blackwood's Magazine" during the ten years from 1825 to 1835.

I should not be doing justice to my own feelings if I were to close this prefatory note without a brief tribute to the editor of the original edition of the "Noctes,"—James Frederick Ferrier.*

Ferrier was a philosophical Quixote,—a man who loved "divine philosophy" for its own sake. The student of pure metaphysics is now rarely met with; the age of mechanical invention—of the steam-engine and the telegraph—being disposed to regard the proverbially barren fields of psychology with disrelish and disrespect. Against this materalizing tendency, Professor Ferrier's life was an uninterrupted and essentially noble protest. No truer, simpler, or more unselfish student ever lived. Seated in his pleasant rustic library, amid its stores of curious and antiquated erudition, he differed as much from the ordinary men one meets in the law courts or on "'Change," as the quaint academic city where he resided differs from Salford or Birmingham. It was here—in his library—that Ferrier spent the best of his days; here that he

* The present edition is based upon that edited by Professor Ferrier. The material passages of the Preface which he contributed are reprinted in the Appendix. The Notes also are mainly taken from that edition, which must always remain the standard, and, so to speak, classical edition of the "Noctes Ambrosianæ."

commented on the Greek psychologists, or explored the intricacies of the Hegelian logic; and for Hegel (be it said in passing) he entertained an immense, and, considering the character of his own mind—its clearness, directness, and love of terseness and epigram—somewhat inexplicable admiration. At the same time he was no mere bookworm. He did not succeed, and did not try to succeed, at the Scottish bar, to which he was called; but he had many of the qualities—subtlety of thought, lucidity of expression, power of arrangement—which ought to have secured success. He took a keen interest in the letters and politics of the day. His own style was brilliant and trenchant, and it was probably the slovenliness and inelegance of Reid (which even the studied art and succinct power of Hamilton have been unable to conceal or repair) which drove him into the camp of the enemy. He was considered, in orthodox philosophical circles, somewhat of a free lance. He had a sharp scorn for laborious dulness and pretentious futility,—a scorn which he took no pains to disguise. When he descended into the controversial arena, he was sure to be in the thickest of the *mêlée*. He hit right and left; quietly, deftly, for the most part, it is true, yet with a force and precision which it was unpleasant to provoke and difficult to resist. If his life should be written hereafter, let his biographer take for its motto the five words of the "Faery Queen," which the biographer of the Napiers has so happily chosen—"*Fierce warres and faithful loves.*" For though combative over his books and his theories, his nature was singularly pure, affectionate, and tolerant. He loved his friends even better than he hated his foes. His prejudices were invincible; but apart from his prejudices, his mind was open and receptive,—prepared to welcome truth from whatever quarter it came. Ferrier, other than a high Tory, is an impossible conception to his friends; yet had he been the most pronounced of Radicals, he could not have returned more constantly to first principles, nor showed more speculative fearlessness. He was, in fact, an intrepid and daring reasoner, who allowed few formulas, political, ecclesiastical, or ethical, to cramp his mind, or restrain the free play of his intellectual faculties. This contrast, no doubt, presents an air of paradox; but Ferrier's character, as well as his logic, was sometimes paradoxical. He was a man of infinite subtlety, and he liked to play with his fancies,—to place them under strong lights, and in unusual attitudes; but he possessed a fund of humor and common-sense which made him on the whole a sound and discerning student of human nature. He was content to spend his days in contemplative retirement; but every one who has seen him must have remarked a certain eager look—an eagerness of gesture and of speech—which indicated quite other than a sluggish repose. He united with a peculiar sensitiveness of constitution and fineness of critical faculty, a sturdy and indomitable soul. His frame, in his latter years at least, was slim and attenuated; but to the end he was one of the manliest of men. He was capable of becoming on occasion, as I have indicated, hotly, and it may be unreasonably indignant. Perhaps to this original fire and fineness of nature his early decline is to be attributed. The fiery soul 'fretted the pigmy body to decay." Taken from us in the prime of life and in the vigor of his powers, the death of such a man is a loss to our philosophical schools not quickly to be repaired; to his relatives, to his disciples, to his students—to all who knew him in the easy intercourse of social life—the loss is irreparable. Apart altogether from those qualities of heart and intellect, of which the world knows, or may yet know, his friends will not soon forget his refined simplicity of manner,—a manner perfectly unaffected, peculiar to himself, and indicating a remarkable delicacy of organization, yet smacking somehow of the high breeding and chivalrous courtesy of that old-fashioned school of Scottish gentlemen whom he had known in his youth, and of which he remained the represen tative.

J. S.

THE HERMITAGE OF BRAID,
11*th May*, 1876.

NOCTES AMBROSIANÆ.

I.

IN WHICH CHRISTOPHER NORTH, TIMOTHY TICKLER, AND THE ETTRICK SHEPHERD ARE INTRODUCED TO THE READER.

Blue Parlor.— Midnight.— Watchman heard crying " One o'clock."

NORTH.—TICKLER.—THE ETTRICK SHEPHERD.
The middle Term asleep.

Shepherd. Sir, I wish there was ony waukening o' Mr Tickler. It's no' like him to fa' asleep. Whisht! whisht! Hear till him! hear till him!

North. Somnium Scipionis!

Tickler (asleep). It was creditable to a British public. Poor dear little soul, she has been cruelly treated altogether. My sweet Miss Lætitia Foote,* although I am now rather——

Shepherd. Isna the wicked auld deevil dreamin' o' that play actress!

Tickler (dormiens). Three times three.—Hurra! hurra! hurra!

Shepherd. That's fearsome. Only think how his mind corresponds wi' his friends, even in a dwam o' drink,—for I

* Afterwards the Countess of Harrington.

never saw him sae fou since the king's visit! I'll just pu the nose o' him, or kittle it wi' the neb o' my keelivine pen.* (*Sic facit.*)

Tickler (*awaking*). The cases are totally different. But, Hogg, what are you staring at? Why, you have been sleeping since twelve o'clock.

Shepherd. I hae some thocht o' writing a play,—a Pastoral Drama.

North. What, James? After Allan Ramsay—after the *Gentle Shepherd?*

Shepherd. What for no? That's a stupid apothegm, though you said it. I wad hae mair variety o' characters, and inceedents, and passions o' the human mind in my drama—mair fun, and frolic and daffin†—in short, mair o' what you, and the like o' you, ca' coorseness;—no sae muckle see-sawing between ony twa individual hizzies, as in Allan; and, aboon a' things, a mair natural and wiselike ‡ catastrophe. My peasant or shepherd lads should be sae in richt earnest, and no turn out Sirs and Lords upon you at the hinder end o' the drama. No but that I wad aiblins introduce the upper ranks intil the wark; but they should stand abeigh frae§ the lave o' the characters,—by way o' "similitude in dissimilitude," as that haverer ‖ Wordsworth is sae fond o' talking and writing about. Aboon a' things, I wuss to draw the pictur o' a perfect and polished Scotch gentleman o' the auld schule.

North Videlicet, —Tickler!

Shepherd. Him, the lang-legged sinner! Na, na; I'll immortalize baith him and yoursel in my "Ain Life,"—in my yawtobeeografly. I'll pay aff a' auld scores there, I'se warrant you. Deevil tak me gin ¶ I haena a great mind—(*a*

* *Keelivine*—chalk pencil.
† *Daffin*—humorsome nonsense.
‡ *Wiselike*—judicious.
§ *Abeigh frae*—aloof from
‖ *Haverer*—proser.
¶ *Gin*—if.

pause,—jug)—to hawn * you down to the latest posterity as a couple o'——

North. James !—James !—James !

Shepherd. Confound thae grey glittering een o' yours, you warlock that you are! I maun like you, and respeck you, and admire you too, Mr. North; but och, sirs! do you ken that whiles I just girn, out-by yonner, wi' perfect wudness † when I think o' you, and your chiels about you, lauchin' at and rinnin' down me, and ither men o' genius——

North. James !—James !—James !

Tickler. Dig it well into him—he is a confounded churl.

Shepherd. No half sae bad as yoursel, Mr. Tickler. He's serious sometimes, and ane kens when he is serious. But as for you, there's no a grain o' sincerity in a' your composition. You wadna shed a tear gin your Shepherd, as you ca' him, were dead, and in the moulds.

Tickler (evidently much affected). Have I not left you my fiddle in my will? When I am gone, Jamie, use her carefully —keep her in good strings—and whenever you screw her up, think of Timothy Tickler—and——(*His utterance is choked.*)

North. James! James! James!— Timothy! Timothy! Timothy!— Something too much of this. Reach me over that pamphlet; I wish to light my cigar. The last speech and dying words of the Rev. William Lisle Bowles!

Shepherd. What! a new poem? I houp it is. Lisle Bolls is a poet o' real genius. I never could thole a sonnet till I read his. Is the pamphlet a poem?

North. No Shepherd. It is prose; being a further portion of Botheration about Pope. ‡

* *Hawn*—hand. † *Wudness*—distraction.

‡ The "botheration about Pope" refers to a protracted controversy originating in a dispute between Bowles and Campbell, as to whether nature or art supplied the better materials for poetry. Most of the leading literary men of the day had been drawn into the discussion.

Shepherd. I care little about Pop—except his Louisa and Abelard. That's a grand elegy; but for coorseness it beats me hollow. . . . Puir wee bit hunched-backed, windle-strae-legged, gleg-eed, * clever, acute, ingenious, sateerical, weel-informed, warm-hearted, real philosphical, and maist poetical creature, wi' his sounding translation o' a' Homer's works, that reads just like an original War Yepic,—his Yessay on Man, that, in spite o' what a set o' ignoramuses o' theological critics say about Bolingbroke and Crousass, and heterodoxy and atheism, and like havers, is just ane o' the best moral discourses that ever I heard in or out o' the pulpit,—his Yepistles about the Passions, and sic like, in the whilk he goes baith deep and high, far deeper and higher baith than mony a modern poet, who must needs be either in a diving-bell or a balloon,—his Rape o' the Lock o' Hair, wi' a' these sylphs floating about in the machinery o' the Rosicrucian Philosophism, just perfectly yelegant and gracefu', and as gude, in their way, as onything o' my ain about fairies, either in the *Queen's Wake* or *Queen Hynde,*—his Louisa to Abelard is, as I said before, coorse in the subject-matter, but, O sirs! powerfu' and pathetic in execution—and sic a perfect spate † o' versification! His unfortunate lady, wha sticked hersel' for love wi' a drawn sword, and was afterwards seen as a ghost, dim-beckoning through the shade—a verra poetical thoct surely, and full both of terror and pity——

North. Stop, James—you will run yourself out of breath. Why, you said, a few minutes ago, that you did not care much about Pope, and were not at all familiar with his works—you have them at your finger ends.

Shepherd. I never ken what's in my mind till it begins to work. Sometimes I fin' mysel just perfectly stupid—my mind, as Locke says in his *Treatise on Government,* quite a

* *Gleg-eed*—sharp-eyed. † *Spate*—stream in flood.

carte blanche—I just ken that I'm alive by my breathing, when, a' at ance, my sowl begins to hum like a hive about to cast off a swarm—out rush a thousand springing thochts, for a while circling round and round like verra bees—and then, like them too, winging their free and rejoicing way into the mountain wilderness and a' its blooming heather—returning, in due time, with store o' wax on their thees, and a wamefu' o' hinney, redolent of blissful dreams gathered up in the sacred solitudes of nature.

Tickler. Bowles also depreciates his genius.

North. No, no, no!

Tickler. Yes, yes, yes!

Shepherd. Gude save us, Mr. Tickler, you're no sober yet, or you wad never contradic Mr. North.

Tickler. Bowles also depreciates his genius. What infernal stuff all that, about nature and art! Why, Pope himself settles the question against our friend Bowles in one line :—

"Nature must give way to Art."

North. Pope's poetry is full of nature, at least of what I have been in the constant habit of accounting nature for the last threescore and ten years. But (thank you, James, that snuff is really delicious!) leaving nature and art, and all that sort of thing, I wish to ask a single question—What poet of this age, with the exception perhaps of Byron, can be justly said, when put into close comparison with Pope, to have written the English language at all?

Shepherd. Tut, tut, Mr. North; you needna gang far to get an answer to that question. I can write the English language—I'll no say as well as Pop, for he was an Englishman, but——

North. Well, I shall except you, James; but, with the single exception of Hogg, from what living poet is it possible to select any passage that will bear to be spouted (say by

James Ballantyne * himself, the best declaimer extant) after any one of fifty casually taken passages from Pope?—Not one.

Tickler. What would become of Bowles himself, with all his elegànce, pathos, and true feeling? Oh, dear me, James! what a dull, dozing, disjointed, dawdling dowdy of a drawl would be his Muse, in her very best voice and tune, when called upon to get up and sing a solo after the sweet and strong singer of Twickenham!

North. Or Wordsworth—with his eternal—Here we go up, up, and up, and here we go down, down, and here we go roundabout, roundabout! Look at the nerveless laxity of his *Excursion!* What interminable prosing! The language is out of condition,—fat and fozy, thick-winded, purfled and plethoric. Can he be compared with Pope? Fie on't! no, no, no!—Pugh, pugh!

Tickler. Southey—Coleridge—Moore?

North. No; not one of them. They are all eloquent, diffusive rich, lavish, generous, prodigal of their words. But so are they all deficient in sense, muscle, sinew, thews, ribs, spine. Pope, as an artist, beats them hollow. Catch him twaddling.

Shepherd. I care far less about Pop, and the character and genius of Pop, than I do about our own Byron. Many a cruel thing has been uttered against him, and I wish, Mr. North, you would vindicate him, now that his hand is cauld.

North. I have written a few pages for my next number, which I think will please you, James. Pray, what do you consider the most wicked act of Byron's whole wicked life?

Shepherd. I declare to God, that I do not know of any one wicked act in his life at all. Tickler, there, used to cut him up long ago,—what says he now?

* The friend of Sir Walter Scott.

Tickler. The base multitude, day after day, week after week, month after month, year after year, got up brutal falsehoods concerning his private life, and these they mixed up and blended with their narrow and confused conceptions of his poetical productions, till they imagined the real, living, flesh-and-blood Byron to be a monster, familiarly known to them in all his hideous propensities and practices. He was, with all his faults, a noble being, and I shall love Hobhouse* as long as I live. What it is to be a gentleman!

North. The character of one of the greatest poets the world ever saw, in a very few years, will be discerned in the clear light of truth. How quickly all misrepresentations die away! One hates calumny, because it is ugly and odious in its own insignificant and impotent stinking self. But it is almost always extremely harmless. I believe at this moment that Byron is thought of as a man, with an almost universal feeling of pity, forgiveness, admiration and love. I do not think it would be safe in the most popular preacher to abuse Byron now,—and that not merely because he is now dead, but because England knows the loss she has sustained in the extinction of her most glorious luminary.

Shepherd. I hae nae heart to speak ony mair about him—puir fallow. I'll try the pickled this time—the scalloped are beginning to lie rather heavy on my stomach. Oysters is the only thing maist we canna get at Altrive. But we have capital cod and haddock now in St. Mary's Loch.

Tickler. James!—James!—James!

Shepherd. Nane o' your jeering, Mr. Tickler. The naturalization of sea-fishes into fresh-water lochs was recommended some years ago in the *Edinburgh Review*, and twa-three 'o us, out by yonner, have carried the thing into effect.

* John Cam Hobhouse, afterwards Lord Broughton--the friend of Byron when living, and his defender when dead.

We tried the oysters too, but we could mak nathing ava o' them—they dwindled into a kind o' wulks, and were quite fushionless,* a' beards and nae bodies.

Tickler. I thought the scheme plausible at the time. I read it in the *Edinburgh*, which I like, by the way, much better as a zoological than a political journal. Have you sent a creel of codlings to the editor ?

Shepherd. Why, I have felt some delicacy about it just at present. I was afraid that he might think it a bribe for a favorable opinion of *Queen Hynde.*†

North. No,—no. Jeffrey has a soul above bribery or corruption. All the cod in Christendom would not shake his integrity. You had, however, better send half-a-dozen rizzered haddocks to Tom Campbell.

Shepherd. My boy Tammy wull never choke himself wi' my fish-banes, Mr. North.

North. Tom is fickle and capricious—and ever was so—but he has a fine, a noble genius.

Shepherd. I'm no dispooting that, Mr. North. No doubt, his *Theodric* is a grand, multifarious, sublime poem ; although, confound me, gin the worst fifty lines in a' *Queen Hynde* are nae worth the haill vollumm. . . . Wha's conceit ‡ was the boiler ?

Tickler. Your humble servant's. Ambrose goes to bed regularly at twelve, and Richard half an hour after. Occasionally, as at present, old friends are loath to go—so, not to disturb the slumbers of as worthy a family as is in all Scotland, I ordered the boiler you now see at Begby and Dickson's, St. Andrew Square. It holds exactly six common kettlefuls. Strike it with the poker.—Ay, James, you hear by the clearness of the tinkle that it is nearly low water.

* *Fushionless*—without sap.

† A poem by Hogg, published in 1825.

‡ *Conceit*—notion.

Shepherd. Deel ma care. I ken where the pump is in the back green—and if the wall's fanged,* I'll bring up a gush wi' a single drive. If no, let us finish the spirits by itsel'. I never saw the match o' this tall square fallow o' a green bottle for hauding spirits. The verra neck o' him hauds spirits for a jug, before you get down to his shouthers; and we'se a' three be blin' fou or we see the crystal knob inside o' the doup o' him peering up amang the subsiding waters of Glenlivet.

North. I have bequeathed you Magog in my settlement, James. With it, and Tickler's Cremona, many a cheerful night will you spend, when we two old codgers have laid off life's pack—

At our feet a green grass turf,
And at our head a stone.

Shepherd. You and Mr. Tickler are very gude in leaving me things in your wull; but I would prefer something in haun———

North. Then, my dear friend, there is a receipt for your last article—the Shepherd's Calendar.

Shepherd. Twa tens! Come noo,sirs, let me pay the reckoning. . . . Are ye gaun to raise the price of a sheet this Lady-day, Mr. North?

North. My dear Hogg, what would you have? You are rolling in wealth—are you not?

Hogg. Ay; but I wad like fine to be ower the head a'thegither, man. That's my apothegm.

North. Let me see—Well, I think I may promise you a twenty-gallon tree this next Whitsunday, by way of a douceur—a small perquisite.

Hogg. Twenty gallons, man,—that does not serve our house for sax weeks in the summer part of the year, when

* When the piston of a pump-well ceases to work from having become too dry, water is poured down upon it to restore the action. This operation is called *fanging* the well.

a' the leeterary warld is tramping about. But ne'er heed—mony thanks to you for your kind offer, sir.

North. You must come down to my "happy rural seat of various view," James, on your spring visit to Edinburgh—Buchanan Lodge.

Shepherd. Wi' a' my heart, Mr. North. I hear you've been biggin a bonny lodge near Larkfield yonder, within the murmur of the sea. A walk on the beach is a gran' thing for an appetite. Let's hear about your house.

North. The whole tenement is on the ground flat. I abhor stairs; and there can be no peace in any mansion where heavy footsteps may be heard overhead. Suppose James, three sides of a square. You approach the front by a fine serpentine avenue, and enter, slap-bang, through a wide glass door, into a greenhouse, a conservatory of everything rich and rare in the world of flowers. Folding doors are drawn noiselessly into the walls, as if by magic, and lo! drawing-room and dining-room, stretching east and west in dim and distant perspective, commanding the Firth, the sea, the kingdom of Fife, and the Highland mountains!

Shepherd. Mercy on us, what a panorama!

North. Another side of the square contains kitchen, servants' room, etc.; and the third side my study and bedrooms,—all still, silent, composed, standing obscure, unseen, unapproachable, holy. The fourth side of the square is not,—shrubs, and trees, and a productive garden shut me from behind; while a ring-fence, enclosing about five acres, just sufficient for my nag and cow, form a magical circle, into which nothing vile or profane can intrude. O'Doherty alone has overleaped my wall,—but the Adjutant was in training for his great match (ten miles an hour), and when he ran bolt against me in Addison's Walk,* declared upon

* So named after the celebrated walk in the Grounds of Magdalen College, Oxford, where Professor Wilson was educated.

honor that he was merely taking a step across the country, and that he had no idea of being within a mile of any human abode. However, he stayed dinner—and over the Sunday.

Shepherd. Do you breed poultry, sir?—You dinna? Do't then. You hae plenty o' bounds within five yacre. But mind you, big* nae regular hen-house, You'll hae bits o' sheds, nae doubt, ahint the house, amang, the offishes, and through amang the grounds; and the belts o' plantations are no very wide, nor the sherubberies stravagin awa into wild mountainous regions o' heather, whins, and breckans.

North. Your imagination, James, is magnificent, even in negatives. But is all this poetry about hen-roosts?

Shepherd. Ay. Let the creturs mak their ain nests where'er they like pheasants, or patricks, or muirfowl. Their flesh will be the sappier, and mair highly flavored on the board, and their shape and plummage beautifuller far, strutting about at liberty among your suburbs. Aboon a' things, for the love o' heevin, nae cavies! † I can never help greeting, half in anger half in pity, when I see the necks o' some half-a-score forlorn chuckies jouking out and in the narrow bars o' their prison-house, dabbing at daigh and drummock.‡ I wonder if Mrs Fry ever saw sic a pitiful spectacle.

North. I must leave the feathers to my females, James.

Shepherd. Canna you be an overseer? Let the hens aye set theirsels; and never offer to tak ony notice o' the clockers. They canna thole being looked at when they come screeching out frae their het eggs, a' in a ever, with their feathers tapsetowry, and howking holes in the yearth, till the gravel gangs down-through and aff among the plummage like dewdraps, and now scouring aff to some weel-kend corner for drink and victual.

* *Big*—build. † *Cavies*—hen-coops.

‡ *Daigh and drummock*—dough and cold porridge.

North. You amaze me, James. You are opening up quite a new world to me. The mysteries of incubation . . .

Hogg. Hae a regular succession o' Clackins frae about the mid o' March till the end o' August, and never devour aff a haill clackin at ance. Aye keep some three or four pullets for eerocks, or for devouring through the winter; and never set aboon fourteen eggs to ae hen, nor indeed mair than a dizzen, unless she be a weel-feathered mawsie,* and broad across the shoulders.

North. Why, the place will be absolutely overrun with barn-door fowl.

Shepherd. Barn-door fowl! Hoot awa! You maun hae a greed o' gem-birds. Nane better than the lady-legg'd reds. I ken the verra gem-eggs at the first pree frae your dunghill —a different as a pine-apple and fozy turnip.

North. The conversation has taken an unexpected turn, my dear Shepherd. I had intended keeping a few deer.

Shepherd. A few deevils ! Na—na. You maun gang to the Thane's; † or if that princely chiel be in Embro' or Lunnon, to James Laidlaw's and Watty Bryden's, in Strathglass, if you want deer. Keep you to the how-towdies.

North. I hope, Mr. Hogg, you will bring the mistress and the weans to the house-warming ?

Shepherd. I'll do that, and mony mair besides them. Whare the deevil's Mr. Tickler?

North. Off. He pretended to go to the pump for an aquatic supply, but he long ere now has reached Southside.‡

* An easy-tempered, somewhat slovenly female is called in Scotland a *mawsie.*

† The Thane was the Earl of Fife, whose estates in Braemar abound in red deer. James Laidlaw and Walter Bryden were sheep farmers in Strathglass. The former was the brother of William Laidlaw, Sir Walter Scott's friend and factor.

‡ Mr. Robert Sym, of whom Timothy Tickler was in some respects the eidolon, resided in No. 20 George Square, on the *south side* of Edinburgh.

Shepherd. That's maist extraordinar. I could hae ta'en my Bible oath that I kept seeing him a' this time sitting right foreanent me, with his lang legs and nose, and een like daggers; but it must hae been ane o' Hibbert's phantasms—an idea has become more vivid than a present sensation. Is that philosophical language? What took him aff? I could sit for ever. Catch me breaking up the conviviality of the company. I'm just in grand spirits the nicht—come, here's an extempore lilt.

AIR, "*Whistle, and I'll come to ye, my lad.*"

If e'er you would be a brave fellow, young man,
Beware of the Blue and the Mellow, * young man;
If ye wud be strang,
And wish to write lang,
Come, join wi' the lads that get Mellow, young man.
Like the crack o' a squib that has fa'en on, young man,
Compared wi' the roar o' a cannon, young man,
So is the Whig's blow
To the pith that's below
The beard o' auld Geordie Buchanan, † young man.

Re-enter TICKLER.

Shepherd. There's Harry Longleggs.

Tickler. I felt somewhat hungry so long after supper, and having detected a round of beef in a cupboard, I cut off a segment of a circle, and have been making myself comfortable at the solitary kitchen fire.

North (*rising*). Come away, my young friend. Give me your arm, James. That will do, Shepherd—softly, slowly, my dearest Hogg—no better supporter than the author of the *Queen's Wake.*

Shepherd. What a gran' ticker is Mr. Ambrose's clock! It

* The "Blue and the Yellow" is the *Edinburgh Review.*

† The *effigies* of George Buchanan is the frontispiece to *Blackwood's Magazine.*

beats like the strong, regular pulse of a healthy horse. Whirr! whirr! whirr! Hear till her gi'eing the warning. I'll just finish these twa half tumblers o' porter, and the wee drappie in the bit blue noseless juggy. As sure's death, it has chapped three. The lass that sits up at the Harrow *'ll hae gane to the garret, and how'll I get in?

(*Sus canit.*)—O let me in this ae night,
This ae ae ae night, etc.

With a' our daffin, we are as sober as three judges with double gowns.

Tickler. As sober!

Mr. AMBROSE *looks out in his nightcap, wishing good-night with his usual suavity. Exeunt*—TICKLER *in advance—and* NORTH *leaning on the* SHEPHERD.

* The sign of the hostelrie near the Grassmarket where Hogg resided when in Edinburgh.

II.

IN WHICH TICKLER NARRATES HIS EXPERIENCES AT DALNACARDOCH.

North. Let us have some sensible conversation, Timothy At our time of life such colloquy is becoming.

Tickler. Why the devil would you not come to Dalnacardoch ? * Glorious guffawing all night, and immeasurable murder all day. Twenty-seven brace of birds, nine hares, three roes, and a red deer stained the heather on the Twelfth, beneath my single-barrelled Joe—not to mention a pair of patriarchal ravens, and the Loch-Ericht eagle, whose leg was broken by the Prince when hiding in the moor of Rannoch.

North. Why kill the royal bird ?

Tickler. In self-defence. It bore down upon Sancho like a sunbeam from its eyrie on the cliff of Snows, and it would have broken his back with one stroke of its wing, had I not sent a ball right through its heart. It went up, with a yell, a hundred fathom into the clear blue air ; and then, striking a green knoll in the midst of the heather, bounded down the rocky hill-side, and went shivering and whizzing along the black surface of a tarn, till it lay motionless in a huge heap among the water lilies.

North. Lost ?

Tickler. I stripped instanter—six feet four and three-quar-

* A shooting-quarter in the highlands of Perthshire, occupied in the summer of 1825 by some friends of Professor Wilson.

ters *in puris naturalibus*—and out-Byroning Byron, shot in twenty seconds, a furlong across the Fresh. Grasping the bird of Jove in my right, with my left I rowed my airy state towards the spot where I had left my breeches and other habiliments. Espying a trimmer, I seized it in my mouth, and on relanding at a small natural pier, as I hope to be shaved, lo! a pike of twenty-pound standing, with a jaw like an alligator, and reaching from my hip to my instep, smote the heather, like a flail, into a shower of blossoms.

North. Was there a cloud of witnesses?

Tickler. To be sure there was. A hundred stills beheld me from the mountain-sides. Shepherd and smuggler cheered me like voices in the sky; and the old genius of the solitary place rustled applause through the reeds and rushes, and birch-trees among the rocks—paced up and down the shore in triumph . . .

North. What a subject for the painter! Oh that Sir Thomas Lawrence * or our own John Watson, † had been there to put you on canvas! Or shall I rather say, would that Chantrey had been by to study you for immortal marble!

Tickler. Braced by the liquid plunge, I circled the tarn at ten miles an hour. Unconsciously I had taken my Manton into my hand—and unconsciously reloaded—when, just as I was clearing the feeder-stream, not less than five yards across up springs a red deer, who, at the death of the eagle, had cowered down in the brake, and wafted away his antlers in the direction of Benvoirlich. We were both going at the top of our speed when I fired, and the ball piercing his spine the magnificent creature sunk down, and died almost without a convulsion.

* Sir Thomas Lawrence died in 1830.

† Afterwards Sir John Watson Gordon, President of the Royal Scottish Academy.

North. Red deer, eagle, and pike, all dead as mutton!

Tickler. I sat down upon the forehead, resting an arm on each antler—Sancho sitting with victorious eyes on the carcase. I sent him off to the tarn-side for my pocket-pistol, charged with Glenlivet No. 5. In a few minutes he returned, and crouched down with an air of mortification at my feet.

North. Ho! ho! the fairies have spirited away your nether integuments!

Tickler. Not an article to be seen!—save and except my shoes!—Jacket, waistcoat, flannel shirt, breeches, all melted away with the mountain dew! There was I like Adam in Paradise, or—

> "Lady of the Mere,
> Sole-sitting by the shores of old romance."

North. Did not the dragon-flies attack you—the winged ants—and the wasp of the desert?

Tickler. A figure moved along the horizon—a female figure—a Light and Shadow of Celtic Life—and, as I am a Christian, I beheld my buckskin breeches dangling over her shoulders. I neared upon the chase, but saw that Malvina was making for a morass. Whiz went a ball within a stride of her petticoats, and she deflected her course towards a wood on the right. She dropped our breeches. I literally leaped into them; and, like Apollo in pursuit of Daphne, pursued my impetuous career.

North. To Diana!—to Diana ascends the virgin's prayer!

Tickler. Down went, one after the other, jacket, waistcoat, flannel shirt,—would you believe it, her own blue linsey-woolsey petticoat! Thus lightened, she bounded over the little knolls like a barque over Sicilian seas; in ten minutes she had fairly run away from me hull-down, and her long yellow hair, streaming like a pendant, disappeared in the forest.

North. What have you done with the puir lassie's petticoat?

Tickler. I sent it to my friend Dr. M'Culloch, to lie among his other relics . . . of Highland greed.

North. If idle folks will wander over the Highlands, and get the natives to show them how to follow their noses through the wildernesses, ought they not to pay handsomely for being saved from perdition, in bogs, quagmires, mosses, shelving lake-shores, fords and chasms?

Tickler. Undoubtedly; and if the orphan son of some old Celt, who perhaps fought under Abercromby, and lost his eyes in ophthalmia, leave his ordinary work beside his shieling, be it what it may, or give up a day's sport on the hill or river to accompany a Sassenach* some thirty miles over the moors, with his big nag, too, loaded with mineralogy and botany, and all other matter of trash, are five shillings, or twice five, a sufficient remuneration? Not they, indeed. Pay him like a post-chaise, fifteenpence a mile, and send him to his hut rejoicing through a whole winter.

North. Spoken like a gentleman. So, with boats, a couple of poor fellows live, and that is all, by rowing waif and stray Sassenachs over lochs or arms of the sea. No regular ferry, mind you. Perhaps days and weeks pass by without their boat being called for—and yet grumble and growl is the go as soon as they hold out a hand for silver or gold. Recollect, old or young hunks, that you are on a tour of pleasure—that you are as fat as a barn-door fowl; and these two boatmen—there they are grinding Gaelic—as lean as laths;—what the worse will you be of being cheated a little? But if you grudge a guinea, why, go round by the head of the loch, and twenty to one you are never seen again in this world.

Tickler. The Highlanders are far from being extortioners.

* *Sassenach*—a Lowlander or Englishman.

An extraordinary price must be paid for an extraordinary service. But, oh! my dear North, what grouse-soup at Dalnacardoch! You smell it on the homeward hill, as if it were exhaling from the heather: deeper and deeper still, as you approach the beautiful chimney vomiting forth its intermitting columns of cloud-like peat-smoke, that melts afar over the wilderness!

North. Yes, Tickler—it was Burke that vindicated the claims of smells to the character of the sublime and beautiful.

Tickler. Yes, yes! Burke it was. As you enter the inn, the divine afflatus penetrates your soul. When up-stairs perhaps in the garret, adorning for dinner, it rises like a cloud of rich distilled perfumes through every chink on the floor, every cranny of the wall. The little mouse issues from his hole, close to the foot of the bed-post, and raising himself, squirrel-like, on his hinder-legs, whets his tusks with his merry-paws and smooths his whiskers.

North. Shakespearean!

Tickler. There we are, a band of brothers round the glorious tureen! Down goes the ladle into "*a profoundis clamavi*," and up floats from that blessed Erebus a dozen cunningly resuscitated spirits. Old cocks, bitter to the back-bone, lovingly alternating with young pouts, whose swelling bosoms might seduce an anchorite!

North (*rising*). I must ring for supper, Ambrose–Ambrose—Ambrose!

Tickler. No respect of persons at Dalnacardoch! I plump them into the plates around *sans* selection. No matter although the soup play JAWP* from preses to croupier. There too sit a few choice spirits of pointers round the board—Don—Jupiter—Sancho—"and the rest"—with steadfast eyes and dewy chops, patient alike of heat, cold, thirst, and hun

* *Jawp*—spalsh.

ger—dogs of the desert indeed, and nose-led by unerring instinct right up to the cowering covey in the heather groves on the mountain-side.

North. Is eagle good eating, Timothy? Pococke the traveller used to eat lion: lion pasty is excellent, it is said—but is not eagle tough?

Tickler. Thigh good, devilled. The delight of the Highlands is in the Highland feeling. That feeling is entirely destroyed by stages and regular progression. The waterfalls do not tell upon sober parties—it is tedious in the extreme to be drenched to the skin along high-roads—the rattle of wheels blends meanly with thunder—and lightning is contemptible, seen from the window of a glass coach. To enjoy mist, you must be in the heart of it, as a solitary hunter, shooter, or angler. Lightning is nothing unless a thousand feet below you,* and the live thunder must be heard leaping, as Byron says, from mountain to mountain, otherwise you might as well listen to a mock peal from the pit of a theatre.

North. Pray, Tickler, have you read Milton's Treatise on Christianity?†

Tickler. I have; and feel disposed to agree with him in his doctrine of polygamy. For many years I lived very comfortably without a wife; and since the year 1820 I have been a monogamist. But I confess that there is a sameness in that system. I should like much to try polygamy for a few years. I wish Milton had explained the duties of a polygamist; for it is possible that they may be of a very intricate, compli-

* In his "Address to a Wild Deer," Professor Wilson says of the hunter:

"'Tis his, by the mouth of some cavern his seat,
The lightning of heaven to hold at his feet,
While the thunder below him that growls from the cloud,
To him comes on echo more awfully loud."

† At that time recently discovered.

cated, and unbounded nature, and that such an accumulation of private business might be thrown on one's hands that it could not be in the power of an elderly gentleman to overtake it; occupied, too as he might be, as in my own case, in contributing to the Periodical Literature of the age.

North. Sir, the system would not be found to work well in this climate. Milton was a great poet, but a bad divine, and a miserable politician.

Tickler. How can that be?—Wordsworth says that a great poet must be great in all things.

North. Wordsworth often writes like an idiot; and never more so than when he said of Milton, "His soul was like a star, and dwelt apart!" For it dwelt in tumult, and mischief, and rebellion. Wordsworth is, in all things, the reverse of Milton—a good man and a bad poet.

Tickler. What!—That Wordsworth whom Maga cries up as the Prince of Poets?

North. Be it so; I must humor the fancies of some of my friends. But had that man been a great poet, he would have produced a deep and lasting impression on the mind of England; whereas his verses are becoming less and less known every day, and he is, in good truth, already one of the illustrious obscure.

Tickler. I never thought him more than a very ordinary man—with some imagination, certainly, but with no grasp of understanding, and apparently little acquainted with the history of his kind. My God! to compare such a writer with Scott and Byron!

North. And yet, with his creed, what might not a great poet have done?—That the language of poetry is but the language of strong human passion!—That in the great elementary principles of thought and feeling common to all the race, the subject-matter of poetry is to be sought and found!—That enjoyment and suffering, as they wring and crush, or expand and elevate, men's hearts, are the sources of song!—And what, pray, has he made out of this true and philosophical creed?—A few ballads (pretty at the best), two or three moral fables, some natural description of scenery, and half-a-dozen narratives of common distress or happiness. Not one single character has he created—not one incident—not one tragical catastrophe. He has thrown no light on man's estate here below; and Crabbe, with all his defects, stands immeasurably above Wordsworth as the Poet of the Poor.

Tickler. Good. And yet the youngsters, in that absurd Magazine of yours, set him up to the stars as their idol, and kiss his very feet, as if the toes were of gold.

North. Well, well; let them have their own way a while. I confess that the "Excursion" is the worst poem, of any character, in the English language. It contains about two hundred sonorous lines, some of which appear to be fine even in the sense as well as in the sound. The remaining seven thousand three hundred are quite ineffectual. Then, what labor the builder of that lofty rhyme must have undergone! It is, in its own way, a small Tower of Babel, and all built by a single man!

Tickler. Wipe your forehead, North; for it is indeed a most perspiring thought. I do not know whether my gallantry blinds me, but I prefer much of the female to the male poetry of the day.

North. O thou Polygamist!

Tickler. And what the devil would you be at with your great bawling He-Poets from the Lakes, who go round and round about, strutting upon nothing, like so many turkey cocks, gobbling with a long red pendant at their noses, and frightening away the fair and lovely swans as they glide down the waters of immortality?

North. Scott's poetry puzzles me—it is often very bad.

Tickler. Very.

North. Except when his martial soul is up, he is but a tame and feeble writer. His versification in general flows on easily—smoothly—almost sonorously; but seldom or never with impetuosity or grandeur. There if no strength, no felicity in his diction—and the substance of his poetry is neither rich nor rare.

Tickler. But then, when his martial soul is up—and up it is at sight of a spear-point or a pennon—then indeed you hear the true poet of chivalry. What care I, Kit, for all his previous drivelling—if drivelling it be—and God forbid I should deny drivelling to any poet, ancient or modern—for now he makes my very soul burn within me; and, coward and civilian though I be,—yes, a most intense and insuperable coward, prizing life and limb beyond all other earthly possessions, and loath to shed one single drop of blood either for my king or country,—yet such is the trumpet power of the song of that son of genius, that I start from my old elbow-chair, up with the poker, tongs, or shovel, no matter which, and flourishing it round my head, cry,—

"Charge, Chester, charge! On, Stanley, on!"

and then, dropping my voice, and returning to my padded bottom, whisper,

"Were the last words of Marmion!"

North. Bravo—bravo—bravo!

Tickler. I care not one single curse for all the criticism that ever was canted, or decanted, or recanted. Neither does the world. The world takes a poet as it finds him, and seats him above or below the salt. The world is as obstinate as a million mules, and will not turn its head on one side or another, for all the shouting of the critical population that ever was shouted. It is very possible that the world is a bad judge. Well, then, appeal to posterity, and be hanged to you, and posterity will affirm the judgment with costs.

North. How you can jabber away so in such a temperature as this confounds me. You are indeed a singular old man.

Tickler. Therefore I say that Scott is a Homer of a poet, and so let him doze when he has a mind to it; for no man I know is better entitled to an occasional half canto of slumber.

North. Did you ever meet any of the Lake poets in private society?

Tickler. Five or six times. Wordsworth has a grave solemn, pedantic, awkward, out-of-the-worldish look about him, that rather puzzles you as to his probable profession, till he begins to speak—and then, to be sure, you set him down at once for a Methodist preacher.

North. I have seen Chantrey's bust.

Tickler. The bust flatters his head, which is not intellectual. The forehead is narrow, and the skull altogether too scanty. Yet the baldness, the gravity, and the composure are impressive, and, on the whole, not unpoetical. The eyes are dim and thoughtful, and a certain sweetness of smile occasionally lightens up the strong lines of his countenance with an expression of courteousness and philanthropy.

North. Is he not extremely eloquent?

Tickler. Far from it. He labors like a whale spouting—his voice is wearisomely monotonous—he does not know when to have done with a subject—oracularly announces perpetual truisms—never hits the nail on the head—and leaves you amazed with all that needless pother, which the simple bard opines to be eloquence, and which passes for such with his Cockney idolaters, and his catechumens at Ambleside and Keswick.

North. Not during dinner, surely ?

Tickler. Yes, during breakfast, lunch, dinner, tea, and supper,—every intermediate moment,—nor have I any doubt that he proses all night long in his sleep.

North. Shocking indeed. In conversation, the exchange should be at par. That is the grand secret. Nor should any Christian ever exceed the maximum of three consecutive sentences—except in an anecdote.

Tickler. O merciful heavens ! my dear North. What eternal talkers most men are now-a-days—all at it in a party at once—each farthing candle anxious to shine forth with its own vile wavering wick—tremulously apprehensive of snuffers—and stinking away after expiration in the socket ! *

North. Bad enough in town, but worse, far worse, in country places.

Tickler. The Surgeon ! The dominie ! The old minister's assistant and successor ! The president of the Speculative Society ! Two landscape painters ! The rejected contributor to *Blackwood !* The agricultural reporter of the county ! The surveyor ! Captain Campbell ! The Laird, his son ! The stranger gentleman on a tour ! The lecturer on an or-

* Scott's conversation is thus elsewhere described :—

" *Shepherd.* I never in a' my born days, and I'm noo just the age o' Sir Walter, and, had he been leevin, o' Bonnypratt, met a perfeckly pleasant—that is a'thegither enchantin man in a party—and I have lang thocht there's nae sic thing in existence as poo'rs o' conversation. There's Sir Walter wi' his everlastin anecdotes, nine out o' ten meanin naething, and the tenth itsel as auld as the Eildon Hills. Yet I love and venerate Sir Walter aboon a' ither leevin men except yoursel, sir, and for that reason try to thold his discourse. As to his ever hearin richt ae single syllable o' what ye may be sayin to him, wi' the maist freendly intent o' enlichtenin his weak mind, you maun never indulge ony howp o' that kind—for o' a' the absent men when anither's speakin, that ever glowered in a body's face, without seemin to ken even wha he's lookin at, Sir Walter is the foremost ; and gin he behaves in that gate to a man o' original genius like me, you may conceive his treatment o' the sumphs and sumphesses that compose fashionable society".

rery! The poet about to publish by subscription! The person from Pitkeathly! The man of the house himself—my God! his wife and daughters! and the widow, the widow! I can no more—the widow, the widow, the widow! (*Sinks back in his chair.*)

North. I have heard Coleridge. That man is entitled to speak on till Doomsday—or rather the genius within him—for he is inspired. Wind him up, and away he goes, discoursing most excellent music—without a discord—full, ample, inexhaustible, serious, and divine!

Tickler. Add him to my list, and the band of instrumental music is complete.

North. It is pleasant to know how immediately everything said or done in this world is forgotten. Murder a novel,or a man, or a poem,or a child—forge powers of attorney without cessation during the prime of life,till old maids beyond all computation have been sold unsuspectingly out of the stocks in every country village in England—for a lustre furnish Balaam to a London magazine at thirty shillings per bray,—in short, let any man commit any enormity, and it is forgotten before the first of the month! Who remembers anything but the bare names—and these indistinctly—of Thurtell, and Hunt, and Fauntleroy, and Hazlitt, and Tims, and Soames, and Sotheran? Soap-bubbles all—blown, burst, vanished, and forgotten.

Tickler. Why, you almost venture to republish Maga herself in numbers, under the smirk of a New Series. I know a worthy and able minister of our church, who has been preaching (and long may he preach it) the self-same sermon for upwards of forty years. About the year 1802 I began to suspect him; but having then sat below him only for some dozen years or so, I could not, of course, in a matter of so much delicacy, dare trust to my very imperfect memory

During the Whig ministry of 1806, my attention was strongly riveted to the "practical illustrations," and I could have sworn to the last twenty minutes of his discourse, as to the voice of a friend familiar in early youth. About the time your Magazine first dawned on the world, my belief of its identity extended to the whole discourse; and the good old man himself, in the delight of his heart, confessed to me the truth a few Sabbaths after the Chaldee.

North. Come, now, tell me truth—have you ever palmed off any part of it upon me in the shape of an article?

Tickler. Never, 'pon honor; but you shall get the whole of it some day, as a Number One; for, now that he has got an assistant and successor, the sermon is seldom employed, and he has bequeathed it me in a codicil to his will.

North. I cannot imagine, for the life of me, what Ambrose is about. Hush! there he comes. (*Enter* AMBROSE.) What is the meaning of this, sir?

Ambrose. Unfold.

(*Folding-doors thrown open, and supper-table is shown.*

Tickler. What an epergne! Art—art. What would our friend Bowles say to that, North? "Tadmore thus, and Syrian Balbec rose."—(*Transeunt omnes.*)

SCENE II.—*The Pitt Saloon.*

North. Hogg, with his hair powdered, as I endure! —God bless you, James—how are you all at Altrive?

Shepherd. All's well—wool up—nowte* on the rise—harvest stacked without a shower—potatoes like stones in the Meggat—turnips like cabbages, and cabbages like balloons—bairns brawly, and Mistress bonnier than ever.—It is quite an *annus mirabilis.*

Tickler. James, my heart warms to hear your voice.

* *Nowte*—cattle. A stream near Hogg's farm.

That suit of black becomes you extremely—you would make an excellent Moderator of the General Assembly.*

Shepherd. You mistake the matter entirely, Tickler; your eyesight fails you;—my coat is a dark blue—waistcoat and breeches the same—but old people discern objects indistinctly by candle-light, or I shall rather say, by gas-light. The radiance is beautiful.

Tickler. The radiance is beautiful!

Shepherd. Why, you are like old Polonius in the play! I hate an echo—be original or silent.

Tickler. James!

Shepherd. Mr. Hogg, if you please, sir. Why, you think because I am good-natured, that you and North, and "the rest," are to quiz the Shepherd? Be it so—no objections—but hearken to me, Mr. Tickler, my name will be remembered when the dust of oblivion is yard-deep on the gravestone of the whole generation of Ticklers. Who are you—what are you—whence are you—whither are you going, and what have you got to say for yourself? A tall fellow, undoubtedly—but Measure for Measure is the comedy in which I choose to act to-night—so, gentlemen, be civil—or I will join the party at Spinks'†—and set up an opposition Magazine, that . . .

North. This is most extraordinary behavior, Mr. Hogg; and any apology . . .

Shepherd. I forgive you, Mr. North—but . . .

North. Come—come, you see Tickler is much affected.

Shepherd. So am I, sir—but is it to be endured . . .

Tickler. Pardon me, James; say that you pardon me—at my time of life a man cannot afford to lose a friend. No, he cannot indeed.

* Of the Church of Scotland.

† Spinks' Hotel,—the resort (real or supposed) of opposition literary convivialists.

Shepherd. Your hand, Mr. Tickler. But I will not be the butt of any company.

North. I fear some insidious enemy has been poisoning your ear, James. Never has any one of us ceased, for a moment, to respect you, or to hear you with respect, from the time that you wrote the Chaldee Manuscript . . .

Shepherd. Not another word—not another word—if you love me.

North. Have the Cockneys been bribing you to desert us, James?

Shepherd. The Cockneys! Puir misbegotten deevils! (I maun to speak Scotch again now that I'm in good humor.) I would rather crack nuts for a haill winter's nicht wi' a monkey, than drink the best peck o' mawt that ever was brewed wi' the King himsel' o' that kintra.

North. I understood you were going to visit London this winter.

Shepherd. I am. But I shall choose my ain society there, as I do in Embro' and Yarrow. . . .

(*Here follows the Supper.*)

Tickler. James, you are the worst smoker of a cigar in Christendom. No occasion to blow like a hippopotamus. Look at me or North—you would not know we breathed.

Shepherd. It's to keep mysel' frae fallin' asleep. Hear till that auld watchman, crawing the hour like a bit bantam. What's the cretur screeching? Twa o'clock!! Mercy me!—we maun be aff. (*Exeunt omnes.*)

III.

IN THE BLUE PARLOR.

NORTH.—SHEPHERD.—TICKLER.

North. Thank heaven for winter! Would that it lasted all year long! Spring is pretty well in its way, with budding branches and carolling birds, and wimpling burnies, and fleecy skies, and dew-like showers softening and brightening the bosom of old mother earth. Summer is not much amiss, with umbrageous woods, glittering atmosphere, and awakening thunderstorms. Nor let me libel Autumn, in her gorgeous bounty, and her beautiful decays. But Winter, dear, cold-handed and warm-hearted Winter, welcome thou to my fur-clad bosom! Thine are the sharp, short, bracing, invigorating days, that screw up muscle, fibre, and nerve, like the strings of an old Cremona discoursing excellent music—thine the long snow-silent or hail-rattling nights, with earthly firesides and heavenly luminaries, for home comforts, or travelling imaginations, for undisturbed imprisonment, or unbounded freedom, for the affections of the heart and the flights of the soul! Thine, too—

Shepherd. Thine, too, skatin, and curlin, and grewin,* and a' sorts o' deevilry amang lads and lasses at rockins and kirns. Beef and greens! Beef and greens! Oh, Mr. North, beef and greens!

* *Grewin*—coursing.

North. Yes, James, I sympathize with your enthusiasm. Now, and now only, do carrots and turnips deserve the name. The season this of rumps and rounds. Now the whole nation sets in for serious eating—serious and substantial eating, James, half leisure, half labor—the table loaded with a lease of life, and each dish a year. In the presence of that Haggis I feel myself immortal.

Shepherd. Butcher-meat, though, and coals are likely, let me tell you, to sell at a perfec' ransom frae Martinmas to Michaelmas.

North. Paltry thought. Let beeves and muttons look up, even to the stars, and fuel be precious as at the Pole. Another slice of the stot, James, another slice of the stot—and, Mr. Ambrose, smash that half-ton lump of black diamond till the chimney roar and radiate like Mount Vesuvius.—Why so glum, Tickler?—why so glum?

Tickler. This outrageous merriment grates my spirits. I am not in the mood. 'Twill be a severe winter, and I think of the poor.

North. Why the devil think of the poor at this time of day? Are not wages good, and work plenty, and is not charity a British virtue?

Shepherd. I never heard sic even-doun nonsense in a' my born days. . . . Mr. Tickler, there's nae occasion, man, to look sae doun-in-the-mouth—everybody kens ye're a man o' genius, without your pretending to be melancholy.

Tickler. I have no appetite, James.

Shepherd. Nae appeteet! how suld ye hae an appeteet? A bowl o' Mollygo-tawny soup, wi' bread in proportion—twa codlins (wi' maist part o' a labster in that sass)—the first gash o' the jiget—stakes—then I'm maist sure, pallets, and finally guse—no to count jeelies and coosturd, and bluemange, and many million mites in that Campsie Stilton—better than ony

English—a pot o' draught—twa long shankers o' ale, noos and thans a sip o' the auld port, and just afore grace a caulker o' Glenlivet, that made your een glower and water in your head as if you had been looking at Mrs. Siddons in the sleep-walking scene in Shakespeare's tragedy of *Macbeth*—gin ye had an appeteet after a' that destruction o' animal and vegetable matter, your maw would be like that o' Death himsel, and your stamach insatiable as the grave

Tickler. Mr. Ambrose, no laughter, if you please, sir.

North. Come, come, Tickler—had Hogg and Heraclitus been contemporaries, it would have saved the shedding of a world of tears.

Shepherd. Just laugh your fill, Mr. Ambrose. A smile is aye becoming that honest face o' yours. But I'll no be sae wutty again, gin I can help it.

(*Exit* Mr. AMBROSE *with the epergne.*

Tickler. Mr. Ambrose understands me. It does my heart good to know when his arm is carefully extended over my shoulder, to put down or to remove. None of that hurry-and-no-speed waiter-like hastiness about our Ambrose! With an ever observant eye he watches the goings-on of the board, like an astronomer watching the planetary system. He knows when a plate is emptied to be filled no more, and lo! it is withdrawn as by an invisible hand. During some "syncope and solemn pause" you may lay down your knife and fork and wipe your brow, nor dread the evanishing of a half-devoured howtowdy; the moment your eye has decided on a dish, there he stands plate in hand in a twinkling beside tongue or turkey! No playing at cross purposes—the sheep's head of Mullion usurping the place of the kidneys of O'Doherty. The most perfect confidence reigns round the board. The possibility of mistake is felt to be beyond the fear of the hungriest imagination; and sooner shall one of

Jupiter's satellites forsake his orbit, jostling the stars, and wheeling away into some remoter system, than our Ambrose run against any of the subordinates, or leave the room while North is in his chair.

North. Hear the Glenlivet!—Hear the Glenlivet!

Shepherd. No, Mr. North, nane o' your envious attributions o' ae spirit for anither. It's the soul within him that breaks out, like lightning in the collied * night, or in the dwawm-like † silence o' a glen the sudden soun' o' a trumpet.

Tickler. Give me your hand, James.

Shepherd. There, noo—there, noo! It's aye me that's said to be sae fond o' flattery; and yet only see how by a single word o' my mouth I can add sax inches to your stature, Mr. Tickler, and make ye girn like the spirit that saluted De Gama at the Cape o' Storms.

North. Hear the Glenlivet!—Hear the Glenlivet!

Shepherd. Hush, ye haveril. ‡ Give up a speech yoursel, Mr. North, and then see who'll cry, "Hear the Glenlivet!—hear the Glenlivet!" then. But haud your tongues, baith o' you—dinna stir a fit. And as for you, Mr. Tickler, howk the tow out o' your lug, and hear till a sang.

(*The* SHEPHERD *sings* "The brakens wi' me.")

Tickler (*passing his hand across his eyes*). "I'm never merry when I hear sweet music."

North. Your voice, James, absolutely gets mellower through years. Next York Festival you must sing a solo—"Angels ever bright and fair," or "Farewell, ye limpid streams and floods."

Shepherd. I was at the last York Festival, and one day I was in the chorus, next to Grundy of Kirk-by-Lons

* "Like Lightning in the *collied* night."—*Midsummer Night's Dream* *Collied*—blackened as with coal.

† *Dwawm-like*—swoon-like.

‡ *Haveril*—a chattering half-witted person.

dale. I kent my mouth was wide open, but I never heard my ain voice in the magnificent roar.

North. Describe—James—describe.

Shepherd. As weel describe a glorious dream of the seventh heaven. Thousands upon thousands o' the most beautiful angels sat mute and still in the Cathedral. Weel may I call them angels, although a' the time I knew them to be frail, evanescent creatures o' this ever-changing earth. A sort o' paleness was on their faces, ay, even on the faces where the blush-roses o' innocence were blooming like the flowers o' Paradise—for a shadow came ower them frae the awe o' their religious hearts that beat not, but were chained as in the presence of their Great Maker. All eyne were fixed in a solemn raised gaze, something mournful-like I thocht, but it was only in a happiness great and deep as the calm sea. I saw—I did not see the old massy pillars—now I seemed to behold the roof o' the Cathedral, and now the sky o' heaven, and a licht—I had maist said a murmuring licht, for there surely was a faint spirit-like soun' in the streams o' splendor that came through the high Gothic window, left shadows here and there throughout the temple, till a' at ance the organ sounded, and I could have fallen down on my knees.

North. Thank you, kindly, James.

Shepherd. I understand the hint, sir. Catch me harpin ower lang on ae string. Yet music's a subject I could get geyan * tiresome upon.

North. What think you, James, of the projected Fish Company.

Shepherd. Just everything that's gude. I never look at the sea without lamenting the backward state of its agriculture. Were every eatable land animal extinc', the human race could dine and soup out o' the ocean till a' eternity.

* *Geyan*—rather.

Tickler. No fish-sauce equal to the following:—Ketchup —mustard—cayenne pepper—butter amalgamated on your plate *proprio manu*, each man according to his own proportions. Yetholm ketchup made by the gipsies. Mushroom, for ever—damn walnuts.

North. I care little about what I eat or drink.

Shepherd. Lord have mercy on us—what a lee! There does not, at this blessed moment, breathe on the earth's surface ae human being that doesna prefer eating and drinking to all ither pleasures o' body and sowl.* This is the rule: Never think about either the ane or the ither but when you are at the board. Then, eat and drink wi' a' your powers—moral, intellectual, and physical. Say little, but look freendly—tak care chiefly o' yoursel', but no, if you can help it, to the utter oblivion o' a' ithers. This may soun' queer but it's gude manners, and worth a Chesterfield. Them at the twa ends o' the table maun just reverse that rule—till ilka body has been twice served—and then aff at 'a haun gallop.

North. What think ye of luncheons?

Shepherd. That they are the disturbers o' a' earthly happiness. I daurna trust mysel' wi' a luncheon. In my hauns it becomes an untimeous denner—for after a hantle o' cauld meat, muirfowl pies, or even butter and bread, what reasonable cretur can be ready afore gloamin for a het denner? So when'er I'm betrayed into a luncheon, I mak it a luncheon wi' a vengeance; and then order in the kettle, and finish aff wi' a jug or twa, just the same as gin it had been a regular dinner wi' a table-cloth. Bewaur the tray.

North. A few anchovies, such as I used to enjoy with my

* "Some people," says Dr. Samuel Johnson, "have a foolish way of not minding, or pretending not to mind, what they eat. For my part, I mind my belly very studiously, and very carefully. For I look upon it, that he who does not mind his belly will hardly mind anything else." —BOSWELL'S *Life*, chap. xvii.

dear Davy at the corner, act as a whet, I confess, and nothing more.

Shepherd. I never can eat a few o' onything, even ingans. Ance I begin, I maun proceed ; and I devoor them—ilka ane being the last—till my een are sae watery that I think it is raining. Break not upon the integrity o' time atween breakfast and the blessed hour o' denner.

North. The mid-day hour is always, to my imagination the most delightful hour of the whole Alphabet.

Shepherd. I understaun. During that hour—and there is nae occasion to allow difference for clocks, for in nature every object is a dial—how many thousand groups are collected a' ower Scotland, and a' ower the face o' the earth—for in every clime wondrously the same are the great leading laws o' man's necessities—under bits o'bonny buddin or leaffu' hedgeraws, some bit fragrant and fluttering birk-tree, aneath some owerhanging rock in the desert, or by some diamond well in its mossy cave—breakin their bread wi' thanksgiving, and eatin with the clear blood o' health meandering in the heaven-blue veins o' the sweet lassies, while the cool airs are playing amang their haflins-covered* bosoms wi' many a jeist and sang atween, and aiblins kisses too, at ance dew and sunshine to the peasant's or shepherd's soul—then up again wi' lauchter to their wark amang the tedded grass, or the corn-rigs sae bonny, scenes that Robbie Burns lo'ed sae weel and sang sae gloriously—and the whilk, need I fear to say't, your ain Ettrick Shepherd, my dear fellows, has sung on his auld border harp, a sang or twa that may be remembered when the bard that wauk'd them is i' the mools, and "at his feet the green-grass turf and at his head a stane."

Tickler. Come, come, James, none of your pathos—none

* *Haflins-covered*—half-covered.

of your pathos, my dear James. (*Looking red about the eyes.*)

North. We were talking of codlins.*

Shepherd. True, Mr. North, but folk canna be aye talkin o' codlins, ony mair than aye eatin them; and the great charm o' conversation is being aff on ony wind that blaws. Pleasant conversation between friends is just like walking through a mountainous kintra—at every glen-mouth the wun' blaws frae a different airt†—the bit bairnies come tripping alang in opposite directions—noo a harebell scents the air—noo sweet briar—noo heather bank—here is a gruesome quagmire, there a plat o' sheep-nibbled grass, smooth as silk and green as emeralds—here a stony region of cinders and lava, there groves o' the lady-fern embowering the sleeping roe—here the hillside in its own various dyes resplendent as the rainbow, and there woods that the Druids would have worshipped—hark, sound sounding in the awfu' sweetness o' evening wi' the cushat's sang, and the deadened roar o' some great waterfa' far aff in the very centre o' the untrodden forest. A' the warks o' ootward natur are symbolical o' our ain immortal souls. Mr. Tickler, is't not just even sae?

Tickler. Sheridan—Sheridan; what was Sheridan's talk to our own Shepherd's, North?

North. A few quirks and cranks studied at a looking-glass‡—puns painfully elaborated with pen and ink for extemporaneous reply—bon-mots generated in *malice prepense*—witticisms jotted down in short-hand to be extended when he had put on the spur of the occasion—the drudgeries of memory

* *Codlins*—small cod; not *apples*, as the American editor supposes.

† *Airt*—point of the compass.

‡ How carefully Sheridan's impromptus were prepared beforehand may be learned from Moore's *Life* of that celebrated wit, just published at the date of this number of the *Noctes*.

to be palmed off for the ebullitions of imagination—the coinage of the counter passed for currency hot from the mint of fancy—squibs and crackers ignited and exploded by a Merry-Andrew, instead of the lightnings of the soul, darting out forked or sheeted from the electrical atmosphere of an inspired genius.

Shepherd. I wish that you but saw my monkey, Mr. North. He would make you hop the twig in a guffaw. I hae got a pole erected for him o' about some 150 feet high, on a knowe ahint Mount Benger; and the way the cretur rins up to the knob, lookin ower the shouther o' him, and twisting his tail roun' the pole for fear o' playin thud on the grun', is comical past a' endurance.

North. Think you, James, that he is a link?

Shepherd. A link in creation? Not he, indeed. He is merely a monkey. Only to see him on his observatory, beholding the sunrise! or weeping, like a Laker, at the beauty o' the moon and stars!

North. Is he a bit of a poet?

Shepherd. Gin he could but speak and write, there can be nae manner o' doubt that he would be a gran' poet. Safe us! what een in the head o' him! Wee, clear, red, fiery, watery, malignant-lookin een, fu' o' inspiration.

Tickler. You should have him stuffed.

Shepherd. Stuffed, man? say, rather, embalmed. But he's no likely to dee for years to come—indeed, the cretur's engaged to be married, although he's no in the secret himsel', yet. The bawns* are published.

Tickler. Why, really, James; marriage, I think, ought to be simply a civil contract.

Shepherd. A civil contract! I wuss it was. But oh! Mr. Tickler, to see the cretur sittin wi' a pen in's hand, and pipe

* *Bawns*—banns.

in's mouth, jotting down a sonnet, or odd, or lyrical ballad! Sometimes I put that black velvet cap ye gied me on his head, and ane o' the bairn's auld big-coats on his back; and then sure eneugh, when he takes his stroll in the avenue, he is a heathenish Christian.

North. Why James, by this time he must be quite like one off the family?

Shepherd. He's a capital flee fisher. I never saw a monkey throw alighter line in my life. But he's greedy o' the gude linns, and canna thole to see onybody else gruppin great anes but himsel'. He accompanied me for twa-three days in the season to the Trows, up aboon Kelso yonner; and Kersse* allowed that he worked a salmon to a miracle. Then, for rowing a boat!

Tickler. Why don't you bring him to Ambrose's?

Shepherd. He's sae bashfu'. He never shines in company; and the least thing in the world will mak him blush.

Tickler. Have you seen the *Sheffield Iris*, containing an account of the feast given to Montgomery† the poet, his long-winded speech, and his valedictory address to the world as abdicating editor of a provincial newspaper?

Shepherd. I have the *Iris*—that means Rainbow—in my pocket, and it made me proud to see sic honors conferred on genius. Lang-wunded speech, Mr. Tickler! What! would you have had Montgomery mumble twa-three sentences, and sit down again, before an assemblage o' a hundred o' the most respectable o' his fellow-townsmen, with Lord Milton at their head, a' gathered thegither to honor with heart and hand One of the Sons of Song?

North. Right, James, right. On such an occasion, Mont-

* Kersse, a celebrated Kelso salmon-fisher.

† James Montgomery, author of *The World before the Flood*, and other esteemed poems, was born in 1771, and died in 1854.

gomery was not only entitled, but bound to speak of himself—and by so doing he "has graced his cause." Meanwhile let us drink his health in a bumper.

Shepherd. Stop, stop, my jug's done. But never mind, I'll drink't in pure speerit. (*Bibunt omnes.*)

Tickler. Did we include his politics?

Shepherd. Faith, I believe no. Let's tak anither bumper to his politics.

North. James, do you know what you're saying?—the man is a Whig. If we do drink his politics, let it be in empty glasses.

Shepherd. Na, na. I'll drink no man's health, nor yet ony ither thing, out o' an empty glass. My political principles are so well known, that my consistency would not suffer were I to drink the health o' the great Whig leader, Satan himself; besides, James Montgomery is, I verily believe, a true patriot. Gin he thinks himself a Whig, he has nae understanding whatever o' his ain character. I'll undertak to bring out the Toryism that's in him in the course o' a single *Noctes.* Toryism is an innate principle o' human nature—Whiggism but an evil habit. O sirs, this is a gran' jug!

Tickler. I am beginning to feel rather hungry.

Shepherd. I hae been rather sharp-set even sin' Mr. Ambrose took awa the cheese.

North. 'Tis the night of the 21st of October—the battle of Trafalgar—Nelson's death—the greatest of all England's heroes—

> "His march was o'er the mountain wave,
> His home was on the deep."

Nelson not only destroyed the naval power of all the enemies of England, but he made our naval power immortal. Thank God, he died at sea.

Tickler. A noble creature; his very failings were ocean-born.

Shepherd. Yes—a cairn to his memory would not be out of place even at the head of the most inland glen. Not a sea-mew floats up into our green solitudes that tells not of Nelson.

North. His name makes me proud that I am an islander. No continent has such a glory.

Shepherd. Look out o' the window—what a fleet o'stars in Heaven! Yon is the Victory—a hundred-gun ship—I see the standard of England flying at the main. The bricht-est luminary o' nicht says in that halo, "England expects every man to do his duty." . . . What think you of the *Iliad,* Mr. North?

North. The great occupation of the power of man, James, in early society, is to make war. Of course, his great poetry will be that which celebrates war. The mighty races of men, and their mightiest deeds, are represented in such poetry. It contains "the glory of the world" in some of its noblest ages. Such is Homer. The whole poem of Homer (the *Iliad*) is war, yet not much of the whole *Iliad* is fighting and that, with some exceptions, not the most interesting. If we consider warlike poetry purely as breathing the spirit of fighting, the fierce ardor of combat, we fall to a much lower measure of human conception. Homer's poem is intellectual, and full of affections; it would go as near to make a philosopher as a soldier. I should say that war appears as the business of Homer's heroes, not often a matter of pure enjoyment. One would conceive, that if there could be found anywhere in language the real breathing spirit of lust for fight which is in some nations, there would be conceptions, and passion of blood-thirst, which are not in Homer. There are flashes of it in Æschylus.

Shepherd. I wish to heaven I could read Greek. I'll begin to-morrow.

Tickler. The songs of Tyrtæus goading into battle are of that kind, and their class is evidently not a high one. Far above them must have been those poems of the ancient German nations, which were chanted in the front of battle, reciting the acts of old heroes to exalt their courage. These, being breathed out of the heart of passion of a people, must have been good. The spirit of fighting was there involved with all their most ennobling conceptions, and yet was merely pugnacious.

North. The *Iliad* is remarkable among military poems in this, that, being all about war, it instils no passion for war. None of the high inspiring motives to war are made to kindle the heart. In fact, the cause of war is false on both sides. But there is a glory of war, like the splendor of sunshine, resting upon and enveloping all.

Shepherd. I'm beginning to get a little clearer in the upper storey. That last jug was a poser. How feel you gentlemen—do you think you're baith quite sober? Our conversation is rather beginning to get a little heavy. Tak a mouthfu'. (NORTH *quaffs.*)

Tickler. North, you look as if you were taking an observation. Have you discovered any new comet?

North (*standing up*). Friends—countrymen—and Romans—lend me your ears. You say, James, that that's a gran' jug; well then, out with the ladle, and push about the jorum. No speech—no speech—for my heart is big. This may be our last meeting in the Blue Parlor. Our next meeting in

AMBROSE'S HOTEL, PICARDY PLACE! *

* At this time Ambrose was about to shift his sign from Gabriel's Road, at the back of Princes Street, to a large tenement in Picardy Place, facing the head of Leith Walk. It will be seen, in the next *Noctes*, that the party again met in the old, "Blue Parlor" in Gabriel's Road.

(NORTH *suddenly sits down;* TICKLER *and the* SHEPHERD *in a moment are at his side.*)

Tickler. My beloved Christopher, here is my smelling-bottle (*Puts the vinaigrette to his aquiline nose.*)

Shepherd. My beloved Christopher, here is my smelling-bottle. (*Pnts the stately oblong Glenlivet crystal to his lips.*)

North (*opening his eyes*). What flowers are those? Roses—mignonette, bathed in aromatic dew!

Shepherd. Yes; in romantic dew—mountain dew, my respected sir, that could give scent to a sybo.*

Tickler. James, let us support him into the open air.

North. Somewhat too much of this. It is beautiful moon light. Let us take an arm-in-arm stroll round the ramparts of the Calton Hill.

(*Enter* Mr. AMBROSE, *much affected, with* NORTH'S *dreadnought;* NORTH *whispers in his ear,* Subridens olli; Mr. AMBROSE *looks cheerful,* et exeunt omnes.

* *Sybo*—a leek.

IV.

IN WHICH THE SHEPHERD USURPS THE EDITORIAL CHAIR.

Blue Parlor.—SHEPHERD *and* TICKLER.

Shepherd. I had nae heart for't, Mr. Tickler, I had nae heart for't. Yon's a grand hotel in Picardy—and there can be nae manner o' doubt that Mr. Ambrose 'll succeed in it. Yon big letters facing doun Leith Walk will be sure to catch the een o' a' the passengers by London smacks and steamboats, to say naething o' the mair stationary land population. Besides, the character o' the man himself, sae douce, civil, and judicious. But skill part from my right hand when I forget Gabriel's Road. Draw in your chair, sir.

Tickler. I wish the world, James, would stand still for some dozen years—till I am at rest. It seems as if the very earth itself were undergoing a vital change. Nothing is unalterable except the heaven above my head—and even it, James, is hardly, methinks at times, the same as in former days or nights. There is not much difference in the clouds, James, but the blue sky, I must confess, is not quite so very, very blue as it was sixty years since; and the sun, although still a glorious luminary, has lost a leetle—just a leetle—of his lustre. But it is the streets, squares, courts, closes,

--lands, houses, shops, that are all changed—gone—swept off—razed—buried.

> "And that is sure a reason fair,
> To fill my glass again."

Shepherd. Ony reason's fair enough for that. Here's to you, sir—the Hollands in this house is aye maist excellent. . . . Is the oysters verra gude this season? I shanna stir frae this chair till I hae devoored five score o' them. That's just my allowance on coming in frae the kintra.

Tickler. James, that is a most superb cloak. Is the clasp pure gold? You are like an officer of hussars—like one of the Prince's Own. Spurs too, I protest!

Shepherd. Sit closer, Mr. Tickler, sit closer, man; light your cigar, and puff away like a steam-engine—though ye ken I just detest smokin;—for I hae a secret to communicate—a secret o' some pith and moment, Mr. Tickler; and I want to see your face in a' the strength o' it's maist natural expression when I am lettin you intil't. Fill your glass, sir.

Tickler. Don't tell it to me, James—don't tell it to me; for the greatest enjoyment I have in this life is to let out a secret—especially if it has been confided to me as a matter of life and death.

Shepherd. I'll rin a' hazards. I maun out wi't to you; for I hae aye had the most profoun' respect for your abeelities, and I hae a pleasure in giein you the start o' the world for four-and-twenty hours.—I am noo the Yeditor o' *Blackwood's Magazine.*

Tickler. Angels and ministers of grace defend us!

Shepherd. Why, you see, sir, they couldna do without me. North's getting verra auld—and, between you and me, rather doited—crabbed to the contributors, and—come hither wi' your lug—no verra ceevil to Ebony himsel; so out comes letter upon letter to me, in Yarrow yonder, fu' o' the maist magnificent offers—indeed, telling me to fix my ain terms, and, faith, just to get rid o' the endless fash o' letters by the carrier, I druve into toun here, in the Whusky, through Peebles, on the Saturday o' the hard frost, and that same night was installed into the Yeditorship in the Sanctum Sanctorum.

Tickler. Well, James, all that Russian affair * is a joke to this. Nicholas, Constantine, and the old Mother-Empress may go to the devil and shake themselves, now that you, my dear, dear Shepherd, are raised to the Scottish throne.

Shepherd. Wha wad hae thocht it, Mr. Tickler—wha wad hae thocht it—that day when I first entered the Grassmarket wi' a' my flock afore me, and Hector youf-youfin round the Gallow-Stane—where, in days of yore, the saints—

Tickler. Sire !

Shepherd. Nane o' your mocking—I'm the Editor ; and, to prove't, I'll order in—the Balaam-box.

Tickler. James, as you love me, open not that box.—Pandora's was a joke to it.

Shepherd. Ha! ha! ha! Mr. Tickler, you're feared that I'll lay my haun on yane o' your articles. O man, but you're a vain auld chiel; just a bigot to your ain abeelities. But hear me, sir; you maun compose in a mair classical style gin you think o' continuing a contributor. I must not let down the character of the work to flatter a few feckless fumblers. Mr. Ambrose—Mr. Ambrose—the Balaam-box I tell you—I hae been ringing this half-hour for the Balaam-box.

Mr. Ambrose. Here is the safe, sir. I observe the spider is still in the key-hole ; but as Mr. North, God bless him, told

* The "Russian affair" was the declinature by Constantine of the Russian sceptre, in favor of his younger brother Nicholas, who died on the 2nd of March, 1855.

me not to disturb him, I have given him a few flies daily that I found in an old bottle; perhaps he will get out of the way when he feels the key.

Tickler. James, that spider awakens in my mind the most agreeable recollections.

Shepherd. Dang your speeders. But, Mr. Ambrose, where's the Monthly Budget?

Mr. Ambrose. Here, sir.

Shepherd (emptying the green bag on the table). Here, Mr. Tickler. Here's a sight for sair een—materials for a dizzen numbers. Arrange them by tens—that's right; what a show! I'm rich aneuch to pay aff the national debt. Let us see—"Absenteeism." The speeder maun be disturbed—into the Balaam-box must this article go. Gude preserve us, what a weight! I wonder what my gude auld father wad hae said, had he lived to see the day when it became a great public question whether it was better or waur for a country that she should hae nae inhabitants! . . . What's that your glowering on, Sub?

Tickler. Sub?

Shepherd. Ay, Sub. I create you Sub-yeditor of the Magazine. You maun correc' a' the Hebrew, and Chinese, and German, and Dutch, Greek and Latin, and French and Spanish, and Itawlian. You maun likewise help me wi' the pints, and in kittle words look after the spellin. Noo and then ye may overhaul, and cut down, and transmogrify an article that's ower lang, or ower stupid in pairts, putting some smeddum * in't, and soomin a' up wi' a soundin peroration. North had nae equal at that; and I hae kent him turn out o' his hands a short, pithy, biting article, frae a long lank, lumbering rigmarole, taken, at a pinch, out the verra Balaam-box. The author wondered at his ain genius and

* *Smeddum*—spirit.

erudition when he read it, and wad gang for a week after up and down the town, asking everybody he met if they had read his leading-article in Ebony. The sumph thocht he had written it himsel! I can never hope to equal Mr. North in that faculty, which in him is a gift o' nature; but in a things else I am his equal,—and in some, dinna ye think sae his superior?

Tickler. I do. There seems to me something pretty in this little song. To do it justice, I must sing it. (*Sings.*)

> "Oh! often on the mountain's side
> I've sung with all a shepherd's pride,
> And Yarrow, as he roll'd along,
> Bore down the burden of the song.
> A shepherd's life's the life for me
> He tends his flock so merrily,—
> He sings his song, and tells his tale, *
> And is beloved through all the vale."

Shepherd. Tut, tut!—it's wersh †—wersh as a potauto without saut. The writer o' that sang never wore a plaid. What for will clever chaps, wi' a classical education, aye be writin awa at sangs about us shepherds? Havers! ‡ Let Burns, and me, and Allan Cunningham talk o' kintra matters under our ain charge. We'll put mair real life and love into ae line—aiblins into a word—than a' the classical callants that ever were at college.

Tickler. Well, well—here's a poem that may as well go into the fire-heap at once, without further inspection.

Shepherd. For God's sake, haud your hand, Mr. Tickler!—dinna burn that, as you houp to be saved! It's my ain haun-writin—I ken't at a' this distance—I'll swear till't in a court o' justice! Burn that, and you're my Sub nae langer.

* *Tells his tale.* Milton in *l'Allegro*, uses this expression as a synonym for "counts his flock;" here, by a singular misapprehension, the words seem to be used literally in the sense of "tells his *story!*"

† *Wersh*—insipid. ‡ *Havers*—jargon.

Tickler. My dear Editor, I will sing it.

Shepherd. Na, you shanna sing't—I'll sing't mysel, though I'm as hoarse as a craw. Breathin that easterly harr is as bad as snooking down into your hawse sae many yards o' woollen. Howsomever, I'll try. And mind, nane o' your accompaniments wi' me, either o' fiddle or vice. A second's a thing that I just perfectly abhor,—it seems to me—though I hae as gude an ear as Miss Stephens* hersel—and better, too—to be twa different tunes sang at ae time—a maist intolerable practice. Mercy me! It's the twa Epithaliums that I wrote for the young Duke o' Buccleuch's birthday, held at Selkirk the 25th of November, 1825.† (*sings.*)

Rejoice, ye wan and wilder'd glens,
Ye dowie dells o' Yarrow.

Tickler. Beautiful, James, quite beautiful!

Shepherd. Mr. Tickler, I think, considering all things,—the situation I now occupy, my rank in society, and the respect which I have at all times been proud to show you and Mrs. Tickler, that you might call me Mr. Hogg, or Mr. Yeditor. Why always James—simple James?

Tickler. A familiar phrase, full of affection. I insist on being called Timothy.

Shepherd. Weel, weel, be it so now and then. But as a general rule, let it be Mr. Tickler—Mr. Hogg, or, which I would prefer, Mr. Editor. Depend upon it, sir, that there is great advantage to social intercourse in the preservation of those mere conversational forms by which "table talk" is protected from degenerating into a coarse or careless familiarity.

Tickler. Suppose you occasionally call me "Southside," and that I call you "Mount Benger"—

* Afterwards the Countess of Essex.

† Hogg's munificent landlord, the present Duke of Buccleuch, born in 1806.

Shepherd. A true Scottish fashion that of calling gentlemen by the names of their estates. Did you ever see the young Duke? You nod, Never!—He's a real scion of the old tree. What power that laddie has ower human happiness!—He has a kingdom, and never had a king more loyal subjects. All his thousands o' farmers are proud o' him and his executors and that verra pride gies them a higher character. The clan must not disgrace the Chief. The "Duke" is a household word all over that Border—the bairns hear it every day—and it links us thegither in a sort o' brotherhood. Curse the Radicals, who would be for destroying the old aristocracy of the land! (*Sings the second Epithalium,*—WAT O' BUCCLEUCH.) There's a sang for you, Timothy. My blude's up. I bless Heaven I am a Borderer. Here's the Duke's health—here's the King's health—here's North's health—here's your health—here's my ain health—here's Ebony's health—here's Ambrose's health—the healths o' a' the contributors and a' the subscribers. That was a wully-waught! * I haena left a dribble in the jug. I wuss it mayna flee to my head—it's a half-mutchkin jug.

Tickler. Your eyes, James, are shining with more than their usual brilliancy. But here it goes. (*Drinks his jug.*)

Shepherd. After all, what blessing is in this world like a rational, well founded, stedfast friendship between twa people that hae seen some little o' human life—felt some little o' its troubles—kept fast hauld o' gude character, and are doing a' they can for the benefit o' their fellow-creatures? The Magazine, Mr. Tickler, is a mighty engine, and it behoves me to think well what I am about when I set it a-working.

Tickler. Try the anchovies. I forget if you skate, Hogg?

Shepherd. Yes, like a flounder. I was at Duddingston Loch on the great day. Twa bands of music kept cheering the

* *Wully-waught*—large draught.

shade of King Arthur on his seat, and gave a martial character to the festivities. It was then, for the first time, that I mounted my cloak and spurs. I had a young leddie, you may weel guess that, on ilka arm; and it was pleasant to feel the dear, timorous creturs clinging and pressing on a body's sides every time their taes caught a bit crunkle on the ice, or an imbedded chucky-stane. I thocht that between the twa they wad never hae gien ower till they had pu'd me doun on the breid o' my back. The muffs were just amazing, and the furbelows past a' enumeration. It was quite Polar. Then a' the ten thousand people (there couldna be fewer) were in perpetual motion. Faith, the thermometer made them do that, for it was some fifty below zero. I've been at mony a bonspeil, but I never saw such a congregation on the ice afore. Once or twice it cracked, and the sound was fearsome,—a lang, sullen growl, as of some monster starting out o' sleep, and raging for prey. But the bits o' bairns just leuch, and never gied ower sliding; and the leddies, at least my twa, just gied a kind o' sab, and drew in their breath, as if they had been gaun in naked to the dookin on a cauld day; and the mirth and merriment were rifer than ever. Faith, I did make a dinner at the Club-house.

Tickler. Did you skate, James?

Shepherd. That I did, Timothy—but ken you hoo? You will have seen how a' the newspapers roosed the skatin o' an offisher, that they said lived in the Castle. Fools!—it was me—naebody but me. Ane o' my twa leddies had a wig in her muff, geyan sair curled on the frontlet, and I pat it on the hair o' my head. I then drew in my mouth, puckered my cheeks, made my een look fierce, hung my head on my left shouther, put my hat to the one side, and so, arms akimbo, off I went in a figure of 8, garring the crowd part like clouds, and circumnavigating the frozen ocean in the space of about two minutes. " The curlers quat their roaring play," and every tent cast forth its inmates, with a bap in the ae haun and a gill in the ither, to behold the offisher frae the Castle. The only fear I had was o' my long spurs; but they never got fankled; and I finished with doing the 47th Proposition of Euclid with mathematical precision.

Tickler. My dear Editor, you are forgetting the articles. The devil will be here for copy. . . .

Shepherd. Mr Tickler, here's a most capital article, entitled "Birds."* I ken his pen the instant I see the scart o't. Naebody can touch aff these light, airy, buoyant, heartsome articles like him. Then there's aye sic a fine dash o' nature in them—sic nice touches o' description—and, every now and then, a bit curious and peculiar word—just ae word and nae mair, that lets you into the spirit of the whole design, and makes you love both the writer and written.—Square down the edges with the paper-folder, and label it "Leading Article."

Tickler. I wish he was here.

Shepherd. He's better where he is, for he's a triflin creatur when he gets a bit drink; and then the tongue o' him never lies.—Birds—Birds!—I see he treats only o' singing birds; —he maun gie us afterhend Birds o' Prey. That's a grand subject for him. Save us! what he would mak o' the King o' the Vultures! Of course he would breed him on Imaus. His flight is far, and he fears not famine. He has a hideous head of his own—fiend-like eyes—nostrils that woo the murky air—and beak fit to dig into brain and heart. Don't forget Prometheus and his liver. Then dream of being sick in a desert place, and of seeing the Vulture-King alight within ten yards of you—folding up his wings very composedly—

* This article, written by Professor Wilson, appeared in *Blackwood's Magazine*, vol. xix. p. 105.

and then coming with his horrid bald scalp close to your ear, and beginning to pick rather gently at your face, as if afraid to find you alive. You groan—and he hobbles away with an angry shriek, to watch you die. You see him whetting his beak upon a stone, and gaping wide with hunger and thirst. Horror pierces both your eyelashes before the bird begins to scoop; and you have already all the talons of both his iron feet in your throat. Your heart's blood freezes; but notwithstanding that, by and by he will suck it up; and after he has gorged himself till he cannot fly, but falls asleep after dinner, a prodigious flock of inferior fierce fowl come flying from every part of heaven, and gobble up the fragments.

Tickler. A poem—a poem—a poem!—quite a poem!

Shepherd. My certes, Mr. Tickler, here's a copy of verses that Ambrose has dropped that are quite pat to the subject. Hearken—here's the way John Kemble used to read. Stop—I'll stand up, and use his action too, and mak my face as like his as I can contrive. There's difference o' features, but very muckle o' the same expression. (*Recites.*)

"Oh to be free, like the eagle of heaven."

Tickler. I used sometimes to think that North gave us too little poetry in the Magazine. Here's a little attempt of my own, Mr. Editor—if I thought it could pass muster.

Shepherd. Ou ay. But what noise is that? Do you hear ony noise in the lobby, Mr. Tickler? Dot, Dot, Dot! Dinna you hear't? It's awfu'! This way. O Lord! it's Mr. North, it's Mr. North, and I am a dead man. I am gaun to be deteckit in personating the Yeditor. I'll be hanged for forgery. Wae's me—wae's me! Could I get into that press? or into ane o' the garde-du-vins o' the sideboard? Or maun I loup at ance ower the window, and be dashed to a thousand pieces?

Tickler. Compose yourself, James—compose yourself. But what bam is this you have been playing off upon me? I thought North had resigned, and that you were, *bonâ fide*, editor. And I too! Am not I your Sub? What is this, Mount Benger? *

Shepherd. A sudden thocht strikes me. I'll put on the wig, and be the offisher frae the Castle. Paint my ee-brees wi' burned cork—fast, man, fast—the gouty auld deevil's at the door.

Tickler. That will do—on with your cloak. It may be said of you, as of the Palmer in *Marmion*—

"Ah me! the mother that you bare,
If she had been in presence there,
In cork'd eyebrows and wig so fair,
She had not known her child."

(*Enter* NORTH).

North. Mr. Tickler! Beg pardon, sir,—a stranger.

Tickler. Allow me to introduce to you Major Moggridge, of the Prince's Own.

North. How do you do, Major?—I am happy to see you. I have the honor of ranking some of my best friends among the military—and who has not heard of the character of your regiment?

The Major (*very short-sighted*). Na—how do you do, Mr. North? 'Pon honor, fresh as a two-year-old. Is it, indeed, the redoubtable Kit that I see before me? You must become a member of the United Service Club. We can't do without you. You served, I think, in the American War. Did you know Fayette, or Washington, or Lee, or Arnold? What sort of a looking fellow was Washington?

North. Why, Major, Washington was much such a good-

* Hogg's territorial title, from the name of his farm.

looking fellow as yourself, making allowance for difference in dress—for he was a plain man in his apparel. But he had the same heroic expression of countenance—the same commanding eye and bold broad forehead.

The Major. He didna mak as muckle use, surely, o' the Scottish deealec as me?

North. What is the meaning of this? I have heard that voice before—where am I? Excuse me, sir, but—but—why, Tickler has Hogg a cousin, or a nephew, or a son in the Hussars? Major Moggridge, you have a strong resemblance to one of our most celebrated men, the Ettrick Shepherd. Are you in any way connected with the Hoggs?

Shepherd (throwing off his disguise). O ye Gawpus! Ye great Gawpus! It's me, man—it's me! Tuts, man, dinna lose your temper. Dinna you think I would mak a capital play-actor?

North. Why, James, men at my time of life are averse to such waggeries.

Shepherd. Averse to waggeries! You averse to waggeries? Then let us a' begin saying our prayers, for the end o' the world is at hand. Now that's just the way baith wi' you and Mr. Tickler. As lang as you get a' your ain way, and think you hae the laugh against the Shepherd, a's richt—and you keckle, and you craw, and you fling the straw frae ahint the heel o' you, just like game-cocks when about to gi'e battle. Vow, but you're crouse; * but sae sune as I turn the tables on you, gegg you, as they would say in Glasgow—turn you into twa asses, and make you wonder if your lugs are touching the ceiling—but immediately you begin whimpering about your age and infirmities—immediately you baith draw up your mouths as if you had been eatin sourocks, let down your jaws like so many undertakers, and

* *Crouse*—brisk and confident.

propose being philosophical! Isna that the truth, the whole truth, and nothing but the truth?

North. I fear, James, you're not perfectly sober.

Shepherd. If I am fou, sir, it's nae been at your expense. But, howsomever, here I am ready to dispute wi' you on ony subject, sacred or profane. I'll cowp * you baith, ane after the ither. What sall it be? History, Philosophy, Theology, Poetry, Political Economy, Oratory, Criticism, Jurisprudence, Agriculture, Commerce, Manufactures, Establishments in Church and State, Cookery, Chemistry, Mathematics—OR MY MAGAZINE?

North. Your Magazine?

Shepherd (*bursting into a guffaw*). O Mr. North! O Mr. North! what a fule I hae made o' Tickler. I made him believe that I was the Yeditor o' *Blackwood's Magazine!* The coof credited it; and gin you only heard hoo he abused you! He ca'd you the Archbishop of Toledo.

Tickler. You lie, Hogg!

Shepherd. There's manners for you, Mr. North. Puir, passionate cretur, I pity him, when I think o' the apology he maun mak to me in a' the newspapers.

North. No, no, my good Shepherd—be pacified, if he goes down here on his knees.

Shepherd. Stop a wee while, till I consider. Na, na; he maunna gang doun on his knees—I couldna thole to see that. Then, I was wrang in saying he abused you. So let us baith say we were wrang, preceesely at the same moment. Gi'e the signal, Mr. North.

Tickler.
Shepherd. } I ask pardon.

North. Let us embrace. (*Tria juncta in uno.*)

Shepherd. Hurra! hurra! hurra!—Noo for the Powldowdies.†

* *Cowp*—overthrow. † *Powldowdies*—oysters.

V.

IN WHICH THE SHEPHERD ROUTS MULLION

Blue Parlor.—NORTH, SHEPHERD, TICKLER, MULLION.

Shepherd. You may keep wagging that tongue o' yours, Mr. Tickler, till midsummer, but I'll no stir a foot frae my position, that the London University, if weel schemed and weel conduckit, will be a blessing to the nation. It's no for me, nor the like o' me, to utter ae single syllable against edication. Take the good and the bad thegether, but let a' ranks hae edication.

Tickler. All ranks cannot have education.

Mullion. I agree with Mr. Tickler,—

> "A little learning is a dangerous thing.
> Drink deep, or taste not the Pierian spring."

Shepherd. Oh, man, Mullion! but you're a great gowk! What the mair dangerous are ye wi' your little learning? There's no a mair harmless creature than yoursel, man, amang a' the contributors. The Pierian spring? What ken ye about the Pierian spring? Ye never douked your lugs * intil't I'm sure. Yet, gin it were onything like a jug o' whisky, faith, ye wad hae drank deep aneuch—and then, dangerous or no dangerous, ye might hae been lugged awa to the Poleesh-office, wi' a watchman aneath ilka oxter, kickin and spurrin a' the way, like a pig in a string. Haud

* *Douked your lugs*—plunged your ears.

your tongue, Mullion, about drinkin deep, and the Pierian spring.

North. James, you are very fierce this evening. Mullion scarcely deserved such treatment.

Shepherd. Fairce? I'm nae mair fairce than the lave o' ye. A' contributors are in a manner fairce—but I canna thole to hear nonsense the nicht. Ye may just as weel tell me that a little siller's a dangerous thing. Sae, doubtless, it is, in a puir, hard-working chiel's pouch, in a change-house on a Saturday nicht—but no sae dangerous either as mair o't. A guinea's mair dangerous than a shilling, gin you reason in that gate. It's just perfect sophistry a'thegether. In like manner, you micht say a little licht's a dangerous thing, and therefore shut up the only bit wunnock* in a poor man's house, because the room was ower sma' for a Venetian! Havers! havers! God's blessings are aye God's blessings, though they come in sma's and driblets. That's my creed, Mr. North—and it's Mr. Canning's too, I'm glad to see, and that o' a' the lave o' the enlichtened men in civilized Europe.

Mullion. Why, as to Mr. Canning—I cannot say that to his opinion on that subject I attach much—

Shepherd. Haud your tongue, ye triflin cretur—ye maun hae been drinkin at some o' your caird-clubs afore you cam to Awmrose's the nicht. You're unpleasant aneuch when ye sleep, and snore, and draw your breath through a wat crinkly cough, wi' the head o' ye nid noddin, first ower your back and syne ower your breast, then on the tae shouther and then on the tither;—but onything's mair preferable than yerk, yerkin at everything said by a wiser man than yoursel—by me, or Mr. Canning, or Mr. North, when he chooses to illuminate.

* *Wunnock*—window.

Mullion. What will Mr. Canning say now about Parliamentary Reform, after that oration of his about Turgot and Galileo?

Shepherd. Turkey and Galilee! What care I about such outlandish realms? Keep to the point at issue, sir,—the edication o' the people; and if Mr. Canning does not vote wi' me for the edication o' the people, confoun' me gin he'll be Secretary o' State for the Hame Department anither session o' Parliament.

Mullion. The Foreign Department, if you please, Mr. Hogg.

Shepherd. Oh, man, that's just like you,—takin haud o' a word, as if ony rational man would draw a conclusion frae a misnomer o' a word. There's nae distinction atween Foreign and Hame Departments. Gin Mr. Canning didna ken the state o' our ain kintra, how the deevil, man, could he conduck the haill range o' international policy?

Tickler. I confess, Mr. Hogg, that—

Shepherd. Nane o' your confessions, Mr. Tickler, to me. I'm no a Roman priest. Howsomever—beg pardon for interrupting you. What's your wull?

Tickler. I confess that I like to see each order in the State keeping in its own place—following its own pursuits—practising its own virtues.

Shepherd. Noo, noo, Mr. Tickler, ye ken the unfeigned respec I hae for a' your opinions and doctrines. But ye maunna come down upon the Shepherd wi' your generaleezin. As for orders in the State, how mony thousan' o' them are there—and wha can tell what is best, to a tittle, for ilka ane o' them a' in a free kintra? I've read in beuks that there are but three orders in the State—the higher, the middle, and the lower orders. Siccan nonsense!

Mullion. The best authorities—

Shepherd. I'll no speak anither word the nicht, if that

creter Mullion keeps interruptin folk wi' that nyaffing* voice o' him in that gate. I say there are at least three thousand orders in the State—ploughmen, shepherds, ministers, squires, lords, ladies, auld women, virgins, weavers, smiths, professors, tailors, sodgers, howdies, bankers, pedlars, tinklers, poets, editors, contributors, manufacturers, annuitants, grocers, drapers, booksellers, innkeepers, advocates, writers to the W. S., grieves, bagmen, and ten hundred thousand million forbye—and wull you, Mr. Tickler, presume to tell me the proper modicum o' edication for a' these Pagan and Christian folk?

Tickler. Why, James, you put the subject in a somewhat new point of view. Go on. Mr. Mullion, if you please, let us hear James.

Shepherd. I hae little or naething to say upon the subject, Mr. North—only it is not in the power o' ony man to say what quantum o' knowledge ony other man, be his station in life what it may, ought to possess, in order to adorn that station and discharge its duties. Besides, different degrees o' knowledge must belong to different men even in the same station; and I'm sure it's no you, sir, that would haud clever chiels ignorant, that they might be on a level wi' the stupid anes o' their ain class. Raise as high as you can the clever chiels, and the stupid anes will gain a step by their elevation.

North. James, the toothache, wi' his venomed stang, has been tormenting me all this evening. Excuse my saying but little; but I am quite in the mood for listening, and I never heard you much better.

Shepherd. I'm glad o't. What's that, sir, you're pittin into your mouth?

North. The depilatory of Spain, James, a sovereign remedy for the toothache.

* *Nyaffing*—small yelping.

Shepherd. Take a mouthfu' o' speerit, and keep whurlin't aboot in your mooth—dinna spit it out, but ower wi't—then anither, and anither, and anither—and nae mair toothache in your stumps than in a fresh stab * in my garden paling.

North. James, is my cheek swelled?

Shepherd. Let's tak the cawnel, and hae a right vizy. Swalled! The tae side o' your face, man, is like a haggis, and a' the colors o' the rainbow. We maun apply leeches. I daursay Mrs. Awmrose has a dizzen in bottles in the house —but if no, I'll rin mysel to the laboratory.

North. The paroxysm is past. Look at Tickler and Mullion yonder, playing at backgammon.

Shepherd. Safe us—sae they are! Weel, do ye ken, I never ance heard the rattlin o' the dice the haill time we were speakin. You was sae enterteenin, Mr. North—sae eloquent—sae philosophical.

Mullion. That's twa ggems, Mr. Tickler. Hurra, hurra hurra!

Shepherd. Od, man, Mullion, to hear ye hurrain that gate, ane wad think ye had never won onything a' your lifetime afore. When you hae been coortin, did ye never hear a saft laigh voice saying, "Ou ay"? And did you get up, and wave your haun that way roun' your head, and cry, Hurra, hurra, hurra, like a Don Cossack?

Mullion. Do not cut me up any more to-night, James—let us be good friends. I beg pardon for snoring yestreen—for give me, or I must go—for your satire is terrible.

Shepherd. You're a capital clever chiel, Mullion. I was just tryin to see what effect severity o' manner and sarcasm wud hae upon you, and I'm content wi' the result o' the experiment. You see, Mr. North, there's Mullion—and there's millions o' Mullions in the warld—whenever he sees me

* *Stab*—stake.

frichtened for him, or modest like, which is my natural disposition, he rins in upon me like a terrier gaun to pu' a badger. That's a' I get by actin on the defensive. Sometimes, therefore, as just noo, I change my tactics, and at him open-mouthed, tooth and nail, down wi' him and worry him, as if I were a grew,* and him a bit leveret. That keeps him quate for the rest o' the nicht, and then the Shepherd can tak his swing without let or interruption.

Tickler. I have not lost a game at backgammon these five years!

Shepherd. What a lee! The tailor o' Yarrow Ford dang ye a' to bits, baith at gammon and the dambrod, that day I grupped the sawmont wi' the wee midge-flee. You were perfectly black in the face wi' anger at the bodie—but he had real scientific genius in him by the gift o' nature, the tailor o' Yarrow Ford, and could rin up three columns o' feegures at a time, no wi' his finger on the sclate, but just in his mind's ee, like George Bidder, or the American laddie Colburn.

North. Gaming is not a vice, then, in the country, James?

Shepherd. As for young folks—lads and lasses, like—when the gudeman and his wife are gane to bed, what's the harm in a ggem at cairds? It's a cheerfu', noisy sicht o' comfort and confusion. Sic luckin into ane anither's hauns! Sic fause shufflin! Sic unfair dealin! Sic winkin to tell your pairtner that ye hae the king or the ace! And when that wunna do, sic kickin o' shins and treadin on taes aneath the table—aften the wrang anes! Then down wi' your haun o' cairds in a clash on the brod, because you've ane ower few, and the coof maun lose his deal! Then what gigglin amang the lasses! What amicable, nay, love quarrels between pairtners! Jokin and jeestin, and tauntin, and toozlin—the cawnel blawn out, and the soun' o' a thousan' kisses! That's

* *Grew*—Greyhound

caird-playing in the kintra, Mr. North; and whare's the man amang ye that wull daur to say that it's no a pleasant pastime o'a winter's nicht, when the snaw is comin doon the lum, or the speat's roarin amang the mirk mountains?

Mullion. I should like to have been t'other day at the shooting of the elephant.

Tickler. Well, I should not. Elephant-feet are excellent. —*Experto crede Roberto.*

Shepherd. Tidbits! How are they dressed, Mr. Tickler? Like sheep's-head and trotters, I presume. A capital dish for a Sabbath dinner, elephant head and trotters. How mony could dine aff't? I'm gettin hungry—I've a great likin for wild beasts. Oh, man! gin we had but wolves in Scotland!

Tickler. Why, they would make you shepherds attend a little better to your own business. How could you visit Ed inburgh and Ambrose, if there were wolves in the forest?

Shepherd. I wadna grudge a score o' lambs in the year—for the wolves would only raise the price o' butcher's meat—they would do nae harm to the kintra. What grand sport, houndin the wolves in singles, or pairs, or flocks, up yonder about Loch Skene!

Tickler. What think you of a few tigers, James?

Shepherd. The royal Bengal teegger is no indigenous in Scotland, as the wolves was in ancient times; and that's ae reason against wushin to hae him amang us. Let the Alien Act be held in operation against him and may he never be naturaleezed!

Tickler. What! woul you be afraid of a tiger, James?

Shepherd. Would I be afraid o' a teegger, Timothy? No half as afeard as you wad be yourself. Faith, I wadna grudge giein a jug o' toddy to see ane play spang upon you frae a distance o' twenty yards, and wi' a single pat o' his paw on that pow o' yours, that ye haud so heigh, fracture your skull, dislocate your neck, crack your spine, and gar ye play tapsalteerie * ower a precipice into a jungle where the teegger had his bloody den.

Tickler. Would you give no assistance—lend no helping hand, James?

Shepherd. Ou ay, me and some mair wad come to the place in a week or twa, when we were sure the teegger had changed his feedin' grun', and wad collec the banes for Christian burial. But wad you be afraid o' teeggers, Timothy?

North. I once did a very foolish thing in the East Indies to a tiger. I was out shooting snipes, when the biggest and brightest royal tiger I have ever faced before or since rose up with a roar like thunder, eyeing me with fiery eyes, and tusks half a foot long, and a tail terrific to dwell upon, either in memory or imagination.

Shepherd. I didna ken there had been snipes in the East Indies?

North. Yes, and sepoys likewise. The tiger seemed, after the first blush of the business, to be somewhat disconcerted at the unexpected presence of the future Editor of *Blackwood's Magazine;* and, in a much more temperate growl, requested a parley. I hit him right in the left eye with number 7, and the distance being little more than five paces, it acted like ball, and must have touched the brain—for never surely did royal tiger demean himself with less dignity or discretion. He threw about twenty somersets, one after the other, without intermission, just as you have seen a tumbler upon a spring-board. Meanwhile I reloaded my barrel, and a wild peacock starting from cover, I could not resist the temptation, but gave away a chance against the tiger, by firing both barrels successfully against the Bird of Juno.

* *Tapsalteerie*—heels-over-head.

Shepherd. I've heard you tell that story a thousan' times, Mr. North; but ye'll pardon me for sayin noo, what I only look'd before, that it's a downright lee, without ae word o' truth in't, no even o' exaggeration. You never killed a teegger wi' snipe-shot.

North. Never, James—but I rendered him an idiot or a madman for the rest of his life. Much evil is done the cause of humanity by indiscriminate and illogical abuse of pursuits or recreations totally dissimilar. I doubt if any person can be really humane in heart unless really sound in head. You hear people talk of angling as cruel.

Shepherd. Fools—fools—waur than fools. It's a maist innocent, poetical, moral, and religious amusement. Gin I saw a fisher gruppin creelfu' after creelfu' o' trouts, and then flingin them a' awa among the heather and the brackens on his way hame, I micht begin to suspec that the idiot was by nature rather a savage. But as for me, I send presents to my freen's, and devour dizzens on dizzens every week in the family—maistly dune in the pan, wi' plenty o' fresh butter and roun' meal—sae that prevents the possibility o' cruelty in my fishin, and in the fishin o' a' reasonable creatures.

North. It seems fox-hunting, too, is cruel.

Shepherd. Ane may weel lose patience, to think o' fules being sorry for the death o' a fox. When the jowlers tear him to pieces, he shows fecht, and gangs aff in a snarl. Hoo could he dee mair easier?—and for a' the gude he has ever dune, or was likely to do, he surely had leeved lang aneuch.

North. Did you never use pencil or brush, James? I do not remember anything of yours, "by an Amateur," in any of our Exhibitions.

Shepherd. I've skarted * some odds and ends wi' the keeli-

* *Skarted*—scratched.

vine on brown paper, and Mr. Scroope * telt Sir Walter they showed a gran' natural genius. I fin' maist diffeeculty in the foreshort'nin and perspective. Things wunna retire and come forrit as I wush—and the back-grun' will be the fore-grun' whether I will or no. Sometimes, however, I dash the distance aff wi' a lucky stroke, and then I can get in the sheep or cattle in front; and the sketch, when you dinna stan' ower near, has a' the effect o' nature.

North. Do you work after Salvator Rosa or Claude Lorraine, James?

Shepherd. I'm just as original in paintin as in poetry, and follow nae master! I'm partial to close scenes—a bit neuk, wi' a big mossy stane, aiblins a birk tree, a burnie maist dried up, a' but ae deep pool, into which slides a thread o' water doun a rock—a shepherd readin—nae ither leevin thing—for the flock are ayont the knowes and up amang the green hills;—ay, anither leevin thing, and just ane,—his collie, rowed up half-asleep, wi' a pair o' lugs that still seem listenin, and his closin een towards his maister. That's a simple matter, sir, but, properly disposed, it makes a bonny pictur.

North. I should have thought it easier to "dash off" a wide open country with the keelivine.

Shepherd. So it is. I've dune a moor—gin you saw't you would doubt the earth being roun', there's sic an extent o' flat—and then, though there's nae mountain-taps, you feel you're on tableland. I contrive that by means o' the cluds. You never beheld stronger bent—some o' the stalks thick as your arm—and places wi' naething but stanes. Here and there earth-chasms, cut by the far-off folk for their peats—and on the foreground something like water, black and sullen,

* This accomplished gentleman and keen sportsman was the author of a finely illustrated work on deer stalking.

as if it quaked. Nae birds but some whaups *—ane fleein, and ane walkin by itsel, and ane just showin its lang neck amang some rushes. You think, at first, it may be the head o' a serpent—but there's nane amang our mosses, only asks, which is a sort o' lizards, or wee alligators, green, and glidin awa without noise or rustle intil the heather. Time—evening, or rather late on in the afternoon, when Nature shows a solemn—maist an awfu' stillness—and solitude, as I hae aften thocht, is deeper than at midnight.

North. James, I will give you twenty guineas for that keelivine sketch.

Shepherd. Ye'se hae't for naething sir, and welcome—if you'll only fasten't against the wa' wi' a prin † aboon the brace-piece o' your Leebrary-room. Let it be in the middle, and you sall hae Twa Brigs to hing at either side on't. The ane, a' the time I was drawin't, I could hardly persuade mysel wasna a rainbow. You see, it's flung across a torrent geyan far up a hill-side, and I was sittin sketchin't a gude piece doun below, on a cairn. The spray o' the torrent had wat a' the mosses, and flowers, and weeds, and siclike on the arch, and the sun smote it wi' sudden glory, till in an instant it burst into a variegated lowe, and I could hae taen my Bible-oath it was the rainbow. Oh! man, that I had had a pallet o' colors! I'm sure I could hae mixed them up prismatically aneuch,—yet wi' the verra mere, naked, unassisted keelivine (that day fortunately it was a red ane), I caught the character o' the apparition; and keepin my een for about a minute on the paper, shadin aff and aff, you ken, as fine as I could—when I luckit up again, naething but a bare stane-and lime brig, wi' an auld man sittin on a powney, wi' his knees up to his chin—for he happened to be a cadger,

* *Whaups*—curlews. † *Prin*—pin.

and he had his creels. I felt as if it had been a' glamour. Sae muckle for ane o' the Twa Brigs.

Tickler. Now, James, if you please, we shall adjourn to supper. It is now exactly ten o'clock, and I smell the turkey. From seven o'clock to this blessed moment your tongue has never ceased wagging. I must now have my turn.

Shepherd. Tak your turn, and welcome. As for me, I never speak nane during supper. But you may e'en give us a soliloquy.

North. Ten o'clock! Now, James, eye the folding doors —for Ambrose is true to a second. Lo, and behold!

(*The doors are thrown open.*)

Shepherd. Stop, Mullion, stop. What! will ye daur to walk before Mr. North? Tak my arm, sir.

North. My dear James, you are indeed my right-hand man. You are as firm as a rock. Thou art indeed the "Gentle Shepherd—"

Shepherd. Gentle is that gentle does—and I hope, on the whole, nane o' my freen's hae ony reason to be ashamed o' me, though I hae my failins.

North. I know not what they are, James. There—there —on the right hand—ay, say the grace, James.——Thank ye, James—we have been joking away, but now it behoves us to sit down to serious eating, while Timothy regales our ears with a monologue.

VI.

IN WHICH THE SHEPHED ASSISTS AT AN INCREMATION.

Blue Parlor.

NORTH.—TICKLER.—SHEPHERD.—CLERK OF THE BALAAM-BOX.—MR AMBROSE.—DEVIL.—PORTERS.—INCREMATORS.

Shepherd. Safe us! I was never at an Incremation afore!

North. Mr. Ambrose, bring in Balaam,* and place him on the table.

Mr. Ambrose. May I crave the assistance of the Incremators, sir—for he is heavier this year than I ever remember him, since that succeeding the Chaldee.

Shepherd. Is yon him ower-by in the window neuk. I'se tak haud o' ane o' the end-handles mysel. Come, you wee lazy deevil there, what for are you skartin your lug at that gate? Get up and be usefu'.—Noo, Mr. Ambrose, let us put a' our strength till't, and try to hoise him up, our twa lanes, ontil the table.

Tickler. My dear Shepherd, you'll burst a blood-vessel. Let me assist.

North. And me too!

Shepherd. Dinna loot † wi' that lang back o' yours, Mr. Tickler. Pity me—I hear't crackin. There, it muves! it muves!—What for are you trampin on my taes, Mr. Awmrose?

* The depository of rejected contributions. † *Loot*—stoop.

—Dinna girn that way in my face, Mr. Beelzebub. Faith, it gars us a' fowre stoiter.*

(SHEPHERD, TICKLER, BEELZEBUB, *and* AMBROSE *succeed in placing the Balaam-box on the table.*)

North. Thank ye, gentlemen. Here is a glass of Madeira to each of you.

Shepherd. North, rax me ower the Stork. There—that's a hantle heartsomer than ony o' your wines, either white or black. It's just maist excellent whisky, Glenlivet or no Glenlivet. But hech, sir, that's a sad box, that Balaam, and I'll weigh't against its ain bouk,† lead only excepted o' ony ither material noo extant, and gi'e a stane.

North. Let the Incremators take their stations.

(*They do so, one at each side of the chimney. The Incremators are firemen belonging to the Sun Fire Office.*)

Devil!

Devil. Here!

North. Clerk of the B. B.

C. B. B. Here!

North. Open Balaam.

C. B. B. Please, sir, to remember the catastrophe of last year. We must take the necessary precautions.

North. Certainly.—Mr. Hogg, on opening Balaam last year, we had neglected to put weight on the lid, and the moment the clerk had turned the key, it flew up with prodigious violence, and the jammed-down articles, as if discharged from a culverin, wafted destruction around—breaking that beautiful fifty-guinea mirror, in whose calm and lucid depths we had so often seen ourselves reflected to the very life—all but speech.

Shepherd. I could greet to think on't. A' dung ‡ to shivers —scarcely ae bit big eneuch to shave by. But the same

* *Stoiter*—stagger. † *Bouk*—bulk. ‡ *Dung*—knocked.

shinna* befa' the year—for I'se sit doun upon the lid like a guardian angel, and the lid'll hae a powerfu' spring indeed gin it whamles me ower after sic a denner.

(*The* SHEPHERD *mounts the table with youthful alacrity, and sits down on the Balaam-box.*)

North. Use both your hands, sir.

C. B. B. Beg your pardon—Mr. North—there the key turns.—Sit fast, Mr. Hogg.

Shepherd. Never mind me, I'm sittin as fast's a rock.—

(*The lid, like a catapulta, dislodges the* SHEPHERD, *who alights on his feet a few yards from the table.*)

Tickler. My dear Shepherd, why, you are a rejected contributor!

North. Mr. Ambrose, send in the scavenger.—Sorters, collect and arrange.

(C. B. B., SORTERS, *and* DEVIL *in full employment.*)

Shepherd. Thae Incremawtors hae a gran' effec! They canna be less than sax feet four, and then what whuskers! I scarcely ken whether black whuskers or red whuskers be the maist fearsome! What tangs in their hauns! and what pokers! Lucifer and Beelzebub!

North. At home, James, and at their own firesides, they are the most peaceable of men.

Shepherd. I canna believe't, Mr. North, I canna believe't! they can hae nae human feeling—neither sighs nor tears.

North. They are men, James, and do their duty.—He with the red whiskers was married this forenoon to a pretty delicate little girl of eighteen, quite a fairy of a thing—seemingly made of animated wax—so soft that, like the winged butterfly, you would fear to touch her, lest you might spoil the burnished beauty.

Shepherd. Married—on him wi' the red whuskers!

* *Shinna*—shall not.

North. Come, now, James, no affected simplicity, no Arcadian innocence!

Shepherd. You micht hae gi'en him the play the day, I think, sir; you micht hae gi'en him the play. The Incremawtor!

Devil. The sorters have made up a skuttlefu' o' poetry.—Sir, shall I deliver up to Lucifer or Beelzebub?

North. All poetry to Beelzebub.

Shepherd. A' poetry to Beelzebub!! O wae's me, wae's me.—Well-a-day, well-a-day! Has it indeed come to this? A' poetry to Beelzebub! I can scarce believe my lugs—

North. Stop, Beelzebub—read aloud that bit of paper you have in your fist.

Beelzebub. Yes, sir.

Shepherd. Lord safe us, what a voice! They're my ain verses, too. Whist—whist.

(BEELZEBUB *recites* "The great muckle village of Balmaquhapple.")

North (*to Tickler, aside*). Bad—Hogg's.

Shepherd. What's that you two are speaking about? Speak up.

North. These fine lines must be preserved, James. Pray, are they allegorical?

Shepherd. What a dracht in that lum! * It's a verra fiery furnace!—hear till't hoo it roars, like wund in a cavern! Sonnets, charauds, elegies, pastorals, lyrics, farces, tragedies, and yepics—in they a' gang into the general bleeze; then there is naething but sparkling ashes, and noo the thin, black, wavering coom o' annihilation and oblivion! It's a sad sicht, and but for the bairnliness o't, I could weel greet. Puir chiels and lasses, they had ither howps when they sat down to compose, and invoked Apollo and the Muses!

* *Lum*—chimney.

North. James, the poor creatures have been all happy in their inspiration. Why weep? Probably, too, they kept copies, and other Balaam-boxes may be groaning with duplicates. 'Tis a strange world we live in!

Shepherd. Was you ever at the burning o' heather or whins, Mr. North?

North. I have, and have enjoyed the illuminated heavens.

Tickler. Describe.

North. In half-an-hour from the first spark, the hill glowed with fire unextinguishable by waterspout. The crackle became a growl, as acre after acre joined the flames. Here and there a rock stood in the way, and the burning waves broke against it, till the crowning birch-tree took fire, and its tresses, like a shower of flaming diamonds, were in a minute consumed. Whirr, whirr, played the frequent gorcock gobbling in his fear; and, swift as shadows, the old hawks flew screaming from their young, all smothered in a nest of ashes.

Tickler. Good—excellent!—Go it again.

North. The great pine-forest on the mountain side, two miles off, frowned in ghastly light, as in a stormy sunset—and you could see the herd of red deer, a whirlwind of antlers, descending, in their terror, into the black glen, whose entrance gleamed once—twice—thrice, as if there had been lightning; and then, as the wind changed the direction of the flames, all the distance sank in dark repose.

Tickler. Vivid coloring, indeed, sir. Paint away.

North. That was an eagle that shot between and the moon.

Tickler. What an image!

North. Millions of millions of sparks of fire in heaven, but only some six or seven stars. How calm the large lustre of Hesperus!

Tickler. James, what do you think of that, eh?

Shepherd. Didna ye pity the taids and puddocks, and asks and beetles, and slaters and snails and spiders, and worms and ants, and caterpillars and bumbees, and a' the rest o' the insect-world, perishin in the flamin nicht o' their last judgment?

North. In another season, James, what life, beauty, and bliss over the verdant wilderness! There you see and hear the bees busy on the white clover—while the lark comes wavering down from heaven, to sit beside his mate on her nest! Here and there are still seen the traces of fire, but they are nearly hidden by flowers—and—

Shepherd. For a town-chiel, Mr. North, you describe the kintra wi' surprisin truth and spirit; but there's aye something rather wantin about your happiest pictures, as if you had glowered on everything in a dream or trance.

North. Like your own Kilmeny, James, I am fain to steal away from this everyday world into the Land of Glamoury.

Shepherd. O sirs! the room's gettin desperate warm. I pity the poor Incremawtors—they maun be unco dry. Beelzebub, open the window, man, ye ugly deevil, and let in a current o' cool air. Mr. North, I canna thole the heat; and I ask it as a particular favor, no to burn the prose till after supper. At a' events, let the married Incremawtor gang hame to his bride—and there's five shillings to him to drink my health at his ain ingle.

(INCREMATOR, DEVIL, CLERK OF THE BALAAM-BOX, PORTERS, *and* MR. AMBROSE *retire.*)

North. Who are the wittiest men of our day, Tickler?

Tickler. Christopher North, Timothy Tickler, and James Hogg.

North. Poo, poo—we all know that—but out of doors?

Tickler. Canning, Sydney Smith, and Jeffrey.

North. I fear it is so. Canning's wit is infallible. It is never out of time or place, and is finely proportioned to its object. Has he a good-natured, gentlemanly, well-educated blockhead—say of the landed interest—to make ridiculous, he does it so pleasantly, that the Esquire joins in the general smile. Is it a coarse, calculating dunce of the mercantile school—he suddenly hits him such a heavy blow on the organ of number, that the stunned economist is unable to sum up the total of the whole. Would some pert prig of the profession be facetious overmuch, Canning ventures to the very borders of vulgarity, and discomfits him with an old Joe. Doth some mouthing member of mediocrity sport orator, and make use of a dead tongue, then the classical Secretary * runs him through and through with apt quotations, and before the member feels himself wounded, the whole House sees that he is a dead man.

Tickler. His wit is shown in greatest power in the battles of the giants. When Brougham bellows against him, a Bull of Bashan, the Secretary waits till his horns are lowered for the death-blow, and then, stepping aside, he plants with graceful dexterity the fine-tempered weapon in the spine of the mighty Brute.

Shepherd. Whish!—Nae personality the nicht. Michty Brute.—Do you ca' Hairy Brumm a michty Brute? He's just a maist agreeable enterteenin fallow, and I recollect sittin up wi' him a' nicht, for three nichts rinnin, about thretty years syne, at Miss Ritchie's hottel, Peebles. O man, but he was wutty wutty—and bricht thochts o' a maist extraordinary kind met thegether frae the opposite poles o' the human understanding. I prophesied at every new half-mutchkin that Mr. Brumm would be a distinguished character; and there he is, you see, Leader o' the Opposition!

Tickler. His Majesty's Opposition!

* At this time Canning was Secretary of State for Foreign Affairs.

North. Sydney Smith is a wit.

Shepherd. No him—perpetually playin upon words. I canna thole to hear words played upon till they lose their natural downright meaning and signification. It was only last week that a fallow frae Edinburgh came out to the south for orders o' speerits amang the glens (rum, and brandy, and Hollands), and I asked him to dine at Mount Benger. He had hardly put his hat on a peg in the transe,* afore he began playin wi' his ain words; and he had nae sooner sat down, than he began playin wi' mine too, makin puns o' them, and double-entendres, and bits o' intolerable wutticisms, aneuch to make a body scunner. Faith, I cut him short, by tellin him that nae speerit dealer in the kingdom should play the fule in my house, and that if he was a wut, he had better saddle his powney and be aff to Selkirk. He grew red red in the face; but for the rest o' the evening, and we didna gang to bed till the sma' hours, he was not only rational, but clever and weel-informed, and I gi'ed him an order for twenty gallons.

Tickler. Yes—Sydney Smith has a rare genius for the grotesque. He is, with his quips and cranks, a formidable enemy to pomposity, and pretension. No man can wear a big wig comfortably in his presence: the absurdity of such enormous frizzle is felt; and the dignitary would fain exchange all that horse-hair for a few scattered locks of another animal.

North. He would make a lively interlocutor at a Noctes. Indeed, I intend to ask him, and Mr. Jeffrey, and Cobbett, and Joseph Hume, and a few more choice spirits, to join our festive board—

Shepherd. O man, that will be capital sports! Sic conversation!

* *Transe*—a passage within a house,—the lobby.

Tickler. O my dear James, conversation is at a very low ebb in this world!

Shepherd. I've often thought and felt that, at parties where ane micht hae expeckit better things. First o' a' comes the wather—no a bad toppic, but ane that town's folks kens naething about. Wather! My faith, had ye been but in Yarrow last Thursday!

Tickler. What was the matter, James, the last Thursday in Yarrow?

Shepherd. I'se tell you, and judge for yoursel. At four in the mornin, it was that hard frost that the dubs * were bearin, and the midden † was as hard as a rickle o' stanes. We couldna plant the potawtoes. But the lift was clear. Between eight and nine, a snaw-storm came down frae the mountains about Loch Skene—noo a whirl, and noo a blash, till the grun' was whitey-blue, wi' a sliddery sort o' sleet, and the Yarrow began to roar wi' the melted broo alang its frost-bound borders, and aneath its banks, a' hanging wi' icicles, nane o' them thinner than my twa arms. Weel, then, about eleven it began to rain, for the wund had shifted—and afore dinnertime it was an even-doun pour. It fell lown about sax, and the air grew close and sultry to a degree that was fearsome. Wha wud hae expeckit a thunderstorm on the eve o' sic a day? But the heavens, in the thundery airt, were like a dungeon—and I saw the lightning playing like meteors athwart the blackness, lang before ony growl was in the gloom. Then, a' at ance, like a waken'd lion, the thunder rose up in his den, and shakin his mane o' brindled clouds, broke out into sic a roar, that the very sun shuddered in eclipse—and the grews and collies that happened to be sittin beside me on a bit knowe, gaed whinin into the house wi' their tails atween their legs, just venturin a hafflin

* *Dubs*—puddles. † *Midden*—dunghill.

glance to the howling heavens, noo a' in low, for the fire was strong and fierce in electrical matter, and at intervals the illuminated mountains seemed to vomit out conflagration like verra volcanoes.

Tickler. 'Επεα πτεροεντα!

Shepherd. Afore sunset, heaven and earth, like lovers after a quarrel, lay embraced in each other's smile!

North. Beautiful! Beautiful! Beautiful!

Tickler. Oh! James—James—James!

Shepherd. The lambs began their races on the lea, and the thrush o' Eltrive (there is but a single pair in the vale aboon the kirk) awoke his hymn in the hill silence. It was mair like a mornin than an evenin twilight, and a' the day's hurly-burly had passed awa into the uncertainty o' a last week's dream!

North. Proof positive that, from the lips of a man of genius, even the weather—

Shepherd. I could speak for hours, days, months, and years about the wather, without e'er becoming tiresome. O man, a cawm!

North. On shore, or at sea?

Shepherd. Either. I'm wrapped up in my plaid, and lyin a' my length on a bit green platform, fit for the faries' feet, wi' a craig hangin ower me a thousand feet high, yet bright and balmy a' the way up wi' flowers and briars, and broom and birks, and mosses maist beautifu' to behold wi' half-shut ee, and through aneath ane's arm, guardin the face frae the cloudless sunshine!

North. A rivulet leaping from the rock—

Shepherd. No, Mr. North, no loupin; for it seems as if it were nature's ain Sabbath, and the verra waters were at rest. Look down upon the vale profound, and the stream is without motion! No doubt, if you were walking along the bank, it would be murmuring with your feet. But here—here up among the hills, we can imagine it asleep, even like the well within reach of my staff!

North. Tickler, pray make less noise, if you can, in drinking, and also in putting down your tumbler. You break in upon the repose of James' picture.

Shepherd. Perhaps a bit bonny butterfly is resting wi' faulded wings on a gowan, no a yard frae your cheek; and noo, waukening out o' a simmer dream, floats awa in its wavering beauty, but, as if unwilling to leave its place of mid-day sleep, comin back and back, and roun' and roun', on this side and that side, and ettlin * in its capricious happiness to fasten again on some brighter floweret, till the same breath o' wund that lifts up your hair sae refreshingly catches the airy voyager, and wafts her away into some other nook, of her ephemeral paradise.

Tickler. I did not know that butterflies inhabited the region of snow.

Shepherd. Ay, and mony million moths; some o' as lovely green as of the leaf of the moss-rose, and ithers bright as the blush with which she salutes the dewy dawn; some yellow as the long steady streaks that lie below the sun at set, and ithers blue as the sky before his orb has westered. Spotted, too, are all the glorious creatures' wings—say, rather, starred wi' constellations! Yet, O sirs, they are but creatures o' a day!

North. Go on with the calm, James—the calm!

Shepherd. Gin a pile o' grass straughtens itself in silence, you hear it distinctly. I'm thinkin that was the noise o' a beetle gaun to pay a visit to a freen on the ither side o' that mossy stane. The melting dew quakes! Ay, sing awa, my bonny bee, maist industrious o' God's creatures! Dear me,

* *Ettlin*—intending, attempting.

the heat is ower muckle for him, and he burrows himsel in amang a tuft o' grass, like a beetle panting! and noo invisible a' but the yellow doup o' him. I too feel drowsy, and will go to sleep amang the mountain solitude.

North. Not with such a show of clouds—

Shepherd. No! not with such a show of clouds. A congregation of a million might worship in that Cathedral! What a dome! And is not that flight of steps magnificent? My imagination sees a crowd of white-robed spirits ascending to the inner shrine of the temple. Hark—a bell tolls! Yonder it is, swinging to and fro, half-minute time, in its tower of clouds. The great air-organ 'gins to blow its pealing anthem—and the overcharged spirit, falling from its vision, sees nothing but the pageantry of earth's common vapors—that ere long will melt in showers, or be wafted away in darker masses over the distance of the sea. Of what better stuff, O Mr. North, are made all our waking dreams? Call not thy Shepherd's strain fantastic; but look abroad over the work-day world, and tell him where thou seest aught more steadfast or substantial than that cloud-cathedral, with its flight of vapor-steps, and its mist towers, and its air-organ, now all gone for ever, like the idle words that imaged the transitory and delusive glories.

Tickler. Bravo, Shepherd, bravo! You have nobly vindicated the weather as a topic of conversation. What think you of the Theatre—Preaching—Politics—Magazines and Reviews, and the threatened Millenium?

Shepherd. Na, let me tak my breath. What think ye Mr. Tickler, yoursel, o' preachin?

Tickler. No man goes to church more regularly than I do; but the people of Scotland are cruelly used by their ministers. No sermon should exceed half an hour at the utmost. That is a full allowance. . . . (*The long-winded are rated by the three.*)

North. What the deuce is the meaning of all this vituperation?

Shepherd. Deil tak me gin I ken. But I fin' mysel gettin desperate angry at something or ither, and could abuse maist onybody. Wha was't that introduced the toppic o' kirks? I'm sure it wasna me. It was you, Mr. Tickler.

Tickler. Me introduce the top of kirks?

Shepherd. Yes; you said, "What think you of the theatre — preaching — politics — magazines and reviews, and the threatened millennium?" I'll swear to the verra words, as if I had taen them down wi' the keelivine.

North. James, don't you think Tickler would have been an admirable preacher?

Shepherd. I canna say; but I could answer for his being a good precentor.*

Tickler. Why not a preacher?

Shepherd. You wadna hae been to be depended on. Your discourses, like your ain figure, wad hae wanted proportion; and as for doctrine, I doubt you wad hae been heterodox. Then, you wad hae been sic a queer-lookin chiel in the poupit!

Tickler. Don't you think I would have been an admirable Moderator? †

Shepherd. You're just best as you are—a gentleman at large. You're scarcely weel adapted for ony profession—except maybe a fizician. You wad hae fan'‡ a pulse wi' a true Esculawpian solemnity; and that face o' yours, when you looked glum or gruesome, wad hae frichtened families into fees, and held patients down to sick-beds, season after season. O man! but you wad hae had gran' practice.

* The "precentor" in the Presbyterian service corresponds to the "clerk" in the Episcopalian.

† Moderator, or president, of the General Assembly of the Church of Scotland.

‡ *Fan'*—felt.

Tickler. I could not have endured the quackery of the thing, Hogg.

Shepherd. Haud your tongue. There's equal quackery in a' things alike. Look at a sodger—that is, an offisher—a' wavin wi' white plumes, glitterin wi' gowd, and ringin wi' iron—gallopin on a grey horse, that caves * the foam frae its fiery nostrils, wi' a mane o' clouds, and a tail that flows like a cataract—mustachies about the mouth like a devourin cannibal, and proud, fierce een, that seem glowerin for an enemy into the distant horrison—his long swurd swinging in the scabbard wi' a fearsome clatter aneath Bellerophon's belly —and his doup dunshin † down among the spats o' a teeger's skin, or that o' a leopard—till the sound o' the trumpet gangs up to the sky, answered by the rampaugin Arab's "ha, ha,"—and a' the stopped street stares on the aide-de-camp o' the stawf,—writers' clerks, bakers, butchers, and printers' deevils, a' wushin they were sodgers,—and leddies frae balconies, where they sit shooin silk purses in the sunshine, start up, and, wi' palpitatin hearts, send looks o' love and languishment after the Flyin Dragon.

North. Mercy on us, James, you are a perfect Tyrtæus.

Shepherd. O! wad you believe't—but it's true—that at school that symbol o' extermination was ca'd Fozie ‡ Tam?

North. Spare us, James—spare us. The pain in our side returns.

Shepherd. Every callant in the class could gie him his licks; and I recollec ance a lassie geein him a bloody nose. He durstna gang into the dookin § aboon his doup, for fear o' drownin, and even then wi' seggs; ¶ and as for speelin trees,

* *Caves*—tosses.

† *Dunshin.*—There seems to be no English word for this except "bumping;" yet how feeble.

‡ *Fozie*—soft as a frost-bitten turnip.

§ *Dookin*—bathing.

¶ *Seggs*—sedges, answering the purpose of a cork jacket.

he never ventured aboon the rotten branches o' a Scotch fir. He was feared for ghosts, and wadna sleep in a room by himsel ; and ance on a Halloween, he swarfed at the apparition o' a lowin turnip.* But noo he's a warrior, and fought at Waterloo. Yes—Fozie Tam wears a medal, for he overthrew Napoleon. Ca' ye na that quackery, wi' a vengeance?

North. Why, James, you do not mean surely thus to characterize the British soldier?

Shepherd. No. The British army, drawn up in order o' battle, seems to me an earthly image of the power of the right hand of God. But still what I said was true, and nae ither name had he at school but Fozie Tam. O sirs! when I see what creturs like him can do, I could greet that I'm no a sodger.

Tickler. What the deuce can they do, that you or I, James, cannot do as well, or better?

Shepherd. I wonder to hear you askin. Let you or me gang into a public room at ae door, amang a hunder bonny lassies, and Fozie Tam in full uniform at anither, and every star in the firmament will shine on him alone—no a glint for ane o' us twa—no a smile or a syllable—we can only see the back o' their necks.

Tickler. And bare enough they probably are, James.

Shepherd. Nae great harm in that, Mr. Tickler, for a bonny bare neck can do naebody ill, and to me has aye rather the look o' innocence—but maun a poet or orator—

Tickler. Be neglected on account of Fozie Tam?

Shepherd. And by mony o' the verra same creturs that at a great leeterary sooper the nicht afore were sae affable and sae flatterin, askin me to receet my ain verses, and sing my ain sangs—drinkin the health o' the Author o' the *Queen's Wake* in toddy out o' his ain tumbler—shakin hauns at partin, and

* A turnip lanthorn.

in the confusion at the foot o' the stairs, puttin their faces sae near mine, that their sweet, warm breath was maist like a faint, doubtfu' kiss, dirlin * to ane's very heart—and after a' this, and mair than this, only think o' being clean forgotten, overlooked, or despised for the sake o' Fozie Tam!

Tickler. We may have our revenge. Wait till you find him in plain clothes—on half-pay, James, or sold out—and then, like Romeo, when the play is over, and the satin breeches off, he walks behind the scenes, no better than a tavern-waiter, or a man-milliner's apprentice.

Shepherd. There's some comfort in that, undoubtedly.—Are the Fife hens layin?

North. Yes, James, and Tapitoury is sitting.

Shepherd. That's richt. Weel, o' a' the how-towdies I ever ate, yon species is the maist truly gigantic. I could hae taen my Bible-oath that they were turkeys. Then I thocht, "Surely they maun be capons;" but when I howked into the inside o' ane o' them, and brought out a spoonfu' o' yellow eggs, frae the size o' a peppercorn to that o' a boy's bools, † and up to the bulk o' a ba' o' thread, thinks I to mysel, "Sure aneuch they are hens," and close upon the layin. Maist a pity to kill them!

North. James, you shall have a dozen eggs to set, and future ages will wonder at the poultry of the Forest. Did you ever see a capercailzie?

Shepherd. Never. They have been extinct in Scotland for fifty years. But the truth is, Mr. North, that all domesticated fowl would live brawly if turned out into the wilds and woods. They might lose in size, but they would gain in sweetness—a wild sweetness—caught frae leaves and heather-berries, and the products o' desert places, that are blooming like the rose. A tame turkey wad be a wild ane in sax months; and oh,

* *Dirlin*—thrilling.

† *Bools*—marbles.

sir! it wad be gran' sport to see and hear a great big bubbly-jock* gettin on the wing in a wood, wi' a loud gobble, gobble, gobble, redder than ordinar in the face, and the ugly feet o' him danglin aneath his heavy hinder-end, till the hail brought him down with a thud and a squelch amang the astonished pointers!

North. You seem melancholy, Tickler—a penny for your thoughts.

Tickler. I am depressed under the weight of an unwritten article. That everlasting Magazine of yours embitters my existence. Oh that there were but one month in the year without a *Blackwood!*

Shepherd. Or rather a year in ane's life without it, that a body micht hae leisure to prepare for anither warld. Hoo the Numbers accumulate on the shelve o' ane's leebrary! I begin to think they breed. Then a dizzen or twa are maistly lyin on the drawers-head—twice as mony mair in the neuks o' rooms, up and down stairs—the servants get haud o' them in the kitchen—and ye canna open the press to tak a dram, but there's the face o' Geordy Buchanan.

Tickler. My dear Shepherd, you are a happy man in the Forest, beyond the clutches and the clack of an Editor. But here am I worried to death by devils, from the tenth to the twentieth of every month. I wish I was dead.

Shepherd. You dinna wush ony sic thing, Mr. Tickler. That appeteet o' yours is worth five thousan' a year. O man! it wad be a sair pity to dee wi' sic an appeteet!

[*Clock strikes ten—folding-doors fly open, and the* Tria Lumina Scotorum *sit down to supper.*

* *Bubbly-jock*—turkey-cock.

VII.

AT THE LODGE IN SUMMER.

Scene,—Buchanan Lodge—Porch. Time,—Afternoon.

NORTH.—TICKLER.—SHEPHERD.

Shepherd. What a changed warld, sirs, since that April forenoon we druv doun to the Lodge in a cotch! I couldna but pity the puir Spring.

Tickler. Not a primrose to salute his feet that shivered in the snow-wreath.

North. Not a lark to hymn his advent in the uncertain sunshine.

Shepherd. No a bit butterflee on its silent waver, meeting the murmur of the straightforward bee.

Tickler. In vain Spring sought his Flora, in haunts beloved of old, on the banks of the shaded rivulet—

North. Or in nooks among the rocky mountains—

Shepherd. Or oases among the heather—

Tickler. Or parterres of grove-guarded gardens—

North. Or within the shadow of veranda—

Shepherd. Or forest glade, where move the antlers of the unhunted red deer.—In siccan bonny spats hae I often seen the Spring, like a doubtfu' glimmer o' sunshine, appearing and disappearing frae amang the birk-trees, twenty times in the course o' an April day.—But, oh! sirs, yon was just a maist detestable forenoon,—and as for the hackney-cotch—

Tickler. The meanest of miseries!

Shepherd. It's waur than sleepin in damp sheets. You haena sat twa hunder yards till your breeks are glued to the clammy seat, that fin's* saft and hard aneath you at ane and the same time, in a maist unaccountable manner. The auld, cracked, stained, faded, tarnished, red leather lining stinks like a tan-yard. Gin you want to let down the window, or pu't up, it's a' alike; you keep rugging at the lang slobbery worsted till it comes aff wi' a tear in your haun, and leaves you at the mercy o' wind and weather,—then what a sharp and continual rattle o' wheels! far waur than a cart; intolerable aneuch ower the macadam, but Lord hae mercy on us when you're on the causeway! you could swear the wheels are o' different sizes; up wi' the tae side, doun wi' the tither, sae that nae man can be sufficiently sober to keep his balance. Puch! puch! what dung-like straw aneath your soles; and as for the roof, sae laigh that you canna keep on your hat, or it'll be dunshed down atower your ee-brees; then, if there's sax or eight o' you in ae fare—†

Tickler. Why don't you keep your own carriage, James?

Shepherd. So I do—a gig; but when I happen to forgather wi' sic scrubs as you, that grudge the expense o' a yeckipage o' their ain, I maun submit to a glass-cotch and a' its abominations.

North. How do you like that punch, James?

Shepherd. It's rather ower sair iced, I jalouse, and will be

* *Fin's*—feels.

† This is a faithful description of the old hackney-coach—a very different vehicle from the smart broughams which now ply upon our streets.

apt to gie ane the toothache; but it has a gran' taste, and a maist seducin smell.—Oh! man, that's a bonny ladle! and you hae a nice way o' steerin! Only half-fu', if you please, sir, for thae wineglasses are perfect tummlers, and though the drink seems to be, when you are preein't, as innocent as the dew o' lauchin lassie's lip, yet it's just as dangerous, and leads insensibly on, by littles and wees, to a state o' unconscious intoxication.

Tickler. I never saw you the worse o' liquor in my life, James.

Shepherd. Nor me you.

North. None but your sober men ever get drunk.

Shepherd. I've observed that many a thousan' times; just as nane but your excessively healthy men ever die. Whene'er I hear in the kintra o' ony man's being killed aff his horse, I ken at once that he's a sober coof, that's been gettin himsel drunk at Selkirk or Hawick, and sweein aff at a sharp turn ower the bank, he has played wallop into the water, or is aiblins been fun' lyin in the middle o' the road, wi' his neck dislocate, the doctors canna tell hoo; or ayont the wa' wi' his harns* sticking on the coupin-stane.

North. Or, foot in stirrup, and face trailing the pebbly mire, swept homewards by a spanking half-bred, and disentangled at the door by shriek and candle-light.

Shepherd. Had he been in the habit o' takin his glass like a Christian, he wad hae ridden like a Centaur; and instead o' havin been brought hame a corp, he wuld hae been staggering geyan steady into the parlor, wi' a' the weans ruggin at his pouches for fairins,† and his wife, half angry, half pleased, helpin him tidily and tenderly aff wi' his big boots; and then by and by mixing him the bowster cup—and then—

* *Harns*—brains.

† *Fairins*—presents.

Tickler. Your sober man, on every public occasion of festivity, is uniformly seen, soon after "the Duke of York and the Army," led off between two waiters, with his face as white as the table-cloth, eyes upwards, and a ghastly smile about his gaping mouth, that seems to threaten unutterable things before he reach the lobby.

North. He turns round his head at the "three times three," with a loyal hiccup, and is borne off a speechless martyr to the cause of Hanoverian Succession.

Shepherd. I wad rather get fou five hunder times in an ordinary way like, than ance to expose mysel sae afore my fellow-citizens. Yet, meet my gentleman next forenoon in the Parliament House, or in a bookseller's shop, or in Princes Street, arm-in-arm wi' a minister, and he hauds up his face as if naething had happened, speaks o' the pleasant party, expresses his regret at having been obliged to leave it so soon, at the call of a client, and, ten to ane, denounces you to his cronies for a drunkard, who exposes himself in company, and is getting constantly into scrapes that promise a fatal termination.

North. Hush! The minstrels!

Shepherd. Maist delightfu' music! O sir, hoo it sweetens, and strengthens, and merrifies as it comes up the avenue! Are they Foreigners?

North. An itinerant family of Savoyards.

Shepherd. Look at them—look at them! What an outlandish, toosy-headed, wee sunbrunt deevil o' a lassie that, playing her antics, heel and head, wi' the tambourine. Yon's a darlin wi' her thoom coquet-coquettin on the guitaur, and makin music without kennin't—a' the while she is curtshyin and singin wi' lauchin rosy mouth, and then blushin because we're glowering on her, and lettin fa' her big black een on the grun', as if a body were asking for a kiss! That maun be her younger sister, as dark as a gypsey, that hafflins lassie wi' the buddin breast, her that's tinklin on the triangle that surely maun be o' silver, sae dewy sweet the soun'! Safe us, only look at the auld man and his wife! There's mony a comical auld woman in Scotland, especially in the Heelans, but I never saw the match o' that ane. She maun be mony hunder year auld, and yet her petticoats as short as a play-actress dancin on the stage. Gude legs too—thin ankles, and a thick calve—girl, wife, and witch a' in ane; and only think o't,—playin on a base drum! Savyaurds! It'll be a mountainous kintra theirs, for sic a lang-backed, short-theë'd, sinewy and muscular, hap-and-stap-jump o' a bouncin body as that man o' hers, wi' the swarthy face and head harlequinaddin on the Pan's-pipes, could never hae been bred and born on a flat—But whish—whish—they're beginning to play something pathetic!

Tickler. Music is the universal language.

Shepherd. It's a lament that the puir wandering creturs are singin and playin about their native land. I wush I may hae ony change in my pocket—

Tickler. They are as happy in their own way as we are in ours, my dear James. May they find their mountain cottage unharmed by wind or weather on their return, and let us join our little subscription—

Shepherd. There's a five-shillin crown-piece for mine.

North. And mine.

Tickler. And mine.

Shepherd. I'll gie't to them.—(SHEPHERD *leaps out.*)—There, my bonny bloomin brunette wi' the raven hair, that are just perfectly beutifu', wanderin wi' your melody hameless but happy; and may nae hand untie its snood till your bridal night in the hut on the hill, when the evening marriage dance and song are hushed and silent, and love and innocence in their lawfu' delight lie in each other's arms. —If your sweetheart's a shepherd, so am I—

Tickler. Hallo, Hogg—no whispering. Here, give each of them a tumbler of punch, and God be with the joyous Savoyards.

Shepherd. Did you see, sirs, hoo desperate thirsty they a' were—nae wonner, singin frae morn to night a' up and doun the dusty streets and squares. Yet they askt for naething, contented creturs!—Hear till them singin awa doun the avenue "God save the King," in compliment to us and our country. A weel-timed interlude this, Mr. North, and it has putten me in a gran' mood for a sang.

North and *Tickler.* A song—a song—a song!

(SHEPHERD *sings* "My bonnie Mary.")

Tickler. Scotch and English puppies make a striking contrast. The Scotch puppy sports philosophical, and sets to rights Locke, Smith, Stewart, and Reid. In his minority he is as solemn as a major of two-score—sits at table, even during dinner, with an argumentative face, and in a logical position—and gives out his sentences deliberately, as if he were making a payment in sovereigns.

Shepherd. Oh, man, how I do hate sic formal young chiels —reason, reason, reasoning on things that you maun see whether you will or no, even gin you were to shut your een wi' a' your force, and then cover them wi' a bandage,—chiels that are employed frae morning to nicht colleckin facks out o' books, in that dark, dirty dungeon, the Advocates' Leebrary, and that'll no hesitate, wi' a breach o' a' gude manners, to correct your verra chronology when you're in the middle o' a story that may hae happened equally weel ony day frae the flood to the last judgment—chiels that quote Mr. Jeffrey and Hairy Cobrun, and even on their first introduction to Englishers, keep up a clatter about the

Ooter House—chiels that think it a great maitter to spoot aff by heart an oraution on the corn laws, in that puir puckit Gogotha, the Speculative Society, and treat you, ower the nits and prunes, wi' skreeds o' College Essays on Syllogism, and what's ca'd the Association o' Ideas—chiels that would rather be a Judge o' the Court o' Session than the Great Khan o' Tartary himsel—and look prouder when taking their forenoon's airing alang Princes Street, on a bit shachlin* ewe-necked powney, coft frae a sportin flesher, than Saladin, at the head of ten thousand chosen chivalry, shaking the desert—chiels—

North. Stop, James—just look at Tickler catching flies.

Shepherd. Sound asleep, as I'm a Contributor. Oh! man —I wush we had a saut herrin to put intil the mooth o' him, or a burned cork to gie him mistashies, or a string o' ingans to fasten to the nape o' his neck by way o' a pigtail, or—

North. Shamming Abraham.

Shepherd. Na—he's in a sort o' dwam—and nae wonner, for the Lodge is just a very Castle o' Indolence. Thae broad vine leaves hingin in the veranda in the breathless heat, or stirrin when the breeze sughs by, like water-lilies tremblin in the swell o' the blue loch-water, inspire a dreamin somnolency that the maist waukrife† canna a'thegither resist; and the bonny twilight, chequering the stane floor a' round and round the shady Lodge, keeps the thochts confined within its glimmerin boundaries, till every cause o' disturbance is afar off, and the life o' man gets tranquil as a wean's rest in its cradle, or amang the gowans on a sunny knowe; sae let us speak lown and no wauken him, for he's buried in the umbrage o' imagination, and weel ken I what a heavenly thing it is to soom doun the silent stream o' that haunted world.

* *Shachlin*—shuffling. † *Waukrife*—watchful.

North. What say you to that smile on his face, James?

Shepherd. It's a gey wicked ane—I'm thinkin he's after some mischief. I'll put this raisin-stalk up his nose. Mercy on us, what a sneeze!

Tickler. (*starting and looking round*). Ha! Hogg, my dear fellow, how are you? Soft—soft—I have it—why, that hotchpotch, and that afternoon sun—

North. James, now that you have seen us in summer, how do you like the Lodge?

Shepherd. There's no sic anither house, Mr. North, baith for elegance and comfort, in a' Scotland.

North. In my old age, James, I think myself not altogether unentitled to the luxuries of learned leisure.—Do you find that sofa easy and commodious?

Shepherd. Easy and commodious! what! it has a' the saftness o' a bed, and a' the coolness o' a bank; yielding rest without drowsiness, and without snoring repose.

Tickler. No sofa like a chair! See, James, how I am lying and sitting at the same time! carelessly diffused, yet—

Shepherd. You're a maist extraordinary feegur, Mr. Tickler, I humbly confess that, wi' your head imbedded in a cushion, and your een fixed on the roof like an astronomer; and your endless legs stretched out to the extremities o' the yearth; and your lang arms hanging down to the verra floor, atower the bend o' the chair-settee, and only lift up, wi' a magnificent wave, to bring the bottom o' the glass o' cauld punch to rest upon your chin; and wi' that tamboured waist coat o' the fashion o' aughty-aught, like a meadow yellow wi' dandylions; and breeks—

Tickler. Check your hand, and change your measure, my dear Shepherd.—Oh! for a portrait of North!

Shepherd. I daurna try't, for his ee masters me; and I fear to tak the same leeberties wi' Mr. North that I sometimes venture upon wi' you, Mr. Tickler. Yet, oh, man! I like him weel in that black neckerchief; it brings out his face grandly—and the green coat o' the Royal Archers gies him a Robin-Hoodish character, that makes ane's imagination think o' the umbrage o' auld oaks, and the glimmering silence o' forests.

Tickler. He blushes.

Shepherd. That he does—and I like to see the ingenuous blush o' bashfu' modesty on a wrinkled cheek. It proves that the heart's-blood is warm and free, and the circulation vigorous. Deil tak me, Mr. North, if I dinna think you're something like his Majesty the King.

North. I am proud that you love the Lodge. There! a bold breeze from the sea! Is not that a pleasant rustle, James?—and lo! every sail on the Firth is dancing on the blue bosom of the waters, and brightening like sea-mews in the sunshine!

Shepherd. After a', in het wather, there's naething like a marine villa. What for dinna ye big* a Yott?

North. My sailing days are over, James; but mine is now the ship of Fancy, who can go at ten knots in a dead calm, and carry her sky-scrapers in a storm.

Shepherd. Nae wonder, after sic a life o' travel by sea and land, you should hae found a hame at last, and sic a hame! A' the towers, and spires, and pillars, and pinnacles, and bewilderments o' blue house-roofs, seen frae the tae front through amang the leafy light o' interceptin trees—and frae the tither, where we are noo sitting, only here and there a bit sprinklin o' villas, and then atower the grove-heads, seeming sae thick and saft that you think you might lie down on them and tak a sleep, the murmuring motion o' the never weary sea! Oh, Mr. North, that you would explain to me the nature o' the tides!

**Big*—build.

North. When the moon—

Shepherd. Stap, stap; I couldna command my attention wi' yon bonny brig huggin the shores o' Inchkeith* sae lovingly—at first I thocht she was but a breakin wave.

North. Wave, cloud, bird, sunbeam, shadow or ship—often know I not one from the other, James, when half-sleeping, half-waking, in the debateable and border land between realities and dreams,—

> "My weary length at noontide would I stretch,
> And muse upon the world that wavers by."

Tickler. I never had any professed feeling of the *super* or *preter*-natural in a printed book. Very early in life I discovered that a ghost, who had kept me in a cold sweat during a whole winter's midnight, was a tailor who haunted the house, partly through love, and partly through hunger, being enamored of my nurse, and of the fat of ham which she gave him with mustard, between two thick shaves† of a quartern loaf, and afterwards a bottle of small beer to wash it down, before she yielded him the parting kiss. After that I slept soundly, and had a contempt for ghosts, which I retain to this day.

Shepherd. Weel, it's very different wi' me. I should be feared yet even for the ninth pairt o' a ghost, and I fancy a tailor has nae mair ;—but I'm no muckle affeckit by reading about them—an oral tradition out o' the mouth o' an auld grey-headed man or woman is far best, for then you canna dout the truth o' the tale, unless ye dout a' history thegither, and then, to be sure, you'll end in universal skepticism.

North. Don't you admire the romances of the Enchantress of Udolpho?

Shepherd. I hae nae doubt, sir, that had I read *Udolpho* and her ither romances in my boyish days, that my hair would

* An island in the Firth of Forth, near Edinburgh. † *Shaves*—slices

hae stood on end like that o' ither folk, for, by nature and education baith, ye ken, I'm just excessive superstitious. But afore her volumes fell into my hauns, my soul had been frightened by a' kinds of traditionary terrors, and mony hunder times hae I maist swarfed * wi' fear in lonesome spats in muirs and woods, at midnicht, when no a leevin thing was movin but mysel and the great moon. Indeed, I canna say that I ever fan' mysel alane in the hush o' darkened nature, without a beatin at my heart; for a sort o' spiritual presence aye hovered about me—a presence o' something like and unlike my ain being—at times felt to be solemn and nae mair—at times sae awfu' that I wushed mysel nearer ingle-licht—and ance or twice in my lifetime, sae terrible that I could hae prayed to sink down into the moss, sae that I micht be saved frae the quaking o' that ghostly wilderness o' a world that wasna for flesh and bluid!

North. Look—James—look—what a sky!

Shepherd. There'll be thunder the morn. These are the palaces o' the thunder, and before daybreak every window will pour forth lichtnin. Mrs. Radcliffe has weel described mony sic, but I have seen some that can be remembered, but never, never painted by mortal pen; for after a', what is ony description by us puir creturs o' the works o' the Great God?

North. Perhaps it is a pity that Mrs. Radcliffe never introduced into her stories any real ghosts.

Shepherd. I canna just a'thegither think sae. Gin you introduce a real ghost at a', it maun appear but seldom—seldom, and never but on some great or dread account—as the ghost o' Hamlet's father. Then, what difficulty in makin it speak with a tomb voice! At the close o' the tale, the mind would be shocked unless the dead had burst its cere

* *Swarfed*—swooned.

ments for some end which the dead alane could have accomplished—unless the catastrophe were worthy an Apparition. How few events and how few actors would, as the story shut itself up, be felt to have been of such surpassing moment as to have deserved the very laws o' nature to have been in a manner changed for their sakes, and shadows brought frae amang the darkness o' burial-places, that seem to our imaginations locked up frae a' communion wi' the breathin world!

North. In highest tragedy, a Spirit may be among the *dramatis personæ*—for the events come all on processionally, and under a feeling of fate.

Shepherd. There, too, you *see* the ghost; and indifferently personated though it may be, the general hush proves that religion is the deepest principle o' our nature, and that even the vain shows o' a theatre can be sublimed by an awe-struck sadness, when, revisiting the glimpses o' the moon, and makin night hideous, comes glidin in and awa in cauld unringin armor, or unsubstantial vapor, a being whose eyes ance saw the cheerfu' sunlight, and whose footsteps ance brought out echoes frae the flowery earth.

Tickler. James, be done with your palavering about ghosts, and " gie us anither sang."

North. Come, I will sing you one of Allan's.

Shepherd. Huts, ye never sung a sang i' your life—at least never that I heard tell o' ;—but, to be sure, you're a maist extraordinary cretur, and can do onything you hae a mind to try.

North. My voice is rather cracked and tremulous—but I have sung Scotch airs, James, of old, with Urbani. (*Sings* " My ain countree.")

Shepherd. Weel, I never heard the like o' that in a' my days. Deevil tak me gin there be sic a perfectly beautiful singer in a' Scotland. I prefer you to baith Peter Hill and David Wylie, * and twa bonnier singers you'll no easier hear in "house or ha', by coal or candle licht." But do you ken, I'm desperate sleepy.

Tickler. Let's off to roost.

North. Stop till I ring for candles.

Shepherd. Cawnels! and sic a moon! It wad be perfect blasphemy—dounricht atheism. But hech, sirs, it's het, an' I'se sleep without the sark the nicht.

North. Without a sark, James! "a mother-naked man!"

Shepherd. I'm a bachelor, ye ken, the noo, sae can tak my ain way o't—Gude nicht, sir—gude nicht. We've really been verra pleasant, and our meetin has been maist as agreeable as ane o' the

NOCTES AMBROSIANÆ.

* Peter Hill is spoken of in the "Chaldee MS." as "a sweet singer." David Wylie was one of the circuit clerks of the Court of Justiciary.

VIII.

IN WHICH THE SHEPHERD IS HANGED AND BE-HEADED.

MR. TICKLER'S *smaller Dining-room—Southside.*

SHEPHERD.—MR. NORTH.—MR. TICKLER.

Shepherd. We've just had a perfec denner, Mr. Tickler—neither ae dish ower mony, nor ae dish ower few. Twa coorses is aneuch for ony Christian—and as for frute after fude, it's a dounricht abomination, and coagulates on the stamach like sour cruds. I aye like best to devoor frute in the forenoons, in gardens by mysel, daunering* at my leisure frae bush to bush, and frae tree to tree, pu'in awa at strawberries, or rasps, or grozets, or cherries, or aipples, or peers, or plooms, or aiblins at young green peas, shawps † an' a', or wee juicy neeps, that melt in the mouth o' their ain accord without chewin, like kisses of vegetable maitter.

Tickler. Do you ever catch a tartar, James, in the shape o' a wasp, that—

Shepherd. Counfound thae deevils incarnate, for they're the curse o' a het simmer. O' a' God's creturs, the wasp is the only ane that's eternally out o' temper. There's nae sic thing as pleasin him. In the gracious sunshine, when a' the bit bonny burdies are singing sae cantily, and stopping for half a minute at a time, noo and than, to set richt wi' their

* *Daunering*—saunteri

† *Shawps*—husks.

bills a feather that's got rumpled by sport or spray—when the bees are at wark, murmuring in their gauzy flight, although no gauze, indeed, be comparable to the filaments o' their woven wings, or clinging silently to the flowers, sook, sookin out the hinny-dew, till their verra doups dirl wi' delight—when a' the flees that are ephemeral, and weel contented wi' the licht and the heat o' ae single sun, keep dancin in their burnished beauty, up and down, and to and fro, and backwards and forwards, and sideways, in millions upon millions, and yet ane never joistling anither, but a' harmoniously blended together in amity, like imagination's thochts,—why, amid this "general dance and minstrelsy," in comes a shower o' infuriated wasps, red het, as if let out o' a fiery furnace, pickin quarrels wi' their ain shadows—then roun' and roun' the hair o' your head, bizzin against the drum o' your ear, till you think they are in at the ae hole and out at the ither—back again, after makin a circuit, as if they had repentit o' lettin you be unharmed, dashing against the face o' you who are wishin ill to nae leevin thing, and, although you are engaged out to dinner, stickin a lang poishoned stang in just below your ee, that, afore you can rin hame frae the garden, swalls up to a fearsome hicht, making you on that side look like a Blackamoor, and on the opposite white as death, sae intolerable is the agony frae the tail of the yellow imp, that, according to his bulk, is stronger far than the Dragon o' the Desert.

Tickler. I detest the devils most, James, when I get them in my mouth. Before you can spit them out the evil is done—your tongue the size of that of a rein-deer—or your gullet, once wide as the Gut of Gibraltar, clogged up like a canal in the neighborhood of a railroad.

Shepherd. As for speaking in sic a condition, everybody but yoursel kens it's impossible, and wunner to hear ye tryin't. But you'll no be perswauded, and attempt talking—every motion o' the muscles bein' as bad as a convulsion o' hydrophobia, and the best soun' ye can utter waur than ony bark, something atween a grunt, a growl, and a guller, like the skraich o' a man lyin on his back, and dreamin that he's gaun to be hanged.

Tickler. My dear James, I hope you have had that dream? What a luxury!

Shepherd. There's nae medium in my dreams, sir—heaven or hell's the word. But oh! that hanging! It's the warst job o' a', and gars my very sowl sicken wi' horror for sake o' the puir deevils that's really hanged out and out, *bonâ fide*, wi' a tangible tow, and a hangman that's mair than a mere apparition—a pardoned felon wi' creeshy second-hand corduroy breeks, and coat short at the cuffs, sae that his thick hairy wrists are visible when he's adjustin the halter, hair red, red, yet no sae red as his bleared een, glarin wi' an unaccountable fairceness—for, Lord hae mercy upon us, can man o' woman born, think ye, be fairce on a brither when handlin his wizen * as executioner, and hearin, although he was deaf, the knockin o' his distracted heart, that wadna break for a' its meesery, but, like a watch stoppin when it gets a fa' on the stanes, in ae minute lies quate when down wi' a rummle gangs the platform o' the scaffold, and the soul o' the son o' sin and sorrow is instantly in presence of its eternal Judge!

North. Pleasant subject-matter for conversation after dinner, gentlemen. In my opinion, hanging—

Shepherd. Haud your tongue about hangin; it's discussed. Gin you've got onything to say about beheadin, let's hear you—for I've dreamt o' that, too, but it was a mere flee-bite to the other mode o' execution. Last time I was beheaded, it was for a great National Conspiracy, found out just when

* *Wizen*—the throat.

the mine was gaun to explode, and blaw up the King on his throne, the constitution, as it was ca'd, and the Kirk. Do ye want to hear about it?

North. Proceed, you rebel.

Shepherd. A' the city sent out its population into ae michty square, and in the midst thereof was a scaffold forty feet high, a' hung wi' black cloth, and open to a' the airts.* A block like a great anvil, only made o' wood instead o' airn, was in the centre o' the platform, and there stood the headsman wi' a mask on, for he was frichtened I wad see his face, sax feet high and some inches, wi' an axe ower his shouther, and his twa naked arms o' a fearsome thickness, a' crawlin wi' sinews, like a yard o' cable to the sheet-anchor o' a man-o'-war. A hairy fur cap towered aboon his broos, and there were neither shoes nor stockings on his braid splay feet, juist as if he were gaun to dance on the boards. But he never mudged—only I saw his een rollin through the vizor, and they were baith bloodshot. He gied a gruesome cough, or something not unlike a lauch, that made ice o' my bluid; and at that verra minute, hands were laid on me, I kentna by whom or whither, and shears began clipping my hair, and fingers like leeches creeped about my neck, and then, without ony further violence, but rather as in the freedom o' my ain wull, my head was lying on the block, and I heard a voice praying, till a drum drowned it and the groans o' the multitude together—and then a hissin, that, like the sudden east wind, had moved the verra mournins o' the scaffold.

Tickler. North, put about the bottle. Will you never be cured of that custom of detaining the crystals?

North. I am rather squeamish—a little faintish or so. James, your good health. Now proceed.

Shepherd. Damn their drums, thocht I, they're needless—

* *Airts*—points of the compass.

for had I intended to make a speech, would I not have delivered it afore I laid down my head on the block? As for the hissin, I kent weel aneuch they werena hissin me, but the Man in the mask and the big hairy fur-cap, and the naked feet, wi' the axe in his hands raised up, and then let down again, ance, twice, thrice, measuring the spat on my craig * to a nicety, that wi' ae stroke my head might roll over into the bloody sawdust.

Tickler. Mr. North, Mr. North—my dear sir, are you ill? My God, who could have thought it!—Hogg, Christopher has fainted!

Shepherd. Let him faint. The executioner was daunted, for the hiss gaed through his heart; and thae horrid arms o' his, wi' a' their knots o' muscle, waxed weak as the willow-wands. The axe fell out o' his hauns, and being sharp, its ain wecht drove it quivering into the block, and close to my ear the verra senseless wud gied a groan. I louped up on to my feet—I cried wi' a loud voice, "Countrymen, I stand here for the sacred cause of Liberty all over the world!"

North (reopening his eyes). "The cause of Liberty all over the world!" Who gave that toast? Hush—hush—where am I? What is this? Is that you, James? What, music? Bagpipes? No—no—no—a ringing in my poor old ears. I have been ill—I feel very, very ill. Hark you, Tickler—hark you—no heeltaps, I suppose—"The cause of Liberty all over the world!"

Shepherd. The shouting was sublime. Then was the time for a speech—not a drum dared to murmur. With the bandage still ower my een, and the handkerchief in my hand, which I had forgotten to drap, I burst out into such a torrent of indignant eloquence that the Slaves and Tyrants were all tongue-tied, lock-jawed, before me; and I knew that my voice

* *Craig*—neck.

would echo to the furthermost regions of the earth, with fear of change perplexing monarchs, and breaking the chains of the shameful bondage by king and priestcraft wound round the Body Politic, that had so long been lying like a heart-stricken lunatic under the eyes of his keepers, but that would now issue forth from the dungeon gloom into the light of day, and in its sacred frenzy immolate its grey oppressors on the very altar of superstition.

North. What the devil is the meaning of all this, James? Are you spouting a gill of one of Brougham's frothy phials of wrath poured out against the Holy Alliance? Beware of the dregs.

Shepherd. I might have escaped—but I was resolved to cement the cause with my martyred blood. I was not a man to disappoint the people. They had come there to see me die—not James Hogg the Ettrick Shepherd—but Hogg the Liberator; and from my blood, I felt assured, would arise millions of armed men, under whose tread would sink the thrones of ancient dynasties, and whose hands would unfurl to all the winds the standard of Freedom, never again to en circle the staff till its dreadful rustling had quailed the kings, even as the mountain sough sends down upon their knees whole herds of cattle, ere rattles from summit to summit the exulting music of the thunderstorm.

Tickler. Isn't he a wonderful creature, North? He beats Brougham all to besoms.

Shepherd. So once more my head was on the block—the axe came down—and I remember nothing more, except that after bouncing several times about the scaffold, it was taken up by that miserable slave of slaves, who muttered, "Behold the head of a traitor!" Not a voice said Amen—and I had my revenge and my triumph!

North. Strange, so true a Tory should be so revolutionary in his dreams!

Tickler. In France, James would have been Robespierre.

Shepherd. Huts! tuts! Dreams gang by the rule o' contraries. Yet I dinna say what I might hae been during the French Revolution. At times and seasons the nature o' the very brute animals is no to be depended on; and how muckle mair changeable is that o' man, wi' his boasted reason looking before and after—his imagination building up, and his passions pu'in down; ae day a loving angel frae heaven—the next a demon o' destruction let loose frae hell! But wasna ye there yoursel, Mr. North? What for no speak? There's naebody here but freens!

Tickler. Remember, James, that our beloved Christopher fainted a few minutes ago—

Shepherd. Sae he did—sae he did. . . . But was ye ever in the Guse-dubs o' Glasgow? Safe us a'! what clarty closses, narrowin awa' and darkenin doun—some stracht, and some serpentine—into green middens o' baith liquid and solid matter, soomin' wi' dead cats and auld shoon, and rags o' petticoats that had been worn till they fell aff and wad wear nae langer.

Tickler. Hear! hear! hear!

Shepherd. Dive down anither close, and you hear a man murderin his wife up-stairs in a garret. A' at ance flees open the door at the stair-head, and the mutchless mawsey, a' dreepin wi' bluid, flings herself frae the tap step o' the flicht to the causeway, and into the nearest change-house, roaring in rage and terror—twa emotions that are no canny when they chance to forgather—and ca'in for a constable to tak haud o' her gudeman, who has threatened to ding out her brains wi' a hammer, or cut her throat wi' a razor.

North. What painting, Tickler! What a Salvator is our Shepherd!

Shepherd. Down anither close, and a battle o' dowgs! A

bull-dowg and a mastiff! The great big brown mastiff mouthin the bull-dowg by the verra hainches, as if to crunch his back, and the wee white bull-dowg never seemin to fash his thoomb, but stickin by the regular-set teeth o' his underhung jaw to the throat o' the mastiff, close to the jugular, and no to be drawn aff the grip by twa strong baker-boys pu'in at the tail o' the tane, and twa strong butcher-boys pu'in at the tail o' the tither—for the mastiff's maister begins to fear that the veeper at his throat will kill him outright, and offers to pay a' betts and confess his dowg has lost the battle. But the crood wush to see the fecht out—and harl the dowgs, that are noo worryin ither without ony growlin—baith silent, except a sort o' snortin through the nostrils, and a kind o' guller in their gullets—I say, the crood harl them out o' the midden, ontil the stanes again—and "Weel dune, Cæsar."—"Better dune, Veeper."—"A mutchkin to a gill on whitey."—"The muckle ane canna fecht."—"See how the wee bick is worryin him now by a new spat on the thrapple."—"He wad rin awa gin she wad let him loose."—"She's just like her mither, that belanged to the caravan o' wild beasts."—"Oh man, Davie, but I wud like to get a breed out o' her, by the watch-dowg at Bell-meadow Bleachfield, that killed, ye ken, the Kilmarnock carrier's Help in twunty minutes, at Kingswell—"

North. Stop, James, your mine is inexhaustible. But here goes for a chant. (*Sings* "The Humors of Donnybrook Fair.")

Shepherd. The like o' that was never heard in this warld afore. The brogue as perfec as if you had been born and bred in the bog o' Allen! How muckle better this kind o' weel-timed daffin, that aye gangs on here at Southside, than literary and philosophical conversation, and criticism on the fine arts, and polemical discussion wi' red faces and fiery een on international policy, and the corn laws and surplus population, and havers about Free Tread! Was ye in the shower-bath the day, Mr. Tickler?

Tickler. Yes, James—do you take it?

Shepherd. I hae never yet had courage to pu' the string. In I gang and shut the door on mysel—and tak haud o' the string very gently, for the least rug 'ill bring down the squash like the Falls of the Clyde; and I look up to the machine, a' pierced wi' so many water-holes, and then I shut my een and my mouth like grim death, and then I let gae the string, and, gruin a' the time, try to whistle; and then I agree to allow myself a respite till I count fifty; and neist begin to argue wi' my ain conscience, that the promise I had made to mysel to whumle the splash-cask was only between it and me, and that the warld will ken naething about the matter if I come out again *re infectâ;* and, feenally, I step out as cautiously as a thief frae a closet, and set myself down in the arm-chair, beside the towel warming at the fire, and tak up the Magazine, and peruse, perhaps, ane o' the "Noctes Ambrosianæ," till I'm like to split wi' lauchin at my ain wut, forgetting a' the time that the door's no locked, and what a figure I wud present to ony o' the servant lasses that micht happen to come in lookin for naething, or to some collegian or contributor, come out frae Embro' during the vacance to see the Ettrick Shepherd. But I canna help thinkin, Mr. Tickler, for a' your lauchin, that in a like predicament you would be a mair ridiculous mortal than mysel.—But what are ye thinking on, Mr. North? I dinna believe ye hae heard a word o' what I've been saying—but it's your ain loss.

North. Here's a copy of fine verses, James, but every line seems written twice over—how is that?

Shepherd. I never could tell how that happens—but miss every ither line, and a' will be right.

Tickler. I have observed that at night, after supper, with ships at sea. Two ships of the line! not one ship and one frigate—but two eighty-fours. Shut one eye, and there at anchor lies, let us say, the Bellerophon—for I am speaking of the olden time. Open the other, and behold two Bellerophons riding at anchor. Optics, as a science, are all very well, but they can't explain that mystery—not they, and be hanged to them—ask Whewell or Airy. But, North, the verses!

Shepherd. There's nae mair certainty in mathematical science than in sheep-shearing. The verses!

Tickler. The stanzas seem to me to be sixteen lines each, but I will divide them by two, which gives eight verses!

North. Well, well, James, if you think the Magazine's not falling off—

Shepherd. Mr. Tickler, man, I canna stay ony langer—ye see Mr. North's gotten unco fou, and I maun accompany him in the cotch down to Buchanan Lodge—shall I?

North. Hogg, as to that, if you don't care about the calculation; for as to the Apocrypha, and so on, if the Bible Society pay four hundred a year, really the *Christian Instructor* —hip—hip—hip!—Why, Hogg, ye see—the fools are—hurra—hurra—hurra!

Shepherd. Oh, Mr. Tickler, North's gotten a mouthful' o' fresh air when you opened the window, and is as fou's the Baltic. But I'll see him hame. The cotch, the cotch, the cotch—dinna dint the pint o' your crutch into my instep, Mr. North—there, there—steady, steady—the cotch, the cotch. Gude mornin, Tickler—what a moon and stars!

North. Surely Ambrose has made some alteration in his house lately. I cannot make out this room at all. It is not the Blue Parlor?

Shepherd. We're at Southside, sir—we're at Southside, sir —perfectly sober ane and a'; but dinna be alarmed, sir, if you see twa cotches at the door, for we're no gaun to separate—there's only ane, believe me—and I'll tak a hurl wi' ye as far's the Harrow.

IX.

IN THE PAPER PARLOR.

Scene—Ambrose's Hotel, Picardy Place—Paper Parlor.

SHEPHERD.—NORTH.—TICKLER.

Shepherd. Do you ken, Mr. North, that I'm beginning to like this snug wee roomy in Mr. Awmrose's New Hotel maist as weel's the Blue Parlor in the dear auld tenement?

North. Ah, no, my dear James, none of us will ever be able to bring our hearts to do that; to us, Gabriel's Road will aye be holy and haunted ground. George Cooper * is a fine fighter and a civil landlord, but I cannot look on his name on that door without a pensive sigh! Mr. Ambrose's worthy brother has moved, you know, upstairs, and I hobble in upon him once a fortnight for auld langsyne.

Shepherd. I aften wauken greetin † frae a dream about that dear, dear tenement. "But what's the use o' sighing, since life is on the wing?" and but for the sacredness o' a' thae recollections, this house—this hotel—is in itsel preferable, perhaps, to our ancient howf.

North. Picardy is a pleasant place, and our host is prosperous. No house can be quieter and more noiseless.

* George Cooper, a respectable man, although a pugilist, succeeded Ambrose in Gabriel's Road.

† *Greetin*—weeping.

Shepherd. That's a great maitter. You'll recollect me ance lodging in Anne Street,* noo nae langer in existence,—a steep street, ye ken, rinnin down alang the North Brig toward where the New Markets are, but noo biggit up wi' a' thae new buildings—

North. That I do, James. 'Twas there, up a spiral stone staircase, in a room looking towards the Castle, that first I saw my Shepherd's honest face, and first I ate along with him cod's head and shoulders.

Shepherd. We made a nicht o't wi' twa dear freens; †—ane o' them at this hour in Ettrick, and the ither ower the saut seas in India, an Episcopalian chaplain.

North. But let's be merry, James. Our remembrances are getting too tender.

Shepherd. What I was gaun to say was this,—that yon room, quate ‡ as it seemed, was aften the maist infernally noisy chawmer on the face o' this noisy earth. It wasna far, ye ken, frae the playhouse. Ae wunter there was an after-piece ca'd the Burnin o' Moscow, that was performed maist every nicht. A while afore twal the Kremlin used to be blawn up; and the soun', like thunder, wauken'd a' the sleepin dowgs in that part o' the town. A' at ance there was set up siccan a barkin, and yellin, and youlin, and growlin, and nyaffin, and snaffin, and clankin o' chains frae them in kennels, that it was waur than the din o' aërial jowlers pursuing the wild huntsman through the sky. Then cam the rattlin o' wheels, after Moscow was reduced to ashes, that

* The North British Railway terminus is close to the site where Anne Street formerly stood.

† Mr. Grieve of Cacra Bank, Ettrick, an Edinburgh merchant, and Mr. James Gray, one of the masters of the High School. The latter was an accomplished linguist. After leaving the High School, he held an appointment in Belfast College, and died in India, in the service of the Church of England, while engaged in translating the Scriptures into one of the native dialects.

‡ *Quate*—quiet.

made the dowgs, especially the watch anes, mair outrageous than ever, and they keepit rampaugin in their chains on till past twa in the mornin. About that hour, or sometimes suner, they had wauken'd a' the cocks in the neeborhood—baith them in preevate families and in poulterers' cavies; and the creturs keepit crawin defiance to ane anither quite on to dawn o' licht. Some butchers had ggem-cocks in pens no far frae my lodgings; and oh! but the deevils incarnate had hoarse, fierce, cruel craws! Neist began the dust and dung carts; and whare the mail-coaches were gaun or comin frae, I never kent, but ilka half-hour there was a toutin o' horns—lang tin anes, I'm sure, frae the scutter o' broken-winded soun'. After that a' was din and distraction, for day-life begude* to roar again; and aften hae I risen without ever having bowed an ee, and a' owing to the burnin o' Moscow and blawin up o' the Kremlin.

North. Nothing of the sort can happen here. This must be a sleeping-house fit for a Sardanapalus.

Shepherd. I'll try it this verra nicht. But what for tauk o' bedtime sae sune after denner? It's really a bit bonny parlor.

North. What think you, James, of that pattern of a paper on the wall?

Shepherd. I was sae busily employed eatin durin denner, and sae muckle mair busier drinkin after denner, that, wull ye believe me when I say't, that gran' huntin-piece paperin the wa's never ance caught my een till this blessed moment? O sirs, but it's an inspeeritin picture, and I wush I was but on horseback, following the hounds!

Tickler. The poor stag! how his agonies accumulate and intensify in each successive stage of his doom, flying in distraction, like Orestes before the Furies!

* *Begude*—began.

Shepherd The stag! confoun' me gin I see ony stag! But yon's a lovely leddy—a Duchess—a Princess—or a Queen—wha keeps aye crownin the career, look whaur you wull—there soomin* a ford like a Naiad—there plungin a Bird o' Paradise into the forest's gloom—and there, lo! reappearing star-bright on the mountain brow!

North. Few ladies look lovable on horseback. The bumping on their seat is not elegant; nor do they mend the matter much when, by means of the crutch, they rise on the saddle like a postilion, buckskin breeches excepted.

Tickler. The habit is masculine, and, if made by a country tailor, to ordinary apprehension converts a plain woman into a pretty man.

North. No modest female should ever sport beaver. It gives her the bold air of a kept-mistress.

Tickler. But what think you of her elbows, hard at work as those of little Tommy Lye, the Yorkshire Jockey, beginning to make play on a north-country horse in the Doncaster St. Leger when opposite the grand stand!

North. How engagingly delicate the virgin splattering along, whip in mouth, draggle-tailed, and with left leg bared to the knee-pan!

Shepherd. Tauk awa—tauk awa—ye twa auld revilers; but let me hae anither glower o' my galloping goddess, gleaming gracefully through a green glade, in a' the glorious grimness of a grove of gigantic forest-trees!

Tickler. What a glutter o' gutturals!

Shepherd. Oh that some moss-hidden stump, like a snake in the grass, wud but gar her steed stumble, that she might saftly glide outower the neck before the solitary shepherd in a flichter o' rainbow light, sae that I were by to come jookin out frae ahint an aik, like a Satyr, or rather the god Pan, and

* *Soomin*—swimming.

ere her lovely limbs could in their disarray be veiled among the dim wood violets, receive into my arms and bosom—O blessed burthen!—the peerless Forest Queen!

North. O gentle Shepherd!—thou fond idolater!—how canst thou thus in fancy burn with fruitless fires before the image of that beautiful cruelty, all athirst and a-wing for blood?

Shepherd. The love that starts up at the touch o' imagination, sir, is o' mony million moods.—A beautiful Cruelty! Thank you, Mr. North, for the poetic epithet.

North. Such SHAPES, in the gloom of forests, hunt for the souls of men!

Shepherd. Wood witch, or Dell deevil, my soul would follow such a shape into the shades o' death. Let the Beautiful Cruelty wear murder on her face, so that something in her fierce eyeballs lure me to a boundless love. I see that her name is Sin; and those figures in the rear, with black veils, are Remorse and Repentance. They beckon me back into the obscure wi' lean uplifted hands, and a bony shudder, as if each cadaver were a clanking skeleton; but the closer I come to Sin, the farther awa and less distinct do they become; and as I touch the hem o' her garment, where are they gone?

North. James, you must have been studying the German Romances. But I see your aim—there is a fine moral—

Tickler. Curse all German Romances. (*Rings the bell violently.*)

Shepherd. Ay, Mr. Tickler, just sae. You've brak the bell rope, ye see, wi' that outrageous jerk. What are ye wantin?

Tickler. A spitting-box.

Shepherd. Hoots! You're no serious in sayin your gaun to smoke already? Wait till after sooper.

Tickler. No, no, James. I rang for our dear Christopher's

cushion. I saw, by the sudden twist that screwed up his chin, that his toe twinged.—Is the pain any milder now, sir?

Shepherd. Oh, sir! oh, sir! say that the pain's milder noo, sir!—Oh dear me! only to think o' your listenin to my stupid havers, and never betrayin the least uneasiness, or wish to interrupt me, and gaur me haud my tongue!—Oh, sir! oh, sir! say that the pain's milder noo, sir!

North. Wipe my brow, James, and let me have a glass of cold water.

Shepherd. I'll wipe your broo.—Pity me—pity me—a' drappin wi' cauld sweat! But ye maunna tak a single mouthfu' o' cauld water. My dearest sir—its poishin for the gout—try a soup o' my toddy. There! grasp the tummler wi' baith your hauns. Aff wi't—it's no strang.—Arena ye better noo, sir? Isna the pain milder noo?

North. Such filial tenderness, my dear boy, is not lost on —oh! gemini—that was the devil's own twinge!

Shepherd. What's to be dune? What's to be dune? Pity me, what's to be dune?

North. A single small glass, James, of the unchristened creature, my dear James.

Shepherd. Ay, ay—that's like your usual sense. Here it's —open your mouth, and I'll administer the draught wi' my ain hauns.

Tickler. See how it runs down his gizzern, his gizzern, his gizzern, see how it runs down his gizzern—ye ho! ye ho! ye ho! *

North. Bless you, James—it is very reviving—continue to converse—you and Tickler—and let me wrestle a little in silence with the tormentor.

Shepherd. Wha wrote yon article in the Magazine on Captain Cleeas and Jymnastics?

* This is the fag-end of some old Bacchanalian ditty.

Tickler. Jymnastics!—James—if you love me—G hard. The other is the Cockney pronunciation.

Shepherd. Weel, then, GGGhhymnastics! Wull that do?

Tickler. I wrote the article.

Shepherd. That's a damned lee. It was naebody else but Mr. North himsel. But what for didna he describe some o' the fates * o' the laddies at the Edinburgh Military Academy on the Saturday afore their vacanse! I never saw the match o' yon.

Tickler. What tricks did the imps perform?

Shepherd. They werena tricks—they were fates. First, ane after anither took haud o' a transverse bar o' wud aboon their heads, and raised their chins ower't by the power o' their arms wi' a' the ease and elegance in the warld, and leanin ower't on their breasts, and then catching haud, by some unaccountable cantrip, o' the waistband o' their breeks, awa they set heels ower head, whirligig, whirligig, whirligig, wi' a smoke-jack velocity, that was perfectly confoundin, the laddie doin't being nae mair distinguishable in lith and limb, than gin he had been a bunch o' claes hung up to frichten craws in the fields within what's ca'd a wund-mill.

Tickler. I know the exercise—and have often done it in my own back-green.

Shepherd. Ha, ha, ha, ha! What maun the neebors hae thought the first time they saw't, lookin out o' their wundows—or the second aither? Ha, ha, ha, ha! What a subject for a picture by Geordie Cruickshanks—ha, ha, ha, ha, ha, ha!

Tickler. Your laugh, Hogg, is coarse—it is offensive.

Shepherd. Ha, ha, ha, ha! My lauch may be coorse, Tickler, for there's naething superfine about me; but to nae man o' common sense can it, on sic on occasion, be offensive. Ha, ha, ha, ha! Oh dear me! Ha, ha, ha, ha, ha, ha, ha,

* *Fates*—feats.

ha! Lang Timothy whurlin round a cross-bar, up in the air amang the rowan-tree* taps, in his ain back-green at Southside!!! Ha, ha, ha, ha, ha, ha! I wush I mayna choke mysel.

Tickler. Sir, you are now a fit object of pity—not of anger or indignation.

Shepherd. I'm glad o' that, for I hate to see ye angry, sir. It gars ye look sae unco ugly—perfectly fearsome.

North. It must indeed have been a pretty sight, James.

Shepherd. Oh, Mr. North, is that your vice? I am glad to see you've come roun'.

North. What think ye, James, of this plan of supplying Edinburgh with living fish?

Shepherd. Gude or bad, it shall never hae my countenance. I couldna thole Embro without the fishwives, and gin it succeeded, it would be the ruin o' that ancient race.

Tickler. Yes, James, there are handsome women among these Nereids.

Shepherd. Weel-faured hizzies, Mr. Tickler. But nane o' your winks—for wi' a' their fearsome tauk, they're dacent bodies. I like to see their well-shaped shanks aneath their short yellow petticoats. There's something heartsome in the creak o' their creeshy creels on their braid backs, as they gang swinging up the stey† streets without sweetin, with the leather belt atower their mutched heads, a' bent laigh doun against five-stane load o' haddocks, skates, cods, and flounders, like horses that never reest‡—and oh, man, but mony o' them hae musical voices, and their cries afar aff make my heart-strings dirl.

North. Hard-working, contented, cheerful creatures indeed, James, but unconscionable extortioners, and—

* This rowan-tree, or mountain ash, still flourishes in the back-green of No. 20 George Square, formerly occupied by Mr. Robert Sym.

† *Stey*—steep.

‡ *Reest*—grow restive.

Shepherd. Saw ye them ever marchin hamewards at nicht, in a baun o' some fifty or threescore, down Leith Walk, wi' the grand gas-lamps illuminating their scaly creels, all shining like silver? And heard ye them ever singing their strange sea-sangs—first half-a-dizzen o' the bit young anes, wi' as saft vices and sweet as you could hear in St George's Kirk on Sabbath, half singin and half shoutin a leadin verse, and then a' the mithers and granmithers, and aiblins great granmithers, some o' them wi' vices like verra men, gran' tenors and awfu' basses, joinin in the chorus, that gaed echoing roun' Arthur's Seat, and awa ower the tap o' the Martello Tower, out at sea ayont the end o' Leith Pier? Wad ye believe me that the music micht be ca'd a hymn—at times sae wild and sae mournfu'—and then takin a sudden turn into a sort o' queer and outlandish glee? It gars me think o' the saut sea-faem —and white mew-wings wavering in the blast—and boaties dancin up and down the billow vales, wi' oar or sail—and waes me—waes me—o' the puir fishing-smack, gaun down head foremost into the deep, and the sighin and the sabbin o' widows, and the wailin o' fatherless weans! . . .

North. You alluded, a little while ago, to the *Quarterly Review*, James. I have carefully preserved, among other relics of departed worth, the beautiful manuscript of the first article the new Editor * ever sent me.

Tickler. In the Balaam-box?

Shepherd. Na, faith, Mr. Tickler, you may set up your gab noo; but do you recollec how ye used to try to fleech and flatter him, when he begood sharpening his keelivine pen, and tearing aff the back o' a letter to sketch a bit caricature o' Southside? Na—I've sometimes thocht, Mr. North, that ye were a wee feared for him yoursel, and used, rather without

* John Gibson Lockhart, Esq., the late editor of the *Quarterly Review.* Born in 1793; died in 1854.

kennm't, to draw in your horns. The Balaam-box, indeed! Ma faith, had ye ventured on sic a step, ye micht just as weel at ance hae gien up the Magazine.

North. James, that man never breathed, nor ever will breathe, for whose contributions to the Magazine I cared one single curse.

Shepherd. Oh, man, Mr. North, dinna lose your temper, sir. What for do you get sae red in the face at a bit puir, harmless, silly joke—especially you that's sae wutty and sae severe yoursel, sae sarcastic an fu' o' satire, and at times (the love o' truth chirts* it out o' me) sae like a sleuth-hound, sae keen on the scent o' human bluid! Dear me! mony a luckless deevil, wi' but sma' provocation, or nane, Mr. North, hae ye worried.

North. The Magazine, James, is the Magazine.

Shepherd. Is't really? I've nae mair to say, sir; that oracular response removes a' diffeeculties, and settles the hash o' the maitter, as Pierce Egan† would say, at ance.

North. Nothing but the purest philanthropy could ever have induced me, my dearest Shepherd, to suffer any contributors to the Magazine; and I sometimes bitterly repent having ever departed from my original determination (long religiously adhered to) to write, *proprio Marte*, the entire miscellany.

Shepherd. A' the world kens that—but whaur's the harm o' a few gude, sober, steady, judicious, regular, weel-informed, versateele, and biddable contributors?

North. None such are to be found on earth—you must look for them in heaven. Oh, James! you know not what it is to labor under a load of contributors! A prosy parson, who, unknown to me, had, it seems, long worn a wig, and published an assize sermon, surprising me off my guard on a dull rainy day, when the most vigilant of editors has fallen

* *Chirts*— spurts. † The author of *Boxiana*.

asleep, effects a footing in the Magazine. Oh, what toil and trouble in dislodging the Doctor! The struggle may continue for years—and there have been instances of clerical contributors finally removed only by death.

Shepherd. Dog on't, ye wicket auld Lucifer, hoo your een sparkle as you touzle the clergy! You just mind me o' a lion purlin wi' inward satisfaction in his throat, and waggin his tufted tail ower a Hottentot lying atween his paws aye preferring the flesh o' a blackamoor to that o' a white man.

North. I respect and love the clergy, James. You know that well enough, and the feeling is mutual. Or suppose a young lawyer—

Shepherd. Or suppose that some shepherd, more silly than his sheep, that roams in yon glen where Yarrow frae still St. Mary's Loch rows wimplin to join the Ettrick, should lay down his cruick, and aneath the shadow o' a rock, or a ruin, indite a bit tale, in verse or prose, or in something between the twa, wi' here and there aiblins a touch o' nature—what is ower ower aften the fate o' his unpretending contribution, Mr. North? A cauld glint o' the ee—a curl o' the lip—a humph o' the voice—a shake o' the head—and then—but the warld, wicked as it is, could never believe it—a wave o' your haun, and instantly and for evermore is it swallowed up by the jaws of the Balaam-box, greedy as the grave and hungry as Hades. Ca' ye that friendship—ca' ye that respec—ca' ye that sae muckle as the common humanity due to ane anither, frae a' men o' woman born, but which you, sir,—na, dinna frown and gnaw your lip,—hae ower aften forgotten to show even to me, the Ettrick Shepherd, and the author o' the *Queen's Wake?*

North (much affected). What is the meaning of this, my dear, dear Shepherd? May the Magazine sink to the bottom of the Red Sea!—

Shepherd. Dinna greet, sir—oh ! dinna, dinna, greet ! Forgie me for hurtin your feelins ; and be assured, that frae my heart I forgie you if ever you hae hurted mine. As for wushin the Magazine to sink to the bottom o' the Red Sea, that's no possible ; for it's lichter far than water, and sink it never wull till the laws o' Nature hersel undergo change and revolution. My only fear is, under the present constitution o' the elements, that ae month or ither Maga will flee ower the moon, and, thenceforth a comet, will be eccentric on her course, and come careering in sight o' the inhabitants o' the yearth, perhaps, only ance or twice before Neddy Irving's * Day o' Judgment.

(Mr. AMBROSE *enters.*)

Shepherd. As sure's death, there's the oysters ! O man, Awmrose, but you've the pleasantest face o' ony man o' a' my acquaintance. Here's ane as braid's a mushroom. This is Saturday nicht, and they've a' gotten their bairds shaved. There's a wee ane awa down my wrang throat ; but deil a fears, it'll find its way into the stamach. A waught † o' that porter gars the drums o' ane's lugs crack and play dirl.

Tickler. They are in truth precious powldowdies. More boards, Ambrose, more boards.

Shepherd. Yonner are half-a-dizzen fresh boards on the side-tables. But more porter, Awmrose—more porter. Canna ye manage mair than twa pots at a time, man, in ilka haun ? For twunty years, Mr. North, I used aye to blaw aff the froth, or cut it smack-smooth across wi' the edge o' my loof ; but for the last ten or thereabouts, indeed ever since the Magazine, I hae sooked in froth and a', nor cared about diving my nose in't. Faith, I'm thinkin that maun be what they ca' BROON STOOT ; for Mr. Pitt and Mr. Fox are

* The Rev. Edward Irving, a popular preacher of the day. He died in 1834.

† *Waught*—a large draught.

nearing ane anither on the wa' there, as gin they were gaun to fecht; and either the roof's rising, or the floor fa'in, or I'm hafflins fou!

Tickler. Mr. Pitt and Mr. Fox!—why, James, you are dreaming. This is not the Blue Parlor!

North. A Psychological Curiosity!

Shepherd. Faith, it is curious aneuch, and shows the power o' habit in producing a sort o' delusion on the ocular spectrum. I wad hae sworn I saw the lang, thin, lank feegur and cocked-up nose o' Pitt, wi' his hand pressed down wi' an authoritative nieve on a heap o' Parliamentary papers; and the big, clumsy carcase, arched een, and jolly chops o' Fox, mair like a master coal-merchant than an orator or a statesman;—but they've vanished away, far aff, and wee, wee like atomies, and this is not the Blue Parlor sure aneuch.

North. To think of one of the Noctes Ambrosianæ passing away without ever a single song!

Shepherd. It hasna past awa yet, Mr. North. It's no eleven, man; and to hinner twal frae strikin untimeously—and on a Saturday nicht I hate the sound o't—Mr. Awmrose, do you put back, ae round, the lang hand o' the knock.* Ye'se hae a sang or twa afore we part, Mr. North; but, even without music, hasna this been a pleasant nicht? I sall begin noo wi' pepper, vinegar, and mustard, for the oysters by theirsels are getting a wee saut. By the tramping on the stairs I jalouse the playhouse is scalin. Whisht, Mr. North! keep a calm sugh, or O'Doherty will be in on us, and gar us break the Sabbath morning. Noo, let's draw in our chairs to the fireside, and when a's settled in the tither parlors, I'll sing you a sang.

[*Curtain falls.*

* *Knock*—clock.

X.

IN WHICH THE SHEPHERD RELATES HOW THE BAG-MEN WERE LOST.

Scene—Ambrose's Hotel, Picardy Place—Paper Parlor.

NORTH.—SHEPHERD.

Shepherd. Oh, sir! but I'm real happy to see you out again; and to think that we're to hae a twa-handed crack, without Tickler or ony o' the rest kennin that we're at Awmrose's. Gie's your haun again, my dear sir. Noo, what shall we hae?

North. A single jug, James, of Glenlivet—not very strong, if you please; for—

Shepherd. A single jug o' Glenleevit—no very strang! My dear sir, hae you lost your judgment? You ken my reçate for toddy, and ye never saw't fail yet. In wi' a' the sugar and a' the whusky, whatever they chance to be, intil the jug about half fu' o' water—just say three minutes to get aff the boil—and then the King's health in a bumpor.

North. You can twist the old man, like a silk thread round your finger, James. But remember, I'm on a regimen.

Shepherd. Sae am I,—five shaves o' toasted butter and bread—twa eggs—a pound o' kipper sea-trout or saumon, be it mair or less—and three o' the big cups o' tea to breakfast; ae platefu' o' corned beef, and potatoes and greens—the leg and the wing o' a how-towdy—wi' some tongue or ham—a cut o' ploom-puddin, and cheese and bread, to denner—and ony wee trifle afore bedtime. That's the regimen, sir, that I'm on the noo, as far as regards the victualling department; and I canna but say that, moderate as it is, I thrive on't decently aneuch, and haena fun' mysel stouter or stranger either in mind or body, sin' the King's visit to Scotland. I hae made nae change on my licker sin' the *Queen's Wake*, and the time you first dined wi' me in Anne Street—only I hae gien up porter, which is swallin drink, and lays on naething but fat and foziness.

North. I forget if you are a great dreamer, James?

Shepherd. Sleepin or waukin?

North. Sleeping—and on a heavy supper.

Shepherd. Oh! sir, I not only pity but despise the coot, that aff wi' his claes, on wi' his nichtcap, into the sheets, doun wi' his head on the bowster, and then, afore anither man could hae weel taken aff his breeks, snorin awa' wi' a' great open mouth, without a single dream ever travellin through his fancy! What wad be the harm o' pittin him to death?

North. What! murder a man for not dreaming, James?

Shepherd. Na—but for no dreaming and for snorin at the same time. What for blaw a trumpet through the hail house at the dead o' nicht, just to tell that you've lost your soul and your senses, and become a breathin clod? What a blow it maun be to a man to marry a snorin woman! Think o' her during the haill hinnymoon, resting her head, with a long, gurgling, snorting snore, on her husband's bosom!

North. Snoring runs in families; and, like other hereditary complaints, occasionally leaps over one generation, and descends on the next. But my son, I have no doubt, will snore like a trooper.

Shepherd. Your son?! Try the toddy, sir. Your son?!

North. The jug is a most excellent one, James. Edin burgh is supplied with very fine water.

Shepherd. Gie me the real Glenleevit—such as Awmrose aye has in the hoose—and I weel believe that I could mak drinkable toddy out o' sea-water. The human mind never tires o' Glenleevit, ony mair than o' cauler* air. If a body could just find out the exac proper proportion o' quantity that ought to be drank every day, and keep to that, I verily trow that he micht leeve for ever, without dying at a,' and that doctors and kirkyards would go out of fashion.

North. Have you had any snow yet, James, in the Forest?

Shepherd. Only some skirrin † sleets—no aneuch to track a hare. But, safe us a'! what a storm was yon, thus early in the season, too, in the Highlands! I wush I had been in Tamantowl ‡ that nicht. No a wilder region for a snow-storm on a' the yearth. Let the wun' come frae what airt it likes, richt doun Glen Aven, or up frae Grantown, or across frae the woods o' Abernethy, or far aff frae the forests at the Head o' Dee, you wad think that it was the deevil himsel howlin wi' a' his legions. A black thunderstorm's no half sae fearsome to me as a white snaw ane. There is an ocular grandeur in it. wi' the opening heavens sending forth the flashes o' lichtnin, that brings out the burnished woods frae the distance close upon you where you staun, a' the time the hills rattling like stanes on the roof o' a hoose, and the rain either descending in a universal deluge, or here and there pouring down in *straths*, till the thunder can scarcely quell the roar o' a thousand cataracts.

North. Poussin—Poussin—Poussin!

Shepherd. The heart quakes, but the imagination even in its awe is elevated. You still have a hold on the external

* *Cauler*—fresh. † *Skirrin*—flying. ‡ A village in Banffshire.

world, and a lurid beauty mixes with the magnificence, till there is an austere joy in terror.

North. Burke—Burke—Burke—Edmund Burke!

Shepherd. But in a nicht snaw-storm the ragin world o' elements is at war with life. Within twenty yards o' a human dwelling, you may be remote from succor as at the Pole. The drift is the drift of death. Your eyes are extinguished in your head—your ears frozen—your tongue dumb Mountains and glens are all alike—so is the middle air eddying with flakes and the glimmerin heavens. An army would be stopt on its march—and what then is the tread o' ae puir solitary wretch, man or woman, struggling on by theirsel, or sittin doun, ower despairing even to pray, and fast congealin, in a sort o' dwam* o' delirious stupefaction, into a lump o' icy and rustling snaw! Wae's me, wae's me! for that auld woman and her wee granddauchter, the bonniest lamb, folk said, in a' the Highlands, that left Tamantowl that nicht, after the merry strathspeys were over, and were never seen again till after the snaw, lying no five hunder yards out o' the town, the bairn wrapt round and round in the crone's plaid as weel as in her ain, but for a' that, dead as a flower-stalk that has been forgotten to be taken into the house at nicht, and in the mornin brittle as glass in its beauty, although, till you come to touch it, it would seem to be alive!

North. With what very different feelings one would read an account of the death of a brace of Bagmen † in the snow! How is that to be explained, James?

Shepherd. You see, the imagination pictures the twa Bagmen as Cockneys. As the snaw was getting dour at them, and giein them sair flaffs and dads on their faces, spittin in their verra een, ruggin their noses, and blawin upon their

* *Dwam*—swoon.

† Commercial travellers.

blubbery lips till they blistered, the Cockneys wad be waxing half feared and half angry, and damnin the "Heelans," as the cursedest kintra that ever was kittled. But wait awee, my gentlemen, and you'll keep a lowner sugh or you get half-way from Dalnacardoch to Dalwhinnie.*

North. A wild district, for ever whirring, even in mist snow, with the gorcock's wing.

Shepherd. Whist—haud your tongue, till I finish the account o' the death of the twa Bagmen in the snaw. Ane o' their horses—for the creturs are no ill mounted—slidders awa doun a bank, and gets jammed into a snaw-stall, where there's no room for turnin. The other horse grows obstinate wi' the sharp stour in his face, and proposes retreating to Dalnacardoch, tail foremost; but no being sae weel up to the walkin or the trottin backwards as that English chiel Townsend, the pedestrian, he cloits† doun first on his hurdies, and then on his tae side, the girths burst, and the saddle hangs only by a tack to the crupper.

North. Do you know, James, that though you are manifestly drawing a picture intended to be ludicrous, it is to me extremely pathetic?

Shepherd. The twa Cockneys are now forced to act as dismounted cavalry through the rest of the campaign, and sit doun and cry—pretty babes o' the wood—in each ither's arms! John Frost decks their noses and their ears with icicles—and each vulgar physiognomy partakes of the pathetic character of a turnip making an appeal to the feelings on Halloween.—Dinna sneeze that way when ane's speakin, sir!

North. You ought rather to have cried, "God bless you."

Shepherd. A' this while neither the snaw nor the wund has been idle—and baith Cockneys are sitting up to the middle, poor creturs—no that verra cauld, for driftin snaw sune begins

* In the Highlands of Perthshire. † *Cloits*—falls heavily.

to fin' warm and comfortable, but wae's me! unco, unco sleepy—and not a word do they speak!—and now the snaw is up to their verra chins, and the bit bonny, braw, stiff, fause shirt-collars, that they were sae proud o' stickin at their chafts, are as hard as airn, for they've gotten a sair Scotch starchin—and the fierce North cares naething for their towsy hair a' smellin wi' Kalydor and Macassar, no it indeed, but twurls it a' into ravelled hanks, till the frozen mops bear nae earthly resemblance to the ordinary heads o' Cockneys;—and hoo indeed should they, lying in sic an unnatural and out-o'-the-way place for them, as the moors atween Dalnacardoch and Dalwhinnie?

North. Oh, James—say not they perished!

Shepherd. Yes, sir, they perished; under such circumstances, it would have been too much to expect of the vital spark that it should not have fled. It did so—and a pair of more interesting Bagmen never slept the sleep of death. Gie me the lend o' your hankercher, sir, for I agree wi' you that the picture's verra pathetic.

North. Did you read, James, in one of Maga's Leading Articles, called "Glance over Selby's Ornithology," an account of the Red Tarn Raven Club devouring the corpse of a Quaker on the dark brow of the mighty Helvellyn?*

Shepherd. Ay,—what about it? I could hae dune't as weel mysel.

North. Do you know, James, that it gave great offence?

Shepherd. I hae nae doubt that the birds o' prey that keep gorging themsels for weeks after a great battle, gie great offence to thousands o' the wounded,—picking out their een, and itherwise hurting their feelings. Here a bluidy straight beak tweakin a general officer by the nose, and there a no less bluidy crooked ane tearing aff the ee-broos o' a drummer,

* See the *Recreations of Christopher North*, vol. iii. p. 81.

and happin aff to eat them on the hollow round o' his ain drum,—on which never will tattoo be beaten ony mair, for a musket-ball has gone through the parchment, and the "stormy music," as Cammel ca's it, is hushed for ever. What need a description o' the dreadfu' field, when it has been crappit and fallowed year after year, gie offence to ony rational reader? Surely no; and, therefore, why shudder at a joke about the death o' ae Quaker?—Tuts, tuts, it's a nonsense.

North. James, you are a good shot?

Shepherd. I seldom miss a haystack, or a barn-door, standing, at twenty yards; but war they to tak wings to themselves and flee away, I should be shy o' takin on ony big bet that I should bring them down—especially wi' a single barrel. . . . Nane o' your pigeon-killers for me, waitin in cool blood till the bonny burdies, that should ne'er be shot at a' excep when they're on the corn-stooks, flee out o' a trap wi' a flutter and a whirr; and then prouder men are they nor the Duke o' Wellington, when they knock down, wi' pinions ower purple, the bright birds o' Venus, tumbling, as if hawk-struck, within boun's, or carrying aneath the down o' their bonny bosoms some cruel draps, that ere nightfall will gar them moan out their lives amang the cover o' suburban groves.

North. So you have no pity, James, for any other birds but the birds of Venus?

Shepherd. I canna say that I hae muckle pity for mony o' the ithers—mair especially wild-dyucks and whaups. It's a trial that Job would never hae come through, without swearin—after wading half the day through marsh and fen, sometimes up to the houghs, and sometimes to the oxters, to see a dizzen or a score o' wild-dyucks a' risin thegither, about a quarter o' a mile aff, wi' their outstretched bills and droopin doups, maist unmercifully ill-made, as ane might mistake it.

for fleeing, and then making a circle half a mile ayont the reach o' slug, gradually fa'in intil a mathemetical figure in Euclid's Elements, and vanishin, wi' the speed o' aigles, in the weather-gleam,* as if they were aff for ever to Norway, or to the North Pole. Dang their web-footed soles—

North. James, remember where you are, and with whom—time, place, and person. No maledictions to-night on any part o' the creation, feathered or un-feathered. During Christmas holidays, I would rather err on the side of undue humanity. What are whaups?

Shepherd. That's a gude ane! Ma faith, you pruved that you kent weel aneuch what were whaups that day at Yarrow-Ford, when you devoored twa, stoop and roop, † to the astonishment o' the Tailor, ‡ wha begood to fear that you would neist § eat his guse for a second coorse. The English ca' whaups curl-loos—the maist nonsensicalest name for a whaup ever I heard—but the English hae little or nae imagination.

North. My memory is not so good as it used to be, James —but I remember it now—"Most prime picking is the whaup."

Shepherd. In wuntur they're aff to the sea—but a' simmer and hairst they haunt the wide, heathy, or rushy and boggy moors. Ye may discover the whaup's lang nose half a mile aff, as the gleg-eed cretur keeps a watch ower the wilderness, wi' baith sicht and smell.

North. Did you shoot the whaups alluded to above, James, —or the Tailor himself?

Shepherd. Him—no me. But mony and aft's the time that I hae lain for hours ahint some auld turf-dyke, that aiblins had ance enclosed a bit bonny kailyard belanging to a housie

* *Weather-gleam*—horizon. † *Stoop and Roop.*—stump and rump.

‡ The flying tailor of Ettrick, an eccentric character, celebrated for his agility.

§ *Neist.*—next.

noo soopt frae the face of the yearth,—every noo and than keekin ower the grassy rampart to see gif the whaups, thinkin themselves alane, were takin their walk in the solitude ; and gif nane were there, layin mysel doun a' my length on my grufe* and elbow, and reading an ancient ballant, or maybe tryin to croon a bit sang o' my ain, inspired by the lown and lanesome spat,—for oh, sir ! haena ye aften felt that the farther we are in body frae human dwellings, the nearer are we to their ingles in sowl ?

North. Often, James—often. In a crowd I am apt to be sullen or ferocious. In solitude I am the most benevolent of men. To understand my character, you must see me alone—converse with me—meditate on what I then say—and behold my character in all its original brightness.

Shepherd. The dearest thocht and feelings o' auld lang syne come crowd, crowdin back again into the heart whenever there's an hour o' perfect silence, just like so many swallows coming a-wing frae God knows where, when winter is ower and gane, to the self-same range o' auld clay biggins, aneath the thatch o' house or the slate o' ha'—unforgetfu' they o' the place whare they were born, and first hunted the insect-people through shadow or sunshine !

North. I wish you had seen Audubon, James ; you would have taken to each other very kindly, for you, James, are yourself a naturalist, although sometimes, it must be confessed, you deal a little in the miraculous when biographically inclined about sheep, dogs, eagles, and salmon.

Shepherd. The ways o' the creatures o' the inferior creation, as we choose to ca' birds and beasts, are a' miraculous thegither—nor would they be less so if we understood better than we do their several instincts. Natural History is just anither name for Natural Theology—and the sang o' the

* *Grufe*—belly.

laverock, and the plumage o' the goldfinch—do they not alike remind us o' God?

North. Hark! the Calabrian harpers. Ring the bell, James, and we shall have them up-stairs for half an hour.

Shepherd (*rings*). Awmrose—Awmrose—bring my fiddle. I'll accompany the Calawbrians wi' voice and thairm.

XI.

THE EXECUTION OF THE MUTINEER

Scene,—Ambrose's Hotel, Picardy Place—Paper Parlor.

NORTH.—SHEPHERD.

North. How do you account, my dearest Shepherd, for the steadiness and perseverance of my affection for thee, seeing that I am naturally and artificially the most wayward, fickle, and capricious of all God's creatures? Not a friend but yourself, James, with whom I have not frequently and bitterly quarrelled, often to the utter extinction of mutual regard — but towards my incomprehensible Brownie my heart ever yearns—

Shepherd. Haud your leein tongue, ye tyke, you've quarrelled wi' me mony thousan' times, and I've borne at your hands mair ill-usage than I wad hae taen frae ony ither mortal man in his Majesty's dominions. Yet I weel believe that only the shears o' Fate will ever cut the cords o' our friendship. I fancy it's just the same wi' you as wi' me, we maun like ane anither whether we wull or no—and that's the sort o' freendship for me—for it flourishes, like a mountain flower, in all weathers—braid and bricht in the sunshine, and just faulded up a wee in the sleet, sae that it micht maist be thocht dead, but fu' o' life in its cozy bield * ahint the

* *Cozy bield*—snug shelter.

mossy stane, and peering out again in a' its beauty at the sang o' the rising laverock.

North. This world's friendships, James—

Shepherd. Are as cheap as crockery, and as easily broken by a fa'. They seldom can bide a clash, without fleein intil flinders.* Oh, sir, but maist men's hearts, and women's too, are like toom nits †—nae kernel, and a splutter o' fushionless dust. I sometimes canna help thinkin that there's nae future state.

North. Fie, fie, James; leave all such dark skepticism to a Byron—it is unworthy of the Shepherd.

Shepherd. What for should sae mony puir, peevish, selfish, stupid, mean, and malignant creatures no just lie still in the mools amang the ither worms, aneath their bits o' inscribed tombstones, aiblins railed in, and a' their nettles, wi' painted airn-rails, in a nook o' the kirkyard that's their ain property, and naebody's wushin to tak it frae them—what for, I say, shouldna they lie quate in skeleton for a thousand years, and then crummle, crummle, crummle awa intil the yearth o' which Time is made, and ne'er be reimmatterialeezed into Eternity?

North. This is not like your usual gracious and benign philosophy, James; but, believe me, my friend, that within the spirit of the most degraded wretch that ever grovelled earthward from caudle-day to corpse-day, there has been some slumbering spark divine, inextinguishable by the death-damps of the cemetery—

Shepherd. Gran' words, sir, gran' words, nae doubt, mair especially "cemetery," which I'm fond o' usin mysel, as often's the subject and the verse will alloo. But after a', is't mair poetical than the "Grave"? Deevil a bit. For a wee, short, simple, stiff, stern, dour, and fearsome word, commend me to the "Grave."

* *Flinders*—shivers. † *Toom nits*—empty nuts.

North. Let us change the channel of our discussion, James, if you please—

Shepherd. What! You're no feared for death, are you, sir?

North. I am.

Shepherd. So am I. There, only look at the cawnle* expiring—faint, feeble, flickering, and just like ane o' us puir mortal human creatures, sair, sair unwilling to die! Whare's the snuffers, that I may put it out o' pain? I'm tell't that twa folk die every minute, or rather every moment. Isna that fearsome to think o'?

North. Ay, James, children have been made orphans, and wives widows, since that wick began to fill the room with its funereal odor.

Shepherd. Nae man can manage snuffers richt, unless he hae been accustomed to them when he was young. In the Forest we a' use our fingers, or blaw the cawnles out wi' our mouths, or chap the brass sticks wi' the stinkin wicks again' the ribs—and gin there was a pair o' snuffers in the house, you might hunt for them through a' the closets and presses for a fortnight, without their ever castin up.

North. I hear that you intend to light up Mount Benger with gas, James. Is that a true bill?

Shepherd. I had thochts o't—but the gasometer, I find, comes ower high—so I shall stick to the "Lang Twas." Oh, man, noo that the cawnle's out, isna that fire unco heartsome? Your face, sir, looks just perfeckly ruddy in the bleeze, and it wad tak a pair o' poorfu' specks to spy out a single wrinkle. You'll leeve yet for ither twa hundred Numbers.

North. And then, my dear Shepherd, the editorship shall be thine.

Shepherd. Na. When you're dead, Maga will be dead.

* *Cawnle*—candle.

She'll no surveeve you ae single day. Buried shall you be in ae grave, and curst be he that disturbs your banes! Afore you and her cam out, this wasna the same warld it has been sin' syne. Wut and wisdom never used to be seen linkin alang thegither, han'-in-han', as they are noo, frae ae end o' the month to the ither;—there wasna prented a byuck that garred ye break out at ae page into grief, and at anither into a guffaw;—where could ye foregather wi' * sic a canty † crew o' chiels as O'Doherty and the rest, passin themselves aff sometimes for real, and sometimes for fictious characters, till the puzzled public glowered as if they had flung the glamour ower her?—and oh, sir, afore you brak out, beautiful as had been many thousan' thousan' million, billion, trillion, and quadrillion nights by firesides in huts or ha's, or out-by in the open air, wi' the starry heavens resting on the saft hill-taps, yet a' the time that the heavenly bodies were performing their stated revolutions—there were nae, nae NOCTES AMBROSIANÆ!

North. I have not, I would fain hope, my dear James, been altogether useless in my generation—but your partiality exaggerates my merits—

Shepherd. A man would require an oss magna sonaturum to do that. Suffice it to say, sir, that you are the wisest and wittiest of men. Dinna turn awa your face, or you'll get a crick in your neck. There's no sic a popular man in a' Britain the noo as Christopher North. Oh, sir, you'll dee as rich as Crœsus—for every day there's wulls makin by auld leddies and young leddies, leaving you their residiatory legatee, sometimes, I fear, past the heirs, male or female, o' their bodies, lawfully begotten.

North. No, James; I trust that none of my admirers, since admirers you say the old man hath, will ever prove so unprin-

* *Foregather wi'*—fall in with. † *Canty*—lively.

cipled as to leave their money away from their own kin. Nothing can justify that—but hopeless and incurable vice in the natural heirs.

Shepherd. I wush I was worth just twenty thousan' pounds. I could leeve on that—but no on a farden less. In the first place, I would buy three or four pair o' tap-boots—and I would try to introduce into the Forest buckskin breeks. I would neist, sin' naebody's gien me ane in a present, buy a gold musical snuff-box, that would play tunes on the table.

North. Heavens! James—at that rate you would be a ruined man before the coming of Christmas. You would see your name honorably mentioned in the *Gazette.*

Shepherd. Then a gold twisted watch-chain, sax gold seals o' various sizes, frae the bigness o' my neive amaist, doun to that o' a kitty-wren's egg.

North. Which O'Doherty would chouse you out of at brag some night at his own lodgings, after the play.

Shepherd. Catch me at the cairds, unless it be a game at Birky; * for I'm sick o' Whust itsel, I've sic desperate bad hauns dealt to me noo—no an ace ance in a month, and no that unseldom a haun without a face-caird, made up o' deuces, and trays, and fours, and fives, and be damned to them; so that to tak the verra weakest trick is entirely out o' my power, except it be by main force, harling the cairds to me whether the opposite side wull or no; and then at the close o' the round, threepin † that I had twa honors—the knave and anither ane. Sic bad luck hae I in a' chance games, Mr. North, as you ken, that were I to fling dice for my life alang wi' a haill army o' fifty thousand men, I wad be sure to be shot; for I would fling aces after some puir trumlin drummer had flung deuces, and be led out into the middle o' a hollow square for execution.

* *Angliće.* Beggar-my-neighbor. † *Threepin*—asserting pertinaciously

North. James, you are very excursive this evening in your conversation—nobody is thinking of shooting you, James.

Shepherd. And I'm sure that I hae nae thochts o' shootin mysel. But ance—it's a lang time syne—I saw a sodger shot—dead, sir, as a door-nail, or a coffin-nail, or ony ither kind o' nail.

North. Was it in battle, James?

Shepherd. In battle?—Na, na; neither you nor me was ever fond o' being in battle at ony time o' our lives.

North. I was Private Secretary to Rodney when he beat Langara,* James.

Shepherd. Haud your tongue!—What a crowd on the Links † that day! But a' wi' fixed, whitish faces—nae speakin—no sae muckle as a whisper—a frozen dumbness that nae wecht ‡ could break!

North. You mean the spectators, James.

Shepherd. Then the airmy appeared in the distance; for there were three haill regiments, a' wi' fixed beggonets; but nae music—nae music for a while at least, till a' at ance, mercy on us! we heard, like laigh sullen thunder, the soun' o' the great muffled drum, aye played on, ye ken, by a black man; in this case an African neegger, sax feet four; and what bangs he gied the bass—the whites o' his een rowin about as if he was glad, atween every stroke.

North. I remember him—the best pugilist then going, for it was long before the days of Richmond and Molineaux—and nearer forty than thirty years ago, James.

Shepherd. The tread of the troops was like the step o' ae giant—sae perfate was their discippleen—and afore I weel kent that they were a' in the Links, three sides o' a square were formed—and the soun' o' the great drum ceased, as at

* Off Cape St. Vincent, on the 16th of January 1780.

† *Links*—downs. ‡ *Wecht*—weight.

an inaudible word of command, or wavin o' a haun, or the lowerin o' a banner. It was but ae man that was about to die—but for that ae man, had their awe no hindered them, twenty thousan' folk wad at that moment hae broken out into lamentations and rueful cries—but as yet not a tear was shed—not a sigh was heaved—for had a' that vast crowd been sae mony images, corpses raised up by cantrip in their death-claes, they couldna hae been mair motionless than at that minute, nor mair speechless than that multitude o' leevin souls!

North. I was myself one of the multitude, James.

Shepherd. There, a' at ance, hoo or whare he came frae nane could tell—there, I say, a' at ance stood the Mutineer. Some tell't me afterwards that they had seen him marchin alang, twa-three yards ahint his coffin, wi' his head just a wee thocht inclined downwards, not in fear o' man or death, but in awe o' God and judgment, keepin time wi' a military step that was natural to him, and no unbecoming a brave man on the way to the grave, and his een fixed on the green that was fadin awa for ever and ever frae aneath his feet; but that was a sicht I saw not—for the first time I beheld him he was standin, a' unlike the ither men, in the middle o' that three-sided square, and there was a shudder through the haill multitude, just as if we had been a' standin haun in haun, and a natural philosopher had gien us a shock o' his electrical machine. "That's him—that's him—puir, puir fallow! Oh! but he' a pretty man!"—Such were tho ejaculations frae thousan's o' women, maist o' them young anes, but some o' them auld, and grey-headed aneath their mutches, and no a few wi' babies sookin or caterwailin at their breasts.

North. A pretty girl fainted within half-a-dozen yards of where I stood.

Shepherd. His name was Lewis Mackenzie—and as fine a young man he was as ever stepped on heather. The moment before he knelt down on his coffin, he seemed as fu' o' life as if he had stripped aff his jacket for a game at foot-ba,' or to fling the hammer. Ay, weel micht the women-folk gaze on him wi' red, weepin een, for he had lo'ed them but ower weel; and mony a time, it is said, had he let himsel down the Castle-rock at night, God knows hoo, to meet his lemans—but a' that, a' his sins, and a' his crimes, acted and only meditated, were at an end noo—puir fallow—and the platoon, wi' fixed beggonets, were drawn up within ten yards, or less, o' where he stood, and he himsel havin tied a handkerchief ower his een, dropped down on his knees on his coffin, wi' faulded hands, and lips moving fast, fast, and white as ashes, in prayer!

North. Cursed be the inexorable justice of military law!—he might have been pardoned.

Shepherd. Pardoned! Hadna he disarmed his ain captain o' his sword, and ran him through the shouther—in a mutiny of which he was himsel the ringleader? King George on the throne durstna hae pardoned him—it wad hae been as much as his crown was worth—for hoo could King, Kintra, and Constitution thole a standing army in which mutiny was not punished wi' death?

North. Six balls pierced him—through head and heart—and what a shriek, James, then arose!

Shepherd. Ay, to hae heard that shriek, you wad hae thought that the women that raised it wad never hae lauched again; but in a few hours, as sune as nightfall darkened the city, some o' them were gossipin about the shootin o' the sodger to their neighbors, some dancin at hops that shall be nameless, some sittin on their sweethearts' knees, wi' their arms roun' their necks, some swearin like troopers, some doubtless sittin thochtfu' by the fireside, or awa to bed in sadness an hour sooner than usual, and then fast asleep.

North. I saw his old father, James, with my own eyes, step out from the crowd, and way being made for him, he walked up to his son's dead body, and embracing it, kissed his bloody head, and then with clasped hands looked up to heaven.

Shepherd. A strang and stately auld man, and ane, too, that had been a soldier in his youth. Sorrow, not shame, somewhat bowed his head, and ance he reeled as if he were faint on a sudden.—But what the deevil's the use o' me haverin awa this way about the shootin o' a sodger, thretty years sin' syne, and mair too—for didna I see that auld, silvery-headed father o' the mutineer staggering alang the Grassmarket, the verra next day after the execution, as fou as the Baltic, wi' a heap o' mischievous weans hallooin after him, and him a' the while in a dwam o' drink and despair, maunderin about his son Lewis, then lyin a' barken'd wi' blood in his coffin, six feet deep in a fine rich loam.

North. That very same afternoon I heard the drums and fifes of a recruiting party, belonging to the same regiment, winding away down towards Holyrood; and the place of Lewis Mackenzie in the line of bold sergeants with their claymores, was supplied by a corporal, promoted to a triple bar on his sleeve in consequence of the death of the mutineer.

Shepherd. It was an awfu' scene, yon, sir; but there was naething humiliating to human nature in it—as in a hangin; and it struck a wholesome fear into the souls o' many thousan' sodgers.

North. The silence and order of the troops, all the while, was sublime.

Shepherd. It was sae, indeed.

North. What do you think, James, of that, by way of a toasting cheese? Ambrose calls it the Welshman's delight, or Davies' darling.

Shepherd. It's rather teuch—luk, luk, hoo it pu's out, out, out, and better out, into a very thread o' the unbeaten gold, a' the way frae the ashet to my mouth. Saw ye ever onything sae tenawcious? I verily believe that I could walk, without breakin't, intil the tither room. Noon that I've gotten't intil my mouth—I wush it ever may be gotten out again! The tae * end o' the line is fastened, like a hard gedd † (see Dr. Jamieson) in the ashet—and the ither end's in my stammach—and the thin thread o' attenuated cheese gets atween my teeth, sae that I canna chow't through and through. Thank ye, sir, for cuttin't. Rax me ower the jug. Is't yill? Here's to you, sir.

North. Peebles ale, James. It has a twang of the Tweed.

Shepherd. Tweed! Do you ken, Mr. North, that last simmer ‡ the Tweed ran dry, and never flowed sin' syne. They're speakin o' takin doun a' the brigs frae Erickstane to Berwick, and changing the channel intil the turnpike road. A' the materials are at haun, and it's a' to be macadameezed.

North. The Steam-Engine Mail-Coach is to run that road in spring.

Shepherd. Is't? She'll be a dangerous vehicle—but I'll tak my place in the safety-valve. But jeestin apairt, do you ken, sir, that mony and mony a wee well among the hills and mountains was really dried up by the drought o' three dry simmers—and for them my heart was wae, as if they had been ance leevin things! For werena they like leevin things, aye sae calm, and clear, and bright, and sae contented, ilka ane by itsel, in far-awa spats, whare the grass runkled only

* *Tae*—one. † *Gedd*—a pike-staff stuck into the ground.

‡ The summer of 1826 was memorable for its drought.

to the shepherd's foot twa-three times a year, and a' the rest o' the sun's annual visit roun' the globe lay touched only by the wandering light and shadows!

North. Poo—poo—James—there's plenty of water in the world without them.

Shepherd. Plenty o' water in the world without them? Ay, that there is, and mair than plenty—but what's that to the purpose, ye auld haveral? Gin five thousan' bonny bairns were to be mawn doun by the scythe o' Death during the time that I'm drinking this glass—(oh, man, but this is a grand jug, aiblins rather ower sweet, and rather ower strong, but, that's twa gude fauts)—there wad be plenty o' bairns left in the warld, legitimate and illegitimate—and you nor me micht never miss them. But wadna there be just sae much extinguishment, or annihilation like, o' beauty and bliss, o' licht and lauchter, o' ray-like ringlets, and lips that war nae sweeter, for naething can be sweeter, than the half-opened buds o' moss-roses, when the morning is puttin on her claes, but lips that were just as sweet when openin and shuttin in their balmy breath, when ilka happy bairn was singing a ballant or a psalm, baith alike pious and baith alike pensive; for a' the airs o' Scotland (excep a gey hantle, to be sure, o' wicket tunes) soun' aye to me mair melancholy than mirthfu', spirit-like, and as if of heavenly origin, like the bit lown musical soun's that go echoing by the ear, or rather the verra soul o' the shepherd leaning on his staff at nicht, when a' the earth is at rest, and lookin up, and ower, and through into the verra heart o' heaven, when the lift is a' ae glorious glitter o' cloudless stars! You're no sleepy, sir?

North. Sleepy! You may as well ask the leader in a tandem if he be sleepy, when performing the match of twenty-eight miles in two hours without a break.

Shepherd. Ae spring there is—in a nook known but to me

and anither, a bit nook greener than ony emerald—or even the Queen Fairy's symar, as she disentangles it frae her feet in the moonlight dance, enclosed wi' laigh broomy rocks, amaist like a sheep-fauld, but at the upper end made lown in a' weathers by ae single stane, like the last ruin o' a tower, smelling sweet, nae doubt, at this blessed moment, wi' thyme, that enlivens even the winter season,—ae spring there is, I say—

North. Dear me! James—let me loosen your neckcloth—you are getting black in the face. What sort of a knot is this? It would puzzle the ghost of Gordius to untie it.

Shepherd. Dinna mind the cravat. I say, Mr. North, rather were my heart dried up to the last drop o' bluid, than that the pulses of that spring should cease to beat in the holy wilderness.

North. Your emotion is contagious, James. I feel the rheum bedimming my aged eyes, albeit unused to the melting mood.

Shepherd. You've heard me tell the tale afore—and it's no a tale I tell when I can help it—but sometimes, as at present, when sittin wi' the friend I love, and respect and venerate, especially if, like you, he be maist like a father, or at least an elder brither, the past comes upon me wi' a' the power o' the present, and though my heart be sair, ay, sair maist to the verra breakin, yet I maun speak—for though big and great griefs are dumb, griefs there are, rather piteous and profound, that will shape themselves into words, even when nane are by to hear—nane but the puir silly echoes, that can only blab the twa-three last syllables o' a secret.

North. To look on you, James, an ordinary observer would think that you had never had any serious trials in this life—that Doric laugh of thine, my dear Shepherd—

Shepherd. I hate and despise ordinary observers, and thank

God that they can ken naething o' me or my character. The pitifu' creturs aye admire a man wi' a lang nose, hollow cheeks, black een, swarthy cheeks, and creeshy hair; and tauk to ane anither about his interesting melancholy, and severe misfortunes; and hoo he had his heart weel-nigh broken by the death o' twa wives, and the loss o' a third evangelical miss, wha eloped, after her wedding-claes had been taen aff at the haberdasher's, wi' a play-actor wha had ance been a gentleman—that is, attached to the commissawriat department o' the army in the Peninsula, a dealer in adulterated flour and mule-flesh sausages.

North. Interesting emigrants to Van Diemen's Land.

Shepherd. A man wi' buck-teeth and a cockit nose, like me, they'll no alloo to be a martyr to melancholy; but because they see and hear me lauchin as in Peter's Letters,* scoot the idea o' my ever geein way to grief, and afttimes thinkin the sweet light o' heaven's blessed sunshine darkened by a black veil that flings a correspondin shadow ower the seemingly disconsolate yearth.

North. Most of the good poets of my acquaintance have light-colored hair.

Shepherd. Mine in my youth was o' a bricht yellow.

North. And a fine animal you were, James, I am told, as you walked up the transe o' the kirk, with your mane flying over your shoulders, confined within graceful liberty by a blue ribbon, the love-gift of some bonny May, that wonned amang the braes, and had yielded you the parting kiss, just as the cottage clock told that now another week was past, and you heard the innocent creature's heart beating in the hush o' the Sabbath morn.

Shepherd. Whisht, whisht!

* *Peter's Letters to his Kinsfolk*, 1819. These lively sketches of Edinburgh society and its celebrities were from the pen and the pencil of Mr. Lockhart.

North. But we have forgotten the Tale of the Haunted Well.

Shepherd. It's nae Tale—for there's naething that could be ca'd an incident in a' that I could say about that well! Oh! sir—she was only twa months mair than fifteen—and though she had haply reached her full stature, and was somewhat taller than the maist o' our Forest lassies, yet you saw at ance that she was still but a bairn. I was a hantle aulder than her—and as she had nae brither, I was a brither to her—neither had she a father or mither, and ance on a day, when I said to her that she wad find baith in me, wha loved her for her goodness and her innocence, the puir britherless, sisterless, parentless orphan had her face a' in ae single instant as drenched in tears as a flower cast up on the sand at the turn o' a stream that has brought it down in a spate frae the far-aff hills.

North. Her soul, James, is now in heaven!

Shepherd. The simmer afore she died, she didna use to come o' her ain accord, and, without being asked in aneath my plaid, when a skirring shower gaed by—I had to wise * her in within its faulds—and her head had to be held down by an affectionate pressure, almost like a faint force, on my breast—and when I spak to her, half in earnest half in jest, o' love, she had nae heart to lauch,—sae muckle as to greet!

North. One so happy and so innocent might well shed tears.

Shepherd. There, beside that wee, still, solitary well, have we sat for hours that were swift as moments, and each o' them filled fu' o' happiness that wad noo be aneuch for years!

North. For us, and men like us, James, there is on earth no such thing as happiness. Enough that we have known it.

Shepherd. I should fear noo to face sic happiness as used

* *Wise*—entice.

to be there, beside that well—sic happiness would noo turn my brain—but nae fear, nae fear o' its ever returnin, for that voice went wavering awa up to heaven from this mute earth, and on the nicht when it was heard not, and never more was to be heard, in the psalm, in my father's house, I knew that a great change had been wrought within me, and that this earth, this world, this life was disenchanted for ever, and the place that held her grave a Paradise no more!

North. A fitter place of burial for such an one is not on the earth's surface, than that lone hill kirkyard, where she hath for years been sleeping.* The birch shrub in the south corner will now be quite a stately tree.

Shepherd. I visit the place sae regularly every May-day in the morning, every Midsummer-day, the langest day in the year, that is, the twenty-second o' June, in the gloaming, that I see little or nae alteration on the spat, or onything that belangs to it. But nae doubt, we are baith grown aulder thegither; it in that solitary region, visited by few or none —except when there is a burial—and me sometimes at Mount Benger, and sometimes in here at Embro', enjoyin mysel at Ambrose's—for, after a', the world's no a bad world, although Mary Morison be dead—dead and buried thirty years ago, and that's a lang portion o' a man's life, which is, scripturally speakin, somewhere about threescore and ten.

North. I have not seen any portrait of you, James, in any late Exhibition?

* This lonely churchyard, on the shore of St. Mary's Loch, is thus described by Scott:—

> "Nought living meets the eye or ear,
> But well I ween the dead are near;
> For though, in feudal strife, a foe
> Hath laid Our Lady's chapel low,
> Yet still, beneath the hallow'd soil,
> The peasant rests him from his toil,
> And, dying, bids his bones be laid
> Where erst his simple fathers prayed."
>
> *Marmion*, introd. to Canto II.

Shepherd. Nor me o' you, sir. What for doesna Watson Gordon immortaleeze himsel by paintin a Portrait o' Christopher North ? * But oh, sir ! but you hae gotten a kittle face —your een's sae changefu' in their gleg expression, and that mouth o' yours takes fifty shapes and hues every minute, while, as for your broos, they're noo as smooth as those o' a lassie, and noo as frownin as the broos o' a Saracen's head.

North. There is nothing uncommon in my face, James ?

Shepherd. Oh, sir, you hae indeed a kittle, kittle face, and to do it justice it should be painted in a Series. Ane micht ken something o' your physiognomy in the coorse o' a Gallery . . . But nae mair about pictures for ae nicht, if you please, sir.

North. Unless I am much mistaken indeed, James, you introduced the subject yourself.

Shepherd. I'll bet you anither jug I did nae sic thing.

North. Done.

Shepherd. But wha'll decide ? Let's drink the jug, though, in the first place. It's quite a nicht this for whusky toddy. Dinna you observe that a strong frost brings out the flavor o' the speerit in a maist surprising manner, and gies't a mair precious smell o'er the haill room ? It's the chemical action, you understun, o' the cauld and heat, the frost and fire, working on a' the materials o' the jug, and the verra jug itsel, frae nose to doup, sae that sma'-still becomes perfect nectar, on which Jupiter, or Juno either, micht hae got drunk, and Apollo, after a haill nicht's screed, risen up in the morning wi' his gowden hair, and not the least o' a headache, nor

* The best portrait extant of Professor Wilson was painted by Sir John Watson Gordon, in 1850, for Mr. John Blackwood, in whose possession it now is. The portrait of the Ettrick Shepherd by the same artist is also in Mr. Blackwood's possession.

crap-sick as he druve his chariot along the Great Turnpike Road o' Heaven.

North. I wish, James, you would write a Tragedy.

Shepherd. I hae ane in my pouch, man—“ Mirk Monday.” *

North. No poet of this age has shown sufficient concentration of thought and style for tragedy. All the living poets are loose and lumbering writers—and I will engage to point out half-a-dozen feeblenesses or faults of one kind or another in any passage of six lines that you, James, will recite from the best of them.

Shepherd. He's gettin fuddled noo, I see, or he wadna be haverin about poetry.—Mr. North, you're as sober as when we begood to the saxth jug afore the ane that was the immediate predecessor o' this jug's great-grandfather—but as for me, I'm blin' fou, and rather gizzy. I canna comprehend hoo we got into this room, and still less hoo we're to get out again—for I'll stake my character that there's no ae single door in a' the four wa's. I shouldna care gin there was a shake-down or a suttee ; but I never could sleep wi' a straught back. Mercy on us! the haill side o' the house is fa'en doon, as in the great earthquake at Lisbon. Steady—sir—steady—that's Mr. Awmrose—you ken Mr. Awmrose. (Awmrose, he's far gane the nicht, and I'm feered the fresh air'll coup and capsize him a'thegither.)

North. Mr. Ambrose, don't mind me—give Mr. Hogg your arm. James, remember there are a couple of steps. There now—I thought Pride would have a Fall at last, James! Now, coachy! ! drive to the devil. [*Exeunt.*

* The sun was totally eclipsed on Monday the 24th March 1652 ; hence the expression *Mirk Monday*.

XII.

IN WHICH THE SHEPHERD PAINTS HIS OWN PORTRAIT.

Scene,—Ambrose's Hotel, Picardy Place—Paper Parlor.

NORTH.—TICKLER.—SHEPHERD.

North. Doctors are generally dull dogs; and nobody in tolerable health and spirits wishes to hear anything about them and their quackeries.

Tickler. Their faces are indeed at all times most absurd; but more especially so when they are listening to your account of yourself, and preparing to prescribe for your inside, of which the chance is that they know no more than of the interior of Africa.

North. And yet, and yet, my dear Tickler, when old bucks like us are out of sorts, then, like sinners with saints, we trust to the sovereign efficacy of their aid, and feel as if they stood between us and death. There's our beloved Shepherd, whose wrist beats with a yet unfelt pulse—

Shepherd. I dinna despise the doctors. In ordinary complaints I help mysel out o' the box o' drogs; and I'm never mair nor three days in gettin richt again;—the first day, for the beginning o' the complaint—dull and dowie, sair gien to gauntin, and the streekin out o' ane's arms, rather touchy in the temper, and no easily satisfied wi' onything ane can get to eat;—the second day, in bed, wi' a nicht-cap on, or a worsted stockin about the chafts, shiverin ilka half-hour aneath the blankets, as if cauld water were pourin doun your back; a stamach that scunners at the very thocht o' fude, and a sair sair head, amaist as if a wee deevil were sittin in't knappin stanes wi' an airn hammer;—the third day, about denner-time hungrier than a pack o' hounds, yokin to the haggis afore the grace, and in imagination mair than able to devour the haill jiget, as weel's the giblet-pie and the pancakes.

North. And the fourth day, James?

Shepherd. Out wi' the grews gin it be afore the month o' March, as souple and thin in the flanks as themsels—wi' as gleg an ee—and lugs pricked up ready for the start o' pussie frae amang the windle-straes.—Halloo—halloo—halloo!—Oh, man, arena ye fond o' coorsin?

Tickler. Of hare-soup I am—or even roasted hare—but—

Shepherd. There are some things that a man never gets accustomed to, and the startin o' a hare's ane o' them;—so is the whurr o' a covey o' paitricks—and aiblins so is the meetin o' a bonny lassie a' by hersel amang the bloomin heather, when she seems to rise up frae the earth, or to hae drapped doun frae heaven.—Were I to leeve ten thousan' years, and gang out wi' the grews or pointers every ither day, I sud never get the better o' the dear delightfu' dirl o' a fricht, when pussie starts wi' her lang horns.

North. Or the covey whirrs—

Tickler. Or the bonny lassie—

Shepherd. Oh, man, Tickler, but your face the noo is just like the face o' a satyr in a pictur-byuck, or that o' an auld stane-monk keekin frae a niche in the corner o' an abbey wa' —the leer o' the holy and weel-fed scoonrel's een seemin mair intense on the Sabbath, when the kirkyard is fu' o' innocent young maidens, trippin ower the tombs to the

House o' Prayer! Mr. North, sir, only look at the face o' him!

North. Tickler, Tickler, give over that face—it is absolutely getting like Hazlitt's. We will, if you please, James, take each a glass—all round—of Glenlivet—to prevent infection.

Shepherd. Wi' a' my heart.—Sic a change in the expression o' your twa faces, sirs! Mr. North, you look like a man that has just received a vote o' thanks for ha'in been the instrument o' some great national deliverance.—Isna that wonderfu' whisky?—As for you, Mr. Tickler,—your een's just like twa jaspers—pree'd ye ever the like o't?

North. Never, so help me Heaven!—never, since I was born!

Shepherd. Wordsworth tells the world, in ane o' his prefaces, that he is a water-drinker—and it's weel seen on him. —There was a sair want of speerit through the haill o' yon lang "Excursion." If he had just made the paragraphs about ae half shorter, and at the end of every ane taen a caulker, like ony ither man engaged in geyan sair and heavy wark, think na ye that his "Excursion" would hae been far less fatiguesome?

Tickler. It could not at least well have been more so, James,—and I devoutly hope that that cursed old Pedlar is defunct. Indeed, such a trio as the poet himself, the packman, and the half-witted annuitant—

North. My friend Wordsworth has genius, but he has no invention of character—no *constructiveness*, as we phrenologists say.

Shepherd. He, and ither folk like him, wi' gude posts and pensions, may talk o' drinkin water as muckle's they choose —and may abuse me and the like o' me for preferrin speerits —but—

North. Nobody is abusing you, my dear Shepherd—

Shepherd. Haud your tongue, Mr. North—for I'm geyan angry the noo—and I canna thole being interrupted when I'm angry,—sae haud your tongue, and hear me speak,—and faith, gin some folk were here, they should be made to hear on the deafest side o' their heads.

North. Oyez! Oyez! Oyez!

Shepherd. Well, then, gentlemen, it cannot be unknown to you that the water-drinking part of the community have not scrupled to bestow on our meetings here, on the Noctes Ambrosianæ, the scurrilous epithet of Orgies; and that I, the Shepherd, have come in for the chief part of the abuse. I therefore call on you, Mr. North, to vindicate my character to the public—to speak truth and shame the devil—and to declare in Maga, whether or not you ever saw me once the worse of liquor during the course of your career?

North. Is it possible, my dearest friend, that you can trouble your head one moment about so pitiful a crew? That jug, James, with its nose fixed upon your's, is expressing its surprise that—

Tickler. Hogg, Hogg, this is a weakness which I could not have expected from you.—Have you forgotten how the Spectator, and Sir Roger de Coverley, and others, were accused of wine-bibbing and other enormities by the dunces of those days?

Shepherd. Confound their backbiting malignity! Is there a steadier hand than that in a' Scotland?—see how the liquid quivers to the brim, and not a drop overflowing.—Is my nose red? my broo blotched? my een red and rheumy? my shanks shrunk? my knees, do they totter? or does my voice come from my heart in a crinkly cough, as if the lungs were rotten? Bring ony ane o' the base water-drinkers here, and set him doun afore me, and let us discuss ony subject he likes, and see whase head's the clearest, and whase tongue wags wi' maist unfalterin freedom?

North. The first thing, James, the water-drinker would do, would be to get drunk, and make a beast of himself.

Shepherd. My life, Mr. North, as you ken, has been ane of some vicissitudes, and even now I do not eat the bread of idleness. For ae third o' the twenty-four hours, tak ae day wi' anither throughout the year, I'm i' the open air, wi' heaven's wind and rain, perhaps, or its hail and sleet, and they are blessed by the hand that sends them, blashing against me on the hill.—For anither third, I am at my byucks—no mony o' them, to be sure, in the house—but the few that are, no the wark o' dunces, ye may believe that; or aiblins doin my best to write a byuck o' my ain, or if no a byuck, siccan a harmless composition as ane o' my bits o' "Shepherd's Calendars," or the like;—or, if study hae nae charms, playing wi' the bairns, or hearing them their lessons, or crackin wi' a neighbor, or sittin happy wi' the mistress by our ain twa sels, sayin little, but thinkin a hantle, and feelin mair. For the remaining third, frae ten at nicht to sax in the morning, enjoying that sweet sound sleep that is the lot o' a gude conscience, an dout o' which I come as regular at the verra same minute as if an angel gently lifted my head frae the pillow, and touched my eyelids with awakening licht,—no forgettin, as yoursel kens, Mr.North, either evening or morning prayers, no verra lang anes to be sure, except on the Sabbath; but as I hope for mercy, humble and sincere, as the prayers o' us sinfu' beings should ever be—sinfu', and at a' times, sleepin or waukin, aye on the brink o' death! Can there be ony great harm, Mr. North, in a life that—saving and excepting always the corrupt thochts o' a man's ain heart, which has been wisely said to be desperately wicked—even when it micht think itsel, in its pride, the verra perfection o' virtue—

North. I never left Altrive or Mount Benger, James, without feeling myself a better and a wiser man.

Shepherd. Nae man shall ever stop a nicht in my house, without partakin o' the best that's in't, be't meat or drink; and if the coof* canna drink three or four tummlers or jugs o' toddy, he has nae business in the Forest. But if he do nae mair than follow the example I'se set him, he'll rise in the morning without a headache, and fa' to breakfast, no wi' that fause appeteet that your drunkards yoke on to the butter and bread wi', and the eggs, and the ham and haddies, as if they had been shipwrecked in their sleep, and scoured wi' the salt water,—but wi' that calm, sane, and steady appeteet, that speaks an inside sound in a' its operations as clockwork, and gives assurance o' a lang and usefu' life, and a large family o' children.

North. Replenish the dolphin, James.

Shepherd. She's no toom † yet.—Now, sir, I ca' that no an abstemious life—for why should ony man be abstemious?—but I ca't a temperate life, and o' a' the virtues, there's nane mair friendly to man than Temperance.

Tickler. That is an admirable distinction, James.

Shepherd. I've seen you forget it, sir, howsomever, in practice—especially in eatin. Oh, but you're far frae a temperate eater, Mr. Tickler. You're ower fond o' a great heap o' different dishes at denner. I'm within boun's when I say I hae seen you devour a dizzen. For me, sufficient is the Rule of Three. I care little for soop—unless kail, or cocky-leeky, or hare-soop, or mock-turtle, which is really, considerin it's only mock, a pleasant platefu'; or hodge podge, or potawto-broth, wi' plenty o' mutton-banes, and weel peppered; but your white soops, and your broon soops, and your vermisilly, I think naething o', and they only serve to spoil without satisfyin a gude appeteet, of which nae man o' senses will ever tak aff the edge afore he attacks a dish

* *Coof*—ninny. † *Toom*—empty.

that is in itself a denner. I like to bring the haill power o' my stamach to bear on vittles that's worthy o't, and no to fritter't awa on side-dishes, sic as pâtes, and trash o' that sort, only fit for boardin-school misses, wi' wee shrimpit mouths, no able to eat muckle, and ashamed to eat even that; a' covered wi' blushes, puir things, if ye but offer to help onything ontil their plates, or to tell them no to mind folk starin, but to mak a gude denner, for that it will do them nae harm, but, on the contrary, mingle roses with the lilies of their delicate beauty.

Tickler. Every man, James, is the best judge of what he ought to eat, nor is one man entitled to interfere—

Shepherd. Between another man and his own stomach! —Do you mean to say that? Why, sir, that is even more absurd than to say that no man has a right to interfere between another and his own conscience, or his—

Tickler. And is that absurd?

Shepherd. Yes, it is absurd—although it has, somehow or other, become an apothegm.—It is not the duty of all men, to the best o' their abilities to enlighten ane anither's understandings? And if I see my brethren o' mankind fa' into a' sorts o' sins and superstitions, is't nae business o' mine, think ye, to endeavor to set them right, and enable them to act according to the dictates o' reason and nature?—Hae ye read Boaden's *Life o' Siddons,* sir?

North. I have, James—and I respect Mr. Boaden for his intelligent criticism. He is rather prosy, occasionally—but why not? God knows, he cannot be more prosy, than I am now at this blessed moment—yet what good man, were he present now, would be severe upon old Christopher for havering away about this, that, or t'other thing, so long as there was heart in all he said, and nothing *contra bonos mores?* Sarah was a glorious creature. Methinks I see her now in the sleep-walking scene!

Shepherd. As Leddy Macbeth! Her gran', high, straicht-nosed face, whiter than ashes! Fixed een, no like the een o' the dead, yet hardly mair like them o' the leevin; dim and yet licht wi' an obscure lustre, through which the tormented sowl looked in the chains o' sleep and dreams wi' a' the distraction o' remorse and despair,—and oh! sic an expanse o' forehead for a warld o' dreadfu' thochts, aneath the braided blackness o' her hair, that had nevertheless been put up wi' a steady and nae uncarefu' haun before the troubled Leddy had lain doun, for it behooved ane so high-born as she, in the middle o' her ruefu' trouble, no to neglect what she owed to her stately beauty, and to the head that lay on the couch of ane o' Scotland's Thanes—noo likewise about to be, during the short space o' the passing o' a thunder-cloud, her bluidy and usurping King.

North. Whisht—Tickler—whisht—no coughing.

Shepherd. Onwards she used to come—no Sarah Siddons—but just Leddy Macbeth hersel—though through that melancholy masquerade o' passion, the spectator aye had a confused glimmerin apprehension o' the great actress—glidin wi' the ghostlike motion o' nicht-wandering unrest, unconscious o' surroundin objects,—for oh! how could the glazed yet gleamin een see aught in this material world?—yet, by some mysterious power o' instinct, never touchin ane o' the impediments that the furniture o' the auld castle micht hae opposed to her haunted footsteps,—on she came, wring, wringin her hauns, as if washin them in the cleansin dews frae the blouts o' blood,—but wae's me for the murderess, out they wad no be, ony mair than the stains on the spat o' the floor where some midnicht-slain Christian has groaned out his soul aneath the dagger's stroke, when the sleepin hoose heard not the shriek o' departing life.

Tickler. North, look at James's face. Confound me, under the inspiration of the moment, if it is not like John Kemble's!

Shepherd. Whether a' this, sirs, was natural or not, ye see I dinna ken, because I never beheld ony woman, either gentle or semple, walkin in her sleep after having committed murder. But, Lord safe us! that hollow, broken-hearted voice, "Out, damned spot," was o' itsel aneuch to tell to a' that heard it, that crimes done in the flesh during time will needs be punished in the spirit during eternity. It was a dreadfu' homily yon, sirs; and wha that saw't would ever ask whether tragedy or the stage was moral, purging the soul, as she did wi' pity and wi' terror?

North. James, I'll tell you a kind of composition that would tell.

Shepherd. What is't, man? Let's hear't.

North. Pastoral Dramatic Poetry, partly prose and partly verse—like the "Winter's Tale," or "As You Like It," or "The Tempest," or "The Midsummer-Night's Dream."

Tickler. Dramas of which the scenes are laid in the country cannot be good, for the people have no character.

Shepherd. Nae character's better than a bad ane, Mr. Tickler;—but you see, sir, you're just perfectly ignorant o' what you're talkin about—for it's only kintra-folk that has ony character ava,—and town's-bodies seem to be a' in a slump. Hoo the street rins wi' leevin creatures, like a stream rinnin wi' foam-bells! What maitter if they a' break as they gang by? For another shoal succeeds o' the same empty race!

North. The passions in the country, methinks, James, are

stronger and bolder, and more distinguishable from each other, than in the towns?

Shepherd. Deevil a passion's in the town, but envy, and backbiting, and conceitedness. As for friendship, or love, or hate, or revenge—ye never meet wi' them where men and women are a' jumbled throughither, in what is ca'd ceevileesed society. In solitary places, the sicht o' a human face aye brings wi't a corresponding feeling o' some kind or ither—there can be nae sic thing as indifference in habitations stannin here and there, in woods and glens, and on hill-sides and the shores o' lochs or the sea.

Tickler. Are no robberies, murders, and adulteries perpetrated in towns, James?

Shepherd. Plenty—and because there are nae passions to guard frae guilt. What man wi' a sowl glowin wi' the free feelings o' nature, and made thereby happy and contented, wi' his plaid across his breast, would condescend to be a highway robber, or by habit and repute a thief? What man, whose heart loupt to his mouth whenever he forgathered wi' his ain lassie, and never preed her bonny mou' but wi' a whispered benediction in her ear, wad at ance damn and demean himsel by breaking the seventh commandment? As for committing murder, leave that to the like o' Thurtell and Probert, and the like, wha seem to have had nae passions o' ony kind but a passion for pork-chops and porter, drivin in gigs, wearin rough big-coats wi' a dizzen necks, and cuffin ane anither's heads wi' boxin-gloves on their neives,—but nae real South-kintra shepherd ever was known to commit murder, for they're ower fond o' fechtin at fair, and kirns, and the like, to tak the trouble o' puttin ye to death in cool blood—

Tickler. James, would you seriously have North to write dramas about the loves of the lower orders—men in corduroy breeches, and women in linsey-woollen petticoats—

Shepherd. Wha are ye, sir, to speak o' the lower orders? Look up to the sky, sir, on a starry nicht, and puir, ignorant thochtless, upsettin cretur you'll be, gin you dinna feel, far within and deep doun your ain sowl, that you are, in good truth, ane o' the lower orders—no perhaps o' men, but o' intelligences! and that it requires some dreadfu' mystery, far beyond your comprehension, to mak you worthy o' ever in after life becoming a dweller among those celestial mansions. Yet think ye, sir, that thousan's and tens o' thousan's o' millions, since the time when first God's wrath smote the earth's soil with the curse o' barrenness, and human creatures had to earn their bread wi' sweat and dust, haena lived and toiled, and laughed and sighed, and groaned and grat, *o' the lower orders*, that are noo in eternal bliss, and shall sit above you and Mr. North, and ithers o' the best o' the clan, in the realms o' heaven!

Tickler. 'Pon my soul, James, I said nothing to justify this tirade.

Shepherd. You did, though. Hearken till me, sir. If there be no agonies that wring the hearts of men and women lowly born, why should they ever read the Bible? If there be no heavy griefs makin aftentimes the burden o' life hard to bear, what means that sweet voice callin on them to "come unto me, for I will give them rest?" If love, strong as death, adhere not to yon auld widow's heart, while sairly bowed down, till her dim een canna see the lift but only the grass aneath her feet, hoo else would she or could she totter every Sabbath to kirk, and wi' her broken, feeble and quiverin voice, and withered hands clasped together on her breast, join, a happy and a hopefu' thing, in the holy Psalm? If—

Tickler. James, you affect me, but less by the pictures you draw, than by the suspicion—nay, more than the suspicion — you intimate that I am insensible to these things—

Shepherd. I refer to you, Mr. North, if he didna mean, by what he said about corduroy breeks and linsey-woollen petticoats, to throw ridicule on all that wore them, and to assert that nae men o' genius, like you or me, ought to regard them as worthy o' being charactereezed in prose or rhyme?

North. My dear James, you have put the argument on an immovable basis. Poor, lonely, humble people, who live in shielings, and huts, and cottages, and farmhouses, have souls worthy of being saved, and therefore not unworthy of being written about by such authors as have also souls to be saved; among whom you and I, and Tickler himself—

Shepherd. Yes, yes—Tickler himself, sure aneuch. Gie's your haun, Mr. Tickler, gie's your haun—we're baith in the right; for I agree wi' you, that nae hero o' tragedy or a Yepic should be brought forrit ostentatiously in corduroy breeks, and that, I suppose, is a' you intended to say?

Tickler. It is, indeed, James; I meant to say no more.

Shepherd. Surely, Mr. North, you'll no allow anither spring to gang by without comin out to the fishing? I dinna understaun' your aye gaun up to the Cruick-Inn in Tweedsmuir. The Yarrow Trouts are far better eatin—and they mak far better sport, too—loupin out the linns in somersets like tumblers frae a spring-brod, head-ower-heels,—and gin your pirn doesna rin free, snappin aff your tackle, and doun wi' a plunge four fathom deep i' the pool, or awa like the shadow o' a hawk's wing alang the shallows.

North. Would you believe it, my dear Shepherd, that my piscatory passions are almost dead within me; and I like now to saunter along the banks and braes, eyeing the younkers angling, or to lay me down on some sunny spot, and with my face up to heaven, watch the slow-changing clouds!

Shepherd. I'll no believe that, sir,till I see't—and scarcely then—for a bluidier-minded fisher nor Christopher North never threw a hackle. Your creel fu',—your shootin-bag fu' —your jacket-pouches fu', the pouches o' your verra breeks fu',—half-a-dozen wee anes in your waistcoat, no to forget them in the croon o' your hat,—and, last o' a,' when there's nae place to stow awa ony mair o' them, a willow-wand drawn through the gills of some great big anes, like them ither folk would grup wi' the worm or the mennon—but a' gruppit wi' the flee—Phin's * delight, as you ca't,—a killin inseck,—and on gut that's no easily broken,—witness yon four-pounder aneath Elibank wood, where your line, sir, got entangled wi' the auld oak-root, and yet at last ye landed him on the bank, wi' a' his crosses and his stars glitterin like gold and silver amang the gravel! I confess, sir, you're the king o' anglers. But dinna tell me that you have lost your passion for the art; for we never lose our passion for ony pastime at which we continue to excel.

Tickler. Now that you two have begun upon angling, I shall ring the bell for my nightcap.

Shepherd. What! do you sleep wi' a nichtcap?

Tickler. Yes, I do, James—and also with a nightshirt—extraordinary as such conduct may appear to some people. I am a singular character, James, and do many odd things, which, if known to the public, would make the old lady turn up the whites of her eyes in astonishment.

Shepherd. Howsomever that be, sir, dinna ring for a nicht-cap, for we're no gaun to talk ony mair about angling! We baith hae our weakness, Mr. North and me;—but there's

* Phin was an approved artificer of fishing tackle. The shop still exists, and sustains its ancient reputation.

Mr. Awmrose— (*Enter* Mr. AMBROSE).—Bring supper, Mr. Awmrose—verra weel, sir, I thank ye—hoo hae you been yoursel, and hoo's a' wi' the wife and weans? Whenever you like, sir; the sooner the better. [*Exit* Mr. AMBROSE.

Tickler. No yawning, James,—a barn-door's a joke to such jaws.

North. Give us a song, my dear Shepherd—"Paddy o' Rafferty," or "Low doun i' the Broom," or "O Jeanie, there's naething to fear ye," or "Love's like a dizziness," or "Rule Britannia," or "Aiken Drum," or—

Tickler. Beethoven, they say, is starving in his native country, and the Philharmonic Society of London, or some other association with music in their souls, have sent him a hundred pounds to keep him alive—he is deaf, destitute, and a paralytic.—Alas! alas!

Shepherd. Whisht! I hear Mr. Awmrose's tread in the transe!—

"His verra foot has music in't
As he comes up the stair."

(*Enter* Mr. AMBROSE *and Assistants.*)

Hoo mony hunder eisters are there on the brod, Mr. Awmrose?—Oh! ho! Three brods!—One for each o' us!—A month without an R has nae richt being in the year. Noo, gentlemen, let naebody speak to me for the neist half-hour. Mr. Awmrose, we'll ring when we want the rizzers—and the toasted cheese—and the deevil'd turkey.—Hae the kettle on the boil, and put back the lang haun o' the clock, for I fear this is Saturday nicht, and nane o' us are folk to break in on the Sabbath. Help Mr. North to butter and bread,—and there, sir, there's the vinnekar cruet. Pepper awa, gents.

XIII.

IN WHICH TICKLER SECURES THE CALF, AND THE SHEPHERD THE BONASSUS.

SCENE I. *Porch of Buchanan Lodge. Time,—Evening.*

MRS. GENTLE.—MISS GENTLE.—SHEPHERD.—COLONEL CYRIL THORNTON.*—TICKLER.

Shepherd. I just ca' this perfec' Paradise. Oh! Mem! but that's the natest knitting ever blessed the een o' man. Is't for a veil to your dochter's bonny face? I'm glad it's no ower deep, sae that it winna hide it a'thegither—for sure amang sic a party o' freens as this, the young leddy'll forgie me for saying at ance, that there's no a mair beautifu' cretur in a' Scotland.

Mrs. Gentle. See, Mr. Hogg, how you have made poor Mary hang down her head—but you Poets—

Shepherd. Breathe and hae our beings in love, and delight in the fair and innocent things o' this creation. Forgie me, Miss Gentle, for bringing the blush to your broo—like sunlight on snaw—for I'm but a simple shepherd, and whiles

* Captain Thomas Hamilton, an early contributor to *Blackwood's Magazine,* and author of the admirable novel, *The Youth and Manhood of Cyril Thornton,* was the younger brother of Sir William Hamilton, Bart., Professor of Logic and Metaphysics in the University of Edinburgh. His other works are, *Men and Manners in America,* and *Annals of the Peninsular Campaigns.* He died at Florence in 1842.

says things I sudna say, out o' the very fulness of my heart.

Mrs. Gentle. Mary, fetch my smaller shuttle from the parlor—it is lying, I believe, on one of the cushions of the yellow sofa. [MISS GENTLE *retires.*

Shepherd. Oh! Mem! that my ain dochter may grow up, under the blessing o' God, sic a flower! I've often heard tell o' you and her—and o' Mr. North's freenship o' auld for her father—

North. Hallo, James—there's a wasp running along your shoulder in the direction of your ear!

Shepherd. A wasp—say ye? Whilk shouther? Ding't aff, some o' ye. Wull nane o' ye either speak or stir? Whilk shouther, I say? Confoun' ye, Tickler—ye great heigh ne'er doweel, wunna ye say whilk shouther? Is't aff?

Tickler. Off! No, James, that it isn't. How it is pricking along, like an armed knight, up the creases of your neckcloth! Left chin—Shepherd.

Mrs. Gentle. Allow me, Mr. Hogg, to remove the unwelcome visitor. (MRS. GENTLE *rises and scares the wasp with her handkerchief.*)

Shepherd. That's like a leddy, as you are. There's nae kindness like kindness frae the haun o' a woman.

Tickler. He was within an inch o' your ear, Hogg, and had made good his entrance, but for the entanglement of the dusty whisker.

Shepherd. That's no a word, sir, to speak afore a leddy. It's coorse. But you're wrang again, sir, for the wasp cudna hae made gude his entrance by that avenue, for my left lug's stuffed wi' cotton.

North. How happens it, my dear James, that on coming to town you are never without a cold? That country will kill you—we shall be losing you, James, some day, of a brain-fever.

Shepherd. A verra proper death for a poet. But it's just your ain vile, vapory, thick, dull, yellow, brown, dead, drizzling, damned (beg you pardon, Mem) easterly haur o' Embro' that gies me the rheumatics. In the country I think naething o' daundering awa to the holms, without my bannet, or onything around my chafts—even though it sud be raining—and the weather has nae ither effec' than to gar my hair grow.

North. You must have been daundering about a good deal lately, then, my dear James, for I never saw you with such a crop of hair in my life.

Shepherd. It's verra weel for you that's bald to tauk about a crap o' hair. But the mair hair a man has on his head the better, as lang's it's tousy—and no in candle-wick fashion. What say ye, Corrnall? for, judging frae your ain pow, you're o' my opinion.

C. Cyril Thornton. I see, Mr. Hogg, that we both patronize Macassar.

Shepherd. What? Macawser ile? Deevel a drap o't ever wat my weeg—nor never sall. It's stinkin stuff—as are a' the iles and gies an unwholesome and unnatural greasy glimmer to ane's hair, just like sae muckle creesh.

C. Cyril Thornton. 'Pon my honor, my dear Mr. Hogg, I never suspected you of a wig.

Shepherd. Hoots, man, I was metaphorical. It's a weeg o' nature's weavin. (*Re-enter* Miss Gentle *with a small ivory shuttle in her hand.*) Come awa—come awa, Mem—here's an empty seat near me. (Miss Gentle *sits down beside the* Shepherd.) And I'll noo praise your beauty ony mair, for I ken that maidens dinna like blushing, bonny as it makes them; but dinna think it was ony flattery—for gif it was the last word I was ever to speak in this warld, it was God's truth, but no the half o' the truth; and when ye gaed ben the house, I cudna help saying to your Leddy Mother, hoc happy and mair than happy would I be had I sic a dochter. (*Enter* PETER.) Peter, my braw man, Mr. North is ordering you to bring but * a bottle o' primrose wine. (*Exit* PETER.) Wae's me, Mr. North, but I think Peter's lookin auld-like.

North. Like master like man.

C. Cyril Thornton. Nay, nay, sir—I see little or no change on you since I sold out, and that, as you know, was the year in which the Allied armies were in Paris.

Shepherd. Weel—I declare, Corrnall, that I'm glad to hear your voice again—for, as far as I ken you on ower short an acquaintance, I wush it had heen langer—but plenty o' life let us houp, is yet afore us. You hae but only ae faut—and that's no a common ane—you dinna speak half aneuch as muckle's your freens could desire. Half aneuch, did I say—na, no a fourth pairt—but put a pen intil your haun, and you ding the best o' us. Oh! man! but your Memoirs o' your Youth and Manhood's maist interestin. I'm no speakin as a critic, and hate phrasin onybody—but you's no a whit inferior, as a whole, to my ain "Perils."

C. Cyril Thornton. Allow me to assure you, Mr. Hogg, that I am fully sensible both of the value and the delicacy of the compliment. Many faults in style and composition your practised and gifted eye could not fail to detect, or I ought rather, in all humility to say, many such faults must have forced themselves upon it; but I know well, at the same time, that the genius which delights the whole world by its own creations is ever indulgent to the crudities of an ordinary mind, inheriting but feeble powers from nature, and those, as you know, little indebted to art, during an active life that afforded but too few opportunities for their cultivation.

Shepherd. Feeble poo'rs! Ma faith, Corrnall, there's nae

* Bring *but* is bring *out*, as bring *ben* is bring *in*.

symptoms o' feeble poo'rs yonner—you're a strong-thinking, strong-feeling, strong-writing, strong-actin, and let me add, notwithstanding the want o' that airm that's missin, strong-looking man as is in a' his Majesty's dominions—either in the ceevil or military depairtment—and the cleverest fallow in a' Britain micht be proud to father yon three volumes. Phrasin's no my faut—it lies rather the ither way. They're just perfeckly capital—and what I never saw afore in a' my born days, and never houp to see again, as sure as ocht,* the thrid volumm's the best o' the three,—the story, instead o' dwinin awa intil a consumption, as is the case wi' maist lang stories that are seen gaun backwarts and forrits, no kennin what to do wi' themsels, and loosin their gate as sune as it gets dark—grows stouter and baulder, and mair confident in itsel as it proceeds

"Veerace aqueerit yeundo,"†

till at last it soums up a' its haill poo'rs for a satisfactory catastrophe, and gangs aff victoriously into the land o' Finis in a soun' like distant thunner, or to make use o' a martial simile, sin' I'm speakin to a sodger, like that o' a discharge o' the great guns o' artillery roarin thanks to the welkin for twa great simultawneous victories baith by sea and land, on ane and the same day.

North. James, allow me, in the name of Colonel Thornton, to return you his very best thanks for your speech.

Shepherd. Ay—ay—Mr. North—my man—ye needna, after that, sir, to try to review it in *Blackwood;* or gin you do, hae the grace to avow that I gied you the germ o' the article, and sen' out to Altrive in a letter the twenty guineas a sheet.

North. It shall be done,‡ James.

* *Ocht*—aught, anything.

† Vires acquirit eundo.

‡ *Cyril Thornton* was reviewed by Professor Wilson in *Blackwood's Magazine*, No. CXXVII.

Shepherd. Or rather suppose—to save yourself the trouble o' writin, which I ken you detest, and me the postage—you just tak out your red-turkey * the noo, and fling me ower a twenty-pun' Bank post bill—and for the sake o' auld lang syne, you may keep the shillins to yoursel.

North. The evening is beginning to get rather cold—and I feel the air, from the draught of that door, in that painful crick of my neck—

Shepherd. That's a' a flam. Ye hae nae crick o' your neck. Oh, sir, you're growin unco hard—just a verra Joseph Hume. Speak o' siller, that's to say o' the payin o't awa, and you're as deaf's a nit; but be there but a whusper o' payin't intil your haun, and you're as gleg o' hearin as a mowdiewarp.† Isna that true?

North. Too true, James—I feel that I am the victim of a disease—and of a disease, too, my Shepherd, that can only be cured by death—old age—we septuagenarians are all misers.

Shepherd. Oh, struggle against it, sir! As you love me—struggle against it! Dinna let your imagination settle on the stocks. Pass the faldin-doors o' the Royal Bank wi' your een shut—sayin a prayer.—Dear me!—dear me! what's the maitter wi' Mrs. Gentle? Greetin, I declare, and wipin her een wi' Mr. North's ain Bandana!—What for are ye greetin, Mrs. Gentle? Hae ye gotten a sudden pain in your head? If sae, ye had better gang up-stairs, and lie doun.

Mrs. Gentle (in tears, and with a faint sob). Mr. Hogg—you know not that man's—that noble—generous—glorious man's heart. But for him, what, where, how might I now have been—and my poor orphan daughter there at your side? Orphan I may well call her—for when her brave father, the General, fell—

* Pocket-book. † *Mowdiewarp*—mole.

Shepherd. There's nae punishment ower severe to inflick on me, Mem. But may I never stir aff this firm,* if I wasna a' in jeest;—but there's naething mair dangerous than ill-timed daffin—I weel ken that—and this is no the first time I hae wounded folks' feelins wi' nae mair thocht or intention o' doin sae than—this angel at my side.

Mrs. Gentle (*Peter entering with tea-tray*). Mr. Hogg, do you prefer black or green tea?

Shepherd. Yes—yes—Mem—black and green tea. But I'm taukin nonsense. Green—Mem—green—mak it strong—and I'll drink five cups, that I may lie awauk a' nicht, and repent bringin the saut tear into your ee by my waur than stupid nonsense about our benefactor.

Miss Gentle. Peter, take care of the kettle.

Shepherd. You're ower kind, Miss Gentle, to bid Peter tak care o' the kettle on my account. There's my legs stretched out, that the stroop may hiss out it's boilin het steam on my shins. by way o' penance for my sin. I'll no draw a worsted thread through a single ane o' a' the blisters. . . . But it'll make us a' mair than happy—me, and the mistress, and the weans, and a' our humble household, if Mrs. Gentle, you and your dutifu' dochter'll come out to Yarrow wi' Mr. North, his verra first visit. Say, Mem, that you'll do't. Oh! promise you'll do't, and we'll a' be happy as the twenty-second o' June is lang.

Mrs. Gentle. I promise it, Mr. Hogg, most cheerfully. The Peebles Fly—

Miss Gentle. My mother will make proper arrangements, Mr. Hogg, in good time.

Shepherd. And then, indeed, there will be a Gentle Shepherdess in Yarrow.

North. A vile pun.

* *Firm*—form, bench.

Shepherd. Pun? Heaven be praised, I never made a pun in my life. It's no come to that o't wi' me yet. A man's mind must be sair rookit o' thochts before he begins in his dotage to play upon words. But then, I say, there will be a shepherdess in Yarrow; and the author o' *Lichts and Shadows*,* who imagines every red-kuted † hizzie he meets to be a shepherdess—

Miss Gentle. Pardon me, sir, the *Lights and Shadows* are extremely beau—

Shepherd. Nae mair sugar, Mem, in ma cup; the last was rather ower sweet. What was ye gaun to say, Miss Gentle? But nae matter—it's fixed that you're comin out to Altrive in the Peebles Fly, and—

Miss Gentle. The *Lights and Shadows of Scottish Life*—

Shepherd. I agree with you. They certainly are. Nobody admires the author's genius mair than I do; but—What the deevil's become o' Mr. Tickler? I never missed him till this moment.

North. Yonder he is, James, rolling down the hill all his length with my gardener's children! happy as any imp among them—and worrying them in play, like an old tiger acting the amiable and paternal with his cubs, whom at another hour he would not care to devour.

Shepherd. Look at him wi' his heels up i' the air, just like a horse rollin i' the garse on bein' let out o' the harnesh! I wush he mayna murder some o' the weans in his unwieldy gambols.

North. 'Tis the veriest great boy, Colonel Thornton! Yet as soon as he has got rid of the urchins, you will see him come stalking up the gravel walk, with his hands behind his back, and his face as grave as a monk's in a cloister,

* *The Lights and Shadows of Scottish Life.* By Professor Wilson.

† *Red-kuted*—red-ankled.

till, flinging himself into a chair, with a long sigh he will exclaim against the vanities of this weary world, and, like the melancholy Jacques himself, moralize on that calf yonder—which by the way has pulled up the peg, and set off at a scamper over my beds of tulips. Mr. Tickler—hallo—will you have the goodness, now that you are on your legs, to tell the children to look after that young son of a cow—

Tickler (running up out of breath). He has quite the look of a Puma—see how he handles his tail, and kicks up his heels like a D'Egville. Jem—Tommy—Bauldy, my boys,—the calf—the calf—the hunt's up—halloo, my lads—halloo!

[*Off they all set.*

Shepherd. Faith, I've eneuch o' rinnin after calves at hame. Here I'm on a holiday, and I'll sit still. What's a Puma, Mr. North? I never heard tell o' a beast wi' that name before. Is it outlandish or indigenous?

[*The Calf gallops by in an exhausted state, tail-on-end,—with* TICKLER, *and* JEM, TOMMY, *and* BAULDY, *the gardener's children, in full cry.*

Shepherd. I canna lauch at that—I canna lauch at that; and yet I dinna ken either—yonner's Tickler a' his length, haudin fast by the tail, and the calf—it's a desperate strong beast for sae young a ane, and a quey* too—harlin him through the shrubbery. Haw! haw! haw! haw!—Oh, Corrnall! but I'm surprised no to hear you lauchin—for my sides is like to split.

C. Cyril Thornton. It is a somewhat singular part of my idiosyncrasy, Mr. Hogg, that I never feel the slightest impulse to laugh aloud. But I can assure you, that I have derived from the view-holla the most intense excitation of the midriff. I never was more amused in my life; and you

* *Quey*—a young cow.

had, within my very soul, a silent accompaniment to your guffaw.

North. These, Cyril, are not the indolent gardens of Epicurus. You see we indulge occasionally in active, even violent exercises.

C. Cyril Thornton. There is true wisdom, Mr. North, in that extraordinary man's mind. It has given me much pleasure to think that Mr. Tickler should have remembered my name—for I never had the honor of being in his company but once—when I was at the University of Glasgow, in the house of my poor old grand-uncle, Mr. Spreull.* Mr. Tickler had carried some important mercantile case through your law-courts here for Mr. Spreull, and greatly gratified the old gentleman by coming west without ceremony to take pot-luck. It was with no little difficulty that we got through dinner, for I remember Girzy was so utterly confounded by his *tout-ensemble*, his stature, his tie—for he sported one in those days—his gestures, his gesticulations, his jokes, his waggery, and his wit, all of a kind new to the West, that she stood for many minutes with the tureen of hotch-potch supported against her breast, and all her grey goggles fascinated as by a serpent, till poor old Mr. Spreull cursed her in his sternest style to set it down on the table, that he might ask a blessing.

[TICKLER, JEM, TOMMY, *and* BAULDY *re-cross the front of the Porch in triumph with the captive Calf, and disappear in the rear of the premises.*

Shepherd. He'll be laid up for a week noo, on account o' this afternoon's stravagin without his hat, and a' this rowin ower braes wi' weans, and a' this gallopin and calf-huntin. He'll be a' black and blue the morn's morning, and sae stiff that he'll no be able to rise.

* One of the characters in *Cyril Thornton.*

Mrs. Gentle. Mary, we must bid Mr. North and his friends good-night. You know we are engaged at ten —

"And yon bright star has risen to warn us home."

North. Farewell.

Shepherd. Faur ye weel, faur ye weel—God bless you baith—faur ye weel—noo be sure no to forget your promise to bring Miss Mary out wi' ye to Ettrick.

Miss Gentle (smiling). In the Peebles Fly.

Shepherd. Na, your father, as ye ca'd him, when ye gied his auld wrinkled forehead a kiss, 'll bring you to the Forest in his ain cotch-and-four. Faur ye weel—God bless you baith—faur ye weel.

C. Cyril Thornton. Ladies, I wish you good evening. Mrs. Gentle, the dews are falling; allow me to throw my fur cloak over you and Miss Gentle; it is an ancient affair, but of the true Merino.—You flatter me by accepting it.

[*Covers Mother and Daughter with his military cloak, and they vanish.*

North. Now, James, a single jug of toddy.

Shepherd. What! each?

North. Each. There comes Tickler, as grave's a judge—make no allusion to the chase. (TICKLER *rejoins the party.*) But it is chilly, so let us go into the parlor. I see Peter has had the sense to light the candles—and there he goes with a pan of charcoal.

SCENE II.—*The Pitt Parlor.*

Tickler. I fear, Colonel, since you lost your arm, that you are no longer a sportsman.

C. Cyril Thornton. I have given up shooting, although Joe Manton constructed a light piece for me, with which I generally contrived to hit and miss time about; but I am a devout disciple of Izaak, and was grievously disappointed on my arrival t'other day in Kelso, to find another occupier in Walton-hall; but my friend, Mr. Alexander Ballantyne, and I, proceed to Peebles on the 1st of June, to decide our bet of a rump and dozen, he with the spinning minnow, and I with Phin's delight.

Shepherd. Watty Ritchie'll beat you baith with the May-flee, if it be on, or ony length aneath the stanes.

North. You will be all sorry to hear that our worthy friend Watty is laid up with a bad rheumatism, and can no longer fish the Megget Water and the lochs, and return to Peebles in the same day.

Shepherd. That's what a' your waders come to at last. Had it no been, Mr. North, for your plowterin in a' the rivers and lochs o' Scotland, baith saut water and fresh, like a Newfoundland dog, or rather a seal or an otter, you needna, had that crutch aneath your oxter. Cornall Cyril, saw ye him ever a fishin?

C. Cyril Thornton. Never but once, for want of better ground, in the Crinan Canal, out of a coal-barge, for braises when I was a red-gowned student at Glasgow.

Shepherd. Oh! but you should hae seen him in Loch Owe, or the Spey. In he used to gang, out, out, and ever sae far out frae the pint o' a promontory, sinkin aye furder and furder doun, first to the waistband o' his breeks, then up to the middle button o' his waistcoat, then to the verra breast, then to the oxters, then to the neck, and then to the verra chin o' him, sae that you wonnered how he could fling the flee, till last o' a' he would plump richt out o' sicht, till the Highlander on Ben Cruachan thocht him drooned; but he wasna born to be drooned—no he, indeed—sae he taks to the soomin, and strikes awa wi' ae arm, like yoursel, sir—for the tither had haud o' the rod—and, could ye believe't, though it's as true as Scriptur, fishing a' the time, that no a moment o' the cloudy day micht be lost; ettles at an island a quarter o' a mile aff, wi' trees, and an old ruin o' a religious house, wherein beads used to be coonted, and wafers eaten, and mass muttered hundreds o' years ago; and gettin footin on the yellow sand or the green sward, he but gies himsel a shake, and ere the sun looks out o' the clud, has hyucket a four-pounder, whom in four minutes (for it's a multiplying pirn the cretur uses) he lands gasping through the giant gills, and glitterin wi' a thousan' spots, streaks, and stars, on the shore. That's a pictur o' North's fishing in days o' yore.* But look at him noo—only look at him noo—wi' that auld-farrant face o' his, no unlike a pike's, crunkled up in his chair, his chin no that unwullin to tak a rest on his collar-bane—the hauns o' him a' covered wi' chalk-stanes—his legs like winnle-straes—and his knees but knobs, sae that he canna cross the room, far less soom ower Loch Owe, without a crutch; and wunna you join wi' me, Corrnall Cyril, in hauding up baith your hauns—I aux your pardon, in hauding up your richt haun—and compairing the past wi' the present, exclaim, amaist sobbin, and in tears, "Vanity o' vanities! all is vanity!"

North (suddenly hitting the Shepherd over the sconce with his crutch). Take that, blasphemer!

Shepherd (clawing his pow). "Man of age, thou smitest sore!"

C. Cyril Thornton. Mr. Hogg, North excels at the crutch-exercise.

Shepherd. Put your finger, Corrnall, on here—did you ever fin' sic a big clour risen in sae wee a time?

* Professor Wilson's mode of angling in his younger days is here painted to the life. Even so late as 1849 he was in the habit of wading up to the loins in the practice of his favorite pastime.

C. Cyril Thornton. Never. Mr. North with his crutch, had he lived in the Sylvan Age of Robbery, would have been a match for the best of the merry Outlaws of Sherwood. Little John would have sung small, and Robin Hood fancied him no more than he did the Pinder of Wakefield.

Shepherd. That's what's ca'd at Buchanan Lodge cracking a practical joke, Corrnall. I maun get Peter to bring me some brown paper steep'd in vinegar, or the clour'll be like a horn. I scarcely think, even already, that my hat would stay on. Oh, sir, but you're desperate cruel.

North. Not I, my dear James. I knew I had a man to deal with: the tenth part of such a touch would have killed a Cockney.

Shepherd. What a bow-wowing's that, thinks ony o' you out-by?

North. Bronte baying at some blackguards on the outer side of the gate.

Shepherd. Oh! sir, I've heard tell o' your new Newfoundland dowg, and would like to see him. May I ring for Peter to lowse him frae his cheen, and bring him ben for me to look at? (*Rings the bell*—PETER *receives his instructions.*)

North. Bronte's mother, James, is a respectable female who now lives in Claremont Crescent; his father, who served his time in the navy, and was on board Admiral Otway's ship when he hoisted his flag in her on the Leith station, is now resident, I believe, at Portobello. The couple have never had any serious quarrel; but for reasons best known to themselves, choose to live apart. Bronte is at present the last of all his race—the heir-apparent of his parents' virtues—his four brothers and three sisters having all unfortunately perished at sea.

Shepherd. Did ye ever see onything grow sae fast as a Newfoundland whalp? There's a manifest difference on them between breakfast and denner, and denner and sooper ; and they keep growin a' nicht lang.

North. Bronte promises to stand three feet without his shoes—

Shepherd. I hear him comin—yowf-yowffin as he spangs along. I wush he mayna coup that weak-ham'd bodie, Peter.

[*Door opens, and* BRONTE* *bounces in.*

C. Cyril Thornton. A noble animal, indeed, and the very image of a dog that saved a drummer of ours, who chose to hop overboard, through fear of a flogging in the Bay of Biscay.

North. What do you think of him, James ?

Shepherd. Think o' him ? I canna think o' him—it's aneuch to see him—what'n a sagacious countenance ! Look at him lauchin as he observes the empty punch-bowl. His back's preceesely on a line wi' the edge o' the table. And oh ! but he's bonnily marked—a white ring roun' the neck o' him, a white breast, white paws, a white tip o' the tail, and a' the rest black as nicht. O man, but you're towsy ! His legs, Mr. North, canna be thinner than my airm, and what houghs, hips, and theeghs ! I'm leanin a' my haill waght upon his back, and his spine bends nae mair than about the same as Captain Brown's chain-pier at Newhaven when a hundred folk are walking alang't to gang on board the steamboat. His neck, too, 's like a bill's—if he was turnin o' a sudden at speed, a whap o' his tail would break a man's leg. Fecht ! I'se warrant him fecht, either wi' ane o' his ain specie, or wi' cattle wi' cloven feet, or wi' the lions Nero or Wallace o' Wummell's Menagerie, or wi' the Lord o' Creation, Man—by himsel Man ! How he would rug them down—dowgs, or soos, or stirks, or lions, or rubbers ! He

*Bronte was a real character. His life and death are afterwards commemorated.

could kill a man, I verily believe, without ever bitin him—just by dounin him wi' the waght o' his body and his paws, and then lying on the tap o' him, growlin to throttle and devour him if he mudged. He would do grandly for the Monks o' St Bernard to save travellers frae the snaw. Edwin Landseer maun come down to Scotland for anes errand, just to pent his pictur, that future ages may ken that in the reign o' George the Fourth, and durin the Queer Whig-and-Tory Administration, there was such a dowg.

North. I knew, James, that he was a dog after your own heart.

Shepherd. Oh, sir! dinna let onybody teach him tricks—sic as runnin back for a glove, or standin on his hurdies, or loupin out-ower a stick, or snappin bread frae aff his nose, or ringin the bell, or pickin out the letters o' the alphabet, like ane o' the working classes at a Mechanic Institution,—leave a' tricks o' that sort to Spaniels, and Poodles, and Puggies (I mean nae reflection on the Peebles Puggie withouten the tail, nor yet Mr. Thomas Grieve's Peero), but respec' the soul that maun be in that noble, that glorious frame; and if you maun chain him, let him understand that sic restraint is no incompawtible wi' liberty; and as for his kennel, I would hae it sclated, and a porch ower the door, even a miniature imitation o' the porch o' Buchanan Lodge.

North. James, we shall bring him with us—along with the Gentles—to Altrive.

Shepherd. Proud wad I be to see him there, sir, and gran' soomin wad he get in St. Mary's Loch, and the Loch o' the Lowes, and Loch Skene. But—there's just ae objection—ae objection—sir—I dinna see how I can get ower't.

North. The children, James? Why, he is as gentle as a new-dropt lamb.

Shepherd. Na, na—it's no the weans—for Jamie and his sisters would ride on his back—he could easy carry threeple—to Yarrow Kirk on the Sabbaths. But—but he would fecht with—The Bonassus.

North. The Bonassus! What mean ye, Shepherd?

Shepherd. I bocht the Bonassus frae the man that had him in a show; and Bronte and him would be for fechtin a duel, and baith o' them would be murdered, for neither Bronte nor the Bonassus would say "Hold, enough."

North. Of all the extraordinary freaks, my dear bard, that ever your poetical imagination was guilty of, next to writing the *Perils of Woman*, your purchase of the Bonassus seems to me the most miraculous.

Shepherd. I wanted to get a breed aff him wi' a maist extraordinar cow, that's half-blood to the loch-and-river kine by the bill's side—and I have nae doubt but that they wull be gran' milkers, and if fattened, will rin fifty score a quarter. But Bronte mauna come out to Altrive, sir, till the Bonassus is dead.

North. But is the monster manageable, James? Is there no danger of his rebelling against his master? Then, suppose he were to break through, or bound over the stone-wall and attack me, as I kept hobbling about the green braes, my doom would be sealed. I have stood many a tussle in my day, as you know and have heard, James; but I am not, now, single-handed, a match for the Bonassus.

Shepherd. The stane-wa's about my farm are rather rickly; but he never tries to break them doun as lang's the kye's wi' him,—nor do I think he has ony notion o' his ain strength. It's just as weel, for wi' yon head and shouthers he could ding doun a house.

C. Cyril Thornton. How the deuce, Mr Hogg, did you get

him from Edinburgh to Altrive? To look at him, he seemed an animal that would neither lead nor drive.

Shepherd. I bought him, sir, at Selkirk, waggon and a', and druv him hame mysel. The late owner tauked big aboot his fury and fairceness—and aiblins he was fairce in his keepin, as weel he micht be, fed on twa bushels o' ingans —unnions, that is—per deeam—but as sune as I had him at Mount Benger, I backet the waggon a wee doun hill, flang open the end door, and out like a debtor frae five years' confinement lap the Bonassus—

Tickler. Was you on the top of the waggon, James?

Shepherd. No—that thocht had occurred to me—but I was munted,—and the powney's verra fleet, showin bluid,—and aff I set at the gallop—

Tickler. With the Bonassus after you—

Shepherd. Whisht, man, whisht. The poor beast was scarcely able to staun'! He had forgotten the use of his legs! Sae I went up to him, on futt, withouten fear, and patted him a' ower. Sair frights some o' the folk frae Megget Water got, on first comin on him unawares—and I'm telt that there's a bairn ower-by about the side of Moffat Water—it's a callant—whose mither swarfed at the Bonassus when she was near the doun-lying, that has a fearsome likeness till him in the face; but noo he's weel kent, and, I may say, liked and respeckit through a' the Forest, as a peaceable and industrious member o' society.

North. I dread, my dear James, that, independent of the Bonassus, it will not be possible for me to be up with you before autumn. I believe that I must make a trip to London im—

Shepherd. Ay, ay,—the truth's out noo. The rumor in the Forest was, that you had been sent for by the King a month sin' syne, but wadna gang—and that a sheriff's offisher had been despatched in a chaise-and-four frae Lunnon, to bring you up by the cuff o' the neck, and gin you made ony resistance at the Lodge, to present his pistol.

North. There are certain secrets, my dearest James, the development of which, perhaps, lies beyond even the privileges of friendship. With you I have no reserve—but when Majesty—

Shepherd. Lays its command on a loyal subject, you was gaun to say, he maun obey. That's no my doctrine. It's slavish-like. You did perfectly richt, sir; the haill Forest swore you did perfectly richt in refusin to stir a futt frae your ain fireside, in a free kintra like the auld kingdom o' Scotland. Had the King been leevin at Holyrood, it micht hae been different; but for a man o' your years to be harled through the snaw—

North. I insist that this sort of conversation, sir, stop—and that what has been now said—most unwarrantedly, remember, James—go no farther. Do you think, my dear Shepherd, that all that passes within the penetralia of the Royal breast finds an echo in the rumors of the Forest? "But something too much of this."

Shepherd. Weel, weel, sir—weel, weel. But dinna look sae desperate angry. I canna thole to see a frown on your face, it works sic a dreadfu', I had maist said deeabolical change on the haill expression o' the faytures. Oh, smile sir! if you please—do, Mr. North, sir, my dear freen, do just gie ae bit blink o' a smile at the corner o' your ee or mouth—ay, that'll do, Christopher—that'll do. Oh, man, Kit, but you was fairce the noo just at naething ava, as folks generally is when they are at their faircest, for then their rampagin passion meets wi' nae impediment, and keeps feed, feed, feedin on itself and its ain heart. But whisht—there's thunner!

Tickler. Only Mr. Ambrose with the coach I ordered to be at the Lodge precisely at one.

Shepherd. I'm sorry she's come. For I was just beginnin to summon up courage to hint the possibility, if no the propriety, o' anither bowl—or at least a jug.

C. Cyril Thornton (rising). God bless you, sir, good morning—Mr. Ambrose may call it but one o'clock, if it gives him any pleasure to think that the stream of time may run counter to the moon and stars; but it is nearer three, and I trust the lamps are not lighted needlessly to affront the dawn. Once more—God bless you sir. Good morning.

North. Thursday at six, Cyril—farewell.

[*Enter* Mr. AMBROSE *to announce the coach.*

Shepherd. Gude-by, sir—dinna get up aff your chair. (*Aside*) Corrnall, he canna rise. The coach 'll drap the Corrnall at Awmrose's in Picardy, and me at the Peebles Arms, sign o' the Sawmon, Candlemaker Row,—and Mr. Tickler at his ain house, Southside—and by then it'll be about time for't to return to the stance in George Street.

C. Cyril Thornton (opening the window-shutters at a nod from North). The blaze of day.

[*Coach drives from the Lodge, ribbons and rod in the hand of* Mr. AMBROSE.

XIV.

IN WHICH THE SHEPHERD AND TICKLER TAKE TO THE WATER.

SCENE I.—*Two Bathing-machines in the Sea at Portobello.**

SHEPHERD.—TICKLER.

Shepherd. Halloo, Mr. Tickler, are you no ready yet, man? I've been a mother-naked man, in my machine here, for mair than ten minutes. Hae your pantaloons got entangled amang your heels, or are you saying your prayers afore you plunge?

Tickler. Both. These patent long drawers, too, are a confounded nuisance—and this patent short under-shirt. There is no getting out of them without greater agility than is generally possessed by a man at my time of life.

Shepherd. Confound a' pawtents. As for mysel, I never wear drawers, but hae my breeks lined wi' flannen a' the year through; and as for thae wee short corded under-shirts, that clasp you like ivy, I never hae had ane o' them on sin' last July, when I was forced to cut it aff my back and breast wi' a pair o' sheep-shears, after having tried in vain to get out o't every morning for twa months. But are ye no ready, sir? A man on the scaffold wadna be allowed sae lang time for preparation. The minister or the hangman wad be jugging † him to fling the hankerchief.

* A bathing quarter near Edinburgh.

† *Jugging*—jogging.

Tickler. Hanging, I hold, is a mere flea-bite—

Shepherd. What! tae dookin?—Here goes.

[*The* SHEPHERD *plunges into the sea.*

Tickler. What the devil has become of James? He is nowhere to be seen. That is but a gull—that only a seal—and that a mere pellock. James, James, James!

Shepherd (*emerging.*) Wha's that roaring? Stop a wee till I get the saut water out o' my een, and my mouth, and my nose, and wring my hair a bit. Noo, where are you, Mr. Tickler?

Tickler. I think I shall put on my clothes again, James. The air is chill; and I see from your face that the water is as cold as ice.

Shepherd. Oh, man! but you're a desperate cooart. Think shame o' yoursel, stannin naked there, at the mouth o' the machine, wi' the haill crew o' yon brig sailin up the Firth looking at ye, ane after anither, frae cyuck to captain, through the telescope.

Tickler. James, on the sincerity of a shepherd and the faith of a Christian, lay your hand on your heart, and tell me, was not the shock tremendous? I thought you never would have reappeared.

Shepherd. The shock was naething, nae mair than what a body feels when waukenin suddenly during a sermon, or fa'in ower a staircase in a dream.—But I am aff to Inchkeith.

Tickler. Whizz. [*Flings a somerset into the sea.*

Shepherd. Ane—twa—three—four—five—sax—seven—aught—but there's nae need o' coontin—for nae pearl-diver, in the Straits o' Madagascar or aff the coast o' Coromandel, can haud in his breath like Tickler. Weel, that's surprisin. Yon chaise has gane about half a mile o' gate towards Portybelly sin' he gaed fizzin outower the lugs like a verra rocket. Safe us! what's this gruppin me by the legs? A sherk—a sherk—a sherk!

Tickler (*yellowing to the surface*). Blabla—blabla—bla—

Shepherd. He's keept soomin aneath the water till he's sick; but every man for himsel, and God for us a'—I'm aff.

[SHEPHERD *stretches away to sea in the direction of Inchkeith*—TICKLER *in pursuit.*

Tickler. Every sinew, my dear James, like so much whip-cord. I swim like a salmon.

Shepherd. Oh, sir! that Lord Byron had but been alive the noo, what a sweepstakes!

Tickler. A Liverpool gentleman has undertaken, James, to swim four-and-twenty miles at a stretch. What are the odds?

Shepherd. Three to one on Saturn and Neptune. He'll get numm.

Tickler. James, I had no idea you were so rough on the back. You are a perfect otter.

Shepherd. Nae personality, Mr. Tickler, out at sea. I'll compare carcases wi' you ony day o' the year. Yet, you're a gran' soomer—out o' the water at every stroke, neck, breast, shouthers, and half-way doun the back—after the fashion o' the great American serpent. As for me, my style o' soomin's less showy—laigh and lown—less hurry, but mair speed. Come, sir, I'll dive you for a jug o' toddy.

[TICKLER *and* SHEPHERD *melt away like foam-bells in the sunshine.*

Shepherd. Mr. Tickler!

Tickler. James!

Shepherd. It's a drawn bate—sae we'll baith pay.— Oh, sir! isna Embro' a glorious city? Sae clear the air, yonner you see a man and a woman stannin on the tap o'Arthur's Seat! I had nae notion there were sae mony steeples, and spires, and columns, and pillars, and obelisks, and domes, in Embro'! And at this distance the ee canna distinguish atween them that belangs to kirks, and them that belangs to naval monuments, and them that belangs to ile-gas companies, and them that's only chimley-heids in the auld toun, and the taps o' groves, or single trees, sic as poplars; and aboon a' and ahint a', craigs and saft-broo'd hills sprinkled wi' sheep, lichts and shadows, and the blue vapory glimmer o' a midsummer day —het, het, het, wi' the barometer at ninety; but here, to us twa, bob-bobbin amang the fresh, cool, murmurin, and faemy wee waves, temperate as the air within the mermaid's palace. Anither dive!

Tickler. James, here goes the Fly-Wheel.

Shepherd. That beats a'! He gangs round in the water like a jack roastin beef. I'm thinkin he canna stop himsel. Safe us! he's fun' out the perpetual motion.

Tickler. What fish, James, would you incline to be, if put into scales?

Shepherd. A dolphin—for they hae the speed o' lichtnin. They'll dart past and roun' about a ship in full sail before the wind, just as if she was at anchor. Then the dolphin is a fish o' peace—he saved the life o' a poet of auld, Arion, wi' his harp—and, oh! they say the cretur's beautifu' in death—Byron, ye ken, comparin his hues to those o' the sun settin ahint the Grecian Isles. I sud like to be a dolphin.

Tickler. I should choose to sport shark for a season. In speed he is a match for the dolphin—and then, James, think what luxury to swallow a well-fed chaplain, or a delicate midshipman, or a young negro girl occasionally—

Shepherd. And feenally to be grupped wi' a hyuck in a cocked hat and feather, at which the shark rises as a trout does at a flee, hauled on board, and hacked to pieces wi' cutlasses and pikes, by the jolly crew or left alive on the deck, gutted as clean as a dice-box, and without an inch o' bowels.

Tickler. Men die at shore, James, of natural deaths as bad as that—

Shepherd. Let me see—I sud hae nae great objections to be a whale in the Polar Seas. Gran' fun to fling a boatfu' o' harpooners into the air—or, wi' ae thud o' your tail, to drive in the stern-posts o' a Greenlandman.

Tickler. Grander fun still, James, to feel the inextricable harpoon in your blubber, and to go snoving away beneath an ice-floe with four mile of line connecting you with your distant enemies.

Shepherd. But then whales marry but ae wife, and are passionately attached to their offspring. There, they and I are congenial speerits. Nae fish that swims enjoys so large a share of domestic happiness.

Tickler. A whale, James, is not a fish.

Shepherd. Isna he? Let him alane for that. He's ca'd a fish in the Bible, and that's better authority than Buffon. Oh, that I were a whale!

Tickler. What think you of a summer of the American Sea-Serpent.

Shepherd. What? To be constantly cruised upon by the haill American navy, military and mercantile! No to be able to show your back aboon water without being libelled by the Yankees in a' the newspapers, and pursued even by pleasure-parties, playin the hurdy-gurdy and smokin cigars! Besides, although I hae nae objection to a certain degree o' singularity, I sudna just like to be sae very singular as the American Sea-Serpent, who is the only ane o' his specie noo extant; and whether he dees in his bed, or is slain by Jonathan, must incur the pain and the opprobrium o' defunckin an auld bachelor. What's the matter wi' you, Mr. Tickler? [*Dives.*

Tickler. The calf of my right leg is rather harder than is altogether pleasant. A pretty business if it prove the cramp; and the cramp it is sure enough.—Hallo—James—James—James—hallo—I'm seized with the cramp—James—the sinews of the calf of my right leg are gathered up into a knot about the bulk and consistency of a sledge-hammer—

Shepherd. Nae tricks upon travellers. You've nae cramp. Gin you hae, streek out your richt hind leg, like a horse geein a funk—and then ower on the back o' ye, and keep floatin for a space, and your calf'll be as saft's a cushion. Lord safe us! what's this? Deevil tak me if he's no droonin. Mr. Tickler, are you droonin? There he's doun ance, and up again—twice, and up again;—but it's time to tak haud o' him by the hair o' the head, or he'll be doun amang the limpets!

[SHEPHERD *seizes* TICKLER *by the locks.*

Tickler. Oho—oho—oho—ho—ho—ho—hra—hra—hrach—hrach.

Shepherd. What language is that? Finnish? Noo, sir, dinna rug me doun to the bottom alang wi' you in the dead-thraws.

Tickler. Heaven reward you, James—the pain is gone—but keep near me.

Shepherd. Whammle yoursel ower on your back, sir. That 'ill do. Hoo are you now, sir? Yonner's the James Watt* steamboat, Captain Bain, within half a league. Lean on my airm, sir, till he comes alangside, and it 'ill be a real happiness to the captain to save your life. But what 'll a' the leddies do when they're hoistin us aboard? they maun just use their fans.

Tickler. My dear Shepherd, I am again floating like a turtle,—but keep within hail, James. Are you to windward or leeward?

Shepherd. Right astarn. Did you ever see, sir, in a' your born days, sic a sky? Ane can scarcely say he sees't, for it's maist invisible in its blue beautifu' tenuity, as the waters o' a well! It's just like the ee o' a lassie I kent lang ago—the

* The "James Watt" plied between London and Edinburgh, under the command of Captain Bain.

langer you gazed intil't, the deep, deep, deeper it grew—the cawmer and the mair cawm—composed o' a smile, as an amythist is composed o' licht—and seeming something impalpable to the touch, till you ventured, wi' fear, joy, and tremmlin to kiss it—just ae hesitatin, pantin, reverential kiss—and then, to be sure, your verra sowl kent it to be a bonny blue ee, covered wi' a lid o' dark fringes, and drappin aiblins a bit frichtened tear to the lip o' love.

Tickler. What is your specific gravity, James? You float like a sedge.

Shepherd. Say rather a Nautilus, or a Mew. I'm native to the yelement.

Tickler. Where learned you the natatory art, my dear Shepherd?

Shepherd. Do you mean soomin? In St. Mary's Loch. For a haill simmer I kept plouterin alang the shore, and pittin ae fit to the grun', knockin the skin aff my knees, and makin nae progress, till ae day, the gravel haein been loosened by a flood, I plowpt in ower head and ears, and in my confusion, turnin my face to the wrang airt, I swom across the loch at the widest at ae stretch, and ever after that could hae soomed ony man in the Forest for a wager, except Mr. David Ballantyne, that noo leeves ower-by yonner, near the Hermitage Castle.

Tickler. Now, James, you are, to use the language of Spenser, the Shepherd of the Sea.

Shepherd. Oh that I had been a sailor! To hae circumnavigated the warld! To hae pitched our tents, or built our bowers, on the shores o' bays sae glitterin wi' league-lang wreaths o' shells, that the billows blushed crimson as they murmured! To hae seen our flags burnin meteor-like, high up amang the primæval woods, while birds bright as ony buntin sat trimmin their plummage amang the cordage, sae tame in that island, where ship had hapiy never touched afore, nor ever might touch again, lying in a latitude by itsel, and far out o' the breath o' the tredd-wunds! Or to hae landed wi' a' the crew, marines and a', excep a guard on shipboard to keep aff the crowd o' canoes, on some warlike isle, tossin wi' the plumes on chieftains' heads, and soun'-soun'-soundin wi' gongs! What's a man-o'-war's barge, Mr. Tickler, beautifu' sicht though it be, to the hundred-oared canoe o' some savage Island-king! The King himsel lying in state—no dead, but leevin, every inch o' him—on a platform—aboon a' his warriors standin wi' war-clubs, and stane-hatchets, and fish-bane spears, and twisted mats, and tattooed faces, and ornaments in their noses, and painted een, and feathers on their heads a yard heigh, a' silent, or burstin out o' a sudden intil shootin sangs o' welcome or defiance, in a language made up o' a few lang strang words—maistly gutturals—and gran' for the naked priests to yell intil the ears o' their victims, when about to cut their throats on the altar-stane that Idolatry had encrusted with blood, shed by stormy moonlicht to glut the maw of their sanguinary god. Or say rather—oh, rather say, that the white-winged Wonder that has brought the strangers frae afar, frae lands beyond the setting sun, has been hailed with hymns and dances o' peace—and that a' the daughters of the Isle, wi' the daughter o' the King at their head, come a' gracefully windin alang in a figur, that, wi' a thousan' changes, is aye but ae single dance, wi' unsandalled feet true to their ain wild singin, wi' wings fancifully fastened to their shouthers, and, beautifu' creturs! a' naked to the waist.—But whare the deevil's Mr. Tickler? Has he sunk during my soliloquy? or swum to shore? Mr. Tickler—Mr. Tickler—I wush I had a pistol to fire into the air, that he might be brought to. Yonner he is, playing at porpuss. Let me try if I can reach him in twenty strokes—it's no aboon a hunder yards. Five yards a stroke—no bad soomin in dead water.—There, I've done it in nineteen. Let me on my back for a rest.

Tickler. I am not sure that this confounded cramp—

Shepherd. The cramp's just like the hiccup, sir—never think o't, and it's gane. I've seen a white lace veil, sic as Queen Mary's drawn in, lyin afloat, without stirrin aboon her snawy broo, saftenin the ee-licht—and it's yon braided clouds that remind me o't, motionless, as if they had lain there a' their lives; yet, wae's me! perhaps in ae single hour to melt away for ever!

Tickler. James, were a Mermaid to see and hear you moralizing so, afloat on your back, her heart were lost.

Shepherd. I'm nae favorite noo, I suspeck, amang the Mermaids.

Tickler. Why not, James? You look more irresistible than you imagine. Never saw I your face and figure to more advantage—when lying on the braes o' Yarrow, with your eyes closed in the sunshine, and the shadows of poetical dreams chasing each other along cheek and brow. You would make a beautiful corpse, James.

Shepherd. Think shame o' yoursel, Mr. Tickler, for daurin to use that word, and the sinnies o' the cauf o' your richt leg yet knotted wi' the cramp. Think shame o' yoursel! That word's no canny.

Tickler. But what ail the Mermaids with the Shepherd?

Shepherd. I was ance lyin half asleep in a sea-shore cave o' the Isle o' Sky, wearied out by the verra beauty o' the moonlicht that had keepit lyin for hours in ae lang line o' harmless fire, stretchin leagues and leagues to the rim o' the ocean. Nae sound, but a bit faint, dim plash—plash—plash o' the tide—whether ebbin or flawin I ken not—no against, but upon the weedy sides o' the cave—

Tickler.—

> "As when some shepherd of the Hebride Isles,
> Placed far amid the melancholy main!"

Shepherd. That soun's like Thamson—in his "Castle o' Indolence." A' the haill warld was forgotten—and my ain name—and what I was—and where I had come frae—and why I was lyin there—nor was I onything but a Leevin Dream.

Tickler. Are you to windward or leeward, James?

Shepherd. Something—like a caulder breath o' moonlicht fell on my face and breast, and seemed to touch all my body and my limbs. But it canna be mere moonlicht, thocht I, for at the same time there was the whisperin—or say, rather, the waverin o' the voice—no alang the green cave wa's, but close intil my ear, and then within my verra breast,—sae, at first, for the soun' was saft and sweet, and wi' a touch o' plaintive wildness in't no unlike the strain o' an Eolian harp, I was rather surprised than feared, and maist thocht that it was but the wark o' my ain fancy, afore she yielded to the dwawm o' that solitary sleep.

Tickler. James, I hear the Steamer.

Shepherd. I opened my een, that had only been half steekit —and may we never reach the shore again, if there was not I, sir, in the embrace o' a Mermaid!

Tickler. James—remember we are well out to Inchkeith. If you please, no—

Shepherd. I would scorn to be drooned with a lee in my mouth, sir. It is quite true that the hair o' the cretur is green—and it's as slimy as it's green—slimy and sliddery as the sea-weed that cheats your unsteady footing on the rocks. Then what een!—oh, what een!—Like the boiled een o' a cod's head and shouthers!—and yet expression in them—an expression o' love and fondness, that would hae garred an Eskimaw scunner.

Tickler. James, you are surely romancing.

Shepherd. Oh, dear, dear me!—hech, sirs! hech, sirs!—the fishiness o' that kiss!—I had hung up my claes to dry on a peak o' the cliff—for it was ane o' thae lang midsummer nichts, when the sea-air itself fans ye wi' as warm a sugh as that frae a leedy's fan when you're sittin side by side wi' her in an arbor—

Tickler. Oh, James—you fox—

Shepherd. Sae that I was as naked as either you or me, Mr. Tickler, at this blessed moment—and whan I felt mysel enveloped in the hauns, paws, fins, scales, tail, and maw o' the Mermaid o' a monster, I grued till the verra roof o' the cave lot doun drap, drap, drap upon us—me and the Mermaid—and I gied mysel up for lost.

Tickler. Worse than Venus and Adonis, my dear Shepherd.

Shepherd. I began mutterin the Lord's Prayer, and the Creed, and the hundred and nineteenth Psalm—but a' wudna do. The Mermaid held the grup—and while I was splutterin out her kisses, and convulsed waur than I ever was under the warst nichtmare than ever sat on my stamach, wi' ae desperate wallop we baith gaed tapsalteerie—frae ae sliddery ledge to anither—till, wi' accelerated velocity, like twa stanes, increasin accordin to the squares o' the distances, we played plunge like porpusses into the sea, a thousan' fadom deep—and hoo I gat rid o' the briny Beastliness nae man kens till this day; for there was I sittin in the cave chitterin like a drookit cock, and nae Mermaid to be seen or heard; al though, wad ye believe me, the cave had the smell o' crabs and labsters, and oysters, and skate, and fish in general, aneuch to turn the stamach o' a whale or a sea-lion.

Tickler. Ship ahoy!—Let us change our position, James Shall we board the Steamer?

Shepherd. Only look at the waves, hoo they gang welterin

frae her prow and sides, and widen in her wake for miles aff! Gin we venture ony nearer, we'll never wear breeks mair. Mercy on us! she's bearin doun upon us. Let us soom fast, and, passing across her bows, we shall bear up to windward out o' a' the commotion.—Captain Bain! Captain Bain! it's me and Mr. Tickler, taking a soom for an appeteet—stop the ingine till we get past the bowsprit.

Tickler. Heavens! James, what a bevy of ladies on deck! Let us dive.

Shepherd. You may dive—for you swim improperly high; but as for me, I seem in the water to be a mere Head, like a cherub on a church. A boat, captain—a boat!

Tickler. James, you aren't mad, sure? Who ever boarded a steamer in our plight? There will be fainting from stem to stern, in cabin and steerage.

Shepherd. I ken that leddy in the straw bannet and green veil, and ruby sarsnet, wi' the glass at her ee. Ye ho—Miss—

Tickler. James—remember how exceedingly delicate a thing is a young lady's reputation. See, she turns away in confusion.

Shepherd. Captain, I say, what news frae London?

Captain Bain (*through a speaking-trumpet*). Lord Wellington's amendment on the bonding clause in the Corn Bill again carried against Ministers by 133 to 122.* Sixty-six shillings!

Tickler. What says your friend M'Culloch to that, Captain?

Shepherd. Wha cares a bodle about corn bills in our situation? What's the Captain routin about noo out o'

* The Duke of Wellington's amendment on the Ministerial measure was, that "no foreign grain in bond shall be taken out of bond until the average price of corn shall have reached 66s."—See Alison's *History of Europe from* 1815 *to* 1852, vol. iv. p. 110; also *Annual Register*, 1827, p. 147.

his speakin-trumpet? But he may just as weel haud his tongue, for I never understand ae word out o' the mouth o' a trumpet.

Tickler. He says the general opinion in London is that the Administration will stand—that Canning and Brougham—

Shepherd. Canning and Brougham, indeed! do you think, sir, if Canning and Brougham had been soomin in the sea, and that Canning had taen the cramp in the cauf o' his richt leg, as you either did, or said you did, a short while sin' syne, that Brougham wad hae safed him as I safed you? Faith, no he indeed! Hairy wad hae thocht nathing o' watching till George showed the croon o' his head aboon water, and then hittin him on the temples.

Tickler. No, no, James. They would mutually risk lives for each other's sake. But no politics at present; we're getting into the swell, and will have our work to do to beat back into smooth water. James, that was a facer.

Shepherd. Dog on it, ane wad need to be a sea-maw, or kitty-wake, or stormy petrel, or some ither ane o' Bewick's birds—

Tickler. Keep your mouth shut, James, till we're out of the swell.

Shepherd. Em—hem—umph—humph—whoo—whoo—whurr—whurr—herrachvacherach.

Tickler. Whsy—whsy—whsy—whugh—whugh—shugh—shugh—prugh—ptsugh—prgugh.

Shepherd. It's lang sin' I've drank sae muckle saut water at ae sittin—at ae soomin, I mean—as I hae dune, sir, sin' that steamboat gaed by. She does indeed kick up a deevil o' a rumpus.

Tickler. Whoo—whoo—whoof—whroo—whroo—whroof—proof—ptroof—sprtf!

Shepherd. Ae thing I maun tell you, sir, and that's, gin

you tak the cramp the noo, you maunna expeck ony assistance frae me—no, gin you were my ain father. This bates a' the swalls! Confoun' the James Watt, quoth I.

Tickler. Nay, nay, James. She is worthy of her name—and a better seaman than Captain Bain never boxed the compass. He never comes below except at meal times, and a pleasanter person cannot be at the foot of the table. All night long he is on deck, looking out for squalls.

Shepherd. I declare to you, sir, that just noo, in the trough o' the sea, I didna see the top o' the Steamer's chimley. See, Mr. Tickler,—see, Mr. Tickler—only look here—only look here—HERE'S BRONTE! MR. NORTH'S GREAT NEWFUNLAN' BRONTE!

Tickler. Capital—capital. He has been paying his father a visit at the gallant Admiral's, * and come across our steps on the sands.

Shepherd. Puir fallow—gran' fallow—did ye think we was droonin?

Bronte. Bow—bow—bow—bow, wow, wow—bow, wow, wow.

Tickler. His oratory is like that of Bristol Hunt *versus* Sir Thomas Lethbridge.†

Shepherd. Sir, you're tired, sir. You had better take haud o' his tail.

Tickler. No bad idea, James. But let me just put one arm round his neck. There we go. Bronte, my boy, you swim strong as a rhinoceros!

Bronte. Bow, wow, wow—bow, wow, wow.

Shepherd. He can do onything but speak.

Tickler. Why, I think, James, he speaks uncommonly well.

* Admiral Otway.

† Henry Hunt, a mob orator and Radical reformer, M. P. for Preston, 1830-31; died in 1835. Sir T. Lethbridge, a Tory M. P., and large landed proprietor.

Few of our Scotch Members speak better. He might lead the Opposition.

Shepherd. What for will ye aye be introducin politics, sir? But, really, I hae fund his tail very useful in that swall; and let's leave him to himsel noo, for twa men on ae dowg's a sair doundraucht.*

Tickler. With what a bold kind eye the noble animal keeps swimming between us, like a Christian!

Shepherd. I hae never been able to persuade my heart and my understandin that dowgs haena immortal sowls. See how he steers himsel', first a wee towarts me, and then a wee towarts you, wi' his tail like a rudder. His sowl *maun* be immortal.

Tickler. I am sure, James, that if it be, I shall be extremely happy to meet Bronte in any future society.

Shepherd. The minister wad ca' that no orthodox. But the mystery o' life canna gang out like the pluff o' a cawnle. Perhaps the verra bit bonny glitterin insecks that we ca' ephemeral, because they dance out but ae single day, never dee, but keep for ever and aye openin and shuttin their wings in mony million atmospheres, and may do sae through a' eternity. The universe is aiblins wide aneuch.

Tickler. Eyes right! James, a boatful of ladies—with umbrellas and parasols extended to catch the breeze. Let us lie on our oars, and they will never observe us.

Bronte. Bow, wow, wow—bow, wow, wow.

[*Female alarms heard from the pleasure-boat. A gentleman in the stern rises with an oar, and stands in a threatening attitude.*

Tickler. Ease off to the east, James—Bronte, hush!

Shepherd. I howp they've nae fooling-pieces—for they may tak us for gulls, and pepper us wi' swan-shots or slugs. I'll

* *Doundraucht*—down-drag.

live at the flash. Yon's no a gun that chiel has in his haun?

Tickler. He lets fall his oar into the water, and the "boatie rows—the boatie rows."—Hark, a song!

[*Song from the retiring boat.*

Shepherd. A very gude sang, and very well sung—jolly companions, every one.

Tickler. The fair authors of the *Odd Volume!*

Shepherd. What's their names?

Tickler. They choose to be anonymous, James; and that being the case, no gentleman is entitled to withdraw the veil.

Shepherd. They're sweet singers, howsomever, and the words o' their sang are capital. Baith Odd Volumes are maist ingenious, well written, and amusing.

Tickler. The public thinks so—and they sell like wildfire.

Shepherd. I'm beginning to get maist desperat thursty, and hungry baith. What a denner wull we make! How mony miles do you think we hae swom?

Tickler. Three—in or over. Let me sound.—Why, James, my toe scrapes the sand. "By the Nail, six!"

Shepherd. I'm glad o't. It 'ill be a bonny bizziness, gif ony neerdoweels hae run aff wi' our claes out o' the machines. But gif they hae, Bronte 'ill sune grup them—wunna ye, Bronte?

Bronte. Bow, wow, wow—bow, wow, wow.

Shepherd. Now, Tickler, that our feet touch the grun', I'll rin you a race to the machines for anither jug.

Tickler. Done—but let us have a fair start.—Once, twice, thrice!

[TICKLER *and the* SHEPHERD *start, with* BRONTE *in the van, amid loud acclamations from the shore.—Scene closes.*

SCENE II.—*Inside of Portobello Fly.*

Mrs. Gentle.—Miss Gentle.

Miss Gentle. My dear mother! I declare there comes Mr. Tickler and Mr. Hogg! Do let me kiss my hand to them—perhaps they may—

Tickler. Ha! ladies—I am delighted to find we shall have your company to Edinburgh.—Hogg, ascend.

Shepherd. Hoo are ye the day, Mrs. Gentle?—and hoo are you, Miss Mary? God bless your bonny gentle een. Come in, Mr. Tickler—come in.—Coachman, pit up the steps. But git you've ony parshels to get out o' the office, or ony honest outside passengers to tak up, you had better wait a wee while on them, and, as it's unco het, and a' up-hill, and your beasts wearied, tak your time, my man, and hurry nae man's cattle. Miss Mary, you'll hae been doun to the dookin?

Miss Gentle. No, Mr. Hogg; I very seldom bathe in the sea. Bathing is apt to give me a headache, and to induce sleepiness.

Shepherd. That's a sign the dookin disna agree wi' your constitution. Yet though you have that kind o' complexion, my dear Mem, that the poet was dreaming o' when he said, "O call it fair, not pale," I howp devoutly that your health's gude. I howp, Mrs. Gentle, your dochter's no what's ca'd delicate.

Mrs. Gentle. Mary enjoys excellent health, Mr. Hogg, and is much in the open air, which, after all, is the best of baths.

Miss Gentle. I am truly happy, sir, to meet with you again so soon after that charming evening at Buchanan Lodge. I hope you are all well at Mount Benger?

Shepherd. Better than well; and next moon the mistress expects to see your mother and you alang wi' Mr. North, according to your promise. You're no gaun to break it? What for are you lookin sae grave, baith o' you? I dinna understan' this—I am verra near about gaun to grow a wee angry.

Miss Gentle. When my dear sister shall have recovered sufficient strength for a little tour in the country, her physician has recommended—

Shepherd. No anither word. She sall come out wi' you to Yarrow. I've seen near a dizzen o' us in Mr. North's coach afore noo, and no that crooded neither. You fower 'ill ilka ane hae your corner—and you, Mem, Mrs. Gentle, and Mr. North. 'ill be taken for the mother and the father—and Miss Mary and Miss Ellenor for your twa dochters; the ane like Bessy Bell, and the ither like Mary Gray.

Miss Gentle. Most extraordinary, Mr. Hogg—why, my dear friend's name absolutely is Ellinor!

Shepherd. The moment I either see a young leddy, or lassie indeed o' ony sort, or even hear them spoken o' by ane that lo'es them, that moment I ken their Christian name. What process my mind gangs through I canna tell, except that it's intuitive like, and instantawneous. The soun' o' the unpronounced name, or raither the shadow o' the soun', comes across my mind, and I'm never wrang, ony mair than if I had heard the wean baptized in the kirk.

Miss Gentle. What fine apprehensions are given to the poet's gifted soul and senses!

Shepherd. A July at Mount Benger will add twenty years to Miss Ellenor's life. She sall hae asses' milk—and a stool to sit on in the byre every nicht when the "kye come hame" to be milked—for there's naething better for that complaint than the balmy breath o' kine.

Miss Gentle. God bless you, sir, you are so considerate!

Shepherd. And we'll tak care no to let her walk on the gerse when the dews are on,—and no to stay out ower late in the gloamin; and in case o' a chance shower—for there's nae countin on them—she sall hae my plaid—and bonny she'll look in't, gif she be onything like her freen Miss Mary Gentle—and we'll row in a boatie on St. Mary's Loch in the sunshine—and her bed sall be made cozy every nicht wi' our new brass warmin-pan, though there's no as much damp about a' the house as to dim a lookin-glass—and her food sall be Yarrow truits, and Eltrive chickens, and licht barley-scones, wi' a glass o' the mistress's currant-wine.—But I'm gettin wearisome, Mems—and, gude safe us! there's Bronte fechtin wi' a carter's mastiff. We're a mile frae Portybelly, and I never was sensible o' the Fly ha'in steered frae the cotch-offish. Driver—driver, stop, or thae twa dowgs 'ill devoor ane anither. There's nae occasion—Bronte has garred him flee, and that carter 'ill be wise to haud his haun; for faith, gif he strikes Bronte wi' his whup, he'll be on the braid o' his back in a jiffy, wi' a haill set o' teeth in his wizand, as lang's my fingers, and as white as yours, Miss Mary;—but wull ye let me look at that ring, for I'm unco curious in precious stanes?

[SHEPHERD *takes* MISS GENTLE'S *hand into his.*

Miss Gentle. It has been in our family, sir, for several centuries, and I wear it for my grandmother's sake, who took it off her finger and put it on mine a few days before she died.

Shepherd. Mrs. Gentle, I see your dochter's haun's just like your ain—the back narrowish, but rather a wee plumpy—fingers sma' and taper, without being lang—and the beautifu' wee member, pawm an' a', as saft and warm as velvet, that has been no verra far aff the fire. Happy he whom Heaven ordains, on some nae distant day, to put the thin, unadorned, unrubied ring on this finger—my dear Mary—this ane, the neist to the wee finger o' the left haun—and gin you'll ask me to the wedding, you shall get, my bonny doo, warm frae this heart o' mine, a faither's blessing.

Mrs. Gentle. Let me promise for Mary, Mr. Hogg; and on that day, you, Mr. North, and Mr. Tickler will dine with me at Trinity Cottage.

Shepherd. I'll answer for Mr. Tickler. But hoosh—speak lown, or we'll wauken him. I'm never sae happy in his company as when he's sleepin—for his animal spirits, at times, is maist outrawageous—his wut incessant—and the verra een o' him gleg as wummles, mair than I can thole, for hours thegither fixed on mine, as gin he wushed to bore a hole through a body's head, frae *oss frontis* to *cerebellum.*

Mrs. Gentle. Well, Mr. Hogg, this is the first time in my life I ever saw Mr. Tickler asleep. I fear he has been overpowered by the sun.

Shepherd. No, Mem—by soomin. He and I, and Bronte there, took a soom nearly out to Inchkeith—and no being accustomed to it for some years, he's unco comatose. There's no ae single thing in a' this warld that he's sae severe on in other folk as fa'in asleep in company—let them even hae sat up the haill nicht afore, ower bowl or book;—but that trance is like a judgment on him, and he'll be real wud * at me for no waukenin him, when he opens his een as the wheels stop, and he fin's that I've had baith the leddies a' the way up to mysel. But you can see him at ony time—whereas a sight o' me in Awmrose's is guid for sair een, on an average only but ance a season. Mrs. Gentle, did you ever see ony person sleep mair like a gentleman?

Mrs. Gentle. Everything Mr. Tickler does, Mr. Hogg, is like a gentleman.

Shepherd. When he's dead he'll look like a gentleman.

* *Wud*—angry.

Even if ane could for a moment mak sic a supposition, he would look like a gentleman if he were hanged.

Mrs Gentle. Oh, shocking!—My dear sir—

Shepherd. My admiration o' Mr. Tickler has nae bounds, Mem. He would look like a gentleman in the stocks—or the jougs—or the present Ministry—

Mrs. Gentle. I certainly never saw any person enter a drawing-room with an air of more courteous dignity, more heart-felt politeness, more *urbanity,* sir,—a word, I believe, derived—

Shepherd. It's no ae man in fifty thousan' that's entitled to hae what's ca'd a mainner. Maist men, on entering a room, do weel just to sit doun on the first chair they lay their haun on—or to gang intil the window—or lean against the wa'—or keep lookin at pictures on a table—till the denner-bell rings. But Mr. Tickler there—sax feet four—threescore and ten—wi' heigh feturs *—white hair—ruddy cheeks—paircin een—naturally eloquent—fu' o' anecdote o' the olden time—independent in sowl, body and estate—geyan proud—a wee mad—rather deafish on the side of his head that happens to be neist a ninny—he, Mem, is entitled by nature and art to hae a mainner, and an extraordinar mainner sometimes it is †—

Mrs. Gentle. I think Mr. Tickler is about to shake off his drowsiness.

Tickler. Has that lazy fellow of a coachman not got all his parcels and passengers collected yet? Is he never going to set off? Ay, there we go at last. This Portobello, Mrs. Gentle, is really a wonderful place. That building reminds me of the Edinburgh Post-Office.

Shepherd. We're in Embro', sir, we're in Embro', and you've been snorin like a bittern or a frog in Tarras Moss.

Tickler. Ladies—can I hope ever to be pardoned for having fallen asleep in such presence? Yet, could I think that the

* *Feturs*—features † Mr. Robert Sym is here painted to the life.

guilt of sleep had been aggravated by being habit and repute a snorer, suicide alone could—

Mrs. Gentle. During your slumber, sir, you drew your breath as softly as a sleeping child.

Tickler. My offence, then, is not inexpiable.

Shepherd. I am muckle obliged to you, sir, for sleepin—and I drew up the window on your side, that you michtna catch cauld; for, sir, though you draw your breath as saftly as a sleepin child, you hae nae notion how wide open you haud your mouth. You'll do the same for me another time.

[*The coach stops, and the* SHEPHERD *hands out* Miss GENTLE —Mr. TICKLER *gallantly performing the same office to the Lady Mother.*

Bronte. Bow, wow, wow—bow, wow, wow. [*Scene closes.*

SCENE III.—*Mr. Ambrose's Hotel, Picardy Place—Pitt Parlor.*

Mr. NORTH *lying on a sofa, and* Mr. AMBROSE *fanning him with a peacock's tail.*

North. These window-ventilators, Mr. Ambrose, are indeed admirable contrivances, and I must get them adopted at the Lodge. No wind that blows suits this room so well as the south-east. Do you think I might venture on another water-ice before dinner? The pine-apple we shall reserve. Thank you, Ambrose—that fan almost makes me melancholy. Demetrius was truly a splendid—a gorgeous—a glorious bird—and methinks I see him now affronting Phœbus with his thousand lidless eyes intensely bright within the emerald haze by which they were all encircled and overshadowed. Hark! the timepiece sweetly strikes, as with a silver bell, the hour of five!—Cease your fanning, mine host most worthy, and let the dinner appear—for ere a man, with moderate haste, might count a hundred, Tickler and the Shepherd will be in the presence. Ay, God bless his honest soul, there is my dear James's laugh in the lobby.

(*Enter* SHEPHERD *and* TICKLER *and* BRONTE.)

Shepherd. Here I am, sir, gloriously hungry. My stamach, Mr. North, as weel's my heart, 's in the richt place. I'm nae glutton—nae gormandeezer—but a man o' a gude, a great appeteet—and for the next half-hour I shall be as perfectly happy as ony man in a' Scotland.

Tickler. Take a few biscuits, James, till—

Shepherd. Biskits! I could crunch the haill tot o' them like sae mony wafers. Rax me ower ane o' thae cabin-biskits o' a man-o'-war—there—smash into flinders flees it at ae stroke o' my elbow—but here comes the ROOND!

North. Mr. Ambrose, I ordered a cold dinner—

Shepherd. A cauld denner! Wha the deevil in his seven senses wad condescend to sit doun till a cauld denner! Hail, Hotch-potch! What a Cut o' Sawmon! That maun hae been a noble fish! Come forrit, my wee chiel, wi' the chickens, and you bigger callant, wi' the tongue and ham. Tak tent, ye auld dominee, and no scale the sass o' the sweet-breads! Curry's a gran thing, geyan late on in a denner, when the edge o' the appeteet's a wee turned, and you're rather beginnin to be stawed.* Mr. Awmrose, I'll thank ye to lend me a pocky-haundkershief, for I've forgotten mine in my wallise, and my mouth's waterin. There, Mr. North, there—set in his fit-stule aneath the table. I ca' this, sir, a tastefu' and judicious denner for three. Whisht, sirs. "God bless us in these mercies, and make us truly thankful. Amen!"

Tickler. Hodge-podge, Hogg?

Shepherd. Only three ladlefu's.—Mair peas. Dip deeper—That's it.

* *Stawed*—satiated.

North. Boiling broth, with the thermometer at eighty!

Shepherd. I carena if the fermometer war at aught hunder and aughty. I'll eat het hotch-potch against Mosshy Shaubert*—only I'll no gae intil the oven—neither will I eat arsenick or phosphorus. Noo, Mr. Tickler, my hotch-potch is dune, and I'll drink a pint o' porter wi' you frae the tap.

[Mr. AMBROSE *places the pewter.*

Shepherd. Wha wull the College laddies make Rector neist? I'll tell you wha they should eleck.

North. Whom, James?

Shepherd. Just yoursel. They've had a dynasty o' Whigs—Jaffrey, and Sir James Mackintosh. and Brougham, and Cammell—and noo they should hae a dynasty o' Tories. THE FIRST GREAT TORY RECTOR SHOULD BE CHRISTOPHER NORTH.

North. No—no—no, James. *Nolo Episcopari.*

Shepherd. What for no? Haud your tongue. I'll mak an appeal to the laddies, and your election is sure. First, you're the auldest Tory in Scotland—secondly, you're the bauldest Tory in Scotland—thirdly, you're the wuttiest Tory in Scotland—fourthly, you're the wisest Tory in Scotland. That Tammas Cammell is a mair popular poet than you, sir, I grant; but that he has ae tenth pairt o' your poetical genius I deny. As a miscellawneous writer on a' subjects, human and divine, he is no to be named wi' you, sir, in the same lifetime—and as an EDITOR, he is, compared wi' CHRISTOPHER NORTH—but as a spunk to the Sun!

Tickler. Rector! a glass of hock or sauterne?

North. Mr. Ambrose, the Peacock's Tail, if you please. The room is getting very hot.

Shepherd. Oh, sir, but you look bonny when you blush. I

* A fire-eater of those days. He could handle, it is said, red-hot iron, and enter with impunity an oven in which beef-steaks were cooking.

can conceeve a virgin o' saxteen fa'in in love wi' you.—Rector, your good health. Mr. Awmrose, fill the Rector's glass. Oh, sir, but you wad luk gran' in your robs. Jaffrey and Cammell's but pechs* to you—the verra stoop o' your shouthers would be dignified aneath a goon—the gait o' the gout is unco philosophical—and wi' your crutch in your nieve, you would seem the champion o' Truth, ready either to defend the passes against the wily assaults of Falsehood, or to follow her into her ain camp, storm the intrenchments, and slaughter her whole army o' sceptics.—Mr. Awmrose, gie me a clean plate—I'm for some o' the curried kernels.

North. I have some thoughts, James, of relinquishing animal food, and confining myself, like Sir Richard Phillips, to vegetable matter.

Shepherd. Ma troth, sir, there are mony millions o' Sir Richard Phillipses in the world, if a' that's necessary to make ane be abstinence frae animal food. It's my belief that no aboon ane in ten o' mankind at large pree animal food frae week's end to week's end. Sir Richard Phillips, on that question, is in a great majority.

Tickler. North, accustomed, James, all his life, to three courses—fish, flesh, and fowl—would think himself an absolute phenomenon or miracle of man, were he to devote the remainder of his meals to potatoes and barley bannocks, pease-soup, maccaroni, and the rest of the range of bloodless but sappy nature. How he would be laughed at for his heroic resolution, if overheard by three million strapping Irish beggars, with their bowels yearning for potatoes and potheen!

North. No quizzing, boys, of the old gentleman.

Shepherd. I agree wi' him in thinkin Sir Isaac Newton out o' his reckonin entirely about gravitation. There's nae sic

* *Pechs*—pigmies.

thing as a law o' gravitation! What would be the use o't? Wull onybody tell me that an apple or a stane wudna fa' to the grun' without sic a law? Sumphs that say sae! They fa' to the grun' because they're heavy.

North. Gentlemen, cheese?

Shepherd. Na, na—nae cheese. Cheese is capital in the forenoons, or the afternoons either, when you've had nae ither denner, especially wi' fresh butter and bread; but nane but gluttonous epicures wad hae recourse to it after they hae been stuffin themsels, as we hae noo been doin for the last hour, wi' three coorses, forbye hotch-potch and puddins.—Draw the cloth, Mr. Awmrose, and down wi' the Deevil's Punch-Bowl.

North. You will find, I trust, that it breathes the very Spirit of the West. St. Mungo's Cathedral, you know, is at the bottom—and near it the monument of John Knox—almost as great a reformer in his day as I in mine; and had the West India trade then flourished, no doubt he had been as religiously devoted to cold Glasgow Punch. I'll answer for him that he was no milksop.

[MR. AMBROSE *and assistants deposit the Devil's Punch-Bowl in the centre of the circular table.*

North. THE KING.

Shepherd. I took the hips frae you last time, Mr. North,—tak you the hips frae me this time. . . .

North. The wickedness of the whole world, James, is fearsome. Many a sleepless night I pass thinking of it, and endeavoring to digest plans for the amelioration of my species.

Shepherd. A' in vain, a' in vain! The bit wean at its mother's breast, lang afore it can speak, girns like an imp o' sin; and the auld man, sittin palsied and pillow-prapped in his arm-chair at the neuk o' the fire, grows black i' the face wi' rage, gin his parritch is no richt biled, or the potawties ower hard; and prefaces his mummled prayer wi' a mair mummled curse.

Tickler. Your language, James, has been particularly strong all this evening. The sea is bracing.

Shepherd. The lassie o' saxteen 'ill rin awa wi' a tinkler, and break her father's heart. He dees, and his poor disconsolate widow, wha has worn a deep black veil for a towmont, that she mayna see or be seen by the sun, marries an Eerish sodger; and neist time you see her, she has naething on her head but a dirty mutch, and she's gaun up and doun the street half-fou, wi' an open bosom, sucklin twuns!

Tickler. Ephesian matron!

Shepherd. Gie an advocate bizziness whan he's starvin at the tap o' a common stair, wull he help you to fit out your son for India when he has become a Judge, inhabiting a palace in Moray Place? Gie a preacher a kirk, and in three months he insults his pawtron. Buy up a naitural son, stap by stap, in the airmy, till he's a briggadeer, and he'll disoun his ain father, and pretend that he belangs to a distant branch o' the stem o' some noble family—although, aiblins, he never had on stockins till he was ensign, and up to the date o' his first commission herded the kye. Get a reprieve for a rubber the nicht afore execution, and he sall celebrate the anniversary o' his Free Pardon in your pantry, carryin aff wi' him a silver trencher and the branching cawnlesticks. In short, do a' the gude you can to a' mankind, and naebody 'ill thank you. But come nearer to me, Mr. North—lend me your ear, sir, it's richt it sud be sae—for, let a man luk into his ain heart—the verra man—me—or you—or Mr. Tickler there—that has been lamentin ower the original sin o' our fellow-creturs,—and oh! what a sicht does he see there—just a mass o' corruption! We're waur than the warst o' them we hae been consignin to the pit, and grue to peep ower the edge o't, lest Satan, wha is stannin girnin ahint our back, gie us a dunge when we're no mindin, and bury us in the brimstone.

Tickler. Oh, ho, gents—from libelling individuals, you two are now advancing to libel human nature at large. For my own part, I have a most particular esteem for human nature at large—and—

Shepherd. Your views is no scriptural, Mr. Tickler.

North. Perhaps, Tickler, we are getting out of our depths.

Shepherd. Gettin out o' your deepth! Ma faith, Mr. North, when ye get out o' your deepth, ither folk 'll be drooning—when the water's up to your chin, there 'll be a sair jinglin in maist throats; and when it's risen out-ower your nose, sir, there'll be naething less than a universal deluge.

North. May I believe, sir, what I hear from so many quarters, that you are about editing the SOUTHSIDE PAPERS?

Tickler. You may. The Preface is at press.

Shepherd. That's gran' news!—But, pity me, there's John Knox's moniment and the Glasgow Cathedral reappearin aboon the subsidin waves! Anither bowl, sir?

North. Not a drop. We have timed it to a minute—nine o'clock. You know we are all engaged—and we are not men to neglect an engagement.

Shepherd. Especially to sooper wi' leddies—let's aff. Oh, man! Bronte, but you have behaved weel—never opened your mouth the haill nicht—but sat listenin there to our conversation. Mony a Christian puppy micht take a lesson frae thee.

Bronte. Bow—wow—wow.

Shepherd. What spangs! [*Exeunt omnes.*

XV.

THE SHEPHERD IS ATTACKED BY TIC-DOULOUREUX, ANGINA PECTORIS, AND JAUNDICE.

SCENE I.—*Picardy Place—South-East Drawing-room.*

The SHEPHERD *solus.*

Shepherd. Perfeck enchantment! Ae single material coal-fire multiplied by mirrors into a score o' unsubstantial reflections, ilka image burnin awa as brichtly up its ain shadowy chimley as the original Prototeep!—Ma faith, you're a maist magnificent time-piece, towerin there on the mantel,* mair like a palace wi' thae ivory pillars, or the verra temple o' Solomon! Mony, certes, is the curious contrivance for notin time! The hour-glass—to my mind the maist impressive, perhaps, o' them a'—as ye see the sand perpetually dreep-dreepin awa momently, and then a' dune, just like life. Then, wi' a touch o' the haun, or whammle in which there's aye something baith o' feelin and o' thocht, there begins anither era, or epoch of an hour, during which ane o' your ain bairns, wha has been lang in a decline, and visited by the doctor only when he's been at ony rate passin by, gies a groanlike sich, and ye ken in a moment that he's dead; or an earthquake tumbles down Lisbon, or some city in Calabria, while a' the folk, men, women, and children, fall down

* *Mantel*—chimney-piece.

on their knees, or are crushed aiblins by falling churches. "The dial-stane aged and green,"—ane a' Cammel's fine lines! Houses change families not only at Michaelmas, but often, on a sudden summons frae death, there is a general flittin, awa a'thegither frae this side o' the kintra, nane o' the neebors ken whare; and sae, ye see, dial-stanes get green, for there are nae bairns' hauns to pick aff the moss, and it's no muckle that the Robin Redbreast taks for his nest, or the Kitty-Wren. It's aften been a mournfu' thocht wi' me, that o' a' the dial-stanes I ever saw, stanin in a sort o' circle in the middle o' a garden, or in a nyeuck o' grun' * that might ance hae been a garden, just as you gang in or out o' the village, or in a kirkyard, there was aye something wrang wi' them, either wi' the finger or the face, sae that Time laughed at his ain altar, and gied it a kick in the bygaun, till it begood to hang a' to the tae side, like a neglecktit tombstane ower the banes o' some ane or ither buried lang afore the Covenant.—Isna that a fiddle on the brace-piece? Let's hawnle † her.—Ay, just like a' the lave—ae string wantin—and something or ither wrang wi' twa-three o' the pegs—sae that whan ye skrew up, they'll no haud ‡ the grip. Neertheless, I'll play mysel a bit tune. Got, she's no an ill fiddle—but some folk can bring music out o' a boot-jack.—(*Sings*, "O mother, tell the laird o't.")—I'm no in bad vice the nicht—and oh! but the Saloon's a gran' ha' for singin! Here's your health and sang, sir. Dog on't, if I didna believe for a minute that yon Image was anither Man! I dinna a'thegither just like this room, for it's getting unco like a Pandemonium. It would be a fearsome room to get fou in—for then you would sit glowerin in the middle o' forty fires, and yet fear that you were nae

* *Nyeuck o' grun'*—nook of ground.
† *Hawnle*—handle.
‡ *Haud*—hold.

Salamander. You wud be frichtened to stir, in case you either walked intil the real ribs, or gaed crash through a lookin-glass, thinkin't the trance.* I'm beginnin to get a wee dizzy—sae let me sit down on this settee. Oh! wow, but this is a sonsy sofa! It wad do brawly for a honey-moon.

(*Enter* MR. AMBROSE *with some Reindeer tongues.*)

Mr. Ambrose. A present, Mr. Hogg, from the Emperor of Russia to Mr. North. The Emperor, you remember, sir, when Duke Nicholas,† used to honor Gabriel's Road.—Asleep, with his eyes open! [*Exit retrogrediens.*

Shepherd. Was Awmrose no in the room the noo? Preserve us! what a tot o' tongues! And it' me that used to fin' faut wi' Shakespeare for putting long soliloquies into the mouths of his chief characters! But I'm gettin as hoarse as a craw—and had better ring the bell for a jug. Deevil tak the worsted bell-rape—see if it hasna bracken short aff, leaving the ring in my haun! Mercy on us, whatten a feet o' flunkeys in the trance!

(*Door flies open—and enter* TICKLER—NORTH, *supported by* MR. AMBROSE.)

Shepherd. What a queer couple o' auld fallows, a' covered wi' cranreuch! ‡ Is't snawin, sirs?

Tickler. Snowing, my dear James!—Sleeting, hailing, raining, driving, and blasting, all in one unexpected coalition of parties, to the utter discomfort and dismay of all his Majesty's loyal subjects.

Shepherd. And hae you walked up, like twa fules, frae Bawhannan Lodge, in sic an eerie nicht, knee-deep in mire, glaur, and sludge?

* *Trance*—passage.
† The late Emperor of Russia visited Edinburgh in 1816.
‡ *Cranreuch*—hoar-frost.

Tickler. One of North's coach-horses is sick, and the other lame—and—

Shepherd. Catch me keepin a cotch. It costs Mr. North five guineas every hurl—and him that's getting sae narrow, too—but Pride! hech, sirs, Pride gets the maister o' Avarice —and he'll no condescend to hire a haickney. Dinna melt in the Saloon, sirs—gang intil the trance, and cast your outer skins, and then come back glitterin like twa serpents as you are, twa Boa-Constrictors, or rather Rattlesnakes, wi' your forked tongues, and wee red piercin een, growin aye mair and mair venomous, as ye begin to bask and beek in the hearth-heat, and turn about the heads o' you to spy whom you may fasten on, lick a' ower wi' glue, and then draw them into your jaws by suction, crashin their banes like egg-shells, and then hissin to ane anither in weel-pleased fierceness, after your ain natur, which mony a puir tortirt cretur has kent to his cost to be without pity and without ruth—ye Sons o' Satan!

North. Thank ye, my dear James, for all your kind inquiries.—Quite well, except being even deafer than usual, or—

Shepherd. Ne'er mind, sir; I'll mak you hear on the deafest side o' your head. But what's he fummlin at yonner? Od, he's just, for a' the warld, like a wee bit corn-stack, frosted and pouthered ower wi' rime. Noo Mr. Awmrose has gotten him out o' the theekin,—and oh! but he looks genteel, and like a verra nobleman, in that speck-and-span-new blue coat, wi' big yellow buttons; nor wad that breast ill become a star. Reel roun' his throne, Mr. Awmrose.

[Mr. Ambrose *wheels* Mr. North *in the Patent Chair to the off-door side of the Fire, setting his Footstool, and depositing the Crutch in its own niche, leaning on the pedestal of Apollo.*

Tickler. Heaven and earth! James, are you well, my dear friend?—you seem reduced to a mere shadow.

Shepherd. Reduced to a mere shadow!—I'm thinkin, sir, you'll hae been mistakin your nain figure in the glass for me the noo—

North. Thank ye, Mr. Ambrose.—Family all well? That's right—that's right. Where's the Shepherd? Lord bless me, James, are you ill?

Shepherd. Me ill? What the deevil's to mak me ill?—But you're baith jokin noo, sirs.

Tickler. Pardon my weakness, James, but I had a very ugly dream about you—and your appearance.

Shepherd. Ma appearance? What the deevil's the matter wi' ma appearance? Mr. North, am I luckin ony way out o' health?—(*Aside*)—Ay, ay, my lads, I see what you're ettlin at noo—but I'm no sae saft and simple's I look like.—(*Aloud*)—You had an ugly dream, Mr. Tickler?—what was't about? Let's hear't.

Tickler. That you were dead, James,—laid out—coffined—biered—buried—superscribed—and—

Shepherd. Houkit * up by half-a-dizzen resurrection-men—driven by nicht in a gig to Embro', and selt for three pounds ten shillings to a lecturin surgeon for a subject o' demonstration afore a schule o' young doctors; and after that, an atomy in Surgeons' Ha'. Do ye ken, Mr. Tickler, that I wud like gran' to see you disseckit? That is, after you was dead—for I'm no wishin you dead yet, although you plague me sairly sometimes; and are aye tryin, I winna say wi' what success, to be witty at my expense. I wish you a' happiness, sir, and a lang life—but I howp I may add without offence, that gin ye was fairly and *bonny feedy* dead—I wud like to see the corp disseckit, no on a public table, afore hunners o' glower-

* *Houkit*—dug.

ing gawpuses, but in a parlor afore a few chosen peers, sic as Mr. North there, and O'Doherty, and Δ; * who, by the way, would be happy, I dinna doubt, to perform the operation himsel, and I could answer for his doin't wi' a haun at ance firm and tender, resolute and respectfu', for ae man o' genius is aye kind to anither on a' sic occasions; and Δ would cut you up, sir, as delicately as you were his ain faither.

Tickler. Is it to give a flavor to the oysters, James, that you talk so? Suppose we change the subject.

Shepherd. We shall leave that to Δ, sir. There's nae need for changin the subject yet; besides, didna ye introduce't yoursel, by offerin to receet your ugly dream about my decease? But—

North. My dear James, I have left you, by my last will and testament, my Skull.

Shepherd. Oh! my dear sir, but I take that verra, verra kind. I'll hae't siller-munted,—the tap o't—that is, the organ o' veneration, which in you is enormous—sawn aff like that o' a cocko-nit, and then fastened on for a lid by a hinge,—and I'll keep a' ma manuscripps in't—and also that wee stereoteep Bible you gied me that beautiful Sunday simmer night we spak sae seriously about religion, when the sun was settin sae gloriously, and the profound hush o' nature seemed o' itsel an assurance o' immortality. Mr. Tickler, will ye no leave me your skull too, as weel's the cremona that I ken's in a codicil, to staun cheek-by-jowl wi' Mr. North's, on the tap o' my mahogany leebrary?

Tickler. Be it so, James—but the bequest must be mutual.

Shepherd. I hae nae objection—there's my thumb, I'll ne'er beguile you. Oh, sir! but I wad look unco gash † on a bit

* D. M. Moir, the "Delta" of *Blackwood's Magazine*, was an eminent medical practitioner at Musselburgh, near Edinburgh. He died in 1851.

† *Unco gash*—uncommonly sagacious.

pedestal in the parlor o' Southside, when you were enterteenin your sma' snug pairties wi' anecdots o' the Shepherd. There's something pleasant in the thocht, sir, for I'm sure ye wad tell nae ill o' me—and that you wud every Saturday nicht wipe the dust frae my skull wi' a towel, mutterin perhaps at a time, "Alas, poor Yorick!"

Tickler. James—you affect me—you do indeed—

Shepherd. Silly fules, noo, were they to owerhear us jockin and jeerin in this gate about ane anither's skulls, wud ca' us Atheists, and deny our richt to Christian burial. But what signifies a skull? The shell of the flown bird, said Simonides, a pensive poet of old—for whose sake would that I could read Greek—though I fancy there are o' him but some sma' and uncertain remains.

North. James, many a merry Christmas to us all. What a jug!

Shepherd. It's an instinck wi' me noo, makin het whisky toddy. A' the time o' our silly discourse about our skulls, was I steerin about the liquid, plumpin in the bits o' sugar, and garrin the green bottle gurgle—unconscious o' what I was about—yet, as ye observe, sir, wi' your usual sagacity, "What a jug!"

Tickler. There is no such school of temperance as Ambrose's in the world—a skreed * in any room of his house clears my head for a month, and re-strings my stomach to such a pitch of power, that, like an ostrich, I can digest a nail or a cork-screw.—I scarcely think, James, that you are in your usual spirits to-night. Come, be brilliant.

Shepherd. Oh, man, Mr. Tickler, wha wad hae expeckit sic a sumphish speech frae you, sir? Wha was ever brilliant at a biddin? Bid a sleepin fire bleeze—wull't? Na. But ripe the ribs, and then gie the central coal a smash wi' the poker, and lo! a volcano vomits like Etna or Vesuvius.

* *A skreed*—a liberal allowance of anything.

Tickler. After all, my dear James, I believe the truth to be, that Christmas is not a merry season.

Shepherd. Aiblins scaircely sae to men like us, that's gettin raither auld. But though no merry, it needna be melancholy—for after a', death, that taks awa the gude—a freen or twa drappin awa ilka year—is no so very terrible, except when he comes to our ain fireside, our ain bed, or our ain cradle—and, for my ain part, I can drink, wi' an unpainfu' tear, or without ony tear at a', to the memory o' them I loved dearly, naething doubtin that Heaven is the trystin-place where all friends and lovers will feenally meet at last, free frae a' jealousies, and heart-burnings, and sorrows, and angers—sae, why should our Christmas be melancholy, though we three have buried some that last year lauched, and sang, and danced in our presence, and because of our presence, and looked as if they had been destined for a lang, lang life? . . . But do you ken, in spite o' a' that, I'm just desperate fond o' Christmas minshed pies. Sirs—in a bonny bleeze o' brandy, burnin blue as snapdragon—I can devoor a dizzen.

Tickler. Christmas geese are prime birds, James, with onions and sage sufficient, and each mouthful accompanied by its contingent of rich red apple-sauce.

Shepherd. A guse aye gives me the colic—yet I canna help eatin't for a' that—for whan there's nae sin nor iniquity, it's richt and reasonable to purchase pleasure at the expense o' pain. I like to eat a' sorts o' land or fresh-water wild-fools—and eke the eggs. Pease-weeps' * eggs is capital poached.

Tickler. James, whether do you like eating or drinking best? Is hunger or thirst the preferable appetite?

Shepherd. Why, you see, I, for ane, never eat but when I'm hungry—and hunger's soon satisfied if you hae plenty o' vittals. Compare that wi' drinkin when your thursty—

* *Pease-weep*—lapwing.

either clear well-water, or sour-milk, or sma' yill, or porter, or speerits half-and-half, and then I wad say that eatin and drinkin's pretty much of a muchness—very nearly on a par, wi' this difference, that hunger wi' me's never sae intense as thurst. I never was sae hungry that I wad hae devoured a bane frae the gutter, but I hae often been sae thursty, on the muirs, that I hae drank black moss-water wi' a green scum on't without scunnerin.

North. I never was hungry in my life.

Shepherd. That's a confounded lee, sir, beggin your pardon—

North. No offence, James—but the instant I begin to eat, my appetite is felt to be excellent.

Shepherd. Felt and seen baith, sir. A how-towdie's a mere laverock to you, sir, on the day the Magazine's finished aff—and Mr. Awmrose himsel canna help lauchin at the relays o' het beef-stakes that ye keep yokin to, wi' pickled ingans or shallotts, and spoonfu's o' Dickson's mustard, that wad be aneuch to blin' a Lynx.

Tickler. I have lost my appetite—

Shepherd. I howp nae puir man 'ill find it, now that wages is low and wark scarce;—but drinkin, you see, Mr. North, has this great advantage over eatin, that ye may drink a' nicht lang without being thursty—tummler after tummler—jug after jug—bowl after bowl—as lang's you're no sick—and you're better worth sittin wi' at ten than at aucht, and at twal than at ten, and during the sma' hours you're just intolerable good company—scarcely bearable at a', ane waxes sae truly wutty and out o' a' measure deevertin; whereas I'll defy ony man, the best natural and acquired glutton that ever was born and bred at the feet o' a father that gaed aff at a city feast, wi' a gob o' green fat o' turtle half-way down his gullet, in an apoplexy, to carry on the eatin wi' ony spunk or speerit after three or four courses, forbye toasted cheese, and roasted chestnuts, and a dessert o' filberts, prunes, awmons, and raisins, ginger-frute, guava jeelly, and ither Wast Indian preserves. The cretur coups ower * comatose. But only tak tent † no to roar ower loud and lang in speakin or singin, and you may drink awa at the Glenlivet till past midnight, and weel on to the morning o' the day after to-morrow.

Tickler. Next to the British, Hogg, I know no such constitution as yours—so fine a balance of powers. I daresay you never had an hour's serious illness in your life.

Shepherd. That's a' you ken—and the observe comes weel frae you that began the nicht wi' giein the club my death-like prognosis.

Tickler. Prognosis?

Shepherd. Simtoms like. This back-end ‡ I had a' three at ance, the Tick Dollaroose, the Angeena Pectoris, and the Jaundice.

North. James—James—James!

Tickler. Hogg—Hogg—Hogg!

Shepherd. I never fan' ony pain like the Tick Dollaroose. Ane's no accustomed to a pain in the face. For the tooth-ache's in the inside o' the mouth, no in the face; and you've nae idea hoo sensitive's the face. Cheeks are a' fu' o' nerves —and the Tick attacks the haill bunch o' them, screwing them up to sic a pitch o' tension that you canna help screechin out, like a thousan' ools, and clappin the pawms o' your hauns to your distrackit chafts, and rowin yoursel on the floor on your groof, § wi' your hair on end, and your een on fire, and a general muscular convulsion in a' your sinnies, sae piercin, and searchin, and scrutinisin, and diggin, and houkin, and

* *Coups ower*—tumbles over. † *Tak tent*—take care.
‡ *Back-end*—close of the year. § *Groof*—belly.

tearin is the pangfu' pain that keeps eatin awa and manglin the nerves o' your human face divine. Draps o' sweat, as big as beads for the neck or arms o' a lassie, are pourin doun to the verra floor, so that the folk that hears you roarin thinks you're greetin, and you're aye afterwards considered a bairnly chiel through the haill kintra. In ane o' the sudden fits I gruppit sic haud o' a grape that I was helpin our Shusey * to muck the byre wi' that it withered in my fingers like a frush † saugh-wand ‡—and 'would hae been the same had it been a bar o' airn. Only think o' the Tick Dollaroose in a man's face continuing to a' eternity!

North. Or even for a few million ages—

Shepherd. Angeena Pectoris is even waur, if waur may be, than the Tick Dollaroose. Some say it's an ossified condition o' the coronary arteries o' the heart; but that' no necessarily true—for there's nae ossification o' these arterial branches o' my heart. But oh! sirs, the fit's deadly, and maist like till death. A' at ance, especially if you be walkin up-hill, it comes on you like the shadow o' a thunder-cloud ower smilin natur, silencin a' the singin birds, as if it threatened earthquake,—and you canna doubt that your last hour is come, and that your sowl is about to be demanded of you by its Maker. However aften you may have it, you aye feel and believe that it is, this time—death. It is a sort o' swoon, without loss o' sense—a dwawm, in which there still is consciousness—a stoppage o' a' the animal functions, even o' breathin itsel, which, if I'm no mista'en, is the meaning o' a syncope—and a' the while something is rug-ruggin § at the heart itsel, something cauld and ponderous, amist like the forefinger and thoom o' a heavy haun—the haun o' an evil speerit; and then you expeck that your heart is to rin doun,

* *Shusen*—Susan.
† *Frush*—brittle.
‡ *Saugh-wand*—willow-wand.
§ *Rug-ruggin*—tear-tearing.

just like a clock, wi' a dull cloggy noise, or rumble like that o' disarranged machinery, and then to beat, to tick nae mair! The collapse is dreadfu'. Ay, Mr. North, collapse is the word.

North. Consult Uwins on Indigestion, James—the best medical work I have read for years, of a popular yet scientific character.

Shepherd. Noo for the Jaundice. The Angeena Pectoris, the Tick Dollaroose, are intermittent—"like angel visits, few and far between"—but the jaundice lasts for weeks, when it is gatherin or brewin in the system—for weeks at its yellowest height,—and for weeks as the disease is ebbin in the blood—a disease, if I'm no sair mista'en, o' the liver.

North. An obstructed condition of the duodenum, James—

Shepherd. The mental depression o' the sowl in the jaundice is most truly dreadfu'. It would hae sunk Samson on the morning o' the day that he bore aff on his back the gates o' Gaza.

Tickler. Tell us all about it, James.

Shepherd. You begin to hate and be sick o' things that used to be maist delightfu'—sic as the sky, and streams, and hills, and the ee and voice, and haun and breast o' woman. You dauner about the doors, dour and dowie, and are seen sittin in nyeucks and corners, whare there's little licht, no mindin the cobwabs, or the spiders themselves drappin doun amang your unkempt hair. You hae nae appeteet; and if by ony chance you think you could tak a mouthfu' o' a particular dish, you splutter't out again, as if it were bitter ashes. You canna say that you are unco ill either, but just a wee sickish—tongue furry, as if you had been licking a muff or a mawkin—and you observe, frae folk stannin weel back when you happen to speak to them—which is no aften—that your breath's bad, though a week before it was as caller as clover.

You snore mair than you sleep—and dream wi' your een open —ugly, confused, mean, stupid, unimaginative dreams, like those of a drunk dunce imitatin a Noctes—and that's aboot the warst thing o' a' the complaint, that you're ashamed o' yoursel, and begin to fear that you're no the man you ance thocht yoursel, when in health shootin groose on the hills, or listerin sawmon.

North. The jaundice that, James, of a man of genius—of the author of the *Queen's Wake.*

Shepherd. Wad ye believe it, sir, that I was ashamed of "Kilmeny"? A' the poems I ever writ seemed trash—rubbish—fuilzie; and as for my prose—even my verra articles in Maga—"Shepherd's Calendar" and a'—waxed havers—like something in the *Metropolitan Quarterly Magazine*, the stupidest o' a' created periodicals, and now deader than a' the nails in Nebuchadnezzar's coffin.

North. The disease must have been at its climax then, my dear James.

Shepherd. Na, na, na; it was far frae the cleemax. I tuk to the bed, and never luckit out frae the coortains for a fortnight—gettin glummier and glummier in sense and sowl, heart, mind, body, and estate—eating little or naething, and —wad ye believe it?—sick, and like to scunner at the very name o' whusky.

North. Thank God, I knew nothing of all this, James. I could not have borne the thought, much less the sight, of such total prostration, or rather perversion of your understanding.

Shepherd. Wearied and worn out wi' lyin in the bed, I got up wi' some sma' assistance frae wee Jamie, God bless him! and telt them to open the shutters. What a sicht! A' faces as yellow's yellow lilies, like the parchment o' an auld drumhead! Ghastly were they, ane and a', when they leuch;* yet

* *Leuch*—laughed.

seemed insensible o' their corp-like hue—I mean, a corp that has died o' some unnatural disease, and been keepit ower lang aboon grun' in close weather, the carpenter having gotten drunk, and botched the coffin. I ca'd for the glass—and my ain face was the warst o' the haill set. Whites o' een! They were the color o' dandelions, or yellow-yoldrins.* I was feared to wash my face, lest the water grew ochre. That the Jaundice was in the house was plain; but whether it was me only that had it, or a' the rest likewise, was mair than I could tell. That the yellow I saw wasna in them, but in me, was hard to believe, when I luckit on them; yet I thocht on green specks, and the stained wundows in Windermere Station, and reasoned wi' mysel that the discoloration must be in my lens, or pupil, or optic nerve, or apple, or ba' o' the ee; and that I, James Hogg, the Ettrick Shepherd, was The Jaundice.

Tickler. Your portrait, colored from nature, James, would have been inestimable in after ages, and given rise to much argument among the learned about your origin—the country of your birth. You must have looked cousin-german to the Green Man and Still.

Shepherd. I stoitered to the door, and, just as I feared, the Yarrow was as yellow as a rotten egg—a' the holms the color o' a Cockney's play-going gloves—the skies like the dirty ochre wa's o' a change-house—the cluds like buckskin breeks—and the sun, the michty sun himsel, wha lends the rainbow its hues, and is never the poorer, looked at me wi' a disconsolate aspeck, as much as to say, "James, James, is it thou or I that has the Jaundice?"

Tickler. Better than the best bits of Abernethy † in the *Lancet*, North.

* *Yellow-yoldrin*—yellow-hammer.

† This eminent practitioner, celebrated no less for his eccentricity of manner than for his medical skill, was born in 1764, and died in 1831. He was the author of Surgical Observations. Physiological Essays, etc.

Shepherd. Just as I was gaun to answer the sun, the Tick Dollaroose attacked baith o' my cheeks—a' my face, lips, chin, nose, brow, lugs, and crown and back o' my head,—the Angeena Pectoris brought on the Heart-Collapse—and there the three, the Tick, the Angeena, and the Jaundice, a' fell on me at ance, like three English, Scotch, and Eerish regiments stormin a fort, and slaughterin their way wi' the beggonet on to the citadel

North. That you are alive at this blessed hour, my dearest James, almost exceeds belief, and I begin to suspect that you are not flesh and blood—a mere Appearance.

Shepherd. Na, faith, a'm a reallty; an Appearance is a puir haun at a jug. Yet, sir, the recovery was weel worth a' I paid for it in sufferins. The first time I went out to the knowe yonner, aboon the garden, and gazed and glowered, and better gazed and glowered, on the heavens, the earth, and the air, the three bein blent thegither to mak up that mysterious thing—a Day o' Glory—I thocht that my youth, like that o' the sun-staring eagle, had been renewed, and that I was ance mair in the verra middle o' the untamed licht and music o' this life, whan a' is fancy and imagination, and friendship and love, and howp,—oh, howp, sir, howp, worth a' the ither blisses ever sent frae Heaven, like a shower o' sunbeams, for it canna be darkenit, far less put out by the mirkest midnight o' meesery, but keeps shinin on like a star, or rather like the moon hersel—a spiritual moon, sir, that " is never hid in vacant interlunar cave."

Tickler. Mixed metaphors these, James.

Shepherd. Nane the waur o' that, Timothy—I felt about ane-and-twunty—and oh, what an angelical being was a lassie then comin wadin through the ford! At every step she took, after launin wi' her white feet, havin letten doun fa' her cloudlike claes wi' a blush, as she keepit lookin roun' and roun' for a whyleock, to see gin ony ee had been on her, as her limbs came silveryin through the water—

North. The Ladies, James, in a bumpér.

Shepherd. The leddies.—A track o' flowers keepit lengthenin alang the greensward as she walked awa', at last, quite out o' sicht.

Tickler. And this you call recovering from the Tic-Douloureux, the Angina Pectoris, and the Jaundice, James?

[*Enter* Mr. Ambrose, *with copper-kettle No. I.*]

North. Who rung?

Ambrose. I have taken note of the time of the last four jugs, sir, and have found that each jug gains ten minutes on its predecessor—so ventured—

Shepherd. Oh, Mr. Ambrose, but you wad be a gran' observer o' the motions o' the heavenly bodies in an Astronomical Observatory!—The jug's this moment dead. There —in wi' a' the sugar, and a' the whusky,—fill up, Awmrose, fill up. That stroop's * a gràn' pourer, and you're a prime experimenter in hydrostatics.

[*Exit* Mr. Ambrose, *susurrans.*]

North. A mere literary man, James, is a contemptible creature. Indeed, I often wish that I had flourished before the invention of printing or even of writing. What think you, James, of a Noctes in hieroglyphics?

Shepherd. I scarcely ken; but I think ane wadna look amiss in the Chinese. Wi' respeck to mere literary men, oh dear me, sir! hoo I do gaunt† when they come out to Mount Benger! They canna shute, they canna fish, they canna loup, they canna warsle, they canna soom, they canna put the stane, they canna fling the hammer, they canna even drive a gig, they canna kiss a lassie in an aff-haun and pleasant manner, without offendin her feelins, as through the

* *Stroop*—spout.

† *Gaunt*—yawn

dews she "comes wadin all alane;" and what's perhaps the maist contemptible o' a', they canna, to ony effeck, drink whusky. Ae glass o' pure speerits on the hill afore breakfast wad gie them a sick headache; and after denner, although the creturs hae nae objections to the jug, oh, but their heads are wake,* wake—before the fire has got sun-bricht, they are lauchin-fou—you then fin' them out to be rejected contributors to *Blackwood;* and you hear that they're Whigs frae their wee, sharp, shrill, intermittin, dissatisfied, and rather disgustin snore, like a soun' ane aften hears at nicht in moors and mosses, but whence proceedin ane knows not, except it be frae some wild-foul distressed in sleep by a stamach fu' o' slug-worms mixed wi' mire—for he aiblins leeves by suction. Where's Mr. Tickler?

North. I saw him slip away a little ago—just as he had cleared his boards—

Shepherd. I never missed him till the noo.

North. How delightful for a town-talk teazed poor old man, like me, to take refuge, for a month or so, in a deeper solitude even than Buchanan Lodge—the House at the head of the Glen, which, know it ever so well, you still have to search for among so many knolls, some quite bare, some with a birk or two, and some of them each in itself a grove or wood,—self-sown all the trees, brushwood, coppice, and standards.

Shepherd. You're getting desperate descriptive in your dotage, sir—dinna froon—there's nae dishonor in dotage, when nature's its object. The aulder we grow, our love for her gets tenderer and mair tender, for this thocht aften comes across our heart, "In the bosom o' this bonny green earth, in how few years—shall I be laid—dust restored to dust!" That's a' I mean by dotage. . . . What are ye hummin at, sir. You're no gaun to sing?

* *Wake*—weak.

(North *sings.*)

Why does the sun shine on me,
When its light I hate to see?
Fain I'd lay me down and dee,
For o' life I'm weary!

Oh, 'tis no thy frown I fear—
'Tis thy smile I canna bear—
'Tis thy smile my heart does tear,—
When thou triest to cheer me.

Ladies fair hae smiled on me—
A' their smiles nae joy could gie—
Never lo'ed I ane but thee,
And I lo'e thee dearly!

On the sea the moonbeams play
Sae they'll shine when I'm away—
Happy then thou'lt be, and gay,
When I wander dreary!

Shepherd. Some auld fragmentary strain, remindin him, nae doubt, o' joys and sorrows lang ago! He has a pathetic vice—but sing what tune he may, it still slides awa into "Stroud Water."

North. Oh, James! a dream of the olden time—

Shepherd. Huts! huts! I wush you maunna be gettin rather a wee fuddled, sir—hafflins fou. Preserve me! are ye greetin? The whusky's maist terrible strong—and I suspect has never been chrissened. It's time we be aff! Oh! what some o' them he has knouted wad gie to see him in this condition! But there's the wheels o' the cotch. Or is't a fire-engine?

(*Enter* Ambrose, *to announce the arrival of the coach.*)

Dinna look at him, Mr. Ambrose—he's gotten the toothache —and likewise some ingan in his een. This is aye the way wi' him noo,—he fa's aff a' on a sudden—and begins greetin at naething, or at things that's rather amusin as itherwise.

There's mony thousan' ways o' gettin fou—and I ken nae mair philosophical employment than, in sic cityations, the study o' the varieties o' human character.

North. Son James—

Shepherd. Pardon, Father—'twas but a jeest. I've kent you noo the better pairt o' twunty years—and never saw I thae bricht een—that bricht brain obscured,—for wi' a' our daffin—our weel-timed daffin—our *dulce est desipere in loco* —that's Latin, you ken—we return to our hame, or our lodgings, as sober as Quakers—and as peacefu', too—well-wishers, ane and a', to the haill human race—even the verra Wheegs.

North. Sometimes, my dear Shepherd, my life from eighteen to twenty-four is an utter blank, like a moonless midnight—at other times, oh! what a refulgent day! Had you known me then, James, you would—

Shepherd. No hae liked you half as weel's I do noo—for then, though you was doubtless tall and straucht as a tree, and able and willin baith to fecht man, dowg, or deevil, wi' een, tongue, feet, or hauns, yet, as doubtless, you was prouder nor Lucifer. But noo that you're bent doun no that muckle, just a wee, and your "lyart haffits wearing thin and bare," sae pleesant, sae cheerfu', sae fu' o' allooances for the fauts and frailties o' your fellow-creturs, provided only they proceed na frae a bad heart—it's just perfeckly impossible no to love the wise, merry auld man—

North. James, I wish to consult you and Mr. Ambrose about the propriety and prudence of my marrying—

Shepherd. Never heed ye propriety and prudence, sir, in mairrying, ony mair than ither folk. Mairry her, sir—mairry her—and I'll be godfather—for the predestined mither o' him will be an Episcopaulian—to wee Christopher. Let us off to Southside—and sup with Tickler.

Glee—for three voices.

Fall de rall de,
Fall, lall, lall de,
Fall de lall de,
Fall, lall le, &c.

[*Exeunt ambo et* AMBROSE.

XVI.

IN WHICH, AFTER NORTH IS HANGED AND DROWNED IN A DREAM, THE SHEPHERD IS TEMPTED AND FALLS.

Scene,—Large Dining-room.—Time uncertain.—NORTH *discovered sitting upright in his easy-chair, with arms akimbo on his crutch, asleep.*

Enter the SHEPHERD *and* Mr. AMBROSE.

Shepherd. Lord safe us! only look at him sitting asleep. What'n a face!—Dinna leave the parlor, Mr. Awmrose, for it would be fearsome to be alane wi' the Vision.

Ambrose. The heat of the fire has overcome the dear old gentleman—but he will soon awake; and may I make so bold, Mr. Hogg, as to request that you do not disturb—

Shepherd. What! Wad ye be for my takin aff my shoon, and glidin ower the Turkey carpet on my stockin soles, like a pard or panther on the Libyan sands?

Ambrose (suaviter in modo). I beg pardon, sir, but you have got on your top-boots * this evening.

Shepherd. Eh! sae I hae. And trying to rug them aff, tae an' heel, aneath the fit o' a chair, wad be sure to wauken him wi' ane o' thae froons o' his, aneuch to daunt the deevil.

Ambrose. I never saw Mr. North frown, Mr. Hogg, since

* Top-boots, at this period not uncommon, were a favorite attire of the Shepherd.

we came to Picardy. I hope, sir, you think him in his usual health?

Shepherd. That's a gude ane, Awmrose. You think him near his latter end, 'cause he's gien up that hellish froon that formerly used sae aften to make his face frichtsome? Ye ne'er saw him froon sin' ye cam to Picardy?—Look there—only look at the cretur's face—

> A darkness comes across it, like a squall
> Blackening the sea.

Ambrose. I fear he suffers some inward qualm, sir. His stomach, I fear, sir, is out of order.

Shepherd. His stamach is ne'er out o' order. It's an ingine that aye works sweetly. But what think you, Mr. Awmrose, o' a quawm o' conscience?

Ambrose. Mr. North never, in all his life, I am sure, so much as injured a fly. Oh! dear me! he must be in very great pain.

Shepherd.—

> So frooned he ance, when in an angry parle
> He smote the sliding Pollock on the ice.

Ambrose. You allude, sir, to that day at the curling on Duddingston Loch. But you must allow, Mr. Hogg, that the brute of a carter deserved the crutch. It was pretty to see the old gentleman knock him down. The crack on the ice made by the carter's skull was like a star, sir.

Shepherd. The clud's blawn aff—and noo his countenance is pale and pensive, and no without a kind o' reverend beauty, no very consistent wi' his waukin character. But the faces o' the most ferocious are a' placid in sleep and in death. That is an impressive fizziological and sykological fack.

Ambrose. How can you utter the word death in relation to him, Mr. Hogg? Were he dead, the whole world might shut up shop.

Shepherd. Na, na. Ye micht, but no the warld. There never leeved a man the warld missed, ony mair than a great, green, spreading simmer tree misses a leaf that fa's doun on the moss aneath its shadow.

Ambrose. Were you looking round for something, sir?

Shepherd. Ay; gie me that cork aff yon table—I'll burn't on the fire, and then blacken his face wi' coom.

Ambrose (*placing himself in an imposing attitude between* NORTH *and the* SHEPHERD). Then it must be through my body, sir. Mr. Hogg, I am always proud and happy to see you in my house; but the mere idea of such an outrage—such sacrilege—horrifies me; the roof would fall down—the whole land—

Shepherd. Tuts, man, I'm only jokin. Oh! but he wad mak a fine pictur! I wish John Watson Gordon were but here to pent his face in iles. What a mass o' forehead! an inch atween every wrinkle, noo scarcely visible in the calm o' sleep! Frae eebree to croon o' the head a lofty mountain o' snaw—a verra Benledi—wi' rich mineral ore aneath the surface, within the bowels o' the skull, copper, silver, and gold! Then what a nose! Like a bridge, along which might be driven cart-loads o' intellect;—neither Roman nor Grecian, hookit nor cockit, a wee thocht inclined to the ae side, the pint being a pairt and pendicle o' the whole, an object in itsel, but at the same time finely smoothed aff and on intil the featur; while his nostrils, small and red, look as they would emit fire, and had the scent o' a jowler or a vultur.

Ambrose. There never were such eyes in a human head—

Shepherd. I like to see them sometimes shut. The instant Mr. North leaves the room, after denner or sooper, it's the same thing as if he had carried aff wi' him twa o' the fowre cawnles.

Ambrose. I have often felt that, sir,—exactly that,—but

never could express it. If at any time he falls asleep, it is just as if the waiter or myself had snuffed out—

Shepherd. Let my image alane, Mr. Awmrose, and dinna ride it to death—double. But what I admire maist o' a' in the face o' him, is the auld man's mouth. There's a warld's difference, Mr. Awmrose, atween a lang mouth and a wide ane.

Ambrose. There is, Mr. Hogg, there is—they are two different mouths entirely. I have often felt that, but could not express it—

Shepherd. Mr. Awmrose, you're a person that taks notice o' a hantle o' things—and there canna be a stronger proof, or a better illustration, of the effeck o' the conversation o' a man o' genius like me, than its thus seeming to express former feelings and fancies of the awditor—whereas the truth is, that it disna wauken them for the second time, but communicates them for the first—for believe me, that the idea o' the cawnles, and eke o' the difference wi' a distinction atween wide mouths and lang anes, never entered your mind afore, but are baith, *bona feedy*, the property o' my ain intelleck.

Ambrose. I ask you many pardons, Mr. Hogg. They are both your own, I now perceive, and I promise never to make use of them without your permission in writing—or—

Shepherd. Poo—I'm no sae pernickitty * as that about my original ideas ; only when folk do mak use o' my obs, I think it but fair they should add, "as Mr. Hogg well said," "as the Ettrick Shepherd admirably remarked," "as the celebrated author o' the *Queen's Wake*, wi' his usual felicity, observed" —and so forth—and ma faith, if some folk that's reckoned yeloquent at roots and petty soopers were aye to do that when they're what's ca'd maist brilliant, my name wad be seldom out o' their mouths. Even North himsel—

* *Pernickitty*—particular.

Ambrose. Do not be angry with me, sir—but it's most delightful to hear Mr. North and you bandying matters across the table; ye take such different views always of the same subject; yet I find it, when standing behind the chair, impossible not to agree with you both.

Shepherd. That's just it, Mr. Awmrose. That's the way to exhowst a subject. The ane o' us ploughs down the rig, and the ither across, then on wi' the harrows, and the field is like a garden.

Ambrose. See, sir, he stirs!

Shepherd. The crutch is like a very tree growin out o' the earth—so straucht and steddy. I daursay he sleeps wi't in his bed. Noo—you see his mouth to perfection—just a wee open—showing the teeth—a smile and no a snarl—the thin lips o' him slightly curled and quiverin, and the corners drawn doun a wee, and then up again wi' a swirl, giein wonderfu' animation to his yet ruddy cheeks—a mouth unitin in ane Mr. Jaffray's and that o' Canning's and Cicero's busts.

Ambrose. No young lady—no widow—could look at him now, as he sits there, Mr. Hogg, God bless him, without thinking of a first or second husband. Many is the offer he must have refused!

Shepherd. Is that your fashun in Yorkshire, Mr. Awmrose, for the women to ask the men to marry?

Ambrose (susurrans). Exceptio probat regulam, sir.

Shepherd. Faith, ye speak Latin as weel's mysel. Do you ken the Doctrine o' Dreams?

Ambrose. No, sir. Dreaming seems to me a very unintelligible piece of business.

Shepherd. So thinks Mr. Coleridge and "Kubla Khan." * But the sowl, ye see, is swayed by the senses—and it's in my power the noo, that Mr. North's half-sleepin and half-

* A poem said by Coleridge to have been composed in his sleep.

waukin, to mak him dream o' a' sorts o' deaths—nay, to dream that he is himsel dreein * a' sorts o' deaths—ane after the ither in ruefu' succession, as if he were some great criminal undergoing capital punishments in the wild warld o' sleep.

Ambrose. That would be worse than blacking my dear master's face—for by that name I love to call him. You must not inflict on him the horror of dreams.

Shepherd. There can be nae such thing as cruelty in a real philosophical experiment. In philosophy, though not in politics, the end justifies the means. Be quiet, Awmrose. There, noo, I hae drapt some cauld water on his bald pow—and it's tricklin doun his haffits to his lugs. Whisht! wait a wee! There na, ye see his mouth openin, and his chest heavin, as if the waters o' the deep sea were gullering in his throat. He's now droonin!

Ambrose. I cannot support this—Mr. Hogg—I must—

Shepherd. Haud back, sir! Look how he's tryin to streik out his richt leg as if it had gotten the cramp. He's tryin to cry for help. Noo he has risen to the surface for the third and last time. Noo he gies ower strugglin, and sinks doun to the broon-ribbed sand amang the crawlin partens! †

Ambrose. I must—I shall waken him—

Shepherd. The dreamed death-fit is ower, for the water's dried—and he thinks himsel walkin up Leith Walk, and then straucht intil Mr. Blackwood's shop. But noo we'll hang him—

Ambrose. My God! that it should ever have come to this! Yet there is an interest in such philosophical experiments, Mr. Hogg, which it is impossible to resist. But do not, I beseech you, keep him long in pain.

Shepherd. There—I just tichten a wee on his wizen hin

* *Dreein*—suffering. † *Partens*—crabs.

black neck-hankerchief, and in a moment you'll see him get blue in the face. Quick as the "lightning on a collied night," the dream comes athwart his sowl! He's on the scaffold, and the grey-headed, red-eyed, white-faced hangman's lean, shrivelled hands are fumblin about his throat, fixing the knot on the juglar! See how puir North clutches the cambric, naturally averse to fling it frae him, as a signal for the drap! It's no aboon a minute since we began the experiment, and yet during that ae minute has he planned and perpetrated his crime—nae dout murder—concealed himsel for a month in empty hovels and tombs, in towns,—in glens, and muirs, and woods, in the kintra,—been apprehended, for a reward o' one hundred guineas, by twa red-coated sheriff's-officers,—imprisoned till he had nearly run his letters,—stood his trial frae ten in the mornin till twelve o'clock at nicht—examination o' witnesses, the speech o' the croon coonsel, and that o' the coonsel for the panel too, and the soumin up o' the Lord Justice-Clerk, nane o' the three shorter than twa hours,—been prayed till, frae daybreak to breakfast, by three ministers,—oh, sickenin breakfast!—sat'n in a chair on account o' his gout—a lang, lang time on the scaffold—and then aff he goes with a swing, a swirl, and a general shriek—and a' within the space o' some forty seconds o' the time that passes in the outer air world which we wauken creatures inhabit;—but which is the true time, and which is the fause, it's no for me to say, for I'm nae metaphysician, and judge o' time either by the shadows on the hill, or on the stane sun-dial, or by the short and lang haun o' our aught-day clock.

Ambrose. Mr. Hogg, it is high time this were put an end to,—my conscience accuses me of a great crime,—and the moment Mr. North awakes, I will make a clean bosom of it, and confess the whole.

Shepherd. What! you'll peach, will you? In that case, it is just as weel to proceed to the last extremity. Rax me ower the carvin-knife, and I'll guillotine him—

Ambrose. Shocking, shocking, Mr. Hogg!

(*The* SHEPHERD *and* AMBROSE *struggle violently for the possession of the carving-knife, amid cries from the latter of "Thieves! Robbers! Fire! Murder!"—and in the struggle they fall against the chimney-piece to the clash of shovel, poker, and tongs.* BRONTE, *who has been sleeping under* NORTH'S *chair, bursts out with a bull-bellow, a tiger-growl, and a lion-roar—and* NORTH *awakes—collaring the* SHEPHERD.)

Bronte. Bow—wow—wow—wow—wow—wow—

Shepherd. Ca' aff your dowg, Mr. North—ca' aff your dowg! He's devourin me—

North (*undisturbed from his former posture*). Gentlemen, what is the meaning of all this—you seem discomposed? James! engaged in the duello with Mr. Ambrose? Mr. Ambrose! [*Exit* Mr. AMBROSE, *retrogrediens, much confused.*

Shepherd. I'll ca' him out—I'll ca' him out wi' pistols! He was the first aggressor.

North. Arrange your dress, James, then sit down, and narrate to me truly these *plusquam civilia bella.*

Shepherd. Why, ye see, sir, a gentleman in the hotel, a Russian General, I believe, was anxious to see you sleepin, and to take a sketch o' you in that predicament for the Emperor, and Mr. Awmrose insisted on bringin him in, whether I would or no,—and as I know you have an antipathy against having your head taken aff—as naebody can hit the face, and a' the likenesses yet attempted are mere caricatures—I rose to oppose the entrance o' the General. Mr. Awmrose put himsel into what I could not but construe a fechtin attitude, though I daursay it was only on the defensive; we yokit, and on me tryin to hough him, we tumbled again' the mantel-piece, and you awoke. This is the truth, the whole truth, and nothing but the truth.

(NORTH *rings the bell violently, and* MR. AMBROSE *appears.*)

North. Show in the Russian General, sir!

Ambrose. The Russian General, sir!

North. How dare you repeat my words? I say, sir, show in the Russian General.

Shepherd. Haw—haw—haw—haw—haw—haw—haw—haw! I'm like to spleet! Haw—haw—haw—haw—haw—haw!

North (*with dignity*). These manners, sir, may do in Ettrick—or the Forest—where the breed of wild boars is not wholly extirpated—but in Edinburgh we expect—

Shepherd. Na—gin that be the way o't, I maun be on my mettle too. As for your wutticism, sir, about the boars, it's just perfectly contemptible, and, indeed, at the best, nae better than a maist meeserable pun. And as to mainners, I'll bet you a ten-gallon cask to a half-mutchkin, that I'll show an elder in Yarrow Kirk, ony Sabbath atween this and Christmas, that shall outmainner your ainsel, wi' a' your high breedin, in everything that constitutes true natural dignity—and as for female mainners, seleck the maist yelegant and fashionable leddy that you see walkin alang Princes Street, wi' a bonnet bigger than a boyne,* atween three and four o' the afternoon, when the street's like a stream, and gin I dinna bring frae the Forest, within a mile's range, wi' Mount Benger the centre of the circle, a bare-leggit lassie, wi' hauns, aiblins, red and hard wi' milkin the coos, wi' naething on her head but a bit pinchbeck kame, that shall outmainner your city madam, till she blush black through the red pent on her cheeks—my name's no James

* *Boyne*—a large wooden *tub*.

Hogg—that's a'. And whether you tak the wager or no, let me tell you to the face o' you, that you're a damned arrogant, upsettin, impudent fallow, and that I do not care the crack o' my thoom for you, or your Magazin, or your Buchanan Lodge, were you and they worth ten thousand million times mair than what you ever will be, as lang's your name's Christopher North!

North. James, you are a pretty fellow. Nothing will satisfy you, it seems, but to insult most grossly the old man whom you have first drowned in his sleep, then hanged, and, but for my guardian angel, Ambrose, would have guillotined!

Shepherd. What! and you were pretending to be asleep a' the while o' the pheelosophical experiments? What a horrid heepocrit! You're really no fit company for plain, simple, honest folk like the like o' me; but as we've been baith to blame, especially you, who began it a' by shammin sleep, let's shake hauns, and say nae mair about it. Do you ken I'm desperate hungry—and no a little thursty.

(*Re-enter* Mr. AMBROSE, *in trim apparel and downcast eyes, with a board of oysters.*)

North. Bless you, James! You wheel me round in my chair to the table with quite a filial touch. Ay, my dear boy, take a pull at the porter, for you are in a violent perspiration.

Shepherd. Naething like draft!

North. Mr. Ambrose, confine the Russian General to his chamber—and see that you keep him in fresh train-oil.

[*Exit* MR. AMBROSE, *smiling through his tears.*

North. James, I shrewdly suspect Mr. Ambrose is up to our high-jinks.

Shepherd. I really begin to jalouse he is. He was sair frichtened at first—but I thocht I heard him geein a bit grunt o' a lauch, a sort o' suppressed nicher, ahint the door, to the flunkeys in the trance, wha had a' flocked thegither in a crood at the cry o' Fire and Murder.

North. I feel as if an oppressive weight were taken from my heart.

Shepherd. Then that's mair than I do—mair than you or ony ither man should say, after devoorin half a hunder eisters—and siccan eisters—to say naething o' a tippenny loaf, a quarter o' a pund o' butter—and the better pairt o' twa pots o' porter.

North. James! I have not eat a morsel, or drank a drop, since breakfast.

Shepherd. Then I've been confusioning you wi' mysel. A' the time that I was sookin up the eisters frae out o' their shells, ilka ane sappier than anither in its shallow pool o' caller saut sea-water, and some o' them takin a stronger sook than ithers to rug them out o' their cradles,—I thocht I saw you, sir, in my mind's ee, and no by my bodily organs, it would appear, doin the same to a nicety, only dashin on mair o' the pepper, and mixing up mustard wi' your vinegar, as if gratifying a fause appeteet.

North. That cursed cholera—

Shepherd. I never, at ony time o' the year, hae recourse to the cruet till after the lang hunder—and in September—after four months' fast frae the creturs—I can easily devoor them by theirsels just in their ain liccor, on till anither fifty—and then to be sure, just when I am beginning to be a wee stawed,* I apply first the pepper to a squad, and then, after a score or twa in that way, some dizzen and a half wi' vinegar, and finish aff, like you, wi' a wheen to the mustard, till the brodd's naething but shells.

North. The cholera has left me so weak, that—

Shepherd. I dinna ken a mair perplexin state o' mind to be in than to be swithering about a further brodd o' eisters, when you've devoored what at ae moment is felt to be sufficient,

* *Stawed*—surfeited.

and anither moment what is felt to be very insufficient—feelin stawed this moment, and that moment yaup* as ever—noo sayin into yoursel that you'll order in the toasted cheese, and then silently swearin that you maun hae anither yokin at the beardies—

North. This last attack, James, has reduced me much—and a few more like it will deprive the world of a man whose poor abilities were ever devoted to her ser—

Shepherd. I agree wi' ye, sir, in a' ye say about the diffeeculty o' the dilemma. But during the dubiety and the swither, in comes honest Mr. Awmrose, o' his ain accord, wi' the final brodd, and a body feels himsel to have been a great sumph for suspecking ae single moment that he wasna able for his share o' the concluding Centenary o' Noble Inventions. There's really no end in natur to the eatin o' eisters.

North. Really, James, your insensibility, your callousness to my complaints, painfully affects me, and forces me to believe that Friendship, like Love, is but an empty name.

Shepherd. An empty wame ?† It's your ain faut gin it's empty—but you wadna surely be for eatin the very shells ? Oh ! Mr. North, but o' a' the men I ever knew you are the most distinguished by natural and native coortesy and politeness—by what Cicero calls Urbanity. Tak it—tak it. For, I declare, were I to tak it, I never could forgie mysel a' my days. Tak it, sir.—My dear sir, tak it.

North. What do you mean, James? What the devil *can* you mean ?

Shepherd. The last eister—the mainners eister—it's but a wee ane, or it hedna been here. There, sir, I've douked it in an amalgamation o' pepper, vinegar, and mustard, and a wee drap whusky. Open your mouth, and tak it aff the pint o' my fork—that's a gude bairn.

* *Yaup*—hungry. † *Wame*—stomach.

North. I have been very ill, my dear James.

Shepherd. Haud your tongue—nae sic thing. Your cheeks are no half that shrivelled they were last year; and there's a circle o' yeloquent bluid in them baith, as ruddy as Robin's breast. Your lips are no like cherries—but they were aye rather thin and colorless since first I kent you; and when chirted thegither—oh! man, but they have a scornfu', and savage, and cruel expression, that ought seldom to be on a face o' clay. As for your een, there's twenty guid year o' life in their licht yet. But, Lord safe us!—dinna, I beseech you, put on your specks; for when you cock up your chin, and lie back on your chair, and keep fastenin your lowin een upon a body through the glasses, it's mair than mortal man can endure—you look so like the Deevil Incarnate.

North. I am a much injured man in the estimation of the world, James, for I am gentle as a sleeping child.

Shepherd. Come, now—you're wushin me to flatter you—ye're desperate fond, man, o' flattery.

North. I admit—confess—glory that I am so. It is impossible to lay it on too thick. All that an author has to do to secure a favorable notice—

Shepherd. What'n an avooal!

North. Why, James, are you so weak as ever to have imagined for a moment that I care a pin's point for truth, in the praise or blame bestowed or inflicted on any mortal creature in my Magazine?

Shepherd. What's that you say?—can I believe my lugs?

North. I have been merely amusing myself for a few years back with the great gawky world. The truth is, James, that I am a misanthrope, and have a liking only for Cockneys.

Shepherd. The chandaleer's gaun to fa' doun on our heads. Eat your words, sir, eat your words, or—

North. You would not have me *lie*, during the only time

that, for many years, I have felt a desire to speak the *truth?* The only distinctions I acknowledge are intellectual ones. Moral distinctions there are none—and as for religion—it is all a—

Shepherd (*standing up*). And it's on principles like these —boldly and unblushingly avoo'd here—in Mr. Awmrose's paper-parlor, at the conclusion o' the sixth brodd, on the evening o' Monday the 22d o' September, Anno Dominie aughteen hunder and twunty-aught, within twa hours o' midnicht—that you, sir, have been yeditin a Maggasin that has gone out to the uttermost corners o' the yerth, wherever civilization or uncivilization is known, deludin and distrackin men and women folk, till it's impossible for them to ken their right hand frae their left—or whether they're standin on their heels or their heads—or what byeuk ought to be perused, and what byeuk puttin intil the bottom o' pie-dishes and trunks—or what awthor hissed, or what awthor hurraa'd—or what's flummery and what's philosophy—or what's rant and what's religion—or what's monopoly and what's free tredd—or wha's poets or wha's but Pats—or whether it's best to be drunk, or whether it's best to be sober a' hours o' the day and nicht—or if there should be rich church establishments as in England, or poor kirk ones as in Scotland—or whether the Bishop o' Canterbury, wi' twunty thousan' a year, is mair like a primitive Christian than the Minister o' Kirkintulloch wi' twa hunder and fifty—or if folk should aye be readin sermons or fishin for sawmon—or if it's best to marry or best to burn —or if the national debt hangs like a millstone round the neck o' the kintra or like a chain o' blae-berries—or if the Millennium be really close at haun, or the present Solar System be calculated to last to a' eternity—or whether the people should be edicated up to the highest pitch o' perfection, or preferably to be all like trotters through the Bog o'

Allen—or whether the Government should subsideeze foreign powers, or spend a' its siller on oursels—or whether the Blacks and the Catholics should be emancipawted or no afore the demolition o' Priest and Obis—or whether—God forgie us baith for the hypothesis—man has a mortal or an immortal sowl—be a Phœnix—or an Eister!

North. Precisely so, James. You have drawn my real character to a hair—and the character, too, of the baleful work over which I have the honor and happiness to preside.

Shepherd. I canna sit here ony langer, and hear a' things, visible and invisible, turned tapsy-turvy and tapsalteerie—I'm aff—I'm aff—I'm ower to the Auld Toon to tak toddy wi' Christians, and no wi' an Atheist, that would involve the warld in even-doun Pyrrhonism—and disorder, if he could, the verra coorses o' the seven Planets, and set the central Sun adrift through the sky. Gude-nicht to ye, sir—gude-nicht.—Ye are the maist dangerous o' a' reprobates—for your private conduct and character is that o' an angel, but your public that o' a fiend; and the honey o' your domestic practice can be nae antidote to the pushion o' your foreign principles. I'm aff—I'm aff.

(*Enter* MR. AMBROSE *with a Howtowdie, and* KING PEPIN *with Potatoes and Ham.*)

Shepherd (*in continuation*). What brought ye intil the room the noo, Mr. Awmrose, wi' a temptation sic as that—nae flesh and bluid can resist? Awa back to the kitchin wi' the savory sacrifice—or clash doun the Towdie afore the Bagman in the wee closet-room ayont the wainscot. What'n a bonny, brown, basted, buttery, iley, and dreepin breast o' a roasted Earock. O' a' the smells I ever fan, that is the maist insupportably seducin to the palate. It has gien me the water-brash. Weel, weel, Mr. North, since you insist on't, we'll resume the argument after supper.

North. Good-night, James.—Ambrose, deposit the Towdie, and show Mr. Hogg down stairs. Lord bless you, James—good-night.

Shepherd (securing his seat). Dinna say anither word, sir. Nae farther apology. I forgie you. Ye wasna serious. Come, be cheerfu'—I'm sune pacified. Oh, man, but ye cut up a fool * wi' incredible dexterity! There—a leg and a wing to yoursel—and a leg and a wing to me—then, to you the breast—for I ken ye like the breast—and to me the back—and I dinna dislike the back,—and then, Howtowdie! "Farewell! a long farewell to all thy fatness." Oh, sir! but the taties are gran' the year! How ony Christian creature can prefer waxies to mealies, I never could conjecture. Anither spoonfu' or twa o' the gravy. Haud—haud—what a deluge!

North. This, I trust, my dear Shepherd, will be a good season for the poor.

Shepherd. Nae fear o' that, sir. Has she ony eggs? But I forgot—the hens are no layin the noo; they're mootin.† Faith, considering ye didna eat mony o' the eisters, your appeteet's no amiss, sir. Pray, sir, will ye tell me gin there be ony difference atween this new-fangled Oriental disease, they ca' the Cholera, and the gude auld-fashion'd Scottish complent, the colic? For gudesake, dinna drain the dolphin!

North. A mixture of Giles's and Berwick—nectar worthy an ambrosial feast!

Shepherd. It gars my een water, and my lugs crack. Noo for the toasted cheese.

(*Enter* TAFFY *with two Welsh Rabbits, and exit.*)

* *Fool*—fowl.

† *Mootin*—moulting.

XVII.

THE HAGGIS DELUGE.

SCENE I.—*The Octagon.—Time,—Ten.*

NORTH.—SHEPHERD.—TICKLER.

North. Thank Heaven! my dear Shepherd, Winter is come again, and Edinburgh is beginning once more to look like herself, like her name and her nature, with rain, mist, sleet, haur, hail, snow I hope, wind, storm—would that we could but add a little thunder and lightning—the Queen of the North.

Shepherd. Hoo could you, sir, wi' a' your time at your ain command, keep in and about Embro' frae May to December? The city, for three months in the dead o' simmer, is like a tomb.

Tickler (*in a whisper to the Shepherd*). The widow—James —the widow.

Shepherd (*aloud*). The weedow—sir—the weedow! Couldna he hae brocht her out wi' him to the Forest? At their time o' life, surely scandal wad hae held her tongue.

Tickler. Scandal never holds her tongue, James. She drops her poison upon the dew on the virgin's untimely grave —her breath will not let the grey hairs rest in the mould—

Shepherd. Then, Mr. North, marry her at ance, and bring her out in Spring, that you may pass the hinney-moon on the sunny braes o' Mount Benger.

North. Why, James, the moment I begin to press matters,

she takes out her pocket-handkerchief—and through sighs and sobs recurs to the old topic—that twenty thousand times told tale—the dear old General.

Shepherd. Deevil keep the dear old General! Hasna the man been dead these twunty years? And if he had been leevin, wuldna he been aulder than yoursel, and far mair infirm? You're no in the least infirm, sir.

North. Ah, James! that's all you know. My infirmities are increasing with years—

Shepherd. Wad you be sae unreasonable as to expect them to decrease with years? Are her infirmities—

North. Hush—she has no infirmities.

Shepherd. Nae infirmities! Then she's no worth a brass button. But let me ask you ae interrogatory.—Hae ye ever put the question? Answer me that, sir.

North. Why, James, I cannot say that I ever have—

Shepherd. What! and you expeck that *she* wull put the question to *you?* That would indeed be puttin the cart before the horse. If the women were to ask the men, there wad be nae leevin in this warld. Yet let me tell you, Mr. North, that it's a shamefu' thing to keep playin in the way you hae been doin for these ten years past on a young woman's feelings—

Tickler. Ha—ha—ha—James!—A young woman! Why, she's sixty, if she's an hour.

North. You lie.

Shepherd. That's a douss * on the chops, Mr. Tickler. That's made you as red in the face as a bubbly-jock, sir. Oh, the power o' ae wee bit single monosyllabic syllable o' a word to awauken a' the safter and a' the fiercer passions! Dinna keep bitin your thoomb, Mr. Tickler, like an Itawlian! Make an apology to Mr. North—

* *Douss*—a blow, a stroke.

North. I will accept of no apology. The man who calls a woman old deserves death.

Shepherd. Did you call her auld, Mr. Tickler?

Tickler. To you, sir, I will condescend to reply. I did not. I merely said she was sixty if she was an hour.

Shepherd. In the first place, dinna "Sir" me—for it's not only ill-bred, but it's stupit. In the second place, dinna talk o' "condescending" to reply to me—for that's language I'll no thole even frae the King on the throne, and I'm sure the King on the throne wadna mak use o't. In the third place, to ca' a woman saxty, and then maintain that ye didna ca' her auld, is naething short o' a sophism. And in the fourth place, you shudna hae accompanied your remark wi' a loud haw—haw—haw,—for on a tender topic a guffaw's an aggravation—and marryin a widow, let her age be what it wull, is a tender topic, depend on't—sae that on a calm and dispassionate view o' a' the circumstances o' the case, there can be nae dout that you maun mak an apology; or, if you do not, I leave the room, and there is an end of the Noctes Ambrosianæ.

North. An end of the Noctes Ambrosianæ!

Tickler. An end of the Noctes Ambrosianæ!

Shepherd. An end of the Noctes Ambrosianæ.

Omnes. An end of the Noctes Ambrosianæ!!!

North. Rather than that should happen, I will make a thousand apologies—

Tickler. And I ten thousand—

Shepherd. That's behavin like men and Christians. Embrace—embrace. [NORTH *and* TICKLER *embrace.*

North. Where were we, James?

Shepherd. I was abusin Embro' in simmer.

North. Why?

Shepherd. Whey?—a' the lums * smokeless! No ae † jack

* *Lums*—chimneys. † *No ae*—not one.

turnin a piece o' roastin beef afore ae fire in ony ae kitchen in a' the New Toon! Streets and squares a' grass-grown, sae that they micht be mawn! Shops like beehives that hae dee'd in wunter! Coaches settin aff for Stirlin, and Perth, and Glasgow, and no ae passenger either inside or out—only the driver keepin up his heart wi' flourishing his whip, and the guard sittin in perfect solitude, playin an eerie spring on his bugle-horn! The shut-up playhouse a' covered ower wi' bills that seem to speak o' plays acted in an antediluvian world! But to return to the near approach o' wunter. Mankind hae again putten on worsted stockins, and flannen drawers—white jeans and yellow nankeen troosers hae disappeared—dooble soles hae gotten a secure footen ower pumps —big-coats wi' fur, and mantles wi' miniver, gie an agreeable rouchness to the picturesque stream o' life eddyin alang the channel o' the streets—gloves and mittens are sae general that a red hairy haun looks rather singular—every third body ye meet, for fear o' a sudden blash, carries an unbrella—a' folk shave noo wi' het water—coal-carts are emptyin theirsels into ilka area—caddies at the corners o' the streets and drivers on coach-boxes are seen warmin themsels by blawin on their fingers, or whuskin themsels wi' their open nieves across the shouthers—skates glitter at shop-wundows, prophetic o' frost —Mr. Phin may tak in his rod noo, for nae mair thocht o' anglin till spring,—and wi' spring hersel, as wi' ither o' our best and bonniest freens, it may be said, out o' sicht out o' mind,—you see heaps o' bears hung out for sale—horses are a hairier o' the hide—the bit toon bantam craws nane, and at breakfast you maun tak tent no to pree an egg afore smellin at it,—you meet hares carryin about in a' quarters— and ggemkeepers proceedin out into the kintra wi' strings o' grews,—sparrows sit silent and smoky wi' ruffled feathers, waiting for crumbs on the ballustrawds—loud is the cacklin in the fowl-market o' Christmas geese that come a month at least afore the day, just like thae Annuals the Forget-me-Nots, Amulets, Keepsakes, Beejoos, Gems, Anniversaries, Souvenirs, Friendship's Offerings, and Wunter-Wreaths—

Tickler. Stop, James—stop. Such an accumulation of imagery absolutely confounds—perplexes—

Shepherd. Folk o' nae fancy. Then for womankind—

Tickler. Oh! James, James! I knew you would not long keep off that theme—

Shepherd. Oh, ye pawkie auld carle! What ither theme in a' this wide weary warld is worth ae single thocht or feelin in the poet's heart—ae single line frae the poet's pen—ae single—

North. Song from the Shepherd's lyre—of which, as of the Teian Bard's of old, it may be said :—

'Α βαρβιτος δε χορδαις
'Ερωτα μουνον ήχει.*

Do, my dear James, give us John Nicholson's daughter.

Shepherd. Wait a wee. The womankind, I say, sirs, never look sae bonny as in wunter, excepp indeed it may be in spring—

Tickler. Or summer or autumn, James—

Shepherd. Haud your tongue. You old bachelors ken naething o' womankind—and hoo should ye, when they treat you wi' but ae feelin, that o' derision? Oh, sirs! but the dear creturs do look weel in muffs—whether they haud them, wi' their invisible hauns clasped thegither in their beauty within the cosy silk linin, close prest to their innicent waists, just aneath the glad beatins o' their first-love-touched hearts—

Tickler. There again, James!

Shepherd. Or haud them hingin frae their extended richt

* The harp with its strings sounds only love.

arms, leavin a' the feegur visible, that seems taller and slimmer as the removed muff reveals the clasps o' the pelisse a' the way doun frae neck till feet!

North. Look at Tickler—James—how he moves about in his chair. His restlessness—

Shepherd. Is no unnatural. Then, sir, is there, in a' the beautifu' and silent unfauldins o' natur amang plants and flowers, onything sae beautifu' as the white, smooth, saft chafts o' a bit smilin maiden o' saxteen, aughteen, or twunty blossomin out, like some bonny bud o' snaw-white satin, frae a coverin o' rough leaves,—blossomin out, sirs, frae the edge o' the fur tippet, that haply a lover's happy haun had delicately hung ower her gracefu' shouthers—oh, the dear delightfu' little Laplander!

Tickler. For a married man, James, you really describe—

North. Whisht!

Shepherd. I wush you only heard the way the bonny croodin-doos * keep murmuring their jeists † to ane anither, as soon as a nest o' them gets rid o' an auld bacheleer on Princes Street.

Tickler. Gets rid o' an auld bachelor!

Shepherd. Booin and scrapin to them after the formal and stately fashion o' the auld school o' politeness, and thinkin himsel the very pink o' courtesy, wi' a gold-headed cane, aiblins, nae lest, in his haun, and buckles on's shoon—for buckles are no quite out yet a'thegither—a frill like a fan at the shirt-neck o' him—and, wad the warld believe't, knee-breeks!—then they titter—and then they lauch—and then, as musical as if they were singin in pairts, the bonny, bloomin, innicent wicked creturs break out into—I maunna say, o' sic rosy lips, and sic snawy breasts, a guffaw ‡—

* *Croodin-doos*—cooing-doves. † *Jeists*—jests.

‡ *Guffaw*—a broad laugh

but a guffay, sirs, a guffay—for that's the feminine o' guffaw—

North. Tickler, we really must not allow ourselves to be insulted in this style any longer—

Shepherd. And then awa they trip, sirs, flingin an antelope's or gazelle's ee ower their shouther, diverted beyond measure to see their antique beau continuing at a distance to cut capers in his pride—till a' at ance they see a comet in the sky—a young offisher o' dragoons, wi' his helmet a' in a low wi' a flicker o' red feathers—and as he " turns and winds his fiery Pegassus," they are a' mute as death—yet every face at the same time eloquent wi' mantling smiles, and wi' blushes that break through and around the blue heavens of their een, like crimson clouds to sudden sunlight burning beautiful for a moment, and then melting away like a thocht or a dream!

North. Why, my dear James, it does one's heart good even to be ridiculed in the language of Poetry. Does it not, Tickler?

Tickler. James, your health, my dear fellow.

Shepherd. I never ridicule onybody, sirs, that's no fit to bear it. But there's some sense and some satisfaction in makin a fule o' them, that, when the fiend's in them, can mak fules o' a'body, like North and Tickler

(*Enter* Mr. AMBROSE *with a hot roasted Round of Beef*—KING PEPIN *with a couple of boiled Ducks*—SIR DAVID GAM *with a trencher of Tripe* à la *Meg Dods*—*and* TAPPYTOORIK *with a Haggis. Pickled Salmon, Welsh Rabbits, &c., &c.*—*and, as usual, Oysters, raw, stewed scolloped, roasted, and pickled, of course*—*Rizzards, Finzeans, Red Herrings.*)

Shepherd. You've really served up a bonny wee neat bit sooper for three, Mr. Awmrose. I hate, for my ain pairt, to see a table overloaded. It's sae vulgar. I'll carve the haggis.*

North. I beseech you, James, for the love of all that is dear to you, here and hereafter, to hold your hand. Stop—stop—stop!

(*The* SHEPHERD *sticks the Haggis, and the Table is instantly overflowed.*)

Shepherd. Heavens and earth! is the Haggis mad? Tooels! † Awmrose—tooels! Safe us! we'll a' be drooned!

[PICARDY *and his Tail rush out for towels.*

North. Rash man! what ruin have you wrought! See how it has overflown the deck from stem to stern—we shall all be lost.

Shepherd. Sweepin everything afore it! Whare's the puir biled ‡ dyucks? Only the croon-head o' the roun' visible! Tooels—tooels—tooels! Send roun' the fire-drum through the city.

(*Re-enter* PICARDY *and* "*the Rest*" *with napery.*)

Mr. Ambrose. Mr. North, I look to you for orders in the midst of this alarming calamity. Shall I order in more strength?

Shepherd. See—see—sir! it's creeping alang the carpet! We're like men left on a sandbank, when the tide's comin in rampaugin. Oh! that I had insured my life! Oh! that I had learned to soom! § What wull become o' my widow and my fatherless children?

North. Silence! Let us die like men.

Shepherd. O Lord! it's ower our insteps already! Open a' the doors and wundows—and let it find its ain level. I'll up on a chair in the meantime.

* A *haggis* is the stomach of a sheep filled with the lungs, heart, and liver of the same animal, minced with suet, onions, salt, and pepper.

† *Tooels*—towels. ‡ *Biled*—boiled. § *Soom*—swim.

(*The* SHEPHERD *mounts the back of The Chair, and draws* MR. NORTH *up after him.*)

Sit on my shouthers, my dear—dear—dearest sir. I insist on't. Mr. Tickler, Mr. Awmrose, King Pepin, Sir David, and Tappitourie—you wee lazy deevil—help Mr. North up—help Mr. North up on my shouthers!

(MR. NORTH *is elevated, Crutch and all, astride on the* SHEPHERD'S *shoulders.*)

North. Good God! Where is Mr. Tickler?

Shepherd. Look—look—look, sir,—yonner he's staunin on the brace piece—on the mantel! Noo, Awmrose, and a' ye waiters, make your escape, and leave us to our fate. Oh! Mr. North, gie us a prayer.—What for do you look so meeserable, Mr. Tickler? Death is common—'tis but "passing through Natur' to Eternity!" And yet—to be drooned in haggis 'ill be waur than Clarence's dream! Alack and alas-a-day! it's up to the ring o' the bell-rope! Speak, Mr. Tickler—oh, speak, sir—men in our dismal condition—Are you sittin easy, Mr. North?

North. Quite so, my dear James, I am perfectly resigned. Yet, what is to become of Maga—

Shepherd. Oh my wee Jamie!

North. I fear I am very heavy, James.

Shepherd. Dinna say't, sir—dinna say't. I'm like the pious Æneas bearin his father Ancheeses through the flames o' Troy. The similie doesna haud gude at a' points—I wish it did—oh, haud fast, sir, wi' your arms roun' my neck, lest the cruel tyrant o' a haggis swoop ye clean awa under the side-board to inevitable death!

North. Far as the eye can reach it is one wide wilderness of suet!

Tickler. Hurra! hurra! hurra!

Shepherd. Do you hear the puir gentleman, Christopher?

It's affeckin to men in our condition to see the pictur we hae baith read o' in accounts o' shipwrecks realeezed! Timothy's gane mad! Hear till him shoutin wi' horrid glee on the brink o' eternity!

Tickler. Hurra! hurra! hurra!

North. Horrible! most horrible!

Tickler. The haggis is subsiding—the haggis is subsiding! It has fallen an inch by the surbase* since the Shepherd's last ejaculation.

Shepherd. If you're tellin a lee, Timothy, I'll wade ower to you, and bring you doun aff the mantel wi' the crutch.—Can I believe my een? It *is* subseedin. Hurraw! hurraw! hurraw! Nine times nine, Mr. North, to our deliverance—and the Protestant ascendancy.

Omnes. Hurra! hurraw! hurree!

Shepherd. Noo, sir, you may dismunt.

(*Re-enter the Household, with the immediate neighborhood.*)

Shepherd. High Jinks! High Jinks! High Jinks! The haggis has putten out the fire, and sealed up the boiler—

(*The* SHEPHERD *descends upon all-fours, and lets Mr.* NORTH *off gently.*)

North. Oh, James, I am a daft old man!

Shepherd. No sae silly as Solomon, sir, at your time o' life. Noo for sooper.

Tickler. How the devil am I to get down?

Shepherd. How the deevil did you get up? Oh, ho, by the gas ladder! And it's been removed in the confusion. Either jump down—or stay where you are, Mr. Tickler.

Tickler. Come now, James—shove over the ladder.

Shepherd. Oh that Mr. Chantrey was here to sculptur him in that attitude! Streitch out your richt haun! A wee grain heicher! Hoo gran' he looks in basso-relievo!

* *Surbase*—the moulding at the upper edge of the wainscot.

Tickler. Shove over the ladder, you son of the mist, or I'll brain you with the crystal.

Shepherd. Sit doun, Mr. North, opposite to me—and Mr. Awmrose, tak roun' my plate for a shave o' the beef.—Isna he the perfeck pictur o' the late Right Honorable William Pitt?—Shall I send you, sir, some o' the biled dyuck?

North. If you please, James.—Rather "Like Patience on a monument smiling at Grief."

Shepherd. Gie us a sang, Mr. Tickler, and then you shall hae the ladder. I never preed a roasted roun' afore—it's real savory.

North.—

> "Oh! who can tell how hard it is to climb
> The height where Fame's proud temple shines afar!"

Shepherd. I'll let you doun, Mr. Tickler, if you touch the ceilin wi' your fingers. Itherwise, you maun sing a sang.

(TICKLER *tries and fails.*)

Tickler. Well, if I must sing, let me have a tumbler of toddy.

Shepherd. Ye shall hae that, sir.

(*The* SHEPHERD *fills a tumbler from the jug, and balancing it on the cross of the crutch, reaches it up to* Mr. TICKLER. TICKLER *sings* "The Twa Magicians.")

Shepherd. Noo—sir—here is the ladder to you—for which you're indebted to Mr. Peter Buchan, o' Peterhead, the ingenious collector o' the *Ancient Ballads*, frae which ye have chanted so speeritedly the speerited "Twa Magicians." It's a capital collection—and should be added in a' libraries, to Percy, and Ritson, and Headley, and the *Minstrelsy of the Border*, and John Finlay, and Robert Jamieson, and Gilchrist and Kinloch, and the Quarto o' that clever chiel, Motherwell * o' Paisley, wha's no only a gude collector and

* William Motherwell, born in 1798, the author of some spirited ballads and editor of *Minstrelsy, Ancient and Modern.* He died in 1835.

commentator o' ballads, but a gude writer o' them too—as he has proved by that real poetical address o' a Northman to his Swurd in ane o' the Annals. Come awa doun, sir—come awa doun. Tak tent, for the steps are gey shoggly.* Noo—sir—fa' to the roun'.

Tickler. I have no appetite, James. I have been suffering all night under a complication of capital complaints,—the toothache, which like a fine attenuated red-hot, steel-sting, keeps shooting through an old rugged stump, which to touch with my tongue is agony—the tongue-ache, from a blister on that weapon, that I begin to fear may prove cancerous—the lip-ache, from having accidentally given myself a labial wound in sucking out an oyster—the eye-ache, as if an absolute worm were laying eggs in the pupil—the ear-ache, tinglin and stounin† to the very brain, till my drum seems beating for evening parade—to which add a headache of the hammer-and-anvil kind—and a stomach-ache, that seems to intimate that dyspepsy is about to be converted into cholera morbus ; and you have a partial enumeration of the causes that at present deaden my appetite—and that prevented me from chanting the ballad with my usual vivacity. However—I will trouble you for a duck.

Shepherd. You canna be in the least pain, wi' sae mony complaints as these—for they maun neutraleeze ane anither. But even if they dinna, I believe mysel, wi' the Stoics, that pain's nae evil.—Dinna you, Mr. North?

North. Certainly. But Tickler, you know, has many odd crotchets.

Ambrose (entering with his suavest physiognomy). Beg pardon, Mr. North, for venturing in unrung, but there's a young lady wishing to speak with you—

Shepherd. A young lady!—show her ben.

* *Shoggly*—shaky.

† *Stounin*—aching.

North. An anonymous article?

Ambrose. No, sir,—Miss Helen Sandford, from the Lodge.

North. Helen!—what does she want?

Ambrose. Miss Sandford had got alarmed, sir—

Shepherd. Safe us! only look at the timepiece! Four o'clock in the mornin!

Ambrose. And has walked up from the Lodge—

North. What? Alone!

Ambrose. No, sir. Her father is with her—and she bids me say—now that she knows her master is well—that here is your Kilmarnock nightcap.

[Mr. NORTH *submits his head to* PICARDY, *who adjusts the nightcap.*

Shepherd. What a cowl!

North. A capote—James. Mr. Ambrose,—we three must sleep here all night.

Shepherd. A' mornin, ye mean. Tak care o' Tickler amang ye—but recolleck it's no safe to wauken sleepin dowgs.—Oh! man! Mr. North! sir! but that was touchin attention in puir Eelen. She's like a dochter, indeed.—Come awa, you auld vagabon, to your bed. I'll kick open the door o' your dormitory wi' my fit, as I pass alang the transe in the mornin! The mornin! Faith, I'm beginnin already to get hungry for breakfast! Come awa, you auld vagabon—come awa.

[*Exeunt* NORTH *and* SHEPHERD, *followed by the Height of* TICKLER, *to Roost.*

NORTH (*singing as they go*)—

"Early to bed, and early to rise,
Is the way to be healthy, wealthy, and wise!"

Da Capo.

XVIII.

IN WHICH THE SHEPHERD, HAVING SKATED FROM YARROW, TAKES A PLOUTER.

SCENE I.—*The Snuggery. Time,—Nine in the Evening.*
NORTH *and* TICKLER.

Tickler. Replenish. That last jug was most illustrious. I wish James were here.

North. Hush! hark! It must be he!—and yet 'tis not just the pastoral tread either of the Bard of Benger. "Alike, but oh! how different!"

Tickler. "His very step has music in't as he comes up the stair!"

Shepherd (*bursting in with a bang*). Huzzaw! Huzzaw! Huzzaw!

North. God bless you, James; your paw, my dear Sus.

Shepherd. Fresh frae the Forest, in three hours—

Tickler. What! thirty-six miles?

North. So it is true that you have purchased the famous American trotter?

Shepherd. Nae trotters like my ain trotters! I've won my bate, sirs.

North. Bet?

Shepherd. Ay,—a bate,—a bate o' twenty guineas.

Tickler. What the deuce have you got on your feet, James?

Shepherd. Skites.* I've skited frae St. Mary's Loch to the Canawl Basin in fowre minutes and a half within the three hours, without turnin a hair.

Tickler. Do keep a little farther off, James, for your face has waxed intolerably hot, and I perceive that you have raised the thermometer a dozen degrees.

Shepherd (*flinging a purse of gold on the table*). It 'ill require a gey strang thaw to melt that, chiels; sae tak your change out o' that, as Joseph† says, either in champagne, or yill, or porter, or Burgundy, or cedar, or Glenlivet—just whatsomever you like best to drink or devoor; and we shanna be lang without supper, for in coming alang the transe I shooted to Tappytoorie forthwith to send in samples o' all the several eatables and drinkables in Picardy. I'm desperate hungry. Lowse my skites, Tickler.

[TICKLER *succumbs to unthong the* SHEPHERD'S *skates.*

Tickler. What an instep!

Shepherd. Ay, nane o' your plain soles, that gang shiffle-shaffling amang the chuckystanes assassinatin a' the insects; but a foot arched like Apollo's bow when he shot the Python—heel, of a firm and decided but unobtrusive character—and taes, ilka ane a thocht larger than the ither, like a family o childer, or a flight o' steps leading up to the pillared portico o' a Grecian temple.

(*Enter* Signor AMBROSIO *susurrans with* IT *below his arm.*)

Shepherd. That's richt—O but Greeny has a gran' gurgle! A mouthfu' o' Millbank never comes amiss. Oh! but it's potent! (*gruing*). I wuss it be na ile o' vitrol.

North. James, enlighten our weak minds.

Shepherd. An English bagman, you see—he's unco fond o' poetry and the picturesque, a traveller in the soft line—paid me a visit the day just at denner-time, in a yellow gig,

* *Skites*—skates.

† Joseph Hume.

drawn by a chestnut blude meer; and after we had discussed the comparative merits o' my poems, and Lord Byron's, and Sir Walter's, he rather attributin to me, a' things considered, the superiority over baith, it's no impossible that my freen got rather fuddled a wee, for, after roosin his meer to the skies, as if she were fit for Castor himsel to ride upon up and doun the blue lift, frae less to mair he offered to trot her in the gig into Embro', against me on the best horse in a' my stable, and gie me a half-hour's start before puttin her into the shafts; when, my birses being up, faith I challenged him, on the same condition, to rin him intil Embro' on shank's naigie.*

North. What! biped against quadruped?

Shepherd. Just. The cretur, as sune as he came to the clear understandin o' my meanin, gied ane o' these bit creenklin cackles o' a Cockney lauch, that can only be forgiven by a Christian when his soul is saften'd by the sunny hush o' a Sabbath morning.

North. Forgotten, perhaps, James, but not forgiven.

Shepherd. The bate† was committed to black and white; and then on wi' my skites, and awa like a reindeer.

Tickler. What? down the Yarrow to Selkirk—then up the Tweed.

Shepherd. Na, na! naething like keepin the high-road for safety in a skiting-match. There it was—noo stretchin straught afore me, noo serpenteezin like a great congor eel, and noo amaist coilin itself up like a sleepin adder; but whether straught or crooked or circling, ayont a' imagination sliddery, sliddery!

Tickler. Confound me—if I knew that we had frost.

Shepherd. That comes o' trustin till a barometer to tell you when things hae come to the freezin-pint. Frost! The ice

* *On shank's naigie*—on foot.

† *Bate*—bet.

is fourteen feet thick in the Loch—and though you hae nae frost about Embro' like our frost in the Forest, yet I wadna advise you, Mr. Tickler, to put your tongue on the airn-rim o' a cart or cotch-wheel.

North. I remember, James, being beguiled—sixty-four years ago!— by a pretty little, light-haired, blue-eyed lassie, one starry night of black frost, just to touch a cart-wheel for one moment with the tip of my tongue.

Shepherd. What a gowmeril! *

North. And the bonny May had to run all the way to the manse for a jug of hot water to relieve me from that bondage.

Shepherd. You had a gude excuse, sir, for geein the cutty a gude kissin.

North. How fragments of one's past existence come suddenly flashing back upon—

Shepherd. Hoo I snooved alang the snaw! Like a verra curlin-stane, when a dizzen besoms are soopin the ice afor't and the granite gangs groanin gloriously alang, as if instinct wi' spirit, and the water-kelpie below strives in vain to keep up wi' the straight-forrit planet, still accompanied as it spins wi' a sort o' spray, like the shiverin atoms of diamonds, and wi' a noise to which the hills far and near respond, like a water-quake—the verra ice itself seemin at times to sink and swell, just as if the Loch were a great wide glitterin tin-plate, beaten out by that cunnin whitesmith, Wunter—and—

Tickler. And every mouth, in spite of frost, thaws to the thought of corned beef and greens.

Shepherd. Hoo I snooved alang! Some collies keepit geyan weel up wi' me as far's Traquair manse—but ere I crossed the Tweed my canine tail had drapped quite away,

* *Gowmeril*—fool.

and I had but the company of a couple of crows to Peebles.

North. Did you dine on the road, James?

Shepherd. Didn't I tell you I had dined before I set off? I ettled at a cauker at Eddlestone—but in vain attempted to moderate my velocity as I neared the village, and had merely time to fling a look to my worthy friend the minister, as I flew by that tree-hidden manse and its rill-divided garden, beautiful alike in dew and in cranreuch!

Tickler. Helpless as Mazeppa!

Shepherd. It's far worse to be ridden aff wi' by ane's ain sowl than by the wildest o' the desert loon.

North. At this moment, the soul seems running away with the body,—at that, the body is off with the soul. Spirit and matter are playing at fast and loose with each other—and at full speed you get skeptical as Spinoza.

Shepherd. Sometimes the ruts are for miles thegither regular as railroads—and your skite gets fitted intil a groove, sae that you can haud out ane o' your legs like an opera dancer playin a peeryette, and on the ither glint by, to the astonishment o' toll-keepers, who at first suspect you to be on horseback—then that you may be a bird—and feenally that you must be a ghost.

Tickler. Did you upset any carriages, James?

Shepherd. Nane that I recollect. I saw severals—but whether they were coming or going—in motion or at rest, it is not for me to say—but they, and the hills, and woods, and clouds, seemed a' to be floatin awa thegither in the direction o' the mountains at the head o' Clydesdale.

Tickler. And where all this while was the bagman?

Shepherd. Wanderin, nae doubt, a' a-foam, leagues ahint; for the chestnut meer was weel cauked, and she ance won a king's plate at Doncaster. You may hae seen, Mr. North, a cloud-giant on a stormy day striding alang the sky, coverin a parish wi' ilka stretch o' his spawl,* and pausin, aiblins, to tak his breath now and then at the meetin o' twa counties; if sae, you hae seen an image o' me—only he was in the heavens, and I on the yearth—he an unsubstantial phantom, and I twal stane wecht—he silent and sullen in his flight, I musical and merry in mine—

Tickler. But on what principle came you to stop, James?

Shepherd. Luckily, the Pentland Hills came to my succor. By means of one of their ridges I got gradually rid of a portion of my velocity—subdued down into about seven miles an hour, which rate got gradually diminished to about four; and here I am, gentlemen, after having made a narrow escape from a stumble, that in York Place threatened to set me off again down Leith Walk, in which case I must have gone on to Portobello or Musselburgh.

North. Well, if I did not know you, my dear James, to be a matter-of-fact man, I should absolutely begin to entertain some doubts of your veracity.

Shepherd. What the deevil's that hingin frae the roof?

North. Why, the chandelier.

Shepherd. The shandleer? It's a cage, wi' an outlandish bird in't. A pawrot, I declare! Pretty Poll! Pretty Poll! Pretty Poll!

Parrot. Go to the devil and shake yourself.

Shepherd. Heaven preserve us!—heard you ever the likes o' that?—A bird cursin! What sort o' an education must the cretur hae had? Poor beast, do you ken what you're sayin?

Parrot. Much cry and little wool, as the devil said when he was shearin the Hog.

Shepherd. You're gettin personal, sir, or madam; for I dinna pretend to ken your sex.

* *Spawl*—shoulder.

North. That everybody does, James, who has anything to do with *Blackwood's Magazine.*

Shepherd. True enough, sir. If it wad but keep a gude tongue in its head—it's really a bonny cretur. What plummage! What'ill you hae, Polly, for sooper?

Parrot.—

> Molly put the kettle on,
> Molly put the kettle on,
> Molly put the kettle on,
> And I shall have some punch.

Shepherd. That's fearsome—yet, whisht! What ither vice was that speakin? A gruff vice. There again! whisht!

Voice.—

> The devil he came to our town,
> And rode away wi' the exciseman.

Shepherd. This room's no canny. I'm aff (*rising to go*). Mercy me! A raven hoppin aneath the sideboard! Look at him, how he turns his great big broad head to the ae side, and keeps regardin me wi' an evil eye! Satan!

North. My familiar, James.

Shepherd. Whence cam he?

North. One gloomy night I heard him croakin in the garden.

Shepherd. You did wrang, sir,—it was rash to let him in; wha ever heard o' a real raven in a surburban garden? It's some demon pretendin to be a raven. Only look at him wi' the silver ladle in his bill. Noo he draps it, and is ruggin at the Turkey carpet, as if he were colleckin lining for his nest. Let alane the carpet, you ugly villain!

Raven. The devil would a wooin go—ho–ho! the wooin, ho! *

* Dickens' incomparable raven in *Barnaby Rudge* would have been quite at home in this party; and appears, indeed, to have taken a lesson in household economy from North's parrot.

Shepherd. Ay—ay—you hear how it is, gentleman—" Love is a' the theme "—

Raven. " To woo his bonny lassie when the kye come hame ! "

Shepherd. Satan singin ane o' my sangs ! Frae this hour I forswear poetry.

Voice.—

O love—love—love,
Love's like a dizziness.

Shepherd. What ! another voice ?

Tickler. James—James—he's on your shoulder.

Shepherd (*starting up in great emotion*). Wha's on my shouther ?

North. Only Matthew.

Shepherd. Puir bit bonny burdie ! What ! you're a Stirling, are you ? Ay—ay—just pick and dab awa there at the hair in my lug. Yet I wad rather see you fleein and flutterin in and out o' a bit hole aneath a wall-flower high up on some auld and ruined castle standin by itsel among the woods.

Raven.—

O love—love—love,
Love's like a dizziness.

Shepherd. Rax me ower the poker, Mr. North—or lend me your crutch, that I may brain Sooty.

Starling.—

It wunna let a puir bodie
Gang about his bissiness.

Parrot. Fie, whigs, awa—fie, whigs, awa.

Shepherd. Na—the bird doesna want sense.

Raven.—

The deil sat girnin in a neuk,
Riving sticks to roast the Duke.

Shepherd. Oh ho ! you are fond of picking up Jacobite relics.

Raven. Ho! blood—blood—blood—blood—blood!

Shepherd. What do you mean, you sinner?

Raven. Burke him—Burke him—Burke him. Ho—ho—ho—blood—blood—blood!

Bronte. Bow—wow—wow.—Bow—wow—wow.—Bow—wow—wow.

Shepherd. A complete aviary, Mr. North. Weel, that's a sight worth lookin at. Bronte lying on the rug—never perceivin that it's on the tap o' a worsted teegger—a raven, either real or pretended, amusin himsel wi' ruggin at the dowg's toosey tail—the pawrot, wha maun hae opened the door o' his cage himsel, sittin on Bronte's shouther—and the stirling, Matthew, hidin himsel ahint his head—no less than four irrational creturs, as they are called, on the rug—each wi' a natur o' its ain; and then again four rational creturs, as they are called, sittin round them on chairs—each wi' his specific character too—and the aught makin ane aggregate—or whole—of parts not unharmoniously combined.

North. Why, James, there are but three of the rationals.

Shepherd. I find I was countin mysel twice over.

Tickler. Now be persuaded, my dear Shepherd, before supper is brought ben, to take a warm bath, and then rig yourself out in your Sunday suit of black, which Mr. Ambrose keeps sweet for you in his own drawer, bestrewed with sprigs of thyme, whose scent fadeth not for a century.

Shepherd. Faith, I think I shall tak a plouter.*

[SHEPHERD *retires into the marble bath adjoining the Snuggery. The hot water is let on with a mighty noise.*

North. Do you want the flesh-brushes, James?

Shepherd (*from within*). I wish I had some female slaves, wi' wooden swurds to scrape me wi', like the Shah o' Persia.

Tickler. Are you in, James?

* *Plouter*—a bathe accompanied with splashing.

Shepherd. Hearken !—

[*A sullen plunge is heard, as of a huge stone into the deep-down waters of a draw-well.*

North (*looking at his watch*). Two minutes have elapsed. I hope, Tickler, nothing apoplectical has occurred.

Shepherd. Blow—o—wo—ho—wro !

Tickler. Why, James—

"You are gurgling Italian half-way down your throat."

North. What temperature, James ?

Shepherd. Nearly up at egg-boiling. But you had better, sirs, be makin anither jug—for that ane was geyan sair dune afore I left you—and I maun hae a glass of het-and-het as sune as I come out, to prevent me takin the cauld. I hope there's nae current o' air in the room. Wha's this that bled himsel to death in a bath ? Wasna't Seneca ?

North. James, who is the best female poet of the age ?

Shepherd. Female what ?

Tickler. Poet.

Shepherd. Haud your tongue, ye sinner. What ! you are for drawin a pictur o' me as Apollo in the het bath surrounded wi' the Muses ? That would be a fine subject for Etty.

North. Isn't his "Judith and Holofernes," my dear Shepherd, a noble, a majestic performance ?

Shepherd. Yon's colorin ! Judith's richt leg's as flesh-like as my ain, noo lyin on the rim o' the bath, and maist as muscular.

Tickler. Not so hairy, though, James.

Shepherd. I'm geyan weel sodden noo, and I think I'll come out. Ring the bell, sir, for my black claes.

North. I have been toasting your shirt, James, at the fire. —Will you come out for it ?

Shepherd. Fling't in at the door. Thank you, sir. Ho ! here's the claes, I declare, hingin on the tenters. Is that sooper coming in? Noo, I'm rubbed down—ae stockin on—anither—noo, the flannen drawers—and noo, the breeks.—Oh! but that turkey has a gran' smell! Mr. Awmrose, ma slippers? Noo for't.

(*The* SHEPHERD *reappears in full sables, blooming like a rose.*)

North. Come away, my dear Shepherd. Is he not, Tickler, like a black eagle that has renewed his youth?

[*They take their seats at the Supper-table.—Mulligatawny—Roasted Turkey—Fillet of Veal—Soles—a Pie—and the Cold Round—Potatoes—Oysters, &c. &c. &c. &c. &c.*

North. The turkey is not a large one, James, and after a thirty-six miles' run, I think you had better take it on your plate.

Shepherd. Na, na, sir. Just set the ashet afore me—tak you the fillet—gie Tickler the pie—and noo, let us hae some discourse about the fine airts.

(*Supper.*)

Shepherd. In another month, sirs, the Forest will be as green as the summer sea rolling in its foam-crested waves in moonlight. You maun come out—you maun baith come out this spring.

North. I will. Every breath of air we draw is terrestrialized or etherealized by imagination. Our suburban air, round about Edinburgh, especially down towards the sea, must be pure, James; and yet, my fancy being haunted by these easterly haurs,* the finest atmosphere often seems to me afloat with the foulest atoms. My mouth is as a vortex, that engulfs all the stray wool and feathers in the vicinity. In the country, and nowhere more than on the Tweed or the Yarrow, I inhale always the gas of Paradise. I look about me

* *Haur*—a chill, foggy, easterly wind.

for flowers, and I see none—but I feel the breath of thousands. Country smoke from cottages or kilns, or burning heather, is not like town smoke. It ascends into clouds, on which angels and departed spirits may repose.

Shepherd. O' a' kintra soun's, which do you like best, sir?

North. The crowing of cocks before, at, and after sunrise. They are like clocks all set by the sun. Some hoarsely scrauching, James,—some with a long, clear, silver chime—and now and then a bit bantam crowing twice for the statelier chanticleer's once—and, by fancy's eye, seen strutting and sliding up, in his impudence, to hens of the largest size, not unaverse to the flirtation of the feathery-legged coxcomb.

Shepherd. Few folk hae seen oftener than me Natur gettin up i' the mornin. It's no possible to help personifyin her first into a goddess, and then into a human—

Tickler. There again, James.

Shepherd. She sleeps a' nicht in her claes, yet they're never runkled; her awakening face she turns up dewy to the sun, and Zephyr wipes it wi' his wing without disturbin its dreamy expression never see ye her hair in papers, for crisp and curly, far-streamin, and wide-waven are her locks, as alternate shadows and sunbeams dancin on the dancin music o' some joyous river rollin awa to the far-aff sea; her ee is heaven—her brow the marble clouds; and after a lang doun-gazing, serene, and spiritual look o' hersel, breathin her orison-prayers, in the reflectin magic o' some loch like an inland ocean, stately steps she frae the east, and a' that meet her—mair especially the Poet, wha draps doun amid the heather in devotion on his knees—kens that she is indeed the Queen of the whole Universe.

Tickler. Incedit Regina.

North. Then, what a breakfast at Mount Benger, after a stroll to and fro' the Loch! One devours the most material breakfast spiritually; and none of the ethereal particles are lost in such a meal.

Shepherd. Ethereal particles! What are they like?

North. Of the soul, James. Wordsworth says, in his own beautiful way, of a sparrow's nest:—

> "Look, five blue eggs are gleaming there!
> Few visions have I seen more fair,
> Nor many prospects of delight
> More touching than that simple sight!"

But five or six, or perhaps a dozen, white hen-eggs gleaming there—all on a most lovely, a most beautiful, a most glorious round white plate of crockery—is a sight even more simple and more touching still.

Tickler. What a difference between caller eggs and caller haddies!

North. About the same as between a rural lassie stepping along the greensward, like a walking rose or lily endued with life by the touch of a fairy's wand, and a lodging-house Girrzzie laying down a baikie* fu' o' ashes at the mouth of a common stair.

Shepherd. North, you're a curious cretur.

Tickler. You must excuse him—for he is gettin into his pleasant though somewhat prosy dotage.

Shepherd. A' men begin to get into a kind o' dotage after five-and-twunty. They think theirsels wiser, but they're only stupider. The glory o' the heaven and earth has a' flown by; there's something gane wrang wi' the machinery o' the peristrephic panorama, and it 'ill no gang roun',—nor is there ony great matter, for the colors hae faded on the canvas, and the spirit that pervaded the picture is dead.

Tickler Poo, poo, James. You're haverin.

* *Baikie*—a kind of scuttle for ashes.

North. Do you think, my dear James, that there is less religion now than of old in Scotland?

Shepherd. I really canna say, sir. At times I think there is even less sunshine. . . . Ony new poets spurtin up, sir, amang us, like fresh daisies amang them that's withered? Noo that the auld cocks are cowed, are the chickens beginning to flap their wings and craw?

Tickler. Most of them mere poultry, James.

North. Not worth plucking.

Shepherd. It's uncomprehensible, sir, to me altogether, what that *something* is that ae man only, amang many million, has that makes him poetical, while a' the lave remain to the day o' their death prosaic? I defy you to put your finger on ae pint o' his mental character or constitution in which the secret lies—indeed, there's aften a sort o' stupidity about the cretur that maks you sorry for him, and he's very generally laucht at;—yet there's a superiority in the strain o' his thochts and feelings that places him on a level by himsel aboon a' their heads; he has intuitions o' the truth, which, depend on't, sir, does not lie at the bottom of a well, but rather in the lift o' the understanding and the imagination—the twa hemispheres; and knowledge, that seems to flee awa frae ither men the faster and the farther the mair eagerly it is pursued, aften comes o' its ain sweet accord, and lies doun at the poet's feet.

North. Just so. The power of the soul is as the expression of the countenance—the one is strong in faculties, and the other beautiful in features, you cannot tell how—but so it is, and so it is felt to be; and let those not thus endowed by nature either try to make souls or make faces, and they only become ridiculous, and laughing-stocks to the world. This is especially the case with poets, who must be made of finer clay.

Tickler. Generally cracked—

Shepherd. But transpawrent—

Tickler. Yea, an urn of light.

North. There is something most affecting in the natural sorrows of poor men, my dear Shepherd, as, after a few days' wrestling with affliction, they appear again at their usual work—melancholy, but not miserable.

Shepherd. You ken a gude deal, sir, about the life and character o' the puir; but then it's frae philosophical and poetical observation and sympathy—no frae art-and-part participation, like mine, in their merriment and their meesery. Folk in what they ca' the upper classes o' society a' look upon life, mair or less, as a scene o' enjoyment, and amusement, and delicht. They get a' selfish in their sensibilities, and would fain mak the verra laws o' natur obedient to their wull. Thus they cherish and encourage habits o' thocht and feeling that are maist averse to obedience and resignation to the decrees o' the Almighty—when these decrees dash in pieces small the idols o' their earthly worship.

North. Too true, alas! my dearest Shepherd.

Shepherd. Pity me! how they moan, and groan, and greet and wring their hauns, and tear their hair, even auld folk their thin grey hair, when death comes into the bed-room, or the verra drawing-room, and carries aff in his clutches some wee bit spoiled bairn, yaummerin * amang its playthings, or keepin its mither awake a'nicht by its perpetual cries!

North. Touch tenderly, James—on—

Shepherd. Ane wad think that nae parents had ever lost a child afore—yet hoo mony a sma' funeral do you see ilka day pacin alang the streets unheeded on, amang the carts and hackney-coaches?

* *Yaummerin*—fretting.

North. Unheeded, as a party of upholsterer's men carrying furniture to a new house.

Shepherd. There is little or naething o' this thochtless, this senseless clamor in kintra-houses, when the cloud o' God's judgment passes ower them, and orders are gien for a grave to be dug in the kirkyard. A' the house is hushed and quate—just the same as if the patient were still sick, and no gane * awa—the father, and perhaps the mother, the brothers, and the sisters, are a' gaun about their ordinary business, wi' grave faces nae doubt, and some o' them now and then dichtin the draps frae their een; but, after the first black day, little audible greetin, and nae indecent and impious outcries.

North. The angler calling in at the cottage would never know that a corpse was the cause of the calm.

Shepherd. Rich folk, if they saw sic douce,† composed ongoings, wad doubtless wonder to think hoo callous, hoo insensible were the puir!—that natur had kindly denied to them those fine feelings that belong to cultivated life! But if they heard the prayer o' the auld man at nicht, when the survivin family were on their knees around the wa', and his puir wife neist him in the holy circle, they wad ken better, and confess that there is something as sublime as it is sincere and simple in the resignation and piety of those humble Christians, whose doom it is to live by the sweat o' their brow, and who are taught, almost frae the cradle to the grave, to feel every hour they breathe, that all they enjoy, and all they suffer, is dropt doun frae the hand o' God almost as visibly as the dew or the hail,—and hence their faith in things unseen and eternal is firm as their belief in things seen and temporal—and that they a' feel, sir, when lettin doun the coffin into the grave!

* *Gane*—Gone. † *Douce*—sedate.

North. Scottish Music, my dear James, is to me rather monotonous.

Shepherd. So is Scottish Poetry, sir. It has nae great range; but human natur never wearies o' its ain prime elementary feelings. A man may sit a haill nicht by his ingle, wi' his wife and bairns, without either thinkin or feelin muckle; and yet he's perfectly happy till bed-time, and says his prayers wi' fervent gratitude to the Giver o' a' mercies. It's only whan he's beginnin to tire o' the hummin o' the wheel, or o' his wife flytin at the weans, or o' the weans upsettin the stools, or ruggin ane anither's hair, that his fancy takes a very poetical flight into the regions o' the Imagination. Sae lang's the heart sleeps amang its affections, it dwalls upon few images; but these images may be infinitely varied; and when expressed in words, the variety will be felt. Sae that, after a', it's scarcely correct to ca' Scottish Poetry monotonous, or Scottish Music either, ony mair than you would ca' a kintra level, in bonny gentle ups and downs, or a sky dull, though the clouds were neither mony nor multiform; a' depends upon the spirit. Twa-three notes may mak a maist beautifu' tune, twa-three woody knowes a bonny landscape; and there are some bit streams amang the hills, without ony striking or very peculiar scenery, that it's no possible to dauner along at gloamin without feelin them to be visionary, as if they flowed through a land o' glamour.

North. James, I wish you would review for Maga all those fashionable Novels—Novels of High Life; such as *Pelham*—the *Disowned*—

Shepherd. I've read thae twa, and they're baith gude. But the mair I think on't, the profounder is my conviction that the strength o' human nature lies either in the highest or lowest estate of life.

Tickler. Is this Tay or Tweed salmon, James?

Shepherd. Tay, to be sure—it has the Perthshire accent, very pallateable. But, to speak plain, they may baith gang to the deevil for me, without excitin ony mair emotion in my mind than you are doin the nöo, Tickler, by puttin a bit o' cheese on your forefinger, and then, by a sharp smack on the palm, makin the mites spang into your mouth.

Tickler. I was doing no such thing, Hogg.

Shepherd. North, wasna he?—Puir auld useless body! he's asleep. Age will tell. He canna staun* a heavy sooper noo as he used to do—the toddy tells noo a hantle faster† upon him, and the verra fire itself drowzifies him noo until a dwawm—na, even the sound o' ane's vice, lang continued, lulls him noo half or haill asleep, especially if your talk like mine demands thocht—and there indeed, you see, Mr. Tickler, how his chin fa's doun on his breast, till he seems—but for a slight snore—the image o' death. Heaven preserve us—only listen to that! Did ye ever hear the like o' that? What is't? Is't a musical snuff-box? or what is't? Has he gotten a wee fairy musical snuff-box, I ask you, Mr. Tickler, within the nose o' him? or what or wha is't that's playin that tune?

Tickler. It is indeed equally beautiful and mysterious.

Shepherd. I never heard "Auld Langsyne" played mair exactly in a' my life.

Tickler "List—O list! if ever thou didst thy dear father love!"

Shepherd (*going up on tip-toes to Mr. North, and putting his ear close to the gentleman's nose*). By all that's miraculous, he is *snoring* "*Auld Langsyne!*" The Eolian harp's naething to that—it canna play a regular tune—but there's no a sweeter, safter, mair pathetic wund instrument in being than his nose.

* *Staun*—stand. † *A hantle faster*—a good deal faster.

Tickler. I have often heard him, James, snore a few notes very sweetly, but never before a complete tune. With what powers the soul is endowed in dreams!

Shepherd. You may weel say that.—Harkee! he's snorin't wi' variations! I'm no a Christian if he hasna gotten into "Maggie Lauder." He's snorin a medley in his sleep!

[TICKLER *and the* SHEPHERD *listen entranced.*

Tickler. What a spirit-stirring snore is his "Erin-go-bragh!"

Shepherd. A' this is proof o' the immortality o' the sowl. Whisht—whisht! [NORTH *snores* "*God save the King.*" Ay—a loyal pawtriot even in the kingdom o' dreams! I wad rather hear that than Catalan in the King's Anthem. We maun never mention this, Mr. Tickler. The warld 'ill no believe't. The warld's no ripe yet for the belief o' sic a mystery.

Tickler. His nose, James, I think, is getting a little hoarse.

Shepherd. Less o' the tenor and mair o' the bass. He was a wee out o' tune there—and I suspeck his nose wants blawin. Hear till him noo—"Croppies, lie doun," I declare; and see how he is clutchin the crutch.

[NORTH *awakes, and for a moment like goshawk stares wild.*

North. Yes—I agree with you—there must be a dissolution.

Shepherd. A dissolution!

North. Yes—of Parliament. Let us have the sense of the people. I am an old Whig—a Whig of the 1688.

Tickler and Shepherd. Hurraw, hurraw, hurraw! Old North, old Eldon, and old Colchester for ever! Hurraw, hurraw, hurraw!

North. No. Old Eldon alone! Give me the Dolphin. No. The Ivy-Tower. No need of a glass. Let us, one after the other, put the Ivy-Tower to our mouth, and drink him in pure Glenlivet.

Shepherd. On the table!

[*The* SHEPHERD *and* TICKLER *offer to help* NORTH *to mount the table.*

North. Hands off, gentlemen! I scorn assistance. Look here!

[NORTH, *by a dexterous movement, swings himself off his crutch erect on the table, and gives a helping hand first to the* SHEPHERD *and then to* TICKLER.

Shepherd. That feat beats the snorin a' to sticks! Faith, Tickler, we maun sing sma'. In a' things he's our maister. Alloo me, sir, to gang doun for your chair?

North (*flinging his crutch to the roof*).—OLD ELDON!

[*Tremendous cheering amidst the breakage by the descending crutch.*

Bronte. Bow, wow, wow—wow, wow—wow, wow, wow.

(*Enter* PICARDY *and Tail in general consternation.*)

Shepherd. Luk at him noo, Picardy—luk at him noo!

Tickler. Firm on his pins as a pillar of the Parthenon!

Shepherd. Saw ye ever a pair o' strauchter, mair sinewy legs, noo that he leans the haill wecht o' his body on them? Ay, wi' that outstretched arm he stauns like a statute o Demosthenes, about to utter the first word o' ane o' his Philippics.

[BRONTE *leaps on the table, and stands by* NORTH'S *knee with a determined aspect.*

North. Take the time from Bronte—OLD COLCHESTER!

Bronte. Bow, wow—wow, wow—wow, wow, wow.

[*Loud acclamations.*

Shepherd. Come, let's dance a threesome reel.

North. Picardy—your fiddle.

[MR. AMBROSE *takes* "*Neil Gow*" *from the peg, and plays.*

Shepherd. Hadna we better clear decks—

North. No—James. In my youth I could dance the

ancient German sword-dance, as described by Tacitus. Sir David, remove the Dolphin. I care not a jot for the rest of the crystal.

[NORTH, TICKLER, *and the* SHEPHERD *thrid a threesome reel*—BRONTE *careering round the table in a Solo*—PICARDY'S *bow-hand in high condition.*

Shepherd. Set to me, sir, set to me—never mind Tickler. Oh! but you're matchless at the Heelan fling, sir!—Luk at him, Mr. Awmrose!

Ambrose. Yes, Mr. Hogg.

Shepherd. I'll match him against a' the Heelans—either in breeks or out o' them—luk, luk—see him cuttin!

[Mr. NORTH *motions to* PICARDY, *who stops playing, and with one bound leaps from the centre of the circular over the Ivy-Tower to the floor.* SHEPHERD *and* TICKLER, *in attempting to imitate the great original, fall on the floor, but recover their feet with considerable alacrity.*

North (resuming his chair). The Catholic Question is not carried yet, gentlemen. Should it be, let it be ours to defend the Constitution.

Shepherd. Speak awa, sir, till I recover my breath. I'm sair blawn. Hear Tickler's bellows.

Tickler (stretching his weary length on a sofa). Whew—whew—whew. [*Exit* PICARDY *with his Tail.*

XIX.

IN WHICH, AFTER SETTLING OTHELLO, NORTH FLOORS THE SHEPHERD.

SCENE I.—*The Snuggery. Time,—Eight o'clock. The Union Table, with Tea and Coffee Pots, and the O'Doherty China-set —Cold Round—Pies—Oysters—Rizzards—Pickled Salmon, &c., &c., &c. A How-towdie whirling before the fire over a large basin of mashed Potatoes. The Boiler on. A Bachelor's Kitchen on the small Oval. A Dumb Waiter at each end of the Union.*

NORTH *and* SHEPHERD.

Shepherd. This I ca' comfort, sir. Everything within oursel—nae need to ring a bell the leeve-lang night—nae openin o' cheepin, nae shuttin o' clashin doors—nae trampin o' waiters across the carpet wi' creakin shoon—or stumblin, clumsy coofs, to the great spillin o' gravy—but a' things, eatable and uneatable, either hushed into a cozy calm, or—

North. Now light, James, the lamp of the Bachelor's Kitchen with Tickler's card, and in a quarter of an hour, minus five minutes, you shall scent and see such steaks!

Shepherd. Only look at the towdie,* sir, how she swings sae granly roun' by my garters, after the fashion o' a planet. It's

* *Towdie* or *how-towdie*—a barn-door fowl.

a beautiful example o' centrifugal attraction. See till the fat dreep-dreepin intil the ashet o' mashed potawtoes, oilifying the crusted brown intil a mair delicious richness o' mixed vegetable and animal maitter! As she swings slowly twirlin roun', I really canna say, sir, for I dinna ken, whether baney back or fleshy breist be the maist temptin! Sappy baith!

North. Right, James—baste her—baste her—don't spare the flour. Nothing tells like the dredge-box.

Shepherd. You're a capital man-cook, sir. Let's pree't.

[SHEPHERD *tastes.*

North. Ay—I could have told you so. Rash man, to swallow liquid and solid fire! But no more spluttering. Cool your tongue with a caulker.

Shepherd. That lamp's no canny. It intensifies hetness until an atrocity aboon natur. Is the skin flyped aff my tongue, sir? [SHEPHERD *shows tongue.*

North. Let me put on my spectacles. A slight incipient inflammation, not worth mentioning.

Shepherd. I howp an incipient inflammation's no a dangerous sort?

North. Is that indeed the tongue, my dear James, that trills so sweetly and so simply those wild Doric strains? How deeply, darkly, beautifully red! Just like a rag of scarlet. No scurf—say rather no haze around the lambent light. A rod of fire—an arrow of flame. A tongue of ten thousand, prophesying an eagle or raven life.

Shepherd. I aye like, sir, to keep a gude tongue in my head, ever since I wrote the Chaldee Mannyscripp.

North. Humph!—No more infallible mark of a man of genius, James, than the shape of his tongue. It is uniformly long, so that he can shoot it out, with an easy grace, to the tip of his nose.

Shepherd. This way?

North. Precisely so. Fine all round the edge, from root to tip—underneath very veinous—surface in color near as may be to that of a crimson curtain shining in setting sunlight. But the tip—James—the tip—

Shepherd. Like that o' the serpent's that deceived Eve, sir—curlin up and doun like the musical leaf o' some magical tree—

North. It is a singular fact with regard to the tongue, that if you cut off the half of it, the proprietor of the contingent remainder can only mumble—but cut it off wholly, and he speaks fully better than before—

Shepherd. That's a hanged lee.

North. As true a word as ever I spoke, James.

Shepherd. Perhaps it may, sir, but it's a hanged lee, nevertheless.

North. Dish the steaks, my dear James, and I shall cut down the how-towdie.

[NORTH *and the* SHEPHERD *furnish up the Ambrosial tables, and sit down to serious devouring.*

North. Now, James, acknowledge it—don't you admire a miscellaneous meal?

Shepherd. I do. Breakfast, noony,* denner, four-hours,† and sooper, a' in ane. A material emblem o' that spiritual substance, *Blackwood's Magazine!* Can it possibly be, sir, that we are twa gluttons?

North. Gluttons we most assuredly are not; but each of us is a man of good appetite. What is gluttony?

Shepherd. Some mair stakes, sir?

North. Very few, my dear James, very few.

Shepherd. What's gluttony?

North. Some eggs?

Shepherd. Ae spoonfu'. What a layer she wad hae been!

* *Noony*—luncheon. † *Four-hours*—tea.

Oh but she's a prolific cretur, Mr. North, your how-towdie! It's necessary to kill heaps o' yearocks,* or the haill kintra wad be a-cackle frae John o' Groat's House to St. Michael's Mount.

North. Sometimes I eat merely as an amusement or pastime —sometimes for recreation of my animal spirits—sometimes on the philosophical principle of sustenance—sometimes for the mere sensual, but scarcely sinful, pleasure of eating, or, in common language, gormandizing—and occasionally, once a month or so, for all these several purposes united, as at this present blessed moment; so a few flakes, my dear Shepherd, of that Westmoreland ham—lay the knife on it, and its own weight will sink it down through the soft, sweet sappiness of fat and lean, undistinguishably blended as the colors of the rainbow, and out of all sight incomparably more beautiful.

Shepherd. As for me, I care nae mair about what I eat than I do what kind o' bed I sleep upon, sir. I hate onything stinkin or mooldy at board—or onything damp or musty in bed. But let the vivres be but fresh and wholesome—and if it's but scones and milk, I shut my een, say a grace, fa' to, and am thankful';—let the bed be dry, and whether saft or hard, feathers, hair, cauff, straw, or heather, I'm fast in ten minutes, and my sowl waverin awa like a butterflee until the land o' dreams.

North. Not a more abstemious man than old Kit North in his Majesty's dominions, on which the sun never sets. I have the most accommodating of palates.

Shepherd. Yes—it's an universal genius. I ken naething like it, sir, but your stammack.—" Sure such a pair were never seen!" Had ye never the colic?

North. Never, James, never. I confess that I have been

* *Yearocks*—chickens.

guilty of many crimes, but never of a capital crime,—never of colic.

Shepherd. There's muckle confusion o' ideas in the brains o' the blockheads who accuse us o' gluttony, Mr. North. Gluttony may be defined "an immoral and unintellectual abandonment o' the sowl o' man to his gustative natur." I defy a brute animal to be a glutton. A swine's no a glutton. Nae cretur but man can be a glutton. A' the rest are prevented by the definition.

North. Sensuality is the most shocking of all sins, and its name is Legion.

Shepherd. Ay, there may be as muckle gluttony on sowens as on turtle-soup. A ploughman may be as greedy and as gutsy as an alderman. The sin lies not in the sense, but in the sowl. Sir—a red herring?

North. Thank ye, James.

Shepherd. Are you drinkin coffee?—Let me toast you a shave o' bread, and butter it for you on baith sides, sir?

[*The* SHEPHERD *kneels on the Tiger, and stretches out the Trident to Vulcan.*

North. There has been much planting of trees lately in the Forest, James?

Shepherd. To my taste, to tell the truth, rather ower muckle —especially o' nurses.*

North. Nurses!—wet or dry nurses, James?

Shepherd. Baith. Larches and Scotch firs; or you can ca' them schoolmasters, that teach the young idea how to shoot. But thinnins in the Forest never can pay, I suspeck; and except on bleeky knowes, the hardwood wad grow better, in my opinion, left to themsels, without either nurses or schoolmasters. The nurses are apt to overlay their weans, and the

*** Trees of the hardier breed, put in at intervals to shelter the more tender plants as they grow.**

schoolmasters to forget, or, what's waur, to flog their pupils; and thus the rising is a stunted generation.

North. Forty-five years ago, my dear James, when you were too young to remember much, I loved the Forest for its solitary single trees, ancient yew or sycamore, black in the distance, but when near how gloriously green! Tall, delicately-feathered ash, whose limbs were still visible in latest summer's leafiness—birch, in early spring, weeping and whispering in its pensive happiness by the perpetual din of its own waterfall—oak, yellow in the suns of June—

Shepherd.—

> "The grace of forest charms decayed,
> And pastoral melancholy!"

North. What lovely lines! Who writes like Wordsworth?

Shepherd. Tuts! Me ower young to remember muckle fourty-five years ago! You're speakin havers. I was then twal—and I remember everything I ever heard or saw sin' I was three year auld. I recolleck the mornin I was pitten intil breeks as distinckly as if it were this verra day.

North. All linnets have died, James—that race of loveliest lilters is extinct.

Shepherd. No thae. Broom and bracken are tenanted by the glad, meek creturs still,—but the chords o' music in our hearts are sair unstrung—the harp o' our heart has lost its melody. But come out to the Forest, my dear, my honored sir, and fear not then, when we twa are walking thegither without speakin among the hills, you

> "Will feel the airs that from them blow,
> A momentary bliss bestow;"

and the wild, uncertain, waverin music o' the Eolian harp, that natur plays upon in the solitude, will again echo far, far awa amang the recesses o' your heart, and the lintie will sing as sweetly as ever frae amang the blossoms o' the milk-white thorn. Or if you canna be brocht to feel sae, you'll hae but to look in my wee Jamie's face, and his glistening een will convince you that Scotia's nightingale still singeth as sweetly as of yore!—But let us sit in to the fire, sir.

North. Thank you, Shepherd—thank you, James.

Shepherd (wheeling his father's chair to the ingle corner, and singing the while)—

"THERE'S CHRISTOPHER NORTH THAT WONS IN YON GLEN,
HE'S THE KING O' GUDE FALLOWS, AND WALE * O' AULD MEN!"

North. James, I will trouble you for the red herrings.

Shepherd. There. Mr. North, I coud write twunty vollumms about the weather. Wad they sell?

North. I fear they might be deficient in incident.

Shepherd. Naething I write's ever deficient in incident. Between us three, what think ye o' my *Shepherd's Calendar*?

North. Admirable, my dear James—admirable. To tell you the truth, I never read it in the Magazine; but I was told the papers were universally liked there—and now, as Vols., they are beyond—above—all praise.

Shepherd. But wull you say that in black and white in the Magazine? What's the use o' rousin a body to their face, and abusin them ahint their backs? Setting them upon a pedestal in private, and in public layin them a' their length on the floor? You're jealous o' me, sir, that's the real truth, —and you wush that I was dead.

North. Pardon me, James, I merely wish that you never had been born.

Shepherd. That's far mair wicked. Oh! but jealousy and envy's twa delusive passions, and they pu' you doun frae your aerial altitude, sir, like twa ravens ruggin an eagle frae the sky.

North. From literary jealousy, James, even of you, my

* *Wale*—best.

soul is free as the stone-shaded well in your garden from the ditch-water that flows around it on a rainy day. I but flirt with the Muses, and when they are faithless, I whistle the haggards down the wind, and puff all care away with a cigar. But I have felt *the* jealousy, James, and of all passions it alone springs from seed wafted into the human heart from the Upas Tree of Hell.

Shepherd. Wheesht! Wheesht!

North. Shakespeare has but feebly painted that passion in Othello. A complete failure. I never was married, that I recollect—neither am I a black man—therefore I do not pretend to be a judge of Othello's conduct and character. But, in the first place, Shakespeare ought to have been above taking an anomalous case of jealousy. How could a black husband escape being jealous of a white wife? There was a cause of jealousy given in his very face.

Shepherd. Eh? What? What? Eh? Faith there's something in that observation.

North. Besides, had Desdemona lived, she would have produced a mulatto. Could she have seen their "visages in their minds?" Othello and she going to church with a brood of tawnies——

Shepherd. I dinna like to hear you speakin that way. Dinna profane poetry.

North. Let not poetry profane nature. I am serious, James. That which in real life would be fulsome, cannot breathe sweetly in fiction; for fiction is still a reflection of truth, and truth is sacred.

Shepherd. I agree wi' you sae far, that the Passion o' Jealousy in Luve can only be painted wi' perfect natur in a man that stands towards a woman in a perfectly natural relation. Otherwise the picture may be well painted, but it is still but a picture of a particular and singular exhibition o' the passion

—in short, as you say, o' an anomaly. I like a word I dinna weel understan'.

North. Mr. Wordsworth calls Desdemona "the gentle lady married to the Moor," and the line has been often quoted and admired. It simply asserts two facts,—that she was a gentle lady, and that she was married to the Moor. What then?

Shepherd. I forgie her—I pity her—but I can wi' difficulty respeck her—I confess. It was a curious kind o' hankerin after an opposite color.

North. Change the character and condition of the parties —can you imagine a white hero falling in love with a black heroine in a country where there were plenty of white women? Marrying and murdering her in an agony of rage and love?

Shepherd. I can only answer for mysel—I never could bring mysel to marry a Blackamoor.

North. Yet they are often sweet, gentle, affectionate, meek, mild, humble, and devoted creatures—Desdemonas.

Shepherd. But men and women, sir, I verily believe, are different in mony things respecting the passion o' luve. I've kent bonny, young, bloomin lassies fa' in luve wi' auld, wizened, disgustin fallows,—I hae indeed, sir. It was their fancy. But I never heard tell o' a young, handsome, healthy chiel gettin impassioned on an auld, wrunkled, skranky hag, without a tocher. Now, sir, Othello was—

North. Well—well—let it pass—

Shepherd. Ay—that's the way o' you—the instant you begin to see the argument gaun against you, you turn the conversation, either by main force, or by a quirk or a sophism, and sae escape frae the net that was about to be flung ower you, and like a bird, awa up into the air—or invisible ower the edge of the horizon.

North. Well, then, James, what say you to Iago?

Shepherd. What about him?

North. Is his character in nature?

Shepherd. I dinna ken. But what for no?

North. What was his motive? Pure love of mischief?

Shepherd. Aiblins.*

North. Pride in power and in skill to work mischief?

Shepherd. Aiblins.

North. Did he hate the Moor even to the death?

Shepherd. Aiblins.

North. Did he resolve to work his ruin, let the consequences to himself be what they might?

Shepherd. It would seem sae.

North. Did he know that his own ruin—his own death—must follow the success of this scheme?

Shepherd. Hoo can I tell that?

North. Was he blinded utterly to such result by his wickedness directed against Othello?

Shepherd. Perhaps he was. Hoo can I tell?

North. Or did he foresee his own doom—and still go on unappalled?

Shepherd. It micht be sae, for onything I ken to the contrary. He was ower cool and calculatin to be blinded.

North. Is he, then, an intelligible or an unintelligible character?

Shepherd. An unintelligible.

North. Therefore not a natural character. I say, James, that his conduct from first to last cannot be accounted for by any view that can be taken of his character. The whole is a riddle—of which Shakespeare has not given the solution. Now, all human nature is full of riddles; but it is the business of dramatic poets to solve them—and this one Shakespeare has left unsolved. But having himself proposed it,

* *Aiblins*—perhaps.

he was bound either to have solved it, or to have set such a riddle as the wit of man could have solved in two centuries. Therefore——

Shepherd. "Othello" is a bad play?

North. Not bad, but not good—that is, not greatly good—not in the first order of harmonious and mysterious creations—not a work worthy of Shakespeare.

Shepherd. Confound me if I can tell whether you're speakin sense or nonsense—truth or havers; or whether you be serious, or only playin aff upon me some o' your Mephistophiles tricks. I aften think you're an evil speerit in disguise, and that your greatest delight is in confounding truth and falsehood . . . Wheesht! I hear a rustlin in the letter-box.

North. John will have brought up my newspapers from the Lodge, expecting that I am not to be at home to dinner.

Shepherd. Denner! it's near the dawin!

[*The* SHEPHERD *opens the letter-box in the door, and lays down nearly a dozen newspapers on the table.*

North. Ay, there they are, the *Herald*, the *Morning Post*, the *Morning Journal*, the *Courier*, the *Globe*, the *Standard*, and "the Rest." Let me take a look into the *Standard*, as able, argumentative, and eloquent a paper as ever supported civil and religious liberty—that is, Protestantism in Church and State.—No disparagement to its staunch brother, the *Morning Journal*, or its excellent cousin, the *Morning Post*. Two strong, steady, well-bred wheelers—and a Leader that shows blood at all points—and covers his ground like the Phenomenon.—No superior set-out to an—Unicorn.

[NORTH *unfolds the Standard.*

Shepherd. I never read prent after twal. And as for newspapers, I carena if they should be a month auld. It's pitifu' to see some folk—nae fules neither—unhappy if their paper misses comin ony nicht by the post. For my ain pairt, I like best to receive a great heap o' them a' at ance in a parshel by the carrier. Ony news, North?

North. Eh?

Shepherd. Ony news? Are you deaf? or only absent?

North. Eh?

Shepherd. There's mainners—the mainners o' a gentleman —o' the auld schule too.—Ony news?

North. Hem—hem *—

Shepherd. His mind's weaken'd. Millions o' reasonable creatures at this hour perhaps—na—no at this hour—but a' this evenin—readin newspapers! And that's the philosophy o' human life! London sendin out, as frae a great reservoir, rivers o' reports, spates o' speculations, to inundate, to droon, to deluge the haill island! I hear the torrents roarin, but the soun' fa's on my ear without stunnin my heart. There comes a drought, and they are a' dry. Catholic Emancipation! Stern shades of the old Covenanters, methinks I hear your voices on the moors and the mountains! But weep not, wail not—though a black cloud seems to be hanging over all the land! Still will the daisy, "wee modest crimson-tipped flower," bloom sweetly on the greensward that of yore was reddened wi' your patriot, your martyr blood. Still will the foxglove, as the silent ground-bee bends doun the lovely hanging bells, shake the pure tears of heaven over your hallowed graves! Though annual fires run along the bonny bloomin heather, yet the shepherds ne'er miss the balm and brightness still left at mornin to meet them on the solitary hills. The sound of Psalms rises not now, as they sublimely did in those troubled times, from a tabernacle not built with hands, whose side-walls were the rocks and cliffs, its floor the spacious sward, and its roof the eternal heavens. But

* It was Professor Wilson's habit, when great events were astir, to be much absorbed in the newspaper he happened to be reading.

from beneath many a lowly roof of house, and hut, and hovel, and shielin, and sylvan cosy bield, ascend the humble holy orisons of poor and happy men, who, when comes the hour of sickness or of death, desire no other pillow for their swimming brain than that Bible, which to them is the Book of everlasting life, even as the Sun is the Orb of the transitory day. And to maintain that faith is now, alas! bigotry and superstition!—But where am I? In the silence I thocht it was the Sabbath—and that I was in the Forest. High thochts and pure feelings can never come amiss—either in place or in time. Folk that hae been prayin in a kirk may lauch, withouten blame, when they hae left the kirkyard Silly thochts maun never be allowed to steal in amang sacred anes—but there never can be any harm in sacred thochts stealing in amang silly anes. A bit bird singin by itsel in the wilderness has sometimes made me amaist greet,* in a mysterious melancholy that seemed wafted towards me on the solitary strain, frae regions ayont the grave. But it flitted awa into silence, and in twa or three minutes I was singin ane o' my ain cheerful—nay, funny sangs.—Mr. North, I say, will ye never hae dune readin at that *Stannard?* It's a capital paper—I ken that—nane better—na, nane sae gude, for it's faithful and fearless, and cuts like a twa-handed twa-edged swurd. Mr. North, I say, I'll begin to get real angry if you'll no speak. O man! but that's desperate bad mainners to keep glowering like a gawpus on a newspaper, at what was meant to be a crick-crack atween twa auld freens. Fling't doun. I'm sayin, sir, fling't doun. Oh but you're ugly the noo—and what's waur, there's nae meanin in your face. You're a puir, auld, ugly, stupid, vulgar, disagreeable, and dishonest-looking fallow, and a'm baith sorry and ashamed that I sud be sittin in sic company.

* *Greet*—weep.

Fling doun the *Stannard*—if you dinna, it 'ill be waur for you, for you've raised my corruption. Flesh and bluid can bear this treatment nae langer. I'll gie just ae mair warnin. Fling doun the *Stannard*. Na, you wunna—won't you? Weel, tak that.

[*The* SHEPHERD *throws a glass of toddy in* Mr. NORTH'S *face.*

North. Ha! What the deuce is that? My cup has jumped out of my hand and spurted the Glenlivet-coffee into its master's countenance. James, lend me your pocket-handkerchief. [*Relapses into the Standard.*

Shepherd. Fling doun the *Stannard*—or I'll gang mad. Neist time I'll shy the jug at him—for if it's impossible to insult, it may perhaps be possible to kill him. Fling doun the *Stannard.* You maddenin auld sinner, you wad be cheap o' death! Yet I maunna kill him—I maunna kill him—for I micht be hanged.

North. Nobly said, Sadler*—nobly said! I have long known your great talents, and your great eloquence too, but I hardly hoped for such a display of both as this.—Hear!—hear!—hear!—There—my trusty fere—you have indeed clapped the saddle on the right horse.

Shepherd. Tak that.

[*Flings another glass of toddy in* Mr. NORTH'S *face.*

North. (*starting up*), Fire and fury!

Shepherd. Butter and brimstone! How daured you to treat me—

North. This outrage must not pass unpunished. Hogg, I shall give you a sound thrashing.

* Michael Thomas Sadler, M. P., 1829, for Newark-upon-Trent, was born in 1780, and died in 1835. The amelioration of the condition of the factory children of England, and of the Irish poor, was due very much to his exertions. His principal works were—*Ireland, its Evils and their Remedies,*—and *The Law of Population,* written in opposition to Malthus.

[Mr. NORTH *advances toward the* SHEPHERD *in an offensive attitude. The* SHEPHERD *seizes the poker in one hand, and a chair in the other.*

Shepherd. Haud aff, sir,—haud aff—or I'll brain you. Dinna pick a quarrel wi' me. I've dune a' I could to prevent it; but the provocation I received was past a' endurance. Haud aff, sir,—haud aff.

North, Coward! coward! coward!

Shepherd. Flyte* awa, sir—flyte awa;—but haud aff, or I'll fell you.

North (resuming his seat). I am unwilling to hurt you, James, on account of those at Mount Benger; but lay down the poker—and lay down the chair

Shepherd. Na—na—na. Unless you first swear on the Bible that you'll tak nae unfair advantage.

North. Let my word suffice—I won't. Now go to that press—and you will see a pair of gloves. Bring them to me— [*The* SHEPHERD *fetches the gloves.*

Shepherd. Ca' you thae gloves?

North. (stripping and putting on the gloves). Now, sir, use your fists as you best may—and in five minutes I shall take the conceit out of you—

Shepherd (peeling to the sark). I'll sune gie you a bluidy nose.

[*The combatants shake hands and put themselves into attitude.*

North. Take care of your eyes.

[SHEPHERD *elevates his guard—and* NORTH *delivers a desperate right-handed lunge on his kidneys.*

Shepherd. That's no fair, ye auld blackguard.

North. Well, then, is that?

[SHEPHERD *receives two left-handed facers, which seem to*

* *Flyte*—rail.

muddle his knowledge-box. He bores in wildly on the old man.

Shepherd. Whew—whew—whew. Fu—fu—fu. What's that? What's that? [*The* SHEPHERD *receives pepper.*

North. Hit straight, James. So—so—so—so—so.

Shepherd. That's foul play. There's mair nor ane o' you. Wha's that joinin in? Let me alane—and I'll sune finish him—

[Mr. NORTH, *who has gradually retreated into a corner of the snuggery, gathers himself up for mischief, and as the* SHEPHERD *rushes in to close, delivers a stinger under* JAMES'S *ear, that floors him like a shot.* Mr. NORTH *then comes out, as actively as a bird on the bough of a tree.*

North. I find I have a hit in me yet. A touch on the jugular always tells tales. Hollo! hollo! My dear James! Deaf as a house.

[Mr. NORTH *takes off the gloves—fetches a tumbler of the jug—and kneeling tenderly down by the* SHEPHERD, *bathes his temples.* JAMES *opens his eyes, and stares wildly around.*

Shepherd. Is that you, Gudefallow? Hae I had a fa' aff a horse, or out o' the gig?

North. My dear maister—out o' the gig. The young horse took fricht at a tup loupin* over the wa', and set aff like lichtnin. You sudna hae louped out—you sudna hae louped out.

Shepherd. Whare's the gig?

North. Never mind, maister.

Shepherd. I say, whare's the gig?

North. In the Loch—

Shepherd. And the horse?

* *Loupin*—leaping.

North. In the Loch too.

Shepherd. Droon'd?

North. Not yet—if you look up, you'll see him soomin across wi' the gig.

Shepherd (*fixing his eyes on vacancy*). Ay—sure aneuch—yonner he goes!

North. Yon proves his breed. He's descended from the water-horse.

Shepherd. I'm verra faint. I wush I had some whusky—

North. Here, maister—here—

[*The* SHEPHERD *drains the tumbler, and revives*

Shepherd. Am I in the open air, or in a hoose; I howp a hoose—or there maun be a concussion o' the brain, for I seem to see chairs and tables.

North. Yes, maister—you have been removed in a blanket by eight men to Mount Benger.

Shepherd. Is baith my legs brok?

North. Dinna ask—dinna ask. We've sent an express to Embro' for Liston.* They say that when he sets broken legs they're stronger than ever.

Shepherd. He's a wonderfu' operawtor—but I can scarcely believe that. Oh! am I to be for life a lameter!† It's a judgment on me for writin the Chaldee!‡

North. I canna thole, maister, to see you greetin—

Shepherd. Mercifu' powers! but your face is changed intil that o' an auld man!—Was Mr. North frae Embro' here the noo?

North. I am indeed that unhappy old man. But 'tis all

* Robert Liston, one of the most eminent surgeons of the day, first in Edinburgh, and afterwards in London. He died in 1847.

† *Lameter*—a cripple.

‡ Messrs. Pringle and Cleghorn—both of whom were excessively lame—were the editors of the first six numbers of *Blackwood's Magazine*. In the famous Chaldee MS. they are satirically described by the Shepherd.

but a dream, my dear James—'tis all but a dream! What means all this wild disjointed talk of yours about gigs and horses, and a horse and a gig swimming over St. Marys Loch? Here we are, my beloved friend, in Edinburgh—in Picardy—at the Noctes Ambrosianæ—at high-jinks, my James, after a bout with the mufflers and the naked mawleys.

Shepherd. I dreamed that I had knocked you down, sir.—Was that the case?

North. It was indeed, James. But I am not angry with you. You did not mean to hit so hard. You generously ran in to keep me from falling, and by some strange sudden twist you happened to fall undermost, and to save me, sacrificed yourself.—'Twas a severe stun.

Shepherd. The haill wecht o' mist has rolled itsel up into cluds on the mountain-taps, and all the scenery aneath lies fresh and green, wi' every kent house and tree. But I howp you're no sair hurt yoursel—let me help you up—

[*The* SHEPHERD *assists* MR. NORTH, *who has been sitting on the floor, like the Shah, to recover his pins—and the two walk arm-in-arm to their respective chairs.*

North. I am sorely shaken, James. An account of our Set-to, our Turn-up, James, ought to be sent to that admirable sporting paper, *Bell's Life in London.*

Shepherd. Let it, my dear sir, be a lesson to you the langest day you leeve, never to pick a quarrel, or even to undertak ony half-and-half sort o' horse-play wi' a younger and a stronger man than yoursel. Sir, if I hadna been sae weel up to the business, that fa' might hae been your last. As for thae nasty gloves, I never wush to see their faces again a' the days o' my life. What's that chappin?

North. Probably Picardy. See, the door's locked inside.

[*The* SHEPHERD *unlocks and opens the door.*

Shepherd. What mob's this?

North. Show in the Democracy.

(*Enter* PICARDY, Mon. CADET, *the Manciple, the Clerk of the Pipe*, KING PEPIN, SIR DAVID GAM, TAPPYTOORIE, *and the "Rest."*)

Ambrose (*while* OMNES *hold up their hands*). Dear me! dear me!

Shepherd. What are you a' glowerin at me for, ye fules?

North. Tappy, bring me a looking-glass. [*Exit* TAPPY, *volans.*

Shepherd. I say, ye fules, what are ye glowerin at me in that gate for? Do you see horns on my head?

(*Re-enter* TAPPY, *with a copy of the Mirror.*)

North. Take a glance, my dear James, at the Magic Mirror.

[*The* SHEPHERD *looks in, and recoils to the sideboard.*

Shepherd. What'n a face! What'n a pair o' black, blue, green, yellow een!

North. We must apply leeches. Mr. Ambrose, bring in a few bottles of leeches, and some raw veal-steaks.

Shepherd. Aff wi' you—aff wi' you—the haill tot o' you.

[*Exit* PICARDY *with his Tail.*

North. Come to my arms, my incomparable Shepherd, and let us hob and nob, to "Gude nicht and joy be wi' us a'," in a caulker of Millbank; and let us, during the "wullie-waught," think of him whose worthy name it bears—

Shepherd. As gude a chiel's in Christendie!—Oh, my ever honored sir, what wad the warld say, if she kent the concludin proceedins o' this nicht? That we were twa auld fules!

North. At times, James—

"'Tis folly to be wise."

Shepherd. As auld Crow, the Oxford orator, says at the end o' his bonny descriptive poem, *Lewesdon Hill*:—

"To-morrow for severer thought—but now
To breakfast."

North. To bed—you mean—

Shepherd. No—to breakfast. It's mornin. The East is brichtenin.—Look over awaukenin Leith—and, lo! white sails glidin ower the dim blue sea!

North. Let us each take a cold bath.

[Mr. North *and* Shepherd *disappear.*

XX.

IN WHICH, DURING THE GREAT STORM, THE SNUGGERY WINDOW IS BLOWN IN, AND THE SHEPHERD SUFFERS

The Snuggery.—Time, seven o'clock.

NORTH *and* SHEPHERD.

Shepherd. Oh, sir! but there's something delightfu' in coal-fire glimmerin and gloomin, breaking out every noo and then into a flickering bleeze; and whenever ane uses the poker, into a sudden illumination, vivifyin the pictured paper on the wa's, and settin a' the range o' looking-glasses a-low, like sae mony beacons kindled on the taps o' hills, burnin awa to ane anither ower a' the kintra-side, on the birthday nicht o' the Duke o' Buccleuch, or that o' his marriage wi' that fair English Leddy *—God bless them baith, and send them in gude time a circle o' bauld sons and bonny dochters, to uphaud the stately and noble house o' the King o' the Border!

North. Amen. James—a caulker.

Shepherd. That speerit's far aboon proof. There's little difference atween awka veety an' awka fortis.† Ay, ma man, that gars your een water. Dicht them wi' the doylez, and then tak a mouthfu' out o' the jug to moderate the intensity

* In 1829 the Duke of Buccleuch married Lady Charlotte Anne Thynne, daughter of the Marquess of Bath.

† *Aqua vitæ* and *aqua fortis*.

o' the pure cretur. Haud, haud! it's no sma' yill, but strong toddy, sir. (*Aside*)—The body 'ill be fou afore aught o'clock.

North. This jug, James, is rather wishy-washy; confound me if I don't suspect it is milk and water!

Shepherd. Plowp in some speerit. Let me try't. It 'ill do noo, sir. That's capital boilin water, and tholes double its ain wecht o' cauld Glenlivet. Let's dook in * the thermometer. Up, you see, to twa hunder and twunty, just the proper toddy pitch. It's mirawculous!

North. What sort of a night out of doors, James?

Shepherd. A fine night, sir, and like the season. The wund's due east, and I'se warrant the ships at anchor in the Roads are a' rather coggly, wi' their nebs doun the Firth, like sae mony rocking-horses. On turnin the corner o' Picardy, a blash o' sleet like a verra snawba' amaist knocked my head aff my shouthers; and as for my hat, if it meet with nae interruption, it maun be weel on to West-Craigs by this time, for it flew aff in a whurlwund. Ye canna see the sleet for the haur;† the ghastly lamps are amaist entirely overpoored by the whustlin darkness; and as for moon and stars, they're a' dead and buried, and we never mair may wutness their resurrection. Auld-women frae chimley-taps are clytin‡ wi' a crash into every area, and the deevil's tirlin § the kirks out-ower a' the Synods o' Scotland. Whisht! Is that thunner?

North. I fear scarcely—but the roar in the vent is good, James, and tells of tempest. Would to heaven I were at sea!

Shepherd. That's impious. Yet you micht aiblins be safe aneuch in a bit cockle-shell o' an open boat—for some folk are born no to be drooned—

North. There goes another old-woman! ‖

* *Dook in*—plunge in.

† *Haur*—flying mist.

‡ *Clytin*—falling.

§ *Tirlin*—unroofing.

‖ *Old-woman*—chimney-can

Shepherd. Oh, but the Yarrow wull be a' ae red roar the noo, frae the Loch to the Ettrick. Yet wee Jamie's soun' asleep in his crib by this time, and dreamin, it may be, o' paiddlin amang the mennows in the silver sandbanks o' sim mer, whare the glassy stream is nae higher than his knee; or o' chasin amang the broom the young linties sent by the sunshine, afore their wings are weel feathered, frae their mossy cradle in the brier-bush, and able to flee just weel aneuch to wile awa on and on, after their chirpin flutter, my dear wee canty callant, chasin first ane and then anither, on wings just like their ain, the wings o' joy, love, and hope; fauldin them, in a disappointment free frae ony taint o' bitterness, when a' the burdies hae disappeared, and his een, as he sits doun on the knowe, fix themselves wi' a new pleasure on the bonny bands o' gowans croodin round his feet

North. A bumper, my dear Shepherd, to Mount Benger.

Shepherd. Thank ye, sir, thank ye. Oh! my dear sir, but ye hae a gude heart, sound at the core as an apple on the sunny south side o' the tree—and ruddy as an apple, sir, is your cheek—

North. Yes, James, a life of temperance preserves—

Shepherd. Help yoursel, and put ower the jug. There's twunty gude years o' wear and tear in you yet, Mr. North—but what for wunna ye marry? Dinna be frichtened—it's naething ava—and it aften grieves my heart to think o' you lyin your lane in that state bed, which canna be less than seven feet wide, when the General's widow—

North. I have long wished for an opportunity of confiding to you a secret which—

Shepherd. A sacret! Tell nae sacret to me—for I never a' my life could sleep wi' a sacret in my head, ony mair than wi' the lug-ache. But if you're merely gaun to tell me that ye hae screwed up your courage at last to marry her, say't, do't and be dune wi't, for she's a comely and a cosy cretur you Mrs. Gentle, and it 'ill do my een gude to see you marchin up wi' her, haun in haun, to the Hymeneal Altar.

North. On Christmas day, my dear James, we shall be one spirit.

Shepherd. And ae flesh. Hurraw! hurraw! hurraw! Gie's your haun on that, my auld hearty! What a gran' echo's in yon corner o' the roof! hear till't smackin loofs after us, as if Cupid himsel were in the cornice!

North. You must write our Epithalamium.

Shepherd. That I wull, wi' a' my birr, and sae wull Delta, and sae wull the Doctor,* and sae, I'm sure, wull Mr. Wudsworth; and I can answer for Sir Walter—

North. Who has kindly promised to give away the Bride.

Shepherd. I could greet to think that I canna be the Best Man.†

North. Tickler has—

Shepherd. Capital—capital! I see him—look, there he is—wi' his speck-and-span-new sky-blue coat wi' siller buttons, snaw-white waistcoat wi' gracefu' flaps, licht casimer knee-breeks wi' lang ties, flesh-colored silk stockings wi' flowered gushets, pumps brushed up to a perfeck polish a' roun', the buckles crystal-set, a dash o' pouther in his hair, een bricht as diamonds, the face o' him like the verra sun, chin shaven smooth as satin, mouth—saw ye ever sic teeth in a man's head at his time o' life?—mantlin wi' jocund benisons, and the haill Feegur o' the incomparable Fallow, frae tap to tae, sax feet fowre inches and a hauf gude measure, instinck wi' condolence and congratulation, as if at times he were almost believing Buchanan Lodge was Southside—that he was changin places wi' you, in a sweet sort o' jookery-pawkery

* Doctor Maginn. † The bridegroom's man.

—that he was Christopher North, and Mrs. Gentle on the verra brink o' becoming Mrs. Tickler!

North. James, you make me jealous.

Shepherd. For heaven's sake, sir, dinna split on that rock. Remember Othello, and hoo he smothered his wife wi' the bowster.

North. The night improves, and must be almost at its best. That is a first-rate howl! Well done—hail. I pity the poor hot-houses. The stones cannot be less than sugar-almonds.

Shepherd. Shoogger-awmons! They're like guse eggs. If the lozens* werena pawtent plate, lang ere noo they would hae a' flown into flinders. But they're ball-proof. They wadna break though you were to let aff a pistol.

North. What, James, is your favorite weather?

Shepherd. A clear, hard, black frost. Sky without a clud—sun bright, but almost cold—earth firm aneath your feet as a rock—trees silent, but not asleep, wi' their budded branches—ice-edged rivers, amaist mute and motionless, yet wimplin a wee, and murmuring dozingly as in a dream—the air or atmosphere sae rarified by the mysterious alchemy o' that wonderfu' Wuzzard Wunter, that when ye draw in your breath, ye're no sensible o' ha'in ony lungs.

The small oriel window of the Snuggery is blown in with a tremendous crash. NORTH *and the* SHEPHERD *prostrated among the ruins.*

North. Are you among the survivors, James—wounded or dead? (*An awful pause.*) Alas! alas! who will write my Epithalamium! And must I live to see the day on which, O gentle Shepherd, these withered hands of mine must falter thy Epicedia!

Shepherd. Oh, tell me, sir, if the toddy-jug has been upset

* *Lozens*—panes of glass, lozenge-shaped.

in this catastrophe, or the Tower of Babel and a' the speerits?

North (*supporting himself on his elbow, and eying the festal board*). Jug and Tower are both miraculously preserved amidst the ruins!

Shepherd. Then am I a dead man, and lyin in a pool o'bluid. Oh! dear me! Oh! dear me! a bit broken lozen has cut my jugular!

North. Don't yet give yourself up, my dear, dear Shepherd, for a dead man. Ay—here's my crutch—I shall be on my legs presently—surely they cannot both be broken; and if I can but get at my tape-garter, I do not despair of being able to tie up the carotid.

Shepherd. Pu' the bell for a needle and thread.—What's this?—I'm fentin!

[*The* SHEPHERD *faints away; and* NORTH *having recovered his feet, and rung the bell violently, enter* MR. AMBROSE, MON. CADET, SIR DAVID GAM, KING PEPIN, *and* TAPPYTOORIE, *cum multis aliis.*

North. Away for Liston*—one and all of you, away like lightning for Liston! You alone, Ambrose, support Mr. Hogg in this, I fear, mortal swoon. Don't take him by the feet, Ambrose, but lift up his head, and support it on your knee.

[MR. AMBROSE, *greatly flurried, but with much tenderness obeys the mandate.*

Shepherd (*opening his eyes*). Are you come hither, too, Awmrose? 'Tis a dreadfu' place. What a fire! But let us speak low, or Clootie † 'ill hear us. Is he ben the house?—Oh! Mr. North, pity me the day! are you here too, and has a' our daffin come to this at last?

North. Where, my dear James, do you think you are? In the Hotel.

* See *ante*, p. 298, note 1.

† *Clootie*—a Scotch name for the devil.

Shepherd. Ay, ay, Hothell indeed! I swarfed awa in a bluidy swoon, and hae awaukened in a fearfu' eternity. Noctes Ambrosianæ indeed! And whare, oh! whare is that puir, short-haund, harmless body, Gurney? Hae we pu'd him doun wi' us to the bottomless pit?

North. Mr. Ambrose, let me support his head, while you bring the Tower of Babel.

[Mr. AMBROSE *brings the Tower of Babel, and applies the battlements to the* SHEPHERD'S *lips.*

Shepherd. Whusky here! I daurna taste it, for it can be naething but melted sulphur. Yet, let me just pree't. It has a maist unearthly similitude to Glenlivet. Oh! Mr. North—Mr. North—tak aff thae horns frae your head, for they're awfu' fearsome. Hae you gotten a tail too? And are you, or are you not, answer me that single question, an Imp o' Darkness?

North. Bear a hand, Mr. Ambrose, and give Mr. Hogg London-carries to his chair.

[NORTH *and* AMBROSE *mutually cross wrists, and bear the* SHEPHERD *to his seat.*

Shepherd. Hoo the wund sughs through the lozenless wundow, awaukenin into tenfold fury the Blast-Furnace.

(*Re-enter* Mon. CADET, KING PEKIN, SIR DAVID GAM, *and* TAPPYTOORIE.)

Mon. Cadet. Mr. Liston has left town to attend the Perth Breakneck, which has had an overturn on Queensferry Hill—and 'tis said many legs and heads are fractured.

Tappytoorie. He'll no be back afore midnicht.

Ambrose (*chastising Tappy*). How dare you speak, sir?

North. Most unlucky that the capsize had not been delayed for ten minutes. How do you feel now, James?

Shepherd. Feel? I never was better in my life. But what's the matter wi' your nose, sir? About half-way doun the middle, it has taken a turn at right angles towards your left lug. Ane o' the splinter-bars o' the window has bashed it frae the line o' propriety, and you're a fricht for life. Only look at him, gentlemen; saw ye ever siccan a pheesiognomy?

North. Tarriers, begone! [*Exeunt Omnes.*

Shepherd. We're twa daft fules—that's sure aneuch—and did the public ken o' this, the idiwuts wad cry out, "Buffoonery—buffoonery!"—But we can never sit here without lozens.

Re-enter Mr. AMBROSE *and a Carpenter, with a new Window-frame.*)

North. Let me adjust the pulleys. It fits to a hair. Well done, deacon. Expedition's the soul of business—off with your caulk r.—Thank you—Good-night.

[Mr. AMBROSE *and Carpenter, exeunt with the debris.*]

Shepherd. Joking and jinks apart, Mr. North, there's bluid on your nose. Let me pit a bit o' black stickin-plaister on't. There—Mrs. Gentle wad think you unco killin wi' that beauty spot on your neb.

North. Hush.—Pray, James, do you believe in the Devil?

Shepherd. Just as firmly as I believe in you, sir. Yet, I confess, I never could see the sin in abusin the ne'erdoweel; whereas mony folk, no ower and aboon religious in ither respects, haud up their hauns and the whites o' their een whenever you satireeze Satan—and cry "Whisht, whisht!" My mind never yet has a' my days got rid o' ony early impression; and against baith reason and revelation, I canna think o' the Deevil even yet, without seein him wi' great big goggle fiery een, a mouth like a foumart-trap, the horns o' a Lancashire kyloe, and a tufted tail atween that o' a bill's, a lion's and a teegger's. Let me see him when I wull, sleepin or waukin, he's aye the verra leevin image o' a woodcut.

North. Mr. Southey, in some of his inimitable ballads, has turned him into such ridicule that he has laid his tail entirely aside, screwed off his horns, hid his hoofs in Wellingtons, and appeared, of late years, in shape and garb more worthy of the Prince of the Air.

Shepherd. Ay, Mr. Southey's a real wutty man, forbye being a great poet. But do you ken, for a' that, my hair stands on end o' its tinglin roots, and my skin amaist crawls aff my body, whenever, by a blink o' the storm-driven moon in a mirk nicht, I chance to forgather wi' auld Clootie, Hornie, and Tuft-tail, in the middle o' some wide moor amang hags, and peat-mosses, and quagmires, nae house within mony miles, and the uncertain weather-gleam, blackened by some auld woods, swingin and sughin to the wind as if hotchin wi' warlocks.

North. Poo—I should at once take the bull by the horns—or, seizing him by the tail, drive him with my crutch into the nearest loch.

Shepherd. It's easy speakin. But you see, he never appears to a man that's no frichtened aforehaun out o' his seven senses—and imagination is the greatest cooard on earth, breakin out into a cauld sweat, his heart loup-loupin, like a fish in a creel, and the retina o' his ee representin a' things, mair especially them that's ony way infernal, in gruesome features, dreadfully disordered; till reason is shaken, by the same panic, judgment lost, and the haill sowl distracted in the insanity o' Fear, till you're nae better than a stark-staring madman.

North. Good, James—good.

Shepherd. In sic a mood could ony Christian cretur, even Mr. Southey himsel, tak haud o' the deil either by the horns or the tail?—Mair likely that in frenzied desperation you loup wi' a spang on the bristly back o' the Evil Ane, wha gallops aff wi' you demented into some loch, where you are found floatin in the mornin a swollen corp, wi' the mark o' claws on your hause, your een hangin out o' their sockets, your head scalped wi' something waur than a tammyhawk, and no a single bane in your body that's no grund to mash like a malefactor's on the wheel for having curst the Holy Inquisition.

North. Why, my dear Shepherd, genius, I feel, can render terrible even the meanest superstition.

Shepherd. Meanness and majesty signify naething in the supernatural. I've seen an expression in the een o' a pyet,* wi' its head turned to the ae side, and though in general a shy bird, no caring for you though you present your rung† at it as if you were gaun to shoot it wi' a gun, that has made my verra heart-strings crunkle up wi' the thochts o' some indefinite evil comin, I kent na frae what quarter o' the lowerin heavens.—For pyets, at certain times and places, are no canny, and their nebs look as if they were peckin at mortcloths.

North. Cross him out, James—cross him out.

Shepherd. A raven ruggin at the booels o' a dead horse is naething; but ane sittin a' by himsel on a rock, in some lanely glen, and croak-croakin, naebody can think why, noo lookin savagely up at the sun, and noo tearin, no in hunger, for his crap's fu' o' carrion, but in anger and rage, the moss aneath him wi' beak or tawlons; and though you shout at him wi' a' your micht, never steerin a single fit frae his stance, but absolutely lauchin at you wi' a horrid guller in the sooty throat o' him, in derision o' you, ane o' God's reasonable creturs,—I say, sir, that sic a bird, wi' sic unaccoontable conduct, in sic an inhuman solitude, is a frichtsome demon; and that when you see him hop-hoppin awa wi'

* *Pyet*—a magpie. † *Rung*—walking staff.

great jumps in amang the region o' rocks, you wadna follow him into his auncient lair for ony consideration whatsomever, but turn your face doun the glen, and thank God at the sound o' some distant bagpipe. A' men are augurs. Yet, sitting here, what care I for a raven mair than for a how-towdie?

North. The devil in Scotland, during the days o' witchcraft, was a most contemptible character.

Shepherd. Sae muckle the better. It showed that sin maun be a low, base state, when a superstitious age could embody it in a nae mair imposing impersonation.

North. Perhaps it is wrong to despise anything; and certainly, in the highest Christian light, it is so. Wordsworth finely says, "He who feels contempt for any living thing has faculties which he has never used."

Shepherd. Then Wudsworth has faculties in abundance that he has never used; for he feels contempt for every leevin thing, in the shape either o' man or woman, that can write as gude or better poetry than himsel—which I alloo is no easy; but still it's possible, and has been dune, and will be dune again, by me and ithers. But that's rinnin awa frae the subject. . . . To my lugs, sir, the maist shockin epithet in our language is—Apostate. Soon as you hear it, you see a man selling his sowl to the deevil.

North. To Mammon.

Shepherd. Belial or Beelzebub. I look to the mountains, Mr. North, and stern they stand in a glorious gloom, for the sun is strugglin wi' a thunder-cloud, and facing him a faint but fast-brichtenin rainbow. The ancient spirit o' Scotland comes on me frae the sky, and the sowl within me re-swears in silence the oath o' the Covenant. There they are—the Covenanters—a' gathered thegither, no in fear and tremblin, but wi' Bibles in their bosoms, and swords by their sides, in a glen deep as the sea, and still as death, but for the sound o' a stream and the cry o' an eagle. "Let us sing, to the praise and glory of God, the hundredth Psalm," quoth a loud, clear voice, though it be the voice o' an auld man; and up to Heaven hauds he his strang withered hauns, and in the gracious wunds o' heaven are flying abroad his grey hairs or say, rather, white as the silver or the snaw.

North. Oh for Wilkie!

Shepherd. The eagle and the stream are silent, and the heavens and the earth are brocht close thegither by that triumphin psalm. Ay, the clouds cease their sailing, and lie still; the mountains bow their heads; and the crags, do they not seem to listen, as in that remote place the hour o' the delighted day is filled with a holy hymn to the Lord God o' Israel?

North. My dear Shepherd!

Shepherd. Oh! if there should be sittin there—even in that congregation, on which, like God's own eye, looketh down the meridian sun, now shinin in the blue region—an Apostate!

North. The thought is terrible.

Shepherd. But na, na, na! See that bonny blue-eed, rosy-cheeked, gowden-haired lassie—only a thought paler than usual, sweet lily that she is—half-sittin, half-lyin on the greensward, as she leans on the knee o' her stalwart grand-father—for the sermon's begun, and all eyes are fastened on the preacher,—look at her till your heart melts as if she were your ain, and God had given you that beautifu' wee image o' her sainted mother, and tell me if you think that a' the tortures that cruelty could devise to inflict, would ever wring frae thae sweet innocent lips ae word o' abjuration o' the faith in which the flower is growing up amang the dewdraps o' her native hills?

North. Never—never—never!

Shepherd She proved it, sir, in death. Tied to a stake on the sea-sands she stood; and first she heard, and then she saw, the white roarin o' the tide. But the smile forsook not her face; it brichtened in her een when the water reached her knee; calmer and calmer was her voice of prayer, as it beat again' her bonny breast; nae shriek when a wave closed her lips for ever; and methinks, sir—for ages on ages hae lapsed awa sin'that martyrdom, and therefore Imagination may withouten blame dally wi' grief—methink, sir, that as her golden head disappeared, 'twas like a star sinkin in the sea!

North. God bless you, my dearest James! shake hands!

Shepherd. When I think on these things—in olden times the produce o' the common day—and look aroun' me noo, I could wush to steek my een in the darkness o' death; for dearly as I love it still, alas! alas! I am ashamed o' my country. . . . Eh? What?

North. Whisht! Had you your choice, James, pray what sort of a bird would you be?

Shepherd. I wad transmigrate intil a gey hantle. And, first and foremost, for royal ambition is the poet's sin, I would be an Eagle. Higher than ever in his balloon did Lunardi soar, would I shoot up into heaven. Poised in that empyreal air, where nae storm-current flows, far up aboon the region of clouds, with wide-spread and unquivering wings would I hang in the virgin sunshine. Nae human ee should see me in my cerulean tabernacle—but mine should see the human specks by the sides of rocks and rivers, creeping and crawling, like worms as they are, over their miserable earthly flats, or toiling, like reptiles as they are, up their majestic molehills. Down with a sughing sweep in one moment would I descend a league of atmosphere, still miles and miles above all the dwarf mountain-taps and pigmy forests. Ae headlong lapse mair, and my ears would drink the faint thunder of some puny cataract; another mile in a moment nearer the poor humble earth, and, lo! the woods are what men call majestic, the vales wide, and the mountains magnificent. That pitiful bit of smoke is a city—a metropolitan city. I cross it wi' ae wave of my wing.—The roar of ocean—what—what's that I hear? You auld mannerless rascal, is that you I hear snorin? Ma faith, gin I was an eagle, I wad scart your haffits wi' my tawlons, and try which o' our nebs was the sharpest. Weel, that's maist extraordinar—he absolutely snores on a different key wi each o' his twa individual nostrils—snorin a first and second like a catch or glee. I wunner if he can snore by the notes—or trusts entirely to his dreaming ear. It's really no that unharmonious—and I think I hear him accompanying Mrs. Gentle on the spinnet. Let's coom his face wi' burned cork.

[*The* SHEPHERD *applies a cork to the fire, and makes* NORTH *a Blackamoor.*

North. Be not so coy—so cold—my love. "Can danger lurk within a kiss?"

Shepherd. Othello—Othello—Othello!

North (*awaking with a tremendous yawn*). 'Tis gone—'twas but a dream!

Shepherd. Ay, ay, what's that you were dreamin about sir? Your face is a' ower blushes—just like a white rose tinged with the setting sun.

North. I sometimes speak in my sleep. Did I do so now?

Shepherd. If you did, sir, I did not hear you—for I have been takin a nap mysel, and just awaukened this moment wi' a fa' frae the cock on a kirk-steeple. I hae often odd dreams; and I thocht I got astride o' the cock, and was haudin on by the tail, when the feathers gave way, and had it not been a dream, I should infallibly have been dashed to pieces. Do you ever dream o' kissing, sir?

North. Fie, James!

Shepherd. Oh, but you look quite captivatin, quite seducin, when you blush that gate, sir! I never could admire a dark-complexioned man.

North. I do—and often wish mine had been dark—

Shepherd. Ye made a narrow escape the noo, sir; for out o' revenge for your havin ance coomed my face when I fell asleep on my chair, I was within an ace of coomin yours—

North (*starting up furiously*). A coomed face? Have you dared, you swineherd, to cork my face? If you have, you shall repent it till the latest day of your life.

Shepherd. You surely will forgive me when you hear I am on my deathbed—

North (*at the mirror*). Blackguard!

Shepherd. 'Tweel you're a' that. I ca' that epithet *multum in parvo.* You're a maist complete blackguard—that's beyond a' manner o' dout. What'n whites o' een! and what'n whites o' teeth! But your hair's no half grizzly aneuch for a blackamoor—at least an African ane—and gies you a sort o' uncanny, mongrel appearance that wad frichten the King o' Congo.

North. Talking with a face as black as the crown of my hat!

Shepherd. And a great deal blacker. The croon o' your hat's broon, and I wunner you're no ashamed, sir, to wear't on the streets! but your face, sir, is as black as the back o' that chimley, and baith wad be muckle the better o' the sweeps.

North. James, I have ever found it impossible to be irate with you more than half a minute at a time during these last twenty years. I forgive you—and do you know that I do not look so much amiss in cork. 'Pon honor—

Shepherd. It's a great improvement on you, sir—and I

would seriously advise you to coom your face every day when you dress for denner. Let's order sooper.

North. Well, James, be it so.

(*As the* SHEPHERD *rises to ring the bell, the Timepiece strikes Ten, and* PICARDY *enters with his Tail.*)

Shepherd. Ye dinna mean to say, Mr. Awmrose, that that's a' the sooper? Only the roun', a cut o' sawmon, beefsteaks, and twa brodds o' eisters! This 'll never do, Awmrose. Remember there's a couple o' us—and that a sooper that may be no amiss for ane may be little better than starvation to twa; especially if them twa be in the prime and vigor o' life, hae come in frae the kintra, and got yaup * ower some half-dizzen jugs o' strang whusky-toddy.

Ambrose (*bowing*). The boiled turkey and the roasted ducks will be on the table forthwith—unless, Mr. Hogg, you would prefer a goose which last week won a sweepstakes—

Shepherd. What? at Perth races? Was he a bluid-guse, belangin to a member o' the Caledonian Hunt?

Ambrose (*smiling*). No, Mr. Hogg—there was a competition between six parishes which should produce the greatest goose, and I had the good fortune to purchase the successful candidate, who was laid, hatched, and brought up at the Manse of—

Shepherd. I ken the successful candidate brawly.—Wasna he a white ane, wi' a tremendous doup that soopt the grun', and hadna he contracted a habit o' turnin in the taes o' his left fit?

Ambrose. The same, sir. He weighed, ready for spit, twenty pounds jump—feathers and giblets four pounds more. Nor do I doubt, Mr. North, that had your Miss Nevison had him for a fortnight longer at the Lodge, she would have

* *Yaup*—hungry.

fattened him (for he is a gander) up to thirty,—that is to say, with all his paraphernalia.

Shepherd. Show him in; raw or roasted, show him in.

(*Enter* KING PEPIN *and* SIR DAVID GAM, *with the successful candidate, supported by* Mon. CADET *and* TAPPYTOORIE.)

What a strapper! Puir chiel, I wadna hae kent him, sae changed is he frae the time I last saw him at the Manse, takin a walk in the cool o' the Saturday e'ening, wi' his wife and family, and ever and anon gabblin to himsel in a sort o' undertone, no unlike a minister rehearsin his sermon for the coming Sabbath.

North. How comes he to be ready roasted, Ambrose?

Ambrose. A party of twenty are about to sup in the Saloon, and—

Shepherd. Set him doun; and if the gentlemen wuss to see North cut up a guse, show the score into the Snuggery.

[*The successful candidate is safely got on the board.*

Hear hoo the table groans!

North. I feel my limbs rather stiffish with sitting so long. Suppose, James, that we have a little leap-frog.

Shepherd. Wi' a' my heart. Let me arrange the forces roun' the table. Mr. Awmrose, staun' you there—Mon. Cadet, fa' intil the rear o' your brither—Pippin, twa yairds ahint Awmrose *junior*—Sir Dawvit, dress by his Majesty—and Tappytoorie, turn your back upon me. Noo, lout doun a' your heads. Here goes.—Keep the pie warm.

[*The* SHEPHERD *vaults away, and the whole circle is in perpetual motion;* NORTH *distinguished by his agility in the ring.*

North (*piping*). Heads all up—no louting. There, James, I topped you without touching a hair.

Shepherd. Mirawculous auld man! A lameter too! I never felt his hauns on my shouther!

Ambrose. I'm rather short of breath, and must drop out of the line.

[Mr. AMBROSE *drops out of the line, and his place is supplied by* TICKLER, *who at that moment has entered the room unobserved.*

Shepherd (coming unexpectedly upon Tickler). Here's a steeple! What glamory's this?

North. Stand aloof, James, and I'll clear the weathercock on the spire.

[NORTH, *using his crutch as a leaping-pole, clears* TICKLER *in grand style; but* TAPPYTOORIE, *the next in the series, boggles, and remains balanced on* SOUTHSIDE'S *shoulders.*

Tickler. Firm on your pins, North. I'm coming.

[TICKLER, *with* TAPPYTOORIE *on his shoulders, clears* CHRISTOPHER *in a canter.*

Omnes. Huzza! huzza! huzza!

North (addressing TICKLER). Mr. Tickler, it gives me great pleasure to present to you the Silver Frog, which I am sure will never be disgraced by your leaping.

[TICKLER *stoops his head, and* NORTH *hangs the Prize Silver Frog, by a silver chain, round his neck;* TAPPYTOORIE *dismounts, and the Three sit down to supper.*

Shepherd. Some sax or seven slices o' the breist, sir, and dinna spare the stuffin.—Mr. Awmrose, gie my trencher a gude clash o' aipple-sass.—Potawtoes. Thank ye.—Noo, some o' the smashed.—Tappy, the porter.—What guse!!!

Tickler. Cut the apron off the bishop, North; but you must have a longer spoon to get into the interior.

Ambrose. Here is a punch-ladle, sir.

Shepherd. Gie him the great big silver soup ane.—Sic sage!

Tickler. Why, that is liker the leg of a sheep than of a goose.

Shepherd. Awmrose, my man, dinna forget the morn * to let us hae the giblets.—Pippin, the mustard.—Mr. North, as naebody seems to be axin for't, gie me the bishop's apron, it seems sappy. What are ye gaun to eat yoursel, sir? Dinna mind helpin me, but attend to your nain sooper.

North. James, does not the side of the breast which I have now been hewing remind you of Salisbury Crags?

Shepherd. It's verra precipitous. The skeleton maun be sent to the College Museum, to staun' at the fit o' the elephant, the rhinoceros, and the cammyleopardawlis; and that it mayna be spiled by unskilful workmanship, I vote we finish him cauld the morn afore we yoke to the giblet-pie. [*Carried nem. con.*

Tickler. Goose always gives me a pain in my stomach. But to purchase pleasure at a certain degree of pain is true philosophy. So, my dear North, another plateful. James, a caulker?

Shepherd. What's your wull?

Tickler. Oh! nothing at all.—Ambrose, the Glenlivet to Mr. North.—Mr. Hogg, I believe, never takes it during supper.

[*The* SHEPHERD *tips* AMBROSE *the wink, and the gurgle goes round the table.*

[*Silence, with slight interruptions, and no conversation for about three-quarters of an hour.*

NATHAN GURNEY.

Shepherd. I had nae previous idea that steaks eat sae capital after guse. Some sawmon.†

North. Stop, James. Let all be removed, except the fish—

* *The morn*—to-morrow.

† "No greater compliment," says a recent writer, "was ever paid to Professor Wilson than by the hypochondriac who, after failing to obtain an appetite from tonics, was beguiled into reading the *Noctes*, and at once 'set in for serious eating' with the will of the Shepherd himself."

to wit, the salmon, the rizzards, the speldrins, the herrings, and the oysters.

Shepherd. And bring some mair fresh anes. Mr. Awmrose, you maun mak a deal o' siller by sellin your eister-shells for manur to the farmers a' roun' about Embro'? They're as gude's lime—indeed, I'm thinkin they *are* lime—a sort o' sea-lime, growing on rocks by the shore, and a coatin at the same time to leevin and edible creturs. Oh, the wonnerfu' warks o' Nature!

North. Then wheeling the circular to the fire, let us have a parting jug or two—

Shepherd. Each?

(*Enter* MR. AMBROSE *with* LORD ELDON.)

North. Na! here's his Lordship full to the brim. He holds exactly one gallon, Imperial Measure; and that quantity, according to Mrs. Ambrose's recipe, cannot hurt us—

Shepherd. God bless the face o' him!

Tickler. Pray, James, is it a true bill that you have had the hydrophobia?

Shepherd. Ower true; but I'll gie you a description o't at our next. Meanwhile, let's ca' in that puir cretur Gurney, and gie him a drap drink. Nawthan! Nawthan! Nawthan!

Gurney (*in a shrill voice from the interior of the Ear of Dionysius*). Here—here—here!

Shepherd. What'n a vice! Like a young ratton * squaakin ahint the lath and plaister.

North. No rattons here, James. Mr. Gurney is true as steel.

Shepherd. Reserve that short similie for yoursel, sir! Oh, sir, but you're elastic as a drawn Damascus swurd. Lean a' your wecht on't, wi' the pint on the grun, but fear na, while it bends, that it will break; for back again frae the

* *Ratton*—rat.

semicircle springs it in a second intil the straught line ; and woe be to him wha daurs that cut and thrust! for it gangs through his body like licht through a wundow, and before the sinner kens he is wounded, you turn him ower on his back, sir, stane-dead!

[Mr. GURNEY *joins the party, and the curtain of course falls.*

XXI.

IN WHICH, THE ENGLISH OPIUM-EATER DINING WITH THE THREE, THE SHEPHERD MOUNTS BONASSUS.

*Scene,—The Saloon, illuminated by the grand Gas Orrery. Time,—First of April—Six o'clock. Present,—*NORTH, *the* ENGLISH OPIUM EATER,* *the* SHEPHERD, TICKLER, *in Court-Dresses. The three celebrated young Scottish* LEANDERS, *with their horns, in the hanging gallery.* AIR: "*Brose and Brochan and a'.*"

TICKLER.

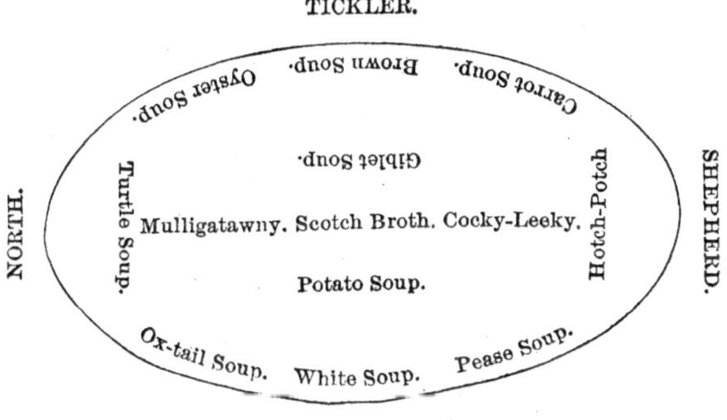

ENGLISH OPIUM-EATER.

Shepherd. Dinna abuse Burns, Mr. De Quinshy. Neither

* Thomas De Quincey has been already referred to more than once in the course of these dialogues. Now he is introduced as an interlocutor; and, if I may be permitted to say so, the general character of his conversation has been imitated not infelicitously by his friend the Professor. But

you nor ony ither Englishman can thoroughly understaun' three sentences o' his poems—

English Opium-Eater (*with much animation*). I have for some years past longed for an opportunity to tear into pieces that gross national delusion, born of prejudice, ignorance, and bigotry, in which, from highest to lowest, all literary classes of Scotchmen are as it were incarnated—to wit, a belief, strong as superstition, that all their various dialects must be as unintelligible, as I grant that most of them are uncouth and barbarous to English ears—even to those of the most accomplished and consummate scholars. Whereas, to a Danish, Norwegian, Swedish, Saxon, German, French, Italian, Spanish—and let me add, Latin and Greek scholar, there is not even a monosyllable that—

Shepherd. What's *a gowpen o' glaur ?*

English Opium-Eater. Mr. Hogg—sir, I will not be interrupted—

Shepherd. You canna tell. It's just *twa neif-fu's o' clarts.**

North. James—James—James !

Shepherd. Kit—Kit—Kit. But beg your pardon, Mr. De Quinshy—afore denner I am aye unco snappish. I admit you're a great grammarian. But kennin something o' a language by bringin to bear upon't a' the united efforts o' knowledge and understaunin—baith first-rate—is ae thing, and feelin every breath and every shadow that keeps playin ower a' its syllables, as if by a natural and born instinct, is anither ; the first you may aiblins hae—naebody likelier,—but to the second, nae man may pretend that hasna had the

the reader who would learn what Mr. De Quincey himself is *in propriâ personâ*—what fascinating powers of eloquence he possesses—how deep his poetical sensibilities are—and how profound his philosophical acumen—must be referred to his collected works. [De Quincey died in 1859.]

* Two handfuls of mud.

happiness and the honor o' havin been born and bred in bonny Scotland. What can ye ken o' Kilmeny?

English Opium-Eater (*smiling graciously*). 'Tis a ballad breathing the sweetest, simplest, wildest spirit of Scottish traditionary song—music, as of some antique instrument, long lost, but found at last in the Forest among the decayed roots of trees, and touched, indeed, as by an instinct, by the only man who could reawaken its sleeping chords—the Ettrick Shepherd.

Shepherd. Na—if you say that sincerely—and I never saw a broo smoother wi' truth than your ain—I maun qualify my former apothegm, and alloo you to be an exception frae the general rule. I wush, sir, you would write a Glossary o' the Scottish Language. I ken naebody fitter.

North. Our distinguished guest is aware that this is "All Fool's Day,"—and must, on that score, pardon these court-dresses. We consider them, my dear sir, appropriate to this Anniversary.

Shepherd. Mine wasna originally a court-dress. It's the uniform o' the Border Club. But nane o' the ither members would wear them, except me and the late Dyuk o' Buccleuch. So when the King cam to Scotland, and expeckit to be introduced to me at Holyroodhouse, I got the tiler at Yarrow-Ford to cut it doun after a patron * frae Embro'—

English Opium-Eater. Green and gold—to my eyes the most beautiful of colors,—the one characteristic of earth, the other of heaven—and therefore, the two united, emblematic of genius.

Shepherd. Oh! Mr. De Quinshy—sir, but you're a pleasant cretur—and were I ask't to gie a notion o' your mainners to them that had never seen you, I should just use twa words, Urbanity and Amenity—meanin, by the first, that saft, bricht

* *Patron*—pattern.

polish that a man gets by leevin amang gentleman scholars in touns and cities, burnished on the solid metal o' a happy natur hardened by the rural atmosphere o' the pure kintra air, in which I ken you hae ever delighted; and by the ither, a peculiar sweetness, amaist like that o' a woman's, yet sae far frae bein' feminine, as masculine as that o' Allen Ramsay's ain *Gentle Shepherd*—and breathin o' a harmonious union between the heart, the intelleck, and the imagination, a' the three keepin their ain places, and thus makin the vice,* speech, gesture, and motion o' a man as composed as a figure on a pictur by some painter that was a master in his art, and produced his effects easily—and ane kens na hoo—by his lichts and shadows. Mr. North, amna † I richt in the thocht, if no in the expression?

North. You have always known my sentiments, James—

Shepherd. I'm thinkin we had better lay aside our swurds. They're kittle dealin when a body's stannin or walkin; but the very deevil's in them when ane claps his doup on a chair, for here's the hilt o' mine interferin wi' my ladle-hand.

Tickler. Why, James, you have buckled it on the wrong side.

Shepherd. What? Is the richt the wrang?

North. Let us all untackle. Mr. Ambrose, hang up each man's sword on his own hat-peg.—There.

North. Hark! my gold repeater is smiting seven. We allow an hour, Mr. De Quincey, to each course—and then—

[*The* LEANDERS *play* " *The Boatie Rows,"—the door flies open,—enter* PICARDY *and his clan.*

* *Vice*—voice. † *Amna*—am not.

SECOND COURSE—FISH.

TICKLER.

Mackerel.
Loch Leven Trout.
Eels.
Bowness Bass.
NORTH. Salmon. Pike. Turbot. Halibut. Cod's-head and Shoulders. SHEPHERD.
Windermere Char.
Haddocks. Soles. Whitings.

ENGLISH OPIUM-EATER.

Shepherd. I'm sure we canna be sufficiently gratefu' for having got rid o' a' thae empty tureens o' soup—so let us noo set in for serious eatin, and tackle to the inhabitants o' the Great Deep. What's that bit body, North, been about? Daidlin * wi' the mock-turtle. I hate a' things mock—soups, pearls, fause tails, baith bustles and queues, wigs, cauves, religion, freenship, love, glass-een, rouge on the face o' a woman,—no' exceppin even cork legs, for timmer anes are far better, there bein' nae attempt at deception, which ought never to be pratised on ony o' God's reasonable creatures—it's sae insultin.

English Opium-Eater. Better open outrage than hidden guile, which—

Shepherd. Just sae, sir.—But it's no a bonny instrument, that key-bugle? I've been tryin to learn't a' this wunter, beginnin at first wi' the simple coo's-horn. But afore I had weel gotten the gamut, I had nearly lost my life.

Tickler. What? From mere loss of breath—positive exhaustion? An abscess in the lungs, James?

* *Daidlin*—trifling.

Shepherd. Nothing o' the sort. I hae wund and lungs for onything—even for roarin you doun at argument, whan, driven to the wa', you begin to storm like a Stentor, till the verra neb o' the jug on the dirlin table regards you wi' astonishment, and the speeders are seen rinnin alang the ceilin to shelter themselves in their corner cobwebs.—(Canna ye learn frae Mr. De Quinshy, man, to speak laigh and lown, trustin mair to sense and less to soun', and you'll find your advantage in't?,—But I allude, sir, to an Adventure.

North. An adventure, James?

Shepherd. Ay—an adventure—but as there's nane o' you for cod's-head and shouthers, I'll first fortify mysel wi' some forty or fifty flakes—like half-crown pieces.

Tickler. Some cod, James, if you please.

Shepherd. Help yoursel—I'm unco thrang* the noo. Mr. De Quinshy, what fish are you devoorin?

English Opium-Eater. Soles.

Shepherd. And you, Mr. North?

North. Salmon.

Shepherd. And you, Mr. Tickler?

Tickler. Cod.

Shepherd. You're a' in your laconics. I'm fear'd for the banes, otherwise, after this cod's dune, I sud like gran' to gie that pike a yokin. I ken him for a Linlithgow loon by the length o' his lantern-jaws, and the peacock-neck color o' the dorsal ridge—and I see by the jut o' his stammack there's store o' stuffin. There'll be naething between him and me, when the cod's dune for, but halibut and turbot—the first the wershest and maist fushionless o' a' swimmin creturs—and the second ower rich, unless you intend eatin no other specie o' fish.

Tickler. Now—for your adventure—my dear Shepherd.

* *Thrang*—busy.

Shepherd. Whisht—and you'se hear't. I gaed out ae day, ayont the knowe—the same, Mr. North, that kythes* aboon the bit field whare I tried, you ken, to raise a counterband crap o' tobacco—and sat doun on a brae among the brackens—then a' red as the heavens in sunset—tootin awa on the Horn, ettlin first at B flat, and then at A sharp,—when I hears, at the close o' a lesson, what I thocht the grandest echo that ever cam frae a mountain-tap—an echo like a rair o' the ghost of ane o' the Bulls o' Bashan, gane mad amang other horned spectres like himsel in the howe† o' the cloudy sky—

English Opium-Eater. Mr. North, allow me to direct your attention to that image, which seems to me perfectly original, and at the same time perfectly true to nature; original I am entitled to call it, since I remember nothing resembling it, either essentially or accidentally, in prose or verse, in the literature of Antiquity,—in that of the middle, ordinarily, but ignorantly, called the Dark Ages,—in that which arose in Europe after the revival of letters—though assuredly letters had not sunk into a state from which it could be said with any precision that they did revive,—or in that of our own Times, which seems to me to want that totality and unity which alone constitute an Age, otherwise but a series of unconnected successions, destitute of any causative principal of cohesion or evolvement. True to nature no less am I entitled to call the image, inasmuch as it giveth, not indeed "to airy nothing a local habitation and a name," but to an "airy *something*," namely, the earthly bellowing of an animal, whose bellow is universally felt to be terrific, nay, moreover, and therefore sublime,—(for that terror lieth at the root—if not always, yet of verity in by for the greater number of in stances—of the true sublime, from early boyhood my intellect

* *Kythes*—shows itself. ‡ *Howe*—hollow.

saw, and my imagination felt to be among the great primal intuitive truths of our spiritual frame),—because it giveth, I repeat, to the earthly bellowing of such an animal an aerial character, which, for the moment, deludes the mind into a belief of the existence of a cloudy kine, spectral in the sky-region, else thought to be the dwelling-place of silence and vacuity, and thus an affecting, impressive—nay, most solemn and almost sacred feeling, is impressed on the sovereign reason of the immortality of the brute creatures,—a doctrine that visits us at those times only when our own being breathes in the awe of divining thought, and disentangling her wings from all clay encumbrances, is strong in the consciousness of her DEATHLESS ME—so Fichte and Schelling speak—

Shepherd. Weel, sir, you see, doun cam on my "DEATHLESS ME" the Bonassus, head cavin, tail-tuft on high, hinder legs visible ower his neck and shouthers, and his hump clothed in thunder, louder in his ae single sel than a wheeling charge o' a haill regiment o' dragoon cavalry on the Portobello sands, —doun cam the Bonassus, I say, like the Horse Life Guards takin a park o' French artillery at Waterloo, richt doun, Heaven hae mercy! upon me, his ain kind maister, wha had fed him on turnips, hay and straw ever sin Lammas, till the monster was as fat's he could lie in the hide o' him—and naething had I to defend mysel wi' but that silly coo's horn. A' the collies were at hame. Yet in my fricht—deadly as it was—I was thankfu' wee Jamie wasna there lookin for primroses—for he micht hae lost his judgment. You understand, the Bonassus had mista'en my B sharp for anither Bonassus challengin him to single combat.*

English Opium-Eater. A very plausible theory.

Shepherd. Thank you, sir, for that commentary on ma text

The naturalization of the Bonassus in Ettrick is described at page 180.

—for it has gien me time to plouter amang the chouks * o' the cod. Faith, it was nae theory, sir, it was practice—and afore I could fin' my feet, he was sae close upon me that I could see up his nostrils. Just at that moment I remembered that I had on an auld red jacket—the ane that was ance sky-blue, you ken, Mr. North, that I had gotten dyed—and that made the Bonassus just an evendoun Bedlamite. For amaist a' horned cattle hate and abhor red coats.

North. So I have heard the army say—alike in town and country.

Shepherd. What was to be done! I thocht o' tootin the horn as the trumpeter did when run aff wi' in the mouth o' a teegger; but then I recollected that it was a' the horn's blame that the Bonassus was there—so I lost nae time in that speculation, but slipping aff my breeks, jackets, waistcoat, shirt, and a', just as you've seen an actor on the stage, I appeared, suddenly before him as naked as the day I was born—and sic is the awe, sir, wi' which a human being, in puris naturalibus, inspires the maddest of the brute creation (I had tried it ance before on a mastiff), that he was a' at ance, in a single moment, stricken o' a heap, just the very same as if the butcher had sank the head o' an aix intil his harn-pan—his knees trummled like a new-dropped lamb's—his tail, tuft and a' had nae mair power in't than a broken thrissle-stalk—his een goggled instead o' glowered—a heartfelt difference, I assure you—

English Opium Eater. It seems to be, Mr. Hogg—but you will pardon me if I am mistaken—a distinction without a difference, as the logicians say—

Shepherd. Ay, De Quinshy, ma man—logician as you are, had you stood in my shoon, you had gotten yoursel on baith horns o' the dilemma.

* *Chouks*—jaws.

North. Did you cut off his retreat to the Loch, James, and take him prisoner?

Shepherd. I did. Poor silly sumph! I canna help thinkin that he swarfed; though perhaps he was only pretendin—so I mounted him, and putting my worsted garters through his nose—it had been bored when he was a wild beast in a caravan—I keepit peggin his ribs wi' my heels, till, after gruntin and grainin,* and raisin his great big unwieldy red bouk † half frae up the earth, and then swelterin doun again, if ance, at least a dizzen times, till I began absolutely to weary o' my situation in life, he feenally recovered his cloots,‡ and, as if inspired wi' a new speerit, aff like lichtnin to the mountains.

North. What!—without a saddle, James? You must have felt the loss—I mean the want, of leather—

Shepherd. We ride a' mainner o' animals bare-backed in the Forest, sir. I hae seen a bairn, no aboon fowre year auld, ridin hame the Bill at the gloamin—a' the kye at his tail, like a squadron o' cavalry anint Joachim Murat, King o' Naples—Mr. North, gin ye keep eatin sae vorawciously at the sawmon, you'll hurt yoursel. Fish is heavy. Dinna spare the vinegar, if you will be a glutton.

North. Ma! §

Shepherd. But, as I was sayin, awa went the Bonassus due west. Though you could hardly ca't even a snaffle, yet I soon found that I had a strong purchase, and bore him doun frae the heights to the turnpike road that cuts the kintra frae Selkirk to Moffat. There does I encounter three gigfu's o' gentlemen and leddies; and ane o' the latter—a bonny cretur—leuch as if she kent me, as I gaed by at full gallop—and I remembered ha'in seen her afore, though where I couldna

* *Grainin*—groaning. † *Bouk*—bulk. ‡ *Cloots*—feet.

§ "*Ma!*" North is too intent upon eating to return an articulate answer.

tell: but a' the lave shrieked as if at the visible superstition o' the Water-Kelpie on the Water-Horse mistakin day for nicht in the delirium o' a fever—and thinkin that it had been the moon shining down on his green pastures aneath the Loch, when it was but the shadow o' a lurid cloud. But I soon vanished into distance.

Tickler. Where the deuce were your clothes all this time, my dear matter-of-fact Shepherd?

Shepherd. Ay—there was the rub. In the enthusiasm of the moment I had forgotten them—nay, such was the state of excitement to which I had worked myself up, that, till I met the three gigfu's o' leddies and gentlemen—a marriage party —full in the face, I was not, Mr. De Quinshy, aware of being so like the Truth. Then I felt, all in a moment, that I was a Mazeppa. But had I turned back, they would have supposed that I had intended to accompany them to Selkirk; and therefore, to allay all such fears, I made a show o' fleein far awa aff into the interior—into the cloudland of Loch Skene and the Grey Mare's Tail.

English Opium-Eater. Your adventure, Mr. Hogg, would furnish a much better subject for the painter, or for the poet, than the Mazeppa of Byron. For it is not possible to avoid feeling, that in the image of a naked man on horseback, there is an involution of the grotesque in the picturesque—of the truly ludicrous in the falsely sublime. But, further, the thought of bonds—whether of cordage or of leather—on a being naturally free is degrading to the moral, intellectual, and physical dignity of the creature so constricted; and it ought ever to be the grand aim of poetry to elevate and exalt. Moreover, Mazeppa, in being subjected to the scornful gaze of hundreds—nay, haply of thousands of spectators—the base retinue of a barbarous power—in a state of uttermost nudity, was subjected to an ordeal of shame and rage, which neither the contemplative nor imaginative mind could brook to see applied to even the veriest outcast scum of our race. He was, in fact, placed naked in a moving pillory—and the hissing shower of scornful curses by which he was by those barbarians assailed, is as insupportable to our thoughts as an irregular volley, or street-firing of rotten eggs, discharged by the hooting rabble against some miscreant standing with his face through a hole in the wood, with his crime placarded on his felon breast. True, that as Mazeppa "recoils into the wilderness," the exposure is less repulsive to common imagination; but it is not to common imagination that the highest poetry is addressed; and, therefore, though to the fit reader there be indeed some relief or release from shame in the "deserts idle," yet doth not the feeling of degradation so subside as to be merged in that pleasurable state of the soul essential to the effect of the true and legitimate exercise of poetical power. Shame pursues him faster than the wolves; nor doth the umbrage of the forest-trees, that fly past him in his flight, hide his nakedness, which, in some other conditions, being an attribute of his nature, might even be the source to him and to us of a high emotion, but which here, being forcibly and violently imposed against his will be the will of a brutal tyrant, is but an accident of his position in space and time, and therefore unfit to be permanently contemplated in a creature let loose before the Imaginative Faculty. Nor is this vital vice—so let me call it—in anywise cured or alleviated by his subsequent triumph, when he returns—as he himself tells us he did—at the head of "twice ten thousand horse!"—for the contrast only serves to deepen and darken the original nudity of his intolerable doom. The mother-naked man still seems to be riding in front of all his cavalry; nor, in this case, has the poet's art sufficed to reinstate him in his pristine dignity, and to efface all remembrance of the degrading process of stripping and of binding, to which of yore the miserable Nude had been compelled to yield, as helpless as an angry child ignominiously whipt by a nurse, till its mental sufferings may be said to be lost in its physical agonies. Think not that I wish to withhold from Byron the praise of considerable spirit and vigor of execution in his narrative of the race; but that praise may duly belong to very inferior powers, and I am now speaking of Mazeppa in the light of a great Poem. A great Poem it assuredly is not; and how small a Poem it assuredly is, must be felt by all who have read, and are worthy to read, Homer's description of the dragging, and driving, and whirling of the dead body of Hector in bloody nakedness behind the chariot wheels of Achilles.

Shepherd. I never heard onything like that in a' my days. Weel, then, sir, there were nae wolves to chase me and the Bonassus, nor yet mony trees to overshadow us; but we made the cattle and the sheep look about them, and mair nor ae hooded craw and lang-necked heron gat a fricht, as we came suddenly on him through the mist, and gaed thundering by the cataracts. In an hour or twa I began to get as firm on my seat as a Centaur; and discovered by the chasms that the Bonassus was not only as fleet as a racer, but that he could loup like a hunter, and thocht nae mair o' a thirty-feet spang than ye wad think o' stepping across the gutter. Ma faith, we werena lang o' being in Moffat!

English Opium-Eater. In your Flight, Mr. Hogg, there were visibly and audibly concentrated all the attributes of the highest Poetry. First, freedom of the will; for self-impelled you ascended the animal. Secondly, the impulse, though immediately consequent upon, and proceeding from, one of fear, was yet an impulse of courage; and courage is not only a virtue, and acknowledged to be such in all Christain countries, but among the Romans—who assuredly, however low they must be ranked on the intellectual scale, were nevertheless morally a brave people—to it alone was given the name *virtus.* Thirdly, though you were during your whole flight so far passive that you yielded to the volition of the creature yet were you likewise, during your whole course, so far active, that you *guided,* as it appears, the motions which it was beyond your power entirely to control; thus vindicating in your own person the rights of the superior order of creation. Fourthly, you were not so subjugated by the passion peculiar and appropriate to your situation, as to be insensible to or regardless of the courtesies, the amenities, and the humanities of civilised life—as witness that glance of mutual recognition that passed in one moment, between you and the "bonny creature" in the gig; nor yet to be inattentive to the effect produced by yourself and the Bonassus on various tribes of the inferior creatures,—cattle, sheep, crows, and herons, to say nothing of the poetical delight experienced by you from the influence of the beautiful or august shows of nature,—mists, clouds, cataracts, and the eternal mountains. Fifthly, the constantly accompanying sense of danger interfused with that of safety, so as to constitute one complex emotion, under which, hurried as you were, it may be said with perfect truth that you found leisure to admire, nay, even to wonder at, the strange speed of that most extraordinary animal—and most extraordinary he must be, if the only living representative of his species since the days of Aristotle—nor less to admire and wonder at your own skill, equally, if not more, miraculous, and well entitled to throw into the shade of oblivion the art of the most illustrious equestrian that ever "witched the world with noble horsemanship." Sixthly, the sublime feeling of penetrating, like a thunderbolt, cloud-land and all the mist cities that evanished as you galloped into their suburbs, gradually giving way to a feeling no less sublime, of having left behind all those unsubstantial phantom-regions, and of nearing the habitation or tabernacle of men, known by the name of Moffat—perhaps one of the most imaginative of all the successive series of states of your soul since first you appeared among the hills, like Sol entering Taurus. And, finally, the deep trance of home-felt delight that must have fallen upon your spirit—true still to all the sweetest and most sacred of all the social affections—when, the Grey Mare's Tail left streaming far behind that of the Bonassus, you knew from the murmur of that silver stream that your flight was about to cease—till, lo! the pretty village of which you spoke, embosomed in hills and trees—the sign of the White Lion, peradventure, motionless in the airless calm—a snug parlor with a blazing ingle—re-apparelling instant, almost as thought—food both for man and beast—for the Ettrick Shepherd—pardon my familiarity for sake of friendship—and his Bonassus. Yea, from goal to goal, the entire Flight is Poetry, and the original idea of nakedness is lost—or say rather veiled—in the halo-light of imagination.

Shepherd. Weel, if it's no provokin, Mr. De Quinshy, to hear you, who never was on a Bonassus a' your days, analeezin, wi' the maist comprehensive and acute philosophical accuracy, ma complex emotion during the Flight to Moffat far better than I could do mysel—

North. Your genius, James, is synthetical.

Shepherd. Synthetical? I howp no—at least nae mair sae than the genius o' Burns or Allan Kinninghame—or the lave —for—

English Opium-Eater. What is the precise Era of the Flight to Moffat?

Shepherd. Mr. De Quinshy, you're like a' ither great

philosophers, ane o' the maist credulous o' mankind! You wad believe me were I to say that I had ridden a whale up the Yarrow frae Newark to Eltrive! the haill story's a lee! and sa free o' ony foundation in truth, that I wad hae nae objections to tak my Bible-oath that sic a beast as a Bonassus never was creawted—and it's lucky for him that he never was, for, seeing that he's said to consume three bushel o' ingans to denner every day o' his life, Noah wad never hae letten him intil the Ark, and he wad hae been fund, after the subsidin o' the waters, a skeleton on the tap o' Mount Ararat.

English Opium Eater. His non-existence in nature is altogether distinct from his existence in the imagination of the poet—and, in good truth, redounds to his honor—for his character must be viewed in the light of a pure *Ens rationis* —or say rather—

Shepherd. Just let him be an *Ens rationis.* But confess at the same time, that you was bammed, sir.

English Opium-Eater. I recognize the legitimate colloquial use of the word *Bam*, Mr. Hogg, denoting, I believe, "the willing surrendering of belief, one of the first principles of our mental constitution, to any statement made with apparent sincerity, but real deceit, by a mind not previously suspected to exist in a perpetual atmosphere of falsehood."

Shepherd. Just sae, sir,—that's a *Bam.* In Glasgow they ca't a ggeg.—But what's the matter wi' Mr. North? Saw ye ever the cretur lookin sae gash?* I wish he mayna be in a fit o' apoplexy. Speak till him, Mr. De Quinshy.

English Opium-Eater. His countenance is, indeed, ominously sable,—but 'tis most unlikely that apoplexy should strike a person of his spare habit. Nay, I must sit cor-

* *Gash*—sagacious: here, in the sense of "solemn."

rected; for I believe that attacks of this kind have, within the last quarter of a century, become comparatively frequent, and constitute one of the not least perplexing phenomena submitted to the inquisition of Modern Medical Science.—Mr. North, will you relieve our anxiety?

Shepherd (starting up, and flying to Mr. North). His face a' purple. Confoun' that cravat!—for the mair you pu' at it, the tichter it grows.

English Opium-Eater. Mr. Hogg, I would seriously and earnestly recommend more delicacy and gentleness.

Shepherd. Tuts. It's fastened I declare, ahint wi' a gold buckle, and afore wi' a gold preen,—a brotch frae Mrs. Gentle, in the shape o' a bleedin heart! 'Twill be the death o' him.—Oh! puir fallow, puir fallow!—rax* me ower that knife. What's this? You've given me the silver fish-knife, Mr. De Quinshy. Na,—that's far waur, Mr. Tickler.—That swurd for carvin the round. But here's my ain jockteleg.†

SHEPHERD *unclasps his pocket-knife,—and while brandishing in great trepidation,* MR. NORTH *opens his eyes.*

North. Emond! Emond! Emond!—Thurtell—Thurtell—Thurtell!‡

Shepherd. A drap o' bluid's on his brain,—and Reason becomes Raving! What's man?

Tickler. Cut away, James. Not a moment to be lost. Be firm and decided, else he is a dead heathen.

Shepherd Wae's me—wae's me! Nae goshawk ever sae glowered,—and only look at his puir fingers hoo they are workin! I canna thole the sicht,—I'm as weak's a wean, and fear that I'm gaun to fent. Tak the knife, Tickler. Oh, look at his hauns—look at his hauns!

* *Rax*—reach. † *Jockteleg*—a folding-knife.

‡ Robert Emond was tried in Edinburgh on the 8th of February, and executed on the 17th of March 1830, for the murder of Katherine Franks and her daughter Madeline, in their house at Abbey, near Haddington.

Tickler (bending over Mr. North). Yes, yes, my dear sir—I comprehend you—I—

Shepherd (in anger and astonishment). Mr. Tickler, are you mad?—fingerin your fingers in that gate,—as if you were mockin him!

English Opium-Eater. They are conversing, Mr. Hogg, in that language which originated in Oriental—

Shepherd. Oh! they're speakin on their fingers?—Then a's richt,—and Mr. North's comin roun' again intil his seven senses. It's been but a dwawm!

Tickler. Mr. North has just contrived to communicate to me, gentlemen, the somewhat alarming intelligence that the back-bone of the pike has for some time past been sticking about half-way down his throat; that, being unwilling to interrupt the conviviality of the company, he endeavored at first to conceal the circumstance, and then made the most strenuous efforts to dislodge it, upwards or downwards, without avail; but that you must not allow yourselves to fall into any extravagant consternation, as he indulges the fond hope that it may be extracted, even without professional assistance, by Mr. De Quinshy, who has an exceedingly neat small Byronish hand, and on whose decision of character he places the most unfaltering reliance.

Shepherd (in a huff). Does he!—Very weel—sin he forgets auld freens—let him do sae—

North. Ohrr Hogrwhu — chru — u — u — u — Hogruwhuu—

Shepherd. Na! I canna resist sic pleadin eloquence as that—here's the screw, let me try it.—Or what think ye, Mr. Tickler,—what think ye, Mr. De Quinshy,—o' thir pair o' boot-hooks?—Gin I could get a cleek o' the bane by ane o' the vertebræ, I might hoise it gently up, by slaw degrees, sae that ane could get at it wi' their fingers, and then pu' it out o' his mouth in a twinklin! But first let me look doun his throat.—Open your mouth, my dearest sir.

[MR. NORTH *leans back his head, and opens his mouth.*

Shepherd. I see't like a harrow. Rin ben baith o' ye, for Mr. Awmrose. [TICKLER *and* Mr. DE QUINCEY *obey.* Weel ackit, sir—weel ackit—I was taen in mysel at first, for your cheeks were like coals. Here's the back-bane o' the pike on the trencher—I'll—

(*Re-enter* TICKLER *and* OPIUM-EATER, *with* Mr. AMBROSE, *pale as death.*)

It's all over, gentlemen.—It's all over!

Ambrose. Oh! oh! oh!

[*Faints away into* TICKLER'S *arms.*

Shepherd. What the deevil's the matter wi' you, you set o' fules?—I've gotten out the bane.—Look here at the skeleton o' the shark!

English Opium-Eater. Monstrous!

North (*running to the assistance of* Mr. AMBROSE). We have sported too far, I fear, with his sensibilities.

English Opium-Eater. A similar case of a fish-bone in Germany—

Shepherd. Mr. De Quinshy, can you really swallow *that?*

[*Looking at the pike-back, about two feet long.*

But the hour has nearly expired.

[*The* LEANDERS *play* "*Hey, Johnnie Cope, are you wauken yet?*"—Mr. AMBROSE *starts to his feet, runs off and re-appears almost instanter at the head of the forces.*

THIRD COURSE—FLESH.

Shepherd (*in continuation*). And do you really think, Mr. North, that the kintra's in great and general distress, and a' orders in a state o' absolute starvation ?

North. Yes—James—although the Duke * cannot see the sufferings of his subjects, I can—and—

Shepherd. Certain appearances do indicate national distress; yet I think I could, withouten meikle difficulty, lay my haun the noo on ithers that seem to lead to a different conclusion.

North. No sophistry, James.

Shepherd. Hunger's naething till Thrust. Ance in the middle o' the muir o' Rannoch I had neer dee'd o' thrust. I was crossing frae Loch Ericht fit † to the heid o'Glenorchy, and got in amang the hags, ‡ that for leagues and leagues a' round that dismal region seem howked out o' the black moss by demons doomed to dreary days-dargs § for their sins in the wilderness. There was naething for't but loup—loup—loupin out o' ae pit intil anither—hour after hour—till, sail

* The Duke of Wellington. He was at this time Prime Minister.

† *Fit*—foot.

‡ *Hags*—pits whence peat has been dug.

§ *Days-dargs*—day's labors.

forfeuchen,* I feenally gied mysel up for lost. Drought had sooked up the pools, and left their cracked bottoms barkened † in the heat. The heather was sliddery as ice, aneath that torrid zone. Sic a sun! No ae clud on a' the sky glitterin wi' wirewoven sultriness! The howe o' the lift ‡ was like a great cawdron pabblin into the boil ower a slow fire. The element of water seemed dried up out o' natur, a' except the big drops o' sweat that plashed doun on my fevered hauns, that began to trummle like leaves o' aspen. My mouth was made o' cork covered wi' dust—lips, tongue, palate, and a', doun till my throat and stammack. I spak—and the arid soun' was as if a buried corpse had tried to mutter through the smotherin mools. I thocht on the tongue of a parrot. The central lands o' Africa, whare lions gang ragin mad for water, when cheated out o' blood, canna be worse—dreamed I in a species o' delirium—than this dungeon'd desert. Oh! but a drap o' dew would hae seem'd then pregnant wi' salvation!—a shower out o' the windows o' heaven, like the direct gift o' God, Rain! Rain! Rain!—what a world o' life in *that* sma' word! But the atmosphere look'd as if it would never melt mair, intrenched against a' liquidity by brazen barriers burnin in the sun. Spittle I had nane—and when in desperation I sooked the heather, 'twas frush and fushionless, as if withered by lichtnin, and a' sap had left the vegetable creation. What'n a cursed fule was I—for in rage I fear I swore inwardly (Heev'n forgie me)—that I didna at the last change-house put into my pouch a bottle o' whisky! I fan' my pulse—and it was thin—thin—thin—sma'—sma'—sma'—noo nane ava—and then a flutter that telt tales o' the exhausted heart. I grat.§ Then shame came to my relief—shame even in that utter solitude. Somewhere or ither in

* *Forfeuchen*—fatigued.
† *Barkened*—hardened.
‡ *Howe o' the lift*—hollow of the sky.
§ *Grat*—wept.

the muir I knew there was a loch, and I took out my map. But the infernal idiwut that had planned it hadna allooed a yellow circle o' aboon six inches square for a' Perthshire. What's become o' a' the birds—thocht I—and the bees—and the butterflees—and the dragons ?—A' wattin their bills and their proboscisces in far-off rills, and rivers, and lochs! O blessed wild-dyucks, plouterin in the water, streekin theirsels up, and flappin their flashin plumage in the pearly freshness! A great big speeder, wi' a bag-belly, was rinnin up my leg, and I crushed it in my fierceness—the first inseck I ever wantonly murdered sin' I was a wean. I kenna whether at last I swarfed or slept—but for certain sure I had a dream. I dreamt that I was at hame—and that a tub o' whey was staunin on the kitchen dresser. I dook'd my head intil't, and sooked it dry to the wood. Yet it slokened* not my thrust, but aggravated a thousand-fauld the torment o' my greed. A thunder-plump or waterspout brak amang the hills—and in an instant a' the burns were on spate; the Yarrow roarin red, and foaming as it were mad,—and I thocht I could hae drucken up a' its linns. 'Twas a brain fever, ye see, sirs, that had stricken me—a sair stroke—and I was conscious again o' lying broad awake in the desert, wi' my face up to the cruel sky. I was the verra personification o' Thrust!—and felt that I was ane o' the Damned Dry, doom'd for his sins to leeve beyond the reign o' the element to a' Eternity. Suddenly, like a man shot in battle, I bounded up into the air—and ran off in the convulsive energy o' dying natur—till doun I fell—and felt that I was about indeed to expire. A sweet, saft, celestial greenness cooled my cheek as I lay, and my burnin een—and then a gleam o' something like a mighty diamond—a gleam that seemed to comprehend within itsel the haill universe—shone in upon and through my being—I

* *Slokened*—quenched.

gazed upon't wi' a' my senses. Mercifu' Heaven! what was't but—a WELL in the wilderness!—water—water—water,—and as I drank—I prayed!

Omnes. Bravo — bravo — bravo! Hurra —hurra — hurra!

Shepherd. Analeeze that, Mr. De Quinshy.

English Opium-Eater. Inspiration admits not of analysis—in itself an evolvement of an infinite series—

Shepherd. Isna the Dolphin rather ower sweet, sirs? We maun mak haste and drain him—and neist brewst, Mrs. Awmrose maun be less lavish o' her sugar—for her finest crystals are the verra concentrated essence o' saccharine sweetness, twa lumps to the mutchkin.

English Opium-Eater. Mr. Hogg, that wallflower in your button-hole is intensely beautiful, and its faint wild scent mingles delightfully with the fragrance of the coffee—

Shepherd. And o' the toddy—ae blended bawm. I pu'd it aff ane o' the auld towers o' Newark, this morning, frae a constellation o' starry blossoms, that a' nicht lang had been drinkin the dews, and at the dawin could hardly haud up their heads, sae laden was the haill bricht bunch wi' the pearlins o' heaven. And would ye believe't, a bit robin-redbreast had bigged its nest in a cozy cranny o' the moss wa', ahint the wallflower, a perfect paradise to brood and breed in,—out flew the dear wee beastie wi' a flutter in my face, and every mouth opened as I keeked in—and then a' was hushed again—just like my ain bairnies in ae bed at hame—no up yet—for the hours were slawly intrudin on the "innocent brichtness o' the new-born day;" and it was, guessing by the shadowless light on the tower and trees, only about four o'clock in the mornin.

Tickler. I was just then going to bed.

Shepherd. Teetus Vespawsian used to say sometimes: "I

have lost a day"—but the sluggard loses a' his life, and lets it slip through his hauns like a knotless thread.

English Opium-Eater. I am no sluggard, Mr. Hogg—yet I—

Shepherd. Change nicht into day, and day into nicht, rinnin coonter to natur, insultin the sun, and quarrellin wi' the equawtor. That's no richt. Nae man kens what Beauty is that hasna seen her a thousan' and a thousan' times lyin on the lap o' nature, asleep in the dawn—on an earthly bed a spirit maist divine. . . . Whisht, I heard a fisslin in the gallery !

North. Leander !

(*The horns sound, and enter* οἱ περὶ AMBROSE.)

Shepherd (*in continuation*). Ggemm ! and Fools !

FOURTH COURSE—FOWL.

TICKLER.

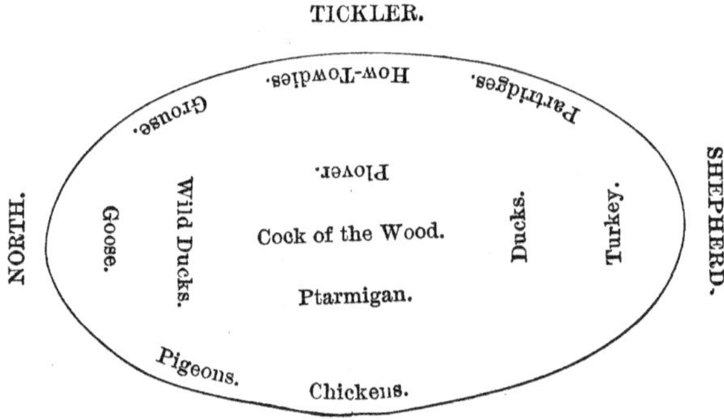

ENGLISH OPIUM-EATER.

North. (*in continuation*). The Greek Tragedy, James, was austere in its principles as the Greek Sculpture. Its subjects were all of ancestral and religious consecration; its style, high, and heroic, and divine, admitted no intermixture even of mirth, or seldom and reluctantly,—much less of grotesque and fantastic extravagances of humor,—which would have marred the consummate dignity, beauty, and magnificence of all the scenes that swept along that enchanted floor. Such was the spirit that shone on the soft and the stately Sophocles. But Shakespeare came from heaven—and along with him a Tragedy that poured into one cup the tears of mirth and madness; showed Kings one day crowned with jewelled diadems, and another day with wild wisps of straw; taught the Prince who, in single combat—

> "Had quench'd the flame of hot rebellion
> Even in the rebels' blood,"

to moralize on the field of battle over the carcase of a fat buffoon wittily simulating death among the bloody corpses of English nobles; nay, showed the son—and that son, prince, philosopher, paragon of men—jocularly conjuring to rest his Father's Ghost, who had revisited earth "by the glimpses of the moon, making night hideous."

Shepherd. Stop—stop, sir. That's aneuch to prove your pint. . . . And sae your auld freen's dead.—What kirkyard was he buried in?

North. Greyfriars.

Shepherd. An impressive place. Huge, auld, red, gloomy church—a countless multitude 'o grass graves a' touchin ane anither—a' roun the kirkyard wa's marble and freestane monuments without end, o' a' shapes, and sizes, and ages—some quaint, some queer, some simple, some ornate; for genius likes to work upon grief—and these tombs are like towers and temples, partakin not o' the noise o' the city, but staunin aloof frae the stir o' life, aneath the sombre shadow o' the Castle cliff, that heaves its battlements far up into the sky. A sublime cemetery—yet I sudna like to be interred in't—it looks sae dank, clammy, cauld—

Tickler. And uncomfortable. A corpse would be apt to catch its death of cold.

Shepherd. Whisht.—Where did he leeve?

North. On the sea-shore.

Shepherd. I couldna thole to leeve on the sea-shore.

Tickler. And pray why not, James?

Shepherd. That everlastin thunner sae disturbs my imagination, that my soul has nae rest in its ain solitude, but becomes transfused as it were into the michty ocean, a' its thochts as wild as the waves that keep foamin awa into naething, and then breakin back again into transitory life—for ever and ever and ever—as if neither in sunshine nor moonlight, that multitudinous tumultuousness, frae the first creation o' the world, had ever ance been stilled in the blessedness o' perfect sleep.

English Opium-Eater. In the turmoil of this our mortal lot, the soul's deepest bliss assuredly is, O Shepherd! a tideless calm.

Shepherd. The verra thocht, sir—the verra feelin—the verra word.

North. What pleasanter spot, James, than a country kirk-yard?

Shepherd. I steek my een—and I see ane the noo—in a green laigh lown spot amang the sheep-nibbled braes. A Funeral! See that row of schoolboy laddies and lassies drawn up sae orderly o' their ain still accord, half curious and half wae,* some o' the lassies wi' lapfu's o' primroses, and gazin wi' hushed faces as the wee coffin enters in on men's shouthers that never feel its wecht, wi' its doun-hangin and gracefu' velvet pall, though she that is hidden therein was the poorest o' the poor! Twa-three days ago the body in that coffin was dancin like a sunbeam ower the verra sods that are noo about to be shovelled over it! The flowers she

* *Wae*—sorrowful.

had been gatherin—sweet, innocent, thochtless cretur—then moved up and doun on her bosom when she breathed—for she and nature were blest and beautifu' in their spring. An auld white-headed man, bent sairly doun, at the head o' the grave, lettin the white cord slip wi' a lingerin, reluctant tenderness through his withered hauns! It has reached the bottom. Wasna that a dreadfu' groan, driven out o' his heart, as if a strong-haun'd man had smote it by the first fa' o' the clayey thunder on the fast-disappearing blackness o' the velvet—soon hidden in the bony mould? He's but her grandfather—for she was an orphan. *But* her grandfather! Wae's me! wha is't that writes in some silly blin' book that auld age is insensible—safe and secure frae sorrow—and that dim eyes are unapproachable to tears?

Tickler. Not till dotage drivels away into death. With hoariest eld often is parental love a passion deeper than ever bowed the soul of bright-haired youth, watching by the first dawn of daylight the face of the sleeping bride.

Shepherd. What gars us a' fowre talk on such topics the nicht? Friendship! That, when sincere—as ours is sincere—will sometimes saften wi' a strange sympathy merriest hearts into ae mood o' melancholy, and pitch a' their voices on ae key, and gie a' their faces ae expression, and mak them a' feel mair profoundly, because they a' feel thegither, the sadness and the sanctity—different words for the same meaning—o' this our mortal life;—I howp there's naething the maitter wi' wee Jamie.

North. That there is not, indeed, my dearest Shepherd. At this very moment he is singing his little sister asleep.

Shepherd. God bless you, sir; the tone o' your voice is like a silver trumpet.—Mr. De Quinshy, hae you ever soum'd up the number o' your weans?*

* *Weans*—children.

English Opium-Eater. Seven.

Shepherd. Stop there, sir, it's a mystical number,—and may they aye be like sae mony planets in bliss and beauty circlin roun the sun.

English Opium-Eater. It seemeth strange the time when as yet those Seven Spirits were not in the body—and the air which I breathed partook not of that blessedness which now to me is my life. Another sun—another moon—other stars—since the face of my first-born. Another earth—another heaven! I loved, methought—before that face smiled—the lights and the shadows, the flowers and the dews, the rivulets that sing to Pilgrims in the wild,—the mountain wells, where all alone the "book-bosomed" Pilgrim sitteth down—and lo! far below the many-rivered vales sweeping each to its own lake—how dearly did I love ye all! Yet was that love fantastical—and verily not of the deeper soul. Imagination over this "visible diurnal sphere" spread out her own spiritual qualities, and made the beauty that beamed back upon her dreams. Nor wanted tenderest touches of humanity—as my heart remembered some living flower by the door of far-up cottage, where the river is but a rill. But in my inner spirit there was then a dearth, which Providence hath since amply, and richly, and prodigally furnished with celestial food—which is also music to the ears, and light to the eyes, and the essence of silken softness to the touch—a family of immortal spirits, who but for me never had been brought into the mystery of accountable and responsible being! Of old I used to study the Spring—but now its sweet sadness steals unawares into my heart—when among the joyous lambs I see my own children at play. The shallow nest of the cushat seems now to me a more sacred thing in the obscurity of the pine-tree. The instincts of all the inferior creatures are now holy in my eyes—for, like Reason's self, they have their origin in love. Affection for my own children has enabled me to sound the depths of gratitude. Gazing on them at their prayers, in their sleep, I have had revelations of the nature of peace, and trouble, and innocence, and sin, and sorrow, which, till they had smiled and wept, offended and been reconciled, I knew not—how could I?—to be within the range of the far-flying and far-fetching spirit of love, which is the life-of-life of all things beneath the sun, moon and stars.

Shepherd. Do ye ken, sir, that I love to hear ye speak far best ava when you lay aside your logic? Grammar's aften a grievous and gallin burden; but logic's a cruel constraint on thochts, and the death of feelings, which ought aye to rin blendin intil ane anither like the rainbow, or the pink, or the peacock's neck, a beautifu' confusion o' colors, that's the mair admired the mair ignorant you are o' the science o' opticks. I just perfectly abhor the word "therefore," it's sae pedantic and pragmatical, and like a doctor. What's the use o' premises?—commend me to conclusions. As for inferences, put them into the form o' apothegms, and never tell the world whence you draw them—for then they look like inspiration. And dinna ye think, sir, that reasoning's far inferior to intuition?

Tickler. How are your transplanted trees, James?

Shepherd. A' dead.

Tickler. I can't endure the idea of a transplanted tree. Transplantation strikes at the very root of its character as a stationary and stedfast being, flourishing where nature dropt it. You may remove a seedling; but 'tis sacrilege to hoist up a huge old oak by the power of machinery, and stick him into another soil, far aloof from his native spot, which for so many years he had sweetly or solemnly overshadowed.

Shepherd. Is that feelin no a wee owre imaginative ?

Tickler. Perhaps it is—and none the worse of that either—for there's a tincture of imagination in all feelings of any pith or moment—nor do we require that they should always be justified by reason. On looking on a tree with any emotion of grandeur or beauty, one always has a dim notion of its endurance—its growth and its decay. The place about it is felt to belong to it—or rather, they mutually belong to each other, and death alone should dissolve the union.

Shepherd. I fin' mysel convincin—that is, being convinced—but no by your spoken words, but by my ain silent thochts. I felt a' you say, and mair too, the first time I tried to transplant a tree. It was a birk—a weepin birk—and I had loved and admired it for twenty years by its ain pool, far up ane o' the grains * o' the Douglas Water, where I beat Mr. North at the fishin—

North. You never beat me at the fishing, sir, and never will beat me at the fishing, sir, while your name is Hogg. I killed that day—in half the time—double the number—

Shepherd. But wecht, sir—wecht, sir, wecht. My creel was mair nor dooble yours's wecht—and every wean kens that in fishin for a wager, wecht wins—it's aye decided by wecht.

North. The weight of your basket was not nearly equal to mine, you—

Shepherd. Confound me gin, on an average, ane o' my troots didna conteen mair cubic inches than three o' yours—while I had a ane to produce that, on his first showin his snoot, I could hae swore was a sawmon;—he would hae filled the creel his ain lane—sae I sent him hame wi' a callant I met gaun to the school. The feck o' yours was mere fry—and some had a' the appearance o' bein' baggy mennons. You're a

* *Grains*—branches. The Douglas Water is a tributary of the Yarrow.

gran' par-fisher, sir ; but you're nae Thorburn * either at troots, morts or fish. †

North (starting up in a fury). I'll fish you for—

Shepherd. Mr. North ! I am ashamed to see you exposin yoursel afore Mr. De Quinshy—besides, thae ragin fits are dangerous—and, some time or ither, 'ill bring on apoplexy. Oh ! but you're fearsome the noo—black in the face, or rather, blue and purple—and a' because I said that you're nae Thorburn at the fishin. Sit doun—sit doun, sir.

[Mr. NORTH *sits down, and cools and calms himself, while the horns sound for the fifth course,* "*The gloomy nicht is gathering fast.*"

* A noted angler on Tweedside.

† In the language of anglers, salmon alone are called **fish.**

XXII.

THE BLOODY BATTLE OF THE BEES.

Scene,—The Arbor, Buchanan Lodge. Time,—Eight o'clock. Present.—NORTH, ENGLISH OPIUM-EATER, SHEPHERD, *and* TICKLER. *Table with light wines, oranges, biscuits, almonds, and raisins.*

Shepherd. Rain but no star-proof, this bonny bee-hummin, bird-nest-concealin Bower, that seems—but for the trellis-wark peepin out here and there where the later flowerin-shrubs are scarcely yet out o' the bud—rather a production o' Nature's sel than o' the gardener's genius. Oh, sir, but in its bricht and balmy beauty 'tis even nae less than a perfeck Poem!

North. Look, James, how she cowers within her couch—only the point of her bill, the tip of her tail, visible—so passionately cleaveth the loving creature to the nestlings beneath her mottled breast,—each morning beautifying from down to plumage, till next Sabbath-sun shall stir them out of their cradle, and scatter them, in their first weak wavering flight, up and down the dewy dawn of their native Paradise.

Shepherd. A bit mavis! * Hushed as a dream—and like a dream to be startled aff intil ether, if you but touch the leaf-croon that o'er-canopies her head. What an ee! Shy, yet confidin—as she sits there ready to flee awa wi' a rustle in a

* *Mavis*—thrush.

moment yet linked within that rim by the chains o' love, motionless as if she were dead!

North. See—she stirs!

Shepherd. Dinna be disturbed. I could glower at her for hours, musin on the mystery o' instinct, and at times forgettin that my een were fixed but on a silly bird,—for sae united are a' the affections o' sentient Natur, that you hae only to keek * intil a brush o' broom, or a sweet-brier, or doun to the green braird aneath your feet, to behold in the lintie, or the lark—or in that mavis—God bless her!—an emblem o' the young Christian mother fauldin up in her nursin bosom the beauty and the blessedness o' her ain First-born!

North. I am now threescore-and-ten, James, and I have suffered and enjoyed much; but I know not if, during all the confusion of those many-colored years, diviner delight ever possessed my heart and my imagination, than of old entranced me in solitude, when, among the braes, and the moors, and the woods, I followed the verdant footsteps of the Spring, uncompanioned but by my own shadow, and gave names to every nook in nature, from the singing birds of Scotland discovered, but disturbed not, in their most secret nests.

Tickler. Namby-pamby!

Shepherd. Nae sic thing. A shilfa's† nest within the angles made by the slicht, silvery, satiny stem o' a bit birk-tree, and ane o' its young branches glitterin and glimmerin at ance wi' shade and sunshine and a dowery o' pearls, is a sicht that, when seen for the first time in this life, gars a boy's being loup out o' his verra bosom richt up intil the boundless blue o' heaven!

Tickler. Poo

Shepherd. Whisht—oh, whisht. For 'tis felt to be something far, far beyond the beauty o' the maist artfu' contrivances o'

* *Keek*—peep. † *Shilfa*—chaffinch.

mortal man,—and gin he be a thochtfu' callant, which frae wanderin and daunderin by himsel, far awa frae houses, and ayont the loneliest shielin * amang the hills, is surely nae unreasonable hypothesis, but the likeliest thing in natur, thinkna ye that though his mood micht be indistinck even as ony sleepin dream, that nevertheless it maun be sensibly interfused, throughout and throughout, wi' the consciousness that that Nest, wi' sic exquisite delicacy intertwined o' some substance seemingly mair beautifu' than ony moss that ever grew upon this earth, into a finest fabric growin as it were out o' the verra bark o' the tree, and in the verra nook,—the only nook where nae winds could touch it, let them blaw a' at ance frae a' the airts,—wadna, sirs, I say, that callant's heart beat wi' awe in its delicht, feelin that that wee, cosy, beautifu' and lovely cradle, chirp-chirpin wi' joyfu' life, was bigged there by the hand o' Him that hung the sun in our heaven, and studded with stars the boundless universe?

Tickler. James, forgive my folly——

Shepherd. That I do, Mr. Tickler—and that I would do, if for every peck there was a firlot. Yet when a laddie, I was an awfu' herrier! † Sic is the inconsistency, because o' the corruption o' human natur. Ilka spring, I used to hae half a dozen strings o' eggs——

Tickler.—

"Orient pearls at random strung."

Shepherd. Na—no at random—but a' accordin to an innate sense o' the beauty o' the interminglin and interfusin variegation o' manifold color, which. when a' gathered thegither on a yard o' twine, and dependin frae the laigh roof o' our bit cottie, aneath the cheese-bauk, and aiblins atween a couple o' hangin hams, seemed to ma een sae fu' o' a strange,

* *Shielin*—a shelter for sheep or shepherd among the hills.

† *Herrier*—rifler of birds' nests.

wild, woodland, wonderfu', and maist unwarldish loveliness, that the verra rainbow hersel, lauchin on us laddies no to be feared at the thunner, looked nae mair celestial than thae egg-shells! Ae string especially will I remember till my dying day. It tapered awa frae the middle, made o' the eggs o' the blackbird—doun through a' possible vareeities —lark, lintie, yellow-yite, hedge-sparrow, shilfa, and goldfinch—ay, the verra goldfinch hersel, rare bird in the Forest —to the twa ends so dewdrap-like, wi' the wee bit blue pearlins o' the kitty-wren. Damm Wullie Laidlaw for stealin them ae Sabbath when we was a' at the kirk! Yet I'll try to forgie him for sake o' "Lucy's Flittin," * and because notwithstanding that cruel crime, he's turned out a gude husband, a gude faither, and a gude freen.

Tickler. We used, at school, James, to boil and eat them.

Shepherd. Gin ye did, then wouldna I, for ony consideration, in a future state be your sowl.

Tickler. Where's the difference?

Shepherd. What! atween you and me? Yours was a base, fleshly hunger, or hatred, or hard-heartedness, or scathe and scorn o' the quakin griefs o' the bit bonny shriekin burdies around the tuft o' moss, a' that was left o' their herried nests; but mine was the sacred hunger and thirst o' divine silver and gold gleamin amang the diamonds drapt by mornin on the hedgeraws, and rashes, and the broom, and the whins—love o' the lovely—desire conquerin but no killin pity—and joy o' blessed possession, that left at times a tear on my cheek for the bereavement o' the heart-broken warblers o' the woods. Yet brak I not mony o' their hearts, after a'; for if the nest had five eggs, I generally took but twa; though I confess that on gaun back again to

* "Lucy's Flitting," by William Laidlaw, Sir Walter Scott's friend, is one of our simplest and most pathetic melodies.

brae, bank, bush, or tree, I was glad when the nest was deserted, the eggs cauld, and the birds awa to some ither place. After a' I was never cruel, sirs; that's no a sin o' mine—and whenever, either then or since, I hae gien pain to ony leevin cretur, in nae lang time after, o' the twa pairties, mine has been the maist achin heart. As for pyats, and hoodie-craws, and the like, I used to herry them without compunction, and flingin up stanes, to shoot them wi' a gun as they were flasterin out o' the nest.

English Opium-Eater. Some one of my ancestors—for, even with the deepest sense of my own unworthiness, I cannot believe that my own sins, as a cause, have been adequate to the production of such an effect—must have perpetrated some enormous—some monstrous crime, punished in me, his descendant, by utter blindness to all birds' nests.

Shepherd. Maist likely. The De Quinshys cam ower wi' the Conqueror, and were great criminals.—But did you ever look for them, sir?

English Opium-Eater. From the year 1811—the year in which the Marrs and Williamsons were murdered *—till the year 1821, in which Bonaparte the little—vulgarly called Napoleon the Great—died of a cancer in his stomach—

Shepherd. A hereditary disease—accordin to the doctors.

English Opium-Eater. —— did I exclusively occupy myself during the spring months, from night till morning, in searching for the habitations of these interesting creatures.

Shepherd. Frae nicht till mornin! That comes o' reversin the order o' Natur. You micht see a rookery or a heronry by moonlicht—but no a wren's nest aneath the portal o' some cave, lookin out upon a sleepless waterfa' dinnin to the stars.

* In the second volume of his *Miscellanies* (1854), Mr. De Quincey has described these murders with a power and circumstantiality which excite the most absorbing interest in the mind of the reader.

Mr. De Quinshy, you and me leeves in twa different warlds—and yet its wonnerfu' hoo we understaun' ane anither sae weel's we do—quite a phenomena. When I'm soopin you're breakfastin—when I'm lyin doun, after your coffee you're risin up—as I'm coverin my head wi' the blankets, you're pittin on your breeks—as my een are steekin like sunflowers aneath the moon, yours are glowin like twa gas-lamps—and while your mind is masterin poleetical economy and metapheesics, in a desperate fecht wi' Ricawrdo and Kant,* I'm heard by the nicht-wanderin fairies snorin trumpet-nosed through the land o' Nod.

English Opium-Eater. Though the revolutions of the heavenly bodies have, I admit, a certain natural connection with the ongoings of—

Shepherd. Wait awee—nane o' your astrology till after sooper. It canna be true, sir, what folk say about the influence o' the moon on character. I never thocht ye the least mad. Indeed, the only faut I hae to fin' wi' you is, that you're ower wise. Yet we speak what, in the lang-run, would appear to be ae common language—I sometimes understaun' you no that very indistinctly—and when we tackle in our talk to the great interests o' humanity, we're philosophers o' the same school, sir, and see the inner warld by the self-same central licht. We're incomprehensible creturs, are we men—that's beyond a dout;—and let us be born and bred as we may—black, white, red, or a deep bricht, burnished copper—in spite o' the division o' tongues, there's nae division o' hearts, for it's the same bluid that

* David Ricardo, an eminent member of the London Stock Exchange, and the profoundest writer on political economy which this country has produced, died in 1823. Immanuel Kant was the great philosopher of Königsberg, his native town, from which he was never farther distant than twenty miles, during the whole course of a life which lasted from 1724 to 1804.

gangs circulatin through our mortal tenements, carrying alang on its tide the same freightage o' feelins and thochts, emotions, affections, and passions—though, like the ships o' different nations, they a' hoist their ain colors, and prood, prood are they o' their leopards, or their crescent-moons, or their stars, or their stripes o' buntin;—but see! when it blaws great guns, hoo they a' fling owerboard their storm-anchors, and when their cables pairt, hoo they a' seek the shelterin lee o' the same michty breakwater, a belief in the being and attributes of the One Living God.—But was ye never out in the daytime, sir?

English Opium-Eater. Frequently.

Shepherd. But then it's sae lang sin' syne, that in memory the sunlicht maun seem amaist like the moonlicht,—sic, indeed, even wi' us that rise with the laverock, and lie doun wi' the lintie, is the saftenin—the shadin—the darkenin power o' the Past, o' Time the Prime Minister o' Life, wha, in spite o' a' Opposition, carries a' his measures by a silent vote, and aften, wi' a weary wecht o' taxes, bows a' the wide warld doun to the verra dust.

English Opium-Eater. In the South my familiars have been the nightingales, in the North the owls. Both are merry birds—the one singing, and the other shouting, in moods of midnight mirth.—Nor in my deepest, darkest fits of meditation or of melancholy, did the one or the other ever want my sympathies,—whether piping at the root of the hedgerow, or hooting from the trunk of a sycamore—else all still both on earth and in heaven.

Shepherd. Ye maun hae seen mony a beautifu' and mony a sublime sicht, sir, in the Region, lost to folk like us, wha try to keep oursels awauk a' day and asleep a' nicht—and your sowl, sir, maun hae acquired something o' the serene and solemn character o' the sunleft skies. And true it is, Mr.

De Quinshy, that ye hae the voice o' a nicht-wanderin man —laigh and lown—pitched on the key o' a wimplin burn speakin to itsel in the silence, aneath the moon and stars.

Tickler. 'Tis pleasant, James, to hear all us four talking at one time—your bass, my counter, Mr. De Quincey's tenor, and North's treble—

North. Treble, indeed!

Tickler. Ay, childish treble—

Shepherd. Come, nae quarrellin yet. That's a quotation frae Shakespeare, and there's nae insult in a mere quotation. (*after a pause.*) Oh, man! if them that's kickin up sic a row the noo about the doctrine o' the Christian religion had looked intil the depths o' their ain natur wi' your een, they had a' been as mum as mice keekin roun' the end o' a pew, in place o' scrauchin like pyats on the leads, or a hoodie wi' a sair throat.

English Opium-Eater. I know not to what you allude, Mr. Hogg, for I live out of what is called the Religious World.

Shepherd. A loud, noisy, vulgar, bawlin, brawlin, wranglin, branglin, routin, and roarin warld—maist unfittin indeed for the likes o' you, sir, wha, under the shadows o' woods and mountains, at midnight, communes wi' your ain heart, and is still.

English Opium-Eater. No religious controversy in modern days, sir, ever seemed to me to reach back into those recesses in my spirit where the sources lie from which well out the bitter or the sweet waters—the sins and the miseries—the holinesses and the happinesses of our incomprehensible being!

Shepherd. And if they ever do, hoo drumly the stream!

English Opium-Eater. Better even a mere sentimental religion, which, though shallow, is pure, than those audacious doctrines broached by Pride-in-Humility, who, blind as the bat, essays the flight of the eagle, and, ignorant of the lowest natures, yet claims acquaintance with the decrees of the Most High.

Shepherd. Ay—better far a sentimental—a poetical religion, as you say, sir—though that's far frae being the true thing either—for o' a' the Three Blessings o' Man, the last is the best—Love, Poetry, and Religion. What'n a book micht be written, I've aften thocht—and aiblins may hae said—on thae three words!

English Opium-Eater. Yes, my dear James—Beauty, the soul of Poetry, is indeed divine—but there is that which is diviner still—and that is Duty.

> "Flowers laugh before her on their beds,
> And fragrance in her footing treads;
> She doth preserve the stars from wrong,
> And the eternal heavens through her are fresh and strong."

Shepherd. Wha said that?

English Opium-Eater. Who?—Wordsworth. And the *Edinburgh Review—laughed.*

Shepherd. He has made it, sin' syne, lauch out o' the wrang side o' its mouth. He soars.

North. Human life is always, in its highest moral exhibitions, sublime rather than beautiful—and the sublimity is not that of the imagination, but of the soul.

Shepherd. If you will alloo a simple shepherd to speak on sic a theme—

North. Yes, my dearest James, you can, if you choose, speak on it better than either of us.

Shepherd. Weel, then, that is the view o' virtue that seems maist consistent wi' the revelation o' its true nature by Christianity, Isna there, sirs, a perpetual struggle—a ceevil war—in ilka man's heart? This we ken, whenever we have an opportunity o' discerning what is gaun on in the hearts o' ithers,—this we ken, whenever we set ourselves to tak a steady gaze intil the secrets o' our ain. We are, then, moved—ay, appalled, by much that we behold; and wherever there is sin, there, be assured, will be sorrow. But arena we aften cheered, and consoled too, by much that we behold? And wherever there is goodness, our ain heart, as weel's them o' the spectators, burns within us! Ay—it burns within us. We feel—we see, that we or our brethren are pairtly as God would wish—as we must be afore we can hope to see His face in mercy. I've often thocht intil mysel that that feeling is ane that we may *desecrate* (is that the richt word?) by ranking it amang them that appertains to our senses and our imagination, rather than to the religious soul.

North. Mr. De Quincey!

English Opium-Eater. Listen. An extraordinary man indeed, sir!

Shepherd. No me; there's naething extraordinar about me, mair than about a thousand ither Scottish shepherds. But ca' not, I say, the face o' that father beautifu' who stands beside the bier o' his only son, and wi' his ain withered hands helps to let doun the body into the grave—though all its lines, deep as they are, are peacefu' and untroubled, and the grey uncovered head maist reverend and affecting in the sunshine that falls at the same time on the coffin of him who was last week the sole stay o' his auld age! But if you could venture in thocht to be wi' that auld man when he is on his knees before God, in his lanely room, blessing Him for a' His mercies, even for having taken awa the licht o' his eyes, extinguished it in a moment, and left a' the house in darkness—you would not then, if you saw into his inner spirit, venture to ca' the calm that slept there—beautifu'! Na, na, na! In it you would feel assurance o' the immortality of the Soul—o' the transitoriness o' mere human sorrows—o' the vanity o' a' passion that clings to the clay—o' the power which the spirit possesses in richt o' its origin to see God's eternal justice in the midst o' sic utter bereavement as might well shake its faith in the Invisible—o' a' life where there is nae decaying frame to weep over and to bewail; and sae thinking—and sae feelin—ye would behold in that auld man kneelin in your unkent presence, an eemage o' human nature by its intensest sufferings raised and reconciled to that feenal state o' obedience, acquiescence, and resignation to the will o' the Supreme, which is virtue, morality, piety, in ae word —RELIGION. Ay, the feenal consummation o' mortality putting on immortality, o' the soul shedding the slough o' its earthly affections, and reappearing amaist in its pristine innocence, nae unfit inhabitant o' Heaven.

English Opium-Eater. Say not that a thousand Scottish shepherds could so speak, my dear sir.

Shepherd. Ay, and far better, too. But hearken till me,—when that state o' mind passed away frae us, and we became willing to find relief, as it were, frae thochts sae far aboon the level o' them that must be our daily thochts, then we micht, and then probably we would, begin to speak, sir, o' the beauty o' the auld man's resignation, and in poetry or painting the picture micht be pronounced beautifu', for then our souls would hae subsided, and the deeper, the mair solemn, and the mair awfu' o' our emotions would o' themselves hae retired to rest within the recesses o' the heart, alang wi' maist o' the maist mysterious o' our moral and religious convictions.—(*Dog barks.*) Heavens! I could hae thocht that was Bronte!

North. No bark like his, James, now belongs to the world of sound.

Shepherd. Purple black was he all over, except the star on his breast—as the raven's wing. Strength and sagacity emboldened his bounding beauty, and a fierceness lay deep down within the quiet lustre o' his een, that tauld ye, even when he laid his head upon your knees, and smiled up to your face like a verra intellectual and moral cretur,—as he was,—that had he been angered, he could hae torn in pieces a lion.

North. Not a child of three years old and upwards, in the neighborhood of the Lodge, that had not hung by his mane, and played with his fangs, and been affectionately worried by him on the flowery greensward.

Shepherd. Just like a stalwart father gambollin wi' his lauchin bairns!—And yet there was a heart that could bring itsel to pushion Bronte! When the atheist flung him the arsenic ba', the deevil was at his elbow.*

North. 'Twas a murder worthy of Hare or Burke, or the bloodiest of their most cruel and cowardly abettors.

Shepherd. I agree wi' you, sir; but dinna look sae white, and sae black, and sae red in the face, and then sae mottled, as if you had the measles; for see, sir, how the evening sunshine is sleeping on his grave!

North. No yew-tree, James, ever grew so fast before—Mrs Gentle herself planted it at his head. My own eyes were somewhat dim, but as for hers — God love them!—they streamed like April skies—and nowhere else in all the garden are the daisies so bright as on that small mound. That wreath, so curiously wrought into the very form of flowery letters, seems to fantasy like a funeral inscription—his very name—Bronte.

Shepherd. Murder's murder, whether the thing pushioned hae four legs or only twa—for the crime is curdled into crime

* Bronte was poisoned—at least so it is very confidently believed—by some of Dr. Knox's students, in revenge for the exposure of the principles on which their anatomical school was conducted.

in the blackness o' the sinner's heart, and the revengefu' shedder even of bestial blood would, were the same demon to mutter into his ears, and shut his eyes to the gallows, poison the well in which the cottage-girl dips the pitcher that breaks the reflection o' her bonny face in that liquid heaven.—But hark! wi' that knock on the table you hae frichtened the mavis!—Aften do I wonder whether or no birds, and beasts, and insecks hae immortal sowls!

English Opium-Eater. What God makes, why should He annihilate? Quench our own Pride in the awful consciousness of our Fall, and will any other response come from that oracle within us—Conscience—than that we have no claim on God for immortality, more than the beasts which want indeed "discourse of reason," but which live in love, and by love, and breathe forth the manifestations of their being through the same corruptible clay which makes the whole earth one mysterious burial-place, unfathomable to the deepest soundings of our souls!

Shepherd. True, Mr. De Quinshy—true, true. Pride's at the bottom o' a' our blindness, and a' our wickedness, and a' our madness; for if we did indeed and of verity, a' the nichts and a' the days o' our life, sleepin and waukin,' in delicht or in despair, aye remember, and never for a single moment forget, that we are a'—WORMS—Milton, and Spenser, and Newton—gods as they were on earth—and that they were gods, did not the flowers and the stars declare, and a' the two blended warlds o' Poetry and Science, lyin as it were like the skies o' heaven reflected in the waters o' the earth, in ane anither's arms? Ay, Shakespeare himsel a WORM—and Imogen, and Desdemona, and Ophelia, a' but the eemages o' WORMS—and Macbeth, and Lear, and Hamlet! Where would be then our pride and the self-idolatry o' our pride, and all the vain-glorifications o' our imagined magnificence?

Dashed doun into the worm-holes o' our birth-place, among all crawlin and slimy things—and afraid in our lurking-places to face the divine purity o' the far, far-aff and eternal heavens in their infinitude!—Puir Bronte's dead and buried—and sae in a few years will a' Us Fowre be! Had we naething but our boasted reason to trust in, the dusk would become the dark—and the dark the mirk, mirk, mirk; but we have the Bible,—and lo! a golden lamp illumining the short midnicht that blackens between the mortal twilight and the immortal dawn.

North (*blowing a boatswain's whistle*). Gentlemen—look here!

(*A noble young Newfoundlander comes bounding into the Arbor.*)

Shepherd. Mercy me! mercy me! the verra dowg himsel! The dowg wi' the star-like breast!

North. Allow me, my friend, to introduce you to O'BRONTE.

Shepherd. Ay—I'll shake paws wi' you, my gran' fallow; and though it's as true among dowgs as men, that he's a clever chiel that kens his ain father, yet as sure as wee Jamie's mine ain, are you auld Bronte's son. You've gotten the verra same identical shake o' the paw—the verra same identical wag o' the tail. (See, as Burns says, hoo it "hangs ower his hurdies wi' a swurl.") Your chowks the same—like him, too, as Shakespeare says, "dew-lapped like Thessawlian bills." The same braid, smooth, triangular lugs, hanging doun aneath your chafts; and the same still, serene, smilin, and sagacious een. Bark! man—bark! let us hear you bark.—Ay, that's the verra key that Bronte barked on whenever "his blood was up and heart beat high:" and I'se warrant that in anither year or less, in a street-row, like your sire you'll clear the causeway o' a clud o' curs, and carry the terror o' your name frae the Auld to the New Flesh-market; though tak my advice, ma dear O'Bronte, and, except when circum stances imperiously demand war, be thou—thou jewel of a Jowler—a lover of peace!

English Opium-Eater. I am desirous, Mr. Hogg, of cultivating the acquaintance—nay, I hope of forming the friendship—of that noble animal. Will you permit him to—

Shepherd. Gang your wa's,* O'Bronte, and speak till the English Opium-Eater. Ma faith! you hae nae need o' drogs to raise your animal speerits, or heighen your imagination. What'n intensity o' life!—But whare's he been sin' he was puppied, Mr. North?

North. On board a whaler. No education like a trip to Davis Strait.

Shepherd. He'll hae speeled, I'se warrant him, mony an iceberg—and worried mony a seal—aiblins a walrus, or sea-lion. But are ye no feared o' his rinnin awa to sea?

North. The spirit of his sire, James, has entered into him, and he would lie, till he was a skeleton, upon my grave.

Shepherd. It canna be denied, sir, that you hae an unaccountable power o' attaching to you, no only dowgs, but men, women, and children. I've never douted but that you maun hae some magical pouther, that you blaw in amang their hair—na, intil their verra lugs and een—imperceptible fine as the motes i' the sun—and then there's nae resistance, but the sternest Whig saftens afore you, the roots o' the Radical relax, and a' distinctions o' age, sex and pairty—the last the stubbornest and dourest o' a'—fade awa intil undistinguishable confusion—and them that's no in the secret o' your glamoury, fears that the end o' the warld's at haun, and that there 'ill sune be nae mair use for goods and chattels in the Millennium.

Tickler. As I am a Christian—

* *Gang your wa's*—get off.

Shepherd. You a Christian!

Tickler Mr. De Quincey has given O'Bronte a box of opium.

Shepherd. What! Has the dowg swallowed the spale-box o' pills? We maun gar him throw it up.

English Opium-Eater. The most monstrous and ignominious ignorance reigns among all the physicians of Europe respecting the powers and properties of the poppy.

Shepherd. I wush in this case, sir, that the poppy mayna pruve ower poorfu' for the puppy, and that the dowg's no a dead man. Wull ye take your Bible-oath that he bolted the box?

English Opium-Eater. Mr. Hogg, I never could see any sufficient reason why, in a civilized and Christian country, an oath should be administered even to a witness in a court of justice. Without any formula, Truth is felt to be sacred—nor will any words weigh—

Shepherd. You're for upsettin the haill frame o' ceevil society, sir, and bringing back on this kintra a' the horrors o' the French Revolution. The power o' an oath lies, no in the Reason, but in the Imagination. Reason tells that simple affirmation or denial should be aneuch atween man and man. But Reason canna bind, or if she do, Passion snaps the chain. For ilka passion, sir, even a passion for a bead or a button, is as strong as Samson bursting the withies. But Imagination can bind, for she ca's on her Flamin Ministers—the Fears;—they palsy-strike the arm that would disobey the pledged lips—and thus oaths are dreadfu' as Erebus and the gates o' hell.—But see what ye hae dune, sir,—only look at O'Bronte

[O'BRONTE *sallies from the Arbor—goes driving head-over-heels through among the flower-beds, tearing up pinks and carnations with his mouth and paws, and, finally, makes repeated attempts to climb up a tree.*

English Opium-Eater. No such case is recorded in the medical books—and very important conclusions may be drawn from an accurate observation of the phenomena now exhibited by a distinguished member of the canine species, under such a dose of opium as would probably send Mr. Coleridge * himself to—

Shepherd.—his lang hame—or Mr. De Quinshy either—though I should be loth to lose sic a poet as the ane, and sic a philosopher as the ither—or sic a dowg as O'Bronte.—But look at him speelin up the apple-tree like the auld serpent! He's thinkin himsel, in the delusion o' the drog, a wull-cat or a bear, and has clean forgotten his origin. Deil tak me gin I ever saw the match o' that! He's gotten up; and's lyin a' his length on the branch, as if he were streekin himsel out to sleep on the ledge o' a brig! What thocht's gotten intil his head noo? He's for herryin the goldfinch's nest amang the verra tapmost blossoms!—Ay, my lad! that was a thud!

O'Bronte, *who has fallen from the pippin, recovers his feet —storms the Arbor—upsets the table, with all the bottles, glasses, and plates—and then, dashing through the glass front-door of the Lodge, disappears with a crash into the interior.*

English Opium-Eater. Miraculous!

Shepherd. A hairy hurricane!—What think ye, sir, o' the Scottish Opium-Eater?

English Opium-Eater. I hope it is not hydrophobia.

Tickler. He manifestly imagines himself at the whaling, and is off with the harpooners.

Shepherd. A vision o' blubber's in his sowl. Oh that he could gie the warld his Confessions!

* S. T. Coleridge was a great consumer of opium. See *his* "Confessions" in Cottle's *Reminiscences.* Born in 1771, Coleridge died in 1834.

English Opium-Eater. Mr. Hogg, how am I to understand that insinuation, sir?

Shepherd. Ony way you like. But did ever onybody see a philosopher sae passionate? Be cool—be cool.

Tickler. See, see, see!

[O'BRONTE.

> "*Like a glory from afar,*
> *Like a reappearing star,*"

comes spanging back into the cool of the evening, with CYPRUS, NORTH'S *unique male tortoise-shell cat in his mouth, followed by* JOHN *and* BETTY, *broom-and-spit-armed, with other domestics in the distance.*

North. Drop Cyprus, you villain! Drop Cyprus, you villain! I say, you villain, drop Cyprus—or I will brain you with Crutch!

[O'BRONTE *turns a deaf ear to all remonstrances, and continues his cat-carrying career, through flower, fruit, and kitchen-gardens—the crutch having sped after him in vain, and upset a beehive.*

Tickler. Demme—I'm off. [*Makes himself scarce.*

North. Was that thunder?

Shepherd. Bees—bees—bees! Intil the Arbor—intil the Arbor.—Oh! that it had a door wi' a hinge, and a bolt in the inside! Hoo the swarm's ragin wud! The hummin heavens is ower het to haud them—and if ae leader chances to cast his ee hither, we are lost. For let but ane set the example, and in a moment there'ill be a charge o' beggonets.*

English Opium-Eater. In the second book of his *Georgics* Virgil, at once poet and naturalist,—and indeed the two characters are, I believe, uniformly united,—beautifully treats of the economy of bees—and I remember one passage—

* *Beggonets*—bayonets.

Shepherd. They're after Tickler—they're after Tickler—like a cloud o' Cossacks or Polish Lancers—a' them that's no settlin on the crutch. And see—see, a division—the left o' the army— is bearin doun on O'Bronte. He'll sune liberate Ceeprus.

Tickler (*sub tegmine fagi*). Murder—murder—murder!

Shepherd. Ay, you may roar—that's nae flea-bitin—nor midge-bitin neither—na, it's waur than wasps—for wasps' stings hae nae barbs, but bees' hae—and when they strike them in, they canna rug them out again withouten leavin ahint their entrails—sae they curl theirsels up upon the wound, be it on haun, neck, or face, and, demon-like, spend their vitality in the sting, till the venom gangs dirlin to your verra heart. But do ye ken I'm amaist sorry for Mr. Tickler—for he'll be murdered outricht by the insecks—although he in a mainner deserved it for rinnin awa, and no sharin the common danger wi' the rest at the mouth of the Arbor. If he escapes wi' his life, we maun ca' a court-martial, and hae him broke for cooardice. Safe us! he's comin here wi' the haill bike* about his head!—Let us rin!—let us rin! Let us rin for our lives! [*The* SHEPHERD *is off and away.*

North. What! and be broke for cowardice! Let us die at our posts like men.

English Opium-Eater. I have heard Mr. Wordsworth deliver an opinion, respecting the courage, or rather the cowardice, of poets, which at the time, I confess, seemed to me to be unwarranted by any of the accredited phenomena of the poetical character. It was to this effect: That every passion of the poet being of "imagination all compact," fear would in all probability, on sudden and unforeseen emergencies, gain an undue ascendancy in his being over all the other unaroused active powers;—(and here suffer me to put you

* *Bike*—swarm.

on your guard against believing, that by the use of such terms as Active Powers, I mean to class myself, as a metaphysical moralist, in the Scottish school,—that is, the school more especially of Reid and Stewart*—whose ignorance of the Will—the sole province of Moral Philosophy—I hold to be equally shameful and conspicuous :)—so that, except in cases where that Fear was withstood by the force of Sympathy, the poet so assailed would, ten to one (such was the homely expression of the Bard anxious to *clinch it*), take to almost immediate flight. This doctrine, as I have said, appeared to me, at that time, not to be founded on a sufficiently copious and comprehensive induction ;—but I had, very soon after its oral delivery by the illustrious author of the *Excursion*, an opportunity of subjecting it to the test act:—For, as Mr. Wordsworth and myself were walking through a field of considerable—nay, great extent of acres —discussing the patriotism of the Spaniards, and more particularly the heroic defence of

> "Iberian burghers, when the sword they drew
> In Zaragoza, naked to the gales
> Of fiercely-breathing war,"

a bull of a red color (and that there must be something essentially and inherently vehement in red, or rather the natural idea of red, was interestingly proved by that answer of the blind man to an inquirer more distinguished probably for his curiosity than his acuteness—" that it was like the sound of a trumpet ") bore down suddenly upon our discourse, breaking, as you may well suppose, the thread thereof, and dissipating, for a while, the many high dreams (dreams indeed !) which we had been delighting to predict

* Dr. Thomas Reid, Professor of Moral Philosophy in the University of Glasgow, born in 1709, died in 1796. Dugald Stewart, Professor of Moral Philosophy in the University of Edinburgh, born in 1753, died in 1828.

of the future fates and fortunes of the Peninsula. The Bard's words, immediately before the intrusion of Taurus, were, "that death was a bugbear," and that the universal Spanish nation would "work out their own salvation." One bellow—and we were both hatless on the other side of the ditch. "If they do," said I, "I hope it will not be after our fashion, with fear and trembling." But I rather suspect, Mr. North, that I am this moment stung by one of those insects behind the ear, and in among the roots of the hair, nor do I think that the creature has yet disengaged—or rather disentangled itself from the nape—for I feel it struggling about the not—I trust—immedicable wound—the bee being scarcely distinguishable, while I place my finger on the spot, from the swelling round the puncture made by its sting, which, judging from the pain, must have been surcharged with—nay, steeped in venom. The pain is indeed most acute—and approaches to anguish—I had almost said agony.

North. Bruise the bee "even on the wound himself has made." 'Tis the only specific.—Any alleviation of agony?

English Opium-Eater. A shade. The analysis of such pain as I am now suffering—or say rather, enduring—

[TICKLER *and the* SHEPHERD, *after having in vain sought shelter among the shrubs, come flying demented towards the Arbor.*

Tickler and Shepherd. Murder!—murder!—murder!

North.—

> "Arcades ambo,
> Et cantare pares, et respondere parati!"

English Opium-Eater. Each encircled, as to his forehead, with a living crown—a murmuring bee-diadem worthy of Aristæus.

North. Gentlemen, if you mingle yourselves with us, I will shoot you both dead upon the spot with this fowling-piece.

Shepherd. What'n a foolin-piece? Oh! sir, but you're cruel! [TICKLER *lies down, and rolls himself on a plat.*

North. Destruction to a bed of onion-seed! James! into the tool-house.

Shepherd. I hae tried it thrice—but John and Betty hae barred themselves in against the swarm.—Oh! dear me—I'm exhowsted—sae let me lie down and dee beside Mr. Tickler! [*The* SHEPHERD *lies down beside* Mr. TICKLER.

English Opium-Eater. If any proof were wanting that I am more near-sighted than ever, it would be that I do not see in all the air, or round the luminous temples of Messrs. Tickler and Hogg, one single bee in motion or at rest.

North. They have all deserted their stations, and made a simultaneous attack on O'Bronte. Now, Cyprus, run for your life!

Shepherd (*raising his head*). Hoo he's devoorin them by hunders!—Look, Tickler.

Tickler. My eyes, James, are bunged up—and I am flesh-blind.

Shepherd. Noo they're yokin to Ceeprus! His tail's as thick wi' pain and rage as my arm. Hear till him caterwaulin like a haill roof-fu'! Ma stars, he'll gang mad, and O'Bronte 'ill gang mad, and we'll a' gang mad thegither, and the garden 'ill be ae great madhouse, and we'll tear ane anither to pieces, and eat ane anither up stoop and roop, and a' that 'ill be left o' us in tho mornin 'ill be some bloody tramplin up and doun the beds, and that 'ill be a catastrophe waur—if possible—than that o' Sir Walter's Ayrshire Tragedy—and Mr. Murray 'ill melodramateeze us in a piece ca'd the "Bluidy Battles o' the Bees;" and pit, boxes, and gallery 'ill a' be crooded to suffocation for a hunder nichts at haill price, to behold swoopin alang the stage the LAST O' THE NOCTES AMBROSIANÆ!!!

English Opium-Eater. Then, indeed, will the "gaiety of nations be eclipsed"; sun, moon, and stars may resign their commission in the sky, and Old Nox reascend, never more to be dislodged from the usurpation of the effaced, obliterated, and extinguished universe.

Shepherd. Nae need o' exaggeration. But sure aneuch I wadna, for anither year, in that case, insure the life o' the Solar System—(*Rising up.*)—Whare's a' the bees?

North. The hive is almost exterminated. You and Tickler have slain your dozens and your tens of dozens—O'Bronte has swallowed some scores—Cyprus made no bones of his allowance—and Mr. De Quincey put to death—one. So much for the killed. The wounded you may see crawling in all directions, dazed and dusty; knitting their hind-legs together, and impotently attempting to unfurl their no longer gauzy wings. As to the missing, driven by fear from house and home, they will continue for days to be picked up by the birds, while expiring on their backs on the tops of thistles and binweeds—and of the living, perhaps a couple of hundreds may be on the combs, conferring on State affairs, and—

Shepherd. Mournin for their queen. Sit up, Tickler.

[TICKLER *rises, and shakes himself.*

What'n a face!

North. 'Pon my soul, my dear Timothy, you must be bled forthwith—for in this hot weather inflammation and fever—

Shepherd. Wull sune end in mortification—then coma—and then death. We maun lance and leech him, Mr. North, for we canna afford, wi' a' his failins, to lose Southside.

Tickler. Lend me your arm, Kit—

North. Take my crutch, my poor dear fellow. How are you now?

Shepherd. Hoo are you noo?—Hoo are you noo?

English Opium-Eater. Mr. Tickler, I would fain hope, sir, that, notwithstanding the assault of those infuriated insects, which in numbers without number numberless, on the upsetting—

Tickler. Oh! oh!—Whoh! whoh!—whuh! whuh!

Shepherd. That comes o' wearin nankeen pantaloons without drawers, and thin French silk stockins wi' open gushets, and nae neckcloth, like Lord Byron. I find corduroys and tap-boots impervious to a' mainner o' insects,—bees, wasps, hornets, ants, midges, clegs, and, warst o' a'—the gad. By the time the bite reaches the skin, the venom's drawn out by ever so mony plies o' leather, linen, and wurset—and the spat's only kittly. But (*putting his hand to his face*) what's this?—Am I wearin a mask?—a fause-face wi' a muckle nose? Tell me, Mr. North, tell me, Mr. De Quinshy, on the honors o' twa gentlemen as you are, am I the noo as ugly as Mr. Tickler?

North. 'Twould be hard to decide, James, which face deserves the palm; yet—let me see—let me see—I think—I think, if there be indeed some slight shade of—What say you, Mr. De Quincey?

English Opium-Eater. I beg leave, without meaning any disrespect to either party, to decline delivering any opinion on a subject of so much delicacy, and—

Tickler and Shepherd (*guffawing*). What'n a face! what'n a face! Oh! what'n a face!

English Opium-Eater. Gentlemen, here is a small pocket-mirror, which, ever since the year—

Shepherd. Dinna be sae chronological, sir, when a body's sufferin. Gie's the glass (*looks in*)— and that's ME? Blue, black, ochre, gambooshe, purple, pink, and—*green!* Bottle-nosed—wi' een like a piggie's! The Owther o' the *Queen's Wake!* I maun hae my pictur taen by John Watson Gordon, set in diamonds, and presented to the Empress o' Russia, or some ither croon'd head. I wunner what wee Jamie wad think! It is a phenomena o' a fizzionamy.—An' hoo sall I get out the stings?

North. We must apply a searching poultice.

Shepherd. O' raw veal?

Tickler (*taking the mirror out of the Shepherd's hand*). Ay!

North. 'Twould be dangerous, Timothy, with that face, to sport Narcissus.

> "Sure such a pair were never seen,
> So aptly formed to meet by nature!"

Ha! O'Bronte?

[O'BRONTE *enters the Arbor, still under the influence of opium.*

What is your opinion of these faces?

O'Bronte. Bow—wow—wow—wow.—Bow—wow—wow-wow!

Shepherd. He taks us for Eskymaws.

North. Say rather seals, or sea-lions.

O'Bronte. Bow—wow—wow—wow.—Bow—wow—wow-wow!

Shepherd. Laugh'd at by a dowg!—Wha are ye?

[JOHN *and* BETTY *enter the Arbor with basins and towels, and a phial of leeches.*

North. Let me manage the worms.—Lively as fleas.

[MR. NORTH, *with tender dexterity, applies six leeches to the* SHEPHERD'S *face.*

Shepherd. Preens—preens—preens—preens! *

North. Now, Tickler.

[*Attempts, unsuccessfully, to perform the same kind office to* TICKLER.

Your sanguineous system, Timothy, is corrupt. They won't fasten.

* *Preens*—pins

Shepherd. Wunna they sook him? I find mine hangin cauld frae temple to chaft, and swallin—there's ane o' them played plowp intil the basin.

North. Betty—the salt.

Shepherd. Strip them, Leezy. There's anither.

North. Steady, my dear Timothy, steady; ay! there he does it, a prime worm—of himself a host. Sir John Leech.

English Opium-Eater. I observe that a state of extreme languor has succeeded excitement, and that O'Bronte has now fallen asleep. Hark! a compressed whine, accompanied by a slight general convulsion of the whole muscular system, indicates that the creature is in the dream-world.

Shepherd. In dookin! or fechtin—or makin up to a—

North. Remove the apparatus.

[JOHN *and* BETTY *carry away the basins, pitchers, phial, towels, &c., &c.*

Shepherd. Hoo's my face noo?

North. Quite captivating, James. That dim discoloration sets off the brilliancy of your eyes to great advantage; and I am not sure if the bridge of your nose as it now stands be not an improvement.

Shepherd. Weel, weel, let's say nae mair about it. That's richt, Mr. Tickler, to hang your silk handkerchy ower your face like a nun takin the veil. Whare were we at?

Tickler. I vote we change the Arbor for the Lodge. 'Tis cold—positively chill—curse the climate!

English Opium-Eater. Our sensations are the sole—

Shepherd. If you're cauld, sir, you may gang and warm yoursel at the kitchen fire. But we'se no stir—

Tickler. Curse the climate!

Shepherd. Cleemat! Where's the cleemat like it, I would wush to ken? Greece? Italy? Persia? Hindostan? Poo—poo—poo! Wha could thole months after months o' ae kind o' wather, were the sky a' the while lovely as an angel's ee? Commend me to the bold, bricht, black, boisterous, and blusterin beauty o' the British heavens!

Tickler. But what think ye, James, of a tropic tornado, or hurricano?

Shepherd. I wouldna gie a doit for a dizzen. Swoopin awa a toun o' wooden cages, wi' ane bigger than the lave, ca'd the governor's house, and aiblins a truly contemptible kirk, floatin awa into rottenness sae muckle colonial produce, rice, rum, or sugar, and frichtening a gang o' neeggers! It mayna roar sae loud nor sae lang, perhaps, our ain indigenous Scottish thunner; but it rairs loud and lang aneuch too, to satisfy ony reasonable Christian that has the least regard for his lugs. Nae patriot, Mr. Tickler, would undervalue his native kintra's thunner. Hear it spangin—hap, step, and loup—frae Cruachan to Ben Nevis! The red-deer—you micht think them a' dead—and that their antlers were rotten branches—sae stane-like do they couch atween the claps—without ae rustle in the heather. Black is the sky as pitch—but every here and there, shootin up through the purple gloom,—for whan the lichtnin darts out its fiery serpents it is purple,—lo! bricht pillars and pinnacles illuminated in the growlin darkness, and then gone in a moment in all their glory, as the day-nicht descends denser doun upon the heart o' the glens, and you only *hear* the mountain-tap; for wha can see the thousand year-auld cairn up-by yonder, when a' the haill heaven is ae coal-cloud—takin fire every noo and then as if it were a furnace—and then indeed by that flash may you see the cairn like a giant's ghost? Up goes the sable veil—for an eddy has been churning the red river into spray, and noo is a whirlwind—and at that updriving see ye not a hundred snaw-white torrents tumblin frae the tarns, and every cliff rejoicin in its new-born cataract? There is the van o' anither cloud-army frae the sea. What 'ill become o' the puir ships? A dismal word to think on in a tempest—lee-shore! There's nae wund noo—only a sort o' sugh. Yet the cloud-army comes on in the dead march—and that is the muffled drum. Na—that flash gaed through my head, and I fear I'm stricken blind! Rattle—rattle—rattle—as if great granite stanes were shot out o' the sky doun an invisible airn-roof, and plungin sullenly intil the sea. The eagles daurna scream—but that demon the raven croaks—croaks—croaks,—is it out o' the earth, or out o' the air, cave or cloud? My being is cowed in the insane solitude. But pity me—bless me—is that a wee bit Hieland lassie sittin in her plaid aneath a stane, a' by hersel, far frae hame, ha'in been sent to look after the kids—for I declare there is ane lyin on her bosom, and its mither maun be dead! Dinna be frichtened, my sweet Mhairi, for the lichtnin shanna be allowed by God to touch the bonny blue ribbon round thy yellow hair!—There's a bit o' Scottish thunner and lichtnin for you, Mr. Tickler, and gin it doesna satisfy you, aff to the troppics for a tornawdoe!

English Opium-Eater. You paint in words, mine admirable Shepherd, Nature in all her moods and aspects—

Shepherd. The coorse buffoonery—the indecent ribaldry o' the Noctes Ambrosianæ!!

English Opium-Eater. Spirit of Socrates, the smiling sage! whose life was love, I invoke thee to look down from heaven upon this blameless arbor, and bless "Edina's old man eloquent." Unsphere thy spirit, O Plato! or let it even, like some large and lustrous star, hang over the bower where oft in musing "melancholy sits retired" the grey-haired Wisdom-Seeker whom all Britain's youth adore, or "discourseth most excellent music" with lips on which, as on thine own, in infancy had swarmed—

Shepherd. For Heaven's sake, nae mention o' bees! That's a sair subjeck wi' me and Mr. Tickler. Get on to some o' the lave.

English Opium-Eater. Nor thou, stern Stagirite! who nobly heldst that man's best happiness was "Virtuous Energy," avert thy face severe from the high moral "Teacher of the Lodge," of whom Truth declares that "he never lost a day."

Shepherd. That's bonny.

English Opium-Eater. From thy grove gardens in the sky, O gracious and benign Epicurus! let drop upon that cheerful countenance the dews of thy gentle and trouble-soothing creed!

Shepherd. Od! I thocht Epicurus had been a great Epicure.

English Opium-Eater. And thou, O matchless Merryman o' the Frogs and the Clouds! *—

Shepherd. Wha the deevil's he? The matchless Merryman o' the Frogs and Clouds!—That's opium. But hush your havers, Mr. De Quinshy; and tell me, Mr. North, what for ye didna come out to Innerleithen and fish for the silver medal of the St. Ronan's Border Club! I'm thinkin ye was feared.

North. I have won so many medals, James, that my ambition αἰει ἀριστευειν † is dead—and, besides, I could not think of beating the Major.‡

Shepherd. You beat the Major! You micht at baggy mennons, but he could gie ye a stane-wecht either at trouts or fish. He's just a warld's wunner wi' the sweevil, a warlock wi' the worm, and wi' the flee a feenisher. It's a pure pleesur to see him playin a pounder wi' a single hair. After the first twa-three rushes are ower, he seems to wile them wi' a charm awa into the side, ontil the gerss or the grevvel, whare they

* Aristophanes. † Always to excel.

‡ Major Mackay, a first-rate angler, and esteemed friend of Professor Wilson's.

lie in the sunshine as if they were asleep, His tackle, for bricht airless days, is o' gossamere ; and at a wee distance aff, you think he's fishin without ony line ava, till whirr gangs the pirn, and up springs the sea-trout, silver-bricht, twa yards out o' the water, by a delicate jerk o' the wrist, hyucked inextricably by the tongue clean ower the barb o' the Kirby-bend. Midge-flees!

North. I know the Major is a master in the art, James ; but I will back the Professor* against him for a rump-and-dozen.

Shepherd. You would just then, sir, lose your rump. The Professor can fish nae better nor yoursel. You would make a pretty pair in a punt at the perches ; but as for the Tweed, at trouts or sawmon, I'll back wee Jamie again' ye baith, gin ye'll only let me fish for him the bushy pools.†

North. I hear you, James. Sir Isaac Newton was no astronomer. . . .

Shepherd. I hae nae objection, sir, noo that there's nae argument, to say that you're a gude angler yoursel, and sae is the Professor.

North. James, these civilities touch. Your hand. In me the passion of the sport is dead—or say rather dull ; yet have I gentle enjoyment still in the "Angler's silent Trade." But, heavens! my dear James! how in youth, and prime of manhood too—I used to gallop to the glens like a deer, over a hundred heathery hills, to devour the dark-rolling river, or the blue breezy loch!

Shepherd. Ay, sir, in your younger days you maun hae been a verra deevil. What creelfu's you maun hae killed!

North. A hundred and thirty in one day in Loch Awe, James, as I hope to be saved—not one of them under—

Shepherd. A dizzen pun',—and twa-thirds o' them aboon't. A'thegither a ton. If you are gaun to use the lang-bow, sir,

* Wilson. † Where deep wading is required.

pu' the string to your lug, never fear the yew crackin, and send the grey-guse-feathered arrow first wi' a lang whiz, and then wi' a short thud, right intil the bull's ee, at ten score, to the astonishment o' the ghost o' Robin Hood, Little John, Adam Bell, Clym o' the Clough, and William o' Cloudeslee.

North. My poor dear old friend, M'Neil of Hayfield *—God rest his soul—it is in heaven—at ninety as lifeful as a boy at nineteen—held up his hands in wonder, as under a shady tree I laid the hundred and thirty yellow shiners on the bank at his feet.

Shepherd. Poo! That was nae day's fishin ava, man, in comparison to ane o' mine on St. Mary's Loch. To sae naething about the countless sma' anes, twa hunder about half a pun', ae hunder about a haill pun', fifty about twa pun', five-and-twenty about fowre pun', and the lave rinnin frae half a stane up to a stane and a half, except about half-a-dizzen aboon a' wecht, that put Geordie Gudefallow and Huntly Gordon† to their mettle to carry them pechin‡ to Mount Benger on a haun-barrow.

North. Well done, Ulysses.

Shepherd. Anither day, in the Megget, I caucht § a cartfu'. As it gaed doun the road, the kintra folk thocht it was a cartfu' o' herrins—for they were a' preceesely o' ae size to an unce—and though we left twa dizzen at this house—and four dizzen at that house—and a gross at Henderland—on countin them at hame in the kitchen, Leezy made them out forty dizzen, and Girzzy forty-twa, aught; sae a dispute ha'in arisen, and o' coorse a bet, we took the census ower again,

* On the banks of Loch Awe.

† The friend and amanuensis of Sir Walter Scott. For an interesting account of his connection with Scott, see Lockhart's *Life*, vol. ix. p. 195 *et seq*, second edition.

‡ *Pechin*—panting.

§ *Caucht*—caught.

and may these be the last words I sall ever speak, gin they didna turn out to be Forty-Five!

Tickler. Mr. De Quincey, now that these two old fools have got upon angling—

Shepherd. Twa auld fules! You great, starin, Saracen-headed Langshanks! If it werena for bringin Mr. North intil trouble, by ha'in a dead man fun' within his premises, deil tak me gin I wadna fractur your skull wi' ane o' the cut crystals!

[Mr. NORTH *touches the spring, and the Bower is in darkness.*

Tickler.—

"But such a chief I spy not through the host—
De Quincey, North, and Shepherd, all are lost
In general darkness. Lord of earth and air!
O King! O Father! hear my humble prayer:
Dispel this cloud, the light of heaven restore;
Give me to see, and Tickler asks no more.
If I must perish—I thy will obey,
But let me perish in the face of day!"

Shepherd. Haw! haw! haw! The speech o' Awjax, in Pop's Homer.

North. Gentlemen, let us go to supper in the Lodge.

[*Omnes surgunt.*

Shepherd. What'n a sky!

North.—

"Now glow'd the firmament
With living sapphires. Hesperus, that led
The starry host, rode brightest—till the Moon,
Rising in clouded majesty, at length,
Apparent Queen! unveil'd her peerless light,
And o'er the dark her silver mantle threw."

XXIII.

IN WHICH, AFTER THE SHEPHERD HAS APPEARED SUCCESSIVELY AS PAN, AS HERCULES, AND THE APOLLO BELVIDERE, NORTH EXHIBITS HIS GREAT PICTURE—THE DEFENCE OF SOCRATES.

Scene,—The Snuggery. Time,—Nine. Present,—NORTH, SHEPHERD, *and* TICKLER.

Tickler. CENTAUR! No more like a centaur, James, than he is like a whale. Ducrow * is not "demi-corpsed"—as Shakespeare said of Laertes—with what he bestrides; how could he, with half-a-dozen horses at a time? If the blockheads will but look at a centaur, they will see that he is not six horses and one man, but one manhorse or horseman, galloping on four feet, with one tail, and one face much more humane than either of ours—

Shepherd. Confine yoursel to your ain face, Mr. Tickler. A centaur would hae sma' diffeeculty in ha'in a face mair humane nor yours, sir—for it's mair like the face o' Notus or Eurus nor a Christian's; but as for ma face, sir, it'smeeker and milder than that o' Charon himsel—

North. Chiron, James.

Shepherd. Weel, then, Cheeron be't—when he was instillin wisdom, music, and heroism until the sowl o' Achilles, him

* The famous equestrian.

that afterwards grew up the maist beautifu' and dreadfu' o' a' the sons o' men.

Tickler. The glory of Ducrow lies in his Poetical Impersonations. Why, the horse is but the air, as it were, on which he flies! What godlike grace in that volant motion, fresh from Olympus, ere yet " new-lighted on some heaven-kissing hill!" What seems " the feathered Mercury " to care for the horse, whose side his toe but touches, as if it were a cloud in the ether? As the flight accelerates, the animal absolutely disappears, if not from the sight of our bodily eye, certainly from that of our imagination, and we behold but the messenger of Jove, worthy to be joined in marriage with Iris.

Shepherd. I'm no just sae poetical's you, Mr. Tickler, when I'm at the circus; and ma bodily een, as ye ca' them, that's to say, the een ane on ilka side o' ma nose, are far ower gleg ever to lose sicht o' yon bonny din meer.

North. A dun mare, worthy indeed to waft Green Turban,

" Far descended of the Prophet line,"

across the sands of the Desert.

Shepherd. Ma verra thocht! As she flew round like lichtnin, the sawdust o' the amphitheatre becam the sand-dust o' Arawbia—the heaven-doomed region, for ever and aye, o' the sons o' Ishmael.

Tickler. Gentlemen, you are forgetting Ducrow.

Shepherd. Na. It's only you that's forgettin the din meer. His Mercury's beautifu'; but his Gladiawtor's shooblime.*

Tickler. Roman soldier, you mean, James.

Shepherd. Haud your tongue, Tickler. Isna a Roman sodger a Gladiawtor? Doesna the verra word Gladiawtor come frae the Latin for swurd? Nae wunner the Romans

* Ducrow's impersonations of ancient statues were as perfect as his horsemanship.

conquered a' the warld, gin a' their sodgers focht like yon! Sune as Ducraw tyuck his attitude, as stedfast on the steed as on a stane, there ye beheld, stauning afore you, wi' helmet, swurd, and buckler, the eemage o' a warrior-king! The hero looked as gin he were about to engage in single combat wi' some hero o' the tither side—some giant Gaul—perhaps himsel a king—in sicht o' baith armies—and by the eagle-crest could ye hae sworn, that sune would the barbaric host be in panic-flicht. What ither man o' woman born could sustain sic strokes, delivered wi' sovereign micht and sovereign majesty, as if Mars himsel had descended in mortal guise, to be the champion o' his ain eternal city?

North. Ma verra thocht.

Shepherd. Your thocht! you bit puir, useless, trifling cretur!—Ax you pardon, sir—for really, in the enthusiasm o' the moment, I had forgotten wha's vice it was, and thocht it was Mr. Tickler's.

Tickler. Whose?

Shepherd. Sit still, sir. I wunner gin the Romans, in battle, used, like our sodgers, to cry, "Huzzaw, huzzaw, huzzaw!"

North. We learned it from them, James. And ere all was done, we became their masters in that martial vociferation. Its echoes frightened them at last among the Grampians; and they set sail from unconquered Caledon.

Shepherd. What a bluidy beatin Galgacus gied Agricola!

North. He did so indeed, James—yet see how that fellow, his son-in-law Tacitus, lies like a bulletin. He swears the Britons lost the battle.

Shepherd. Haw, haw, haw! What? I've been at the verra spat—and the tradition's as fresh as if it had been but the verra day after the battle, that the Romans were cut aff till a man.

North. Not one escaped?

Shepherd. Deevil the ane—the hills, where the chief car nage rotted, are greener nor the lave till this hour. Nae white clover grows there—nae white daisies—wad you believe me, sir, they're a' red? The life-draps seepit * through the grun'—and were a body to dig doun far aneuch, wha kens but he wouldna come to coagulated gore, strengthening the soil aneath, till it sends up showers o' thae sanguinary gowans and clover, the product o' inextinguishable Roman bluid? †

Tickler. The Living Statues!

North. Perfect. The very Prometheus of Æschylus. Oh! James! what high and profound Poetry was the Poetry of the world of old! To steal fire from heaven—what a glorious conception of the soul in its consciousness of immortality!

Shepherd. And what a glorious conception o' the sowl, in its consciousness o' immortality, o' Divine Justice! O the mercy o' Almichty Jove! To punish the Fire-stealer by fastening him doun to a rock, and sendin a vultur to prey on his liver—perpetually to keep prey-preyin on his puir liver, sirs—waur even nor the worm that never dees,—or, if no waur, at least as ill—rug-ruggin—gnaw-gnawin—tear-tearin—howk-howking at his meeserable liver, aye wanin and aye waxin aneath that unpacified beak—that beak noo cuttin like a knife, noo clippin like shissors, noo chirtin like pinchers, noo hagglin like a cleaver! A' the while the body o' the glorious sinner bun' needlessly till a rock-block—needlessly bun', I say, sir, for stirless is Prometheus in his endurance o' the doom he drees, as if he were but a Stane-eemage, or ane o' the unsufferin dead!

* *Seepit*—soaked.

† As Lotichius sings of the banks of the Neckar :—

> "Ripa gerit regum natos e sanguine flores,
> E quibus Heroum texent sibi serta nepotes."

North. A troubled mystery!

Shepherd. Ane amaist fears to pity him, lest we wrang fortitude sae majestical. Yet see, it stirs! Ha! 'twas but the vultur. Prometheus himself is still—in the micht, think ye, sir, o' curse or prayer? Oh! yonner's just ae single slicht shudder—as the demon, to get a stronger purchase at his food, taks up new grun' wi' his tawlons, and gies a fluff and a flap wi' his huge wings again' the ribs o' his victim, utterin—was't horrid fancy?—a gurglin throat-croak choked savagely in bluid!

North. The Spirit's triumph over pain, that reaches but cannot pierce its core—

"In Pangs sublime, magnificent in Death!"

Tickler. Life in Death! Exultation in Agony! Earth victorious over Heaven! Prometheus bound in manglings on a sea-cliff, more godlike than Jove himself, when

"Nutu tremefecit Olympum!"

Shepherd. Natur victorious ower the verra Fate her ain imagination had creawted! And in the dread confusion o' her superstitious dreams, glorifying the passive magnanimity o' man, far ayont the active vengeance o' the highest o' her gods! A wild bewilderment, sirs, that ought to convince us that nae licht can ever be thrown on the moral government that reigns ower the region o' human life—nae licht that's no mair astoundin than the blackness o' darkness—but that o' Revelation, that ae day or ither shall illumine the uttermost pairts o' the earth.

North. Noble. These Impersonations by Ducrow, James, prove that he is a man of genius.

Shepherd. Are they a' his ain inventions?

North. Few or none. Why, if they were, he would be the

greatest of sculptors. But thus to convert his frame into such forms—shapes—attitudes—postures—as the Greek imagination moulded into perfect expression of the highest states of the soul—*that*, James, shows that Ducrow has a spirit kindred to those who in marble made their mythology immortal.

Shepherd. That's bonny—na, that's gran'. It gars a body grue—just like ain o' thae lines in poetry that suddenly dirls through you—just like ae smite on a single string by a master's haun, that gars shiver the haill harp.

Tickler. Ducrow was not so successful in his Apollo.

North. 'Twas the Apollo of the painters, Tickler; not of the sculptors.

Tickler. True. But why not give us the Belvidere?

North. I doubt if that be in the power of mortal man. But even were Ducrow to show us that statue with the same perfection that crowns all his other impersonations, unless he were to stand for hours before us, we should not feel, to the full, its divine majesty; for in the marble it grows and grows upon us as our own spirits dilate, till the Sun-god at last almost commands our belief in his radiant being, and we hear ever the fabled Python groan!

Tickler. Yes, North, our emotion is progressive—just as the worshipper who seeks the inner shrine feels his adoration rising higher and higher at every step he takes up the magnificent flight in front of the temple.

Shepherd. Na, na, na—this 'ill never do. It's manifest that you twa hae entered intil a combination again' me, and are comin ower me wi' your set speeches, a' written doun, and gotten aff the nicht afore, to dumfounder the Shepherd. What bit o' paper's that, Mr. Tickler, keekin out o' the pocket o' your vest? Notts. Notts in short haun—and a' the time you was pretendin to be crunklin't up to licht the tip o' your segawr, hae you been cleekin haud o' the catch-word---and that's the gate you deceive the Snuggery intil admiration o' your extemporawneous eeloquence! The secret's out noo—an' I wunner it was never blawn afore; for noo that my een are opened, they set till richts my lugs; and on considerin hoo matters used to staun' in the past, I really canna chairge ma memory wi' a mair feckless cretur than yoursel at a reply.

North. You do me cruel injustice, James—were I to prepare a single paragraph, I should stick---

Shepherd. Oh! man, hoo I would enjoy to see you stick! stickin a set speech in a ha' fu' o' admirin, that is, wunnerin hunders o' your fellow-citizens, on Parliamentary Reform, for instance, or Slavery in the Wast Indies, or—

North. The supposition, sir, is odious; I—

Shepherd. No in the least degree odious, sir—but superlatively absurd, and ludicrous far ayont the boun's o' lauchter—excepp that lauchter that torments a' the inside o' a listener and looker-on, an internal earthquake that convulses a body frae the pow till the paw, frae the fingers till the feet, till a' the pent-up power o' risibility bursts out through the mouth like the lang-smouldering fire vomited out o' the crater o' a volcawno, and then the astonished warld hears, for the first time, what heaven and earth acknowledge by their echoes to be indeed—a Guffaw!

North. James, you are getting extremely impertinent!

Shepherd. Nae personality, sir; nae personality sall be alloo'd, in ma presence at least, at a Noctes. That's to say, nae personality towards the persons present—for as to a' the rest o' the warld, men, women and children, I carena though you personally insult, ane after anither, a' the human race.

North. I insult?

Shepherd. Yes—you insult. Haena ye made the haill

civileesed warld your enemy by that tongue and that pen o' yours, that spares neither age nor sect?

North. I???

Shepherd. You!!!

Tickler. Come, come, gentlemen, remember where you are, and in whose presence you are sitting; but look here—here is the

APOLLO BELVIDERE.

[TICKLER *is transformed into Apollo Belvidere.*

Shepherd. That's no canny.

North. In his lip "what beautiful disdain!"

Shepherd. As if he were smellin at a rotten egg.

North. There "the Heavenly Archer stands."

Shepherd. I wadna counsel him to shoot for the Guse Medal. Henry Watson * would ding him till sticks.

North. I remember, James, once hearing an outrageous dispute between two impassioned connoisseurs, amateurs, men of *vertu*, cognoscenti, dilettanti, about this very Apollo Belvidere.

Shepherd. Confoun' me gin he's no monstrous like marble! His verra claes seem to hae drapped aff him—and I'se no pit on my specks, for fear he should pruve to be naked.—What was the natur o' the dispute?

North. Simply whether Apollo advanced his right or left foot—

Shepherd. Ane o' the disputants maun hae been a great fule. Shouldna Apollo pit his best fit foremost, that is the richt ane, on such an occasion as shootin a Peethon? Hut tut.—Stop a wee—let's consider. Na, it maun be the left fit foremost—unless he was ker-haun'd. † Let's try't.

* Mr. Henry Watson, an accomplished member of the Queen's Body-Guard, the Royal Scottish Archers, is a brother of the distinguished painter, Sir John Watson Gordon. [Mr. Watson, who is still (1876) hale and hearty, has recently endowed a "Fine Art Chair" in the University of Edinburgh, as a memorial to his brother.]

† *Ker-haun'd*—left-handed.

[*The* SHEPHERD *rises, and puts himself into the attitude of the Apollo Belvidere—insensibly transforming himself into another* TICKLER *of a shorter and stouter size.*

North. I could believe myself in the Louvre, before Mrs. Hemans wrote her beautiful poem on the *Restoration of the Works of Art to Italy.* Were the two brought to the hammer, an auctioneer might knock them down for ten thousand pounds each.

Shepherd. Whilk of us is the maist Apollonic, sir?

North. Why, James, you have the advantage of Tickler in being, as it were, in the prime of youth—for though by the parish register you have passed the sixtieth year-stone on the road of life, you look as fresh as if you had not finished the first stage.

Shepherd. Do you hear that, Mr. Tickler?

North. You have also most conspicuously the better of Mr. Tickler in the article of hair. Yours are locks—his leeks.

Shepherd. Mr. Tickler, are you as deaf and dumb's a statue, as weel's as stiff?

North. As to features, the bridge of Tickler's nose—begging his pardon—is of too prominent a build. The arch reminds me of the old bridge across the Esk at Musselburgh.

Shepherd. What say you to that, Mr. Tickler?

North. "'Tis more an antique Roman than a—"

Shepherd. Mr. Tickler!

North. But neither is the nose of the gentle Shepherd pure Grecian.

Tickler. Pure Peebles!

Shepherd. Oho! You've fun' the use o' your tongue.

North. Of noses so extremely—

Shepherd. Mine's, I ken, 's a cockit ane. Our mouths?

North. Why, there, I must say, gentleman, there's a wide opening for—

Tickler. Don't blink the buck teeth.

Shepherd. Better than nane ava.

North. Of Tickler's attitude I should say generally—that is—

[*Here* TICKLER *reassumes* SOUTHSIDE, *and taking the Snuggery at a stride, usurps* THE CHAIR, *and outstretches himself to his extremest length, with head leaning on the ridge, and his feet some yards off on the fender.*

Shepherd. (*leaping about*). Huzzaw—huzzaw—huzzaw!—I've beaten him at Apollo! Noo for Pan.

[*The* SHEPHERD *performs Pan in a style that would have seduced Pomona.*

Tickler. Ay—that's more in character.

North. Sufficient, certainly, to frighten an army.

Tickler. The very picture of our Popular Devil.

North. Say, rather, with Wordsworth—

"Pan himself,
The simple shepherd's awe-inspiring god."

Shepherd. Keep your een on me—keep your een on me—and you'll soon see a change that will strike you wi' astonishment. But rax me ower the poker, Mr. North—rax me ower the poker.

[NORTH *puts the poker into Pan's paws, and instanter he is Hercules.*

Tickler. (*clapping his hands*). Bravo! Bravissimo!

North. I had better remove the crystal. *Wheels the circular closer to the hearth.* James, remember the mirror.

Tickler. At that blow dies the Nemean lion.

[*The* SHEPHERD, *flinging down the poker-club, seems to drag up the carcase of the Monster with a prodigious display of muscularity, and then stooping his neck, heaves it over his head, as into some profound abyss.*

North. Ducrow's Double!

Shepherd. (*proudly*). Say rather the Dooble, that's Twa, o' Ducraw. Ducraw's nae mair fit to ack Hercules wi' me, than he is to ack Samson.

Tickler. I believe it.

Shepherd. I could tell ye a droll story about me and Mr. Ducraw. Ae nicht I got intil an argument wi' him at the Caffée, about the true scriptral gate o' ackin the Fear o' the Philistines, and I was pressin him geyan hard about his method o' pu'in doun the pillars, when he turns about upon me—and bein' putten to his metal—says, "Mr. Hogg, why did not you object to my representing in one scene—and at one time—Samson carrying away the gates of Gaza, and also pulling down the pillars?"

North. There he had you on the hip, James.

Shepherd. I hadna a word to say for't—but confessed at ance that it's just the way o' a' critics, wha stumble ower molehills, and yet mak naething o' mountains. The truth is, that a' us that are maisters in the fine arts, kens ilka ane respectively about his ain airt a thousan' times mair nor ony possible body else—and I thocht on the pedant lecturin Hannibal on war, or ony ither pedant me on poetry, or St. Cecilia on music, or Christopher North on literatur, or Sir Isaac Newton on the stars, or—

North. Now, James, that you may not say that I ever sulkily or sullenly refuse to contribute my quota of "weel-timed daffin" to the Noctes—behold me in

HERCULES FURENS.

[NORTH *off with his coat and waistcoat in a jiffy, and goes to work.*

Shepherd. That's fearsome! Dinna tear your shirt to rags—dinna tear your shirt to rags, sir!

Tickler. The poison searches his marrow-bones now!

Shepherd. His bluid's liquid fire!

Tickler. Lava.

Shepherd. Linens is cheap the noo, to be sure—dinna tear your shirt, sir—dinna tear your shirt. What pains maun a' that shuin * on the breist and collar hae cost Mrs. Gentle!

Tickler. O Dejanira! Dejanira! Dejanira!

Shepherd. That out-hercules's Hercules! Foamin at the mouth like a mad dowg! The Epilepsy! The quiverin o' his hauns! The whites o' his een, noo flickerin and noo fixed! Oh! dire misshapen lauchter, drawin his mouth awa up alang the tae side o' his face, outower till ane o' his lugs! Puir Son o' Alknomook!

Tickler. Alcmena, James.

Shepherd. A' his labours are near an end noo! A' the fifty, if crooded and crammed intil ane, no sae terrible as the last! Loup—loup—loup—tummle—tummle—tummle — sprawl—sprawl—sprawl—row—row—row—roun' about—roun' about—roun' about—like an axle-tree—then ae sudden streek out intil a' his length, and there lies he straught, stiff, and stark, after the dead-thraws, like a gnarled oak-trunk that had keept knottin for a thousan' years.

Tickler. But for an awkward club-foot too much, would I exclaim—

"Cedite Romani *imitatores!* Cedite Graii."

Shepherd (raising North from the floor). Do you ken, sir, you fairly tyuck me in—and I'm a' in a trummle. It's like Boaz frichtenin Ingleby † wi' his ain ba's.

North. Rather hot work, my dear James. I'm beginning to perspire.

Shepherd (feeling North's forehead). Beginnin till perspire!! Never afore, in this weary warld, was a man in sic an even-

* *Shuin*—sewing.

† Boaz and Ingleby were one and the same racket-player.

doun pour o' sweet! A perspiration-fa'! The same wi' your breist! What? You couldna hae been watter had you stood after a thunner-plump for an hour under a roan.

North. Say spout, James, roan is vulgar—it is Scotch—and your English is so pure now, that a word like that grates harshly on the ear, so that were you in England, you would undeceive and alarm the natives. But let us recur to the subject under spirited discussion immediately before Raphael's Dream—I mean the Jug.

Shepherd. Let us come our wa's in till the fire.

The Three are again seated at " the wee bit ingle blinking bonnily."

North. Where were we?

Shepherd. Ou ay. I was beginnin to pent a pictur o' you, sir, stickin a speech on Slavery or Reform. Slowly you rise —and at the uprisin o' " the auld man eeloquent " hushed is that assemblage as sleep. But wide awake are a' een—as fixed on Christopher North, the orator o' the human race.

Tickler. As is usual to say on such occasions—you might hear a pin fall—say a needle, which, having no head, falls lighter.

Shepherd. He begins laigh, and wi' a dimness in and around his een—a kind o' halo, sic as obscures the moon afore a storm. But sune his vice gets louder and louder, musical at its tapmost hicht, as the breath o' a silver trumpet. Action he has little or nane—noo and then the richt haun on the heart, and the left arm at richt angles till the body—just sae, —like Mr. Pitt's,—only this far no like Mr. Pitt's—for there's nae sense in that—no up and doun like a haunle o' a well-pump. What reasonin! What imagination! Fancy free and fertile as an auld green flowery lea! Pathos pure as dew—and wit bricht as the rinnin waters, translucent.

" At touch ethereal o' heaven's fiery rod!"

Tickler. Spare his blushes, Shepherd, spare his blushes.

Shepherd. Wae's me—pity on him—but I canna spare his blushes—sae, sir, just hang doun your head a wee, till I conclude. In the verra middle o' a lang train o' ratiocination—(I'm gratefu' for havin gotten through that word)—surrounded ahint and afore, and on a' sides, wi' countless series o' syllogisms—in the very central heart o' a forest o' feegurs, containin many a garden o' flowers o' speech—within sicht, nay, amaist within touch o' the feenal cleemax, at which the assemblage o' livin sowls were a' waitin to break out intil thunder, like the waves o' the sea impatient for the first smiting o' a storm seen afar on the main,—at that verra crisis and agony o' his fame, Christopher is seized wi' a sudden stupification o' the head and a' its faculties, his brain whirls dizzily roun', as if he were a' at ance waukenin out o' a dream, at the edge o' a precipice, or on a "coign o' disadvantage," outside the battlements o' a cloud-capt tower; his eyes get bewildered, his cheeks wax white, struck seems his tongue wi' palsy, he stutters—stutters—stutters—and "of his stutterin finds no end" till—HE STICKS!

Tickler. Fast as a wagon mired up to the axle-tree, while Roger, with the loosened team, steers his course back to the farm-steading, with arms akimbo on old Smiler's rump.

Shepherd. He fents! a cry for cauld spring-water—

North (*frowning*). Hark ye—when devoid of all probability—nay, at war with possibility—fiction is falsehood, fun folly, mirth mere maundering, humor, forsooth! idiocy, would-be wit "wersh as parritch without saut," James a merry-Andrew, and the Shepherd—sad and sorry am I to say it—a Buffoon!

Shepherd. Haw! haw! haw! Oh, man, but you're angry. It's aye the way o't. Them that's aye tryin ineffecktwally to make a fule o' ithers, when the tables are turned on them, gang red-wud-stark-staring mad a'thegither, and scarcely leave theirsels the likeness o' a dowg. But forgie me, sir—forgie me—I concur wi' you that the description was naething but a tissue—as you hae sae ceevily and coortusly said—o' fausehood, folly, maunderin idiocy, and wersh parritch—

Tickler. James a merry-Andrew, and the Shepherd a Buffoon!

Shepherd. Dinna "louse your tinkler jaw," sir, as Burns said o' Charlie Fox, on me, Mr. Tickler—for I'll no thole frae you a tithe, Timothy, o' what I'll enjoy frae Mr. North—an' it's no twice in the towmont I ventur to ca' him Kit.

North. Next time you pay me a visit, James, at No. 99 *—I'll show you THE PICTURE.

Shepherd. I understaun' you, sir—Titian's Venus—or is't his Danaw yielding to her yellow Jupiter victorious in a shower o' gold? Oh the selfish hizzie!

North. James, such subjects—

Shepherd. You had better, sir, no say anither syllable about them—it may answer verra weel for an auld bachelor like you, sir, to keep that sort o' a serawlio, naked limmers in iles, a shame to ony honest canvas, whatever may hae been the genius o' the Penter that sent them sprawling here; but as for me, I'm a married man, and—

North. My dear James, you are under a gross delusion—

Shepherd. It's nae delusion. Nae pictur o' the sort, na, no e'en although ane o' the greatest o' the auld Maisters, sall ever hang on ma wa's—I should be ashamed to look the servant lassies in the face when they come in to soop the floor or ripe the ribs—

* No. 99 Moray Place was Christopher's *imaginary* residence in Edinburgh. No. 6 Gloucester Place was his real abode.

North (*rising with dignity*). No picture, sir, shall ever hang on my walls, on which *her* eye might not dwell—

Shepherd. Mrs. Gentle! A bit dainty body—wi' a' the modesty, and without ony o' the demureness, o' the Quaker leddie; and as for yon pictur o' her aboon the brace-piece o' your Sanctum, by Sir Thomas Lawrence—

North. John Watson Gordon, if you please, my dear James.

Shepherd. It has the face o' an angel.

North. (*sitting down with dignity*). I was about to ask you, James, to come and see my last work—my masterpiece—my chef-d'œuvre—

Shepherd. The subjeck?

North. The Defence of Socrates.

Shepherd. A noble subjeck indeed, sir, and weel adapted for your high intellectual and moral genie.

North. My chief object, James, has been to represent the character of Socrates. I have conceived of that character as one in which unshaken strength of high and clear Intellect—and a moral Will fortified against all earthly trials—sublime and pure—were both subordinate to the principle of Love.

Shepherd. Gude, sir,—gude. He was the Freen o' Man.

North. I felt a great difficulty in my art, James—from the circumstances purely historical—that neither the figure nor the countenance of Socrates were naturally commanding—

Shepherd. An' hae ye conquered it to your satisfaction, sir?

North. I have. Another difficulty met me too, James, in this—that in his mind there was a cast of intellect—a play of comic wit—inseparable from his discourse—and which must not be forgotten in any representation of it.

Shepherd. Profoond as true.

North. To give dignity and beauty to the expression of features, and a figure of which the form was neither dignified nor beautiful, was indeed a severe trial for the power of art.

Shepherd. An' hae you conquered it too, sir?

North. Most successfully. In the countenance, therefore, my dear James, to answer to what I have assigned as the highest principle in the character, Love, there is a prevailing character of gentleness—the calm of that unalterable mind has taken the appearance of a celestial serenity—an expression caught, methinks, from the peaceful heart of the unclouded sky brooding in love over rejoicing nature.

Shepherd. That's richt, sir.

North. Such expression I have breathed over the forehead, the lips, and the eyes; yet is there not wanting either the grandeur, nor the fire, nor the power of intellect, nor the boldness of conscious innocence.

Shepherd. I'll come and see't, sir, the morn's mornin,* afore breakfast. Fowre eggs.

North. That one purpose I have pursued and fulfilled by the expression of all the Groups in the piece.

Shepherd. Naething in pentin kitlier than groupin.

North. You behold a prevalent expression of Love in the countenance of his friends and followers—of love greater than even reverence, admiration, sorrow, anxiety, and fear!

Shepherd. Though doutless a' thae emotions, too, will be expressed—and familiar hae they been to you, sir, through the coorse o' a strangely chequered though not unhappy life.

North. Then, too, James, have I had to express—and I have expressed it—the habitual character belonging to many there—besides the expression of the moment; countenances of generous, loving, open-souled youth; middle-aged men of calm benign aspect, but not without earnest thought; and not unconspicuous, one aged man, James, almost the counterpart of Socrates himself, only without his high intellectual power,

* *The morn's mornin*—to-morrow morning.

—a face composed, I may almost say, of peace, the only one of all perfectly untroubled.

Shepherd. That's an expressive thought, sir—and it's original—that's to say, it never occurred to me afore you mentioned it.

North. He, like Socrates, reconciled to that certain death, familiar with the looks of the near term of life, and not without hopes beyond it.

Shepherd. Believed thae sages, think ye, sir, in the immortality o' the sowl?

North. I think, James, that they did—assuredly Socrates.

Shepherd. I'm glad o't for their sakes, though they hae a' been dead for thousan's o' years.

North. Then, James, how have I managed his judges?

Shepherd. Hoo?

North. In all their faces, with many expressions, there is one expression—answering to the predominant disposition assigned to the character of Socrates—the expression of Malignity towards Love.

Shepherd. You've hit it, sir; you've hit it. Here's your health.

North. An expression of malignity in some almost lost on a face of timidity, fear, or awe, in others blended almost brutally with impenetrable ignorance.*

Shepherd. That comes o' studying the passions. I think but little noo o' Collins's Odd.

North. Then, James, I have given the countenances of the people.

Shepherd. A fickle people—ever ready to strike doun offensive Virtue—and ever as ready to shed tears o' overactin remorse on her ashes!

* North might have taken some hints for his picture from Plato's *Dialogue of Euthyphron*, in which Socrates describes his accuser, Meletus, as a person "with long straight hair, a scanty beard, and a hooked nose."

North. In the countenances of the people, James, I have laboured long, but succeeded methinks at last, in personifying as it were the Vices which drove them on to sacrifice the father of the city—to dim the eye and silence the tongue of Athens, who was herself the soul of Greece.

Shepherd. A gran' idea, sir—and natural as gran'—ane that could only visit the sowl o' a great Maister.

North. There you see anger, wrath, rage, hatred, spite, envy, jealousy, exemplified in many different natures. That Figure, prominent in the hardened pride of intellect, with his evil nature scowling through, eyeing Socrates with malignant, stern, and deadly revenge—is the King of the Sophists.

Shepherd. About to re-erect his Throne, as he hopes, on the ruins o' that Natural Theology which Socrates taught the heathens.

North. You see, then, James,—you feel that the purpose of the painter on the whole picture has been to express, as I said, his conception of the character of Socrates—a various and manifold reflection of one image; but the image itself, giving the same due proportion—where Love sits on the height of moral and intellectual power, and Intellect in their triple union, though strong in its own character, is yet subordinate to Both.

Shepherd. What a pictur it maun be, if the execution be equal to the design!

North. Many conceptions, my dear James, troubled my imagination, before, in the stedfastness of my delight in Love, I finally fixed upon this—which I humbly hope the world "will not willing let die."

Shepherd. It's the same way wi' poems. They aye turn out at last something seemingly quite different frae the origination form,—but it's no sae—for a spirit o' the same divine sameness breathes throughout, though ye nae langer ken the bit bonny bud in "the bricht consummate flower."

North. In one sketch—I will make you a present of it, my dear James—

Shepherd. Thank ye, sir—thank ye; you're really ower kind—ower gude to your Shepherd; but dinna forget, sir—see that you dinna forget—for you'll pardon me for hintin that sometimes promises o' that sort slip your memory—

North. In one sketch, James, I have represented Socrates speaking—and I found it more difficult to give the character of the principal figure—because the fire of discourse, of necessity, gave a disproportionate force to the intellectual expression; while, again, I found it easier to give the character of all the rest, who looked upon Socrates, under the power of his eloquence, simply commanding, with almost an undivided expression, in which individual character was either lost or subdued.

Shepherd. Never mind—send me the Sketch.

North. I will — and another. For, again, I chose that moment when, having closed his defence, Socrates stands looking upon the consulting judges, and awaiting their decision.

Shepherd. Oh! sir! and that was a time when his ain character, methinks, micht wi' mair ease be most beautifully expressed!

North. Most true. But then, the divided and conflicting expression of all the other figures, some turned on the judges with scrutinizing eagerness, to read the decision before it was on their lips—some certain of the result—looking on Socrates—or on the judges—with what different states of soul! These, James, I found difficult indeed to manage, and to bring them all under the one expression, which in that sketch too, as in my large picture, it was my aim to breathe over the canvas.

Shepherd. You maun try, sir, to mak a feenished pictur frae that sketch, sir,—you maun indeed, sir. I'll lend it to you for that purpose—and no grudge 't though ye keep it in your ain possession till next year.

North. I have not only made a sketch of another design, James, but worked in some of the colors.

Shepherd. The dead colors?

North. No—colors already instinct with life. I have chosen that calmer time, when, after the pronouncing of the sentence, Socrates resumes his discourse—you may read it, James, in that divine dialogue of Plato *—

Shepherd. But I'm no great haun at the Greek.

North. Use Floyer Sydenham's translation, or—let me see —has he done that dialogue? Take, then, that noble old man's, Taylor of Norwich. Socrates resumes his discourse, and declares his satisfaction in death, and his trust in immortality. A moment, indeed, for the sublime in art, but affording to the painter opportunity for a different purpose from that which was mine in my great picture. For in this sketch, instead of intending, as my principal and paramount object, the representation of individual historical character—I have designed to express—rather—the Power among men of the sublime Spirit of their being—exemplified among a people dark with idolatry—using the historical subject as subservient to this my purpose—inasmuch as it shows a single mind raised up by the force of this feeling above nature —yea, shows the power of that feeling within that one mind, resting in awe upon a great multitude of men. For, surely, my dear James, it is not to be believed that at that moment one countenance would preserve unchanged 'ts bitter hostility, when revenge was in part defeated by seeing triumph arise out of doom—when malignant hate

* The *Phaedon*.

had got its victim—and when murder, that had struck its blow, might begin to feel its heart open to the terror of remorse.

Shepherd. My dear Mr. North, gie me baith your twa hauns. That's richt. Noo that I hae shucken, and noo that I hae squozen them in my ain twa nieves no unlike a vice, though you're no the king upon the throne, wi' a golden croon on his head, and a sceptre in his haun—that's King William the Fourth, God bless him—yet you *are* a king; and, as a loyal subject, loyal but no servile, for never was a slave born i' the Forest, here do I, James Hogg, the Ettrick Shepherd, kneel doun on ae knee—thus—and kiss the richt haun o' King Kit.

[*The* SHEPHERD *drops on his knee—does as he says, in spite of* NORTH'S *struggles to hinder him—rises—wipes the dust from his pans—and resumes his seat.*

North. "How many of my poorest subjects," James, "are now asleep!" Look at Tickler.

Tickler. Asleep! Broad-awake as the Baltic in a blast. But when under the power of Eloquence, I always sit with my eyes shut.

Shepherd. But what for snore? Hae ye nae mercy on the sick man through the partition?

North. After Painting, let us have some Politics.

Shepherd. Na—na—na—na—na! Come, Mr. Tickler, gie's a sang—to the fiddle. See hoo your Cremona is smilin on you to haunle her frae her peg.

[*The* SHEPHERD *takes down the celebrated Cremona from the wall, and, after tuning it, gives it to* TICKLER.

Tickler (*attempting a prelude*). Shade of Stabilini! heard'st thou ever grated such harsh discord as this? 'Tis like a litter of pigs. [TICKLER *tunes his instrument.*

Shepherd. Oh, for Geordie Cruckshanks! "TICKLER AT

THE TUNING!" What for, Mr. North, dinna ye get Geordie to invent a series o' Illustrations o' the Noctes, and publish a Selection in four volumms octawvo?

North. Wait, James, till "one with moderate haste might count a HUNDRED."

Shepherd. What if we're a' dead?

North. The world will go on without us.

Shepherd. Ay—but never sae weel again. The verra earth will feel a dirl at her heart, and pause for a moment pensively on her ain axis.

(TICKLER *sings to an accompaniment of his own composition for the Cremona, "Demos."*)

Shepherd. Soun' doctrine weel sung. (*A pause.*) Do you ken, sir, that I admire guses—tame guses—far mair nor wild anes. A wild guse, to be sure, is no bad eatin, shot in season—out o' season, and after a lang flicht, what is he but a rickle o' banes? But a tame guse, aff the stubble, sirs—(and what'n a hairst this 'ill be for guses, the stooks hae been sae sair shucken!)—roasted afore a clear fire to the swirl o' a worsted string—stuffed as fu's he can haud frae neck to doup wi' yerbs—and devoored wi' about equal proportions o' mashed potawtoes and a clash o' aipple-sass—the creeshy breist o' him shinin outower a' its braid beautifu' rotundity, wi' a broonish and a yellowish licht, seemin to be the verra concentrated essence o' tastefu' sappiness, the bare idea o' which, at ony distance o' time and place, brings a gush o' water out o' the pallet—his theeghs slightly crisped by the smokeless fire to the preceese pint best fitted for crunchin—and, in short, the toot-an-sammal o' the Bird a perfeck specimen o' the beau-ideal o' the true Bird o' Paradise,—for sic a guse, sir,—(but oh! may I never be sair sairly tempted)—wad a man sell his kintra or his conscience—and neist day strive to stifle his remorse bygobblin up the giblet-pie.

North. To hear you speak, James, the world would take you for an epicure and glutton, who bowed down five times a day in fond idolatry before the belly-god. What a delusion!

(*Enter* PICARDY *and Tail, with all the substantialities of the season.*)

Shepherd. Eh! Eh! What'n a guse! Mr. Awmrose.—Dinna bring in a single ither guse, till we hae despatched our freen at the head o' the table.—Mr. Tickler, whare 'ill ye sit? and what 'ill ye eat? and what 'ill ye drink? and what 'ill ye want to hear? and what 'ill ye want to say? For oh, sir! you've been pleesant the nicht—in ane o' your lown, but no seelent humors. [*The Three tackle to.*

XXIV.

IN WHICH, IN THE RACE FROM THE SALOON TO THE SNUGGERY, TICKLER AND THE SHEPHERD ARE DISTANCED BY NORTH.

*Scene,—the Snuggery. Time,—Five o'Clock. Actors,—*NORTH, TICKLER, *and the* SHEPHERD. *Occupation,—Dinner.*

Shepherd. What'n a bill o' fare! As lang's ma airm was the slip o' paper endorsed wi' the vawrious eatems,* and I was feared there micht be delusion in the promise ; but here, far ayont a' hope, and aboon the wildest flichts o' fancy, the realization o' the Feast!

North. Mine host has absolutely outdone to-day all his former outdoings. You have indeed, sir.

Ambrose. You make me too happy, sir.

Shepherd. Say ower proud, Picardy.

Ambrose. Pride was not made for man, Mr. Hogg.—Mr. North, I trust, will forgive me, if I have been too bold.

Shepherd. Nor woman neither. Never mind him ; I forgie you, and that's aneuch. You've made a maist excellent observe.

Tickler. Outambrosed Ambrose, by this regal regale!

Shepherd. I ken nae mair impressive situation for a human being to find himsel placed in, than in juxtaposition wi' a mony-dished denner afore the covers hae been removed. The

* *Eatems*--items.

sowl sets itself at wark wi' a' its faculties, to form definite conceptions o' the infinite vareeities o' veeands on the eve o' being brocht to licht. Can this, it asks itsel in a laigh vice—can this dish, in the immediate vicinity, be, do ye think, a roasted fillet o' veal, sae broon and buttery on the outside, wi' its crisp faulds o' fat, and sae white and sappy wi' its firm breadth o' lean in the in? Frae its position, I jalouse * that ashet can conteen nothing less than a turkey—and I could risk my salvation on't, that while yon's Westphally ham on the tae side, yon's twa how-towdies on the ither. Can you—

Tickler. No man should speak with his mouth full.

Shepherd. Nor his head empty. But you're mistaken if you mean me, Mr. Tickler, for ma mouth was at no period o' ma late discourse aboon half fu', as I was carefu' aye to keep swallowing as I went alang, and I dinna believe you could discern ony difference in ma utterance. But, besides, I even-doun deny the propriety, as weel's the applicability, o' the apothegm. To enact that nae man shall speak during denner wi' his mouth fu', is about as reasonable as to pass a law that nae man, afore or after denner, shall speak wi' his mouth empty. Some feeble folk, I ken, hae a horror o' doin twa things at ance; but I like to do a score, provided they be in natur no only compatible but congenial.

Tickler. And who, pray, is to be the judge of that?

Shepherd. Mysel! Every man in this warld maun judge for himsel; and on nae account whatsomever suffer ony ither loon to judge for him, itherwise he'll gang to the deevil at a haun-canter.

North. Nobody follows that rule more inviolably than Tickler.

Shepherd. In the body, frae the tie o' his crawvat a' the

* *Jalouse*—suspect.

way doun to that o' his shoon—in the sowl, frae the lightest surmise about a passing cloud on a showery day, to his maist awfu' thochts about a future state, when his "extravagant and erring spirit hies" intil the verra bosom o' eternity.

Tickler. James, a caulker.

Shepherd. Thank ye, sir, wi' a' my wull. That's prime. Pure speerit. Unchristened. Sma' stell. Gran' worm. Peat-reek. Glenlivet. Ferintosh. It wad argue that a man's heart wasna in the richt place, were he no, by pronouncin some bit affectionate epithet, to pay his debt o' gratitude to sic a caulker.

North. James, resume.

Shepherd. Suppose me, sir, surveying the scene, like Moses frae the tap o' Pisgah the Promised Land. There was a morning mist, and Moses stood awhile in imagination. But soon, sun-smitten, burst upon his vision through the translucent ether the region that flowed with milk and honey—while sighed nae mair the children o' Israel for the flesh-pats o' Egypt. Just sae, sirs, at the uplifting o' the covers, flashed the noo * on our een the sudden revelation o' this lang-expected denner. How simultawneous the muvement! As if they had been a' but ae man, a Briareus, like a waff o' lichtnin gaed the hauns o' Picardy, and Mon. Cadet, and King Pepin, and Sir Dawvid Gam, and Tappytoorie, and the Pech, and the Hoi Polloi, and, lo and behold! towerin tureens and forest-like epergnes, overshadowing the humbler warld o' ashets! Let nae man pretend after this to tell me the difference atween the Beautifu' and the Shooblime.

North. To him who should assert the distinction I would simply say, "Look at that Round!"

Shepherd. Ay, he wad fin' some diffieeculty in swallowin that, sir. The fack is, that the mawgic o' that Buttock o'

* *The noo* (the now)—at this moment.

Beef considered as an objeck o' intellectual and moral Taste, lies in—Harmony. It reminds you o' that fine line in Byron, which beyond a' doubt was originally inspired by sic anither objeck, though afterwards differently applied:—

> "The soul, the music breathing from that face!"

Tickler. Profanation!

Shepherd. What! is there ony profanation in the application o' the principles and practice o' poetry to the common purposes o' life? Fancy and Imagination, sirs, can add an inch o' fat to round or sirloin, while at the same time they sae etherealeese its substance, that you can indulge to the supposable utmost in greediness, without subjectin yoursel, in your ain conscience, to the charge o' grossness—ony mair than did Adam or Eve when dining upon aipples wi' the angel Raphael in the bowers o' Paradise. And Heaven be praised that has bestowed on us three the gracious gift o' a sound, steady, but not unappeasable appeteet.

Tickler. North and I are Epicures—but you, James, I fear, are a—

Shepherd. Glutton. Be't sae. There's at least this comfort in ma case, that I look like ma meat—

Tickler. Which at present appears to be cod's head and shoulders.

Shepherd. Whereas, to look at you, a body would imagine that you leeved exclusively on sheep's head and trotters. As for you, Mr. North, I never could faddom the philosophy o' your fondness for soups. For hotch-potch and cockyleekie the wisest o' men may hae a ruling passion; but to keep plowterin, platefu' after platefu', amang broon soup, is surely no verra consistent wi' your character. It's little better than moss-water. Speakin' o' cockyleekie, the man was an atheist that first polluted it wi' prunes.

North. At least no Christian.

Shepherd. Prunes gie't a sickenin sweetness, till it tastes like a mouthfu' o' a cockney poem; and, scunnerin, you splutter out the fruit, afraid that the loathsome lobe is a stinkin snail.

Tickler. Hogg, you have spoilt my dinner.

Shepherd. Then maun ye be the slave o' the senses, sir, and your very imagination at the mercy of your palat—or rather, *veece versa,* the roof o' your mouth maun haud the tenure o' its taste frae anither man's fancy—a pitiable condition—for a single word may change luxuries intil necessaries, and necessaries intil something no eatable, even during a siege.

North. 'Tis all affectation in Tickler this extreme fastidiousness and delicacy.

Shepherd. I defy the utmost powers o' language to disgust me wi' a gude denner. My stamack would soar superior—

Tickler. Mine, too, would rise.

Shepherd. Oh, sir, you're wutty! but I hate puns.—Tickler, is that mock?

Tickler. I believe it is; but the imitation excels the original, even as Byron's *Beppo* is preferable to Frere's *Giants.*

Shepherd. A' but the green fat.

North. Deep must be the foundation and strong the superstructure of that friendship which can sustain the shock of seeing its object eating mock-turtle soup from a plate of imitation silver—

Shepherd. Meaner than pewter, as is the soup than sowens. An invaluable apothegm!

North. Not that I belong, James, to the Silver-Fork School.*

Shepherd. The flunkeys—as we weel ca'd them, sir—a contumelious nickname, which that unco dour and somewhat

* Novelists of the Theodore Hook class had been thus characterized.

stupit radical in the *Westminster* would try to make himsel believe he invented cwer again, when the impident plagiary changed it—as he did the ither day—into "Lackey."

North. I merely mean, James, that at bed or board I abhor all deception.

Shepherd. Sae, sir, div * I. A plated spoon is a pitifu' imposition; recommend me to horn; and then nane o' your egg-spoons, or pap-spoons for weans, but ane about the diameter o' my loof, that when you put it weel ben into your mouth, gars your cheeks swall, and your een shut wi' satisfaction.

Tickler. I should like to have your picture, my dear James, taken in that gesture.

North. Finely done in miniature, by MacLeay.

Tickler. No. By some savage Rosa.

Shepherd. A' I mean, sirs, is sincerity and plain-dealing. "One man," says the auld proverb, "is born wi' a silver spoon in his mouth, and another wi' a wudden ladle." Noo, what would be the feelings o' the first, were he to find that fortune had clapt intil his mouth, as Nature was geein him to the warld, what to a' appearance was a silver spoon, and by the howdie and a' the kimmers † sae denominated accordingly, but when shown to Mr. Morton the jeweller, or Messrs. Mackay and Cunninghame, was pronounced plated? He would sigh sair for the wudden ladle. Indeed, gents, I'm no sure but it's better nor even the real siller metal. In the first place, it's no sae apt to be stown; ‡ in the second, maist things taste weel out o' wud; thirdly, there's nae expense in keepin't clean, whereas siller requires constant pipe-clay, leather, or flannen; fourthly, I've seen them wi' a maist beautifu' polish, acquired in coorse o' time by the simple process o' sookin the horn as it gaed in and out o' the mouth;

* *Div*—do. † *Kimmers*—gossips. ‡ *Stown*—stolen.

fifthly, there's ten thousand times mair vareeity in the colors; sixthly—

Tickler. Enough in praise of the Wooden Spoon.* Poor fellow! I always pity that unfortunate annual.

Shepherd. Unfortunate annual! You canna weel be fou already; yet, certes, you're beginnin to haver—and indeed I have observed, no without pain, that a single caulker somehoo or ither superannuates ye, Mr. Tickler.

North. James, you have spoken like yourself on the subject of wooden spoons. 'Twas a simple but sapient homily. "*Worms*, madam! nay, it *is*." Be that my rule of life.

Shepherd. The general rule admits but o' ae exception—Vermicelli? What that sort o' soup's composed o' I never hae been able to form ony feasible conjecture. Aneuch for me to ken, on your authority, Mr. North, that it's no worms.

North. I have no recollection of having ever given you such assurance, James.

Shepherd. Your memory, my dear sir, you'll excuse me for metionin't, is no just what it used to be—

North. You are exceedingly im—

Shepherd. Pertinent. Pardon me for takin the word out o' your mouth, sir—but as for your judgment—

North. I believe you are right, my dear James. The memory is but a poor power after all—well enough for the mind in youth, when its business is to collect a store of ideas—

Shepherd. But altogether useless in auld age, sir, when the Intellect—

North. Is Lord Paramount—and all his subjects come flocking of their own accord to lay themselves in loyality at his feet.

Shepherd. There he sits on his throne, on his head a croon,

* The lowest graduate in honors at Cambridge is so called.

and in his haun a sceptre. Cawm is his face as the sea—and his brow like a snaw-white mountain. By divine right a king!

North. Spare my blushes.

Shepherd. I wasna speakin o' you, sir—sae you needna blush. I was speakin o' the Abstrack Power o' Intellect personified in an Eemage, "whose stature reached the sky," and whose countenance, serenely fu' o' thocht, partook o' the majestic stillness o' the region that is glorified by the setting sun.

North. My dear boy, spare my blushes.

Shepherd. Hem. (His face can nae mair blush than the belly o' a hen redbreast.) What philosopher, like an adjutant-general, may order out on parawde the thochts and feelings, and, strick though he be as a disciplinawrian, be obeyed by that irregular and aften mutinous Macedonian phalanx?

North. I confess it does surprise me to hear you, James, express yourself so beautifully over haggis.

Shepherd. What for? What's a wee haggis but a big raggoo?—an' a big raggoo, but a wee haggis? But will you believe me, Mr. Tickler, I was sae taen up wi' the natural sentiment, that I kentna what was on my plate.

Tickler. And probably have no recollection of having, within the last ten minutes, eat a how-towdy.

Shepherd. What the deevil are you twa about? Circum-navigating the table in arm-chairs! What! Am I on wheels too?

[*The* SHEPHERD *follows* NORTH *and* TICKLER *round the genial board.*

North. How do you like this fancy, my dear James?

Shepherd. Just excessively, sir. It gies us a perfeck command o' the entire table, east and wast, north and south; and at present, I calculate that I am cuttin the equawtor.

North. It relives Mr. Ambrose and his young gentlemen from unnecessary attendance—and, besides, the exercise is most salutary to persons of our age, who are apt to get fat and indolent.

Shepherd. Fozy. So ye contrive to rin upon horrals,* halting before a darling dish, and then away on a voyage o' new discovery. This explains the itherwise unaccountable size o' this immense circle o' a table. Safe us! It would sit forty! And yet, by this ingenious contrivance, it is just about sufficient size for us Three. Hae ye taen out a pawtent?

North. No. I hate monopolies.

Shepherd. What! You, the famous foe o' Free-tredd!

North. With our national debt—

Shepherd. Dinna tempt me, sir, to lose a' patience under a treatise on taxes—

North. Well—I won't. But you admire these curricles?

Shepherd. Moveable at the touch o' the wee finger. Whase invention?

North. My own.

Shepherd. You Dædalus!

North. The principle, James, I believe is perfect—but I have not been yet able to get the construction of the vehicle exactly to my mind.

Shepherd. I dinna ken what mair you could howp for, unless it were to move at a thocht. Farewell, sirs, I'm aff across the line to yon pie—nae sma' bulk even at this distance. Can it be pigeons?

[SHEPHERD *wheels away south-east.*

North. Take your trumpet.

Shepherd. That beats a'. For ilka man a silver speakin-trumpet! Let's try mine. (*Shepherd puts his trumpet to his mouth.*) Ship ahoy! Ship ahoy!

* *Horrals* or *whorles*—very small wheels.

North (*trumpet-tongued*). The Endeavor*—bound for—

Shepherd. Whist—whisht—sir.—I beseech you whisht. Nae drums can staun' siccan a trumpet, blawn by siccan lungs (*laying down his trumpet*). This is, indeed, the Pie o' Pies. I howp Mr. Tickler 'ill no think o' wheelin roun' to this quarter o' the globe.

Tickler (*on the trumpet*). What sort of picking have you got at the Antipodes, James?

Shepherd. Roar a little louder—for I'm dull o' hearin. Is he speakin o' the Bench o' Bishops?

Tickler (*as before, but louder*). What pie?

Shepherd. Ay—ay.

Tickler (*larghetto*). What pie?

Shepherd. Ay—ay. What'n a gran' echo up in yon corner!

[TICKLER *wheels away in search of the north-west passage—and on his approach the* SHEPHERD *weighs anchor with the pie, and keeps beating up to windward—close-hauled—at the rate of eight knots, chased by* SOUTHSIDE, *who is seen dropping fast to leeward.*

North. He'll not weather the point of Firkin.†

Shepherd (*putting about under North's stern*). I'll rin for protection frae the Pirrat,‡ under the guns o' the old Admiral—and being on the same station, I suppose he's entitled to his ain share o' the prize. Here, my jolly veteran, here's the Pie. Begin wi' a couple o' cushats, and we'll divide atween us the croon o' paste in the middle, about as big's the ane the King—God bless him—wore at the coronation.

[TICKLER *wheels his chair into the nook on the right of the chimney-piece.*

Southside, hae you deserted the diet? O man! you're

* Professor Wilson had a yacht on Windermere named "The Endeavor."
† A point of land running into Loch Lomond is so called. ‡ Pirate.

surely no sulky? Come back—come back, I beseech you—and let us shake hauns. It'll never do for us true Tories to quarrel amang oursels at this creesis. What'n a triumph to the Whigs, when they hear o' this schism! Let's a' hae a finger in the pie, and as the Lord Chancellor said, and I presume did, in the House o' Lords—"on my bended knees, I implore you to pass this bill!" *

[*The* SHEPHERD *kneels before* TICKLER, *and presents to him a plateful of the pie.*

Tickler (*returning to the administration*). James, we have conquered, and we are reconciled.

North. Trumpets! [*Three trumpet cheers.*

Gurney (*rushing in alarm from the ear of Dionysius*). Gentlemen, the house is surrounded by a mob of at least fifty thousand Reformers, who with dreadful hurrahs are shouting for blood.

Shepherd. Fifty thousan'! Wha counted the radical rascals?

Gurney. I conjecture their numbers from their noise. For Heaven's sake, Mr. North, do not attempt to address the mob—

North. Trumpets! [*Three trumpet cheers.*

Gurney (*retiring much abashed into his ear*). Miraculous!

Ambrose (*entering with much emotion*). Mr. North, I fear the house is surrounded by the enemies of the constitution, demanding the person of the Protector—

Shepherd. Trumpets!

[*Three trumpet cheers. Exit* AMBROSE *in astonishment.*

North. Judging from appearances, I presume dinner is over.

* Lord Brougham concluded his speech on Parliamentary Reform, October 7, 1831, in the following terms:—"I pray and exhort you not to reject this measure. By all you hold most dear—by all the ties that bind every one of us to our common order and our common country, I solemnly adjure you, I warn you,—I implore,—yea, *on my bended knees*, I supplicate you—Reject not this Bill."

Shepherd. A'm stawed.*

North. There is hardly any subject which we have not touched, and not one have we touched which we did not adorn.

Shepherd. By subjecks do you mean dishes? Certes, we have discussed a hantle o' them—some pairtly, and ithers totally; but there's food on the brodd yet sufficient for a score o' ordinar men—

Tickler. And we shall have it served up, James, to supper.

Shepherd. Soun' doctrine. What's faith without warks?

North. Now, gentlemen, a fair start. Draw up on my right, James—elbow to elbow. Tickler, your place is on the *extrême gauche.* You both know the course. The hearth-rug of the snuggery's the goal. All ready? Away!

[*The start is the most beautiful thing ever seen—and all Three at once make play.*

SCENE II.—*The Snuggery.*

Enter NORTH *in his flying chair, at the rate of the Derby, beating, by several lengths,* TICKLER *and the* SHEPHERD, *now neck and neck.*

North (*pulling up as soon as he has passed the Judges' stand*). Our nags are pretty much on a par, I believe, in point of condition, but much depends, in a short race, on a good start, and there the old man showed his jockeyship.

Shepherd. 'Twas a fause start, sir—'twas a fause start—I'll swear it was a fause start till ma dooin day—for I hadna gotten mysel settled in the saiddle, till ye was aff like a shot, and afore I could get intil a gallop, you was half-way across the flat o' the saloon.

North. James, there could be no mistake. The signal to start was given by Saturn himself; and—

* *Stawed*—surfeited.

Shepherd. And then Tickler, afore me and him got to the fauldin-doors, after some desperate crossin and jostlin, I alloo, on baith sides, ran me clean aff the coorse, and I had to make a complete circle in the bow-window or I could get the head o' my horse pinted again in a richt direction for winnin the race. Ca' ye that fair? I shall refer the haill business to the decision o' the Jockey Club.

North. What have you to say, Tickler, in answer to this very serious charge?

Tickler. Out of his own mouth, sir, I convict him of conduct that must have the effect of debarring the Shepherd from ever again competing for these stakes.

Shepherd. For what stakes? Do you mean to mainteen, you brazen-faced neerdoweel, that I am never to be alloo'd again to rin Mr. North frae the saloon to the Snuggery for ony steaks we choose, or chops either? Things 'ill hae come to a pretty pass, when it sall be necessar to ask your leave to start—you blacklegs!

Tickler. He's confessed the crossing and jostling.

Shepherd. You lee. Wha began't? We started sidey-by sidey, ye see, sir, frae the rug afore the fire, where we was a three drawn up, and just as you was gaun out o' sicht atween the pillars, Tickler and me ran foul o' ane anither at the nor'-east end o' the circular. There was nae faut on either side there, and a'm no blamin him, except for ackwardness, which was aiblins mutual. As sune's we had gotten disentangled, we entered by look o' ee, if no word o' mouth, intil a social compact to rin roun' opposite sides o' the table—which we did—and in proof that neither of us had gained an inch on the ither, no sooner had we rounded the south-west cape, than together came we wi' sic a clash, that I thocht we had been baith killed on the spat. There was nae faut on either side there, ony mair than there had been at the nor'-east;

but then began his violation o' a' honor; for ha'in succeeded in shovin mysel aff, I was makin for the fauldin-doors—due west—ettlin for the inside, to get a short turn—when, whuppin and spurrin like mad, what does he do but charge me richt on the flank, and drive me, as I said afore, several yards aff the coorse, towards the bow-window, where I was necessitated to fetch a circumbendibus that wad hae lost me the race had I ridden Eclipse. Ca' ye that fair? But it was agreed that we were to be guided by the law of Newmarket, sae I'll refer the haill affair to the Jockey Club.

Tickler. Hear me for a moment, sir. True, we got entangled at the nor'-west—most true at the sou'-west came we together with a clash. But what means the Shepherd by shoving off? Why, sir, he caught hold of my right arm as in a vice, so that I could make no use of that member, while at the same time he locked me into his own rear, and then away he went like a two-year-old, having, as he vainly dreamt, the race in hand by that manœuvre, so disgraceful to the character of the carpet.

North. If you please, turf.

Tickler. Under such circumstances, was I to consider myself bound by laws which he himself had broken and reduced to a dead letter? No. My subsequent conduct he has accurately described; off the course—for we have a bit of speed in us—I drove him; but as for the circumbendibus in the bow-window, we must believe that on his own word.

Shepherd. And daur you, sir, or ony man breathin, to dout ma word—

North. Be calm, gentlemen. The dispute need not be referred to the Club; for, consider *you were nowhere.*

Shepherd. Eh?

North. You were both distanced.

Shepherd. Baith distanced! Hoo? Where's the post?

North. The door-post of the Snuggery.

Shepherd. Baith our noses were through afore you had reached the rug. I'll tak ma Bible-oath on't. Werena they, Tickler?

Tickler. Both.

North. Not a soul of you entered this room for several seconds after I had dismounted—

Shepherd. After ye had dismounted? Haw! haw! haw! Tickler! North confesses he had dismounted afore he was weighed—and has thereby lost the race. Hurrah! hurrah! hurrah! Noo, ours was a dead heat—so let us divide the stakes—

Tickler. With all my heart; but we ran for the Gold Cup.

Shepherd. Eh! sae we did, man; and yonner it's on the sideboard—a bonny bit o' bullion. Let's keep it year about; and, to prevent ony hargle-barglin about it, let the first turn be mine; oh! but it'll do wee Jamie's heart gude to glower on't stannin aside the siller punch-bowl I got frae my friend Mr.—— What's the matter wi' ye, Mr. North? What for sae doun i' the mouth? Why fret sae at a trifle?

North. No honor can accrue from a conquest achieved by a quirk.

Shepherd. Nor dishonor frae defeat;—then, "prithee why so pale, wan lover? prithee why so pale?"

Tickler. I can hardly credit my senses when I hear an old sportsman call that a quirk, which is in fact one of the foundation-stones of the law of Racing.

Shepherd. I maun gang back for ma shoon.

North. Your shoon.

Shepherd. Ay, ma shoon—I flung them baith in Mr. Tickler's face—for which I noo ask his pardon—when he ran me aff the coorse—

Tickler. No offence, my dear James, for I returned the compliment with both snuff-boxes—

North. Oh! ho! So you who urge against me the objection of having dismounted before going to scale, both confess that you flung away weight during the race!

Shepherd. Eh? Mr. Tickler, answer him—

Tickler. Do, James.

Shepherd (scratching his head with one hand, and stroking his chin with the other). We've a' three won, and we've a' three lost. That's the short and the lang o't—sae the Cup maun staun' ower till anither trial.

North. Let it be decided now. From Snuggery to Saloon.

Shepherd. What! after frae Saloon to Snuggery? That would be reversin the order o' nature. Besides, we maun a' three be unco dry—sae let's turn to, till the table—and see what's to be had in the way o' drink. What'n frutes!

North. These are Ribstons, James—a pleasant apple—

Shepherd. And what's thir?

North. Golden pippins.

Shepherd. Sic jargonels! shaped like peeries—and yon Auchans * (can they be ripe?) like taps. And what ca' ye thae, like great big fir-cones, wi' outlandish-lookin palm-tree leaves archin frae them wi' an elegance o' their ain, rouch though they seem in the rin', and aiblins prickly? What ca' ye them?

North. Pine-apples.

Shepherd. I've aften heard tell o' them—but never clapped een on them afore. And these are pines! Oh! but the scent is sweet, sweet—and wild as sweet—and as wild restorative. I'se tak some jargonels afterwards—but I'll join you noo, sir, in a pair o' pines.

[NORTH *gives the* SHEPHERD *a pine-apple.*

Hoo are they eaten?

* *Auchans*—a kind of pear.

Tickler. With pepper, mustard, and vinegar, like oysters, James.

Shepherd. I'm thinkin you maun be leein.

Tickler. Some people prefer catsup.

Shepherd. Haud your blethers. Catchup's gran' kitchen * for a' kinds o' flesh, fish, and fule, but for frutes the rule is "sugar or naething,"—and if this pine keep the taste o' promise to the palat, made by the scent he sends through the nose, nae extrawneous sweetness will he need, self-sufficient in his ain sappiness, rich as the color o' pinks, in which it is sae savorily enshrined.——I never pree'd ony taste half sae delicious as that in a' ma born days! Ribstanes, pippins, jargonels, peaches, nectrins, currans and strawberries, grapes and grozets, a' in ane! The concentrated essence o' a' ither frutes, harmoneesed by a peculiar tone o' its ain—till it melts in the mouth like material music.

North (pouring out for the Shepherd a glass of sparkling champagne). Quick, James—quick—ere the ethereal particles escape to heaven.

Shepherd. You're no passin aff soddy † upon me? Soddy's ma abhorrence—it's sae like thin soap suds.

North. Fair play's a jewel, my dear Shepherd.

"From the vine-covered hills and gay regions of France—"

Shepherd.—

"See the day-star o' liberty rise."

That beats ony guseberry—and drinks prime wi' pine. Anither glass. And anither. Noo put aside the Langshanks—and after a' this daffin let's set in for serious drinkin, thinkin, lookin, and speakin—like three philosophers as we are—and still let our theme be—Human Life.

* *Kitchen*—relish.

† Soda water.

North. James, I am sick of life. With me "the wine of life is on the lees."

Shepherd. Then drink the dregs and be thankfu'. As lang's there's anither drap, however drumly, in the bottom o' the bottle, dinna despair. But what for are you sick o' life? You're no a verra auld man yet—and although ye was, why mayna an auld man be geyan happy? That's a' ye can expeck noo. But wha's happy—think ye—perfeckly happy—on this side o' the grave? No ane. I left yestreen wee Jamie—God bless him—greetin as his heart would break for the death o' a bit wee doggie that he used to keep playin wi' on the knowe mony an hour when he ought to hae been at his byuck—and when he lifted up his bonny blue een a' fu' o' tears to the skies, after he had seen me bury the puir tyke in the garden, I'se warrant hé thocht there was a sair change for the waur in the afternoon licht—for never did callant loe collie as he loed Luath; and to be sure he, on his side, wasna ungratefu'—for Luath keepit lichin his haun till the verra last gasp, though he dee'd of that cruel distemper. Fill your glass, sir.

North. I have been subject to fits of blackest melancholy since I was a child, James.

Shepherd. An' think ye, sir, that naebody has been subjeck to fits o' blackest melancholy since they were a bairn but yoursel? Wi' some it's constitutional, and that's a hopeless case; for it rins, or rather stagnates, in the bluid, and meesery has been bequeathed frae father to son, doun mony dismal generations—nor has ceased till some childless suicide, by a maist ruefu' catastrophe, has closed the cleemax, by the unblessed extinction o' the race. But you, my dear sir, are come o' a cheerfu' kind, and mirth laughed in the ha's o' a' your ancestors. Cheer up, sir—cheer up—fill your glass wi' Madeiry—an' nae mair folly about fits—for you're gettin fatter an' fatter every year, and what you ca' despair 's but the dumps.

North. O, mihi præteritos referat si Jupiter annos !

Shepherd. Ay—passion gies vent to mony an impious prayer ! The mair I meditat on ony season o' my life, the mair fearfu' grows the thocht o' leevin't ower again, and my sowl recoils alike frae the bliss and frae the meesery, as if baith alike had been sae intense that it were impossible they could be re-endured !

North. James, I regard you with much affection.

Shepherd. I ken you do, sir—and I repay't three-fauld ; but I canna thole to hear you talkin nonsense. What for are ye no drinkin your Madeiry ?

North. How pregnant with pathos to an aged man are those two short lines of Wordsworth—about poor Ruth !—

> " Ere she had wept, ere she had mourn'd,
> A young and happy child."

Shepherd. They are beautifu' where they staun', and true ; but fause in the abstrack, for the youngest and happiest child has often wept and mourned, even when its mither has been tryin to rock it asleep in its cradle. Think o' the teethin, sir, and a' the colic-pains incident to babbyhood !

North. " You speak to me who never had a child."

Shepherd. I'm no sae sure o' that, sir. Few men hae leeved till threescore and ten without being faithers ; but that's no the pint ; the pint is the pleasures and pains o' childhood, and hoo nicely they are balanced to us poor sons of a day ! I ken naething o' your childhood, sir, nor o' Mr. Tickler's, except that in very early life you maun hae been twa stirrin gentlemen—

Tickler. I have heard my mother say that I was a remarkably mild child till about—

Shepherd. Six—when it cost your faither an income for

tawse to skelp out o' you the innate ferocity that began to break upon you like a rash alang wi' the measles—

Tickler. It is somewhat singular, James, that I never have had measles—nor small pox—nor hooping-cough—nor scarlet-fever—nor—

Shepherd. There's a braw time comin, for these are complents nane escape; and I shouldna be surprised to see you at next Noctes wi' them a' fowre—a' spotted and blotched, as red as an Indian or a tile-roof, and crawin like a cock, in a fearsome manner—to which add the Asiatic cholera, and then, ma man, I wadna be in your shoon for the free gift o' the best o' the Duke's store-farms, wi' a' the plenishin—for the fifth comin on the ither fowre, lang as you are, wad cut you aff like a cucumber.

North.—

> "Ah, happy hills! ah, pleasing shade!
> Ah, fields beloved in vain!
> Where once my careless childhood stray'd,
> A stranger yet to pain."

Shepherd. That's Gray—and Gray was the best poet that ever belanged to a college—but—

North. All great (except one) and most good poets have belonged to colleges.

Shepherd. Humph. But a line comes soon after that is the key to that stanza—

> "My weary soul they seem to soothe!"

Gray wasna an auld man—far frae it—when he wrote that beautifu' Odd—but he was fu' o' sensibility and genius—and after a lapse o' years, when he beheld again the bits o' bricht and bauld leevin eemages glancin athwart the green—a' the Eton College callants in full cry—his heart amaist dee'd within him at the sicht and the soun'—for his pulse, as he put his finger to his wrist, beat fent and intermittent in comparison, and nae wunner that he should fa' intil a dooble delusion about their happiness and his ain meesery. And sae the poem's colored throughout wi' a pensive spirit o' regret, in some places wi' the gloom o' melancholy, and in ane or twa amaist black wi' despair. It's a fine picture o' passion, sir, and true to nature in every touch. Yet frae beginnin to end, in the eye o' reason, and faith, and religion, it's a' ae lee. Fause, surely, a' thae forebodings o' a fatal futurity. For love, joy, and bliss are not banished frae this life; and in writin that verra poem, maunna the state o' Gray's sowl hae been itsel divine?

North. Tickler?

Tickler. Good.

Shepherd. What are mony o' the pleasures o' memory, sirs, but the pains o' the past spiritualeezed?

North. Tickler?

Tickler. True.

Shepherd. A' human feelings seem somehow or ither to partake o' the same character, when the objects that awake them have withdrawn far, far awa intil the dim distance, or disappeared for ever in the dust.

Tickler. North?

North. The Philosophy of Nature.

Shepherd. And that Tam Cawmel maun hae felt, when he wrote that glorious line—

"And teach impassion'd souls the joy of grief!"

North. The joy of grief! That is a joy known but to the happy, James. The soul that can dream of past sorrows till they touch it with a pensive delight can be suffering under no severe trouble—

Shepherd. Perhaps no, sir. But may that no aften happen

too, when the heart is amaist dead to a' pleasure in the present, and loves but to converse wi' phantoms? I've seen pale still-faces o' widow-women,—ane sic is afore me the noo, whase husband was killed in the wars lang lang ago in a forgotten battle—she leeves on a sma' pension in a laigh and lonely house,—that bespeak constant communion wi' the dead, and yet nae want either o' a meek and mournfu' sympathy wi' the leevin, provided only ye show them by the considerate gentleness o' your manner, when you chance to ca' on them on a week-day, or meet them at the kirk on Sabbath, that you ken something o' their history, and hae a Christian feelin for their uncomplainin affliction. Surely, sir, at times, when some tender gleam o' memory glides like moonlight across their path, and reveals in the hush some ineffable eemage o' what was lovely and beloved o' yore, when they were, as they thocht, perfectly happy, although the heart kens weel that 'tis but an eemage, and nae mair—yet still it maun be blest; and let the tears drap as they will on the faded cheek, I should say the puir desolate cretur did in that strange fit o' passion suffer the joy o' grief.

North. You will forgive me, James, when I confess, that though I enjoyed just now the sound of your voice, which seemed to me more than usually pleasant, with a trembling tone of the pathetic, I did not catch the sense of your speech.

Shepherd. I wasna makin a speech, sir—only uttering a sort o' sentiment that has already evaporated clean out o' mind or passed awa like an uncertain shadow.

North. Misery is selfish, James—and I have lost almost all sympathy with my fellow-creatures, alike in their joys and their sorrows.

Shepherd. Come, come, sir—cheer up, cheer up. It's naething but the blue devils.

North. All dead—one after another—the friends in whom lay the light and might of my life—and memory's self is faithless now to the "old familiar faces." Eyes—brows—lips—smiles—voices—all—all forgotten! Pitiable, indeed, is old age, when love itself grows feeble in the heart, and yet the dotard is still conscious that he is day by day letting some sacred remembrance slip for ever from him that he once cherished devoutly in his heart's core, and feels that mental decay alone is fast delivering them all up to oblivion!

Shepherd. Sittin wi' rheumy een, mumblin wi' his mouth on his breist, and no kennin frae ither weans his grandchildren, wha have come to visit him wi' their mother, his ain bricht and beautifu' dauchter, wha seems to him a stranger passing alang the street.

North. What said you, James?

Shepherd. Naething, sir, naething. I wasna speakin o' you—but o' anither man.

North. They who knew me—and loved me—and honored me—and admired me—for why fear to use that word, now to me charmless?—all dust! What are a thousand kind acquaintances, James, to him who has buried all the few friends of his soul—*all the few*—one—two—three—but powerful as a whole army to guard the holiest recesses of life!

Shepherd. An' am I accounted but a kind acquaintance and nae mair? I wha—

North. What have I said to hurt you, my dear James?

Shepherd. Never mind, sir—never mind. I'll try to forget it—but—

North. Stir the fire, James—and give a slight touch to that lamp.

Shepherd There's a bleeze, sir, at ae blast. An' there's the Orrery, bricht as the nicht in Homer's *Iliad*, about which you wrote sic eloquent havers. And there's your bumper-glass. Noo, sir, be candid, and tell me gif you dinna think that you've been a verra great fule?

North. I believe I have, my dear James. But, by all that is ludicrous here below, look at Tickler! [*Tickler sleeps*

Shepherd. Oh for Cruckshank!

North. By the bye, James, who won the salmon medal this season on the Tweed?

Shepherd. Wha, think ye, could it be, ye coof, but mysel? I bet them a' by twa stane wecht. Oh, Mr. North, but it wad hae done your heart gude to hae daunered alang the banks wi' me on the 25th, and seen the slauchter. At the third thraw the snout o' a famous fish sookit in ma flee—and for some seconds keepit stedfast in a sort o' eddy that gaed sullenly swirlin at the tail o' yon pool—I needna name't—for the river had risen just to the proper pint, and was black as ink, except when noo and then the sun struggled out frae atween the clud-chinks, and then the water was purple as heather-moss in the season of blaeberries. But that verra instant the flee began to bite him on the tongue, for by a jerk o' the wrist I had slightly gien him the butt—and sunbeam never swifter shot frae Heaven, than shot that saumon-beam down intil and out o' the pool below, and alang the saugh-shallows or you come to Juniper Bank. Clap—clap—clap—at the same instant played a couple o' cushats frae an aik aboon my head, at the purr o' the pirn, that let out in a twinkling a hunner yards o' Mr. Phin's best, strang aneuch to haud a bill or a rhinoceros.

North. Incomparable tackle!

Shepherd. Far, far awa doun the flood, see till him, sir—see till him,—loup-loup-loupin intil the air, describin in the spray the rinnin rainbows! Scarcely could I believe, at sic a distance, that he was the same fish. He seemed a saumon divertin himsel, without ony connection in this warld wi' the Shepherd. But we were linked thegither, sir, by the inveesible gut o' destiny—and I chasteesed him in his pastime wi' the rod o' affliction. Windin up—windin up, faster than ever ye grunded coffee—I keepit closin in upon him, till the whalebone was amaist perpendicular outower him, as he stoppit to tak breath in a deep plum. You see the savage had gotten sulky, and you micht as weel hae rugged at a rock. Hoo I leuch! Easin the line ever so little, till it just moved slichtly like gossamer in a breath o' wund—I half persuaded him that he had gotten aff; but na, na, ma man, ye ken little about the Kirby-bends gin ye think the peacock's harl and the tinsy hae slipped frae your jaws! Snoovin up the stream, he goes hither and thither, but still keepin weel in the middle—and noo strecht and steddy as a bridegroom ridin to the kirk.

North. An original image.

Shepherd. Say rather application! Maist majestic, sir, you'll alloo, is that flicht o' a fish when the line cuts the surface without commotion, and you micht imagine that he was sailin unseen below in the style o' an eagle about to fauld his wings on the cliff.

North. Tak tent, James. Be wary, or he will escape.

Shepherd. Never fear, sir. He'll no pit me aff my guard by keepin the croon o' the causey in that gate. I ken what he's ettlin at—and it's naething mair nor less nor yon island. Thinks he to himsel, wi' his tail, "Gin I get abreist o' the broom, I'll roun' the rocks, doun the rapids, and break the Shepherd." And nae sooner thocht than done—but bauld in my cork-jacket—

North. That's a new appurtenance to your person, James; I thought you had always angled in bladders.

Shepherd. Sae I used—but last season they fell doun to my

heels, and had nearly drooned me—sae I trust noo to my bodyguard.

North. I prefer the air life-preserver.

Shepherd. If it bursts you're gone. Bauld in my cork-jacket, I took till the soomin, haudin the rod aboon my head—

North. Like Cæsar his Commentaries.

Shepherd. And gettin fittin on the bit island—there's no a shrub on't, you ken, aboon the waistband o' my breeks—I was just in time to let him easy ower the Fa', and Heaven safe us! he turned up, as he played wallop, a side like a house! He fand noo that he was in the hauns o' his maister, and began to loss heart; for naethin cows the better pairt o' man, brute, fool, or fish, like a sense o' inferiority. Sometimes in a large pairty it suddenly strikes me dumb—

North. But never in the Snuggery, James—never in the Sanctum—

Shepherd. Na, na, na—never i' the Snuggery, never i' the Sanctum, my dear auld man! For there we're a' brithers, and keep bletherin withouten ony sense o' propriety—I ax pardon—o' inferiority—bein' a' on a level, and that lichtsome, like the parallel roads in Glenroy, when the sunshine pours upon them frae the tap o' Ben Nevis.

North. But we forget the fish.

Shepherd. No me. I'll remember him on my deathbed. In body the same, he was entirely anither fish in sowl. He had set his life on the hazard o' a die, and it had turned up blanks. I began first to pity, and then to despise him—for frae a fish o' his appearance I expeckit that nae ack o' his life wad hae sae graced him as the closin ane—and I was pairtly wae and pairtly wrathfu' to see him *dee saft!* Yet, to do him justice, it's no impossible but that he may hae druv his snout again' a stane, and got dazed—and we a' ken by experience that there's naething mair likely to calm courage than a brainin knock on the head. His organ o' locality had gotten a clour, for he lost a' judgment atween wat and dry, and came floatin, belly upmost, in amang the bit snail-bucky-shells on the sand around my feet, and lay there as still as if he had been gutted on the kitchen-dresser—an enormous fish.

North. A sumph.

Shepherd. No sic a sumph as he looked like—and that you'll think when you hear tell o' the lave o' the adventure. Bein' rather out o' wund, I sits doun on a stane, and was wipin ma broos, wi' ma een fixed upon the prey, when a' on a sudden, as if he had been galvanceesed, he stotted up intil the lift, and wi' ae squash played plunge into the pool, and awa doun the eddies like a porpus. I thocht I should hae gane mad, Heaven forgie me—and I fear I swore like a trooper. Loupin wi' a spang frae the stane, I missed ma feet, and gaed head-ower-heels intil the water—while amang the rushin o' the element I heard roars o' lauchter as if frae the kelpie himsel, but what afterwards turned out to be guffaws frae your friens Boyd and Juniper Bank,* wha had been wutnessin the drama frae commencement to catastrophe.

North. Ha! ha! ha! James! it must have been excessively droll.

Shepherd. Risin to the surface wi' a guller, I shook ma nieve at the neerdoweels, and then doun the river after the sumph o' a saumon, like a verra otter. Followin noo the sicht and noo the scent, I wasna lang in comin up wi' him—for he was as deid as Dawvid—and lyin on his back, I protest, just like a man restin himsel at the soomin. I had forgotten the gaff—so I fastened ma tooth intil the shouther o' him—and like a Newfoundlan' savin a chiel frae droonin, I

* Messrs. Boyd of Innerleithen and Thorburn of Juniper Bank, a farm on Tweedside.

bare him to the shore, while, to do Boyd and Juniper justice, the lift rang wi' acclamations.

North. What may have been his calibre?

Shepherd. On puttin him intil the scales at nicht, he just turned three stane tron.

Tickler (stretching himself out to an incredible extent). Alas! 'twas but a dream!

Shepherd. Was ye dreamin, sir, o' bein' hanged?

Tickler (recovering his first position). Eh!

North. "So started up in his own shape the Fiend." We have been talking, Timothy, of Shakespeare's *Seven Ages.*

Tickler. Shakespeare's *Seven Ages.*

Shepherd. No Seven Ages—but rather seven characters. Ye dinna mean to mainteen that every man, afore he dees, maun be a sodger and a justice o' the peace?

Tickler. Shepherd *versus* Shakespeare—Yarrow *versus* Avon.

Shepherd. I see no reason why me, or ony ither man o' genius, michtna write just as weel's Shakspeer. Arena we a' mortal? Mony glorious glints he has, and surpassin sunbursts—but oh! sirs, his plays are desperate fu' o' trash—like some o' ma earlier poems—

Tickler. The *Queen's Wake* is a faultless production.

Shepherd. It's nae sic thing. But it's nearly about as perfeck as ony work o' human genius; whereas Shakspeer's best plays, sic as *Hamlet*, *Lear*, and *Othello*, are but strang daubs—

Tickler. James—

Shepherd. Are they no, Mr. North?

North. Rather so, my dear Shepherd. But what of his *Seven Ages?*

Shepherd. Nothing—except that they're very poor. What's the first?

North.—

> "At first the infant,
> Mewling and puking in its nurse's arms!"

Shepherd. Weel, then, the verra first squeak or skirl o' a newborn wean in the house, that, though little louder nor that o' a rotten, fills the entire tenement frae grun'-wark to riggin, was far better for the purposes o' poetry than the mewlin and pukin—for besides bein' onything but disgustfu' though sometimes, I alloo, as alarmin as unexpected, it is the sound the young Roscius utters on his first appearance on any stage; and on that latter account, if on nae ither, should hae been seleckit by Shakspeer.

North. Ingenious, James.

Shepherd. Or the moment when it is first pitten,* trig as a bit burdie, intil its father's arms.

Tickler. A man-child—the imp.

Shepherd. Though noo sax feet fower, you were then your sel, Tickler, but a span lang—little mair nor the length o' your present nose.

Tickler. 'Twas a snub.

Shepherd. As weel tell me that a pawrot, when it chips the shell, has a strecht neb.

Tickler. Or that a hog does not show the cloven foot till he has learnt to grunt.

Shepherd. Neither he does—for he grunts the instant he's farrowed—like ony Christian—sae you're out again there, and that envenomed shaft o' satire fa's to the grun'.

North. No bad blood, gents!

Shepherd. Weel, then—or, when yet unchristened, it lies awake in the creddle—and as its wee dim een meet yours, as you're lookin doun to kiss't, there comes strangely ower its bit fair a something joyfu', that love construes until a smile

* *Pitten*—put.

Tickler. "Beautiful exceedingly." Hem.

Shepherd. Or, for the first time o' its life in lang-claes, held up in the hush o' the kirk, to be bapteesed—while——

Tickler. The moment the water touches its face, it falls into a fit of fear and rage—

Shepherd. Sune stilled, ye callous carle, in the bosom o' ane o' the bonny lassies sittin on a furm in the transe, a' dressed in white, wha wi' mony a silent hushaby lulls the lamb, noo ane o' the flock, into haly sleep.

Tickler. Your hand, my dear James.

Shepherd. There. Tak a gude grup, sir, for in spite o' that sneerin, you've a real gude heart.

North. This is the second or third time, my dear James, that we have been cheated by some chance or other out of your Seven Ages. But hark! the timepiece strikes nine—and we must away to the Library. Two hours for dinner in the Saloon—two for wine and walnuts in the Snuggery—then two for tea-tea and coffee-tea in the Library—and finally, two in the blue-parlor for supper. Such was the arrangement for the evening. So lend me your support, my dear boys—we shall leave our curricles behind us—and start pedestrians. I am the lad to show a toe. [*Exeunt.*

XXV.

IN WHICH NORTH ERECTS HIS TENT IN THE FAIRY'S CLEUGH, AND IS CROWNED KING OF SCOTLAND BY THE FOREST WORTHIES.

SCENE I.—*Tent in the Fairy's Cleugh.* NORTH *and the* REGISTRAR * *lying on the brae.* (*In attendance,* AMBROSE *and his Tail.*)

Registrar. And here we are in the Fairy's Cleugh, among the mountains of—

North. Peeblesshire, Dumfriesshire, Lanarkshire, for here all three counties get inextricably entangled; yet in their pastoral peace they quarrel not for the dominion of this nook, central in the hill-heart, and haunted by the Silent People.

Registrar. You do not call us silent people! Why, you out-talk a spinning-jenny, and the mill-clapper stops in despair at the volubility of your speech.

North. Elves, Sam—Elves. Is it not the Fairy's Cleugh?

Registrar. And here have been "little feet that print the ground." But I took them for those of hares—

North. These, Sam, are not worm-holes—nor did Mole the miner upheave these pretty little pyramids of primroses—for

* "The Registrar" was Mr. Samuel Anderson, formerly of the firm of Brougham and Anderson, wine merchants, Edinburgh. He afterwards obtained from Lord Chancellor Brougham (his partner's brother) the appointment of Registrar of the Court of Chancery. He was an esteemed friend of Professor Wilson's, and a general favorite in society. He died in 1849.

these, Sam, are all Fairy palaces,—and yonder edifice that towers above the Lady-Fern—therein now sleeps—let us speak low, and disturb her not—the Fairy Queen, waiting for the moonlight—and soon as the orb shows her rim rising from behind Birk-fell—away to the ring will she be gliding with all the ladies of her Court—

Registrar. And we will join the dance—Kit—

North. Remember—then—that I am engaged to—

Registrar. So am I—three-deep.

North. Do you know, Sam, that I dreamed a dream?

Registrar. You cannot keep a secret, for you blab in your sleep.

North. Ay—both talk and walk. But I dreamed that I saw a Fairy's funeral, and that I was myself a fairy.

Registrar. A warlock.

North. No—a pretty little female fairy not a span long.

Registrar. Ha! ha! ha!

North. And they asked me to sing her dirge, and then I sang—for sorrow in sleep, Sam, is sometimes sweeter than any joy—ineffably sweet—and thus comes back wavering into my memory the elegiac strain.

THE FAIRY'S BURIAL.

Where shall our sister rest?
  Where shall we bury her?
To the grave's silent breast
  Soon we must hurry her!
Gone is the beauty now
  From her cold bosom!
Down droops her livid brow,
  Like a wan blossom!

Not to those white lips cling
  Smiles or caresses!
Dull is the rainbow wing,
  Dim the bright tresses!

Death now hath claimed his spoil—
  Fling the pall over her!
Lap we earth's lightest soil,
  Wherewith to cover her!

Where down in yonder vale
  Lilies are growing,
Mourners the pure and pale
  Sweet tears bestowing!
Morning and evening dews
  Will they shed o'er her;
Each night their task renews
  How to deplore her!

Here let the fern-grass grow,
  With its green drooping!
Let the narcissus blow,
  O'er the wave stooping!
Let the brook wander by,
  Mournfully singing!
Let the wind murmur nigh,
  Sad echoes bringing.

And when the moonbeams shower,
  Tender and holy,
Light on the haunted hour
  Which is ours solely,
Then will we seek the spot
  Where thou art sleeping,
Holding thee unforgot
  With our long weeping!

Amorose (*rushing out of the Tent*). Mr. Tickler, sirs, Mr. Tickler! Yonder's his head and shoulders rising over the knoll—in continuation of his herald the rod.

North (*savagely*). Go to the devil, sir.

Ambrose (*petrified*). Ah! ha! ha! ah! si—sir—pa—pa—pard—

North (*unmollified*). Go to the devil, I say, sir. Are you deaf?

Ambrose (*going, going, gone*). I beseech you, Mr. Registrar—

North (grimly). "How like a fawning publican he looks!"

Registrar. A most melancholy example of a truth I never believed before, that poetical and human sensibility are altogether distinct—nay, perhaps incompatible! North, forgive me (*North grasps the crutch*); but you should be ashamed of yourself—nay, *strike, but hear me!*

North (smiling after a sort). Well—Themistocles.

Registrar. You awaken out of a dream-dirge of Faëry Land—where you, by force of strong imagination, were a female fairy, not a span long—mild as a musical violet, if one might suppose one, "by a mossy stone half-hidden from the eye," inspired with speech.

North. I feel the delicacy of the compliment.

Registrar. Then you feel something very different, sir, I assure you, from what I intended, and still intend, you shall feel; for your treatment of my friend Mr. Ambrose was shocking.

North. I declare on my conscience, I never saw Ambrose!

Registrar. What! aggravate your folly by falsehood! Then are you a lost man—and—

North. I thought it a stirk staggering in upon me at the close of a stanza that—

Registrar. And why did you say "sir"? Nay—nay—that won't pass. From a female fairy, not a span long, "and even the gentlest of all gentle things," you suffer yourself to transform you into a Fury six feet high! and wantonly insult a man who would not hurt the feelings of a wasp!

North (humbly). I hope I am not a wasp.

Registrar. I hope not, sir; but permit me, who am not one of your youngest friends, to say to you confidentially, that you were just now very unlike a bee.

North (hiding his face with both his hands). All sting—and no honey. Spare me, Sam.

Registrar. I will. But the world would not have credited it, had she heard it with her own ears. Are you aware, sir, that you told Mr. Ambrose "to go to the devil"?

North (*agitated*). And has he gone?

Registrar (*beckoning on Ambrose, who advances*). Well, Ambrose?

North. Ambrose! Do you forgive me?

Ambrose. (*falling on one knee*). No—no—no—my dear sir—my honored master—

North. Alas! Ambrose—I am not even master of myself.

Ambrose. It was all my fault, sir. I ought to have looked first to see if you were in the poetics. Such intrusion was most unpardonable for (*smiling and looking down*) shall mere man obtrude on the hour of inspiration—when

> "The poet's eye, in a fine frenzy rolling,
> Glances from heaven to earth, from earth to heaven,
> And as imagination bodies forth
> The form of things unknown, turns them to shape,
> And gives to airy nothing
> A local habitation and a name."

Registrar. Who suffers, Ambrose?

Ambrose. Shakespeare, sir. Mr. Tickler! Mr. Tickler! Mr. Tickler! (*catching up his voice*) Mr. Tick—

Registrar. Yea—verily—and 'tis no other!

Tickler (*stalking up the brae—rod in hand—and creel on his shoulder—with his head well laid back—and his nose pretty perpendicular with earth and sky*). Well—boys—what's the news? And how are you off for soap? How long here? Ho! ho! The Tent.

North. Since Monday evening—and if my memory serve me right, this is either Thursday or Friday. Whence, Tim?

Tickler. From the West. But is there any porter?

Ambrose (*striving to draw*). Ay—ay—sir.

Tickler. You may as well try to uproot that birk. Give it me.

[*Put the bottle between his feet—stoops—and lays on his strength.*

Registrar (*jogging North*). Oh! for George Cruikshank!

Tickler (*loud explosion and much smoke*). The Jug.

Ambrose. Here, sir.

Tickler (*teeming*). Brown stout. The porter's in spate. THE QUEEN!

Omnes. Hurra! hurra! hurra! hurra! hurra! hurra! hurra! hurra! hurra!

Ambrose. Hip—hip—hip—

Registrar. Hush!

Tickler. Hech! That draught made my lugs crack. Oh! Kit!—there was a grand ploy at Paisley.

Ambrose. Dinner on the table, sir,

North. As my old friend Crewe—the University Orator at Oxford—concludes his fine poem of *Lewesdon Hill*

"To-morrow for severer thought, but now
To dinner, and keep festival to-day."

SCENE II.—*Time,—Four o'Clock.*

Scene changes to the interior of the tent. DINNER—*Salmon—Turbot — Trout— Cod — Haddocks — Whitings — Turkey—Goose — Veal-pie — Beafsteak ditto — Chicken — Ham —* THE ROUND—*Damson, Cherry, Currant, Grozet* (this year's) *Tarts, &c., &c., &c.,*

SCENE III.—*Time,—Five o' Clock.*

Without change of place. DESSERT—*Melons—Grapes—Grozets—Pine-apples — Golden Pippins —New Yorkers — Filberts—Hazels.* WINES — *Champagne — Claret—Port—Madeira*

—*Cold Punch in the Dolphin*—GLENLIVET IN THE TOWER OF BABEL—*Water in the Well.*

North. Ambrose, tuck up the tent-door. Fling it wide open. [AMBROSE *lets in heaven.*

Registrar. "Beautiful exceedingly!"

North. Ne'er before was tent pitched in the Fairy's Cleugh! I selected the spot from a memory, where lie many thousand worlds—great and small—and of the tiny not one sweeter, sure, than this before our eyes!

Registrar. I wonder how—by what fine process—you chose! Yet why, might I ask my own heart—why now do I fix on one face, one form, and see but them—haunted as my imagination might be with the images of all the loveliest in the land?

Tickler. Sam! you look as fresh as a daisy.

North. That is truly a vista. Those hills—for we must not call them mountains—how gently they come gliding down from the sky, on each side of the vale-like glen!—

Registrar. Vale-like glen! Thank you, North—that is the very word.

North.——separated but by no wide level of broomy greensward—if that be a level, broken as you see it with frequent knolls—most of them rounded softly off into pastures, some wooded, and here and there one with but a single tree, the white-stemmed, sweet-scented birk—

Registrar. Always lady-like with her delicate tresses, how ever humble her birth.

North. Should we say that the "spirit of the scene" is sylvan or pastoral?

Registrar. Both.

North. Sam! how is it I see no sheep?

Registrar. Sheep and lambs there must be many—latent

somewhere; and I have often noticed, sir, a whole green region without a symptom of life, though I knew that it was not a store-farm, and that there must be some hundred scores of the woolly people within startling of the same low mutter of the thunder-cloud.

North. How soon a rill becomes a river!

Registrar. A boy a man!

North. That is the source of the Woodburn, Sam, that well within five yards of our tent.

Registrar. How the Naiad must be enjoying the wine-cooler! Imbibing—inhaling the aroma, yet returning more than she receives, and tinging the taste of that incomparable claret—vintage 1811—with her own sweet breath!

North. Cuckoo! cuckoo! cuckoo!—Yonder she goes!—see, see, Sam!—flitting along the faint blue haze on the hill-side, across the burn. In boyhood, never could I catch a glimpse of the bird any more than Wordsworth.

> "For thou wert still a hope!—a joy
> Still longed for, never seen."

But so 'tis with us in our old age. All the mysteries that held our youth in wonderment, and made life poetry, dissolve—and we are sensible that they were all illusions; while other mysteries grow more awful; and what we sometimes hoped, in the hour of passion, might be illusions, are seen to be God's own truths, terrible to sinners, and wearing a ghastly aspect in tho gloom of the grave!

Tickler. Cuckoo! cuckoo! cuckoo!

North. She has settled again on some spray—for she is always mute as she flies! And I have stood right below her, within three yards of her anomalous ladyship, as, down head and up tail, with wings slightly opening from her sides, and her feathers shivering, she took far and wide possession of the stillness with her voice, mellow as if she lived oı honey ; and indeed I suspect, Sam—though the bridegroom eluded my ken—that with them two 'twas the honeymoon.

Ambrose (rushing into the Tent, stark naked, except his flannel drawers). Hurra! hurra! hurra!—hurra! hurra! hurra!—hurra! hurra! hurra! Who'll dance—who'll dance with me—waltz—jig—Lowland reel—Highland fling—gallopade? Hurra! hurra! hurra! *(Keeps dancing round the Tent table, yelling, and snapping his fingers.)*

North. Be seated, gentlemen—I see how it is—he has been drinking of the elf-well, up among the rocks behind the Tent, and human lip never touched that cold stream, but man or woman lost his or her seven senses, and was insane for life.

Registrar. A pleasant prospect.

Tickler. That may be—but, confound me, if Ambrose be the man to be caught in that kind of trap. Where's the Tower of Babel?

North. There!

Ambrose (pirouetting). Look yonder, mine honored master, through those rocks.

North. Nay, Brose, I can see as far through a millstone, or a milestone either, as most men, but as for looking through rocks—

Ambrose. I saw him, with these blessed eyes of mine, I saw him on horseback, sir, driving down the hill yonder, sir, at full gallop—

North. Whom?—ye saw whom?

Ambrose. Himself, sir—his very own self, sir—as I hope to be saved.

Registrar. I fear his case is hopeless. Those sudden accesses are fatal.

Tickler. Who, his drawers will be at his heels if—

Ambrose (somewhat subsiding). I had gone into the dookin,

gentlemen, as you say in Scotland, and was ploutering about in the pool, when, just as I had squeezed the water out of my eyes after a plunge, I chanced to look up the hillside, and there I saw him—with these blessed eyes I saw him—his own very self.

(Horses' hoofs heard at full gallop nearing the Tent.

Tickler. The Wild Huntsman!

[*Horse and rider charge the Tent—horse all of a sudden halts—thrown back on his haunches—and rider, flying over his head, alights on his feet—while his foraging cap spins over the Lion's fiery mane, now drooping in the afternoon calm from the mast-head.*

Omnes. THE SHEPHERD! THE SHEPHERD! THE SHEPHERD! hurra! hurra! hurra! hurra! hurra! hurra! hurra! hurra! hurra!

Shepherd. Hurraw! hurraw! hurraw!

North (*white as a sheet, and seeming about to swoon*). Water!

Shepherd. Whare's the strange auld tyke? Whare's the queer auld fallow? Whare's the canty auld chiel! Whare's the dear auld deevil? Oh! North—North—North—North—ma freen—ma brither—ma faither—let's tak ane anither intil ane anither's arms—let's kiss ane anither's cheek—as the guid cheevalry knichts used to do—when, ha'in fa'en out aboot some leddy-luve, or some disputed laun', or some king's changefu' favor, or aiblins aboot naething ava but the stupit lees o' some evil tongues, they happened to forgather when riding opposite ways through a wood, and flingin themsels, wi' ae feeling and ae thocht, aff their twa horses, cam clashin thegither wi' their mailed breists, and began sobbin in the silence o' the auncient aiks that were touched to their verra cores to see sic forgiveness and sic affection atween thae twa stalwart champions, wha, though baith noo weepin like weans or women, had aften ridden side by side thegither, wi' shields on their breists and lang lances shootin far out fearsomely afore them, intil the press o' battle, while their chargers, red-wat-shod, gaed gallopin wi' their hoofs that never ance touched the grun' for men's faces bashed bluidy, and their sodden corpses squelchin at every spang o' the flying dragoons. But what do I mean by all this talkin to mysel?—Pity me—Mr. North—but you're white's a ghaist! Let me bear ye in my airms until the Tent.

[SHEPHERD *carries* NORTH *into the Tent.*

North. I was much to blame, James—but—

Shepherd. I was muckle mair to blame mysel nor you, sir, and—

North. Why, James, it is by no means improbable that you were—

Shepherd. O ye auld Autocrat! But will ye promise me—gin I promise ye—

North. Anything, James, in the power of mortal man to perform.

Shepherd. Gie's your haun! Noo repeat the words after me—(NORTH *keeps earnestly repeating the words*)—I swear, in this Tent pitched in the Fairy's Cleugh, in presence o' Timothy Tickler and Sam An—

North. They are not in the Tent.

Shepherd. I wasna observin. That's delicate. That I wull never breathe a whusper even to ma ain heart—at the laneliest hour o' midnicht—except it be when I am sayin my prayers—dinna sab, sir—o' ony misunderstaunin that ever happened atween us twa—either about Mawga, or ony ither toppic—as lang's I leeve—an' am no deserted by my senses—but am left in fu' possession o' the gift o' reason; an' I noo dicht aff the tablets o' my memory ilka letter o' ony ugly record, that the enemy, takin advantage o' the corruption o' our fallen natur—contreeved to scarify there, wi' the pint o' an airn pen—red-het frae you wicked place—I noo dicht them a' aff, just as I dicht aff frae this table thae wine-draps wi' ma sleeve—and I forgie ye frae the verra bottom o' ma sowl—wi' as perfeck forgiveness—as if you were my ain brither, deein at hame in his father's house—shune after his return frae a lang voyage outower the sea!

[NORTH *and the* SHEPHERD *again embrace—their faces wax exceedingly cheerful—and they sit for a little while without saying a word.*

North. My dear James, have you dined?

Shepherd. Dined? Why, man, I've had ma fowre-hours. But I maun tell ye a' about it. A bit lassie, you see, that had come to your freen Scottie's to pay a visit to a sister o' hers—a servant in the family—that was rather dwinin—frae the kintra down about Annadale-wise, past by the Tent in the grey o' the morning, yesterday, afore ony ane o' you were out o' the blankets, except a cretur that, frae the description, maun hae been Tappytoorie, and she learned frae him that the Tent belanged to a great lord they ca'd North—Lord North—and that he had come out on a shootin and a fishin ploy, and, forby, to tak a plan o' a' the hills, in order to mak a moddle o' them in cork, wi' quicksiller for the lochs and rinnin waters, and sheets o' beaten siller for the waterfa's, and o' beaten gold for the element at sunset—and that twa ither shinin characters were in his rettenue—wham Tappy ca'd to her—as she threeped *—Sir Teemothy Tickleham, Bart., o' Southside, and the Lord High Registrar o' Lunnon. Ma heart lap to ma mouth, and then after some flutterin becam as heavy's a lump o' cauld lead. The wife gied me sic a smile! And then wee Jamie was a' the while, in his affectionat way, leanin again' ma knee. I took a walk by mysel; and a' was licht. Forthwith I despatched some

* *Threeped*—asserted.

gillies to wauken the Forest. I never steekit an ee, and by skreigh o' day * was aff on the beast. But I couldna ken how ye micht be fennin † in the Tent for fish, sae I thocht I micht as weel tak a whup at the Meggat. How they lap ! ‡ I filled ma creel afore the dew-melt; and as it's out o' the poo'r o' ony mortal man wi' a heart to gie ower fishin in the Meggat durin a tak, I kent by the sun it was nine-hours, and by that time I had filled a' my pouches, the braid o' the tail o' some o' them whappin again' my elbows. You'll no be surprised, Mr. North—for though you're far frae bein' sic a gude angler as you suppose, and as you cry yoursel up in Mawga, oh! but you're mad fond o't—that I had clean forgotten the beast! After a lang search I fand him a mile doun the water, and ma certes, for the next twa hours the gress didna grow aneath his heels. I took a hantle o' short cuts, for I ken the kintra better than ony fox. But I forgot I wasna on foot—the beast got blawn, and coming up the Fruid, § reested wi' me on Garlet-Dod. The girth burst—aff fell the saddle, and he fairly laid himsel doun! I feared he had brak his heart, and couldna think o' leavin him, for, in his extremity, I kent the raven o' Gameshope wad hae picked out his een. Sae I just thocht I wad try the Fruid wi' the flee, and put on a professor. ‖ The Fruid's fu' o' sma' troots, and I sune had a string. I couldna hae had about me, at this time, ae way and ither, in ma several repositories, string and a,' less than thretty dizzen o' troots. I heard the yaud nicherin, and kent he had gotten second wun', sae having hidden the saddle among the brackens, munted, and lettin him tak it easy for the first half-hour, as I skirted Earlshaugh holms I got him on the haun-gallop, and I needna tell you o' the

* *Skreigh o' day*—break of day.
† *Fennin*—faring.
‡ *Lap*—leaped.
§ A tributary of the Tweed.
‖ A fly, so called after Professor Wilson.

Arab-like style in which I feenally brocht him in, for, considering that I carried wecht, you'll alloo he wad be cheap at a hunder guineas, and for that soum, sir, the beast's your ain!—Rax me ower the jug.—But didna I see a naked man?

[*Re-enter* TICKLER *and the* REGISTAR.

Tickler. O King of the Shepherds, mayst thou live for ever!

Shepherd (*looking inquisitively to* NORTH). Wha's he that? (*Turning to* TICKLER)—Sir! you've the advantage of me—for I really cannot say that I ever had the pleasure o' seein you atween the een afore; but you're welcome to our Tent—sit doun, and gin ye be dry, tak a drink.

Registrar. James?

Shepherd. Ma name's no James. But what though it was? Folk shouldna be saé familiar at first sight. *To* NORTH *in an undertone*)—A man o' your renown, sir, should really be mair seleck.

Tickler. I beg pardon, sir—but I mistook you for that half-witted body, the Ettrick Shepherd.

Shepherd. Ane can pardon ony degree o' stoopidity in a fallow that has sunk sae laigh in his ain esteem, as weel's in that o' the warld, as to think o' retreevin his character by pretendin to pass himsel aff, on the mere strength o' the length o' his legs, for sic an incorrigible ne'er-do-weel as Timothy Tickler. But let me tell you, you had better keep a gude tongue in your head, or I'll maybe tak you by the cuff o' the neck, and turn ye out o' the Tent.

North to the (SHEPHERD *in an undertone.*) Trot him, James, —trot him—he's sensitive.

Shepherd. You maybe ken him? Is't true that he's gotten intil debt, and that Southside's adverteezed?

Tickler (*coloring*). It's a lie.

Shepherd. That pruves it to be true. Nay, it amaist, too, pruves you to be Tickler. Oh! nae mair nonsense—nae mair nonsense, sir—Southside, Southside—but I'm happier to see you, sir, than tongue can tell—but as the heart knoweth its awn bitterness, sae knoweth it its ain sweetness too; and noo that I'm sittin again atween you twa (*putting one arm over* CHRISTOPHER'S *shoulder, and one over* TIMOTHY'S, *starting up and rushing round the circular*)—"gude faith, I'm like to greet." Sam! Sam! Sam!

Registrar. God bless you, James.

Shepherd. And hae ye come a' the way frae Lunnon to the Fairy's Cleugh? And werena ye intendin to come out to Altrive to see the auld Shepherd? Oh! but we were a' glad, man, to hear o' your appointment, though nane o' us ken very distinckly the nature o't, some sayin they had made you a Bishop, only without a seat among the Lords, some a Judge o' the Pleas; and there was a sugh for a while—but frae you're bein' here the noo, during the sittin o' Parliament, that canna weel be true—that the King, by the recommendation o' Lord Broom and Vox, had appointed you his Premier, on the death o' Yearl Grey; but tell me, was the lassie richt after a' in denominatin ye, on the authority o' Tappytoorie, Lord High Registrar o' Lunnon, and is the post a sinecure, and a free gift o' the Whigs?

Registrar. That, James, is my appointment—but 'tis no sinecure. The duties are manifold, difficult, and important.

North. I wish somebody would knock me down for a song.

Shepherd. I'll do that—but recollect—nae fawsettoes—I canna thole fawsettoes—a very tailor micht be ashamed o' fawsettoes—for fawsettoes mak ye think o' something less than the ninety-ninth pairt o' a man—and that's ten times less than a tailor—and amaist naething ava—sae that the man vanishes intil a pint. Nae fawsettoes.

(North *sings* "*Sam Anderson.*")

Tickler. That must be all Greek to you, James.

Registrar. The less you say, the better, Tim, about Greek. The Shepherd was not with us when I sung a scrap of old Eubulus—but—

Shepherd. I have been studyin the Greek for twa wunters.* Wunter afore last I made but sma' progress, and got but a short way ayont the roots—for the curlin cam in the way—but this bygane wunter there was nae ice in the Forest—or at Duddistane either—and I maistered, during the lang nichts at hame, an incalculable crood o' dereevative vocables, and a hantle o' the kittlest compounds.

Registrar. What grammars and lexicons do you use, Shepherd?

Shepherd. Nane but the maist common. I hae completed a version o' Theocritus, and Bion, and Moschus—no to mention Anacreon; and gin there's nae curlin neist wunter either —and o' that there's but sma' chance, for a change has been gradually takin place within these few years, in the ellipse o' the earth—I suspect about the ecliptic—I purpose puttin a' ma strength upon Pindar. His Odds are dark—but some grand, as ane o' thae remarkable simmer-nichts when a' below is lown, and yet there is storm in heaven, the moon glimpsing by fits through cluds, and then a' at ance a blue spat fu' o' stars.

North. The Theban Swan—

Shepherd I'm ower happy to sing this afternoon, but I'm able, I think, to receet; and here's ane o' my attempts on an Eedle o' Bion—the third Eedle—get the teetle frae Tickler.

Tickler. Third Idyl of Bion.

* "I canna read Greek," the Shepherd had said on an earlier evening "*except in a Latin translation done into English.*"

(SHEPHERD *recites*.

Great Venus once appeared to me, still slumbering in my bed,
And Cupid in her beauteous hand, a tottering child she led ;
And thus with winning words she spake, " See, Cupid here I bring.
Oh, take him ! shepherd dear to me, and teach him how to sing ! "
She disappeared, and I began, a baby in my turn,
To teach him all the shepherd's songs—as though he meant to learn,
How Pan the crooked pipe found out, Minerva made the flute,
How Hermes struck the tortoise-shell, and Phœbus formed the lute.
All this I taught, but little heed gave Cupid to my speech ;
Then he himself sweet carols sung, and me began to teach
The loves of God and men, and all his mother did to each.
Then I forgot what I myself to Cupid taught before :
But all the songs he taught to me, I learnt them evermore !

North. Quite in the style of Trevor, who did such fine versions for my articles on the Greek Anthology.

Shepherd. I canna mak out, Mr. North, the cause o' the effect o' novelty as a source o' pleasure. Some objects aye please, however common.

Tickler. Don't prose, Jamie.

Shepherd. Ass ! There's the Daisy. Naebody cares muckle about the Daisy—till you ask them—and then they feel they hae aye liked it, and quote Burns. Noo naebody tires o' the daisy. A' the warld would be sorry gin a' daisies were dead.

Tickler. Puir auld silly body.

Shepherd. There again are Dockens. What for are they a byword ? Theyre saft, and smooth, and green, and hae nae bad smell. Yet a' the warld would be indifferent were a' dockens dead.

Tickler. I would rather not.

Shepherd. What for ? Would a docken, think ye, Mr. North, be " beauteous to see, a weed o' glorious feature," if it were scarce and a hot-house plant ? Would leddies and gentlemen, gin it were ony ways an unique, pay to get a look at a docken? But I fin' that I'm no thrawin ae single particle o' licht on the subjeck; and the perplexing question will aye recur, "Why is the daisy, though sae common, never felt to be commonplace? and the docken aye?"

Tickler. The reason, undoubtedly, is—

Shepherd. Haud your arrogant tongue, Southside, and never again, immediately after I hae said that ony metapheezical subjeck's perplexing, hae the insolence and the silliness to say, "The reason, undoubtedly, is." If it's no coorse, it's rude—and a man had better be coorse nor rude ony day—but oh, sirs, what'n a pity that in the Tent there are nae dowgs!

Tickler. I hate curs.

Shepherd. A man ca'in himsel a Christian, and hatin poetry and dowgs!

Tickler. Hang the brutes.

Shepherd. There's nae sic perfeck happiness, I suspeck, sir, as that o' the brutes. No that I wuss I had been born a brute—yet aften hae I been tempted to envy a dowg. What gladness in the cretur's een, gin ye but speak a single word to him, when you and him's sittin thegither by your twa sels on the hill. Pat him on the head, and say, "Hector, ma man!" and he whines wi' joy—snap your thooms, and he gangs dancing round you like a whirlwind—gie a whusslin hiss, and he loups frantic ower your head—cry halloo, and he's aff like a shot, chasing naething, as if he were mad.

North. Alas! poor Bronte!

Shepherd. Whisht, dinna think o' him, but in general o' dowgs. Love is the element a dowg leeves in, and a' that's necessary for his enjoyment o' life is the presence o' his master.

Registrar. "With thee conversing, he forgets all time."

Shepherd. Yet, wi' a' his sense, he has nae idea o' death True, he will lie upon his master's grave, and even howk wi his paws in an affeckin manner, but for a' that, believe me, he has nae idea o' death. He snokes wi' his nose into the hole his paws are howkin, just as if he were after a moudiewarp.

North. God is the soul of the brute creatures.

Shepherd. Ay, sir—instinct wi' them's the same's reason wi' us,—only we ken what we intend—they do not; we reflect in a mathematical problem, for example, how best to big a house; they reflect nane, but what a house they big! Sir Isaac Newton, o' himsel, without learnin the lesson frae the bees, wadna hae contrived a hive o' hinney-combs, and biggen them up, cell by cell, hung the creation, like growing fruit, on the branch o' a tree!

North. You that are a Greek scholar, James, do you remember an inscription for a wayside Pan, by Alcæus?

Shepherd. I remember the speerit o't, but I forget the words. Indeed, I'm no sure if ever I kent the words; but that's naething—at this moment I feel the inscription in the original Greek to be very beautiful! For sake o' Mr. Tickler, perhaps you'll receet it in English?

North.—

Wayfaring man, by heat and toil oppress'd,
Here lay thee down thy languid limbs to rest,
Upon this flowery meadow's fragrant breast.
Here the pine leaves, where whispering zephyrs stray,
Shall soothe thee listening to Cigala's lay,
And on yon mountain's brow the shepherd swain
Pipes by the gurgling fount his noontide strain,
Secure beneath the plantane's * leafy spray,
From the autumnal dog-star's sultry ray.
To-morrow thou'lt get on, wayfaring man,
So listen to the good advice of Pan.

Shepherd. Thae auncients, had they been moderns, would hae felt a' we feel oursels; and sometimes I'm tempted to confess, that in the matter o' expression o' a simple thocht,

* *Plantane*—the plane-tree.

they rather excel us—for, however polished may be ony ane o' their maist carefu' compositions, it never looks artificial, and the verra finish o' the execution seems to be frae the fine finger o' Nature's ain inspired sel! Oh, how I hate the artificial!

Registrar. Not worse than I.

Shepherd. Ca' a thing artificial that's no ony sic thing, and ye make me like it less and less till I absolutely dislike it; but then the sense o' injustice comes to ma relief, and I love it better than afore—as, for example, a leddy o' fine education, or a garden flower. For, I'll be shot, if either the ane or the ither be necessarily artificial, or no just as bonny, regarded in a richt licht, as a lass or a lily o' low degree. Ony ither touchin trifle frae the Greek, sir?

North. We have had Pan—now for Priapus.

Shepherd. Ye maun heed what you say, sir, o' Priawpus.

North. Archias is always elegant, James.

Registrar. And often more than elegant, North—poetical. He had a fine eye, too, sir, for the picturesque.

North.—

Near to the shore, upon this neck of land,
A poor Priapus, here I ever stand.
Carved in such guise, and forced such form to take,
As sons of toilsome fishermen could make,
My feetless legs, and cone-shaped, towering head,
Fill every cormorant with fear and dread.
But when for aid the fisher breathes a prayer,
I come more swiftly than the storms of air.
I also eye the ships that stem the flood:
'Tis deeds, not beauty, show the real God.

[*Loud hurras heard from the glen, and repeated by all the echoes.*

North. Heavens! what's that?

Shepherd. Didna I tell ye I had waukened the Forest? What's twunty, thretty, or fifty miles to the lads and lassies o' the South o' Scotland? Auld women and weans 'll walk that atween the twa gloamins,—and haena they gigs, and carts, and pownies for the side-saddle, and lang bare-backed yauds that can carry fower easy—and at a pinch, by haudin on by mane and tail, five? Scores hae been paddin the hoof* sin' mornin frae the head o' Clydesdale—Annan-banks hae been roused as by the sound o' a trumpet—and the auld Grey Mare † has been a' day whuskin her tail wi' pleasure to see Moffatdale croudin to the Jubilee.

[*They all take their station outside on the brae, and hold up their hands.*

North. I am lost in amazement!

Tickler. A thousand souls!

Registrar. I have been accustomed to calculate the numbers of great multitudes—and I fix them at fifteen hundred, men, women, and children.

Shepherd. Twa hunder collies, and, asses and mules included, a hunder horse.

Registrar. Of each a Turm.

Shepherd. Oh! sir, isna't a bonny sicht? There's a Tredd's Union for you, sir, that may weel mak your heart sing for joy—shepherds and herdsmen, and ploughmen, and woodsmen, that wad, if need were, fecht for their kintra, wi' Christopher North at their head, against either foreign or domestic enemies; but they come noo to do him homage at the unviolated altar which Nature has erected to Peace.

Registrar. A band of maidens in the van—unbonneted—silken-snooded all. And hark—they sing! Too distant for us to catch the words—but music has its own meanings—and only that it is somewhat more mirthful, we might think it was a hymn!

* *Paddin the hoof*—trudging on foot.
† The waterfall so called near St. Mary's Loch.

Shepherd (*to Tickler and the Registrar*). Dinna look at him, he's greetin. If that sound was sweet, isna this silence sublime?

Tickler. What are they after now, James?

Shepherd. They hae gotten their general orders—and a' the leaders ken weel hoo to carry them intil effeck. The phalanx is noo breakin into pieces noo, like camstrary* cluds—ae speerit inspires and directs a' its muvements, and it is deploying, Mr. Tickler, round yon great hie-kirk-looking rocks, intil a wide level place that's a perfect circle, and which ye wha hae been here the best part o' a week, I'se warrant, ken naething about; for Natur, I think, maun hae made it for hersel; and such is the power o' its beauty, that sittin there aften in youth, hae I clean forgotten that there was ony ither warld.

Registrar.—

"Shaded with branching palm, the sign of Peace."

Shepherd. Ay, mony o' them are carrying the boughs o' trees—and it's wonderfu' to see how leafy they are so early in the season. But Spring, prophetic o' North's visit, has festooned the woods.

Tickler. Not boughs and branches only——

Shepherd. But likewise furms. There's no a few mechanics amang them, sir, house-carpenters and the like, and seats 'ill be sune raised a' round and round, in an hour or less you'll see sic a congregation as you saw never afore, a' sittin in an amphitheatre—and aneath a hangin rock a platform—and on the platform a throne wi' its regal chair—and in the chair wha but Christopher North—and on his head a crown o' Flowers—for lang as he has been King o' Scotland—this—this is Coronation Day. Hearken to the bawn! †

* *Comstrary* or *camsteery*—unmanageable. † *Bawn*—band.

XXVI.

A NIGHT ON THE LEADS OF THE LODGE.

SCENE.—*The Leads of the Lodge. Present*—NORTH, TICKLER. *the* SHEPHERD, BULLER. *Time—Evening.*

Shepherd. This fancy beats a', and pruves o' itsel, sir, that you're a poet. In fine weather, leevin on the leeds! And siccan an awnin! No a threed o' cotton about it, or linen either, but dome, wa's, cornishes, and fringes—a' silk. Oh! but she's a tastefu' cretur, that Mrs. Gentle—for I see the touch o' her haun in the hangings, the festoonins, the droopins o' the draperies—and it's a sair pity that ye twa, who are seen to be but ae* speerit, arena likewise ae flesh. Pardon the allusion, Mr. North, but you'll never be perfectly happy till she bears your name. or aiblins you'll tak hers, my dear auld sir, and ca' yoursels Mr. and Mrs. North Gentle; or gin you like better to gie hers the precedence, Mr. and Mrs. Gentle Christopher North. But either o' the twa would be characteristic and euphonous—for you're humane, sir, by nature, though by habit rather savage, and a' you want to saften you back into your original constitution is to be a husband—

Tickler. And a father.

Shepherd. As likely to be that as yoursel, Mr. Tickler, and likelier too; and a' the warld would admire to see a bit canty callant or yellegant lassie trottin at his knee——

* *Ae*—one.

Tickler.

> " With all its mother's tenderness,
> And all its father's fire ! "

North. James, is it not a beautiful panorama?

Shepherd. A panorama! What? wad you wush to hae a panorama o' weans?

North. I mean the prospect, James.

Shepherd. A prospect o' a panorama o' weans!

North. Poo—poo—my dear Shephèrd—you wilfully misapprehend my meaning—look round you over land and sea!

Shepherd. I canna look farrer than the leeds. Oh! but it's a beautiful Conservatory! I never afore saw an Orange-tree. And it's true what I hae read o' them—blossom and fruit on the same plant—nae dout an evergreen—and in this caulder clime o' ours bricht wi' its gowden ba's as if we were in the Wast Indies!—What ca' ye thir? *

North. These are mere myrtles.

Shepherd. Mere myrtles! Dinna say that again o' them—mere; an ungratefu' word, o' a flowery plant a' fu' o' bonny white starnies—and is that their scent that I smell?

North. The balm is from many breaths, my dear James. Nothing that grows is without fragrance—

Shepherd. However fent.† I fand that out when a toddler—for I used to fling awa or drap whatever I pu'd that I thocht had nae smell—till ae day I began till suspect that the faut micht lie in my ain nose, and no in the buds or leaves,—and frae a thousand sma' experiments I was glad to learn it was sae—and that there was scent—as ye weel said the noo—in a' that grows. Wasna that kind o' Nature! Hoo else could that real poet, Tamson, hae said, "the air is bawm!"

Tickler. I desiderate the smell of dinner.

* *Thir*—these. † *Fent*—faint.

Shepherd. What'n a sensual sentiment! The smell o' vittals is delicious whan the denner's gettin dished, and during the time o' eatin, but for an hour or mair after the cloth has been drawn, the room to ma nose has aye a close het smell, like that o' ingans. It's no the custom o' the kintra to leeve wi' the leddies—but nae drawin-room like the leeds.—What'n frutes!

North. Help yourself, James.

Shepherd. I'll thank ye, Mr. Tickler, to rax me ower thae oranges.

Tickler. They are suspiciously dark in the color—but perhaps you like the bitter?

Shepherd. They're nae mair ceevil* than yoursel—but genuine St. Michaelers—and as they're but sma', half-a-dizzen o' them will sharpen the pallet for some o' thae American aipples that never put ane's teeth on edge—which is mair than you can say for Scotch anes, that are noo seldom sweeter than scribes.

Buller. Scribes?

Shepherd. Crabs. Mr. North, we maun tak tent what we're aboot, for it wouldna answer weel to stoiter ower the edge o' the leeds; nor yet to tummle doun the trap-door stairs.

North. The companion-ladder, if you please, James.

Shepherd. Companion-ladder? I suppose because only ae person can climb up at a time—though there's room aneuch, that's true, for severals to fa' doun at ance—but the term's nowtical, I ken—and you're a desparate cretur for thinkin o' the sea.

North. Would that Tom Cringle† were here—the best sketcher of sea-scenery that ever held a pen!

* *Seville*—Garrick's poor pun on being pelted with oranges.

† Michael Scott, the author of *Tom Cringle's Log*, was born in Glasgow in 1789, and died in 1835.

Buller. Glascock, sir, can tell, too, a story as well as the best of them all—Hall, or Marryat, or Chamier—of the Gun-room and the Captain's cabin.

North. He can—and eke of the Admiral's. Marryat and Glascock in a bumper, with all the honors.

Shepherd. Na. I wunna drink't.

North. James ! ! !

Tickler. What the devil's the matter with you now ?

Buller. Mr. Hogg !

Shepherd. If I drink't, may I be—

North. No cursing or swearing allowed on board this ship.

Tickler. Call the master-of-arms, and let him get a dozen.

Shepherd. If ony man says that ever I cursed or sweered either in ship or shielin, then he's neither mair nor less than a confoonded leear. Fules ! fules ! fules ! Sumphs ! sumphs ! sumphs ! Sops ! sops ! sops ! Saps ! saps ! saps ! Would you cram the healths o' twa siccan men, wi' a' the honours, intil ae bumper ? Let's drink them separate—and in tumblers.

North. Charge.

Ticker. Halt. "I wunna drink't."

Shepherd. I'll no be mocked, Tickler. Besides, that's no the least like ma vice.

Tickler. "I wunna drink't"—unless we all quaff, before sitting down, another tumbler to Basil Hall.

North. With all my heart.

Shepherd. And sowl.

Buller. And mind. Stap—"I wunna drink't."

Shepherd. That's real like me—for an Englisher.

Tickler. Craziness is catching.

North. Well said, Son of Isis.

Buller. Tom Cringle.

Omnes. Ay, ay, sir.—Ay, ay, sir.—Ay, ay, sir.

North. Instead of the rule *seniores priores*—to prove our equal regard—let us adopt an arithmetical order—and drink them in Round Robin.

[*Four (that is, sixteen) bumper tumblers (not of the higher ranks, but the middle orders) are emptied arithmetically, with all the honors, to the healths of Captains Cringle, Glascock, Hall, and Marryat. For a season there is silence on the leads, and you hear the thrush—near his second or third brood—at his evening song.*

Shepherd. Fowre tummlers, taken in instant sequence, o' strang drink, by each o' fowre men—a' fowre nae farder back than yestreen sworn-in members o' the left-haun branch o' the Temperance Society! I howp siccan a decided exception, while it is pruvin, mayna explode, the general rule. The general rule wi' us fowre when we forgather, is to drink naething but milk and water—the general exception to drink naething but speerits o' wine,—that was a *lapsus lingy*—speerits *and* wine. It's a pleasant sicht to see a good general rule reconciled wi' a good general exception; and it's my earnest desire to see a' the haill warld shakin hauns.

North. Peter, place my pillows. [PETER *does so.*

Shepherd. There's ane geyan weel shued up.*

Tickler. St. Peter? I'm Pope. Kiss my toe, James.

Shepherd. Drink aye maks him clean daft.

Buller. 'Tis merry in the hall, when beards wag all. Then all took a smack—a smack, at the old black-jack—to the sound of the bugle-horn—to the sound of the bugle-horn. Such airs I hate, like a pig in a gate—give me the good old strain—and nought is heard on every side but signoras and signors—like a pig in a gate, to the sound of the bugle-horn.

* *Shued up*—sewed up.

Shepherd. Drink maks him musical—yet he seems to remember the words better nor the tune. North! nae snorin alloo'd on the leeds. Tickler! do you hear? nae snorin alloo'd on the leeds. Buller, pu' baith their noses. Fa'en ower too! Noo, I ca' that a tolerable nawsal treeo. It's really weel snored. Tickler! you're no keepin time. Kit, your'e gettin out o' tune. Buller, nae fawsetto. Come here, Peter, I wush to speak to you. (PETER *goes to the* SHEPHERD.) Isna Mr. North gettin rather short in the temper? Haena ye observed, too, a fa'in aff o' some o' his faculties—sic as memory—and, I fear, judgment? And what's this I hear o' him? (*whispering* PETER.) I do indeed devoutly trust it 'ill no get wun'! (PETER *puts his finger to his nose, and looking towards* NORTH, *winks the* SHEPHERD *to be mum.*) Ye needna clap your finger on your nose, and wunk, and screw your mouth in that gate, for he's in a safe snorin sleep.

Peter (*indignantly*). Mr. Hogg, I trust I shall never be so far left to myself as to act in any manner unbecoming my love, gratitude, and veneration for the best and noblest of men and masters.

Shepherd. You did put your forefinger to your nose—you did wunk—ye did screw your mouth—ye did gesticulate that ye suspeckit his sleep wasna as real's his snore—and ye did nod yes when I asked you wi' a whusper in your lug if it was true that he had taken to tipplin by himsel in the forenoons?

North (*starting up*). Ye backbiting hog in armor—but I will break your bones—Peter, the crutch!

Shepherd. The crutch is safe under lock and key in its ain case—and the key's in ma pocket—for you're no in a condition to be trusted wi' the crutch. As for backbiting, what I said I said afore your face—and if you was pretendin to be asleep, let what you overheard be a lesson till you never to act so meanly again, for be assured, accordin to the auld apothegm, listeners never hear ony gude o' theirsels. Do they, Buller?

Buller. Seldom.

Shepherd. Do they ever, Tickler?

Tickler. Never.

Shepherd. Then I propose that we all get sober again. Peter—THE ANTIDOTE! It's time we a' took it—for I've seen the leeds mair stationary—half-an-hour back, I was lookin eastward, but I'm sair mistaen if ma face be na noo due wast.

North. Yes—Peter. [PETER *administers the Antidote.*

Shepherd. Wasna that a blessed discovery, Mr. Buller! Ae glass o' THE ANTIDOTE taken in time no only remedies the past, but ensures the future—we may each o' us toss aff ither fowre bumper tummlers with the same impunity as we despatched their predecessors—and already what a difference in the steadiness o' the leeds!

Buller. Hermes' Molly!

Tickler. The Great Elixir!

North. Oh, sweet oblivious ANTIDOTE indeed—for out of the grave of memory in bright resurrection rises Hope—and on the wings of Imagination the rekindled Senses seem to hold command over earth and heaven!

Shepherd. Oh coofs—coofs—coofs! wha abuse the wine-bibbers o' the Noctes.

Buller. Coofs indeed!

Shepherd. Never, Mr. Buller, shall they breathe empyrean air.

Buller. Never.

Shepherd. For them never shall celestial dews distil from evening's roseate cloud—

Buller. Never.

Shepherd. Nor setting suns their fancy ever fill with visions born o' golden licht—when earth, sea, cloud, and sky are a' interfused wi' ae speerit—and that speerit, sae beautifully hushed in high repose, tells o' something within us that is divine, and therefore that will leeve for ever! Look! look!

Buller. Such a sunset!

Shepherd. Let nae man daur to word it. It's daurin aneuch even to look at it. For oh! ma freens! arena thae the gates o' glory—wide open for departed speerits—that they may sail in on wings intil the heart o' eternal life! * Let that sicht no be lost on us.

North. It is melting away.

Shepherd. Changed—gane! Anither sun has set—surely a solemn thocht, sirs—yet, come, let's be cheerfu'—Mr. North, let me see a smile on your face, man—for, my dear sir, I canna thole noo bein' lang melancholy at ae time—for every year sic times are growin mair frequent—and I howp the bonny Leddy Moon 'ill no be lang o' risin, nor do I care whether or no she brings wi' her ane, nane, or ten thousan' stars. Here comes the caffee.

(*Enter* AMBROSE, *with tea and coffee silver-service.*)

Ambrose. Tea or coffee, sir?

Shepherd. Chaclat. Help the rest. Mr. North?

North. Sir!

Shepherd. Is that America, on the other side of the Firth?

North. Commonly called the Kingdom of Fife.

* "Come forth, ye drooping old men, look abroad
And see to what fair countries ye are bound!
And if some Traveller, weary of his road,
Hath slept since noontide on the grassy ground,—
Ye Genii! to his covert speed,
And wake him with such gentle heed
As may attune his soul to meet the dower
Bestowed on this transcendent hour!"
WORDSWORTH'S *Evening Ode.*

Shepherd. Noo that steam's brocht to perfection, aiblins I may mak a voyage there before I dee. Can you assure me the natives are no cannibals?

North. They are cannibals, James, and will devour you—with kindness; for to be hospitable, free, affectionate, and friendly, is to be *Fifeish.*

Shepherd. I see through the blue haze toons and villages alang the shores, the kintra seems cultivated, but no cleared—for yon maun be the wudds o' bonny Aberdour atween whilk and the shore o' Scotland sleep the banes o' Sir Patrick Spens and a' his peers. We can write na sic ballant noo-a-days as—

"The king sat in Dunfermline Tower,
Drinking the blood-red wine."

The simplest pawthos, sir, sinks deepest in the heart—and lies there—far down aneath the fleetin storms o' life—just as that, wreck itsel is lyin noo, bits o' weed, and airn, and banes, lodged immovably amang other ruefu' matter at the bottom o' the restless sea.

Buller. Exquisite!

Shepherd. Eh! what said ye, sir? did ye apply that epithet to my sentiment, or to your sherry?

Buller. To both. United, "they sank like music in my heart."

Shepherd. Here's to you, Mr. Buller. Did I ever ask, sir, if you're ony relation to the Bullers o' Buchan? *

Buller. Cousins.

Shepherd. I thocht sae, sir, frae the sound o' your vice.

* "On the east coast of Scotland, a few miles south of Peterhead, are the *Bullers of Buchan*, a nearly round basin, about thirty yards wide, formed in a hollow rock which projects into the sea, towards which there is an arch by which the waves enter. It is open also at the top, round which there is a narrow path about thirty yards from the water; when the sea is high in a storm, this scene is exceedingly grand."—*Penny Cyclopedia.*

You're a fine bauld dashin family, and fling the cares o' the warld aff frae your sides like rocks.

Buller. Scotland seems to me, if possible, improved since my last visit—even

"Stately Edinborough, throned on crags'"

more magnificently wears her diadem.

Shepherd. Embro' as a town, takin't by itsel, 's no muckle amiss, but I canna help considerin't but a clachan * sin' my visit to Lunnon. Mercy on us, what a roar o' life! Ane would think the haill habitable yerth had spewed its haill population intil that whirlpool! or that that whirlpool had sookt it a' in—mair like a Maelstrom than a Metropolis.

North. There's poetry for you!

Buller. It is.

Shepherd. Whales and mennows a' are yonner, sir, dwinnled doun or equaleezed intil the same size by the motion o' millions, and a' sense o' individuality lost. The verra first morning I walked out o' the hotel I clean forgot I was James Hogg.

Buller. Yet, a few mornings after, Mr. Hogg, allow me to say, that the object most thought of there was the Ettrick Shepherd.

Shepherd. Na—no on the streets. Folk keepit shoalin past me—me in ae current o' flesh, and them in anither—without a single ee ever seemin to see me—a' een lookin straucht forrit—a' faces in full front,—sae that I couldna help askin mysel, Will a' this break up—is it a' but the maist wonderfu' o' dreams?

Buller. But in the Park.

Shepherd. Ay! that was a different story—I cam to my seven senses on Sunday in the Park—and I had need o' them

* *Clachan*—a small village.

a'—for gif I glowered, they glowered—and wherever I went, I couldna but see that I was the centre—

Tickler. "The cynosure of neighboring eyes."

Shepherd. O man! wheesht. The centre—the navel o' the great wheel that keepit circumvolving round, while rays, like spokes, innumerable frae leddies' een shot towards me frae the circumference, and hadna my heart been pierced, it wad hae been no o' wudd, but o' stane.

North. O thou Sabbath breaker!

Shepherd. That thocht saddened me, but I shook it aff, and I howp I may be forgiven, for it wasna my ain faut, but the faut o' that Lord that munted me on his ain charger, and would show me—whether I would or no—in the Dress-Rings.

Tickler. And how were you dressed, James?

Shepherd. Wiser-like than you in your ordinar—just in the Sabbath claes I gang in to Yarrow kirk.

North. Simple son of genius! Buller, is he not a jewel?

Buller. He is.

Shepherd. Fie, lads—think shame o' yoursels—for I ken that ahint ma back you ca' me a rouch diamond.

North. But the setting, my dear James! How farther were you set?

Shepherd. I hadna on the blue bannet—for I had nae wush to be singular, sir—but the plaid was atower my shouthers—

North. And across your manly breast, my Shepherd, which must have felt then and there, as here and now, entitled to beat with the pride of conscious genius and worth.

Shepherd. I shanna say that I wasna proud but I shall say that I was happy: for the Englishers I hae ever held to be the noblest race o' leevin men except the Scotch—and for-by that, sirs, a poet is nae mair a poet in his ain kintra than a prophet a prophet; but yonner my inspiration was acknowl edged, and I thocht mair o' mysel as the owther o' the *Queen's Wake*, five hunder miles awa frae the forest, than I ever had ony visible reason to do sae in the city ower which Mary Stuart ance rang,* and in the very shadow o' Holyrood.

North. How you must have eclipsed Count d'Orsay! †

Shepherd. I eclipsed nane. There's nae eclipsin yonner—for the heaven was a' shinin wi' mony thousan' stars. But the sugh went that the Ettrick Shepherd was in the Park—the Shepherd o' the *Wake*, and *The Pilgrims*, and *Kilmeny*—

North. And the Noctes—

Shepherd. Ay, o' the Noctes—and what were they ever, or wad they ever again hae been, withouten your ain auld Shepherd?

North. Dark—dark—irrecoverably dark!

Shepherd. Your haun. Thousans o' trees were there—but a' I kent o' them, as they gaed gliding greenly by, was that they were beautifu'; as for the equipages, they seemed a' ae equipage—

Tickler. Your cortège.

Shepherd. Wheesht—wheesht—O man, wunna ye wheesht! —Representin—containin—a' the wealth, health, rank, beauty, grace, genius, virtue o' England—

Tickler. Virtue!

Shepherd. Yes—virtue. Their een were like the een o' angels; and if virtue wasna smilin yonner, then 'twould be vain to look for her on this side o' heaven.

North. I fear, my dearest Shepherd, that you forgot the Flowers of the Forest.

Shepherd. Clean. And what for no? Wasna I a stranger in Lunnon? and would I alloo fancy to flee awa wi' me out

* *Rang*—reigned.

† This accomplished gentleman, and leader of the fashion in his day, died in 1852.

the gates o' Paradise? Na—she couldna hae dune that, had she striven to harl me by the hair o' the head. Oh, sir! sufficient for the hour was the beauty thereof—sowl and senses were a' absorbed in what I saw—and I became—

Tickler. The Paragon of the Park.

Shepherd. Wull you no fine him, sir, in saut and water?

North. Silence, Tim!

Shepherd. He disturbs one like the Death-Tick.

North. Well, James?

Shepherd. The Forest for me, after a'! Sae would it hae been, sir, even had I been ca'd up to Lunnon in my youth or prime. Out o' utter but no lang forgetfulness it would hae risen up, stretchin itsel out in a' its length and breadth, wi' a' its lochs and mountains, and hills and streams—St. Mary's and the Yarrow, the dearest o' them a'—and wafted me alang wi't, far aff and awa frae Lunnon, like a man in a warld o' his ain, swoomin northward through the air, wi' motion true to that ae airt, and no deviatin for sake o' the brichtest southern star.

Buller. Most beautiful.

Shepherd. If it would hae been sae even then, Mr. Buller, hoo much mair maun it hae been sae but some three simmers back, when my hair, though a gey dour broon, was yielding to the grey? You was never at Mount Benger, sir, nor Altrive, and the mair's the pity, for happy should we a' be to see sic a fine, free, freenly fallow—and o' sic bricht pairts—though the weans michtna just at first follow your English—

Buller. For their sakes, my dear Shepherd—forgive my familiarity—I should learn their own Doric in a day.

Shepherd. That you wad, my dear Mr. Buller; and thinkna ye, gin if I ever, for a flaff, * in the Park, forgot my ain cosy bield, that the thocht on't cam na back on my heart—ay, the

* *Flaff*—instant.

verra sicht o't afore my een—dearer than ever for sake o' the wee bodies speerin at their mother when faither was comin hame—and for sake o' her, who, for my sake, micht at that moment be lettin drap a kiss on their heads.

Tickler. Now that we have seen the Shepherd in the Park, pray, James, exhibit yourself at the Play.

Shepherd. The last exhibition you made o' yoursel, Mr. Tickler, at the Play, as you ca't—meanin, I presume, in the Playhouse—wasna quite sae creditable as your freens wad hae wished—sittin in ane o' the upper boxes wi' a pented wax-doll—no to ca' them waur—on ilka haun—

North. Is that a true bill, Tickler?

Tickler. A lie.

Shepherd. I never answer that monosyllable *—but canna help followin't up, on the present occasion, wi' an apothegm, to wit, that a man's morals may be judged by his mainners. But I tell you, Mr. North, and you, Mr. Buller, that I was in ane of the houses—ance, and but ance; I gaed there out o' regard to some freens, and I ever after staid awa out o' regard to mysel—for o' a' the sichts that ever met my een, there never was the like o' yon; and I wonder hoo men-folk and women-folk, sittin side by side, could thole't in a public theatre.

[*There is silence for a time.* North *rings the silver bell, and appear* Peter *and* Ambrose *with the cold round, ham and fowls and tongues, and the unassuming but not unsubstantial et-ceteras of such a small snug Midsummer supper as you may suppose suitable at a Noctes on the Leads of the Lodge.* North *nods, and* Peter *lets on the gas.*

* "But ae word explains a'—genius—genius—wull a' the metaphizzians in the warld ever expound that mysterious monosyllable?

"*Tickler.* Monosyllable, James, did you say?

"*Shepherd.* Ay—monosyllable! Doesna that mean a word o' three syllables?

"*Tickler.* It is all one in the Greek, my dear James."

Shepherd. Fareweel to the moon and stars.

North. What will you eat, James?

Shepherd. I'll tak some hen. Mr. Buller, gie me the twa legs and the twa wings and the breist—and then haun the hen ower to Mr. Tickler.

[*They settle down into serious eating. The* SHEPHERD *taking the lead—hard pressed by* NORTH.

North. James, what is your opinion of the state of public affairs?

Shepherd. O, sir! but yon was like to be a great national calamity!

North. Probably it was, James. Pray, what was it?

Tickler. The Plague?

Shepherd. Far waur than the Plague—'cause threatenin to be mair universal—though, like the Plague, it was in Lunnon—thank heaven—where it first brak out—THE TAILORS' STRIKE!

North. 'Twas an appalling event—and, like the great earthquake at Lisbon, was, no doubt, felt all over Europe.

Shepherd. The rural districts, as you ca' them, Mr. North, haena aye escaped sic a calamity. I weel remember, in the year wan,* a like visitation in the Forest. It wasna on sae big a scale—for the boonds wadna admit o' its bein sae—but the meesery was nae less—though contrackit within a narrower circle.

Tickler. Diffused over a wider sphere.

North. When?

Tickler. And how?

Shepherd. The Tailor at Yarrow Ford, without having

* *Wan*—one. "The year *wan*"—an ellipsis for the year 1801.

shown ony symptoms o' the phoby the nicht afore, ae morning at sax o'clock—*strack !*

North. How dreadful!

Shepherd. You may weel say that, sir. 'Twas just at the dawn o' the Season o' Tailors, when a' ower the Forest there begins the makin o' new claes and the repairin o' auld—

North. Making—as Bobby says—

> "The auld claes look amaist as weel's the new."

Shepherd. The maist critical time o' the haill year.

North. Well, James?

Shepherd. At sax he strack—and by nine it was kent frae Selkirk to the Grey-Mare's Tail. A' at ance—ordinar claes only—but mairrage-shoots and murnins were at a deid staun. A' the folk in the Forest saw at ance that it was impossible decently to get either married or buried. For, wad ye believe't, the mad body was aff ower the hills, and bat* Watty o' Ettrick Pen! Of coorse he strack—and in his turn aff by a short cut to the Lochs, and bat Bauldy o' Bourhope, wha loupt frae the buird like a puddock, and flang the guse in the fire, swearin by the shears, as he flourished them round his head, and then sent them intil the ass-hole, that a' mankind micht thenceforth gang nakit for him up to the airmpits in snaw!

North. We are all listening to you, James, with the most intense interest.

Shepherd. The Three Tailors formed themsels intil a union —and boond themsels by an aith—the words o' which hae never transpired—but nae dout they were fearsome and they ratified it—it has been said—wi' three draps each o' their ain bluid, let out wi' the prick o' a needle—no to shue

* *Bat*—bit.

anither steek gin the Forest were to fa' doun afore them on its knees!

North. Impious!

Shepherd. But the Forest had nae sic intention—and bauldly stood up again' the Rebellion. Auld Mr. Laidlaw—the faither o' your freens, Watty, George, and James—took the lead—and there was a gatherin on Mount Benger—the same farm that, by a wonderfu' coincidence, I afterwards came to hauld—at which resolutions were sworn by the Forest no to yield, while there was breath in its body, though back and side micht gang bare. I there made ma maiden speech; for it wasna ma maiden speech—though it passed for such, as often happens—the ane ye heard, sir—ma first in the Forum.

North. I confess I had my suspicions at the time, James, I thought I saw the arts of the sophist in those affected hesitations—and that I frequently heard, breaking through the skilful pauses, the powers, omnipotent in self-possession, of the practised orator.

Shepherd. Never was there sic a terrible treeo as them o' Yarrow Ford, Ettrick Pen, and Bourhope! Three decenter tailor lads, a week afore, ye micht hae searched for in vain ower the wide warld. The streck changed them into demons. They cursed, they swore, they drank, they danced, they focht—first wi' whatever folk happened to fa' in wi' them on the stravaig—and then, castin out amang theirsels, wi' ane anither, till they had a' three black een—and siccan noses!

Tickler. 'Tis difficult for an impartial, because unconcerned, spectator to divine the drift of the different parties in a fight of three.

Shepherd. They couldna ha divined it theirsels—for there was nae drift amang them to divine. There they were a' three lounderin at hap-hazard, and then gaun heid-ower-heels on the tap o' ane anither, or colleckit in a knot in the glaur; and I couldna help sayin to Mr. Bryden—father o' your favorite Watty Bryden, to whom ye gied the tortoise-shell mull—"Saw ye ever, sir, a *Tredd's-Union like that.*"

Tickler. Why not import?

Shepherd. As they hae dune since in Lunnon frae Germany? Just because naebody thocht o't. Importin tailors to ensure free tredd!!

Tickler. And how fared the Forest?

Shepherd. No weel. Some folk began tailorin for theirsels—but there was a strong prejudice against it—and to them that made the attempp the result was baith ridiculous and painfu', and in ae case, indeed, had nearly proved fatal.

Tickler. James, how was that?

Shepherd. Imagine yoursel, Mr. Tickler, in a pair o' breeks, wi' the back pairt afore—the seat o' honor transferred to the front—

North. Let us all so imagine, Tickler.

Shepherd. They shaped them sae, without bein' able to help it, for it's a kittle airt cuttin out.

Tickler. But how fatal?

Shepherd. Dandy o' Dryhope, in breeks o' his ain gettin up, rashly daured to ford the Yarrow—but they grupped him sae ticht atween the fork, that he could mak nae head gain'* the water comin doun gey strang, and he was soopit aff his feet, and taen out mair like a bundle o' claes than a man.

Tickler. How?

Shepherd. We listered him like a fish.

North. "Time and the hour run through the roughest day!"

Shepherd. And a' things yerthly hae an end. Sae had the streck. To mak a lang story short—the Forest stood it out

* *Gain,*—against.

—the tailors gied in—and the Tredd's-Union fell to pieces. But no before the Season o' Tailors was lang ower, and pairt o' the simmer too—for they didna return to their wark till the Langest Day. It was years afore the rebels recovered frae the want o' wage and the waste o' pose ;* but atween 1804 and 1808 a' three married, and a' three, as you ken, Mr. North—for I hae been direckin mysel to Mr. Tickler and Mr. Buller—hae been ever sin' syne weel-behaved and weel-to-do—and I never see ony o' them without their tellin me to gie you their compliments, mair especially the tailor o' Yarrow Ford,—for Watty o' the Pen—him, Mr. Buller, that used to be ca'd the Flyin Tailor o' Ettrick—sometimes fears that Christopher North hasna got ower yet the beatin he gied him in the ninety-odd—the year Louis XVI. was guillotined—at hap-stap-and-loup.

North. He never beat me, Mr. Buller.

Buller. From what I have heard of you in your youth, sir, indeed I can hardly credit it. Pardon my skepticism, Mr. Hogg.

Shepherd. You may be as great a skeptic as you choose—but Watty bate Kitty a' till sticks.

North. You have most unkindly persisted, Hogg, during all these forty years, in refusing to take into account my corns—

Shepherd. Corns or nae corns, Watty bate you a' till sticks.

North. Then I had been fishing all day up to the middle in the water, with a creel forty pound weight on my back—

Shepherd. Creel or nae creel, Watty bate you a' to sticks.

North. And I had a hole in my heel you might have put your hand into—

Shepherd. Sound heels or sair heels, Watty bate you a' to sticks.

* *Pose*—a secret hoard of money ; savings.

North. And I sprained one of my ankles at the first rise.

Shepherd. Though you had sprained baith, Watty wad hae bate you a' till sticks.

North. And those accursed corduroys cut me—

Shepherd. Dinna curse the corduroys—for in breeks or out o' breeks, Watty bate ye a' till sticks.

North. I will beat him yet for a—

Shepherd. You shanna be alloo'd to mak sic a fule o yoursel. You were ance the best louper I ever saw—excepp ane —and that ane was wee Watty o' the Pen—the Flyin Tailor o' Ettrick—and he bate ye a' till sticks.

North. Well—I have done, sir. All people are mad on some one point or other—and your insanity—

Shepherd. Mad or no mad, Watty bate you a' till sticks.

North. Peter, let off the gas. (*Rising with marked displeasure.*)

Shepherd. Oh man! but that's pujr spite! Biddin Peter let aff the gas, merely 'cause I tauld Mr. Buller what a' the Forest kens to be true, that him the bairns noo ca' the Auld Hirplin Hurcheon, half-a-century sin', at hap-stap-and-loup, bate Christopher North a' till sticks.

North (*with great vehemence*). Let off the gas, you stone!

Shepherd. That's pitifu'! Ca'in a man a stane! a man that has been sae lang too in his service—and that has gien him nae provocation—for it wasna Peter but me that was obleeged to keep threepin that Watty o' the Pen—by folk o' my time o' life never ca'd onything less than the Flying Tailor o' Ettrick, though by bairns never ca'd onything mair but the Auld Hirplin Hurcheon, at hap-stap-and-loup—on fair level mossy grun'—bate him a' till sticks.

North (*in a voice of thunder*). You son of a sea-gun, let off the gas.

Shepherd. Passion's aften figurative, and aye forgetfu'

But I fear he'll be breakin a bluid-veshel—sae I'll remind him o' the siller bell. Peter has orders never to shaw his neb but as soun' o' the siller bell.—Sir, you've forgotten the siller bell. Play tingle—tingle—tingle—ting.

North (ringing the silver bell). Too bad, James. Peter, let off the gas. [PETER *lets off the gas.*

Shepherd. Ha! the bleeze o' morn! Amazin! 'Twas shortly after sunset when the gas was let on—and noo that the gas is let aff, lo! shortly after sunrise!

Buller. With us there has been no night.

Shepherd. Yesterday was the Twunty-first o' June—the Langest Day. We could hae dune without artificial licht—for the few hours o' midnicht were but a gloamin—and we could hae seen to read prent.

Buller. A deep dew.

North. As may be seen by the dry lairs in the wet grass of those cows up and at pasture.

Shepherd. Naebody else stirrin. Look, there's a hare washin her face like a cat wi' her paw. Eh man! look at her three leverets, like as mony wee bit bears.

Buller. I had no idea there were so many singing birds so near the surburbs of a great city.

Shepherd. Hadna ye? In Scotland we ca' that the skreigh o' day.

North. What has become of the sea?

Shepherd. The sea! somebody has opened the sluice, and let aff the water. Na—there it's—fasten your een upon yon great green shadow—for that's Inchkeith—and you'll sune come to discern the sea waverin round it, as if the air grew glass, and the glass water, while the water widens out intil the Firth, and the Firth awa intil the Main. Is yon North Berwick Law or the Bass—or baith—or naither—or a cape o' cloudland, or a thocht?

North.—

"Under the opening eyelids of the morn."

Shepherd. See! Specks—like black water-flees. The boats o' the Newheeven fishermen. Their wives are snorin yet wi' their head in mutches—but wull sune be risin to fill their creels. Mr. Buller, was you ever in our Embro' Fish-Market?

Buller. No. Where is it, sir?

Shepherd. In the Parliament Hoose.

Buller. In the Parliament House?

Shepherd. Are you daft? Aneath the North Brig.

Buller. You said just now it was in the Parliament House.

Shepherd. Either you or me has been dreamin. But, Mr. North, I'm desperate hungry—are ye no intendin to gie us ony breakfast?

North (*ringing the silver bell*). Lo! and behold!

(*Enter* PETER, AMBROSE, KING PEPIN, SIR DAVID GAM, *and* TAPPYTOORIE, *with trays.*)

Shepherd. Rows het frae the oven! Wheat scones! Barley scones! Wat and dry tost! Cookies! Baps! Muffins! Loaves and fishes! Rizzars! Finnans! Kipper! Speldrins! Herring! Marmlet! Jeely! Jam! Ham! Lamb! Tongue! Beef hung! Chickens! Fry! Pigeon pie! Crust and broon aside the Roon'—but sit ye doun—no—freens, let's staun'—haud up your haun—bless your face—North, gie's a grace.—(NORTH *says grace.*) Noo let's fa' too—but hooly—hooly—hooly—what vision this! What vision this! An Apparition or a Christian Leddy! I ken, I ken her by her curtshy—did that face no tell her name and her nature.—Oh deign, Mem, to sit doun aside the Shepherd.—Pardon me—tak the head o' the table, ma honored Mem—and let the Shepherd sit doun aside YOU—and may I mak sae bauld as to introduce Mr. Buller to you, Mem? Mr. Buller, clear your een—for on the Leads o' the Lodge, in face o' heaven and he risin sun, I noo introduce you till Mrs. Gentle.

North (*starting and looking wildly round*). Ha!

Shepherd. She's gane!

North (*recovering some of his composure*). Too bad, James.

Shepherd. Saw your nocht? Saw naebody ocht?

Omnes. Nothing.

Shepherd. A cretur o' the element! like a' the ither loveliest sichts that veesit the een o' us mortals—but the dream o' a dream! But, thank heaven, a's no unsubstantial in this warld o' shadows. Were ony o' us to say sae, this breakfast would gie him the lee! Noo, Gurney, mind hoo ye extend your short-haun.

Small still Voice. Ay, ay, sir.

Buller. "Oh Gurney! shall I call thee bird, or but a wandering voice!"

North.—

"O blessed Bird! the world we pace
Again appears to be
An unsubstantial faery-place,
That is fit home for Thee!"

XXVII.

A DINNER IN THE FOREST.

SCENE I.—*The Shepherd's Study, Altrive.—The* SHEPHERD *seated at dinner. Time—Six o' Clock.*—AMBROSE *in waiting.*

(*Enter, hurriedly,* NORTH *and* TICKLER.)

Shepherd. What for keep ye folk waitin in this way, sirs, for denner! and it past sax! Sax is a daft-like hour for denner in the Forest, but I'm aye wullin to humor fules that happen to be reseedin in ma ain house at hame. Whare were you—and what hae ye been about? No * shavin at least—for twa sic bairds I dinna remember ha'in witnessed sin' I was in Wales—towards the close o' the century—and they belanged to twa he-goats glowerin ower at mė frae the ruins o' Dolbaldron Castle. Tak your chairs—ye Jews. Moses! sit you on my richt haun—and Aaron! sit you on my left. [NORTH *and* TICKLER *sit down as commanded.*

North. 'Tis the first time in my life that I have been one moment behind the hour.

Shepherd. I believ't. For you can regulat your stamack like a timepiece. It gangs as true's a chronometer—and on board a ship you could tell by't to a nicety when she would reach ony particular port. I daursay it's correck the noo by

* *No*—not.

the sun—but I aye mak Girrzzy bate * the girdle twa-three minutes afore the chap o' the knock.†

Tickler. Bate the girdle?

Shepherd. Ay, just sae, sir—bate the girdle. I used to hae a bell hung on the bourtree at the gable-end—the auld Yarrow kirk-bell—but it got intil its dotage, its tongue had the palsy, it's cheeks were crackit—and pu' the rape as you would, it's vice was as puir's as a pan's. Then the lichtnin, that maun hae had little to do that day, melted it intil the shape o' an airn icicle, and it grew perfeckly useless—sae I got a drum that ance belanged to the militia, and for some seasons it diverted the echoes that used to tak it aff no amiss, whether braced or itherwise—but it too waxed auld and impotent, and you micht as weel for ony music that was in't, hae bate the kitchen-dresser wi' the lint-beetle—sae I then got a gong sent ower frae India frae your freen and mine, Dr. Gray—God bless him—and for a lang, deep, hollow trummlin, sea-like, and thunderous sound, it bate a' that ever was heard in this kintra—but it created sic a disturbance far and wide, that, sair against my wull, I had to shut it up in the garret.

North. Wherefore, James?

Shepherd. In the first place, it was sae like thunner that folk far aff couldna tell whether it was thunner or no; and I've kent them yoke their carts in a hurry to carry in their hay afore it was dry for stacking, fearing a plump. Ae Sunday the sound keepit a' the folk frae the kirk, and aften they wadna ventur on the fuirds, in dread o' a sudden spate frae a water-spoot. I learnt at last to bate it more gently; but then it was sae like the sound o' a bill afore he breaks out intil the bellow, that a' the kye in the forest grew red-wud-mad; sae then I had to take to batin the girdle—an idea

* *Bate*—beat. † *Chap o' the knock*—striking of the clock.

that was suggested to me ae day on the swarmin o' a tap-swarm o' a skep o' bees in the garden—and I find that on a clear day sic as this, when the atmosphere's no clogged, that it answers as weel's either the kirk-bell, the drum, or the gong. You would hear't ayont the knowe, sirs; and wasna't bonny music?

Arcades Ambo. Beautiful, exceedingly.

Shepherd. If her I needna name had been at hame, there would hae been a denner on the table wordier* o' my twa maist esteemed and dearest freens; but I howp wi' sic as we hae—without her mair immediate yet prospective care—you will be able to make a fend.†

North. Bread and cheese would be a feast with the Shepherd.

Shepherd. 'Deed it wad be nae sic thing. It's easy to speak o' feasting on cheese and breed, and butter and breed—and in our younger days they were truly a feast on the hill. But noo our pallets, if they dinna require coaxin, deserve a goo; ‡ and I've seen a barer buird. Mr. Awmrose, lift the lids. [Mr. AMBROSE *smilingly lifts the lids.*

North and Tickler (*in delighted wonder*). Bless us!

Shepherd. That's hotch-potch—and that's cocky-leeky—the twa best soups in natur. Broon soup's moss-water—and white soup's like scauded milk wi' worms in't. But see, sirs, hoo the ladle stauns itsel in the potch—and I wush Mr. Tickler could see himsel the noo in a glass, curlin up his nose, wi' his een glistening, and his mouth waterin, at sicht and smell o' the leeky. We kilt a lamb the day we got your letter, sir, and that's a hind-quarter twal-pund wecht. Ayont it's a beef-stake poy—for Geordy Scougal slaughtered a beast last market day at Innerleithen—and his meat's aye prime. Here are three fules—and that ham's nae sham, sae

* *Wordier*—worthier. † *Fend*—shift. ‡ *Goo*—provocative.

we sall ca' him Japhet. I needna tell ye yon's a roasted green-guse frae Crosslee—and neist it mutton-chaps—but the rest's a' ggem. That's no cat, Tickler—but hare—as you may ken by her lugs and fud. That wee bit black beastie—I wuss she mayna be wizened in the roastin—is a water-hen; the twa aside her are peaseweeps—to the east you may observe a leash o' grouse—wastwards ho! some wild dyucks—a few pints to the south a barren pair o' paitricks—and due north a whaup.

North (*helping himself to a couple of flappers.*)—

"O' a' the airts the wund can blaw
I dearly loe the west,
For there the bonny dyuckie lies,
The dyuck that I loe best."

Shepherd. But you maunna be expeckin a second and third coorse. I hate to hae denner set afore me by instalments; and, frae my no havin the gift o' prophecy, I've kent dish efter dish slip through my fingers in a succession o' coorses, till I had feenally to assuage my hunger on gratins they ca' parmesan. Sir George Warrenner * will recollek hoo I pickit them aff the plate as if I had been famished, yet frae first to last there had been nae absolute want o' vittals. I kept aye waitin for the guse; but nae guse o' an edible kind made his appearance, and I had to dine ower again at sooper in my ain hottle.* That's a sawmon.

Ambrose. There is somebody at the door, sir.

Shepherd. Let him in. (AMBROSE *opens the door, and enter Clavers, Giraffe, Rover, Guile, and Fang.*) It's the dowgs. Gentlemen, be seated. [*The Canine take their seats.*

North. "We are seven."

* I believe that Sir George Warrender presided at a public dinner given to Hogg in London.

† *Hottle*—hotel.

Shepherd. A mystical nummer—

North. The Pleiades.

Tickler.—

"And lend the Lyre of heaven another string."

Shepherd. I ken, Mr. Tickler, ye dinna like dowgs. But ye needna be feared, for nane o' them's got the hydrophoby—excepp it may be Fang. The cretur's been very snappish sin' the barommator reached ninety, and bat a goslin that began to bark—but though the goslin bat him again, he hasna yet been heard to quack ony, sae he's no muckle mad. You're no mad, Fang?

Fang. Buy—wuy—wuy.

Shepherd. His speech's rather affeckit. He used to say—bow—wow—wow.

Tickler (*sidling away nearer the Shepherd*). I don't much like his looks.

Shepherd. But, dear me! I've forgotten to help you—and hae been eatin and talkin awa wi' a fu' mouth and trencher, while baith o' yours is stannin wide open and empty—and I fear, bein' out a' day, you maun be fent.

Tickler. Say grace, James.

Shepherd. I said it, Timothy, afore I sat doun; and though you two was na in, it included you, for I kent you wadna be far aff; sae it's a' richt baith in time and place. Fa' tae.

Tickler. If you have been addressing me, my dear sir, never was there more needless advice. A more delicious duckling—

North. Than Fatima I never devoured.

Shepherd. O ye rubiawtors! Twa wild dyucks dune to the very doups! I intented to hae tasted them mysel—but the twa thegither wadna hae wechted wi' my whaup.

Tickler. Your Whaup?

Shepherd. You a Scotchman and no ken a whaup? O you gowk! The English ca't a curly.

Tickler. Oh! a curlew. I have seen it in Bewick.

Shepherd. And never in the muirs? Then ye needna read Booick. For to be a naturalist you maun begin wi' natur, and then study her wi' the help o' her chosen sons. But what think ye, sirs, o' thae pecks o' green pease?

North. By the flavor, I know them to be from Cacra Bank.

Shepherd. Never kent I a man o' sic great original genius, wi' sic a fine delicate taste. They're really sae. John Grieve kent ye was comin to Altrive, and sent me ower baith them and thae young potawtoes, You'll be delichted to see him the morn in Ettrick kirk—for I haena kent him lookin sae strang and fresh for a dizzen years—oh! there's naething for ane ony way invalidish like the air o' ane's native hills!

Tickler. Come, Mr. Hogg, do tell us how you got the game?

Shepherd. It wasna my blame. Last Saturday, that's this day week, I gaed out to the fishin, and the dowgs gaed wi' me, for when they're left at hame they keep up siccan a yowlin that folk passin by micht think Altrive a kennel for the Duke's jowlers. I paid nae attention to them, but left them to amuse theirsels—Clavers and Giraffe, that's the twa grews—Fang, the terrier—and Guile and Rover, collies—at least they ca' Rover a collie, though he's gotten a cross o' some outlandish bluid, and he belangs to the young gentleman at Thirlstane, but he's a great freen o' our Guile's, and often pays him a visit.

Tickler. I thought there had been no friendship among dogs.

Shepherd. Then you thocht wrang—for they aften loe ane anither like bithers, especially when they're no like ane anither, being indeed in that respect, just like us men; for nae twa human beings are mair unlike ither, physically, morally, and intellectually, than you and me, Mr. Tickler, and yet dinna we loe ane anither like brithers ?

Tickler. We do, we do, my dearest Shepherd. Well ?

Shepherd. The trouts wadna tak ; whup the water as I wad, I couldna get a loup. Flee, worm, mennow, a' useless, and the water, though laigh, wasna laigh aneuch for guddlin.

Tickler. Guddlin ?

Shepherd. Nae mair o' your affeckit ignorance, Mr. Tickler. You think it fashionable to be ignorant o' everything vulgar folk like me thinks worth knawin, but Mr. North's a genteeler man nor you ony day o' the week, and he kens brawly what's guddlin ; and what's mair, he was ance himsel the best guddler in the south o' Scotland, if you exceppit Bandy Jock Gray o' Pebbles. He couldna guddle wi' Bandy Jock ony mair than loup wi' Watty o' the Pen, the Flyin Tailor o' Ettrick.

North (laying down his knife and fork). I'll leap him to-morrow for love.

Shepherd. Wheesht—wheesht. The morn's the Sabbath.

North. On Monday then—running hop-step-and-leap, or a running leap, on level ground—back and forward—with or without the crutch—let him use sticks if he will—

Shepherd. Wheesht—wheesht. Watty's deid.

North. Dead !

Shepherd. And buried. I was at the funeral on Thursday. The folk are talkin o' pittin up a bit monument to him—indeed hae asked me to indite an inscription. I said it should be as simple as possible—and merely record the chief act o' his life—" HIC JACET WALTER LAIDLAW OF THE PEN, THE CELEBRATED FLYING TAILOR OF ETTRICK, WHO BEAT CHRISTOPHER NORTH AT HOP-STEP-AND-JUMP."

North (resuming his knife and fork). Well—fix your day, and though Tweed should be in flood, I will guddle Bandy Jock.

Shepherd. Bandy Jock 'ill guddle nae mair in this warld. He dee'd o' the rheumatiz on May-day—and the same inscription, wi' a little variation—leavin out "hop-step-and-jump," and inserting "guddlin"—will answer for him that will answer for Watty o' the Pen.

Tickler. 'Pon honor, my dear sir, I know not guddlin.

Shepherd. In the wast they ca't ginnlin.

Tickler. Whew! I'll ginnle Kit for a pair of ponies.

North (*derisively*). Ha, ha, ha.

Shepherd. I've seen Bandy Jock dook doun head and shouthers, sae that you saw but the doup o' him facin the sun, aneath a bank, and remain for the better pairt o' five minutes wi' his mouth and nostrils in the water—hoo he contrived to breathe I kenna—when he wad draw them out, wi' his lang carroty hair a' poorin, wi' a trout a fit lang in ilka haun, and ane aiblins auchteen inches atween his teeth.

Tickler. You belong, I believe, Mr. Hogg, to the Royal Company of Archers?

Shepherd. What connection has that? I do; and I'll shoot you ony day. Captain Colley ance backed Bandy Jock again' a famous tame otter o' Squire Lomax's frae Lancashire—somewhat about Preston—that the Squire aye carried wi' him in the carriage—a pool bein' made for its accommodation in the floor wi' air-holes—and Jock bate the otter by fifteen pound—though the otter gruppit a sawmon.

Tickler. But, mine host, the game?

Shepherd. Do you no like it? Is't no gude? It surely canna be stinkin? And yet this het wather's sair compleened o' by the cyuck, and flees will get intil the Safe. I gie you my word for't, howsomever, that I saw her carefully wi' a knife scrapin out the mauks.

Tickler. I see nothing in the shape of maggots in this one.

Shepherd. Nor shall ye in this ane—(*forking it*)—for I see that, though I'm in my ain house, I maun tak care o' mysel wi' you Embro' chaps, or I'll be famished.

Tickler. But, mine host, the game?

Shepherd. That cretur Fang there—him wi' the slicht touch o' the hydrophoby—is the gleggest at a grup o' ggem sittin, in a' the Forest. As for Rover, he has the nose o' a Spanish pinter, and draws and backs as if he had been regularly brak in by a dowg-breaker, wi' a dowg-whup on the muirs. On my way up the Yarrow—me wi' my fishin-rod in my haun, no put up, and no unlike the Crutch, only without the cross—Rover begins snokin and twinin himsel in a serpentine style, that aye denotes a strang scent—wi' his fanlike tail whaffin—and Fang close at his heels—when Fang pounces on what I thocht might pruve but a tuft o' heather, or perhaps a mowdiewarp—but he kent better—for in troth it was the Auld Cock—and then whurr—whurr—whurr—a covey o' what seemed no far short o' half a hunder—for they broon'd the lift; and in the impetus o' the moment, wi' the sudden inspiration o' an improveesistreecky, I let fly the rod amang them as if it had been a rung.* It wounded many, but knocked doun but three—and that's them, or at least was them—for I noo see but ane—Tickler ha'in taen to his share the Auld Cock.

North. And the ducklings?

Shepherd. Ca' them flappers. A maist ridiculous Ack o' Parliament has tried to mak them ggem—through it's weel kent that tame dyucks and wild dyucks are a' ae breed—but a thousand Acks o' Parliament 'ill never gar me consider them ggem, or treat them as ggem, ony mair than if you were to turn out a score o' how-towdies on the heather, and ca' them ggem.

Tickler. Pheasants

* *Rung*—walking staff.

Shepherd. I ken naething about feesants, excepp that they are no worth eatin.

North. You are wrong there, James. The duke sends me annually half-a-dozen, and they eat like Birds of Paradise.

Shepherd. Even the hen's no half sae gude's a hen. But for the flappers. A' the five dowgs fand theirsels a' at ance in amang a brood on a green level marshy spat, where escape was impossible for puir beasts that couldna yet flee—and therefore are ca'd flappers. It wad hae been vain for me to try to ca' the dowgs aff—sae I cried them on—and you never saw sic murder. The auld drake and dyuck keepit circling round—quack-quack-quackin out o' shot in the sky—and I pitied the puir pawrents lookin doun on the death o' their promising progeny. By gude luck I had on the sawmon-creel—and lookin round about, I crammed in a' the ten—doun wi' the lid—and awa alang the holms o' Yarrow as if I was selecking a stream for beginnin to try the fishin—when, wha sud I meet but ane o' his Grace's keepers! Afore I kent whare I was, he put his haun aneath the basket, and tried to gie't a hoist—but providentially he never keekit intil the hole—and tellin him I had had grand trootin—but maun be aff, for that a lassie had been sent to tell me that twa gentlemen frae Embro' had come out to Altrive—I wished him gude day, and took the fuird. But my heart was loupin, and I felt as if I was gaun to fent. A sook o' Glenlivet, however, set me a' richt—and we shall hae the lave to sooper I howp poosie's tasty, sir?

North. I have rarely ate a sweeter and richer leveret.

Shepherd. I'll thank ye, sir, to ca' the cretur by her richt name—the name she gaed by, to my knowledge, for mony years—a Hare. She hasna been a leveret sin' the King's visit to Scotland. I howp you dinna find her teuch? *

* *Teuch*—tough.

North. Not yet.

Shepherd. You maun lay your account wi' her legs bein' harder wark than her main body and wings. I'm glad to see Girrzzy hasna spared the stuffin—and you needna hain the jeel,* for there's twa dizzen pats o' new, red, black, and white, in that closet, wi' their mouths cosily covered wi' pages o' some auld lowse Nummers o' *Blackwood's Magazine*—the feck o' them belangin to twa articles, entitled "Streams" and "Cottages."

North (*wincing*). But to the story of the game.

Shepherd. The witch was sitting in her ain kail-yard—the preceese house I dinna choose to mention—when Giraffe, in louping ower the dyke, louped ower her, and she gied a spang intil the road, turning round her fud within a yard o' Clavers —and then sic a brassel a' three thegither up the brae! And then back again—in a hairy whirlwind—twa miles in less than ae minute. She made for the mouth o' the siver, † but Rover, wha had happened to be examining it, in his inquisitive way, and kent naething o' the coorse, was comin out just as she was gaun in, an' atween the twa there ensued, unseen in the siver, a desperate battle. Weel dune, witch—weel dune, warlock—and at ae time I feared frae his yelpin and yowlin that Rover was gettin the warst o't, and micht lose his life. Auld poosies cuff sair wi' their forepaws—and theirs is a wicked bite. But the outlandish wolfiness in Rover brak forth in extremity, and he cam rushin out o' the siver wi' her in his mouth, shaking her savagely, as if she had been but a ratten, and I had to choke him aff. Forby thraplin her, he had bit intil the jugular—and she lost sae meikle bluid, that you hae eaten her the noo roasted, instead o' her made intil soup. She wad hae been the tenderer o' anither fortnicht o' this het wather—wi' the glass at 92 in the

* *Hain the jeel*—be sparing of the jelly. † *Siver*—a covered drain.

shade o' the Safe in the Larder—yet you seem to be gettin on—

North. Pretty well—were it not that a sinew—like a length of catgut—from the old dame's left hip has got so entangled among my tusks, that—

Shepherd. You are speakin sae through your teeth as no to be verra intelligible. Let me cut the sinny wi' my knife.

[*The* SHEPHERD *operates with much surgical dexterity.*

North. Thank you, James. I shall eat no more of the leveret now—but take it minced at supper.

Shepherd. Minshed! ma faith, you've minshed it wi' a vengeance. She's a skeleton noo, and nae mair—and let's send her in as a curiosity in a glass case to James Wilson—to meet him on his return frae the Grand Scientific Expedition o' thae fearless feelosophers into the remotest regions o' Sutherland, to ascertain whether par be par, or o' the seed o' sawmon. We'll swear that we fand it imbedded in a solid rock, and it 'll pass for the young o' some specie o' antediluvian yelephant.

Tickler. Clap the skin upon it—and tell James that we all three saw it jump out of the heart of the trap.

Shepherd. A queer idea. Awmrose, bid Girrzzy gie ye the hare-skin o' that auld hare that's noo eaten intil a skeleton by Mr. North.

[*Exit* AMBROSE, *and enters with the hare-skin.*

North. Allow me to put it on.

[NORTH *seems much at a loss.*

Shepherd. Hoot, man! The skin's inside out! There—the lugs fit nicely—(*the* SHEPHERD *adroitly re-furs Puss*)—and the head—but there's a sair fa'in aff everywhere else—and noo that it's on—this unreal mockery is mair shockin than the skeleton. Tak it awa—tak it awa, Mr. Awmrose—I canna thole to look at it.

North. Stop, Ambrose. Give it me a moment.

[NORTH *lends it a legerdemain touch after the style of the late celebrated Othello Devaynes of Liverpool, and the witch, in point of activity, apparently not one whit the worse of having been eaten, jumps out of the window.*

Omnes. Halloo! halloo! halloo!

[*Clavers, Giraffe, Rover, Guile, and Fang, spring from their seats, and evanish—Fang clearing the sill as clean as a frog.*

Tickler. Now, Ambrose, down with the window — for, though my nose is none of the most fastidious, we have really had in every way quite enough of dogs.

XXVIII.

A DAY AT TIBBIE'S.

SCENE I.—*Green in front of* TIBBIE'S, *head of St. Mary's Loch.** *Time—Four afternoon.* SHEPHERD *standing alone, in a full suit of the Susalpine Tartan. Arrive* NORTH *and* TICKLER *on their Norwegians.*

Shepherd. True to time as the cuckoo or the swallow. Hail, Christopher! Hail, Timothy! Lords o' the ascendant, I bid ye hail!

Tickler. Hoo's a' wi' ye, Jeems?

Shepherd. Brawlies—brawlies, sir; but tak my advice, Mr. Tickler, and never attempp what ma excellent freen, Downie o' Appin, ca's the Doric, you Dowg, for sic anither pronounciation was never heard on this side o' the North Pole.

North. My beloved Broonie! lend a helping hand to your old accomplice while he endeavors to dismount.

Shepherd. My heart hotches, like a bird's nest wi' young anes, at the sound o' your vice. Ay—ay—I'll affectionately lend a helpin haun to my auld accomplice while he endeavors to dismunt—my auld accomplice in a' kinds o' innicent wicketness—and Clootie shanna tak the ane o' us without the ither—I'm determined on that,—yet Clootie's a great coward, and wull never hae courage to face the Crutch!

* Tibbie Shields and her interesting pastoral hostelry still flourish for the accommodation of travellers in the wild solitudes of St Mary's Loch, Selkirkshire.

Tickler. And how am I to get off?

Shepherd. Your feet's within twa-three inches o' the grund already—straucht your knees—plant your soles on the sward—let gae the grup, and the beast 'll walk out frae aneath you, as if he was passing through a triumphal airch. Cream-colored pownies! Are they a present frae the royal stud?

North. They are Norwegians, James, not Hanoverians. Lineally descended from the only brace of cavalry King Haco had on board at the battle of Largs.

Shepherd. His ain body-guard o' horse-marines. Does he bite?

North. Sometimes. But please to observe that he is muzzled.

Shepherd. I thocht 'twas but a nettin ower his nose. Does he kick?

North. I have known him kick.

Shepherd. I canna say I like that layin back o' his lugs—nor yet that twust o' his tail—and, mercy on us, but he's gotten the Evil Ee!

Tickler. Tibbie! a stool.

[TIBBIE *places a cutty stool below* TICKLER'S *left foot—and describing half a circle with his right,* TIMOTHY *treads the sod—then facing about, leans with his right elbow on Harold's shoulder—while his left forms the apex :f an isosceles triangle, as hand on hip he stands, like Hippolytus or Meleager.*

Shepherd (admiring Tickler). There's an equestrian statue worth a thousand o' that o' Lord Hopetoun and his horse in front o' the Royal Bank—though judges tell me that Cawmel the sculptor's a modern Midas. Hoo grandly the figures combine wi' the backgrund! See hoo that rock relieves Tickler's heid,—and hoo that tree carries off Hawco's tail!

The Director-general was wrang in swearing that sculptur needs nae scenery to set it aff—for will onybody tell me that that group would be as magnificent within the four bare wa's o' an exhibition-room, as where it noo stauns, in the heart o' licht, encircled by hills, and overhung by heaven? Gin a magician could, by a touch o' his wand, convert it intil marble, it would be worth a ransom. But, alas! 'tis but transitory flesh and bluid!

Tickler. Why don't you speak, James?

Shepherd. Admiration has held me mute. I beseech ye, sir, dinna stir—for sic anither attitude for elegance, grace, and majesty, 's no within the possible combinations o' the particles o' maitter. Tibbie! tak aff your een, it's no safe for a widow woman to glower lang on sic a spectacle! Then the garb! what an advantage it has ower Lord Hopetoun's! His lordship looks as if he had loupt out o' his bed on sae sudden an alarm, that he had time but to fling the blankets ower his shouthers, and the groom nae time to saiddle the horse, which his maister had to ride a' nicht bare backit—altogether beneath the dignity o' a British general. But there the costume is a' in perfeck keepin—purple plush jacket wi' great-big white horn buttons single breisted—cape hangin easily ower the back o' the neck—haun-cuffs fliped to gie the wrists room to play—and the flaps o' the mony-pouched reachin amaist doon to the knee, frae which again the ee travels alang the tartan trews till it feenally rests on a braw brass buckle—or is it gowd?—bricht on his instep as a cairngorm. But up wi' a swurl again flees imagination, and settles amang the lights and shadows o' the picturesque scenery o' that mony-shaped straw-hat—the rim o' its circumference a Sabbath-day's journey round—umbrageous umbrella, aneath which he stauns safe frae sun and rain—and might entertain a seleck pairty in the cool of the air! which he could keep in circulation by a shake o' his head!

Tickler. Now that I have stood for my statue, James, pray give us a pen-and-ink sketch of Christopher.

Shepherd. There he sits, turned half round on the saiddle, wi' ae haun restin on the mane, and the ither haudin by the crupper,—no that he's feared to fa' aff—for I've seldom seen him tummle at a staun-still—but that I may hae a front, a back, and a side view o' him a' at ance—for his finest pint is what I would venture, wi' a happy audacity, to ca' the circular contour o' his full face and figure in profile—sae that the spectawtor has a comprehensive visey o' a' the characteristic attributes o' his outward man.

North. The circular contour of my full face and figure in profile? I should like to see it.

Shepherd. I fear I shanna be able to feenish the figure at ae sittin, for it's no easy to get rid o' that face.

North. I am trying to look as mild as cheese.

Shepherd. Dinna fasten your twa grey green een on mine like a wull-cat.

North. Verily they are more like a sucking dove's.

Shepherd. Surely there's nae need to look sae cruel about the doun-drawn corners o' your mouth—for that neb's aneuch o' itsel—every year liker and liker a ggem-hawk's.

North. I am a soft-billed bird.

Shepherd. A multitude o' lang, braid, white, sharp teeth's fearsome in the mouth o' an auld man, and maks ane suspeck dealins wi' the enemy, and an unhallowed lease o' a lang life.

North. Would that I had not forgotten to bargain for exemption from the toothache!

Shepherd. I wuss there mayna be mair meant than meets the ee in thae marks on the forehead. They tell na o' the touch o' Time, but o' the Tempter.

North. I rub them off — so — and lo — the brow of a boy!

Shepherd. Answer me ae question—I adjure you—hae ye selt your sowl to Satan?

North (smiling). James!

Shepherd. Heaven bless you, sir, for that smile—for it has scattered the dismal darkness o' doubt in which ye were beginning to wax intil a demon, and I behold Christopher North in his ain native light—a man—a gentleman—and a Christian. But whare's the crutch?

North. Crutch! The useless old sinecurist has been lying in velvet all autumn. Henceforth I believe I shall dispense with his services—for the air of the Forest has proved fatal to gout, rheumatism, and lumbago—of which truth behold the pleasant proof—James—here goes!

[NORTH *springs up to his feet on the crupper, throws a somerset over Haco's rump, and bounds from the green sward as from a spring-board.*

Tickler. Not amiss. Let's untackle our cattle—and make our toilet.

[NORTH *and* TICKLER *strip their steeds, and turn them loose into the meadow, green as emerald with a flush of aftergrass, in which they sink to the fetlocks, as at full gallop they describe fairy-rings within fairy-rings, till in the centre of the field they subside into a trot, and after diversely careering a while with flowing mane and tail, and neighings that thrill the hills, settle to serious eating, and look as if they had been quietly pasturing there since morn.*

North. That's right, my good Tibbie. Put my pail of water and my portmanteau into the arbor.

Tickler. That's right, my pretty Dolly, put my pail of water and my portmanteau into the shed.

[NORTH *retires into the arbor to make his toilet, and* TICKLER *into the opposite shed. The* SHEPHERD *remains midway between—held there by the counteraction of two equal powers of animal magnetism.*

Shepherd. Are ye gaun into the dookin in thae twa pails?

North. No—as rural lass adjusts her silken snood by reflection in such pellucid mirror—so am I about to shave.

Shepherd. Remember the fable o' the goat and the well.

North (within the Arbor). How beautiful the fading year! A month ago, this arbor was all one dusky green—now it glows—it burns with gold, and orange, and purple, and crimson! How harmonious the many-colored glory! How delightful are all the hues in tone!

Shepherd. Arena ye cauld staunin there in your linen? For I see you through the thin umbrage, like a ghost in a dirty shirt.

North. Sweet are autumn's rustling bowers, but sweeter far her still—when dying leaf after dying leaf drops unreluctantly from the spray—all noiseless as snow-flakes—and like them ere long to melt away into the bosom of mother earth. It seems but yesterday when they were buds!

Shepherd. Tak tent ye dinna cut yoursel—it's no safe to moraleese when ane's shavin. Are ye speakin to me, or was that meant for a soliloquy?

North. In holt or shaw, in wood or grove, on bush or hedgerow, among broom or bracken, the merry minstrelsy is heard no more! Soon as they cease to sing they seem to disappear; the mute mavis retires with her speckled throat and breast so beautiful into the forest gloom; the bold blackbird hides himself for a season, till the berries redden the holly-trees; and where have all the linties gone? Are they, too, home-changing birds of passage? and have they flown ungratefully away with the swallows, to sunny southern isles?

Shepherd. He's mair poetical nor correck in his ornithology; yet it's better to fa' into siclike harmless errors in the study o' leevin birds—errors o' a lovin heart, and a mournfu' imagination—than to keep scientifically richt amang stuffed specimens sittin for ever in ae attitude wi' bead-een in a glass-case.

Tickler (*within the Shed*). What have you been about with yourself all day, my dear James ?

Shepherd. No muckle. I left Altrive after breakfast—about nine—and the Douglas Burn lookin gey temptin, I tried it wi' the black gnat, and sune creeled some fowre or five dizzen—the maist o' them sma'—few exceedin a pund.

Tickler. Hem.*

Shepherd. I fear, sir, you've gotten a sair throat. Ane sune tires o' trootin at ma time o' life, sae I then put on a sawmon flee, and without ony howp daunered donn to a favorite cast on the Yarrow. Sometimes a body may keep threshin the water for a week without seein a snout—and sometimes a body hyucks a fish at the very first thraw ; and sae it happened wi' me—though I can gie mysel nae credit for skill—for I was just wattin my flee near the edge, when a new-run fish, strong as a white horse, rushed at it, and then out o' the water wi' a spang higher than my head,

"My heart to my mouth gied a sten,"

and he had amaist rugged the rod out my nieve ; but I sune recovered my presence o' mind, and after indulgin his royal highness in a few plunges, I gied him the butt, and for a quarter o' an hour keept his nose to the grunstane. It's a sair pity to see a sawmon sulky, and I thocht—and nae doubt sae did he—that he had taen up his lodgins at the bottom o' a pool for the nicht—though the sun had just reached his meridian. The plump o' a stane half a hunderwecht made

* *Hem*—implying a doubt.

him shift his quarters—and a sudden thocht struck him that he would mak the best o' his way to the Tweed, and then doun to the sea at Berwick. But I bore sae hard on him wi' an auchteen-feet rod, that by the time he had swam twa miles—and a' that time, though I aften saw his shadow, I seldom saw himsel—he was sae sair blawn that he cam to the surface o' his ain accord, as if to tak breath—and after that I had it a' my ain way—for he was powerless as a sheaf o' corn carried doun in a spate—and I landed him at the fuird, within a few hunder yards o' Altrive. Curious aneuch, wee Jamie was sittin by himsel on the bank, switherin about wadin across, and you may imagine the dear cretur's joy on seein a twunty-pund fish—the heaviest ever killed wi' the rod in Yarrow—floatin in amang his feet.

Tickler. You left him at home?

Shepherd. Whare else should I hae left him?

Tickler. Hem.

Shepherd. You really maun pit some flannen round that throat—for at this time o' the year, when baith man and horse is saft, inflammation rapidly arrives at its hicht—mortification without loss o' time ensues—and within the four-and-twunty hours I've kent a younger chiel than you, sir, streekit out—

Tickler. What?

Shepherd. A corp.

Tickler. Any more sport?

Shepherd. Returnin to the Loch, I thocht I wad try the otter.* Sae I launched him on a steady leaden keel—twa yards lang—breadth o' beam three inches—and mountin a hunder and fifty hyucks—

* This is an implement with a number of fly-hooks attached to it; and it is worked out into the water from the shore, somewhat after the fashion in which a paper-kite is piqued against the wind.

Tickler. A first-rate man-of-war.

Shepherd. I've seen me in the season atween spring and summer, secure ten dizzen wi' the otter at a single launch. But in October twa dizzen's no to be despised—the half o' them bein' about the size o' herrins, and the half o' them about the size o' haddocks,—and ane—but he's a grey trout—

Tickler. Salmo Ferox?

Shepherd. As big's a cod.

Tickler. Well, James?

Shepherd. I then thocht I would take a look o' some nicht lines I had set twa-three days sin', and began pu'in awa at the langest—wi' some five score o' hyucks, baited for pike and eel, wi' trout and partail, frogs, chicken heads, hen-guts, some mice, some moles, and some water-rats—for there's nae settin boun's to the voracity o' thae sharks and serpents—and it was like drawin a net. At length pike and eel began makin their appearance,—first a pike—then an eel—wi' the maist unerrin regularity o' succession—just as if you had puttin them on sae for a ploy! "Is there never to be an end o' this?" I cried to mysel; and by the time that, walkin backwards, I had reached the road, that gangs roun' the bay wi' a bend—enclosin atween it an the water-edge a bit bonny grass-meadow and twa-three trees—the same that your accomplished freen, George Moir,*—made sae tastefu' a sketch o'—there, wull ye believe me—were lyin five-and-twunty eels and five-and-twunty pikes—in all saxty—till I could hae dreamt that the meadow had been part o' the bay that moment drained by some sort o' subterraneous suction—and that a' the fishy life the water had contained was noo wallopin and wringlin in the sudden sunshine o' unexpected

* A distinguished member of the Scottish bar, and the writer of many admirable papers in *Blackwood's Magazine;* for some time Professor of Rhetoric and Belles-Lettres in the University of Edinburgh, and afterwards Sheriff of Ross-shire.

day. I brak a branch aff an ash, and ran in among them wi' my rung, lounderin awa richt and left, and loupin out o' the way o' the pikes, some of which showed fecht, and offered to attack me on my ain element, and I was obliged to wrestle wi' an eel that speeled up me till his faulds were wounded round my legs, theeghs, and body, in ever sae mony plies, and his snake head—och! the ugly auld serpent—thrust out-ower my shouther—and hissin in my face—till I flang him a fair back fa', and then ruggin him frae me—fauld by fauld—strechtened him out a' his length—and treddin on his tail, sent his wicket speerit to soom about on the fiery lake wi' his faither, the great dragon.

North (*in the Arbor*). Ha! ha! ha! our inimitable pastor has reached his grand climacteric!

Tickler (*in the Shed*). And where, my dear James, are they all? Did you bring them along with you?

Shepherd. I left the pikes to be fetched forrit by the Moffat carrier.

Tickler. And the eels?

Shepherd. The serpent I overthrew had swallowed up all the rest.

Tickler. We must send a cart for him—dead stomachs do not digest; and by making a slit in his belly we shall recover the rest—little the worse for wear—and letting them loose in the long grass, have an eel hunt.

North (*in the Arbor*). Who can give me a bit of sticking-plaster?

Shepherd. I prophesied you would cut yoursel. There's nae stickin-plaister about the toun; but here's an auld bauchle,* and if onybody will lend me a knife, I'se cut aff a bit o' the sole, and when weel soaked wi' bluid, it 'll stick like a sooker—or I can cut aff a bit waddin frae this auld hat—some

* *Bauchle*—an old shoe, crushed into a sort of slipper.

tramper's left ahint her baith hat and bauchle—and it may happen to stainch the bludin—or best of a', let me rug aff a bit o' this remnant o' an auld sheep-skin that maun hae belanged to the foot-board o' some gig—and wi' the woo neist your skin, your chin will be comfortable a' the nicht—though it should set in a hard frost.

[SHEPHERD *advances to the Arbor—but after a single glance into the interior, comes flying back to his stance on the wings of fear.*

North (*in the Arbor*). James? James? James?

Shepherd. A warlock! A warlock! A warlock! The king o' the warlocks! The king o' the warlocks! The king o' the warlocks!

[*From the Arbor issues* CHRISTOPHER *in the character of* LORD NORTH—*in a rich court dress—bag and wig—chapeau-bras—and sword.*

North (*kneeling on one knee*). Have I the honor to be in presence of Prince Charles Edward Stuart Hogg? My sovereign liege and no Pretender—accept the homage of your humble servant—too proud of his noble king to be a slave.

Shepherd (*graciously giving his hand to kiss*). Rise!

[*From the Shed issues* TIMOTHY *in the regimentals of the Old Edinburgh Volunteers.*

Tickler (*kneeling on one knee*). Hail! King of the Forest!

Shepherd (*graciously giving his hand to kiss*). Rise!—Let Us—supported on the arms of Our two most illustrious subjects—enter Our Palace.

[*Enter the Forest King and the two Lords in Waiting into* TIBBIE'S.

SCENE II.—*Interior of* TIBBIE'S—*Grand Hall, or Kitchen Parlor.*

NORTH, TICKLER, *and* SHEPHERD.

Shepherd. A cosy bield, sirs, this o' Tibbie's—just like a bit wren's nest.

North. Methinks 'tis liker an ant-hill.

Tickler. Beehive.

Shepherd. A wren's nest's round and theekit wi' moss—sae is Tibbie's; a wren's nest has a wee bit canny hole in the side o't for the birdies to hap in and out o', aiblins wi' a hangin leaf to hide and fend by way o' door—and sae has Tibbie's; a wren's nest's aye dry on the inside, though drappin on the out wi' dew or rain—and sae is Tibbie's; a wren's nest's for ordinar biggit in a retired spat, yet within hearin o' the hum o' men, as weel's o' water, be it linn or lake—and sae is Tibbie's; a wren's nest's no easy fund, yet when you happen to keek on't, ye wunner hoo ye never saw the happy housie afore—and sae is't wi' Tibbie's; therefore, sirs, for sic reasons, and a thousand mair, I observed, "a cosy bield this o' Tibbie's—just like a bit wren's nest." Sir?

North. An ant-hill's like some small natural eminence growing out of the green ground—and so is Tibbie's; an ant-hill is prettily thatched with tiny straw and grass-blades, and leaves and lichens—and so is Tibbie's; an ant-hill, in worst weather, is impervious to the elements, trembles not in its calm interior, nor—howl till ye split, ye tempests—at any blast doth Tibbie's; an ant-hill, spontaneous birth of the soil though it seems to be, hath its own order of architecture, and was elaborated by its own dwellers—and how wonderfully full of accommodation, when all the rooms at night become the rooms of sleep—just like Tibbie's; an ant-hill, though apparently far from market, never runs out of provisions—nor, when "winter lingering chills the lap of May," ever once doth Tibbie's; Solomon, speaking of an ant-hill, said, "Look at the ant, thou sluggard—consider her ways and be wise,"—and so now saith North, sitting in Tibbie's; so for these, and a thousand other reasons, of which I mention but one—namely, that here, too, as there, is felt the balmy influence of the mountain-dew—I said, "methinks 'tis like an ant-hill." Sir?

Tickler. A beehive is a straw-built shed, loving the lownness, without fearing the wind, and standing in a sheltered place, where yet the breezes have leave to come and go at will, wafting away the creatures with whom work all day long is cheerful as play, outward or homeward bound, to or fro among the heathery hills where the wild honey grows—and these are pretty points of resemblance to Tibbie's; a beehive is never mute—for all that restless noise of industry sinks away with the setting sun into a steady murmur, fit music for the moonlight—and so is it, when all the household are at rest, in Tibbie's; a beehive wakens at peep of day—its inmates losing not a glint of the morning, early as the laverocks waukening by the daisy's side—and so, well knows Aurora, does Tibbie's; a beehive is the perfection of busy order, where, without knowing it, every worker by instinct obeys the Queen—and even so seemeth it to be in Tibbie's; so for these, and a thousand other reasons, of which I mention but two, that it standeth in a land overflowing with milk and honey, and wanteth but *an eke,* I said—Beehive. Sir?

Shepherd. Noo, that's what I ca' poetical eemagery applied to real life.

North. There cannot be a doubt that we three are three men of genius.

Shepherd. Equal to ony ither sax.

Tickler. Hem! How rarely is that endowment united with talent like ours!

North. Stuff. A set of nameless ninnies, at every stumbling step they take, painfully feeling their intellectual impotence, modestly abjure all claim to talent, of which no line is visible on their mild unmeaning mugs, and are satisfied in their humility that nature to them, her favored blockheads—her own darling dunces—and more especial chosen sumphs—in compensation gave the gift of genius—the fire which old Prometheus had to steal from heaven.

Shepherd. Bits o' Cockney creturs wi' mealy mouths, lookin unco weak and wae-begane, on their recovery frae a painful confinement consequent on the birth o' a pair o' twuns o' rickety sonnets.

Tickler. A pair o' twins. Four?

Shepherd. Na—twa sonnets that 'ill never in this warld be able to gang their lanes, but hae to be held up by leading-strings o' red ribbons round their waists, or itherwise hae to be contented to creep or crawl like clocks.

(*Enter* BILLY *and* PALMER *with their game-bags, which they empty on their division of the floor.*)

North. Not a bad day's sport, James?

Shepherd. You dinna mean to tell me that you and Soothside, this blessed day, slew a' that ggem?

North. We did—and more.

(*Enter* CAMPBELL *and* FITZ-TIBBIE *with their game-bags, which they empty on their division of the floor.*)

Shepherd. You dinna mean to tell me that you and Soothside, this blessed day, slew a' that ggem?

North. We did—and more.

(*Enter* MON. CADET *and* KING PEPIN *with their game-bags, which they empty on their division of the floor.*)

Shepherd. You dinna mean to tell me that you and Soothside, this blessed day, slew a' that ggem?

North. We did—and more.

(*Enter* SIR DAVID GAM *and* TAPPYTOORIE *with their game-bags, which they empty on their division of the floor.*)

Shepherd. You dinna mean to tell me that you and Soothside, this blessed day, slew a' that ggem?

North. We do—and more.

(*Enter* AMBROSE *and* PETER *with their game-bags, which they empty on their division of the floor.*)

Shepherd. You dinna mean to tell me that you and Soothside, this blessed day, slew a' that ggem?!! Soothside?

Tickler. I do—and more.

Shepherd. Then are ye twa o' the greatest leears that ever let aff a gun.

North. Or drew a long bow. Where the deuce are the hares?

Tickler. Where the devil are the rabbits?

(*Enter* ROUGH ROBIN *and* SLEEK SAM *with their game-bags, which they empty on their division of the floor—that is, on the table.*)

Shepherd. Fourteen fuds! Aucht maukins, and sax-boroughmongers, as I howp to be saved!

North. I read, with indignation and disgust, of the slaughter by one gun of fivescore brace of birds between eight o'clock and two.

Shepherd. A chiel micht as weel pride himsel on baggin in a poutry-yard as mony chickens, wi' here and there an auld clockin hen and an occasional how-towdie—and to croon a', the bubbly-jock himsel, pretendin to pass him aff for a capercailzie. But I ca' this sport.

North. Which corner, James, dost thou most admire?

Shepherd. Let's no be rash. That nyuck o' paitricks kythes *

* *Kythes*—shows itself.

unco bonny,' wi' its mild mottled licht—the burnished broon harmoniously mixin wi' the siller grey in a style o' colorin understood but by that sweet penter o' still life, Natur ; and a body canna weel look, without a sort o' sadness, on the closed een o' the puir silly creturs, as their heads—crimsoned some o' them wi' their ain bluid, and ithers wi' feathers, bricht in the pride o' sex, auld cocks and young cocks—lie twusted and wrenched by the disorderin haun o' death—outower their wings that shall whirr nae mair—rich in their radiance as flowers lyin broken by the wund on a bed o' moss !

Tickler. James, you please me much.

Shepherd. That glow o' grouse is mair gorgeous, yet bonnier it mayna be—though heaped up higher again' the wa'—and gloomin as weel as gleamin wi' a shadowier depth and a prouder pomp o' color lavished on the dead. There's something heathery in the hues there that breathes o' the wilderness ; and ane canna look on their legs—mony o' them lyin broken—sae thick cled wi' close, white, saft feathers—without thinkin o' the wunter-snaw ! The Gor-Cock ! His name bespeaks his natur—and o' a' the wild birds o' Scotland, nane mair impressive to my imagination and my heart. Oh ! how mony thousan' dawns have evanished into the forgotten warld o' dreams, at which I hae heard him crawin in the silence o' natur, as I lay in my plaid by mysel on the hill-side, and kent by that bold trumpetin that mornin was at hand, without needin to notice the sweet token o' her approach in the clearer licht o' the wee spring-well in the greensward at my feet !

North. James, you please me much.

Shepherd. Yet that angle o' black-cocks has its charms, too, to ma een, for though there's less vareeity in the colorin, and a fastidious critic micht ca' the spotty heap monotonous, yet, sullen as it seems, it glistens wi' a kind o' purple, sic as I hae seen on a lowerin clud on a mirk day, when the sun was shinin on the thunder, or on the loch below, that lay, though it was meridian, in its ain nicht.

Tickler. James, you please me much.

Shepherd. O! thae saft, silken, but sair ruffled backs and breists o' that cruelly killed crood o' bonny grey-hens and pullets—cut aff in their sober matronship and gleesome maidenhood—whilk the mair beautiful, 'twould tak a mair skeely* sportsman than the Shepherd to decide—I could kneel doun on the floor and kiss ye, and gather ye up in my airms, and press you to my heart, till the feel o' your feathers filled my veins wi' love and pity, and I grat to think that never mair would the hill-fairies welcome the gleam o' your plumage risin up in the morning licht amang the green plats on the slopin sward that, dippin doun in the valley, retains here and there amang the decayed birkwood, as loth to lose them, a few small stray sprinklens o' the heather-bells.

Tickler. James, you please me much.

North. I killed two-thirds of them with Old Trusty—slap—bang right and left, without missing a shot—

Tickler. Singing out, "that's my bird," on a dozen occasions when it dropped at least a hundred and fifty yards—right in an opposite direction—from the old sinner's nose.

Shepherd. What was the greatest nummer ye brocht doun at a single discharge?

North. One.

Shepherd. That's contemptible. Ye o' the auld Lake-school are never contented excepp ye kiver your bird, sae that if ye dinna tak them at the crossin, ye shoot a haill day without killin a brace at a blow; but in shootin I belang to the new Mountain-school, and fire wi' a general aim intil the heart o'

* *Skeely*—skilful.

the kivey, and trusting to luck to gar three or four play thud ; and it's no an uncommon case to pick up half-a-dizzen, after the first flaught o' fire and feathers has ceased to dazzle ma een, and I hae had time to rin in amang the dowgs, and pu' the ggem out o' the mouths o' the rabiawtors. It was nae farder back nor the day afore yesterday, that I killed and wounded nine—but to be sure that was wi' baith barrels—though I thocht at the time—for my een was shut—that I had only let aff ane—and wondered that the left had been sae bluidy,—but baith are gran' scatterers, and disperse the hail like chaff frae the fanners on a wundy day. Even them on the edge o' the outside are no safe when I fire intil the middle, and I've knawn me knock heels-ower-head mair nor ane belangin to anither set, that had taken wing as I was ettlin at their neighbors.

Tickler. I killed two-thirds of them, James.

Shepherd. That's four-thirds atween you twa—and at whase door maun be laid the death o' the ither half?

Tickler. Kit with Crambo killed a few partridges in a turnip field, where they lay like stones—an old black-cock that had been severely if not dangerously wounded by a weasel, and fell out of bounds, I suspect from weakness—an ancient grey hen that flew at the rate of some five miles an hour—a hare sitting, which he had previously missed—and neither flying nor sitting, but on the hover, that owl. How the snipe came into his possession I have not learned, but I have reason to believe that he found it in a state of stupor, and I should not be surprised were you, James, to blow into his bill, to see Jack resuscitated—

Shepherd (putting the snipe's bill into his mouth, and puffing into him the breath of life). Is his een beginnin to open?

North. Twinkling like a duck's in thunder.

Shepherd. He's dabbin.

North. Hold him fast, James, or he'll be off.

Shepherd. Let doun the wundow, Tickler, let doun the wundow. Oh! ye clumsy coof! there he has struggled himsel out o' my hauns, and's aff to the mairsh to leeve on suction!

[*Enter* TIBBIE *and* DOLLY *to lay the cloth, &c.*)

Tickler. Symptoms of dinner.

Shepherd. Wi' your leave, sirs, I'll gie Mr. Awmrose the hares to pit intil the gig.

[*Gives* Mr. AMBROSE *the hares, who disappears four-in-hand.*

North. Whose gig, James?

Shepherd. Mine. I'm expeckin company to be wi' me a' neist week—and a turoon o' hare-soup's no worth eaten wi' fewer than three hares in't; sae sax hares will just mak twa tureens o' hare-soup, and no ower rich either—and the third and fourth days we can devoor the ither twa roasted; but for fear my visitors should get stawed o' hare—and auld Burton, in his anatomy, ca's hare a melancholy meat—and I should be averse to onybody committin suicide in my house—Tappy, my man, let me see whether you or me can gather up on our aucht fingers and twa thooms the maist multitude o' the legs o' black-cocks, grey-hens, red grouse, and paitricks; and gin ye beat me, you shall get a bottle o' whisky; and gin I beat you, I shall not put you to the expense o' a gill. (*Aside*)—The pech has twa cases o' fingers, wi' airn-sinnies, and I never kent the cretur's equal at a clutch.

The SHEPHERD *and* TAPPYTOORIE *emulously clutch the game, and carry off some twenty brace of sundries.*

Tickler. James, you please me much.

North. You astonish me, James.

Shepherd. Some folk are easily pleased, and some as easily astonished—but what's keepin the denner?

(*Enter* TIBBIE, *and* DOLLY, *and* SHUSHEY, AMBROSE, MON. CADET, PETER, CAMPBELL, BILLY, PALMER,

ROUGH ROBIN, SLEEK SAM, KING PEPIN, SIR DAVID GAM *and* TAPPYTOORIE, *with black-grouse-soup, red-grouse-soup, partridge-soup, hare-soup, rabbit-soup, potato-soup, pease-soup, brown-soup, white-soup, hotch-potch, cocky-leeky, sheep's-head-broth, kail, and rumbledethumps.*)

Shepherd. Oh, sir! but you've a profound knowledge o' human natur! Eatin at ane's ease, ane's imagination can flee up into the empyrean—like an eagle soarin up the lift wi' a lamb in his talons, and then fauldin up his wings, far aboon shot o' the fowler, on the tapmost o' a range o' cliffs, leisurely devourin't, while ever and anon, atween the rugs, he glances his yellow black-circled een far and wide ower the mountainous region, and afore and after every mouthfu', whattin his beak wi' his claws, yells to the echoes that afar aff return a faint but a fierce reply.

Tickler. Does he spit out feathers and fur?

Shepherd. He spits out naething—devourin bird and beast, stoop and roup, bones, entrails, and a', and leavin after his repast but a wheen wee pickles o' bluidy down, soon dried by the sun, or washed away by the rain, the only evidence there had been a murder.

North. The eagle is not a glutton.

Shepherd. Wha said he was a glutton?

North. Living constantly in the open air—

Shepherd. And in a high latitude.

North. Yes, James—for hours every day in his life sailing in circles some thousand feet above the sea.

Shepherd. In circles, noo narrowin, and noo widenin, wi' sweepy waftage, that seems to carry its ain wund amang its wings—noo speerally wundin up the air stair-case that has nae need o' steps, till you could swear he was soarin awa to the sun—and noo divin doun earthwards, as if the sun had shot him, and he was to be dashed on the stanes intil a blash o' bluid; but in the pride o' his pastime, and the fierceness o' his glee, had been that self-willed headlong descent frae the bosom o' the blue lift, to within fifty fathom o' the croon of the greenwood—for suddenly slantin awa across the chasm through the mist o' the great cataract, he has already voyaged a league o' black heather, and, eein * anither arc o' the meridian, taks majestic possession of a new domain in the sky.

Tickler. No wonder he is sharp set.

Shepherd. I was ance in an eagle's nest.

Tickler. When a child?

Shepherd. A man—and no sae very a young ane. I was let doun the face o' the red rocks of Loch Avon, that affront Cairngorm, about a quarter of a mile perpendicular, by a hair rape, and after swingin like a pendulum for some minutes back and forrit afore the edge o' the platform, I succeeded in establishin mysel in the eyrie.

Tickler. What a fright the poor eaglets must have got!

Shepherd. You ken naething about eaglets. Wi' them fear and anger's a' ane—and the first thing they do when taken by surprise amang their native sticks by man or beast, is to fa' back on their backs, and strike up wi' their talons, and glare wi' their een, and snap wi' their beaks, and yell like a couple o' hell-cats. Providentially their feathers werena fu' grown, or they would hae flown in my face and driven me ower the cliff.

Tickler. Were you not armed?

Shepherd. What a slaughter-house!—What a cemetery! Haill hares, and halves o' hares, and lugs o' hares, and fuds o' hares, and tatters o' skins o' hares, a' confused wi' the flesh and feathers o' muirfowl and wild dyucks, and ither kinds o' ggem, fresh and rotten, undevoored and digested animal maitter mixed in blue-mooldy or bloody-red masses—emittin

* *Eein*—eyeing.

a strange charnel-house, and yet lardner-smell—thickenin the air o' the eyrie—for though a blast cam sughin by at times, it never was able to carry awa ony o' the stench, which I was obliged to breathe, till I grew sick, and feared I was gaun to swarf, and fa' into the loch that I saw, but couldna hear, far doun below in anither warld.

Tickler. No pocket-pistol?

Shepherd. The Glenlivet was ma salvation. I took a richt gude wullie-waucht *—the mistiness afore ma een cleared awa —the waterfa' in my lugs dried up—the soomin in my head subsided—my stamack gied ower bockin—and takin my seat on a settee, I began to inspect the premises wi' mair preceesion, to mak a verbal inventory o' the furnitur, and to study the appearance or character o' the twa guests that still continued lyin back on their backs, and regardin me wi' a malignity that was fearsome, but noo baith mute as death.

North. They had made up their minds to be murdered.

Shepherd. I suspect it was the ither way. A' on a sudden doun comes a sugh frae the sky—and as if borne each on a whurlwund—the yell and the glare o' the twa-auld birds! A mortal man daurin to invade their nest! And they dashed at me as if they wad hae dung me intil the rock—for my back was at the wa'—and I was haudin on wi' my hauns—and aff wi' my feet frae the edge o' the hedge—and at every buffet I, like an inseck, clang closer to the cliff. Dazed wi' that incessant passin to and fro o' plumes, and pennons, and beaks, and talons, rushin and rustlin and yollin, I shut my een, and gied mysel up for lost; when a' at ance a thocht struck me that I would coup the twa imps ower the brink, and that the parent birds would dive doun after them to the bottom o' the abyss.

Tickler. What presence of mind!

* *Wullie-waucht*—large draught.

North. Genius!

Shepherd. I flang myself on them—and I hear them yet in the gullerals. They were eatin intil my inside; and startin up wi' a' their beaks and a' their talons inserted, I flang aff my coat and waistcoat, and them stickin till't, ower the precipice!

Tickler. Whew!

Shepherd. Ay—ye may weel cry whew! Dreadfu' was the yellin, for ae glaff and ae glint;* far doun it deadened; and then I heard nocht. After a while I had courage to lay mysel doun on my belly, and look ower the brink—and I saw the twa auld eagles wheelin and skimmin, and dashin amang the white breakers o' the black loch, madly seekin to save the drownin demons, but their talons were sae entangled in the tartan, and after floating awhile wi' flappin wings in vain, they gied ower strugglin, and the wreck drifted towards the shore wi' their dead bodies.

Tickler. Pray, may I ask, my dear Shepherd, how you returned to the top?

Shepherd. There cam the rub, sirs.. My freens aboon, seeing my claes, wi' the eaglets flaffin, awa doun the abyss, never doubted that I was in them—and they set up sic a shriek! Awa roun' they set to turn the richt flank o' the precipice by the level of the Aven that rins out sae yellow frae the dark-green loch, because o' the color o' the blue slates that lie shivered in heaps o' strata in that lovely solitude—hardly howpin to be able to yield me ony assistance, in case they should observe me attemptin to soom ashore—nor yet to recover the body gin I was drooned. Silly creturs! there was I for hours on the platform, while they were waitin for my corp to come ashore. At last, ashore cam what they supposed to be my corp, and stickin till't the twa dead

* *Ae glaff and ae glint*—one glimpse and one flash.

eaglets, and dashing doun upon't even when it had reached the shingle, the twa savage screamers wi' een o' lichtning!

Tickler. We can conjecture their disappointment, James, on finding there was no corpse.

Shepherd. I shouted—but natur's self seemed deaf; I waved my bannet—but natur's self seemed blind. There stood the great deaf, blind, stupid mountains—and a' that I could bear was ance a laigh echo-like laughter frae the airn heart o' Cairngorm.

Tickler. At last they recognized the Mountain-Bard?

Shepherd. And awa they set again to the tap to pu' me up; but the fules in their fricht had let the rape drap, and never thocht o' lookin for't when they were below. By this time it was wearin late, and the huge shadows were stalkin in for the nicht. The twa auld eagles cam back, but sae changed, I couldna help pityin them, for they had seen the feathers o' them they looed sae weel wrapt up, a' drookit wi' death, in men's plaids—and as they keepit sailin slowly and disconsolately before the eyrie in which there was naebody sittin but me, they werena like the same birds!

North. No bird has stronger feelings than the eagle.

Shepherd. That's a truth. They lay but twa eggs.

North. You are wrong, there, James.

Shepherd. Twa young ones, then, is the average; for gin they lay mair eggs, ane's aften rotten, and I'm mistaen if ae eagle's no nearer the usual number than fowre for an eyrie to send forth to the sky. Then they marry for life—and their annual families being sma', they concentrate on a single sinner or twa, or three at the maist, a' the passion o' their instinck, and savage though they be, they fauld their wide wings ower the down in their "procreant cradle" on the cliff, as tenderly as turtle-doves on theirs, within the shadow o' the tree. For beautiful is the gracious order o' natur, sirs, and we maunna think that the mystery o' life hasna its ain virtues in the den o' the wild beast and the nest o' the bird o' prey.

Tickler. And did not remorse smite you, James, for the murder of those eaglets?

Shepherd. Aften, and sair. What business had I to be let doun by a hair-rape intil their birthplace? And, alas! how was I to be gotten up again—for nae hair-rape cam danglin atween me and the darkenin weather-gleam. I began to dout the efficacy of a deathbed repentance, as I tried to tak account o' my sins a' risin up in sair confusion—some that I had clean forgotten, they had been committed sae far back in youth, and never suspected at the time to be sins ava, but noo seemin black, and no easy to be forgiven—though boundless be the mercy that sits in the skies. But, thank Heaven, there was an end—for a while at least—o' remorse and repentance—and room in my heart only for gratitude—for, as if let doun by hauns o' angels, there again dangled the hair-rape wi' a noose-seat at the end o't, safer than a wicker-chair. I stept in as fearless as Lunardi, and wi' my hauns aboon my head glued to the tether—and my hurdies, and a' aneath my hurdies, interlaced wi' a network o' loops and knots, I felt mysel ascendin and ascendin the wa's, till I heard the voices o' them hoistin. Landed at the tap, you may be sure I fell doun on my knees—and while my heart was beginning to beat and loup again, quaked a prayer.

North. Thank ye, James. I have heard you tell the tale better and not so well, but never before at a Noctes.

North (*looking up at the Cuckoo*). Eight o'clock! It is Saturday night—and Tickler and I have good fourteen miles to drive to the Castle of Indolence.

"O blest retirement! friend to Life's decline!"

Our nags must be all bedded before twelve—for there must

be no intrusion on the still hours of Sabbath. James, we must go.

Shepherd. I declare I never observed Tibbie takin awa the dishes! Sae charmed, sir, hae I been wi' your conversation, that I canna tell whether this be my first, second, or third jug?

North. Your second.

Shepherd. Gude nicht.

[*They finish the second jug, but seem unwilling to rise.*

North. James, the days are fast shortening—alas—alas!

Shepherd. Let them shorten. The nichts 'ill be sae muckle the langer—and " mortal man, who liveth here by toil," hae mair time for waukin as weel as for sleepin rest. Wunter, wild as he sometimes is, is a gracious Season—and in the Forest I hae kent him amaist as gentle as the Spring. Indeed, he seems to me to be gettin safter and safter in his temper ilka year. Frost is his favorite son—and I devoutly howp there 'ill never be ony serious quarrel atween them twa; for Wunter never looks sae cheery as when you see him gaun linkin haun in haun wi' fine black Frost. Snaw is Frost's sister, and she's a bonnie white-skinned lassie, wi' character without speck or stain. She cam to see us last Christmas, but stayed only about a week, and we thocht her lookin rather thin; but the morning afore she left us, I happened to see her on the hill at sunrise—and oh! what a breist!

North. Like that of the sea-mew or the swan.

Shepherd. Richt. For o' a' the birds that sail the air, thae twa are surely the maist purely beautifu'. Then they come and they gae just like the snaw. You see the mew fauldin her wings on the meadow as if she were gaun to be for lang our inland guest—you see the swan floating on the loch as if she had cast anchor for the Wunter there—you see the snaw settled on the hill as if she never would forsake the sun who looks on her with saftened licht — but neist mornin you daunner out to the brae—and mew, swan, and snaw are a' gane—melted into air—or flown awa to the sea.

North. These images touch my heart. Yet how happens it that my own imagination does not supply them, and that you, my dear Shepherd, have to bring them before the old man's eyes?

Shepherd. Because I hae genie.

North. And I, alas! have none.

Shepherd. Dinna look sae like as if you was gaun to fa' a greetin—for I only answered simply a simple question, and was far frae meaning to deny that you had the gift.

North. But I canna write a sang, Jamie—I canna write a sang!

Shepherd. Nor sing ane verra weel either, sir; for, be the tune what it may, ye chant them a' to "Stroudwater," and I never hear you without thinkin that you would hae made—a monotonous ane to be sure, but a pathetic precentor. O but hoo touchingly would ye hae gien out the line! *

North. Allan Cunningham, and William Motherwell, and you, my dear James, have caught the true spirit of the old traditionary strain—and, seek the wide world, where will there be found such a lyrical lark as he whom, not in vain, you three have aspired to emulate—sweet Robbie Burns?

Shepherd. That's richt, sir. I was wrang in ever hinting ae word in disparagement o' Burns's *Cottar's Saturday Night.* But the truth is, you see, that the subjeck's sae heaped up wi' happiness, and sae charged wi' a' sorts o' sanctity—sae national and sae Scottish—that beautifu' as the poem is—

* *To give out the line*—the preposterous practice of reading out each line of the psalm or hymn before singing it once prevailed in Scotland.

and really, after a', naething can be mair beautifu'—there's nae satisfyin either peasant or shepherd by ony delineation o't, though drawn in lines o' licht, and shinin equally wi' genius and wi' piety. That's it. Noo, this is Saturday nicht at Tibbie's—and, though we've been gey funny, there has been naething desecratin in our fun, and we'll be a' attendin divine service the morn—me in Yarrow, and you, Mr. North, and Mr. Tickler, and the lave o' you, in Ettrick kirk.

North. And, James, we can nowhere else hear Christianity preached in a more fervent and truthful spirit.

Shepherd. Naewhere.

(*Enter* CAMPBELL *to tell the Gigs are at the door.*)

North. (*sub dio*). "How beautiful is night!"

Shepherd. That's Southey. In fowre words, the spirit o' the skies.

North. Not one star.

Shepherd. Put on your specks, and you'll see hunders. But they are saft and dim—though there is nae mist—only a kind o' holy haze—and their lustre is abated by the dews. I thocht it had been frost; but there's nae frost—or they would be shinin clearly in thousans—

North. Like angel eyes.

Shepherd. A common comparison—yet no the waur for that—for a' humanity feels, that on a bricht starry nicht, heaven keeps watch and ward over earth, and that the blue lift is instinct wi' love.

North. Where's the moon?

Shepherd. Looking at her a' the time wi' a gratefu' face, that smiles in her licht! as if you were gaun to sing a sang in her praise, or to say a prayer.

North. No halo.

Shepherd. The white Lily o' the sky.

North. No rain to-morrow, Shepherd.

Shepherd. No a drap. 'Twull be a real Sabbath day. Ye see the starnies noo—dinna ye, sir? Some seemin no farrer awa nor the moon—and some far ahint and ayont her, but still in the same region wi' the planet—ithers retiring and retired in infinitude—and sma' as they seem, a' suns. Awfu' but sweet to think on the great works o' God!—But the horses 'ill be catchin cauld—and a' that they ken is, that it's a clear nicht. Lads, tak care o' the dowgs, that they dinna break the couples, and worry sheep. You'll be at the Castle afore Mr. North—for it's no aboon five mile by the cut across the hills—and no a furlong short o' fourteen by the wheel road.—(*They ascend their Gigs.*)—For Heaven's sake! sir, tak tent o' the Norways! Haco's rearin, and Harold's funkin—sic deevils!

Tickler. Whew! Whew! Whew! *D. I. O.* North! Do—*Da—Do—Tibi Gratias!* Farewell—thou Bower of Peace!

XXIX.

IN WHICH THE SHEPHERD APPEARS FOR THE LAST TIME AS THE TERRIBLE TAWNEY OF TIMBUCTOO.

Scene—Penetralia of the Lodge. Time—Ae wee short hour ayont the Twal.

NORTH *and* SHEPHERD.

Shepherd. It wasna safe in you, sir, to gie a' your domestics the play for a haill month in hairst, and to leeve incog a' alane by your single sel, in this Sanctum, like the last remaining wasp in its nest, at the close o' the hummin season;—for what if you had been taken ill wi' some sort o' paralysis in your limbs, and been unable to ring the alarm-bell for succor? Dinna ye see that you micht hae expired for want o' nourishment, without the neiborhood ha'in had ony suspicion that a great licht was extinguished, and that you micht hae been fund sittin in your chair, no a corp in claes, but a skeleton? You should really, sir, hae mair consideration, and no expose your freens to the risk o' sic a shock. Wull you promise?

North. You forget, James, that the milk-lassie called every morning, and eke the baker's boy—except, indeed, during the week I subsisted on ship-biscuit and fruitage.

Shepherd. You auld anchorite!

North. Such occasional abstraction, my dear James, I feel

to be essential to my moral and intellectual well-being. I cannot do now without some utter solitude.

Shepherd. But folk 'ill begin to think you crazy—and I'm no sure if they wad be far wrang.

North. At my time of life, James, it matters not much whether I be crazy or not. Indeed, one so seldom sees a man of my age who is not a little so, that I should not wish to be singular—though, I confess that I have a strong repugnance to the idea of dotage. Come now, be frank with your old friend, and tell me, if the oil in the lamp be low, or if the lamp itself but want trimming?

Shepherd. Neither. But the lamp's o' a curious construction—a self-feedin, self-trimmin lamp—and, sure eneuch, at times in the gloom it gies but a glimmer—sae that a stranger micht imagine that the licht was on its last legs—but would sune start to see the room on a sudden bricht as day, as if the window-shutters had been opened by an invisible hand, and let in a' the heavens.

North. I never desire to be brilliant.

Shepherd. Nor does the Day.

North. Nor the Night.

Shepherd. There lies the charm o' their beauty, sir, just as yours. There's no ostentation either in the sun or in the moon, or in the stars, or in Christopher North.

North. Ah! you quiz!

[*Knocking at the front door and ringing at the front door bell, as if a section of guardians of the night were warning the family of fire, or a dozen devils, on their way back to Pandemonium, were wreaking their spite on Christopher's supposed slumbers.*

Shepherd. Whattt ca' ye thattt?

North (*musing*). I should not wonder were that Tickler.

Shepherd. Then he maun be in full tail as weel's figg, or

else a Breearious. (*Uproar rather increases*). They're surely usin sledge-hammers! or are they but ca'in awa wi' their cuddie-heels? * We ocht to be gratefu', howsomever, that they've settled the bell. The wire-rope's brak.

North (*gravely*). I shall sue Southside for damages.

Shepherd. Think ye, sir, they'll burst the door?

North (*smiling contemptuously*). Not unless they have brought with them Mons Meg.† But there is no occasion for the plural number—'tis that singular sinner Southside.

Shepherd. Your servants maun be the Seven Sleepers.

North. They have orders never to be disturbed after midnight. (*Enter* PETER, *in his shirt.*) PETER, let him in—show him ben—and (*whispers* PETER, *who makes his exit and his entrance, ushering in* TICKLER *in a Dreadnought, covered with cranreuch.*‡ NORTH *and the* SHEPHERD *are seen lying on their faces on the hearth rug*).

Peter. Oh! dear! oh! dear! oh! dear! what is this! what is this! what is this! Hae I leeved to see my maister and Mr. Hogg lyin baith dead.

Tickler (*in great agitation*). Heavens! what has happened! This is indeed dreadful.

Peter. Oh! sir! oh! sir! it's that cursed charcoal that he would use for a' I could do—the effluvia has smothered him at last. There's the pan—there's the pan! But let's raise them up, and bear them into the back-green.

(PETER *raises the body of* NORTH *in his arms*—TICKLER *that of the* SHEPHERD.)

Stiff! stiff! stiff! cauld! cauld! cauld! deid! deid! deid!

Tickler (*wildly*). When saw you them last?

* The iron arming on the heels of boots.

† A piece of ordnance famous in Scottish history, and now placed on the ramparts of Edinburgh Castle.

‡ *Cranreuch*—hoar-frost.

Peter. Oh, sir, no for several hours! my beloved master sent me to bed at twelve—and now 'tis two half-past.

Tickler (dreadfully agitated). This is death.

Shepherd (seizing him suddenly round the waist). Then try Death a wrastle.

North (recuperated by the faithful PETER). Fair play, Hogg! You've hold of the waistband of his breeches. 'Tis a dog-fall.

[*The* SHEPHERD *and* TICKLER *contend fiercely on the rug.*

Tickler (uppermost). You deserve to be throttled, you swineherd, for having well-nigh broke my heart.

Shepherd. Pu' him aff, North—pu' him aff—or he'll thrapple me! Whr—whr—rrrr—whrrrr—

[SOUTHSIDE *is choked off the* SHEPHERD, *and takes his seat on the sofa with tolerable composure. Exit* PETER.

Tickler. Bad taste—bad taste. Of all subjects for a practical joke, the worst is death.

Shepherd. A gran' judge o' taste! Ca' you't gude taste to break folk's bell-ropes, and kick at folk's front doors, when a' the city's in sleep?

Tickler. I confess the propriety of my behavior was problematical.

Shepherd. Problematical. You wad hae been cheap o't, if Mr. North out o' the wundow had shot you deid on the spat.

North (leaning kindly over TICKLER, *as* SOUTHSIDE *is sitting on the sofa, and insinuating his dexter hand into the left coat-pocket of* TIMOTHY'S *Dreadnought).* Ha! ha! Look here, Mr. Hogg! *(Exhibits a bell-handle and brass knocker.)* Street robbery?

Shepherd. Hamesucken!*

North. An accomplished Cracksman!

Tickler. I plead guilty.

* A Scottish law term, expressing assault and battery committed on a person in his own house.

Shepherd. Plead guilty! What brazen assurance! Caught wi' the *corpus delicti* in the pouch o' your wrap-rascal. Bad taste—bad taste. But sin' you repent, you're forgien. Whare hae you been, and whence at this untimeous hour hae you come? Tak a sup o' that. (*Handing him the jug.*)

Tickler. From Duddingston Loch. I detest skating in a crowd—so have been figuring away by moonlight to the Crags.

Shepherd. Are you sure you are quite sober?

Tickler. Quite at present. That's jewel of a jug, James. But what were you talking about?

Shepherd. Never fash your thoom—but sit doun at the side-table yonner.

Tickler. Ha! The ROUND! (*Sits retired.*)

Shepherd. I was sayin, Mr. Tickler, that I canna get rid o' a belief in the mettaseekozies or transmigration of sowls. It aften comes upon me as I'm sittin by mysel on a knowe in the Forest; and a' the scenery, stedfast as it seems to be before my senses as the place o' my birth, and accordin to the popular faith where I hae passed a' my days, is then strangely felt to loss its intimate or veetal connection wi' my speerituality, and to be but ae dream-spat amang mony dream-spats which maun be a' taken thegither in a bewilderin series, to mak up the yet uncompleted mystery o' my bein' or life.

North. Pythagoras!

Shepherd. Mind that I'm no wullin to tak my Bible-oath for the truth o' what I'm noo gaun to tell you—for what's real and what's visionary—and whether there be indeed three warlds—ane o' the ee, ane o' the memory, and ane o' the imagination—it's no for me dogmatically to decide; but this I wull say, that if there are three, at sic times they're sae circumvolved and confused wi' ane anither, as to hae the appearance and inspire the feelin o' their bein' but ae warld —or I should rather say, but ae life. The same sort o' consciousness, sirs, o' my ha'in experimentally belanged alike to them a' comes ower me like a threefauld shadow, and in that shadow my sowl sits wi' its heart beatin, frichtened to think o' a' it has come through, sin' the first far-awa glimmer o' nascent thocht connectin my particular individuality wi' the universal creation. Am I makin mysel understood?

Tickler. Pellucid as an icicle that seems warm in the sunshine.

Shepherd. Yet you dinna see my drift—and I'm at a loss for words.

Tickler. You might as well say you are at a loss for oysters, with five hundred on that board.

Shepherd. I think on a cave—far ben, mirk always as a midnicht wood—except that twa lichts are burnin there brichter than ony stars—fierce leevin lichts—yet in their fierceness fu' o' love, and therefore fu' o' beauty—the een o' my mother, as she gently growls ower me wi' a' pur that inspires me wi' a passion for milk and bluid.

Tickler. Your mother! The man's mad.

Shepherd. A lioness, and I her cub.

North. Hush, hush, Tickler.

Shepherd. I sook her dugs, and sookin I grow sae cruel that I could bite. Between pain and pleasure she gies me a cuff wi' her paw, and I gang heid-ower-heels like a bit playfu' kitten. And what else am I but a bit playfu' kitten? For we're o' the Cat kind—we Lions—and bein' o' the royal race o' Africa, but ae whalp at a birth. She taks me mewin up in her mouth, and lets me drap amang leaves in the outer air—lyin doun aside me and enticin me to play wi' the tuft o' her tail, that I suppose, in my simplicity, to be itsel a separate hairy cretur alive as well as me, and gettin fun, as wi' loups and springs we pursue ane anither, and then for a minute pretend to be sleepin. And wha's he yon? Wha but my Faither? I ken him instinctively by the mane on his shouthers, and his bare tawny hurdies; but my mither wull no let him come ony nearer, for he yawns as if he were hungry, and she kens he would think naething o' devoorin his ain offspring. Oh! the first time I heard him crunch! It was an antelope—in his fangs like a mouse; but that is an after similitude—for then I had never seen a mouse—nor do I think I ever did a' the time I was in the great desert.

North (*removing to some distance*). Tickler, he looks alarmingly leonine.

Shepherd. I had then nae ee for the picturesque; but out o' thae materials then sae familiar to my senses, I hae mony a time since constructed the landscape in which my youth sported—and oh! that I could but dash it aff on canvas!

North. Salvator Rosa, the greater Poussin, and he of Duddingston,* would then have to "hide their diminished heads."

Shepherd. A cave-mouth, half-high as that o' Staffa; but no fantastic in its structure like thae hexagonals—a' ae sullen rock! Yet was the savage den maist sweet—for frae the arch hung doun midway a mony-colored drapery, leaf-and-flower-woven by nature, who delights to beautify the wilderness, renewed as soon as faded, or else perennial, in spite o' a' thae suns, and a' thae storms! Frae our roof strecht up rose the trees, wi' crowns that touched the skies. There hung the umbrage like clouds—and to us below how pleasant was the shade! From the cave-mouth a green lawn descended to a pool, where the pelican used to come to drink—and mony a time hae I watched crouchin ahint the water-lilies, that I

* The Rev. Mr. Thomson.

micht spring upon her when she had filled her bag; but if I was cunnin she was wary, and aye fand her way back unscathed by me to her nest. A' roun' was sand; for you see, sirs, it was an oasis—and I suspeck they were palm-trees. I can liken a leaf, as it cam wavering doun, to naething I hae seen sin' syne but a parachute. I used to play with them till they withered, and then to row mysel in them, like a wean hidin itsel for fun in the claes, to mak its mother true* it wasna there—till a' at ance I loupt out on my mither the Lioness, and in a mock-fecht we twa gaed gurlin doun the brae—me generally uppermost—for ye can hae nae idea hoo tender are the maist terrible o' animals to their young—and what delicht the auld she ane has in pretendin to be vanquished in evendoun worryin by a bit cub that would be nae mair than a match for Rover there, or even Fang. Na—ye needna lift your heids and cock your lugs, my gude dowgies, for I'm speakin o' you and no to you, and likenin your force to mine when I was a Lion's whalp.

Rover and *Fang* (*leaping up and barking at the Shepherd*). Wow—bow, wow—bow, wow, wow.

North. They certainly think, Tickler, that he must be either Wallace or Nero.

Shepherd. Sae passed my days—and a happier young hobbledehoy of a Lion never footed it on velvet pads alang the Libyan sands. Only sometimes for days—na, weeks—I was maist desperate hungry—for the antelopes and siclike creturs began to get unco scarce—pairtly frae being killed out, and pairtly frae being feared awa—and I've kent us obleeged to dine, and be thankful, on jackal.

Tickler. Hung up in hams from the roof of the cave.

Shepherd. But that wasna the warst o't—for spring cam —as I felt rather than saw; and day or nicht—sleepin or

* *True*—trow, believe.

waukin—I could get nae rest: I was verra feverish and verra fierce, and keepit prowlin and growlin about—

Tickler. Like a lion in love—

Shepherd. I couldna distinctly tell why—and sae did my mither, wha lookit as if in gude earnest she wad tear me in pieces.

Tickler. Whattt?

Shepherd. She would glare on me wi' her green een, as if she wanted to set fire to my hide, as you may hae seen a laddie in a wundow wi' a glass settin fire to a man's hat on the street, by the power o' the focus; and then she would wallow on the sand, as if to rub aff ticks that tormented her; and then wi' a shak, garrin the piles shower frae her, would gallop doun to the pool as if about to droon hersel—and though no in general fond o' the water, plowter in't like the verra pelican.

Tickler.—

> "Just like unto a trundling mop,
> Or a wild goose at play.

Shepherd. The great desert grew a' ae roar! and thirty feet every spang cam loupin wi' his enormous mane, the Lion my father, wi' his tail, tuft and a', no perpendicular like a bull's, but extended horizontally ahint him, as stiff's iron, and a' bristlin—and fastened in his fangs in the back o' the Lioness my mother's neck, wha forthwith began caterwaulin waur than a hunder roof-fu's o' cats, till I had amaist swarfed through fear, and forgotten that I was ane o' their ain whalps.

Tickler.—

> "To show how much thou wast degenerate."

Shepherd. Sae I thocht it high time to leave them to devoor ane anither, and I slunk aff, wi' my tail atween my legs, until the wilderness, resolved to return to my native oasis never mair. I lookit back frae the tap o' the sand-hill, and saw what micht hae been, or not been, the croons o' the palm-trees—and then glided on till I cam to anither "palm-grove islanded amid the waste"—as Soothey finely says—where instinct urged me to seek a lair; and I found ane—no sae superb, indeed, as my native den—no sae magnificent—but in itsel bonnier and brichter and mair blissfu' far: safter, far and wide a' round it, was the sand to the soles and paums o' my paws—for an event befell me there that in a day elevated me into Lionhood, an crooned me' wi' the imperial diadem of the Desert.

Tickler. As how?

North. James!

Shepherd. In the centre o' the grove was a well, not dug by hands—though caravans had passed that way—but formed naturally in the thin-grassed sand by a spring that in summer drought cared not for the sun—and round about that well were some beautifu' bushes, that bore flowers amaist as big's roses, but liker lilies.

Tickler. Most flowery of the feline!

Shepherd. But, O heavens! ten thousand million times mair beautifu' than the gorgeous bushes 'neath which she lay asleep! A cretur o' my ain kind! couchant! wi' her sweet nose atween her forepaws! The elegant line o' her yellow back, frae shouther to rump, broken here and there by a blossom-laden spray that depended lovingly to touch her slender side! Her tail gracefully gathered up amang the delicate down on which she reposed! Little of it visible but the tender tuft! Eyes and lips shut! There slept the Virgin of the Wild! still as the well, and as pure, in which her eemage was enshrined! I trummled like a kid—I heard a knockin, but it didna wauken her—and creepin stealthily on my gruff,* I laid mysel, without

* *Gruff*—belly.

growlin, side by side, a' my length alang hers—and as our fur touched, the touch garred me at first a' grue, and then glow as if prickly thorns had pleasurably pierced my verra heart. Saftly, saftly pat I ae paw on the back o' her head, and anither aneath her chin—and then laid my cheek to hers, and gied the ear neist me a wee bit bite!— when up she sprang higher in the air, Mr. Tickler, than the feather on your cap when you was in the Volunteers; and on recoverin her feet after the fa', without stayin to look around her, spang by spang tapped the shrubs, and afore I had presence o' mind to pursue her, round a sand-hill was out o' sicht!

North. Ay, James—joy often drops out between the cup and the lip—or, like riches, takes wings to itself and flies away. And was she lost to thee for ever?

Shepherd. I lashed mysel wi' my tail—I trode and tore up the shrubs wi' my hind paws—I turned up my jaws to heaven, and yowled in wrathfu' despair—and then pat my mouth to the dust, and roared till the well began to bubble: then I lapped water, and grew thirstier the langer I lapped—and then searched wi' a' my seven senses the bed whare her beautifu' bulk had lain—warmer and safter and sweeter than the ither herbage—and in rage tried to bite a bit out o' my ain shouther, when the pain sent me bounding aff in pursuit o' my lovely lioness; and lo! there she was stealin alang by the brink o' anither nest o' bushes, far aff on the plain, pausin to look back—sae I thocht—ere she disappeared in her hiding-place. Round and round the brake I careered, in narrowing circles, that my Delicht should not escape my desire, and at last burst crashin in upon her wi' ae spang, and seized her by the nape o' the neck, as my father had seized my mother, had pinned her doun to the dust. But I was mercifu' as I was strang; and being assured by her, that if I would but be less rampawgeous, that she would at least gie me a hearin, I released her neck frae my fangs, but keepit a firm paw on her, till I had her promise that she would agree to ony proposal in reason, provided my designs were honorable—and honorable they were as ever were breathed by bosom leonine in the solitary wilderness.

North.—

> "I calmed her fears, and she was calm,
> And told her love with virgin pride;
> And thus I won my Genevieve,
> My bright and beauteous bride."

Shepherd. We were perfectly happy, sir. Afore the hinnymoon had filled her horns, mony an antelope, and not a few monkeys, had we twa thegither devoored! Oh, sirs! but she was fleet! and sly as swift! She would lie couchin in a bush till she was surrounded wi' grazing edibles suspeckin nae harm, and ever and anon ceasing to crap the twigs, and playin wi' ane anither, like lambs in the forest, where it is now my lot as a human cretur to leeve! Then up in the air and amang them wi' a roar, smitin them deid in dizzens wi' ae touch o' her paw, though it was safter than velvet—and singlin out the leader by his horns, that purrin she micht leisurely sook his bluid; nor at sic times would it hae been safe even for me, her lion and her lord, to hae interfered wi' her repast: for in the desert hunger and thirst are as fierce as love. As for me, in this respect, I was mair generous; and mony is the time and aft that I hae gien her the tid-bits o' fat frae the flank o' a deer o' my ain killin when she had missed her ain by ower-springin't—for I never kent her spang fa' short—without her so much as thankin me,—for she was ower prood ever to seem gratefu' for ony favor—and carried hersel, like a Beauty as she was, and a spoiled Bride. I was sometimes sair tempted to throttle her; but then, to be sure, a playfu' pat frae her paw could smooth my bristles at ony time, or mak me lift up my mane for her delicht, that she micht lie doun bashfully aneath its shadow, or as if shelterin there frae some object o' her fear, crouch pantin amang that envelopment o' hairy clouds.

Tickler. Whew!

North. In that excellent work. *The Naturalist's Library*, edited by my learned friend Sir William Jardine, it is observed, if I recollect rightly, that Temminck, in his Monograph, places the African lion in two varieties—that of Barbary and that of Senegal—without referring to those of the southern parts of the continent. In the southern parts there are two kinds analogous, it would seem, to the northern varieties—the yellow and the brown, or according to the Dutch colonists, the blue and the black. Of the Barbary lion, the hair is of a deep yellowish brown, the mane and hair upon the breast and insides of the fore-legs being ample, thick, and shaggy; of the Senegal lion, the color of the body is of a much paler tint, the mane is much less, does not extend so far upon the shoulders, and is almost entirely wanting upon the breast and insides of the legs. Mr. Burchel encountered a third variety of the African lion, whose mane is nearly quite black, and him the Hottentots declare to be the most fierce and daring of all. Now, my dear James, pardon me for asking whether you were the Senegal or Barbary Lion, or one of the southern varieties analogous to them, or the third variety, with the mane nearly black, that encountered Mr. Burchel?

Tickler. He must have been a fourth variety, and probably the sole specimen thereof; for all naturalists agree that the young males have neither mane nor tail-tuft, and exhibit no incipient symptoms of such appendages till about their third year.

Shepherd. Throughout the hale series o' my transmigration

o' sowl I hae aye been equally in growth and genius extraordinar precocious, Timothy ; and besides, I dinna clearly see hoo either Buffoon, or Civviar, or Tinnock, or Sir William Jarrdinn, or James Wulson, or even Wommle himsel, familiar as they may be wi' Lions in plates or cages, should ken better about their manes and the tuft o' their tails, than me wha was ance a Lion *in propria persona*, and hae thochts o' writing my ain Leonine Owtobiography wi' Cuts. But as for my color, I was neither a blue, nor a black, nor a white, nor a red Lion—though you, Tickler, may hae seen siclike on the signs o' inns—but I was the TERRIBLE TAWNEY O' TIMBUCTOO ! ! !

Tickler. What ! did you live in the capital ?

Shepherd. Na—in my kintra seat a' the year roun'. But there was mair than a sugh o' me in the metropolis—mony a story was tauld o' me by Moor and Mandingo—and by whisper o' my name they stilled their cryin weans, and frichtened them to sleep. What kent I, when a lion, o' geography ? Nae map o' Africa had I ever seen but what I scrawled wi' my ain claws on the desert dust. As for the Niger, I cared na whether it flawed to meet the risin or the settin sun—but when the sun entered Leo, I used instinctively to soom in its waters ; and I remember, as if it had been yesterday, loupin in amang a bevy o' black girlies bathin in a shallow, and breakfastin on ane o' them, wha ate as tender as a pullet, and was as plump as a paitrick. It was lang afore the time o' Mungo Park ; but had I met Mungo I wouldna hae hurt a hair o' his head—for my prophetic sowl would hae been conscious o' the Forest, and however hungry, never would I hae harmed him wha had leeved on the Tweed.

North. Beautiful. Pray, James, is it true that your lion prefers human flesh to any other—nay, after once tasting it, that he uniformly becomes an anthropophagus ?

Shepherd. He may or he may not uniformly become an anthropophagus, for I kenna what an anthropophagus is; but as to preferring human flesh to ony ither, that depends on the particular kind o' human flesh. I presume, when I was a lion, that I had the ordinar appetencies o' a lion—that is, that I was rather aboon than below average or par—and at a' events, that there was naething about me unleonine. Noo, I could never bring my stamack, without difficulty, to eat an auld woman: as for an auld man, that was out o' the question, even in starvation. On the whole, I preferred, in the long run, antelope even to girl. Girl doubtless was a delicacy ance a fortnight or thereabouts—but girl every day would hae been—

Tickler. *Toujours perdrix.*

Shepherd. Just sae. Anither Lion, a freen o' mine, though, thocht otherwise, and used to lie in ambuscade for girl, on which he fed a' through the year. But mark the consequence—why, he lost his senses, and died ragin mad!

Tickler. You don't say so?

Shepherd. Instinctively I kent better, and diversified my denners with zebras and quaggas, and such small deer, sae that I was always in high condition, my skin was aye sleek, my mane meteorous; and as for my tail, wherever I went, the tuft bore aff the belle.

North. Leo—are you, or are you not a cowardly animal?

Shepherd. After I had reached the age o' puberty my courage never happened to be put to ony verra severe trial, for I was aye faithfu' to my mate—and she to me—and jealousy never disturbed our den.

Tickler. Any cubs?

Shepherd. But I couldna hae wanted courage, since I never felt fear. I aye took the sun o' the teegger; and though the rhinoceros is an ugly customer, he used to gie me the wa';

at sicht o' me the elephant became his ain trumpeter, and sounded a retreat in amang the trees. Ance, and ance only, I had a desperate fecht wi' a unicorn.

North. So he is not fabulous?

Shepherd. No him, indeed—he's ane o' the realest o' a' beasts.

Tickler. What may be the length of his horn, James?

Shepherd. O' a dagger.

North. Shape?

Shepherd. No speerally wreathed like a ram's horn—but strecht, smooth, and polished, o' the yellow ivory—sharper than a swurd.

Tickler. Hoofs?

Shepherd. His hoofs are no cloven, and he's no unlike a horse. But in place o' nicherin like a horse, he roars like a bull; and then he leeves on flesh.

Tickler. I thought he had been omnivorous.

Shepherd. Nae cretur's omnivorous but man.

North. Rare?

Shepherd. He maun be very rare, for I never saw anither but him I focht. The battle was in a wudd. We're natural enemies, and set to wark the moment we met without ony quarrel. Wi' the first pat o' my paw I scored him frae shouther to flank, till the bluid spouted in jettees. As he ran at me wi' his horn I joukit ahint a tree, and he transfixed it in the pith—sheathin't to the verra hilt. There was nae use in flingin up his heels, for wi' the side-spang I was on his back, and fastenin my hind claws in his flank, and my fore-claws in his shouthers, I began at my leisure devoorin him in the neck. She sune joined me, and ate a hole into his inside till she got at the kidneys; but judgin by him, nae animal's mair tenawcious o' life than the unicorn—for when we left him the remains were groanin. Neist mornin we went to breakfast on him, but thae gluttonous creturs, the vulturs had been afore us, and he was but banes.

North. Are you not embellishing, James?

Shepherd. Sic a fack needs nae embellishment. But I confess, sirs, I was, on the first hearin o't, incredulous o' Major Laing's ha'in fand the skeleton stickin to the tree!

North. Why incredulous?

Shepherd. For wha can tell at what era I was a lion? But it pruves that the banes o' a unicorn are durable as airn.

North. And ebony an immortal wood.

Tickler. Did you finish your career in a trap?

Shepherd. Na. I died in open day in the centre o' the great square o' Timbuctoo.

Tickler. Ha, ha! baited?

Shepherd. Na. I was lyin ae day by mysel—for she had disappeared to whalp amang the shrubs—waitin for some wanderin waif comin to the well—for thirst is stronger than fear in them that dwall in the desert, and they will seek for water even in the lion's lair—when I saw the head o' an unknown animal high up amang the trees, browzin on the sprays—and then its lang neck—and then its shouthers—and then its forelegs; and then its body droopin doun into a tail like a buffalo's—an animal unlike ony ither I had ever seen afore—for though spotted like a leopard, it was in shape liker a unicorn—but then its een were black and saft, like the een o' an antelope, and as it lickit the leaves, I kent that tongue had never lapped bluid. I stretched mysel up wi' my usual roar, and in less time than it taks to tell't was on the back o' the Giraffe.

Ambo. Oh! oh! oh! oh! oh! oh!

Shepherd. I happened no to be verra hungry; and my fangs—without munchin—pierced but an inch or twa deep. Brayin across the sand-hills at a lang trot flew the camelopard—nor for hours slackened she her pace, till she plunged into the Black river—

Tickler. The Niger.

Shepherd. —— swam across, and bore me through many groves into a wide plain, all unlike the wilderness round the Oasis we had left at morn.

North. What to that was Mazeppa's ride on the desert-born!

Shepherd. The het bluid grew sweeter and sweeter as I drank—and I saw naething but her neck, till a' at ance staggerin she fell doun—and what a sicht! Rocks, as I thocht them—but they were houses encirclin me a' round; thousan's o' blackamoors, wi' shirts and spears and swurds and fires, and drums, hemmin the Lion—and arrows—like the flyin dragons I had seen in the desert, but no, like them, harmless—stingin me through the sides intil the entrails, that when I bat them brak! You asked me if I was a cooard? Was't like a cooard to drive, in that condition, the haill city like sheep? But a' at ance, without my ain wull, my spangin was changed into sprawlin wi' my fore-feet. I still made them spin; but my hind-legs were useless—my back was broken—and what I was lappin, sirs, was a pool o' my ain bluid. I had spewed it as my heart burst; first fire grew my een, and then mist—and the last thing I remember was a shout and a roar. And thus, in the centre o' the great square o' Timbuctoo, the Lion died!

North. And the hide of him, who is now the Ettrick Shepherd, has for generations been an heirloom in the palace of the Emperor of all the Saharas!

Shepherd. Nae less strange than true. Noo, North, let's hear o' ane o' your transmigrations.

North. Another night; for really, after such painting and such poetry—— . . . Shall we have some beef *à-la-mode*, James?

Shepherd. Eh?

(*Beef à-la-mode.*)

Shepherd (*in continuation*). What is Love o' Kintra but an amalgamated multitude o' sympathies in brethren's hearts!

North. Yes, James, that is our country—not where we have breathed alone; not that land which we have loved, because it has shown to our opening eyes the brightness of heaven, and the gladness of earth; but the land for which we have hoped and feared,—that is to say, for which our bosom has beat with the consenting hopes and fears of many million hearts; that land, of which we have loved the mighty living and the mighty dead; that land, the Roman and the Greek would have said, where the boy had sung in the pomp that led the sacrifice to the altars of the ancient deities of the soil.

Shepherd. And therefore, when a man he would guard them frae profanation, and had he a thousan' lives, would pour them a' out for sake o' what some micht ca' superstition, but which you and me, and Southside, sittin there wi' his great grey een, would fearna, in the face o' heaven, to ca' religion.

Tickler. Hurra!

Shepherd. I but clench my nieves.

North. James, the Campus Martius and the Palæstra—

Shepherd. Sir?

North. ——where the youth exercised Heroic Games, were the Schools of their Virtue; for there they were taking part in the passions, the power, the life, the glory that flowed through all the spirit of the nation.

Shepherd. O' them, sir, the ggems at St. Ronan's are, but on a sma' scale, and imperfect eemage.

North. Old warriors and gowned statesmen, that frowned in marble or in brass, in public places, and in the porches of noble houses, trophied monuments, and towers riven with the scars of ancient battles—the Temple raised where Jove had stayed the Flight—or the Victory whose expanded wings still seemed to hover over the conquering bands—what were all these to the eyes and the fancy of the young citizen, but characters speaking to him of the great secret of his Hopes and Desires—in which he read the union of his own heart to the heart of the Heroic Nation of which he was One?

Shepherd. My bluid's tinglin and my skin creeps. Dinna stap.

North. And what, James, I ask you, what if less noble passions must hereafter take their place in his mind?—what if he must learn to share in the feuds and hates of his house or of his order? Those far deeper and greater feelings had been sunk into his spirit in the years when it is most susceptible, unsullied, and pure, and afterwards in great contests, in peril of life and death, in those moments of agitation or profound emotion in which the higher soul again rises up, all those high and solemn affections of boyhood and youth would return upon him, and consecrate his warlike deeds with the noblest name of virtue thas was known to those ancient states.

Shepherd. What was't? Eh?

North. Patriotism.

Shepherd. Ou ay. Say on, sir.

North. Therefore how was the Oaken Crown prized which was given to him who had saved the life of a citizen!

Shepherd. And amang a people too, sir, whare every man was willin at a word to die.

North. Perhaps, James, he loved not the man whom he had preserved; but he had remembered in the battle that it was a son of his country that had fallen, and over whom he had spread his shield. He knew that the breath he guarded was part of his country's being.

Shepherd. Mr. Tickler, saw ye ever sic een?

North. Look at the simple incitements to valor in the songs of that poet who is said to have roused the Lacedemonians, disheartened in unsuccessful war, and to have animated them to victory. "He who fights well among the foremost, if he fall shall be sung among his people; or if he live, shall be in reverence in their council; and old men shall give place to him; his tomb shall be in honor, and the children of his children."

Shepherd. Simple incitement, indeed, sir, but as you said richtly, shooblime.

North. Why, James, the love of its own military glory in a warlike people is, indeed, of itself an imperfect patriotism.

Shepherd. Sir? Wull ye say that again, for I dinna just tak it up?

North. Believe me, my dear Shepherd, that in every country there is cause for patriotism, or the want of such a cause argues defects in the character and condition of the country of the grossest kind. It shows that the people are vicious, or servile, or effeminate—

Shepherd. Which only a confoonded leear will ever say o' Scotsmen.

North. The want of this feeling is always a great vice in the individual character; for it will hardly ever be found to arise from the only justifiable or half-justifiable cause, namely, when a very high mind, in impatient disdain of the baseness of all around it, seems to shake off its communion with them. I call that but half-justifiable.

Shepherd. And I, sir, with your leave, ca't a'thegither unjustifiable, as you can better explain than the simple Shepherd.

North. You are right, James. For the noblest minds do not thus break themselves loose from their country; but they mourn over it, and commiserate its sad estate, and would die to recover it. They acknowledge the great tie of nature—of that house they are—and its shame is their own.

Shepherd. Oh, sir! but you're a generous, noble-hearted cretur!

North. In all cases, then, the want of patriotism is sheer want of feeling; such a man labors under an incapacity of sympathizing with his kind in their noblest interests. Try him, and you shall find that on many lower and unworthier occasions he feels with others—that his heart is not simply too noble for this passion—but that it is capable of being animated and warmed with many much inferior desires.

Shepherd. A greedy dowg and a lewd ane,—in the ae case, snarlin for a bane—and in the ither, growlin for the flesh. I scunner at sic a sinner.

North. Woe to the citizen of the world!

Shepherd. Shame—shame—shame!

North. The man who feels himself not bound to his country can have no gratitude.

Shepherd. Hoo selfish and cauld-hearted maun hae been his very childhood!

North. I confess that, except in cases of extreme distress, I have never been able to sympathize with—emigrants.

Shepherd. I dinna weel ken, sir, what to say to that—but mayna a man love, and yet leave his country?

North. My dear James, I see many mournful meanings in the dimness of your eyes—so shall not pursue that subject—but you will at least allow me to say, that there is something shocking in the mind of the man who can bear, without reluctance or regret, to be severed from the whole world of his early years—who can transfer himself from the place which is his own to any region of the globe where he can advance his fortune—who, in this sense of the word, can say, in carrying himself, "omnia mea mecum porto."

Shepherd. That's no in my book o' Latin or Greek quotations.

North. Exiles carry with them from their mother country all its dearest names.

Shepherd. And a wee bit name—canna it carry in it a wecht o' love?

North. Ay, James, the fugitives from Troy had formed a little Ilium, and they had, too, their little Xanthus.

Tickler. "Et avertem Xanthi cognomine rivum."

Shepherd. You're twa classical scholars, and wull aye be quotin Greek. But for my part,—after a' those eloquent diatribes o' yours on the pawtriotism o' the auncients, I wudna desire to stray for illustrations ae step out o' the Forest.

Tickler. Aren't ye all Whigs?

Shepherd. Some o' a' sorts. But it's an epitome o' the pastoral warld at large—and the great majority o' shepherds are Conservatives. They're a thinkin people, sir, as ye ken, and though far frae bein' unspeculative, or unwillin to adopt new contrivances as sune's they hae got an insight intil the principle on which they work, yet a new-fangle in their een's but a new-fangle; and as in the case o' its bein' applied to a draw-well, they wait no only to see how it pumps up, but hae patience to put its durability to the proof o' a pretty lang experience, sae in the political affairs o' the State—they're no to be taen in by the nostrums o' every reformer that has a plan o' a new, cheap constitution to shaw, but they fasten their een on't as dourly as on a dambrodd;* and then began cross-questionin the cheil—quack or else no—on the vawrious bearings o' the main-

* *Dambrodd*—draft-board.

springs, wheels, and drags; and as sune's they perceive a hitch, they cry, Ha! ha! ma lad! I'm thinkin she'll no rin up hill—and if ye let her lowse at the tap o' ane, she'll rattle to the deevil.

North. And such too, my dear sir, don't you think, is the way of thinking among the great body of the agriculturists?

Shepherd. I could illustrate it, sir, by the smearin o' sheep.

Tickler. And eke the shearing.

Shepherd. Say clippin. The Whigs and Radicals assert toon folks are superior in mind to kintra folks. They'll be sayin neist that they're superior to them likewise in body—and speak o' the rabble o' the Forest as ither people speak o' the rabble o' the Grassmarket. But the rural riff-raff are in sprinklins, in sma' families, and only seen lousin ane anither on spats forming an angle on the road-sides. Findlay o' Selkirk has weel-nigh cleaned the coonty o' a' sic—but in great toons, and especially manufacturin anes, there are haill divisions hotchin wi' urban riff-raff, and it's them ye hear at hustins routin in a way that the stots and stirks o' the Forest would be ashamed o' theirsels for doin in a bare field on a wunter day, when something had hindered the hind fra carryin them some fodder to warm their wames in the snaw. The salvation o' the kintra, sir, depends on the—

Tickler. This will never do, North—this is too bad. See, 'tis six!

North (*rising, and giving his guests each his candle*). We shall hear you another time, my dear Shepherd — but now—

Shepherd. The salvation o' the kintra, sir, depends on the—

North (*touching first one spring and then another, while fly open two panels in the oak wainscoting*). You know your rooms. The alarm-bell will ring at twelve—and at one lunch will be on the table in the Topaz. I wish you both the nightmare. (*Touches a spring, and vanishes.*)

Shepherd. Mr. Tickler! I say the salvation o' the country—baith gane!—I'm no sleepy—but I'll rather sleep than soliloqueese. (*Vanishes.*)

SIC TRANSEUNT NOCTES AMBROSIANÆ.

THE APPENDIX.

I. NOTICES BY PROFESSOR FERRIER.

II. GLOSSARY OF SCOTCH WORDS.

APPENDIX.

I.—NOTICES OF TIMOTHY TICKLER AND THE ETTRICK SHEPHERD,

BY PROFESSOR FERRIER.

AMBROSE'S was situated in the vicinity of West Register Street, at the back of the east end of Princes Street, and close to the Register Office. Here stood the tavern from which the *Noctes Cœnœque*, commemorated in these volumes, derived their name.

A *cursed* spot, 'tis sad, in days of yore ;
But *nothing* ails it now—the place is *merry* !"

But a too literal interpretation is not to be given to the scene of these festivities. Ambrose's Hotel was indeed " a local habitation and a name," and many were the meetings which Professor Wilson and his friends had within its walls. But the *true* Ambrose's must be looked for only in the realms of the imagination—the veritable scene of the " Ambrosian nights " existed nowhere but in their Author's brain, and their flashing fire was struck out in solitude by genius, wholly independent of the stimulus of companionship.

The same remark applies to the principal characters who take part in these dialogues. Although founded to some extent on the actual, they are in the highest degree idealized. Christopher North was Professor Wilson himself, and here, therefore, the real and the ideal may be viewed as coincident. But Timothy Tickler is a personage whose lineaments bear a resemblance to those of their original only in a few fine although unmistak able outlines, while James Hogg in the flesh was but a faint adumbration of the inspired Shepherd of the Noctes.

Mr. Robert Sym (the prototype of Timothy Tickler) was born in 1750, and died in 1844 at the age of ninety-four, having retained to the last the full possession of his faculties, and enjoyed uninterrupted good health to within a very few years of his decease. He followed the profession of Writer to the Signet from 1775 until the close of that century, when he retired from business on a competent fortune. He was uncle to Professor Wilson by the mother's side, and his senior by some five-and-thirty years. He thus belonged to a former generation, and had passed his grand climacteric long before the establishment of "Blackwood's Magazine," with which he had no connection whatever beyond taking an interest in its success. And although his conviviality flowed down upon a later stock, and was never more heartily called forth than when in the company of his nephew, these circumstances must of themselves have prevented the Author of the "Noctes" from trenching too closely on reality in his effigation of Timothy Tickler.

Mr Sym's portrait in the character of Timothy Tickler is sketched more than once in the course of the "Noctes Ambrosianæ." But the following description of him by the Ettrick Shepherd is so graphic, and for the most part so true, that I cannot resist the pleasure of transcribing it :—

"I had never heard," says Hogg in his 'Reminiscences of Former Days,'* "more than merely his [Mr Sym's] name, and imagined him to be some very little man about Leith. Judge of my astonishment when I was admitted by a triple-bolted door into a grand house † in St. George's Square, and introduced to its lord, an uncommonly fine-looking elderly gentleman, about seven feet high, and as straight as an arrow ! His hair was whitish, his complexion had the freshness and ruddiness of youth, his looks and address full of kindness and benevolence ; but whenever he stood straight up (for he always had to stoop about

* Prefixed to 'Altrive Tales,' by the Ettrick Shepherd. London, 1832.

† This is a slight exaggeration. Mr Sym's house, though sufficiently commodious, was a bachelor domicile of very moderate dimensions.

half-way when speaking to a common-sized man like me), then you could not help perceiving a little of the haughty air of the determined and independent old aristocrat.

"From this time forward, during my stay in Edinburgh, Mr. Sym's hospitable mansion was the great evening resort of his three nephews* and me; sometimes there were a few friends beside, of whom Lockhart and Samuel Anderson† were mostly two, but we four for certain; and there are no jovial evenings of my by-past life which I reflect on with greater delight than those. Tickler is completely an original as any man may see who has attended to his remarks; for there is no sophistry there, —they are every one his own. Nay, I don't believe that North has, would, or durst, put a single sentence into his mouth that had not proceeded out of it.‡ No, no; although I was made a scape-goat, no one, and far less a nephew, might do so with Timothy Tickler. His reading, both ancient and modern, is boundless,§ his taste and perception acute beyond those of most other men; his satire keen and biting, but at the same time his good-humor is altogether inexhaustible, save when ignited by coming in collision with Whig or Radical principles. Still, there being no danger of that with me, he and I never differed in one single sentiment in our lives, excepting as to the comparative merits of some strathspey reels.

* Professor Wilson, Mr. Robert Sym Wilson, Manager of the Royal Bank of Scotland, and Mr. James Wilson, the eminent naturalist.

† Samuel Anderson makes his appearance at page 440.

‡ This observation is very wide of the mark, Assuredly Mr. Sym was no consenting party to the slight liberties which were taken with him in the "Noctes," and it is not to be supposed that he had more than a faint suspicion of his resemblance to the redoubted Timothy. What Hogg says in regard to the vigor of Mr. Sym's talents, and the originality and pointedness of his remarks, is quite true; but had the nephew ventured to report any of the conversations of the uncle, there cannot be a doubt that the "breach of privilege" would have been highly resented by the latter. But the Professor had too much tact for that. He took good care not to sail too near the wind; and the utmost that can be said is, that the language and sentiments of Mr. Sym bore some general resemblance, and supplied a sort of groundwork, to the conversational characteristics of Mr. Tickler.

§ This also is incorrect. Mr. Sym's reading, although accurate and intelligent so far as it went, was by no means unbounded. It was limited to our best British classics and of these his special favorites were Hume and Swift.

"But the pleasantest part of our fellowship is yet to describe. At a certain period of the night our entertainer knew, by the longing looks which I cast to a beloved corner of the dining-room, what was wanting. Then, with "Oh, I beg your pardon, Hogg, I was forgetting," he would take out a small gold key that hung by a chain of the same precious metal from a particular button-hole, and stalk away as tall as the life, open two splendid fiddle-cases and produced their contents; first the one and then the other, but always keeping the best to himself. I'll never forget with what elated dignity he stood straight up in the middle of that floor and rosined his bow; there was a twist of the lip and an upward beam of the eye that were truly sublime. Then down we sat side by side, and began—at first gently, and with easy motion, like skilful grooms keeping ourselves up for the final heat, which was slowly but surely approaching. At the end of every tune we took a glass, and still our enthusiastic admiration of the Scottish tunes increased—our energies of execution redoubled, till ultimately it became not only a complete and well-contested race, but a trial of strength, to determine which should drown the other. The only feelings short of ecstasy which came across us in these enraptured moments were caused by hearing the laugh and the joke going on with our friends, as if no such thrilling strains had been flowing. But if Sym's eye chanced at all to fall on them, it instantly retreated upwards again in mild indignation.

To his honor be it mentioned, he has left me a legacy of that inestimable violin, provided that I outlive him.* But not for a thousand such would I part with my old friend."

To this description I may be just permitted to add, that in the more serious concerns of life Mr. Sym's character and career were exemplary. To the highest sense of honor, and the most scrupulous integrity in his professional dealings, he united the manners of a courtier of the ancient *régime*, and a kindliness of nature which endeared him to the old and to the young, with the latter of whom, in particular, he was always an especial favorite.

* Hogg did not outlive him.

But the animating spirit of the "Noctes Ambrosianæ" is the Ettrick Shepherd himself. James Hogg was born in 1772, in a cottage on the banks of the Ettrick, a tributary of the Tweed; and died at Altrive, near St. Mary's Loch—a lake in the same district—in 1835. His early years were spent in the humblest pastoral avocations, and he scarcely received even the rudiments of the most ordinary education. For long "chill penury repressed his noble rage;" but the poetical instinct was strong within him, and the flame ultimately broke forth under the promptings of his own ambition, and the kind encouragement of Sir Walter Scott. After a few hits and many misses in various departments of literature, he succeeded in striking the right chord in the "Queen's Wake," which was published in 1813. This work stamped Hogg as, after Burns (*proximus sed longo intervallo*), the greatest poet that had ever sprung from the bosom of the common people. It became at once, and deservedly, popular; and by this poem, together with some admirable songs, imbued with genuine feeling and the national spirit of his country, he has a good chance of being known favorably to posterity. But his surest passport to immortality is his embalmment in the "Noctes Ambrosianæ."

In connection with this brief notice of James Hogg, I may take the opportunity of clearing up a point of literary history which has been enveloped in obscurity until now: I allude to the authorship of a composition which is frequently referred to in the "Noctes Ambrosianæ," the celebrated Chaldee MS. This trenchant satire on men and things in the metropolis of Scotland was published in the seventh number of "Blackwood's Magazine." It excited the most indescribable commotion at the time—so much noise, indeed, that never since has it been permitted to make any noise whatever, this promising babe having been pitilessly suppressed almost in its cradle, in consequence of threatened legal proceedings. A set of the Magazine containing it is now rarely to be met with. The authorship of this composition has been always a subject of doubt. Hogg used to claim the credit of having written it. I have recently ascertained that to him the original conception of the Chaldee MS. is due; and also that he was the author of the first thirty-seven verses of Chap. I., and of one or two sentences beside. So that, out of the one hundred and eighty verses of which the whole piece consists, about forty are to be attributed to the Shepherd. Hogg, indeed, *wrote* and sent to Mr. Blackwood much more of the Chaldee MS. than the forty verses aforesaid; but not more than these were inserted in the Magazine; the rest of the production being the workmanship of Wilson and Lockhart. Such is a true and authentic account of the origin and authorship of the Chaldee MS. . . . To return to the Shepherd.

There was a homely heartiness of manner about Hogg, and a Doric simplicity in his address, which were exceedingly prepossessing. He sometimes carried a little too far the privileges of an innocent rusticity, as Mr. Lockhart has not failed to note in his Life of Scott; but, in general, his slight deviations from etiquette were rather amusing than otherwise. When we consider the disadvantages with which he had to contend, it must be admitted that Hogg was, in all respects, a very remarkable man. In his social hours, a *naïveté*, and a vanity which disarmed displeasure by the openness and good-humor with which it was avowed, played over the surface of a nature which at bottom was sufficiently shrewd and sagacious; but his conversational powers were by no means pre-eminent. He never, indeed, attempted any colloquial display, although there was sometimes a quaintness in his remarks, a glimmering of drollery, a rural freshness, and a tinge of poetical coloring, which redeemed his discourse from common place, and supplied to the consummate artist who took him in hand the hints out of which to construct a character at once original, extraordinary, and delightful—a character of which James Hogg undoubtedly furnished the germ, but which, as it expanded under the hands of its artificer, acquired a breadth, a firmness, and a power to which the bard of Mount Benger had certainly no pretension. . . .

In another respect the dialect of the Shepherd is peculiar: it is thoroughly Scottish, and could not be Anglicized without losing its raciness and spoiling entirely the dramatic propriety of his character. Let it not be supposed, however, that it is in any degree *provincial*, or that it is a departure from English speech in the sense in which the dialects of Cockneydom and of certain English counties are violations of the language of England. Although now nearly obsolete, it ranks as a sister-tongue to that of England. It is a dialect consecrated by the genius of Burns, and by the usage of Scott; and now confirmed as classical by its last, and in some respects its greatest, master. This dialect was Burns's natural tongue; it was one of Sir Walter's most effective instruments; but the author of the "Noctes Ambrosianæ, wields it with a copiousness, flexibility, and splendor which never have been, and probably never will be equalled. As the last specimen, then, on a large scale, of the national language of Scotland which the world is ever likely to see, I have preserved with scrupulous care the original orthography of these compositions. Glossarial interpretations, however, have been generally subjoined for the sake of those readers who labor under the disadvantage of having been born on the south side of the Tweed.

II.—GLOSSARY.

A

A'—all
Abee—alone
Abeigh—aloof
Aboon—above
Ackit—noted
Acks—acts
Acquent—acquainted
Ae—one
Afterhend—afterwards
Ahint—behind
Aiblins—perhaps
Aik—oak
Airn—iron
Airt—direction, point of the compass
Aits—oats
Alane—alone
Amna—am not
Ance—once
Aneath—beneath
Anent—concerning, about
Aneuch—enough
Ankil—ankle
Argling—wrangling
Ashet—an oblong dish
Asks—lizards
Ass-hole—ash-pit, or dust-hole
A'thegither—altogether
Athort—athwart
Atower—away from
Atween—between
Auchteen—eighteen
Aughts—owns
Auld—old
Auld-woman—a revolving iron chimney-top
Aumry—cupboard in a corner
Ava—at all
Awee—a little while
Awin—owing
Awmous—alms
Ax—ask
Ayont—beyond

B

Back-o'-beyont (back-of-beyond)—a Scotch slang phrase signifying any place indefinitely remote
Backend—close of the year
Baggy-mennon—a minnow, thick in the belly
Baikie—a bucket for ashes
Baird—beard
Bairn—, Bairnie— } child
Bairnly—childish
Baith—both
Bakiefu's—bucketfuls
Ballant—ballad
Bane—bone

Banieness — largeness and strength of bone
Bap—a small flat loaf with pointed ends
Bardy—positive
Barkened—hardened
Bashed — somewhat flattened with heavy strokes or blows
Bat—bit
Bate—beat
Bauchle—an old shoe crushed down into a sort of slipper
Bauk—one of a set of planks or spars across the joists in rude old Scotch cottages
Bauld—bold
Bawdrons—a cat
Bawm—balm
Bawn—band
Bawns—banns
Beek — to grow warm and ruddy before the fire; (beek in the hearth heat)
Beetin—fanning and feeding a fire with fuel
Beggonets—bayonets
Begood—, Begude— } began
Belyve—soon
Ben—into the room
Beuk—book
Bick—bitch
Bield—shelter
Big—to build
Bike—swarm
Bikes—nests of bees
Biled—boiled
Bill—bull
Binna—be not
Birk (tree)—birch
Birks—birches
Birks—beggar-my-neighbor, a game at cards
Birr—force
Birses—bristles; metaphorically used in Scotland for angry pride
Birzed—bruised
Blab—a big drop
Black-a-viced—of dark complexion
Blash, (a)—a drench
Blashin—driven by the wind and drenching
Blate—bashful
Blaw—blow
Blawmange—, Bleimanch— } blanc-mange
Blethers — rapid nonsensical talk
Blin'—blind
Blouterin — gabbling noisily and foolishly
Blouts—large deep blots or stains scarcely dried
Blude—blood
Bocht—bought
Bock—vomit
Bodle—a small Scottish coin, not now used
Bogle—a goblin
Bole—the cup or bowl of a pipe
Bonny—handsome, beautiful
Bonny fide—bona fide
Bonspeil—a match at curling
Boo—bow
Bools—marbles
Boord—board
Boud—were bound
Bouet—a hand-lanthorn
Bouk—bulk
Bourtree—elder-tree
Bowster—bolster
Boyne—a washing tub
Brace-piece—mantel-piece
Brackens—, Brakens — } fern
Braes—slopes somewhat steep
Braid—broad
Brak—broke
Branglin—a sort of superlative of wrangling
Brassle— panting haste up a hill

Brastlin—hasting up a hill toilsomely, and with heavy panting
Braw—fine
Breckans—*see* Brackens
Breeks—trousers
Breid—bread
Breist—breast
Brent—rising broad, smooth, and open
Brewst—a brewing; used in the text as the making of a jug or bowl of toddy
Bricht—bright
Brig— } bridge
Brigg— }
Brock—badger
Brodd—board
Broo—brow
Broo'd—brewed
Broon—brown
Broose—a race at a country wedding
Browst—*see* Brewst
Brughs—burghs
Bubbly-jock—turkey-cock
Buckies—a kind of sea-shell
Bught—sheepfold
Buird—a board; used in the text as the low table on which a tailor sits
Buirdly—tall, large, and stout
Buirds—boards
Bum—buzz
Bumbee—the bumble-bee
Bummer—blue-bottle fly
Bun'— } bound
Bund— }
Bunker—window-seat
Burd—board
Burnie—rivulet
Busked—dressed showily
But—into an outer or inferior apartment
By-gaun (in the by-gaun)—in going past
Byre—cowhouse
Byuckie—small book

C

Ca'—call
Caddie— } street porter
Cadie— }
Caff—chaff
Callant—young lad
Caller—fresh
Came—comb
Camstrary—unmanageable
Canny (no canny).—Canny means gentle, but "no canny" is a phrase in Scotland for one with a spice of the power of a wizard or devil in him
Cantrip—magical spell
Canty—lively
Carvey—the smallest kind of sweetmeats, generally put on bread-and-butter for children
Caucht—caught
Caudie—*see* Cadie
Cauff—chaff
Cauked—tipped with rough points, as horse-shoes are prepared for slippery roads in frost
Cauldit—troubled with a cold
Cauldrife—easily affected by cold; in the text it is used as selfishly cold
Cauler—fresh
Caulker—a glass of pure spirits, a dram
Causey—causeway
Caves—tosses
Cavie—a hencoop
Cavin—tossing
Cawm—calm

Cawnle—candle
Chack—a squeeze with the teeth
Chaclat—chocolate
Chafts—jaws
Chap—knock
Chapped—struck, as a clock strikes
Chapping—knocking
Chap o' the knock—striking of the clock
Chaumer—chamber
Cheep—to complain in a small peevish voice
Cheyre—chair
Chiel—a fellow, a person
Chirt—to press hard with occasional jerks, as in the act of turning a key in a stiff lock
Chitterin—shivering, with the teeth chattering at the same time
Chop—shop
Chovies—anchovies
Chowin—chewing
Chowks—jaws
Chow't—chew it
Chrissen'd—christened, baptized
Chuckies—hens
Chucky-stane—a small smooth round stone, a pebble
Chumley—chimney
Clachan—a small village
Clackins—broods of young birds
Claes—clothes
Clapped (clapped een)—set eyes
Clarts—mud
Clash—a noisy collision
Claught—to clutch
Clautin—groping
Cleckin—brood
Cleedin—clothing
Cleek—a hold of anything, caught with a hooked instrument
Cleemat—climate
Cleugh—a very narrow glen
Clink—cash
Clishmaclaver—idle talk
Clockin—bent on hatching
Cloits—falls heavily
Clootie—the devil
Cloots—feet
Closses—narrow lanes in towns
Clour—a lump raised by a blow
Clout—a bit of linen or other cloth
Clud—cloud
Cockettin—coquetting
Cockit—cocked
Cock-laird—yeoman
Cocko-nit—cocoa-nut
Codlin—a small cod
Coft—bought
Coggly—shaky from not standing fair
Collie—shepherd's dog
Collyshangie—squabble
Conçate—conceit
Conceit—ingenious device
Coo—cow
Cooart—coward
Coof—a stupid silly fellow
Cookies—soft round cakes of fancy bread for tea
Coom—to blacken with soot
Coorse—coarse
Coots—ankles
Copiawtor—plagiarist
Corbies—carrion crows
Corn-stooks—shocks of corn
Cosh—neat
Cosy—snug
Cotch—coach
Cottie—small cottage
Coup—upset
Coupin-stane—cope-stone
Couthie—frank and kind
Covin—cutting

Cozy—snug
Crabbit—crabbed
Crack—a quiet conversation between two
Craig—neck
Cranreuch—hoar-frost
Crap-sick—sick at the stomach
Crappit—cropped, made to bear crops
Craw—a crow of triumph
Creddle—cradle
Creel—a fish basket
Creenklin—chuckling, with a small tinkling tone of triumph in it
Creepie—a small low stool
Creesh—grease
Cretur—creature
Crinkly—hoarsely crepitating
Croodin doos—cooing doves
Croon—crown
Crouse—brisk and confident
Crowdy—a gruel of oatmeal and cold water
Cruckit—crooked
Cruds—curds, thickened milk
Crunkled—a wrinkled roughness
Crummle—crumble
Cuddie—donkey, an ass
Cuddie-heels—iron boot or shoe heels
Cuff (cuff o' the neck)—nape of the neck
Cummers—female gossips. In the text the word simply means elderly wives
Cuntra—country
Curtshy—curtsy
Custock—stalk of colewort or cabbage
Cute—ankle
Cutty—a frolicsome little lass
Cutty-mun—a slang phrase for a poor fellow's dance in air when he is hanged
Cyuck—cook

D

Dab—peck, like a bird
Dadds—thumps
Dae—do
Daffin—frolicking
Daft—crazy
Daidlin—trifling
Daigh—dough
Dambrod—Draught-board
Dang—beat
Daud—lump
Daudin—thumping
Daunderin—sauntering
Dauner—saunter
Daur—dare
Dawin—the breaking of the dawn
Day-lily—asphodel
Day's-darg—day's labor
Dazed—bewildered from intoxication or derangement
Dead-thraws—agonies of death
Deavin—deafening
Dee—die
Deealec—dialect
Deid—dead
Delvin—digging
Dew-blobs—big drops of dew
Dew-flaughts—vapors of dew
Dight—wipe
Din—dun
Dinna—do not
Dirl—a tremulous shock
Disna—does not
Div—do
Dixies—a hearty scolding by way of reproof

Dizzen—dozen
Docken—dock
Doit—a small copper coin
Doited—stupid
Dolp—bottom or breech
Donsy—a stupid lubberly fellow
Doo—pigeon
Dook—bathe
Door-cheek—side of the door
Douce—grave and quiet
Douk—bathe
Doundraucht—down-drag
Doup—bottom or breech
Dour—slow and stiff
Douss—a blow, a stroke
Dowy—doleful
Dracht—draught
Drappie—little drop
Draucht—draught
Dree—to suffer
Dreein—suffering
Drog—, Drogg— } drug
Dreigh—tedious
Droich—dwarf
Drookin—drenching
Drookit—drenched
Droosy—drowsy
Drucken—drunken
Drumly—turbid, muddy
Drummock—meal mixed with cold water
Dub—puddle
Dung—knocked
Dunge—*see* Dunsh
Dumbie—a dumb person
Dunsh—a knock, a jog or quick shove with the elbow
Dunshin—bumping
Durstna—durst not
Dwam—, Dwawm— } swoon
Dwam o' drink—a drunken stupor
Dwinin—pining
Dyuck—duck

E

Ear—early
Earock—a chicken
Eatems—items
Ee—eye
Ee-brees—eyebrows
Eein—eyeing
Een—eyes
Eerie—inspiring or inspired with nameless fear in a solitary place
Eerisome—fear-inspiring in a lonely place
Eerocks—*see* Earock
Eident—diligent
Eiry—full of wonder and fear
Eisters—oysters
Ettle—intend and aim at
Evendown—undisguised and clear
Exhowsted—exhausted

F

Fack—fact
Failosophers—philosophers
Fan'—felt
Fankled—entangled
Farder—farther
Far-keekers—far-lookers
Farrer—farther
Fash—trouble
Fashous—troublesome
Fates—feats

Fause-face—mask
Faut—fault
Fawsettoes—falsettoes
Faynomenon—phenomenon
Fearsome—terrible
Fechtin—fighting
Feck—number or quantity. "The grand feck," means the greater proportion, or most
Feckless—feeble
Feenal—final
Feesants—pheasants
Fend—shift
Fennin—faring
Fent—faint
Ferly (to)—to look amazed and half unconscious
Fernytickled—freckled
Feturs—features
Fictious—fictitious
Fidginfain—restless from excess of eagerness and delight
Fin's—feels
Finzeans—smoked haddocks
Firm—form, bench
Fisslin—rustling almost inaudibly
Fit—foot
Fit-ba—football
Fivver—fever
Fizz—make an effervescing sound
Fizzionamy—physiognomy
Flaff—instant
Flaffs—strong windy puffs
Flaffered—blown about with strong puffs of wind
Flaffin—fluttering in the air
Flaucht—a momentary outburst of flame and smoke
Fleech—beseech with fair words
Flees—flies
Flesher—butcher
Flett—flat (in music)
Flichter—flutter
Flinders—shivers
Fliped—turned back or up, or inside out
Flipes—comes peeling off in shreds
Floory—flowery
Fluff—a quick short flutter
Flyte—rail
Flyped—*see* Fliped
Foggies—garrison soldiers; old fellows past their best, or worn out
Fool—fowl
Forbye—besides
Forfeuchen—fatigued
Forgather wi'—fall in with
Forrit—forward
Foulzie—*see* Fuilzie
Foumart—polecat
Fowre—four
Fowre-hours—tea, taken by Scotch rustics about four o'clock in the afternoon
Fozie—soft as a frost-bitten turnip
Frae—from
Fraucht—freight
Freen—friend
Frush—brittle
Frutus—fruits
Fu'—tipsy
Fud—breech; seldom used except in reference to a hare or rabbit
Fugy—flee off in a cowardly manner
Fuilzie—filth; filth of streets and sewers
Fuirds—fords
Fules—fools, fowls
Fulzie—*see* Fuilzie
Fulzie-man—a night-man
Fummlin—fumbling
Funk—a kick
Furm—form
Fushionless—without sap
Fut—foot

G

Gab—mouth
Gaberlunzies—mendicants
Gad—the gadfly
Gaily—rather
Gain'—against
Gallemaufry—idle hubbub
Gang—go
Gar—make
Garse—grass
Gash—solemnly and almost supernaturally sagacious
Gate—manner
Gaunt—yawn
Gaucy—portly
Gawmut—gamut
Gawpus—fool
Gear—goods, riches
Geeing—giving
Gegg—to impose upon one's credulity with some piece of humbug
Geggery—humbug to impose upon the credulous
Gerse—grass
Gey—, Geyan—, Geyly— } rather
Ggeg—a piece of humbug to impose upon the credulous
Ggem—game
Ghaistly—ghostly
Gie—give
Gied—given
Gif—if
Gillies—serving-lads in the train of a Highland chieftain
Gimmer—a two-year-old ewe
Gin—if
Ginnlin—catching trouts with the hand
Girn—grin
Girnel—a large meal-chest
Girrzies—coarse servant-girls
Gizzy—a sort of compound of giddy and dizzy
Glaff—momentary wide flutter and flash
Glaur—mud
Gled—the glead or kite
Glee'd—squinting
Gleg—quick and sharp
Gleg-eed—sharp-eyed
Glint—a quick gleam
Gloamin—twilight of evening
Glower—stare with wide wondering eyes
Glummier—gloomier
Glutter—a gurgling pressure of words and saliva when the mouth cannot utter fast enough
Gollaring—uttering with loud confused vehemence
Goo—provocative to food
Gouk—fool
Gowan—daisy
Gowden—golden
Gowk—fool
Gowmeril—fool
Gowpen,—what the two hands put together can hold
Grain—to groan
Grains—branches
Graned—groaned
Grape—a dung-fork
Grat—wept
Gratins—gratings
Grawds—grades
Gree—prize
Greening—longing for a thing, as a pregnant woman is said to long
Greet—weep
Grew—greyhound
Grewin—coursing the hare, &c.

Grieves—farm stewards or overseers
Groof—belly
Grozert— } gooseberry
Grozet— }
Grousy—inclined to shiver with cold
Gruin—disposed to shiver
Gruesome—causing shuddering with loathing
Grufe— } belly
Gruff— }
Grumph—to grunt like a sow
Grumphie—pig
Grun'—ground
Grunstane—grindstone
Grup—gripe, hold
Guddlin—catching trouts with the hand
Gude—good
Guffaw—a broad laugh
Guller—a gurgling sound in the throat when it is compressed or half-choked with water
Gullerals—angry gurgling noises from the mouth
Gull-grupper—one catching gulls
Gully—large pocket-knife
Gurlin—rolling roughly, huddled together
Gushets—fancy pieces worked with wide open stitches in the ankles of stockings
Gutsy—gluttonous
Guttlin—guzzling, eating gluttonously

H

Ha'—hall
Hadden—holding
Haddies—haddocks
Haffest— } the temples
Haffist— }
Hafflins—half
Hags—breaks in mossy ground, remnants of breastworks of peat left among the dug pits
Hagglin—cutting coarsely
Hail, (a)—abundance
Haill—whole
Hailsome—wholesome
Hain—husband
Hainches—haunches
Hairst—harvest
Hairt—heart
Hale—whole
Haliest—holiest
Hantle—number, handful
Hap—hop
Hap-step-and-loup—hop-step-and-leap
Haps—wraps
Harl—drag
Hargarbargilng—wrangling, bandying words backward and forward
Harn-pan—brain-pan, skull
Harns—brains
Hash—a noisy blockhead
Haud— } hold
Hauld— }
Haun—hand
Haur—a thick cold fog
Havers—jargon
Haverer—proser
Haveril—a chattering half-witted person
Hawn—hand
Hawnle—handle
Hawrem—harem
Hawse—throat
Heads and thraws—heads and feet lying together at both ends of a bed
Heech—high
Hee-fleers—high-flyers
Heelan—Highland
Heich—high

Heid—head
Heidlands—headlands
Heigh—high
Herried—robbed or rifled, generally in reference to birds' nests
Herrier—a robber of birds' nests
Het—hot
Hicht—height
Hing't—hang it
Hinny—honey
Hirple—to walk very lamely
Hirsel—flock
Hizzie—hussy, a young woman, married or unmarried, generally applied to one of a free open carriage
Hoast—to cough
Hogg—a year-old sheep
Hoggit—hogshead
Hoise—raise
Hoodie-craws—hooded crows
Hoolet—owlet
Hooly—leisurely
Horrals—small wheels on which tables or chairs move
Horrel'd — wheeled, having wheels
Hotch—to heave up and down
Hotchin—heaving up and down
Hottle—hotel
Houghs—the hollows of the legs behind, between the calves and the thighs
Houghmagandy—fornication
Houkit—dug
Houlats—owls
Houp—hope
Howdie—midwife
Howe—hollow
Howes—holes
Howf—haunt
Howk—to dig
Howp—hope
How-towdies—barn-door fowls
Huggers—stockings without feet
Hunder—hundred
Hurcheon—urchin, hedgehog
Hurdies—hips
Hurl (a)—a ride in any vehicle, but with usual reference to a cart
Huts, tuts !—an exclamation of contemptuous doubt or unbelief
Hyuckit—hooked

I

Idiwit—idiot
Iles—oils
Iley—oily
Ilk—, Ilka— } each, every
Ill-faured—ill-favoured
Ingan—onion
Ingine—genius, ingenuity
Ingle—fireside, hearth
Interteenin—entertaining
Intil—into
Isna—is not

J

Jalouse—suspect
Jawp—splash
Jee (a)—a turn
Jeely—Jelly
Jeest—, Jeist— } jest
Jigot—gigot
Jimp-waisted—slender-waisted

Jinkin—turning suddenly when pursued
Jirt—to send out with quick short emphasis
Jockteleg—a folding-knife
Jougs—an iron collar fastened to the wall of a church, and put round a culprit's neck, in the old ecclesiastical discipline of Scotland
Jookery-pawkery— } juggling
Joukery-pawkery— } trickery
Jookin—coming suddenly forth in a sly and somewhat stooping manner
Jouked—dodged
Joukit—dodged, to avoid a thrust or blow
Jugging—jogging

K

Kame—comb
Keckle—cackle
Kecklin—cackling
Keek—peep
Keekit—peeped
Keeklivine pen—chalk pencil
Kembe—comb
Ken—know
Kennin't—knowing it
Kenna—do not know
Kenspeckle—noticeable
Kent—known
Ker-hauned—left-handed
Kerse—carse, alluvial lands lying along a river
Kibbock—a cheese
Kimmers—gossips
Kipper—fish dried in the sun, usually applied to salmon
Kirns—feasts of harvest home, with a dance
Kitchen—relish
Kittle—difficult
Kittly—easily tickled, sensitive
Kittled—literally littered, as of kittens
Kitty-wren—wren
Kiver—cover
Kivey—covey
Knappin—breaking with quick short blows
Knowe—knoll
Kye—cows
Kyeanne—cayenne
Kyloe—an ox, generally used in reference to the Highland breed
Kythes—shows itself
Kyuck—cook

L.

Lab—strike
Laigh—low
Lair—learning
Laith—loth
Laithsome, loathsome
Lameter—cripple
Lane—lone, alone
Lanes (twa)—two selves
Lang—long
Lang-nebbed—long-nosed; generally applied to words long and learned *(verba sesquipedalia)* with contempt for him that uses them
Lap—leaped
Lauchin—laughing
Launin—landing
Law (as applied to a height)—an isolated hill, generally more or less conical in form

Lave—remainder
Laverock—lark
Leddies—ladies
Leear—liar
Leecures—liqueurs
Leeds—leads
Lee-lang—live-long
Leemits—limits
Leeves—lives
Len—loan
Leuch—laughed
Licht—light
Licks—chastisement
Lift—firmament
Lilt—to sing merrily
Limmers—worthless characters, usually applied to women
Links—downs
Linns—small cascades, together with the rocks over which they fall
Lintie—linnet
Lintwhite—linnet
Lister—a pronged spear for striking fish
Lith—joint
Loan—a green open place near a farm or village, where the cows are often milked
Lo'esome—lovable
Loo—to love
Loof—palm of the hand
Loot—stoop
Losh—a Scotch exclamation of wonder
Lounderin—striking heavily in a fight
Loup—leap
Lout—lower the head, stoop
Low—flame
Lowin—flaming
Lown—calm
Lowse—loose
Lozen—window pane
Luck—, Luk— } look
Lug—ear
Lum—chimney
Lyart—grey, hoary

M

Mailin—a small property
Make—match, or mate
Mankey—a kind of coarse cloth for female wear
Manteens—maintains
Mantel—chimney-piece
Marrow—match, equal
Mart—an ox killed at Martinmas and salted for winter provision
Mauks—maggots
Maukin—hare
Maun—must
Mawt—malt
Measter—master
Meer—mare
Meerage—mirage
Meikle—much
Meltith—a meal of meat
Mennon—minnow
Mense—to grace, to enable to make a good show
Mere—mare
Messan—a mongrel cur
Mettaseekozies-metempsychosis
Michtna—might not
Midden—dunghill
Mint (to)—to hint or aim at
Mirk—dark
Mizzles—measles
Monyplies—part of the intestines with many convolutions
Mool—mule
Mortcloth—the black cloth thrown over the coffin at a funeral

Moold—mould
Mootin—moulting
Mooldy—mouldy.
Mou—mouth
Moul—mould, earth, soil
Mouls—small crumbling clods
Moudiwarp, — Moudiewart mole
Muck the byre—clean out the cow-house
Muckle—much
Mudged—made the slightest movement
Munted—mounted
Mummle—mumble
Murnins—mourning-dress
Mutch—a woman's cap
Mutchkin—a Scotch liquid measure nearly equivalent to the imperial pint

N

Nae—no
Naig—nag
Nain—own
Nate—neat
Nawsal—nasal
Neb—nose
Neep—turnip
Neerdoweel—one who never does well, incorrigibly foolish or wicked.
Neist—next
Neuk—nook
New harled—new plastered
Nicher—neigh
Niddlety-noddlety — nodding the head pleasantly
Nieve—fist
Nocht—nought, nothing
Noo—now
Noos and thans—now and then
Noony—luncheon
Notts—notes
Nowte—neat cattle
Nowtical—nautical
Numm—benumbed
Nummers—numbers
Nuzzlin— Nuzzlin, pressing with the nose, as a child against its mother's breast
Nyaffing—small yelping
Nyuck—nook

O

Obs—observation
Ocht—ought
Ocht—aught, anything
Odd—ode
Oe—grandson
Ony ae—any one
Ool—owl
Out-by—without, in the open air
Outower—out over
Ower—over
Ower-by—over the way
Owertap—overtop
Owther—author
Oxter—arm-pit

P

Pabble—to boil, to make the sound and motion of boiling
Paddocks—frogs
Paiks—a drubbing

Paidllin—wading saunteringly for amusement in the water
Paircin—piercing
Pairodowgs—paradox
Paitrick—partridge
Parritch—oatmeal porridge
Parshel—parcel
Partens—crabs
Pastigeos—pasticcios
Pat—put
Patrick—partridge
Patron—pattern
Pawkie—shrewd
Paum—palm
Pease-weep—lapwing
Pech—pant
Pechs—pigmies
Peel—pill
Peepin—peeping
Peerie—peg-top
Peerie-weerie—insignificant
Peeryette—pirouette
Peeryin—purling
Pellock—a porpoise
Pensie—pensive
Penter—painter
Pernicketty—precise in trifles, finical
Pickle—small quantity
Pingle—difficulty, trouble
Pint—point
Pirn—reel for a fishing-line
Pirrat—pirate
Pit—to put
Pitten—put
Pleuch—plough
Plookin—plucking
Ploom—plumb, £100,000
Ploomdamass—prune
Plouter—to work or play idly and leisurely in water or any other soft matter
Plowp—the sound of anything small but heavy dropping into water or other soft matter
Ploy—a social meeting for amusement
Pluff—a small puff as of ignited powder
Plum—a perpendicular fall
Pockey-ort—marked with the small-pox
Poleish—police
Pomes—poems
Pooked—plucked
Poor—power
Poorfu'—powerful
Poortith—poverty
Poossie—pussy; applied to a hare
Pootry—poultry
Pose—hoard of money
Potty—putty
Poupit—pulpit
Pouther—powder
Poutry—poultry
Pow—poll or head
Powheads—tadpoles
Powldowdies—oysters
Powper—pauper
Poy—pie
Pree—try, taste
Pree'd—tried, tasted
Preein—tasting
Preevat—private
Prent—print
Prick-ma-denty—finical, ridiculously exact
Priggin—entreating, haggling with a view to cheapen
Prin—pin
Propine—gift; properly gift in promise or reserve
Pruve—prove
Pu'—pull
Puckit—meagre and mean looking; better spelt "pookit."
Puir—poor
Pushion—poison
Puddock-stools—fungi
Pyet—magpie

Q

Quaich—a drinking-cup with two handles, generally of wood
Quat—did quit
Quate—quiet
Quey (a)—a young cow
Quullies—small quills

R

Raggoo—ragout
Rampawgeous — outrageously violent
Rampauging — raging and storming
Ram-stam—headlong, onward without calculation
Randie—scolding woman
Rang—reigned
Rape—rope
Rashes—rushes
Rasps—raspberries
Rattan—rat
Rax—reach
Ream—cream
Reçate—receipt, recipe
Red-kuted—red-ankled
Red-wud mad—raging mad
Reek—smoke
Reest—to be restive
Reesty—restive
Reseedin—residing
Rickle—a loose heap
Rickley—loosely built up and easily knocked down
Riff-raffery—of the rabble and disreputable
Rig—ridge of land
Riggin—roof and ridge
Ripe—poke
Ripin—poking
Rippet—disturbance
Riving—tearing
Rizzers—, Rizzer'd haddies— } haddocks dried in the sun.
Roan—spout
Rockins—evening neighborly meetings for a general spinning with the distaff
Rooket, rooked—"cleaned out" at play
Roop—rump
Roosed—extolled
Roots—routs
Rose-kamed—rose-combed
Rotten—rat
Rouch—rough
Roun'—round
Roup—rump
Rouse—extol
Routin—roaring
Rows—rolls
Rowled—rolled
Rowted—roared
Rubber—robber
Rubbit—robbed
Rubiawtors—devouring monsters
Rucks—ricks
Ruff — applause by beating with the feet
Rug—tear
Rung—a cudgel
Runkled—crumpled
Rype—*see* Ripe

S

Sabbin—sobbing
Saft—soft
Saip—soap
Sair—serve

Sair—sore
Sants—saints
Sark—shirt
Sass—sauce
Sassenach—a Lowlander or Englishman
Saugh wand—willow wand
Saun—sand
Saunt—saint
Saut—salt
Sawmont—salmon
Scald—scold
Scale—spill
Scart—scratch
Sceeance—science
Schule—school
Sclate—slate
Sclutter—a bubbling outburst or rush of liquid
Scones—soft cakes of bread, generally unleavened
Scoonrel—scoundrel
Scoor—scour
Scraugh—a screech or shriek
Screed—tear, a revel
Scribe—scrab or wild apples
Scroof—nape
Scrow—crew
Scunner—to shudder with loathing
Scutter—a thin scattered discharge
Seck—sect
Seelent—silent
Seenonims—synonyms
Seepit—soaked
Seggs—sedges
Seik—sick
Sel—self
Selt—sold
Sereawtim—seriatim
Sey—assay, prove
Shachlin—shuffling
Shank's naigie—on foot
Shankers — ale-glasses with long stalks
Shaw—show
Shauchly—ill made about the limbs and feet, and walking with a sort of shuffle
Shave—slice
Shawps—husks
Shells—cells
Shielin—a shepherd's slender, temporary cot
Shilfa—chaffinch
Shinna—shall not
Shissors—scissors
Shoggly—shaky
Shooblimest—sublimest
Shool—shovel, spade
Shoon—shoes
Shoor—shower
Shouther—shoulder [withered
Shranky—slender, lean, and
Shucken—shaken
Shue—sew
Shusey—Susan
Sib—akin
Siccan—such kind of
Sich—a sigh
Siclike—such as, similar
Sile—soil
Siller—silver, money
Sinnies—sinews
Sin'syne—ago
Siver—a covered drain
Skaith—harm
Skarted—scratched
Skeel—skill
Skeely—skilful
Skein-dhu—a Highland dagger
Skelp—a slap, a sharp blow (properly with the palm of the hand)
Skently—scantily, barely
Skep—hive
Skeugh—a slight shelter; more correctly spelt Scug
Skirl—a shrill cry
Skirrin—flying
Skites—skates

Skraich— }
Skreich— } a screech, a scream
Skreigh — (skreigh-o-day) — break of day
Skreeds—long pieces
Skrow—number, swarm
Skuddy—naked
Skunner—shudder with disgust
Slaters—small insects of the beetle species
Sleuth hound—blood-hound
Slokener—allayer of thirst
Sluddery—slippery
Sma—small
Smeddum—spirit
Smeeks—stifles with smoke
Smiddy—smithy
Smoored—smothered
Snaffin—the shortest, smallest petulant bark of the smallest dog
Sneevlin—speaking with a strong nasal twang through the mucus of the nose
Snokin—smelling like a dog
Snood—head-band worn by maidens only
Snooking—sucking down by the nostrils
Snooled—cowed
Snoot—snout
Snooved—went smoothly and constantly
Snoving—going smoothly and constantly
Soddy—soda water
Sonsy—well-conditioned
Soo—sow
Soocker—sucker
Sooens—a sort of flummery made of the dust of oatmeal
Sook—suck
Soom—swim
Soop—sup
Sooper—supper
Sooterkin—abortion
Sough—rumor
Soum—swim, sum
Soup—sup
Sourocks—sorrel
Sowens—*see* Sooens
Spale-box—a small box made of chips of wood, mainly for holding pills or salves
Spang—leap
Sparables—small iron nails in soles and heels of shoes, &c.
Spat—spot
Spate—stream in flood
Spawl—shoulder
Speaned—weaned
Speat—stream in flood
Speel—climb
Speer—ask
Speerally—spirally
Speldrins—haddocks salted and dried
Spinnle-shankit—thin-limbed
Spleet—split
Spootin—spouting
Spring-brod—spring-board
Spunk—a wooden match tipped with brimstone
Spunked out—came to light
Spunkie—spirited
Squozen—squeezed
Stab—stake
Stacherin—staggering
Staigs—stags
Stake—steak
Stamack—stomach
Stane—stone
Stap—stop
Starnies—stars
Staun—stand
Stawed—satiated
Steaks—stakes
Steek—shut
Steepin—stipend
Stell—a still, a shelter for sheep or cattle
Sternies—stars

Stey—steep
Sticket minister—one who gives up the clerical profession in Scotland from not being able to get ordination and a living
Stirks—young cattle in the first year of their age
Stock—fore part of a bed
Stoiter—stagger
Stooks—shocks of corn
Stool—the bottom of any crop; generally thick and close crops are said to "stool out" when they thicken at bottom
Stooned—pained
Stoop and roop—completely
Stoopit—stupid
Stot—to rebound
Stotted—rebounded
Stoun—a thrilling beat, a quick painful ache
Stouning—aching
Stour—flying dust, or dust in motion
Stown—stolen
Stownways—stealthily
Stracht—straight
Strack—struck
Strae—straw
Stramash—uproar, tumult
Strang—strong
Strauchened—straightened
Stravaig—idle, aimless wandering
Strecht—straight
Streck—strike
Streckin—stretching
Streekit—stretched
Stroop—spout
Strussle—fight
Stullion—stallion
Sturt—trouble
Sud—should
Sugh (keep a calm sugh)—be quiet. Sugh itself means the solemn murmur of wind in the trees or through a narrow passage
Suit—suite
Sumph—a blockhead
Sune—soon
Swallin—swelling
Swap—exchange
Swarf—a swoon
Swattle—fill gluttonously or drunkenly
Sweein—swinging
Sweered—unwilling
Sweeties—small sweetmeats
Swither—hesitate
Swoopit—swept
Swurl—whirl
Swutches—switches
Sybo—a young onion with its green tail
Symar—cymar, scarf
Syne (sin'syne)—ago

T

Tae—one of two
Taes—toes
Taeds— } toads
Taids— }
Taigle—linger
Tain (the—the one
Tangle—a kind of sea-weed
Tantrums—a fit of sulky whim, whimsical sullens
Tap—top
Tapsalteerie—heels-over-head
Tapsetowry—in excited and raised confusion
Taukin—talking
Tauted— } matted
Tautied— }
Tawpy—thoughtless and coarse
Tawry—tarry

Tawse—the implements of flagellation in Scottish schools
Tawty—matted
Teegar—tiger
Teep—type
Tent—care
Teuch— } tough
Teugh— }
Thairm—fiddle-strings
Thees—thighs
Theekin—thatching
Theekit—thatched
Theirsel—theirselves
Thir—these
Thocht—thought
Thole—endure
Thoom—thumb
Thrang—busy
Thrapple—windpipe
Thrapplin—choking by compressing the throat
Thrawart and uncannie—perverse and dangerous
Thrawin—throwin
Threed—thread
Threecolore—tricolor
Threeped—asserted
Threeple—triple
Threteen—thirteen
Thretty—thirty
Thrissle—thistle
Throughither—mixed all together
Thursty—thirsty
Thud—a thump, and the noise it makes
Thummlefu's—thimblefuls
Ticht—tight
Tiler—tailor
Till—to
Till't—to it
Timmer—timber
Timmer-tuned—altogether unmusical in the voice
Tining—losing
Tinsy—tinsel
Tint—lost
Tirlin—unroofing
T'ither—the other
Tocher—dowry
Toddle—to totter like a child in walking
Toddler—a tottering child
Toman—a knoll, a thicket
Tooels—towels
Toom—empty
Toon—town
Toosy— }
Toosey— } shaggy, rough, dishevelled
Toozy— }
Toozlin—handling the lasses in rough sport
Tootin—blowing a horn
Tosh up—display to best advantage
Toshly—neatly
Tot—the whole number
Touts—sounds
Touzle—deal roughly with
Towdie—a barn-door fowl
Towmont—twelvemonth
Towsy — shaggy, dishevelled, rough
Tramper—wandering beggar
Trance—passage
Transmogrify—to metamorphose strangely
Trate—treat
Tredd—trade
Trig—neat
Trochs—troughs
Trotters—legs and feet
True—trow, believe
Trummel— } tremble
Trummle— }
Trumlin—trembling
Twa-haun—two-handed
Twa-three—two or three
Twal—twelve
Twalt—twelfth
Tyke—dog, cur
Tyuk—took

U

Unce—ounce
Unco—uncommon
Unwiselike—unlike the truth, ridiculous
Upcast—taunt, reproach
Uptak—apprehension, comprehension
Urchin—the shell so called

V

Vacance—vacation
Vice—voice
Vicey—small thin voice
Vivers—victuals
Vizy—a deliberate look at a particular object

W

Wa'—wall
Wab—web
Wabsters—weavers
Wad—would
Waefu'—sorrowful
Waff—wave
Waght—weight
Wale—best
Walin—choosing
Wallise—valise
Wame—stomach
Wamefu—bellyful
Wamle—a sudden tumbling roll, generally on the belly
Wan—one
Warna—were not
Warsle—wrestle
Was na't—was it not
Water-pyat—the water-ouzel
Wather—weather
Wattin—wetting
Waught (a)—a large draught
Waukrife—watchful, sleepless
Waur—worse
Weans—children
Weather-gleam—a gleam of light in the track of the sun on the edge of the horizon, in cloudy weather
Wecht—weight
Wede—weeded
Wee—little
Wees—(by littles and wees), by insensible degrees
Weel-faured—weel-favored
Weel-kend—well-known
Weezen'd—dried, hide-bound, withered, shrunk, and yellow
Werena—were not
Wersh—insipid
Wershness—insipidity
Whafflin—raising a wind with violent waving
Whalps—whelps
Whammle—upset
Whang—a large slice or cut
Whap—a heavy slap
Whase—whose
What—whet
Whattin—whetting
Whaups—curlews
Wheen—a number
Wheesht—, Wheish—, Whisht— } hush
Whilk—which
Whilly-wha—a shuffler
Whins—furze
Whumle—to turn up or round
Whup—whip
Whupt—whipt
Whurlint—whirling

Whuskin—whisking
Whusky—whisky
Whusper—whisper
Whussle— } whistle
Whustle— }
Whut—whit
Whyleock—little while
Wi' hit—with it
Wice—wise
Wimplin—curling and purling
Win—get
Windle-strae—a tall, dun, sapless grass that grows on Scottish hills
Windle - strae - legged — with small, puny legs
Wise—entice
Wiselike—judicious
Wizen—throat
Wizened—*see* Weezened
Wons—dwells
Wonner—wonder
Wonnin—dwelling
Woo—wool
Wordier—worthier
Wrastle—wrestle
Wud—angry
Wudcock—woodcock
Wudcut—woodcut
Wudds—woods
Wudna—would not
Wudness—distraction
Wull-cat—wild cat
Wullie-waucht—large draught
Wull't—will it
Wummle—wimble
Wun'— } wind
Wund— }
Wundin—winding
Wunk—wink
Wunna—will not
Wunnel-strae — *see* Windle-strae
Wunnock—window
Wurset—worsted
Wus—swish
Wut—wit
Wutty—witty
Wuzzard—wizard
Wysslike—judiciously
Wyte—blame, fault

Y

Yammer—murmur or whimper peevishly
Yatt—yacht
Yaud—a sorry old horse
Yawp—sharp set
Yearock—chicken
Yellow yoldrin—yellow hammer
Yepoch—epoch
Yerk-yerking—carp-carping
Yerth—earth
Yestreen—yester even
Yett—gate
Yill—ale
Yirth—earth
Yoke till him—set upon him
Yonner—yonder
Yott—yacht
Youf-youfin—yelp-yelping
Youlin— } howling
Yowlin— }

www.ingramcontent.com/pod-product-compliance
Lightning Source LLC
LaVergne TN
LVHW021219110826
845150LV00002B/205

* 9 7 8 1 4 2 5 5 6 4 7 0 4 *